Topias and Utopias in Health

# World Anthropology

*General Editor*

SOL TAX

*Patrons*

CLAUDE LÉVI-STRAUSS
MARGARET MEAD
LAILA SHUKRY EL HAMAMSY
M. N. SRINIVAS

MOUTON PUBLISHERS · THE HAGUE · PARIS
DISTRIBUTED IN THE USA AND CANADA BY ALDINE, CHICAGO

# Topias and Utopias in Health

## Policy Studies

*Editor*

**STANLEY R. INGMAN**
**ANTHONY E. THOMAS**

MOUTON PUBLISHERS · THE HAGUE · PARIS

DISTRIBUTED IN THE USA AND CANADA BY ALDINE, CHICAGO

For men are not determined entities, like rocks and trees. They have minds. Human beings can, and do, react AGAINST the past. They are affected BY the past, in so far as they absorb behaviour-patterns of their culture. But they also have the faculties of imagination and creativity; they innovate as well as receive and absorb, they revolt as well as continue. They step outside the structural framework of the existing order and the intellectual framework of received ideas to create NEW ideas and NEW ways of ordering their relationships with one another. In order to understand human behaviour, then, we have to be sensitive not only to the past and the present, but also to the future, to make a place in our thinking about society for what people want to be, to have, and to do — in a word, for Mannheim's "utopian" element. To put it paradoxically, perhaps, society is a product of the FUTURE, as much as the past and present.

PETER WORSLEY, *The Third World*

# General Editor's Preface

Insofar as sicknesses are influenced by sociocultural systems, so are means of maintaining the health of individuals. Although much in illness is universal and biological, the health system within any culture is as artificial and changeable as anything else in human society. Indeed, the systems we take for granted can be related to special circumstances of the past century or two. It is the function of anthropology to free us to think about radical changes in our own societies by showing us the many different models which humans have elsewhere developed. The present book does just this, using the forum of an international Congress to discuss also the directions of change.

Like most contemporary sciences, anthropology is a product of the European tradition. Some argue that it is a product of colonialism, with one small and self-interested part of the species dominating the study of the whole. If we are to understand the species, our science needs substantial input from scholars who represent a variety of the world's cultures. It was a deliberate purpose of the IXth International Congress of Anthropological and Ethnological Sciences to provide impetus in this direction. The *World Anthropology* volumes, therefore, offer a first glimpse of a human science in which members from all societies have played an active role. Each of the books is designed to be self-contained; each is an attempt to update its particular sector of scientific knowledge and is written by specialists from all parts of the world. Each volume should be read and reviewed individually as a separate volume on its own given subject. The set as a whole will indicate what changes are in store for anthropology as scholars from the developing countries join in studying the species of which we are all a part.

The IXth Congress was planned from the beginning not only to include as many of the scholars from every part of the world as possible, but also with a view toward the eventual publication of the papers in high-quality volumes. At previous Congresses scholars were invited to bring papers which were then read out loud. They were necessarily limited in length; many were only summarized; there was little time for discussion; and the sparse discussion could only be in one language. The IXth Congress was an experiment aimed at changing this. Papers were written with the intention of exchanging them before the Congress, particularly in extensive pre-Congress sessions; they were not intended to be read at the Congress, that time being devoted to discussions — discussions which were simultaneously and professionally translated into five languages. The method for eliciting the papers was structured to make as representative a sample as was allowable when scholarly creativity — hence self-selection — was critically important. Scholars were asked both to propose papers of their own and to suggest topics for sessions of the Congress which they might edit into volumes. All were then informed of the suggestions and encouraged to re-think their own papers and the topics. The process, therefore, was a continuous one of feedback and exchange and it has continued to be so even after the Congress. The some two thousand papers comprising *World Anthropology* certainly then offer a substantial sample of world anthropology. It has been said that anthropology is at a turning point; if this is so, these volumes will be the historical direction-markers.

As might have been foreseen in the first post-colonial generation, the large majority of the Congress papers (82 percent) are the work of scholars identified with the industrialized world which fathered our traditional discipline and the institution of the Congress itself: Eastern Europe (15 percent); Western Europe (16 percent); North America (47 percent); Japan, South Africa, Australia, and New Zealand (4 percent). Only 18 percent of the papers are from developing areas: Africa (4 percent); Asia-Oceania (9 percent); Latin America (5 percent). Aside from the substantial representation from the U.S.S.R. and the nations of Eastern Europe, a significant difference between this corpus of written material and that of other Congresses is the addition of the large proportion of contributions from Africa, Asia, and Latin America. "Only 18 percent" is two to four times as great a proportion as that of other Congresses; moreover, 18 percent of 2,000 papers is 360 papers, 10 times the number of "Third World" papers presented at previous Congresses. In fact, these 360 papers are more than the total of ALL papers published after the last International Congress of Anthropological and Ethnological Sciences which was held in the United States (Philadelphia, 1956). Even in the beautifully organized Tokyo Congress in 1968 less than a third as many members from developing nations, including those of Asia, participated.

The significance of the increase is not simply quantitative. The input of scholars from areas which have until recently been no more than subject matter for anthropology represents both feedback and also long-awaited theoretical contributions from the perspectives of very different cultural, social, and historical traditions. Many who attended the IXth Congress were convinced that anthropology would not be the same in the future. The fact that the next Congress (India, 1978) will be our first in the "Third World" may be symbolic of the change. Meanwhile, sober consideration of the present set of books will show how much, and just where and how, our discipline is being revolutionized.

This book is one of several in "medical anthropology," including one with that title. They range from studies of reproduction and population to mental health, drug and alcohol use, and witchcraft; and from primate behavior and physiological evolution to psychological anthropology; and include, of course, description of cultures in all parts of the world.

*Chicago, Illinois*                                          SOL TAX
*July 16, 1975*

# Table of Contents

# Introduction

This introduction reproduces, in an edited form, the proceedings of the symposium "Topias and Utopias in Health" at the IXth ICAES in Chicago, 4 September 1973. Comments have been edited by the organizers, Stanley R. Ingman and Anthony E. Thomas, and the contributors.

The opening remarks by Anthony Thomas introduce the major topics of discussion: "Interest groups and the allocation of health care," "Topias, utopias, and counter-utopias in health care," and "Social science in health reserach and action." These topics are then presented by Carlos Ramos, Stephen Schensul, and Sally Guttmacher in the light of the papers included in this volume. Following these presentations are comments from the audience and summary statements by Amafume Onoge, Alanagh Raikes, and Stanley R. Ingman.


## INTRODUCTORY REMARKS

ANTHONY E. THOMAS: In reference to our first topic of discussion, "Interest groups and allocation of health care," there is generally an emphasis on analyzing how health systems or components of health systems work. The idea here is to have a collection of papers which would analyze, and in some cases criticize, the processes of the various health systems or components of these systems.

Regarding the second topic, "Topias, utopias, and counter-utopias in health care," there has been an effort to focus on experimental and new socialist systems of health care. That is, there is a greater emphasis on the construction of new kinds of health systems and new methods in training within a total system of health workers rather than just a focus on one particular category such as physicians or mid-level people.

Stan Ingman and I chose the title, "Topias, utopias, and counter-utopias" for this subsection so that we could deal with both continuity and change. Or perhaps from a critical standpoint, we wanted to provoke discussion of stagnation or change in contemporary health systems. We have felt that these terms serve as useful concepts to discuss change in both the health systems and in the larger nation-state systems within which health systems are embedded.

The term "topia" in English has probably only been used in the writings of Karl Mannheim, the well-known pioneer in the sociology of knowledge. Mannheim used the term, topia, in the 1920's in three essays written in German which then became part of a larger book for English publication, *Ideology and utopia* (1936). The book itself was published a decade later in a more conservative stage in Mannheim's life — the early years of his exile in Great Britain. Mannheim borrowed the term, topia, from Gustav Landauer, author of *Die Revolution* (1923) and socialist leader in Bavaria. Mannheim took the term topia in order to develop a certain kind of dialectical analysis in *Ideology and utopia*.

Numerous scholars have utilized Thomas More's fictitious place name Utopia with a capital U. Mannheim's intention, however, in *Ideology and utopia* (1936) was to decapitalize, and perhaps, to demythologize Thomas More's term Utopia so it could be used to express plans and efforts for real rather than mythical change. "Topia," then, following Mannheim's impressive essays, is any conventional system (from the Greek word TOPOS meaning "a place"), and "utopia" is any serious plan for its replacement. "Counter-utopia," then, is roughly equivalent to counter-insurgency.

Many persons of the 1970's might smile in recalling that when Karl Mannheim left Germany in 1933 and went to England, he became very conservative and ceased to refer to Marxist scholars in his writings. When Mannheim wrote those original three essays, he was a colleague of Georg Lukàcs in Heidelberg. At least for an "establishment sociologist" at that time, he was quite critical of the conventional order and could be given credit, in those circles, of being radical; but later he joined the faculty of the London School of Economics and changed his orientation considerably.

One of the very useful concepts that Karl Mannheim developed is "utopia blindness" — "the representatives of a given order will label as utopian all conceptions of existence which FROM THEIR POINT OF VIEW can in principle never be realized" (1936: 196). Those who generally support the *status quo* or who advocate only minimal reformist change will usually assess plans for radical change in their own institutions or in the American health care system as impractical or unrealizable, i.e. Utopian in the folk meaning of that word.

The following is an example of utopia blindness. Spiro Agnew, as spokesman for the current regime in America, has continually dwelled on the unrealizability and impracticality of the many utopian plans proposed by those politically to the left of the Nixon/Agnew regime. This mode of attack was particularly annoying prior to Agnew's present difficulties.

On July 30, 1973, only two weeks prior to the first public exposure of Agnew's political corruption, Stewart Alsop wrote a column entitled, "President Agnew?" in which he quoted and paraphrased former Vice-President Agnew's two most important expressed concerns:

1. "The cost of government is controllable only as the density of population is controllable."
2. "The greatest problem facing the country today is that we have become utopians. We are never satisfied with the achievable, measurable gains. We insist on utopia."

An example of utopianism, says Mr. Agnew, is the American attitude toward poverty. It is NOT ENOUGH that there are fewer poor people than ever before in any country's history (1973: 76; emphasis added).

I think Agnew's comments provide an important illustration of the conservative utopia blindness that Mannheim was talking about. This is the natural reluctance among conservatives to recognize the distinctive merits of any design which transcends the limits of the *status quo.*

Turning politically to the left we find that most Marxists avoid the term utopia in discussing a serious socialist effort. Perhaps this avoidance is understandable considering the unenviable association of utopia with such paternalistic and anti-egalitarian socialism as the projects of Robert Owen and other Utopian socialists in the nineteenth century. The terms conventional order, revolution, and counter-revolution are indeed less ambiguous and more aggressive than Mannheim's analogous terms. However, Paul Baran, the well-known Marxist economist, did not shy away from using the term utopian in his discussions of the construction of a socialist environment. I rather like this short comment by Paul Baran in a collection of his writings entitled *The longer view*:

For what is, in my opinion, central to the Marxian position is ... the combination of historical vision and the courage to be utopian — with the vision sternly disciplined by an analysis of tendencies discernible at the present time, and with the utopia rendered concrete by the identification of the social forces that may be expected to further its realization (1969: v).

## DISCUSSANTS' COMMENTS

### Interest Groups and the Allocation of Health Care

CARLOS G. RAMOS: The papers under discussion present a diversity of approaches and areas of interest on the part of social scientists as regards health services and/or systems. I will attempt to outline the analytical perspectives used by the various authors. The first of these defines the client within a particular cultural, economic, or geographical context. These units serve as points of reference to analyze the implementation, impact, or effectiveness of particular health care programs. This approach is illustrated by the work of Epling, Vandale, and Steuart entitled "Beyond the individual for the practice of medicine" and Urdaneta's study on "Fertility and the 'pill' in a Texas barrio."

Once the basic elements have been defined, it is possible to utilize them in order to structure or implement health care at the regional or national levels. This approach attempts to provide solutions to the problems regarding the distribution of health services. These obstacles are viewed as being essentially administrative ones that hinder effective planning and functioning of health programs. Elling's paper on "Regionalization of health services: sociological blocks to realization of an ideal" falls within this category.

It should be noted that the first two analytical approaches are concerned with reorganizing particular subunits within a given socioeconomic system. The third approach is primarily concerned with the restructuring of total systems. Although the unit of analysis of this methodological perspective is the subsystem, it is primarily interested in analyzing the distribution and dynamics of power within the social structure, and its consequences on the nature and functioning of the system's subunits. This analysis is characteristic of the papers presented by Schoepf on "Human relations vs. social relations in medical care," Yee on "Dialectical materialism and community health programs," and Schoen on "Uses and abuses of innovations in the delivery of dental care."

Finally, a group of colleagues has utilized historical analyses to explain those factors that have influenced the development of ideological positions and responses to specific public health programs and/or systems. This type of analysis stresses interest group interaction and the motives or intentions of these groups in proposing certain health care schemes. The papers by Polgar on "Birth planning: between neglect and coercion," Henderson and Ramos on "Political ideology and population policy in Puerto Rico," Raikes on "Medical education in transition: Tanzania," and Ingman on "Static dynamics of medical care organization" are examples of this perspective.

The diversity of analytical approaches based on diverse intellectual and ideological schools of thought raise a number of questions. First, as scientists and citizens, can we continue to participate in social research intended to inform health policy, which is formulated in a social vacuum, without taking into account the structure and functioning of total systems? Second, can or should the social scientist continue to maintain a relativist position regarding the various types of socioeconomic systems, or should he commit himself to a particular system that is better able to deal with the distribution of necessary health services?

The papers presented also suggest discussion of the role of the scientist within a social system. Hitherto, the social scientist has been assigned or has assumed the role of critic or advocate of his society. Both roles have their pitfalls. The first can alienate him, while the second can absorb him as a functional element. It thus seems necessary to broach the issue regarding the possibility of synthesizing the already-mentioned alternatives.

Finally, we must decide whether we are to continue to view the client or consumer as a passive agent to whom we bring or on whom we impose a program or service, or whether the client should be viewed as an active agent who molds and determines the kinds of services which he requires.

### Topias, Utopias, and Counter-Utopias in Health Care

STEPHEN SCHENSUL: The eight papers reviewed for this section clearly agree on what good health care or, in our terms, utopian health care systems are all about. First of all, they agree that standard American private practice in the one-to-one physician-patient model is close to antithetical to utopian health care systems. The authors of each of these papers also agree that medical practice should be community, neighborhood, and family oriented rather than placing the emphasis on the individual treatment-care model. Utopian health care systems should have, in these authors' view, an emphasis on prevention rather than on the band-aid approach to health care problems. The utopian system should have strong citizen participation and control. In a utopian system there should be equality of health care in that all citizens in a national system should have equal access to health services. The authors believe that a utopian system of health care is one that is centralized and coordinated and that the orientation should be toward group practice rather than the private practitioner model. Health care should be eliminated as a tool of political and social oppression of minority groups and Third World people. Finally, each of the papers agree that health care systems must have an awareness and sensitivity to the language and culture of the consumers of health care services.

Although these papers deal with health care systems in a number of different countries the message we get is that the authors are quite pessimistic concerning the transformation of their particular country's health care into a utopian system. Segovia and Gómez describe the Argentinian Health Care system as "loose, unorganized, and chaotic." In this kind of situation positive innovation for better health care is extremely difficult. James says that the Canadian system works extremely smoothly in terms of payments but little else in the system works. Epling, Vandale, and Steuart discussed the need for household kin networks as an intermediate strategy for health care intervention between the community and the individual. However, they doubt that such a practice would develop because of the vested interests of the health care establishment in the kinds of training usually offered in medical schools. Falk and Hawkins go so far as to dream about what it would be like if the United States had a Chinese Health Care policy. Onoge describes health care as a "colonial political tool" in Africa, and Urdaneta describes the insensitivity of Anglo institutions to Chicano health care needs.

Thus, the overwhelming impression from these papers is that the topia is awfully difficult to transform into the utopia. These authors are particularly pessimistic about the possibility of change because they feel there must first be a concomitant change in the society as a whole. Two papers present the health care situation in Cuba — a society which has undergone such change. Both papers support the view that Cuba is well on its way to establishing a utopian health care system. Danielson shows that the development of equal rural and urban health care, preventative health on a community basis, and the adjustment in health care to fit the needs of the people were dependent on such societal changes as the tossing out of the conservatives, the restructuring of medical schools, the change in the socioeconomic structure, and the centralization of the health care system. I suspect that numbers of health care systems can undergo radical change if we can get that kind of societal revolution. However, we're not going to get that kind of revolution in a large number of countries in which the topian health care system is currently providing inadequate care. What can be done to make positive changes in health care systems in the absence of revolutionary societal change?

There are many programs in the United States that at least superficially have similar goals to those described for health programs in Cuba. Community health, community mental health, and community psychiatry are all efforts to make health care accessible to, controlled by, and sensitive to consumers. However, it is clear that these programs become easily sabotaged by the very institutions that develop them. Since these programs by their very nature threaten the existence of the broader health care system, every effort is made once they are established to see that they are blocked in achieving their goals. This may partially account for why medical anthropologists and other applied social scientists have such a difficult time in relating even to these "new community oriented health programs."

Guttmacher and Garcia describe a much greater integration between social science research and health care practice in the post-revolutionary stage. They believe that the health care system is much more open to the input of medical social scientists as it reflects ways to more effectively provide health care services to the people. Based on their paper it is clear that when we can transform the societal and health care system, we as medical social scientists can have a much greater role in the post-revolutionary society, if we are still around, of course.

The papers on Cuba, because they are expansive reviews of the health care system, fail to give us a real sense of what health care means on an everyday basis in a particular locale. Both articles are completely positive in their evaluation of Cuba's health care system. Surely there are some negative elements of health care even after the revolution has taken place.

Another point made in this group of papers is the role of culture in understanding health practices and beliefs for a consumer population. Onoge and Urdaneta make the point that culture is overrated as an explanative device for why traditional populations do not accept new kinds of health practices. Their view is that the attitudes and cultural practices of Africans and Chicanos are the primary explanative device for why health innovations are not readily accepted. As a result the failure to adopt Western medical practices produces a situation described by Onoge as "blaming the victim." This view asks the consumer: "How can you possibly turn down this perfectly brilliant health care system that we have made available for you?" There must be something in the consumers' culture, says this approach, which keeps them from accepting this new development in health care.

We as medical social scientists are frequently asked to answer just this question: "What cultural factors keep our health service system from being accepted in this community?" I would like to suggest, and I think I would be supported by both these authors, that if we were to do more consumer-oriented research, more advocacy research, we wouldn't be asking this kind of question at all. We would rather be seeking answers to the question of how we can get societal and health care institutions to provide the kind of health services that the consumers themselves feel they need. Onoge rightfully points to the fact that because medical social scientists receive their support from establishment societal institutions they get stuck in seeking answers to institution-oriented questions rather than doing research on consumer-oriented questions. Perhaps such an orientation on the part of medical social scientists can create positive and utopian changes in the delivery of health care while we wait for revolutionary societal change.

*Social Science in Health Research*

SALLY GUTTMACHER: In reading the papers in this section it becomes obvious that attempted solutions to health problems reflect political ideology, and will differ, depending in part upon the degree of centralized social and economic planning. I have chosen for discussion a few points that I personally find interesting among the many made in these papers.

First, I will consider the problem of affecting MOTIVATIONS toward positive health behavior. In the paper by Reitz, "The use of social research in population programs in India," motivation related to family planning is examined. India's largely unchecked population growth is commonly seen as a major hindrance to her development. It is hardly controversial to state that family planning in India has not been a resounding success. Reitz discusses the use of social science studies in predicting the effectiveness of proposed policies and in evaluating existing programs. He points out that different approaches to the problem depend upon the target population. Reitz dichotomizes this population into one segment which is, to some extent, motivated to have fewer children but lacks the knowledge and techniques to act, and the other segment which lacks motivation as well as knowledge. The problem, in motivating the latter group, is to choose the most effective type of incentive for a largely illiterate, non-unified population. Decreasing population growth is in the interest of India's national development, but not clearly in the immediate self-interest of the group whose family planning behavior is seen by experts as less than optimal. It is hardly likely that the enormous gap which exists in India between the small wealthy class and the rest of the population will be narrowed in the foreseeable future by the poor having fewer children. It is also uncertain that the economic and social development of the country will be of benefit chiefly to those toward whom family planning programs are directed, as opposed, for example, to the large landholders or industrialists.

Given India's overall social and economic orientation, then, the use of economic incentives as a tool for motivating the rural and indigent poor to have fewer children is perhaps realistic and possibly feasible. The benefits derived from a change in behavior patterns will at least be perceived to be in the immediate self-interest of the target population. However, one might worry about both practical and human implications when material incentives are seen as the only effective vehicle for changing popular behavior patterns. For example, a program which relies on economic incentives may prove too expensive for a poor country to maintain on a national scale. It is doubtful that there would be any permanent effects on behavior if such a program cannot be maintained consistently for such a substantial period of time that the induced behavior becomes the acceptable social norm. Further, the reliance on immediate self-interest may foster the development of an individual rather than a social orientation.

Although Cuba uses both material and moral incentives, she has chosen to minimize the use of the former and instead to motivate socially conscious behavior largely through the use of public recognition and educational programs. An example of the mix can be seen in the area of health where the allocation of diapers and baby bottles (material incentives) is carried out at pre-natal clinics when mothers come in for their check-ups. However, under the moral incentive system, workers are also given points toward awards for merit and distinction for attending annual health check-ups. The interesting point is that programs aimed at motivating socially desirable behavior, including health behavior, are a function of ideology and social and economic development.

In the paper on "The role of applied research in the development of health services in a Chicano community in Chicago," Schensul and Bymel also touch on problems of motivation of health behavior; however, in this case the focus is on the community rather than the individual. The paper examines the dynamics involved in the evolution of a community mental health center. One of the initial problems in the establishment of the center was that of community interest and involvement. Although it was not the anthropologists' responsibility to improve the functioning of the center, they did find a way to make a positive contribution to its development by offering technical expertise in the formation of proposals for government funding. This kind of participant observation has unique implications for future social responsibility of researchers in applied social science.

The anthropologists suggest that the center's success in funding was largely political, due to the fact that the militancy of the community had become perceived as a political threat. If such funding is largely politically motivated, then it is in danger of being terminated for the same type of reasons. For example, there is always a threat of funding being cut or terminated if community activism becomes diverted or lessens. The result of this situation is that often more time and energy go into getting such programs funded and operating and in maintaining the funding than go into developing and delivering services. In addition, a community which is well-enough organized to apply for funding and to be perceived as a political threat may have less real need than people of a similar economic level who lack the expertise, organization, and leadership to articulate their needs. That services in the United States are too frequently set up in response to reasons other than greatest need is a result of the lack of centralized planning.

The final area I want to touch upon is evaluation research. The theory and methodology of evaluation research has been a recent major interest for applied social science in the United States. Although much good work has already been carried out in this relatively new field, as Ricci and Nesbit point out in their paper, "Policy/evaluation research: some methodological and political issues," initiation, funding, and termination of a program are too often based on political determinants rather than on the results of good research. If most of us involved in this research agree that this is the case, then should we not devote some energy to reversing this trend? We must constantly ask ourselves: is the effort we extend really intended to benefit the recipients of services and programs, or is it to benefit ourselves, the evaluation researchers, in terms of data and publications?

## AUDIENCE COMMENTS

LAWRENCE MALCOLM: The following are some health planning procedures that we've engaged in Papua, New Guinea. I'm speaking as an epidemiologist and head of the health planning unit of Papua New Guinea. We've embarked on the development of a health plan this year to provide for comprehensive health care for the whole country. The process we have adopted tries to involve people as much as possible in the planning for their future. We've been given the support of a strong government framework for this and the government of Papua has given us a motto which I think is very similar to the Tanzanian motto — "Equality and Self-Help" — as the basis within which health planning is to be established. The procedure so far has been to define health in local anthropological terms, a definition of health and a concept of health which have a very large social component. That is, we define the problems impairing health and well-being as they have been defined, and set up a series of objectives and priorities. This includes prominently the importance of traditional medicine within this set of objectives and the integration of traditional medicine with the Western model. Recognizing important elements of traditional medicine which can be utilized in improving and maintaining health in the community, community participation plays an important part in the integration of curative and preventive medicine in the design of their health plan. We have involved the health professionals as much as possible. A series of committees has been set up so that people will be involved in making decisions about the system, in other words choosing their own future and sorting out the needs as they see them within the health system. We have been fortunate in New Guinea to have "barefoot" doctors for more than 25 years. The use of auxiliaries has been an important element in the system. It has been important in the past and will certainly play a significant role in the future. Perhaps I'm not describing what might be a utopian system but certainly we've been very fortunate in this country to be able to make choices about our future health care system which have not been possible in some other countries.

Ross Danielson: I am struck with the impression that the review of my paper sounded rather like myself when I returned from Cuba, that is, speaking in broad general terms that make the health system in a country which parades a lot of ideological trappings seem unreal to outsiders. This is necessarily true — because how else can one define a new system except in terms of models, abstract categories, and maybe slogans and clichés? It is for this reason that I should emphasize what I discovered after trying to use the clichés: The clichés have meaning because they exist in a historical context that is just impossible to communicate in the simple structural models. What is significant is that the models grew out of a process of social antagonism. In trying to see present models as the product of pre-revolutionary social antagonisms and consequent change, we are fortunate to have the very fine analysis by Segovia and Gómez of the incredible system which survives today in Argentina, for present-day Argentina is rather like pre-revolutionary Cuba. Services vary greatly by social class of the patient, and the entrepreneurial medical profession ranges from the familiar push-cart solo practitioner to a more advanced push-cart industry of clinics and pre-paid medical plans, a petty capitalism of services where an elite of owner-physicians stands apart from a larger mass of worker-physicians. So in Cuba, the present structural model is real because it has been defined in a process of resolving real contradictions — between rural scarcity and urban disorganized concentration, between sophisticated and unsophisticated services, and so forth. Models are real in history and there is still going to be history. There are today contradictions and difficulties, and these problems in the present system are the point of departure for tomorrow. But the irony underlying my argument is that our UNAVOIDABLE language of models tends to ignore or even to hide the PROCESS of history — the very substance which lends reality to models in the first place.

STEVE SCHENSUL: In Chicago, every health, mental health, and "helping" program produces a general description of its services. From these general descriptions, every program looks fantastic and it becomes awfully difficult for us to criticize these "perfect" programs. However, their actual operation is less than perfect and in many cases pretty awful. There is no question that Cuba has developed a revolutionary health care system. However, we know it's not perfect. It seems to me that as medical social scientists we must produce something more than publicity releases. I think your paper was much more extensive but it does not include enough information on HOW the system actually works. What I'm interested in is the next instalment in which you would present the health care system in context. In other words, I would like to see how one health clinic operates in a neighborhood in Havana or in a village in a rural area.

ROSS DANIELSON: I was surprised to discover this year that in the very same year that I went to visit Cuba (1968) a colleague of mine was busy consulting in South Vietnam. He was a volunteer, in conjunction with USAID, the American Medical Association, and the Thieu regime volunteering to help South Vietnam. I think that this is another contrast in our discussion of topias and utopias, for what does this anthropologist have to say? Well, this anthropologist, after several visits to South Vietnam, has said "no" to child health clinics, idealistically and even successfully planned in other poor nations by medical anthropologists. He said "no" because the clinics would fit into the "unstable" social elements that will create greater contradictions for the regime in South Vietnam. This is the appropriate kind of contrast to our "utopias" for it helps us keep in mind the social context that underlies the real possibilities in the health sector.

## SUMMARY STATEMENTS

OMAFUME ONOGE: I want to make a brief comment and begin by reminding comrades here of what Marx and Engels wrote in the *Communist manifesto* (I will just quote an excerpt) — "the bourgeoisie has stripped off its halo every occupation hitherto honored and looked up to with reverent awe. It has converted the physician, the lawyer, the priest, the poet, the man of science into its paid wage laborer." I think in many cases this is very crucial, if we as medical sociologists or anthropologists want to move beyond utopia to the radical utopian conceptions of health care. I want to make one small point which is critical, which I think will help us to alleviate the pessimism which Stephen Schensul has been indicating in his remarks. Here we can rely on bourgeois medical anthropologists. In pre-capitalist societies, concerning the issue of public health, I think there is strong evidence to support the premise that the only limitation, the only disability which the people living in pre-capitalist communities experienced, was the limitation of knowledge, i.e. technological. For example, if a society does not have the technology to make a microscope, it cannot have a germ theory of disease. So the limits were limits of knowledge — technical knowledge. But whatever limited amount of medical knowledge was available, it was accessible to every member of the community. Now, in the capitalist societies in which we find ourselves in this epoch, we find that this is no longer so. Although there is now an increase in the fund of medical knowledge and public health care techniques, a major disability has arisen. Accessibility to that growth in human knowledge is now restricted to the client that can pay. The profit motive intervenes and interrupts the humane motive of wanting to make people well. Take America — as far as I know the American society, the American nation has enough resources, enough know-how to double its medical and para-medical personnel almost overnight. I think in terms of cash and technological know-how — America has it. But we know that it will not do this and it has not done it precisely because the profit motive continues to intervene in the process. The American Medical Association is not going to allow that kind of dabbling. In the drug industry, there is research that shows that even when a new drug has been developed it is suppressed until the old stock of inferior drugs has been sold out. In the new colonies in the Third World the situation is even more desperate. We find ourselves spending a lot of money to buy anti-malarial drugs made from herbs which grow in our own environment. There are now plantations owned by foreign monopoly capitalists. The herbs have to be transported to the West, reduced into tablets, and then we buy them back at expensive prices. Our environments are being poisoned in various ways. This is not a question of cultural nationalism. What I am focusing on is capitalism. Capitalist relationships in a country like Nigeria render all our utopian dreams of improved health care impossible. Indications we get from places like China, Cuba, and perhaps Tanzania are that the whole of medical knowledge and social science knowledge about improved health care is being made available to the people. We must also be involved in the talk in reorganizing the social system of those places. The social organization has to be taken care of, and I think right now we have to supersede it in the Third World. Within Africa we must supersede capitalist societies. It is only in replacement of capitalist societies, that is capitalist relationships where the profit motive does not intervene in the humane ways for improving the health of people, that our utopian prescription or models can work. I conclude by saying again, in disagreement with Schensul, the situation is not pessimistic at all. I think the capitalist world order is creaking and cracking, and whether we like it or not, the people will overcome it.

ALANAGH RAIKES: Innovations in health care in capitalist societies have come about through wars and epidemics. In Britain the public health services and concern grew up in the epidemics that took place in the nineteenth and twentieth centuries. It was only then that water sanitation became important because death through plague and disease did not respect social class. People who were in the nobility were dying the same as poor people. Innovations in health care in the capitalist system today have come about during wars, when countries want to keep their soldiers healthy. There are countries where the whole social system has changed through a revolutionary process. When a revolutionary process has taken place, the health services as a subunit within the system can be radically changed. People can choose, and they have chosen in the countries that we've talked about. In Tanzania, the country that I have been working in, they have made choices. They have articulated the costs of health care and the priorities of the nation. Tanzania has nearly 14 million people, and is one of the poorest countries in the world and one of the poorest countries in Africa. They've decided to spend their very limited resources on preventive health care for the majority of the population. At the time of independence in Tanzania, which was just 10 years ago, there were fourteen doctors. That was after many, many years of colonial rule. Today they're spending what little resources they have on preventive medicine, that is, on health education and on immunization campaigns. There isn't a success story yet, but they are aiming at having a socialist health policy.

STAN INGMAN: The remaining papers in the anthology all point to the actual or potential gains to be derived from people, or client-oriented health care systems, in contradistinction to professional, or expert-dominated systems. While these papers can be viewed as anti-professional in emphasis, more fundamentally the remaining papers demonstrate contradictions between service and social stratification. Many professionals, employing the mystique of their expertise to obtain power and position, have permitted themselves to be coopted into the alienation of the social class struggle. In so doing, they became incapacitated, and even at times unwilling, to serve their fellow citizens with their full measure.

In colonial Tanzania, described by Janaki N. Tschannerl, the health care system, though limited to a relatively sophisticated curative system of medical care services, was primarily designed for and utilized by the colonizers and their local assistants. Historically, it is important to note that only years after independence did Tanzania shed the value systems that had served to legitimate the previous focus on curative medical care services. As Omafume Onoge points out, many African countries, although independent, still adhere to these prior "world views" and madly continue to struggle to develop sophisticated surgical and medical care specialties. As can be deduced from Ian Lawson's paper, India too suffers from the same misplaced national priorities. Although India has more medical schools than most developing societies, they actually function as inhibitive on the country and its health care system. The medical educational systems in India, Africa, and the United States, while under professional domination, serve to train and socialize young physicians in such a way as to make them unable and unwilling to serve the needs of the general population, whether in the cities or the rural areas.

Philip Singer and Enrique Araneta critically analyze the role of WHO in stimulating the growth of irrelevant psychiatric services in a country like Guyana. They call for a merger between the forces of community development, public health, and psychiatry. While a community focus is understood by WHO, the authors show how the program they support still remains a "static, service-oriented" one. Singer and Araneta point to the uncritical acceptance of the "medical, dyadic helping relationship" which they see as the antithesis to community psychiatry. They point to a program in a mental hospital in Guyana where policies were altered to meet community and cultural expectations. A basic policy shift was instituted in the power relationship between therapists and patients as well as between the hospital and the community. The boundaries between the two "worlds" became less marked and local healers were integrated into the therapeutic process.

Similarly, Rance Lee in "Toward the convergence of modern and traditional Chinese medical services in Hong Kong" documents the extent of convergence between the two medical care systems and examines the potentialities for their further integration. The past and present domination of Hong Kong by Western administrations and Western thought is shown to be one of the major obstacles inhibiting the transformation of the present order or topia. Another illustration of the colonizers' inability to provide the fundamental and requisite changes is seen in Frank Kehl's description of public housing policy in Hong Kong. He gradually illustrates how bourgeois solutions (counter-utopian) continually failed to improve the overall life of the squatters. Hong Kong's social planners did manage to protect many generations of colonizers from being expelled, even though the housing situation became more and more exasperating. As Kehl indicates, a convincing parallel can be drawn between the housing policy in 20th-century Hong Kong and housing programs of 19th-century Europe.

While British colonialism in Hong Kong is explicit in its impact, Anthony Thomas shows how newly independent countries presently suffer from their past colonial history. Even with "radical changes in the façade," Kenya after a decade of political independence still retains the structures of the pre-colonial period. While a regional structure from primary to tertiary care units exists on paper, essentially a two-class care system still exists. The neighborhood health centers where the lower class receive their care remain essentially isolated and undersupervised. Few referrals are made to the next level of services and many illegal home treatment centers exist where "modern" controlled medicine is dispensed. Thomas, unlike Rance Lee, argues that the British colonial policy was served by protecting local healers as a part of an attempt to arrest the acculturation and to suppress the development of modern felt needs in the native population. For other reasons today the policy still seems to exist in Kenya. Instead of allowing the present pluralistic-non-system to continue, Thomas sees that a blend of centralization and decentralization ought to be instituted so that responsibility and accountability can be determined. As in Tanzania, Nigeria, and India, Kenya must not continue to maintain a sophisticated, curative level of medical care services directed to its upper classes. This commitment can and should be reflected in its medical educational program, as discussed by Tschannerl, Raikes, Onoge, and Danielson.

As Thomas sees the need for accountability in Kenya, Elling points to the problems encountered in establishing regional authorities where public responsibility becomes viable and institutionalized. Robert Dyck displays some of the potential gains which are realizable under strong regional organization and which, to some extent, are realized in Slovenia, Yugoslavia, a relatively old socialist system: (1) improved preventive medical care; (2) functional integration of health with other programs; (3) combined health care and environmental health program planning; and finally, (4) realization of Stampar's elusive concept of "positive" health.

As Dyck underscores the importance of the balanced decentralization in Slovenia, Ian Lawson compares India, Scotland, and the United States with respect to their individual ability to deliver and organize medical care services. A reliable indicator of the quality of these different systems is their ability to provide medical care for unpopular clients, i.e. elderly, poor, and the chronically ill. It became quite clear that some type of regional authority which controls health care resources and sets priorities is crucial and must be established. Public accountability can, at least, help prevent so-called "marginal medicine" from falling into the crack.

## REFERENCES

ALSOP, STEWART
    1973   "President Agnew?" *Newsweek* (July 30):76.
BARAN, PAUL
    1969   *The longer view: essays toward a critique of political economy.* New York: Monthly Review Press.
LANDAUER, GUSTAV
    1923   *Die Revolution*, volume thirteen: *Die Gesellschaft*. Edited by Martin Buber. Frankfurt.
MANNHEIM, KARL
    1936   *Ideology and utopia.* New York: Harcourt, Brace and World.
MARX, KARL, FRIEDRICH ENGELS
    1948   *The communist manifesto.* New York: International.

PART ONE

*Interest Groups and the Allocation of Health Care*

# Birth Planning:
# Between Neglect and Coercion

STEVEN POLGAR

Between 1962 and 1972, large-scale programs for natality regulation have changed from something that few people would support (or even talk about) to a major policy instrument of the United States government for poor people both inside the country and abroad. Several European countries, particularly Britain, Sweden, Holland, and Denmark, as well as the United Nations and its associated agencies, have also become involved in population and family planning programs. This rapid metamorphosis is indeed astonishing. International funds available for bilateral and multilateral efforts in this field are fast approaching the magnitude of expenditures for all other health programs, and, within the United States Agency for International Development, have already surpassed them. Why has this change occurred?

Some would look to "factual" and humanitarian causes: that population was growing in a number of countries almost as fast as average income; that the export of "death control" from the metropolitan countries was a double-edged sword if "birth control" was not exported as well; that new techniques of contraception made mass programs feasible; that surveys showed families in many "developing" countries wanted fewer births than was the average they would have by the end of the childbearing period; that infant mortality could be reduced if births took place further apart; and so on.

Others see less praiseworthy reasons: the preservation of the privileged status of the industrialized countries; a distraction from efforts to liberate and develop the economies of ex-colonial nations; the brainchild of a small interlocking directorate of reactionaries and their helpmates; the prelude to a new wave of colonization from the rich countries occupying sparsely populated areas in the Third World; an attack on the virility and femininity of politically emergent people; a cheap substitute for more positive types of international assistance; and so forth.

To answer my own question about the causes for this sudden change I first will take a quick and rather ethnocentric[1] excursion into the history of birth planning,[2] and then analyze some of the forces operating on the current scene. It is appropriate, I think, before proceeding, to sketch in my own background in this field. In 1956 while I was studying public health, one of my professors argued, convincingly to me, that the population problem was the most important problem in public health. When I joined the faculty of a school of public health in 1959 I wanted to do a study on family planning. My boss demurred because both the head of the university and the governor of the state were Catholics; if we wanted to be accepted as behavioral scientists in this school, family planning would be a poor topic for research. So the study came to focus on prenatal care, but I did ask some questions about prior contraceptive use. In 1963 I joined the Planned Parenthood Federation of America as its Director of Research. And since 1967 I have been affiliated with the Carolina Population Center, working for the last two years mainly with universities in Africa. Thus I think it is fair to say that I am an "insider" in population family planning circles. But as birth planning has attracted an increasingly large and vocal following, I have come to feel more and more a member of a shrinking minority of "non-Malthusians" within this circle.


BIRTH PLANNING BEFORE 1800


The cultural regulation of reproduction, as I have stressed elsewhere (Polgar 1972), has been a very long-standing feature of human groups. In the gathering-hunting stage of evolution, apart from the increases when new ecological zones were entered, cultural and biological forces kept natality close to the replacement level. With the change to food production, local birth rates increased perhaps as much as a hundredfold over a period of a few thousand years. The development of state societies,

---

[1]   I will concentrate on Britain and the United States because I am most familiar with the literature in English, because Malthusianism is most prominent in these two countries, and because of the Anglo-American influence in the Third World today on population matters.
[2]   "Birth planning" is a term coined by Edward Pohlman (1969); it combines birth control and population planning. The two latter concepts should be clearly distinguished in many contexts; sometimes, however, it is efficient to combine them.

empires, colonialism, and mercantilism spurred further increases, but due to the less radical alteration of the subsistence base and to the ravages of great epidemics, populations increased "only" about tenfold. Industrialization and economic colonialism in recent times have led to further growth — at a rate which is now causing much alarm.

The proselytizing religions which developed in state societies all include exhortations such as "be fruitful and multiply and replenish the earth" to promote natality. Notice the term "replenish" which is presumably a reference to catastrophic population losses. But more fundamental, I think, is the pressure exerted by the central authority in a redistribution system to expand the numbers of those paying tribute, taxes, and tithes. Economic decisions are largely centralized, but reproduction, necessarily, still takes place in individual conjugal units.

The Judeo-Christian tradition has an additional feature that is relevant here because it is the tradition of Malthus and of most population/family planning advocates today. This has to do with sexuality. Although pronatalist statements occur in all the major religions, the Judeo-Christian tradition has been unique in linking contraception to "immorality." The Biblical passage on Onan, for example, can be interpreted as showing divine displeasure with a man who refuses to follow the rules of the levirate, but most commentators have regarded the "sin" at issue as contraception (coitus interruptus, in particular, although many use "onanism" to refer to masturbation). A major impetus against contraception in Christianity came with the influence of Thomas Aquinas, who strongly argued that intercourse not aimed at the generation of offspring was a vice against nature. The opposition from Christian denominations was unbroken until 1925 when the Quakers declared themselves in favor of birth control under certain conditions. Then in 1929 the Federal Council of Churches of Christ in America advocated fewer children for each mother and in 1930 the highly significant Lambeth Conference of Anglican Bishops held the sex act to be as important for marital love as for procreation (a theological position adopted also by the Second Vatican Conference three decades later).

Egyptian developments from before 1000 B.C. are customarily accorded a place by Western writers in the history of their own civilization. Thus Himes's monumental review of contraception (1963) starts the chapter on "Contraceptive technique in antiquity (Western World)" with descriptions of Egyptian papyri that contain information on vaginal plugs and other contraceptives. The "ancient" Greeks discussed the question of ideal population size, as well as contraception and abortion, in quite a few writings (Hutchinson 1967: 9–13). The prohibition on prescribing an abortifacient, preserved in the modern-day Hippocratic oath, referred to post-"animation" abortions only and was apparently one of several conflicting opinions on the subject. Of the many Greek and Roman writers of "antiquity," Himes is most impressed with Soranus of Ephesus who described many methods of birth control, distinguished between contraception and abortion, and discussed indications and contra-indications for each (1963: 88–92).

In the Middle Ages the scientific tradition with which Westerners identify was maintained by Islamic scholars who also wrote quite a bit on birth control. Ibn Sina (Avicenna) was clearly among those who "considered the prevention of conception a legitimate part of medical practice" (Himes 1963: 142). In European writings from the Middle Ages and through the eighteenth century, Himes was able to find little more than magical means for preventing conception, and he turned instead to the folk traditions of peasants in the late nineteenth and twentieth centuries and to the history of the condom, which was used to prevent infection rather than pregnancy (1963: 170–206). In their extensive search of the French literature Bergues et al. (1960: 75–119) found medical writings on the mechanisms of conception, the causes of sterility and abnormal offspring, and the determination of gender and accidental abortions, but nothing on birth control. Evidence that induced abortion, contraception, and infant abandonment were practiced at this time, mostly in illicit unions before the seventeenth century and increasingly among married couples thereafter, can be found in other types of historical sources (Bergues, et al. 1960: 121–189; Fryer 1966: 24–32).

## MALTHUS, POVERTY, AND INDUSTRIAL CAPITALISM

I noted that population dynamics had been discussed by some "ancient" Greeks; it was also a topic for Islamic scholars such as ibn-Khaldun in the Middle Ages, Machiavelli, and many others. The symbolic significance of Malthus, however, for our current population policies in the Western world surpasses that of all previous writers as well as of most subsequent ones (see Hutchinson 1967 for a review of population theories in the Western tradition prior to 1900). Malthus's writings on population theory were by no means original, but his ideas found large receptive audiences from 1800 on for reasons I will try to indicate.

Malthus's primary concern was not the regulation of population in general, but the regulation of the poor (Beales 1959; Meek 1971). In contrast to some utopians of his day (against whose arguments he explicitly aimed the first edition of his *Essay on the principle of population* published in 1798) Malthus wrote that poverty stems from the laws of nature. The discrepancy, he argued, between the powers of reproduction and the possible expansion of food production will inevitably frustrate all attempts at obtaining equality among men. To give relief to the poor would only encourage them to have more children; rather they should be exhorted to delay marriage. Malthus saw population control as important to forestall revolutions such as the one of 1789 in France.

Demographers and economic historians have argued endlessly about whether the growth of population in England after 1740 was due to a rising birth rate or a falling death rate and whether it was stimulated by industrialization or allowed industrialization to happen (see Glass and Eversley 1965). One of the most convincing analyses of population growth during this period is that of Langer (1963) who assigns a major role to the spread of potato cultivation. Langer shows that despite numerous epidemics and the widespread abandonment of infants, population grew from 1750 to 1850, very fast relative to earlier periods, not just in England but also in many European countries which did not industrialize until quite a bit later.

Malthus's writings should be seen in the context of this spurt in population and of the rise of industrial capitalism. Polanyi (1944) has argued that by 1800 both land and money, but not yet human labor, had been transformed into market commodities. As the feudal system became weaker, the cultivators started to move away from the manor, both socially and physically. In the towns the guilds had little ability to absorb new entrants beyond their own descendants. The Elizabethan poor laws were stretched to cover more people, including many who were able-bodied, and at the same time vagrancy laws were made more severe and workers' associations were prohibited (Beales 1959; Chambliss 1964). As more and more of the commons came under enclosure and as agricultural prices, colonialist successes, and long-distance trade fluctuated, the problem of unemployment became worse. On the manor the peasants may have starved, but they were not categorized as "poor." Poverty was not only a low level of consumption, but also the social condition of being unattached. Punitive laws, aid-in-wages, and make-work schemes were only stop-gap measures.

When Malthus wrote his *Essay* industrial capitalism even in England had not yet fully developed. Colonialism and mercantilism, together with the enclosure movement and the rise in population, were crucial in the transformation of human labor into a commodity:

The explanation [of increasing poverty] lies primarily in the excessive fluctuations of trade in early times which tended to cover up the absolute increase in trade. While the latter accounted for the rise in employment, the fluctuations accounted for the much bigger rise in unemployment. But while the increase in the general level of employment was slow, the increase in unemployment and underemployment would tend to be fast. Thus the building up of what Friedrich Engels called the industrial reserve army outweighed by much the creation of the industrial army proper (Polanyi 1944:91).

The final and necessary step in creating a working class and a market economy was the poor law reform of 1834:

The new law provided that in the future no outdoor relief should be given.... Aid-in-wages was, of course, discontinued. The workhouse test was reintroduced, but in a new sense. It was now left to the applicant to decide whether he was so utterly destitute of all means that he would voluntarily repair to a shelter which was deliberately made into a place of horror.... (Polanyi 1944:101–102).

Malthus's influence, both through the general arguments of his *Essay* and through his specific opposition to Samuel Whitehead's reform bill (Malthus 1959), was "the spirit behind the Poor Law Amendment Act" (Beales 1959).

Engels and Marx, in numerous places in their writings between 1841 and 1882, condemned Malthus as a plagiarist, an advocate for the interests of the landed aristocracy and, for the most part, a shoddy economist. For them a "superfluous" population (the "reserve army of the unemployed") was both a product of capitalism (through mechanization, boom-and-bust cycles, urban migration, etc.) and essential to its system of exploiting workers (Meek 1971).

## MALTHUSIANS AND NEO-MALTHUSIANS IN BRITAIN AND THE UNITED STATES: 1797–1939

Malthus, of course, was adamantly opposed to contraception. But not so some of his contemporaries. Jeremy Bentham in 1797, a year before the first edition of Malthus's *Essay* was published, advocated the use of birth control (with the sponge method) to reduce the birth rates of the poor (Himes 1963:211). Francis Place, who published "Illustrations and proofs of the principle of population" in 1822 and a number of handbills addressed to working people, was, according to Himes, the founder of the birth control movement (1963:212). Although Place, who started as a journeyman breeches-maker and later became a prosperous tradesman, repeated some of Malthus's arguments, he not only recommended several methods of contraception, but also asserted that birth limitation would help raise the workers' wages, reduce hours of work, and allow earlier marriage without fear of having too many children (Fryer 1966: 45–57). Some of Place's immediate followers were working-class reformers of a radical bent, such as Carlile, Hassell, and Campion, who were sent to jail on free-thought charges, but not for advocating birth control (Himes 1963: 220–222).

Several people in the United States were influenced by Place and Carlile. Most prominent among them were Robert Dale Owen (son of Robert Owen) who published *Moral physiology* in 1830 and Charles Knowlton (a philosophical materialist and physician who was prosecuted several times). Knowlton's *Fruits of philosophy* was probably the most important publication on contraception in the nineteenth century. R. D. Owen saw contraception as a step in the progress of mankind toward rational liberty; Knowlton advocated it on medical, eugenic, social, and economic grounds (Himes 1963: 224–230; Fryer 1966: 99–106).

Judging by the literature in English he had researched, Himes felt that "with the passage of the Reform Bill in 1832 and the Poor Law in 1834, the public agitation for birth control died down" (1963: 231). Population growth, colonial expansion, and the development of industrial capitalism all accelerated in the next half century. With the demand for cheap labor growing both in the industrializing countries and in the colonies, it is not surprising that attention to death control was much greater than to birth control. And working-class people, while buying some of the pamphlets on contraception, saw unionization (Chartism) as a more relevant solution to their most pressing problems (Fryer 1966: 107).

Upwardly mobile middle-class families in England in the latter half of the nineteenth century intensified their efforts to reduce childbearing (Banks 1954) as did some groups of small landowners in several areas on the continent (Carlsson 1966; Demeny 1968). In France, of course, the birth rate had been declining steadily since the 1770's, with large segments of the population joining the new trend toward smaller families after the 1789 revolution. In neither France nor Britain, however, was there much heard from the medical profession, the one exception being George Drysdale who advocated Malthusianism on economic grounds but was a radical on the subject of marriage (Himes 1963: 233).

In 1873 the federal Comstock Law was passed in the United States (followed by many similar state laws) which included literature on contraception and abortion among obscene materials whose dissemination was prohibited. Edward Bliss Foote, a doctor who had started out as a printer, was prosecuted and fined in 1876 for advocating contraception in various publications (Himes 1963: 277). In England in 1877 and 1878, Edward Truelove (an elderly free-thought publisher), Charles Bradlaugh (a publisher and member of Parliament), and Annie Besant (a writer) were brought to trial on charges connected with disseminating Knowlton's *Fruits of philosophy* The publicity related to these trials apparently helped to increase greatly the sale of this and other writings on birth planning.

The Malthusian League was founded shortly after the trial in 1878, with Dr. Charles Drysdale (brother of George) and Mrs. Besant its first officers. The League sponsored lectures and distributed pamphlets. Although no medical services were given, a Medical Branch was formed and an International Medical Congress held in London in 1881 (Himes 1963: 256–257). Drysdale, Foote, Bradlaugh, Besant, and their associates were clearly "Neo-Malthusian" in orientation, combining a concern for overpopulation, particularly among the poor, with strong advocacy of contraception. They also had some ties with the feminist movement, e.g. the active part taken in the Malthusian League by Dr. Alice Drysdale-Vickery, who was married to Dr. Charles Drysdale (however, see Banks and Banks [1964] on the divergent programs of the two groups in Victorian England).

Despite the interest of a few physicians, including at least one highly placed figure in Holland (Himes 1963: 258), official medical circles ranged from neutral to hostile on the issue of contraception, not only in the nineteenth century (Himes 1963: 282–284; Fryer 1966: 119–131) but well into the twentieth (Fryer 1966: 198–199; Kennedy 1970: 172–217).

The story of Margaret Sanger is well known. Daughter of an upstate New York stonemason, trained nurse, briefly an eclectic socialist, she became a tireless crusader for birth control (an expression she and a group of friends originated). By her own account, the turning point that launched her on this crusade was the death, from an attempted abortion, of Sadie Sachs, a resident of a tenement on New York's Lower East Side (Kennedy 1970: 16–17). Margaret Sanger was influenced by the radical ideas of Emma Goldman, Rosa Luxemburg, and Anatole France, tutored in the history of Malthusianism and contraception by Havelock Ellis, and swayed by Dr. Johannes Rutgers of The Hague to favor the Mensinga diaphragm fitted in birth control clinics (Kennedy 1970: 20–32). From a "woman rebel," advocating sexual liberation and scorning the bourgeois capitalist order of society, Margaret Sanger moved rapidly to the right in the 1920's and 1930's, using Malthusian arguments on overbreeding among the poor and eugenicist appeals about the "menace of the feebleminded"; she even spoke for the substitution of the "efficient technique of stock-breeding" for welfare legislation (Kennedy 1970: 112–117). Yet she remained steadfast to the idea that birth control was an essential and powerful factor in the sexual emancipation of women (Kennedy 1970: 127–135).

In England the Malthusian League concentrated on antinatal propaganda until just before World War I, when it finally started to disseminate information on contraceptive methods (Fryer 1966: 235–240). Marie Stopes, botanist, poet, and playwright, was above all interested in freeing women to use their bodies as they saw fit; she opened the first birth control clinic in Britain in 1921, where the stress was on healthy children, and a somewhat anti-Malthusian position was taken (Fryer 1966: 223–234).

Holland was probably the country where systematic clinical work in contraception started (Himes 1963: 309). A great deal was published in nineteenth century Germany, both on Malthusianism and birth control (Himes 1963: 322–323). In Austria it is noteworthy that some anarchists (as in France, Britain, and the United States) were strongly favorable to birth control during the 1910's and 1920's (Himes 1963: 325).

## PHYSICIANS, CLINICS, AND TAX-SUPPORTED SERVICES

Despite the handful of physicians in the ranks of the Malthusian movement, the existence of clandestine medical abortionists, and the important role of a few pioneers in developing new methods of contraception, it is clear that the medical contribution to the spread of natality regulation prior to 1960 was small. Himes wrote that "the failure of the medical profession to accept leadership in contraceptive instruction has undoubtedly played a part in the tremendous increase in recent years in the commercial and sometimes anti-social dissemination of such advice" (1963: 326). Even as late as 1957, among women in metropolitan areas of the United States, only 16 percent of those using a method of contraception said they chose it because of a physician's recommendation (Westoff, et al. 1961: 364).

A study of private physicians in six localities in the northern part of the country by Cornish, Ruderman, and Spivack (1963) produced congruent results: only 27 percent of the medical men themselves thought most women got their information on contraception from doctors (1963: 19); only 29 percent of non-Catholic physicians (and 4 percent of the Catholics) thought providing contraceptive advice and information should be a standard procedure in the practice of medicine (1963: 31); and only 40 percent of non-Catholics (and 10 percent of Catholics) said they often or very frequently introduced the subject of contraception in the course of the premarital medical examination (1963: 48). In sum, this study showed that physicians were reluctant to provide help with family planning unless the patients specifically asked them and the patients in turn were reluctant to ask (1963: 66–67).

A survey of British physicians ten years later (Cartwright 1968) showed that only 23 percent would introduce the subject of birth control themselves with a woman just getting married, although 90 percent would do so with one who was married, had mitral stenosis, and two children. More recent studies in the United States, however, show considerable change in favor of a more active role among some groups of physicians (Wright, et al. 1968).

Kennedy (1970: 172–217) attributes the resistance to family planning among physicians in the United States in the 1920's and 1930's to a combination of factors: their attempt to build themselves up as scientific practitioners (trying to live down the widespread nineteenth-century criticism of quackery while birth control was associated with "troublemakers" like Margaret Sanger); their middle-class attitudes toward sexuality; their fear of being prosecuted under the Comstock laws; and the lack of contraceptives of proven safety and effectiveness. The sole methods they favored were abstinence ("Let Jake sleep on the roof" the doctor had said to Sadie Sachs, according to Margaret Sanger) and sterilization.

With accumulating knowledge about such methods as rhythm and the diaphragm and in response to the enormous growth in commercial sales of birth control materials, physician opposition relented somewhat in the 1930's, particularly in the prescription of birth control where "medical indications" were present. Such indications, of course, had been found with great facility when it came to performing hysterectomies on poor and black women. Sterilization as a "eugenic" measure has long enjoyed the favor of Social Darwinists in the United States (Hofstadter 1955; Paul 1967). Constructive (to use Marie Stopes' phrase) family planning services in tax-supported health facilities, in contrast, are still not accessible to many poor people. Clandestine abortion, meanwhile, has been widespread and those who could afford it could obtain it from qualified physicians.

In the United States, the number of birth control clinics affiliated with the Clinical Research Bureau and the American Birth Control League increased slowly from 1923 to 1939, when the two organizations merged. Then, with the war years, there was a sharp decline. In 1959 the Planned Parenthood Federation of America had ninety-four local affiliates while at the time of the merger the two organizations between them had 417 local units (Rein 1962: 17).

The various attempts to run family planning clinics in the United States, Britain, continental Europe, and elsewhere fell far short of expectations. In most cases the clientele consisted of women with a higher average level of income and education than the clinics' sponsors would have liked. Some clients were working class or poor but their numbers remained small until quite recently. (I have tried to show that this was largely due to factors in the methods offered and other aspects of the services, rather than to "lack of motivation" to plan births [Polgar 1966]; see also the critiques of clinics by Lafitte [1962]; Stycos [1963]; and Chandrasekaran and Kuder [1965].)

With federal funds appropriated for maternal and child health (and some support from Dr. Clarence Gamble's Pathfinder Fund) in 1937 and 1938, seven Southern states and Puerto Rico started to offer family planning services through local health departments. The number of people attracted to these tax-supported services remained very small. New clients admitted to the combined Charlotte and Mecklenburg County Health Departments in North Carolina, for example, fluctuated between 139 and 339 annually in the 1945–1961 period, but then rose quickly to over 1,500 in 1965 following the introduction of orals and IUD's (Corkey 1966).

A significant political battle was fought in New York City in the late 1950's concerning the unwritten ban on providing contraceptive services (and even discussing family planning) in municipal facilities. Sterilizations, of course, were done in most hospitals. Starting with quiet efforts by Dr. Louis M. Hellman to provide services in Kings County Hospital, Brooklyn, and a series of articles by Joseph Kahn in the *New York Post*, the controversy developed into an open confrontation between a broad alliance of medical, religious, and other community leaders orchestrated by Planned Parenthood versus the Catholic Archdiocese and ended with the lifting of the ban (Best 1959). But by the time the ban was lifted, the diabetic woman with two Caesarian sections who was the "test case" in the dispute had been sterilized. Spurred on by this victory and under an increasingly professionalized leadership, the Planned Parenthood Federation of America launched a nationwide campaign to stimulate more health departments to offer family planning services. Some prominent members of the American Public Health Association and other medical, religious, and welfare organizations were also instrumental in this effort. Responses to a questionnaire sent to state health departments show a gradual expansion of such services in the middle 1960's, particularly in the South and in California (Eliot, et al. 1966). Yet, the first really comprehensive review of the extent to which needed services were being met by organized programs shows that by 1967–1968 in two-thirds of the 3,072 counties in the nation, public health departments still provided no services (Center for Family Planning Program Development 1968: 8). Even in those counties where some services were reportedly offered, the number of clients usually remained very small.

Realizing that obstetric clinics might be a superior channel for reaching a large number of clients, both Planned Parenthood (Jaffe 1964, 1967) and the Population Council (Taylor and Berelson 1968) started to focus on large hospitals. In 1967–1968, however, of the nation's 4,305 nonprofit general care hospitals only 435 reported offering regular family planning services (Center for Family Planning Program Development 1969: 8). In the five years since this time substantial progress has been made, particularly in the large metropolitan areas. Thus, combining the reports for public and private clinics, hospitals, and private physicians, it was estimated that about one-half of all low-income women in need of subsidized services for family planning in the United States were receiving some medical help in 1971–1972 (Guttmacher 1973).

The fascinating combination of advocacy, indifference, and opposition to the expansion of family planning services is illustrated in a 1969 study of ten North Carolina counties. The author, a Canadian physician, identified eleven leaders who were instrumental in promoting the programs: six welfare officials, four health professionals and one president of a women's club (Measham 1972: 43). County commissioners approved of public family planning care because they thought it would reduce the cost of public assistance ('welfare'); in this context discriminatory attitudes were directed more toward the poor in general than specifically toward blacks (1972: 49–52). Opposition to the programs came from private physician groups who were concerned about the possible decrease of their income, and disliked "government medicine," although they favored family limitation for the indigent (1972: 52–54).

In Britain, the advocates of birth control services show a similar mixture of intentions. Secularism and anarchism provided the underlying philosophy for Richard Carlile and Guy Aldred, women's emancipation for Marie Stopes, liberalism for H. G. Wells, utilitarianism for Jeremy Bentham, and reactionary Malthusianism for Charles Drysdale and many others. There was a slow growth of private clinics in the 1920's (Fryer 1966: 250–256), but a campaign was also started to include family planning at government maternity and child welfare centers.

In 1924 two London boroughs controlled by the Labour Party set up birth control clinics in their maternity centers, but were stopped by the

Ministry of Health (Dowse and Peel 1965: 184–185). A bill in the House of Commons, introduced by a Labour member of Parliament in 1926, obtained 40 percent of Conservative, 47 percent of Labour and 33 percent of Liberal votes in favor of disseminating birth control through maternity and child welfare centers (Dowse and Peel 1965: 187). In 1930 these centers were permitted to give contraceptive advice to married women on medical indications, and the newly merged birth control organizations set about to persuade local councils to translate policy into action.

While the number of clinics increased and indications for service were liberalized in subsequent years, Dowse and Peel conclude that once it came close to achieving the goals set decades earlier, the family planning movement was reluctant to relinquish its control over services. And, as in the United States, surveys show that until recently clinics and physicians probably had a very limited impact on the contraceptive behavior of most British couples (Lewis-Fanning 1949: 50–55).

## COERCION, POPULATION CONTROL AND THE NEW COLONIALISM

(Le) paternalisme colonial crée les mêmes réflexes malthusiens que le paternalisme familial ou national: *du moment que les sujets deviennent des charges, l'accroissement de leur nombre devient un sujet de préoccupation;* une limitation pârait souhaitable, sinon du nombre lui-même, du moins du rythme de son développement. (Sauvy 1963:145. Original emphasis.)

The idea of using various kinds of constraints to prevent people from having children is, of course, not new. Although castration was not done for Malthusian purposes and chastity belts had nothing to do with the "iron law" of wages, C. A. Weinhold, a German Malthusian of early nineteenth-century vintage, urged that boys be required to wear a kind of ring over the penis from the age of fourteen until they had sufficient income to marry and have children (Himes 1963: 320).

In Britain and the United States the boundaries between eugenic and Malthusian proposals were not always distinct. There is indeed a close similarity between arguments put forward in the 1920's, like the one of the Committee to Study and Report on the Best Means of Cutting Off the Defective Germ-Plasm of the American Population that "Society must look upon germ-plasm as belonging to society and not merely to the individual who carries it" (see Paul 1967: 295), and those of current spokesmen such as Garrett Hardin:

How can we reduce reproduction?... But in the long run a purely voluntary system selects for its own failure: noncooperators outbreed cooperators. So what restraints shall we employ? A policeman under every bed?... We need not titillate our minds with such horrors, for we already have at hand an acceptable technology: sterilization.... If parenthood is only a privilege, and if parents see themselves as trustees of the germ plasm and guardians of the rights of future generations, then there is hope for mankind (Hardin 1970; see also Hardin 1968).

It is easy to guess, even if one did not know what Hardin was saying in private, that he is hinting that the white middle- and upper-class majority should impose sterilization on the poor, the blacks, and other minorities. Reviewing the history of sterilization in the United States in the twentieth century, Julius Paul (1967, 1968) shows how its intended victims are being shifted from the presumably feebleminded or mentally ill to parents receiving Aid for Dependent Children, particularly if the children are "illegitimate." While none of the punitive sterilization laws introduced in many state legislatures have so far been enacted and most judicial decisions on giving mothers a choice between being sterilized or going to jail were overturned, the agitation against AFDC and for "Zero Population Growth" has so intensified in the last five years that such proposals might well succeed in the near future.

There can be no doubt that racism has played an important part in the movement to expand birth control in the United States. Several large private donors to Planned Parenthood (including some members of the Mellon and Du Pont families) earmarked their gifts for "inner city" programs or for the hiring of Spanish-speaking staff. The first appropriation in Congress in 1962 for an explicitly designated family planning program was for Washington, D.C. (Piotrow 1973: 119); it was pushed through by the congressional committee on the District of Columbia on which bigoted Southerners are heavily represented. One should never forget, however, that liberals like Senator Gruening and Congressman Scheuer also played big roles in federal legislation in support of family planning (Piotrow 1973: 103–111). Time and again, political battles on natality regulation have brought together some strange bedfellows!

For a long time, most academics concerned with demographic phenomena have remained largely aloof from those trying to provide organized services for family planning. At the 1927 World Population Conference in Geneva, from which the International Union for the Scientific Study of Population emerged (Fryer 1966: 219), Margaret Sanger was given no official recognition even though she was the primary organizer, and the topic of contraception was barred from the agenda (Kennedy 1970: 103). During the first ten years of its existence the Population Council, brought into being by John D. Rockefeller III in 1952 (Piotrow 1973: 13), acted for the most part as if family planning services existed only on the planet Venus. And Robert Cook of the Population Reference Bureau characteristically printed a report on the important 1960 Growth of American Families study totally ignoring the half of the volume which dealt with contraception (Solomon and Cook 1966).

Apart from the distaste of most academic demographers (like that of most physicians) for the open political battles of Margaret Sanger and her group, many are also convinced that the means by which natality regulation is accomplished are of no consequence — only the motivation to limit births matters (see Polgar 1968). This conclusion is ostensibly based on their studies of nineteenth-century Europe and of natality trends during the 1930's in the United States. The bitter attacks by Davis (1967) and Blake (1969) on family planning services are very much in this tradition. Davis decries the emphasis on voluntary action at the family level in programs abroad and misrepresents the program planners as promoting a purely technological approach. Blake insists, despite voluminous evidence to the contrary (see Harkavy, et al. 1969), that the goal of family planning services in the United States is population control, obfuscates the difference between opinions and actions, and favors an attack on the family because it enforces pronatalist norms. Davis and Blake also advocate the creation of extrafamilial roles for women, but manage to transform even this progressive policy into a punitive one by extolling its virtue in creating role conflict for the mother. (I hold no special brief for the modern Western form of the family myself, but I do deplore policies that deliberately advocate widespread suffering.)

The Davis-Blake brand of repression is relatively mild, but it adds to the political strength of the social Darwinists like Hardin and the latest group of strident Malthusians, the bug-killer types. The climate of public opinion has apparently been so well prepared that one can now openly publish articles on the "earthpest" explosion (Corbet 1970) and on " man the pest" (Eyre 1971).

The concept of the population "bomb" has been publicized for quite a few years by Hugh Moore, founder of the Dixie Cup Company (Piotrow 1973: 18). The picture of our planet as a bomb, which decorated his pamphlets and advertisements, was symbolic of Moore's shock tactics. Also prominent in the campaign he started right after World War II was the linking of the population "explosion" with the threat of communism. I never saw this man at a Planned Parenthood meeting, but he was a strong supporter of the Population Reference Bureau and the major force behind the disgusting newspaper publicity of the Campaign to Check the

Population Explosion (analyzed by Barclay, et al. 1970). He was also instrumental in convincing the formidable General Draper and many other businessmen to join the population control movement (Piotrow 1973: 18, 37–38).

What Hugh Moore has done in the world of big business, the lepidopterist Paul Ehrlich did, perhaps even more successfully, in academic circles. His *Population Bomb* (Ehrlich 1968), with the help of advertisements paid for by Moore, quickly became a basic text of the young "eco-freaks" and "ZPG-ers" (ecology freaks and Zero Population Growthers). Although Ehrlich clearly thinks of himself as a political liberal (he opposed the Vietnam war, for example) he extolled William and Paul Paddock's *Famine 1975!* ("the Paddocks deserve immense credit for their courage and foresight in publishing *Famine 1975!*, which may be remembered as one of the most important books of our age" (Ehrlich 1968: 161), and adopted their proposal of using the military triage concept for allocating U.S. assistance in food. *Famine 1975!* ought to be quoted from the original:

Before the end of the 1970's the interplay of power politics will be based on who is starving and who is not, who has extra food to send to others and who has not. Food will be the basis for power. Here the sophistication will lie in the need for the "food nations" to select which countries, out of the many hungry ones, will receive its limited food stock, which countries will be left in the miseries of their starvation...

During the coming Age of Food that nation which has the most food will be, if it uses that food as a source of power, the strongest nation. This will be, then, clearly an era which the United States can dominate — if the United States picks up the challenge (Paddock and Paddock 1967:232).

This sophisticated vision of grainboat diplomacy had its trial run when Nixon held up food shipments to India two years ago.

Typically, Paul Ehrlich has done almost nothing to encourage the provision of voluntary family planning services; on the contrary, he is clearly enthusiastic about the negative and coercive writings of Blake, Davis, Hauser, and Ketchel, and disdainful towards Harkavy, Jaffe, and "Wishnick" (Ehrlich and Ehrlich 1970: 233-258, especially 257–258).

Government actions regarding international aspects of population can best be understood in the light of commercial, military, and labor force considerations. These concerns, after all, antedate Malthus, Ibn Khaldun, and Plato and are still very much with us today. Early empires depended on tribute and slaves coming in and soldiers and administrators going out. Slavery was eventually supplanted by indentured and contract labor, colonial wars were fought over trading areas, and migratory workers nowadays provide a large part of the manpower for the mines of South

Africa, the factories of West Germany, and the produce fields of southern California.

In the wake of the disastrous population declines set off by early European expansion, a primary concern of colonial administrators became the supply and productivity of labor on plantations and in the mines. Theologians, meanwhile, debated the status of the laborers' souls. Once Western Europe, the United States, and Japan became industrialized, a new consideration emerged: the market for manufactured products. Despite the rapid demise of administrative colonialism after 1945, the metropolitan powers remained anxious to find new customers for their exports as well as safeguard their sources of cheap raw materials and maintain opportunities for highly profitable foreign investments.

The post-World War II foreign aid program of the United States (particularly the Marshall plan) however, was not mainly designed to serve these ends; altruism and the expiation of guilt were probably more important. But if famine relief and health programs in the past had been a response to both humanitarian motives and the need to maintain labor pools for the production of cheap raw materials, the latter purpose had become largely irrelevant under postwar conditions. Many synthetic substitutes had been developed for the raw materials whose imports were uncertain during the war, and the trend towards automation had accelerated even in the foreign-owned production facilities in the Third World. And some Westerners like Hugh Moore had come to believe that population growth in Asia, Africa, and Latin America was contributing to political discontent, which might help the interests of the Soviet Union (see the discussion by Barclay, Enright, and Reynolds [1970] which is among the better recent leftist critiques of Malthusian programs, despite the naiveté of its analysis of the population lobby). And, last but not least, the poverty of the masses in the Third World precluded any great expansion there in the sales of manufactured products. The subjects have become burdens!

Piotrow's highly detailed account (1973: 55–65) of how population policy was handled in the State Department and the Agency for International Development during the early 1960's makes but the briefest mention of one development I consider highly significant. Economists at this time were beginning to attack the foreign aid expenditures for health programs because, by increasing the rate of population growth, mortality reduction was hindering the possibility of raising the average level of income (and purchasing power). Piotrow may be superficially correct in linking the sharp reduction in AID assistance for health programs to the bureaucratic reorganization ordered by the Kennedy administration (1973: 63).

But she hints at a more important factor, I believe, when she notes that the reorganization "put priority on government-directed income and job-producing investments" (1973: 63). In other words, the Keynesian economists were put in charge! The Truman Point Four program of reconstruction and humanitarian assistance was largely over, the bad conscience of the United States over its destructive acts appeased, and the "foreign aid" program could settle down to the major business of helping the interests of American capital.

I have already noted that the first direct appropriation by Congress for birth control in 1962 was for the District of Columbia, where over half of the population is black. Students of internal colonialism will be interested in another "first" three years later:

American Indians, Eskimos and natives of the islands the United States holds in trust in the Pacific have been made the beneficiaries of the first Federal program offering direct help in family planning and birth control. The announcement by Secretary of the Interior Udall that contraceptive advice and services will be made available, where desired, on reservations and in trust territories encourages hope that the taboo against birth control programs will also crumble in such domestic undertakings as the war on poverty (*New York Times*, June 21, 1965).[3]

The irony of Secretary Udall's policy was not lost on the Navajo:
"We had Washington's stock reduction program forced on us, now it would seem that they are trying to sell us a people reduction program" *(Indian Voices* 1965). And in the same year, Langston Hughes wrote in his column on how his protagonist "Simple" was reading the papers

"... in which I see a lot these days about the population explosion and how we ought to be doing something about it"
"What we?" I asked.
"We white folks," said Simple...
"Suppose ... they sent a Sterilization Wagon to Harlem ... They better send that Sterilization Wagon to Viet Nam ..."
"But suppose the Viet Cong captured a lot of our Sterilization Wagons and then used them against American troops?" I said.
"Negotiations for peace would begin at once," said Simple.
"White folks are not thinking about being sterilized, neither in war nor peace. It is India, China, Africa and Harlem they is considering ..." (Hughes 1965).

By attending family planning service units in large numbers, once the orals and IUD's became available, Amerindians and blacks have demonstrated that they do want to regulate their own natality, but, as sociologist

---

[3]   That "taboo" did indeed soon crumble, but recently Nixon, on the one hand, killed the Office of Economic Opportunity (OEO) altogether and, on the other, prohibited the medical corps of the U.S. armed services from performing abortions for servicewomen and dependents.

Charles Willie has stressed in his testimony to the Commission on Population Growth and the American Future, if a national population policy is to

gain the cooperation of black people, such a policy must gather up the goals which blacks themselves have identified as important. A national population policy must demonstrate that it is more concerned about the HEALTH and WEALTH of black people than it is about the number of children they have. (Willie 1972:2. Original emphasis.)

Many United States officials (like their British counterparts) regard Third World people as "*des charges*" — to refer back again to the quotation from Sauvy at the beginning of this section — and the current political situation has selected out or silenced those who might favor a partnership aimed at making substantial improvements in the "health and wealth" of the Third World masses.

From 1965 to 1972 the budget for population activities at the disposal of the United States Agency for International Development rose from two million to one hundred million dollars. As the political base of support increased and included more and more people outside of the family planning lobby, Congress and AID defined the work to be done in increasingly Malthusian terms.

As money is poured into the birth control programs of those countries and agencies that are willing to accept a definition of the population problem in terms of the Malthusian analysis, the leadership of the more humanitarian, health-oriented people is being challenged by those who favor mass campaigns of "motivation," incentive schemes, and even compulsory sterilization. But fortunately the field has not yet been completely preempted by the Malthusians. Some organizations involved in international assistance, including the Swedish International Development Agency, the Canadian International Development Agency, the (Quaker) Friends Service Committee, and the World Health Organization have concentrated on positive programs involving family planning services and medical education. Furthermore, opposition to externally stimulated population control has come not only in the form of nationalist exhortations (from both the political right and the left) but is also based on non-Malthusian philosophical and economic analyses of a scholarly nature (e.g. Amin 1971; Bahri, et al. 1971; Pradervand 1970; Raulet 1970).[4]

---

[4] I will not attempt here to even indicate the various policies pursued by socialist countries or the directions of the writings from these countries on population and family planning. I am simply not well enough informed to do so at this time.

## CONCLUSION

Birth planning as such, I would submit, is neither a progressive nor a reactionary idea; to evaluate it one has to look at the context in which it is pursued. The deliberate modification of natality by an individual, a couple or a kinship unit, i.e. family planning, has a very long history in human evolution. Physicians have often been concerned with family planning and in recent years have made great contributions to the improvement of its technology. That European (and American) medical men were unconcerned with, and even hostile to, contraception and abortion from the thirteenth to well into the twentieth century can be attributed to the influence of the Judeo-Christian tradition and to the changing status of their profession in society. The almost complete failure to provide voluntary family planning services through public medical care channels has been quite injurious to poor people who wanted to regulate their own childbearing, but did not even have recourse to the relatively safe (but expensive) abortions performed by clandestinely practicing physicians. By the same token, poor people were quite frequently sterilized without their prior knowledge or consent.

Voluntary parenthood by safe and effective means has a very important role in family health and welfare and particularly for the liberation of women. Many of the pioneers in the birth planning movement recognized this and so do most socialists today. By contrast, birth control offered in the context of Malthusian schemes of regulating the poor, with only a superficial veneer of charity, and provided on a voluntary basis only because more compulsory programs are not considered politically feasible at the time, is a cruel hoax.

Population control, like natality regulation, is not a new idea. Unlike family planning, however, its history is more closely tied to repression than to liberation. Malthus's ideas originally became popular among the European elite just after the French revolution and as the process of transforming human labor into a marketable commodity was culminating. Today, as Third World people are fighting for and beginning to win their freedom from political and economic exploitation by the big industrial powers, another wave of Malthusian reaction is pouring forth. "Overpopulation" is once again blamed as the cause of poverty, crime, hunger, and war. And there is a new ingredient: the concern for the environment. The sincere worry of many people about the damage of pollution and resource depletion is being manipulated by Malthusians and industrialists who hope to deflect attention from the fact that it is the rapacious and thriftless processes of extraction, manufacturing, and selling by the metropolitan powers which are the major causes of environmental degradation.

Population policies can be regarded as progressive if aimed, for example, at slowing the rate of influx to large cities where employment is scarce and public services are not yet adequate or if concerned with slowing growth rates while educational facilities are still insufficient. In the future, if the distribution of resources becomes more equitable, stabilizing population in order to maintain environmental quality for all the people and to preserve the complex biosphere of the earth will also be a positive measure. None of these population policies, however, can be seen as progressive if isolated from, or put ahead of, more comprehensive measures to promote human equality and the development of people's creative potential.

So why did the policies concerning population and family planning programs change so drastically in the last decade? As in late eighteenth-century Britain, population has been growing rapidly. The expanding numbers of Third World people, who are no longer dutiful subjects toiling in their mines and fields and are not consumers either for an ever-expanding flow of manufactured products, have become a burden for the industrial powers. They are not only a burden, but also a threat, for, as in the time of Malthus, a great revolution is taking place.

But there is another side also. New freedoms have been declared: from all-too-frequent illness and death, from the oppression of women by men, from the high risks of clumsy abortions and the cruel pain of burying an infant. Among the pioneers of family planning there were idealists and anarchists, not just elite privilege seekers. By 1962 the rich already had a number of relatively safe and effective ways to plan their families — and humanitarians wanted to offer this opportunity also to the poor.

The uneasy alliance of rightist and democratic forces has succeeded in greatly increasing attention to birth planning. Today, as the voices of the population "hawks" rise louder and louder demanding that coercion be instituted and that all is lost if birth rates do not immediately tumble, the alliance is no longer tenable. Were the humanitarians used as a tool by the reactionaries? When I visit a well-run family planning service, I don't think so. When I read of an "earthpest explosion" I despair. In another ten years, perhaps, we may have a clearer answer as to what really happened in the 1960's.

# REFERENCES

AMIN, SAMIR
  1971   "Population policies and development strategies: underpopulated Africa." Paper given at the meeting on Population Dynamics and Educational Development in Africa, Dakar, November 29 to December 4, 1971. UNESCO Regional Office for Education in Africa, Dakar, Senegal.
BAHRI, AHMED, *et al.*
  1971   "A new approach to population research in Africa: ideologies, facts and policies." Position paper given at the African Population Conference, UNESCO, Accra, Ghana, December 9 to 18, 1971.
BANKS, J. A.
  1954   *Prosperity and parenthood: a study of family planning among the Victorian middle classes.* London: Routledge.
BANKS, J. A., OLIVE BANKS
  1964   *Feminism and family planning.* Liverpool: Liverpool University Press.
BARCLAY, W., J. ENRIGHT, R. T. REYNOLDS
  1970   Population control in the Third World. *North American Congress on Latin America Newsletter* 4:1–18.
BEALES, H. L.
  1959   "The historical context of the *Essay* on population," in *Introduction to Malthus.* Edited by D. V. Glass, 1–24. London: Frank Cass.
BERGUES, H. *et al.*
  1960   *La prévention des naissances dans la famille.* Institut National d'Etudes Démographiques, Travaux et Documents, Cahier 35. Paris.
BEST, W., *editor*
  1959   *The anatomy of a victory.* New York: Planned Parenthood Federation of America.
BLAKE, J.
  1969   Population policy for Americans: is the government being misled? *Science* 164:522–529.
CARLSSON, G.
  1966   The decline of fertility: innovation or adjustment process? *Population Studies* 20:149–174.
CARTWRIGHT, A.
  1968   General practitioners and family planning. *The Medical Officer* 120: 43–46.
CENTER FOR FAMILY PLANNING PROGRAM DEVELOPMENT
  1969   *Need for subsidized family planning services: United States, each state and county, 1968.* New York: Planned Parenthood Federation of America.
CHAMBLISS, W. J.
  1964   A sociological analysis of the law of vagrancy. *Social Problems* 12: 67–77.
CHANDRASEKARAN, C., K. KUDER
  1965   *Family planning through clinics.* Bombay: Allied Publishers.
CORBET, P. S.
  1970   "Pest management: objectives and prospects on a global scale," in

*Concepts of pest management.* Edited by R. L. Rabb and F. E. Guthrie, 191–208. Raleigh: North Carolina State University.

CORKEY, E. C.
1966 "The birth control program in the Mecklenburg County Health Department," in *Public health programs in family planning.* Edited by S. Polgar and W. B. Cowles. *American Journal of Public Health* 56 (2): 40–47.

CORNISH, M. J., F. A. RUDERMAN, S. S. SPIVACK
1963 *Doctors and family planning.* National Committee on Maternal Health Publication 19, New York.

DAVIS, K.
1967 Population policy: will current programs succeed? *Science* 158:730–739.

DEMENY, P.
1968 Early fertility decline in Hungary: a lesson in demographic transition. *Daedalus* (Spring): 502–522.

DOWSE, R. E., J. PEEL
1965 The politics of birth control. *Political Studies* 13:179–197.

EHRLICH, P. R.
1968 *The population bomb.* New York: Ballantine.

EHRLICH, P. R., A. H. EHRLICH
1970 *Population resources environment: issues in human ecology.* San Francisco: W. H. Freeman.

ELIOT, J. W., C. HOUSER, R. WHITE
1966 "The development of family planning services by state and local health departments in the United States," in *Public health programs in family planning.* Edited by S. Polgar and W. B. Cowles. *American Journal of Public Health* 56 (2):4–16.

EYRE, S. R.
1971 "Man the pest: the dim chance of survival." *New York Review of Books* (November 18, 1971): 18–27.

FRYER, P.
1966 *The birth controllers.* New York: Stein and Day.

GLASS, D. V., D. E. C. EVERSLEY, *editors*
1965 *Population in history.* Chicago: Aldine.

GUTTMACHER, A. F.
1973 *President's Newsletter* 65:3. New York: Planned Parenthood Federation of America.

HARDIN, G.
1968 The tragedy of the commons. *Science* 162:1243–1248.
1970 Parenthood: right or privilege? *Science* 169:427.

HARKAVY, O., F. S. JAFFE, S. M. WISHIK
1969 Family planning and public policy: who is misleading whom? *Science* 165:367–373.

HIMES, N. E.
1963 *Medical history of contraception.* New York: Gamut Press. (Originally published 1936.)

HOFSTADTER, R.
   1955   *Social Darwinism in American thought* (revised edition). Boston: Beacon Press.

HUGHES, L.
   1965   "Population explosion." *New York Post*, December 10.

HUTCHINSON, E. P.
   1967   *The population debate.* Boston: Houghton Mifflin.

INDIAN VOICES
   1965   Rosebud Herald speaks out on birth control. *Indian Voices* (August): 4–5.

JAFFE, F. S.
   1964   Family planning and poverty. *Journal of Marriage and the Family* 26: 467–470.
   1967   Family planning, public policy and intervention strategy. *Journal of Social Issues* 23:145–163.

KENNEDY, D. M.
   1970   *Birth control in America: the career of Margaret Sanger.* New Haven: Yale University Press.

LAFITTE, F.
   1962   *Family planning and family planning clinics today.* Birmingham: Birmingham University.

LANGER, W. L.
   1963   Europe's initial population explosion. *American Historical Review* 69: 1–17.

LEWIS-FANNING, E.
   1949   *Report on an enquiry into family limitation and its influence on human fertility during the past fifty years.* Papers of the Royal Commission on Population 1. London: His Majesty's Stationery Office.

MALTHUS, T. R.
   1959   "A letter to Samuel Whitehead Esq., M.P., on the proposed bill for the amendment of the poor laws," in *Introduction to Malthus.* Edited by D. V. Glass, 183–205. London: Frank Cass. (Originally published 1807. London: J. Johnson.)

MEASHAM, A. R.
   1972   *Family planning in North Carolina: the politics of a lukewarm issue.* Carolina Population Center Monograph 17. Chapel Hill: University of North Carolina.

MEEK, R. L.
   1971   *Marx and Engels on the population bomb* (second edition). Berkeley: Ramparts Press.

NEW YORK TIMES
   1965   "More headway on birth control." *New York Times*, June 21.

PADDOCK, W., P. PADDOCK
   1967   *Famine 1975 !* Boston: Little, Brown.

PAUL, J.
   1967   Population "quality" and "fitness for parenthood" in the light of state eugenic sterilization experience, 1907–1966. *Population Studies* 21: 295–299.

1968    The return of punitive sterilization proposals: current attacks on ille-
        gitimacy and the AFDC program. *Law and Society Review* 3:77–106.

PIOTROW, P. T.
1973    *World population crisis: the United States response.* New York: Praeger.

POHLMAN, E.
1969    *The psychology of birth planning.* Cambridge, Massachusetts: Schenk-
        man.

POLANYI, K.
1944    *The great transformation: the political and economic origins of our time.*
        Boston: Beacon Press.

POLGAR, S.
1966    Sociocultural research in family planning in the United States: review
        and prospects. *Human Organization* 25:321–329.
1968    "Malthus, magic and motivation." Chapel Hill: University of North
        Carolina, Carolina Population Center (processed).
1972    Population history and population policies from an anthropological
        perspective. *Current Anthropology* 13:203–211.

PRADERVAND, P.
1970    Les pays nantis et la limitation des naissances dans le tiers monde.
        *Développement et Civilisations* 39–40:4–40.

RAULET, H. M.
1970    "Population policy, economic development, and social structure in
        South Asia: a critique of the neo-Malthusian perspective." Paper
        given at the Annual Meeting of the American Anthropological
        Association, San Diego, November 1970.

REIN, M.
1962    "An organizational analysis of a national agency's local affiliates in
        their community contexts: a study of the Planned Parenthood Feder-
        ation of America" (excerpts from doctoral dissertation). New York:
        Planned Parenthood Federation of America (processed).

SAUVY, A.
1963    *Théorie générale de la population,* volume one. Paris: Presses Universi-
        taires de France.

SOLOMON, G., R. C. COOK
1966    "Boom babies" come of age: the American family at the crossroads.
        *Population Bulletin* 22:61–79.

STYCOS, J. M.
1963    Obstacles to programs of population control — facts and fancies.
        *Journal of Marriage and the Family* 25:5–13.

TAYLOR, H. C., B. BERELSON
1968    Maternity care and family planning as a world program. *American
        Journal of Obstetrics and Gynecology* 100:885–893.

WESTOFF, C. F., *et al.*
1961    *Family growth in metropolitan America.* Princeton: Princeton Univer-
        sity Press.

WILLIE, C. V.
1972    A position paper, presented to the President's Commission on Popu-

lation Growth and the American Future. Population Reference Bureau Selection 37.

WRIGHT, N. H., G. JOHNSON, D. MEES

1968    "Report on a survey on physicians' attitudes in Georgia toward family
planning services, prescribing contraceptives, sex education, and therapeutic abortion," in *Advances in planned parenthood*, volume three.
Edited by A. J. Sobrero and S. Lewit, 37–46. Excerpta Medica Foundation, International Congress Series 156. Amsterdam.

# Political Ideology and Population Policy in Puerto Rico

CARLOS RAMOS, PETA HENDERSON

## INTRODUCTION

It is a fact well known to anthropologists and others that human populations have long found means to control their reproduction (Polgar 1972; Faris 1973). The issue is thus not that of birth control *per se*, but of its conscious use by the state to control population growth concomitant with explicit national goals. During the past three decades Puerto Rico has attempted to achieve rapid economic growth through industrialization. This effort has led policy makers and planners to direct their attention to the population variable in relation to economic development. During the same period, public and private agencies have been involved in providing birth control facilities and services for Puerto Ricans. Vehement and vocal opposition to these programs has been voiced through the years by the island's *independentista* 'pro-independence' groups. The ideological basis of this opposition has shifted over time from its earlier predominantly Catholic-nationalist orientation to its present socialist manifestations. The prevailing majority position accepts contraception as an individual need, but strong criticism continues to be voiced about birth control programs as a policy of a colonial government.

In this paper we are interested in analyzing the major trends in opposition to population control and family planning in Puerto Rico, and in particular the *independentista* position based on a socialist ideology. In the context of Puerto Rico's present political status (a Commonwealth within the United States Federal system), the socialist approach to birth control must be viewed as a statement of policy for a future society rather than as a program that is potentially realizable under existing political conditions. Therefore, this paper is concerned with an analysis of changing ideologies with respect to population control rather than with an ongoing health care program. We believe that the *independentista* position is important both because it presents a radical alternative for future family planning services and because it has had significant influence on the formulation of present birth control policies in Puerto Rico.

We will first review briefly the evolution of population theories and policies in the socialist countries. This will provide a comparative framework within which to locate the Puerto Rican experience. The second section of the paper provides a historical summary of the birth control movement in Puerto Rico in order to elaborate the objective conditions which gave rise to the socialist critique by the island's *independentista* groups. We will then analyze in some detail the disparate trends in population ideology, which may be seen to provide continuity with what we discern to be the basis of present *independentista* theories on the subject. In conclusion we attempt to evaluate the similarities and differences of the Puerto Rican case vis-à-vis current population theories and policies in the socialist countries.

While our emphasis here is on the evolution of socialist IDEOLOGIES of population control, we want to stress the point that we do not view ideologies as "evolving" except in interaction with the objective conditions which generate them and which they reflect. Unfortunately space does not permit detailed attention to these conditions except in the Puerto Rican case with which we are primarily concerned. The Puerto Rican data are drawn from historical and documentary sources, supplemented by interviews with leading members of the Puerto Rican Independence Party (PIP) and the Puerto Rican Socialist Party (PSP). Confidentiality prevents us from identifying by name the individuals who have provided us with our data. The analysis therefore represents our own distillation of the views expressed.

## THE EVOLUTION OF SOCIALIST THEORIES OF POPULATION AND BIRTH CONTROL POLICIES

The Marxist rebuttal of the well-known proposition of Malthus that human populations grow in geometric ratio while food supply can grow only in arithmetical ratio is directed at both its theoretical and practical policy implications. From a theoretical standpoint, the basis of Marx and Engels' criticism was Malthus' attribution of poverty to natural causes, which are thus irreversible, rather than to concrete man-made structures, which are capable of transformation. As Marx clearly realized, if population is subject to natural laws, then socialism cannot abolish poverty but can only redistribute it. The issue is thus whether the apparent excess of people in industrialized society is a "population problem" or a problem of economic organization. Engels' statement that "only one-third of the earth can be described as cultivated, and ... the productivity of this third could be increased sixfold and more merely by applying the improvements which are already known" (Landstreet 1971: 91) finds its echo in the assertions of current Latin American writers that in relation to actual and potential resources, Latin America is underpopulated (Consuegra 1969: 95). The question posed, then, is whether an absolute scarcity of resources ever exists such that a country may be termed overpopulated, or whether the so-called excess of people may not be attributed to a specific socioeconomic formation, namely capitalism.

In response to the Malthusian thesis, Marx attempted to formulate his own law of population growth under capitalism. Its crux lies in the distinction he makes between the "means of employment" and the "means of subsistence." Malthus, he said, clearly confused the two. Under capitalism, the key to population growth lies in the dynamics of an economic system that places primacy on the accumulation of capital. With the advance of technology, the investment of capital in the means of production (constant capital) inevitably increases at the expense of capital outlays in wages and salaries to the producer (variable capital). Thus, by simply selling his labor, the worker inevitably produces the means for his own displacement. Over a period of time, capitalism thus generates a surplus labor force of increasing size, an industrial reserve army which can be called upon in time of capital scarcity, but which is dispensable in times of technological acceleration and plenty. The increasing concentration of this army of unemployed and underemployed in the urban areas, and its marginality to the economic system, is the principal contradiction of the capitalist system because it represents unlimited revolutionary potential. From this standpoint, then, population growth is a necessary prerequisite to the social and economic transformation, without which labor productivity and the general standard of living cannot be raised. This line of argument clearly provides a PRONATALIST rationale.

Marx and Engels did not articulate a principle of population growth under socialism and communism. However, Engels, at least, believed that communist social organization would be naturally conducive to lower fertility, although he indicated that even under communism some form of birth control might have to be introduced. Lenin, while condemning neo-Malthusianism as "the hypocrisy of the ruling classes," believed in the principle that families have the right to decide on the number of children they will have, and even favored the legalization of abortion (Landstreet 1971: 93). In 1920, abortions were legalized in the Soviet Union and were performed free of charge in state hospitals. However, in 1936 the law was reversed, and throughout the Stalinist era a generally hard line against any attempt to limit births was taken as being "incompatible with the Marxist approach to these questions" (Landstreet 1971: 131). Since 1955 abortion has again been legal in the Soviet Union on request by the woman, and some effort has been made to promote contraception (Landstreet 1971: 94). However, the fact that Russia is not a densely populated country has made the formulation of a national population policy aimed at a reduction in fertility a matter of lesser urgency than in other areas of the world. In fact, there is some evidence that Soviet demographers fear a depopulation of Russia's Slavic areas in relation to population increases in the Central Asian region. As a consequence, differential (e.g. regional and ethnic) population policies have been proposed as a solution (*Family Planning Studies* 1972: 263).

The real shift in socialist ideology with respect to population control has centered around the theoretical problem of population growth and economic development in the Third World. The logic of the Marxist analysis of the capitalist system, as we have seen, favors a pronatalist, anti-birth-control stance. In the case of Marxist-oriented writers in the underdeveloped world, this is reinforced by nationalist, anti-imperialist and in some cases Catholic sentiment. José Consuegra's *El control de la natalidad* is devoted in its entirety to a refutation of neo-Malthusian propaganda in Latin America, stressing the importance of the "human factor as motor force and reason for economic development" (1969: 10, 97). From this perspective the "population explosion" is the major impulse to structural and institutional change; and attempts to control it by the imperialist powers, in particular the United States, can only be interpreted as antipathetic to the autonomous economic development of Latin America. Such efforts are seen as prompted by racism and fear of popular movements leading to socialism and communism. The theme is further developed that the "overpopulation," such as it exists at the present stage of historical developments, is not an overpopulation with respect to natural resources, but rather with respect to the organization of present productive institutions and technology (Consuegra 1969: 90).

Some Soviet analysts, however, have recognized the contradiction between long-term revolutionary strategy and short-time economic development. In the face of growing evidence that birth rates do not automatically decline with increased urbanization and industrialization, they have begun to talk in terms of optimum RATES of population increase concomitant with desired rates of economic growth. While always stressing the primacy of the need for economic reorganization toward a more rational and equitable use and distribution of resources, the question as to the inhibitory effect of large numbers on growth rates has been faced by demographers and others in the socialist countries. It has been recognized that to talk in terms of population density in absolute relation to potential resources evades the central problem of the effects on future economic growth of high RATES of population increase. Two factors have been emphasized in the debate: investment and the burden of dependency (NACLA 1970: Part 2). With respect to the former, it is argued that high rates of population increase divert resources from productive investment into the consumption and service sectors. In other words, there is an inverse relationship between a high rate of population increase and the rate of investment. The second factor concerns the proportion of the population engaged in production as compared to the proportion in the dependent age groups. A large dependent sector likewise limits the rate of investment.

Given the above considerations, a Soviet economist has concluded:

These countries of the "Third World" must follow a policy of spreading family planning and of the transition to a small family system. Underdevelopment for a considerable part of people in these countries means that generations of people throughout their lives consume more than they produce, and this lessens the possibility of improving the economy of these countries and raising the standard of living of their populations ... (*Family Planning Studies* 1970).

Thus, although the demographic variable is never viewed as "causing" poverty and underdevelopment, population growth is now recognized by analysts in the Soviet Union as an important factor in slowing the rate of economic development. Some form of artifical control of fertility therefore seems desirable in order to facilitate the short-term goals of economic development rather than waiting for a "natural" decline in birth rates such as has accompanied the rise in the standard of living in the industrialized nations. The Soviet position on this matter has been summarized as follows:

On the Soviet side, then, it would appear that the main recent changes in attitude involve a recognition that "population problems" do exist, in the sense of being attributable at least in part to high fertility levels. Furthermore, there is a recognition that while, in the long run, fertility levels are determined by broad socio-economic forces, in the short run they can also be influenced by the activities of family planning programs (making contraceptives available and engaging in propaganda for their use) ... (Landstreet 1971: 104).

The Chinese have gone even further in their evolution from a traditional Marxist pronatalist position. Since the mid-fifties, they have sponsored several national birth control campaigns, including promotion of contraceptives, abortion, and sterilization. The Chinese government's rationale for these policies is made explicit in the following article appearing in a San Juan newspaper:

Communist China's birth control efforts have resulted in a decline in the birth rate, a Peking broadcast said Monday, but it gave no figures on the subject.

The official Hsinhua news agency said women, now enjoying equal political and economic rights with men, want to lighten their family rearing chores so "they can do more in building socialism." Other purposes of the birth control program, Hsinhua said, are to "protect the health of mothers and children and regulate population increase so that it corresponds with the development of the Socialist planned economy." Men are encouraged not to marry before age 25 and women before age 23, the agency said (*San Juan Star*, March 6, 1973).

The Chinese position on birth control indicated above appears to be a synthesis of the various trends which have led to a modification of socialist ideologies of population control: first, the recognition that rapid population increase may impede the realization of economic planning goals; second, the transformation of the family and changing roles of women in the development of socialist society; and third, the emphasis in socialist societies on comprehensive health care, which takes into account the social and economic as well as the purely symptomatic and physical aspects of health.

In Cuba, however, there is no OFFICIAL policy of population control. This may be attributed in part to the demographic impact of massive emigration following the 1959 Revolution, which is perceived to have caused a labor shortage (*Avance*, February 26, 1973: 18). This policy vacuum must also be viewed in the context of Cuba's struggle against United States imperialism and its interest in promoting the revolutionary aspirations of other Latin American nations. Fidel Castro, himself, while recognizing the problem of population in some countries, foresees a revolutionary solution in the abolition of archaic and repressive socioeconomic institutions and in the development of natural and human resources. Regulating numbers is not the solution (Landstreet 1972: 6). In one speech he put it this way:

The population is going to keep on growing. And revolution is the inevitable result as in an elementary mathematical equation (Landstreet 1971: 126).

In practice, contraceptive services are widely available in Cuba through its free health system; these services are not, however, being actively publicized. Cuba justifies family planning services on grounds of maternal health and the emancipation of women for productive work in society. The logic of its past and present political status, however, inhibits any explicit linking of fertility "regulation" with national goals of economic development. At the same time it should be noted that a recent analyst of the Cuban scene has observed in Castro's speeches a growing concern for the problem of numbers versus availability of social services as well as a decline in overt attacks on United States-sponsored population control programs. This commentator has suggested the possibility of an endorsement of population control by Cuba in the near future (Landstreet 1972: 8).

From the foregoing, we discern a pattern of development in socialist ideologies of population control and policy. In response to analyses of the workings of capitalism in its early stage, there was first an outright rejection of birth control as national policy. However, at a later stage in the historical development of capitalism (imperialism), there is a growing tendency among socialist analysts to recognize the existence of a "population problem" at least insofar as the underdeveloped countries are concerned. While there is a continued rejection of the implications of neo-Malthusianism as a weapon of imperialism, the reevaluated position places short-term economic development ahead of a revolutionary solution. Furthermore, in the development of socialist society at home, the changing role of the woman and the concept of health as socially and environmentally determined provide additional rationales for the modification of earlier pronatalist policies. The synthesis of these trends is found in the Chinese case, in which both rapid population growth and socialist development dictate the formulation of a national policy of birth control. The Soviet Union, while endorsing family planning services, has stopped short of a national policy of population control due to disparate demographic conditions. Its writers have indicated, however, great interest in the problem of numbers in relation to economic development in the Third World. In general, these writers have espoused a nonrevolutionary approach to these questions, and in many respects their analyses and solutions approximate those of United States advocates of population control in the underdeveloped world.

Cuba also permits birth control services, but rejects a national population control policy primarily on grounds of its role in the anti-imperialist and revolutionary struggle of the Latin American nations. We suggest that past or present colonial status is a determining factor inhibiting an explicit policy of fertility control. We would therefore expect to find a parallel between the Cuban position on birth control and that of Puerto Rico's socialist groups. We will turn now to an analysis of the evolution of birth control policy and practice in Puerto Rico and of the ideological critiques and alternatives which have been articulated by these groups.

## BRIEF HISTORY OF BIRTH CONTROL IN PUERTO RICO

As early as 1925, a group of young, middle-class professionals, headed by Dr. Lanauze of Ponce, established the island's first birth control organization, the Puerto Rican Birth Control League. The League was not a service-oriented organization but rather an educational one. Its members were interested in arousing public opinion regarding overpopulation and its adverse socioeconomic effects on Puerto Rican society. More importantly, they stressed the right of parents to determine freely the number of children desired in light of the families' economic situation. In the absence of free choice and resources to insure the proper rearing of children, the League argued that all women should have the right and freedom to control their reproductive capacity (Alvarado and Teitze 1947: 15).

The League and its organizers were the subject of a series of rather hostile attacks from the combined forces of Catholic and *independentista* groups on the island. The basic argument presented against the League was that their work was offensive to God's law and to the morality of a Christian nation (*El Piloto*, July 8, 1926). Given Roman Catholic opposition, lack of adequate financial resources, and public indifference, these initial attempts by private groups to organize a birth control movement were rendered ineffective.

In the early 1930's, Puerto Rico received substantial United States government funding to alleviate the effects of economic depression on the island. The federal programs included birth control as a primary objective. Thus in 1934 with the aid of the local federal relief agency (the Puerto Rican Emergency Relief Administration [PRERA]), the School of Tropical Medicine established a clinic in San Juan as a pilot project. With the termination of the PRERA program in 1936, a new federal agency (the Puerto Rican Reconstruction Agency [PRRA]) was created to continue its functions. Under the auspices of the new agency, birth control services were expanded, resulting in a network of fifty-three clinics that serviced 10,000 couples over a two-year period.

Unable to curtail the birth control activities of the PRRA effectively at the local level, the island's Catholic hierarchy enlisted the support of various Catholic groups on the mainland. This political pressure at the continental level during a presidential election year was successful in terminating the PRRA's birth control programs (Cofresi 1968: 34–40).

Shortly thereafter, members of the defunct Puerto Rico Birth Control League organized the Maternal and Child Health Association. The Association had a two-fold purpose: to reestablish a birth control program and to wage a campaign to abolish legislation impeding the birth control movement. The Association achieved its aims through an intensive campaign among Puerto Rican legislators (majority pro-statehood) and the vigorous support of Blanton Winship, the island's federally appointed governor, and of James Beverly, a former governor and vice-president of the Association (*Boletín Mensual de la Asociación por Bienestar de la Familia* 1937).

As a result of these efforts, in 1937 the Puerto Rican legislature passed Laws numbers 116, 133, and 136. These established a Eugenics Board, legalized the entrance and distribution of contraceptive information and devices on the island, and empowered the Puerto Rican Department of Health to provide contraceptive services to married and consensually united couples. From 1940–1944 the insular government effectively assumed and vigorously expanded the operations of the privately organized Maternal and Child Health Association's clinics (Cofresi 1968: 38).

During the latter part of the decade of the forties and the fifties, Puerto Rico's public birth control programs were effectively neutralized. The overwhelming victory of the Popular Democratic Party in 1944 ushered in a policy of benevolent neglect toward the island's public birth control program. This policy can be explained by various factors: the reformist nature of the Popular ideology and continued Church and *independentista* opposition. The Popular Party and its leader, Luis Muñoz Marin, set the tone for the future of Puerto Rico's birth control program. In the tradition of Latin American reformist movements, overpopulation was not seen as an obstacle to economic development, but rather its main incentive (Stycos 1955: 194–197). The goal of the Muñoz government was not to limit the number of persons on the island, but to increase production. Given this attitude, industrialization was given top priority, while birth control was seen as a complementary device for achieving economic development. The mass migration of Puerto Ricans to the mainland during the 1950's enabled the *Populares* to sustain their faith in industrialization (*San Juan Star*, July 3, 1973). The reduction in the population growth rate, resulting from massive emigration, had the effect of virtually eliminating official support for the existing birth control programs on the island.

Although the Muñoz administration during this period made no concerted effort to implement existing birth control legislation vigorously, it
also made no effort to abolish the birth control laws or programs. The
Church's opposition to the Muñoz government is partially explained by
the government's continued tolerance of public and private birth control
activities. (To this must be added the legislation enacted under Muñoz
legalizing divorce, and the government's refusal to aid religious schools
financially or to permit religious education in the public schools). These
actions were interpreted by the island's Church hierarchy as immoral
acts by an immoral government and against the interests of a Christian
society. This reasoning finally led in 1960 to the formation by the Catholic
Church of the Christian Action Party (PAC), which was intended to
challenge the moral neutrality of the Popular Party.

The formation of the PAC generated a political alliance between the
Catholic Church and certain Catholic *independentista* leaders. Several of
the latter became members and/or candidates of the PAC. On the other
hand, the majority of the more progressive elements among the *independentistas* refused to associate themselves with the PAC. Some construed
the party's platform and intent as Church interference in national politics. Moreover, the Cuban revolution of 1959 had attracted growing
numbers of young *independentistas* who had begun to view the Church in
Marxian terms as an arm of colonial oppression. Furthermore, the leading spokesman for the PAC at this time was Bishop James MacManus,
who had on numerous occasions expressed his political preference for
eventual statehood for the island and his vehement opposition to socialism. This position was diametrically opposed to the avowed political
objectives of the independence movement.

The outcome of the 1960 election, which pitted the Muñoz administration against the PAC, was rather adverse for the latter. Muñoz obtained
the largest plurality of his political career and was reelected to his fourth
term of office. The PAC received only 6 percent of the total vote, which
entitled only two of its candidates to seats in the Puerto Rican legislature.
However, the legislature refused to seat the PAC representatives because
of alleged electoral fraud. The price paid by the Church to achieve a
reconciliation with Muñoz was the replacement of the island's North
American bishops by native Puerto Rican clergy (*New York Times*,
November 10, 1960). This satisfied the demands of *independentista* groups
for native control of Church affairs. On the other hand, in the interest of
its future relations with the Church, the ruling Popular Democratic Party
under Muñoz Marin (1960–1964) and Sánchez Villella (1964–1968) did
not push a strong birth control program during the sixties. This was

explained to the writers by a former Popular governor as attributable to a reluctance on the part of the government to implement an island-wide program which could be construed as an act of vengeance against the Church.

Under the Sánchez Villella administration, however, the Health Department with the aid of federal funds embarked on a pilot maternal and infant care program in its northeastern area. The program had a comprehensive health orientation, which included family planning. The success of this pilot project, a further infusion of federal funds specifically for family planning, and close personal ties between the New Progressive Party and the Catholic Church contributed to the establishment by the Ferre administration (1968–1972) of an island-wide family planning program. This was the first official government-sponsored island-wide program in the island's history. It stresses the voluntary nature of birth control services, but is quite specific in indicating that these services are intended to reduce population growth in the interest of economic development:

The objective of family planning is to help better the socio-economic conditions of the country through the planning of the number and frequency of children. Towards these ends, medical services are provided towards the reduction of fertility on a voluntary basis (*Presupuesto para el Gobierno de Puerto Rico* 1973: 17).

In the 1972 election, the Ferre pro-statehood party was defeated and the *Populares* were returned to office under the governorship of Rafael Hernández Colón. In a recent press conference, Governor Hernandez indicated his continued support for a governmental family planning program. He announced plans for reorganizing present services in order to achieve maximum effectiveness (*El Mundo*, April 1, 1973).

## THE EVOLUTION OF *INDEPENDENTISTA* IDEOLOGIES OF POPULATION CONTROL AND FAMILY PLANNING

As has been indicated, the Roman Catholic Church and *independentista* groups were vigorously opposed to private and public birth control programs. Their opposition must be understood in terms of the nature of the arguments being put forward by early pro-birth-control forces. These rest upon two basic lines of reasoning, health and eugenics, as illustrated in the following passage:

It is known that the restriction of fertility among the select classes ... aggravates the problem. Every time that these groups reduce their births, they condone the uncontrolled genetic instinct of the hordes. Thus we will end up by eliminating our select classes and creating a nation of morons, irresponsible individuals, and inferior beings, who lack direction and are at the mercy of any adventurer who wishes to submit them to his servitude... In addition, the eugenic laws ... promote the health of the offspring and responsible motherhood, which would enable the human family to purge itself of the bondage of misery and contribute to the purification of the race (*El Diluvio*, April 17, 1937).

The health and eugenics arguments for birth control were further reinforced by those who took the position that "overpopulation" was impeding the island's economic development. This explicit linking of demography and economic growth is characteristic of the opinion of United States federal officials (Beverly 1932–1933; Winship 1937; *Chardon Report* 1935), as well as of those sectors of Puerto Rican opinion which favored the continued development of Puerto Rico within the United States economic framework. Thus, an anti-birth-control position was equated with an anti-United States stance, and those who opposed it were accused of being subversive to the true interests of Puerto Rico.

Those that oppose birth control are none other than those always interested in using the population ... for their political purposes, which are full of violence, hate, fratricide and anarchy (*El Diluvio*, May 8, 1937).

It is as a response to this kind of polemic that the Catholic-Nationalist views on birth control must be interpreted. The basis of the Catholic-Nationalist opposition, of course, was the natural law argument against contraception. This doctrinal argument, based on moral and religious grounds, was reinforced by nationalist sentiment. This viewed the independence struggle as a means of reaffirming a Hispanic cultural tradition threatened by the imposition of "Anglo-Saxon" values and institutions. The positive need and value of a large population in combating this threat is the rationale for a pronatalist nationalist position. Furthermore, high fertility is seen as necessary to counteract the effects of large-scale migration promoted by both United States and Puerto Rican officials. Birth control and encouragement of migration are thus interpreted as cultural genocide. A very early statement of this point of view is expressed in the following passage:

Why are there so many? In these naive words it is affirmed that Puerto Ricans are a nuisance in Puerto Rico: that our population density which is the wall that resists the destruction of our personality and race should be destroyed (De Diego 1970).

A modern version of the same analysis is contained in the recent abortion statement issued by Antulio Parrilla Bonilla, a Catholic bishop and *independentista* (*Claridad*, March 11, 1973):

Abortion on demand, and then sterilization, euthanasia and suicide would precipitate moral deterioration which in turn would contribute to a process of disintegration of our nationality through the decrease and displacement of Puerto Ricans. All of these presuppose the gradual destruction of all our remaining national values.

With the initiation of "Operation Bootstrap," Puerto Rico's attempt to transform its economy through industrialization, the issue of economic development became more central in the evolution of *independentista* ideology. The principal architect of "Operation Bootstrap," Teodoro Moscoso, was himself an advocate of family planning as a necessary means of achieving a balance between fertility rates and a rise in the standard of living. While migration tended to take priority over birth control as the chief instrument of official population policy at the time (coupled with the "battle of production"), family planning services were available in public and private clinics. These were offered at the discretion of the medical directors on the basis of a philosophy of maternal and child health. A more explicitly economic and demographic rationale underlies the philosophy of the private Puerto Rican Family Planning Association, which was actively promoting birth control with heavy reliance on sterilization. Between the years 1947–1948 and 1953–1954, the percentage of sterilized women in the reproductive age groups increased from 6.6 percent (Hatt 1952: 444) to 16.5 percent (Hill, et al. 1959: 167). In 1965 the figure was put at 33 percent (Presser 1969: 343–361)[1] and in 1968 at 34 percent (Vázquez Calzada n.d.). Additionally, experiments with contraceptive foams and jellies and the oral contraceptive were carried out on Puerto Rican women.

The attempt to aid Puerto Rico's economic development through birth control programs was interpreted by Catholic-Nationalist groups as immoral, racially suicidal, and irrelevant to the true causes of underdevelopment. As early as 1926, these groups had argued that the problem of poverty in Puerto Rico was primarily determined by the maldistribution of socioeconomic resources (*El Piloto*, July 15, 1926). This line of reasoning has persisted in *independentista* thought, and its clearest statement is to be found in a series of articles written by Bishop Parrilla, a portion of which we extract here (*Claridad*, April 5, 1972):

[1] Initially popular among Puerto Rican doctors as the only viable solution to high fertility, female sterilization appears to have been adopted by many Puerto Rican women as the BEST solution. Demand now exceeds ability of the system to provide this service, at least in the public sector.

Among the fallacies propagated by the neo-malthusians when they particularly consider economically underdeveloped countries is the one that affirms that the high birth rates that exist in these nations are the cause of underdevelopment ... it is also true that careful analysis has not been given to the degree to which population growth stimulates economic growth.

Some *independentista* analysts, however, incline toward acceptance of the thesis of overpopulation in relation to available resources. These advocate population control in conjunction with a more rational distribution of resources, although they argue that overpopulation must be viewed as a symptom rather than the cause of underdevelopment (Vázquez Calzada 1966).

This sector is strongly critical of an industrialization policy which on the one hand exports its unskilled labor supply while failing to control in-migration of foreign skilled workers. The conclusion drawn is that the benefits of industrialization accrue to aliens rather than to the Puerto Rican labor force (Vázquez Calzada 1963). Moreover, some would argue that it is illogical to consider Puerto Rico as being overpopulated in the absence of effective insular control over in-migration. Puerto Rico's impotence in this regard reflects the fact that migration policy directives are under federal control (*La Hora*, August 11, 1972).

To summarize, the position of *independentista* groups in Puerto Rico concerning birth control programs has been one of rejection and opposition. Throughout the history of the birth control movement this opposition has been based on moral, religious, and nationalist grounds. There has also been a tendency to emphasize the positive aspects of population growth for economic development, although some have conceded a need for some form of fertility control in view of the island's scarcity of natural resources.

In the decade of the sixties, the independence movement in Puerto Rico adopted a more explicitly socialist ideology. This was formalized in the electoral platform statement of the PIP in May 1971, and in earlier declarations of the Movimiento pro Independencia (MPI) which became the PSP in 1971 (PIP 1971; PSP 1972b; MPI 1969). It is important to note that this was a gradual transition, and that many of the Catholic-Nationalist positions, noted earlier, can readily be adapted to a Marxist framework. A class analysis is implicit in the rejection of birth control as a menace to national identity and an effort aimed at cultural assimilation. These are easily equated with the neo-Marxist tenet that imperialist-sponsored birth control programs are racially inspired and aimed at the poor. The pronatalist thesis that numbers are wealth approximates the Marxist position that population pressure is a precondition of transformation of capitalist social and economic structures. The fusion of these two ideological streams is clearly stated in the following article published in an *independentista* journal:

The United States public birth control policy is very clear. It is predominantly racial and cultural on a purely national level [against unassimilated ethnic minorities] and imperialist and defensive [against Third World countries] for reasons of economy and security at the international level (*Claridad*, February 20, 1972).

The adoption of explicitly socialist platforms by the two major independence parties can be attributed to internal developments within Puerto Rico as well as to external influences. In the first place, the persistence of social and economic inequality despite rapid economic growth requires explanation, and this is provided by the Marxian concept of structured inequality within a capitalist colonial situation (Nieves Falcón 1971; Ramírez, et al. 1972). Disillusionment with the promises and outcomes of Operation Bootstrap necessitated a theoretical reformulation which would take into account the island's structural position vis-à-vis the United States and other countries, as well as its purely "national" problems of loss of cultural identity. Secondly, counterbalancing forces to the Catholic tradition within the movement have in recent years made themselves felt. These forces have included an infusion of Protestant influence into the leadership and membership structure, as well as growing secularism in the society at large. In March 1973, of the nine members of the Executive Committee of the PIP, six were either Protestant ministers or came from Protestant families.

The Cuban Revolution of 1959 and its aftermath also had considerable influence on *independentista* ideology and strategy. There were historical links between the independence movements of Cuba and Puerto Rico (Maldonado-Denis 1972: 47, 235, 255), and Cuba's success acted as a catalyst to the reevaluation of the ideological direction of the Puerto Rican independence movement. Additionally, the exposure of *independentista* party members to international currents of thought through travel and study opportunities abroad has had the effect of broadening the scope of analysis of Puerto Rico's problems. More specifically, with respect to the issue of population and family planning programs, the articulation of the concept of the "colonial experience" of Third World nations (Fanon 1963) has tended to reinforce the rejection of "imperialist" birth control programs. On the other hand, information has also been disseminated to Puerto Rico about the more recent population theories and policies which, as we have seen, have been implemented in many of the socialist countries including Cuba, the Soviet Union, and China. Finally, the growing influence of the movement for the liberation of women cannot be discounted even in this Latin culture where *machismo* is acknowledged as a way of life. (Zayas and Silen 1972).

## SOCIALIST FAMILY PLANNING UTOPIAS IN PUERTO RICO

The policy statement of the PIP with respect to population control and family planning is contained in its 1972 party platform (Partido Independentista Puertorriqueño 1971).[2] This argues that:

1. Puerto Rico has an "apparent" population problem due to the misuse and irrational distribution of its existing resources, rather than to a real disequilibrium between resources and population.
2. The maldistribution of resources is an inherent aspect of a political and economic system based on structured inequality.
3. A contributing factor to the apparent overpopulation problem is the lack of control over foreign immigration.
4. Puerto Rico lacks a coherent plan of economic development which truly corresponds to the needs of the Puerto Rican people, and as a result suffers from geographical maldistribution of its population.
5. The Puerto Rican woman's free choice in controlling her reproduction has been inhibited by her unequal status in the society. Her freedom to make decisions affecting her own life has been limited further by lack of adequate information and education concerning the "population problem."

On the basis of the foregoing analysis, the PIP platform concludes that Puerto Rico does not presently have a real population problem. However, it will be necessary in the future to "stabilize" population growth rates in order to strike a balance between the number of inhabitants and economic development. The measures proposed by PIP relevant to population control are:

1. A universal comprehensive health system, emphasizing preventive care, and abolishing the elitist and profit-making concepts of the medical profession.
2. Within this comprehensive health system a voluntary family planning service and intensive educational campaigns. The platform specifically rejects coercive mass programs, particularly those involving sterilization and abortion.

[2] See especially the sections on "Population and Family" and "Health Services" in PIP Program.

3. Recognizing the fact that no voluntary family planning program will be successful without a fundamental restructuring of family relations, various programs and services are proposed (e.g. child care centers, divorce laws on a consensual basis, etc.) to aid in the redefinition of the role of women in future socialist society.

It should be clear that the PIP policy statement views family planning as part of a total comprehensive health system within the framework of a restructured economy, and not as an isolated program aimed at fertility control. A reduction in fertility becomes a consequence or by-product of a healthier and better educated population. The stress is on voluntarism within the context of a society dedicated to the creation of "the new (wo)man." In this scheme, the woman is assigned an active role in constructing socialist society, and thus she comes to perceive her own potential contribution as something broader than the homemaker/child-bearer function. Through the resocialization process, the individual's desire and need to limit the number of children born becomes coincident with the needs and goals of the state. Thus a philosophy of voluntarism is not in contradiction with collective national goals.

The PSP, newly reorganized from the MPI in 1971, has not yet participated in an election, nor has it published a platform.[3] Statements by the party to date avoid the subject of contraceptive services and reiterate the nationalist, anti-imperialist position described earlier. However, the party recognizes the right of women and men to control their reproduction, as may be seen in the following declaration:

The PSP-MPI denounces and combats the official policy of the colonial government of Puerto Rico and its programs of birth control, because under the present conditions they constitute an aggressive form of genocide and grave danger to the physical and mental health of the Puerto Rican woman. On the other hand, let it be noted that the PSP-MPI defends the right of all women to equality in all respects. Therefore it defends the right of women as well as men to know and control the integrity of their body. For this reason the PSP promotes a scientific program of sexual education and orientation in every respect so that every person can responsibly exercise his reproductive faculties (Partido Socialista Puertorriqueño 1972: 10–11).

This PSP statement is less specific in its approach to family planning SERVICES. In fact no detailed blueprint for the future has yet been issued by the party, which is still in the initial stage of structural organization. However, given its socialist ideology (based on Marxist-Leninist principles), we predict that a comprehensive health system will be included in

---

[3] It should be explained that the PSP did not participate in the 1972 elections because at this time it was not a registered political party.

their program. We can conclude, further, that family planning services would be available given their explicit reference to "sexual orientation and education." They appear to be in basic agreement with the PIP on the question of the role of women and in their rejection of present efforts at birth control within the context of United States colonialism.

## CONCLUSIONS

We perceive a certain ambivalence in the positions taken by the independence parties on the issue of the relationship between a population control policy and the provision of family planning services. Where the former implies conscious control by the state of the various factors affecting the demographic structure of the population in the interest of planned economic goals, the latter may exist in a society without any specific linkage with national goals. In our opinion, when the PIP refer to "population control," they in fact mean voluntary family planning although in their reference to population "stabilization," they implicitly suggest that in the future such a linkage will have to be made.

We suggest that this ambivalence is an aspect of the tension arising from a rejection on ideological (Marxist-nationalist) grounds of family planning programs as these are presently being administered in (colonial) Puerto Rico, and yet the tacit acceptance in principle of a need for birth control on an individual basis. The latter can be explained in terms of the *independentistas'* perception of present socioeconomic needs and their ideological acceptance of female equality. It is also a pragmatic response to political reality, in that the Puerto Rican electorate clearly accepts and demands contraceptive services.

The resolution of the above contradictions in the *independentista* approach to population control and family planning represents, in fact, a compromise between the Catholic-Nationalist ideological position, which has persisted within the movement, and its new socialist orientation. In deference to the nationalist position it takes an anti-imperialist stance and avoids the issue of overpopulation by labeling it "apparent." It follows the lead of the socialist countries by adopting new rationales for birth control (individual rights, comprehensive health services) while postponing an explicit linkage of family planning programs with national economic goals.

This solution to the tension created by divergent ideological trends within the movement and pragmatic considerations of present reality in Puerto Rico is closely akin to Cuba's policy, outlined previously. It appears to us that as long as the colonial experience informs the development of ideology, this is the only viable population policy that can be adopted by those of socialist persuasion in the Third World. The perspective of the Soviet Union approximates too closely that of the United States in proposing one solution, based on short-range fertility control in the interest of economic development, for the underdeveloped countries and another for themselves. The Chinese posture which explicitly relates birth control programs to national economic goals is inappropriate in colonial and neocolonial contexts where such programs have been viewed as an "arm of imperialism" with strong racial and class bias and as being aimed at thwarting goals of national liberation. In the absence of political self-determination in Puerto Rico, the *independentista* "population control" program must continue to be a blueprint for the socialist utopia rather than a realizable alternative under the present system. It seems probable that even in a Puerto Rican socialist republic, population policy would continue to be influenced by anti-imperalist sentiment, as has been the case in Cuba.

## REFERENCES

ALVARADO, CARMEN R., CHRISTOPHER TEITZE
    1947    Birth control in Puerto Rico. *Human Fertility* 12:15.
*Avance*
    1973    Article on February 26th.
BEVERLY, JAMES
    1932–1933    *Addresses* to the Puerto Rican Legislature.
*Boletín mensual de la Asociacion por bienestar de la familia*
    1937    Article on September 15th.
*Chardon report*
    1935    *Report of the Puerto Rico Policy Commission.* San Juan.
*Claridad*
    1972a    Article on April 5th.
    1972b    Article on February 20th.
    1973    Article on March 11th.
COFRESI, EMILIO
    1968    *Maltusianismo y neo-maltusianismo.* San Juan: Editorial Cultural.
CONSUEGRA, JOSÉ
    1969    *El control de la natalidad como arma del imperialismo.* Buenos Aires: Editorial Galerna.
DE DIEGO, JOSÉ
    1970    "Speech of 1901," in *El Mundo,* April 30.
*El Diluvio*
    1937a    Article on April 17th.
    1937b    Article on May 8th.

*El Mundo*
1973 Article on April 1st.
*El Piloto*
1926a Article on July 8th.
1926b Article on July 15th.
*Family Planning Studies*
1970 Volume 49. New York: The Population Council.
1972 Volume 3. New York: The Population Council.
FANON, FRANTZ
1963 *The wretched of the earth.* New York: Grove Press.
FARIS, JAMES C.
1973 "Social evolution, population and production." Unpublished manuscript, Department of Anthropology, University of Connecticut, Storrs.
HATT, PAUL H.
1952 *Backgrounds of human fertility in Puerto Rico.* Princeton: Princeton University Press.
HILL, REUBEN, *et al.*
1959 *The family and population control.* Chapel Hill: University of North Carolina Press.
*La Hora*
1972 Article on August 11th.
LANDSTREET, BARENT, JR.
1971 "Marxists," in *Ideology, faith and family planning in Latin America.* Edited by J. Mayone Stycos. New York: McGraw-Hill.
1972 "Cuba." Paper presented at Seminar on Population Policies in the Caribbean, Cornell University, November, Mimeographed.
MALDONADO-DENIS, MANUEL
1972 *Puerto Rico, a socio-historical interpretation.* New York: Vintage.
MPI
1969 *Presente y futuro de Puerto Rico.* Movimiento Pro Independencia.
MPI-PARTIDO SOCIALISTA PUERTORRIQUEÑO
1972 *Declaración general de la asamblea constituyente.* Ediciones Puerto Rico.
NACLA (NORTH AMERICAN CONGRESS ON LATIN-AMERICA)
1970 Population control in the third world. *Newsletter* 4.
*New York Times*
1960 Article on November 10th.
NIEVES FALCON, LUÍS
1971 *Diagnóstico de Puerto Rico.* Río Piedras: Editorial Universitaria.
PARILLA BONILLA, ANTULIO
1972 Article in *Claridad,* April 5.
1973 Article in *Claridad,* March 11.
PIP (PARTIDO INDEPENDENTISTA PUERTORRIQUEÑO)
1971 *Independencia socialismo democracía, único camino ...*
PSP (PARTIDO SOCIALISTA PUERTORRIQUEÑO)
1972a "La situación de la mujer en Puerto Rico." Paper presented at the Congress of Socialist Women, Chile. Mimeographed.
1972b Declaración general de la asamblea constituyente del MPI.

POLGAR, STEVEN
 1972 Population history and population policies from an anthropological perspective. *Current Anthropology* 13:203–211.

PRESSER, HARRIET B.
 1969 The role of sterilization in controlling Puerto Rican fertility. *Population Studies* 23:343–361.

*Presupuesto*
 1973 *Presupuesto para el Gobierno de Puerto Rico, 1974* [Budget proposal for Puerto Rican Department of Treasury]. San Juan.

RAMÍREZ, RAFAEL, *et al.*
 1972 *Problemas de desigualdad social en Puerto Rico.* Río Piedras: Ediciones Librería Internacional.

*San Juan Star*
 1973 Article on March 6th.
 1973 Article on July 3rd.

STYCOS, J. MAYONE
 1955 *Family and fertility in Puerto Rico.* New York: Columbia University Press.

VÁZQUEZ CALZADA, JOSÉ L.
 1963 "La emigración Puertorriqueña: solución o problema." Mimeographed.
 1966 "El desbalance entre recursos y población en Puerto Rico." Mimeographed.
 n.d. "La esterilización feminina in Puerto Rico." Unpublished manuscript.

WINSHIP, BLANTON
 1937 Address to Puerto Rican Legislature.

ZAYAS, NANCY, JUAN A. SILEN
 1972 *La mujer en la lucha hoy.* Río Piedras, Puerto Rico: Ediciones Kiriki.

# Fertility and the "Pill" in a Texas Barrio

MARÍA-LUISA URDANETA

Mexican-Americans constitute the second largest ethnic minority in the United States. They are descendants of Spanish-speaking groups, primarily of New World origin, and the majority are of Mexican descent. Of the eight million Spanish-speaking peoples in the United States today the large majority reside in the Southwest in an area generally corresponding to the area ceded to the United States by Mexico in 1848.

In this paper the word *Anglo* designates the English-speaking white American of non-Mexican origin; Spanish-speaking residents of the Southwest are referred to as Mexican-Americans or Chicanos. Only in the last decade has the Chicano population begun to be systematically studied. They constitute an extremely heterogeneous socioeconomic and ethnic group whose most salient characteristics today are Mexican descent coupled with a relatively low income and educational attainment. They also have unusually high fertility — their birth rate is about 50 percent greater than that of the American population as a whole (U. S. Commission on Civil Rights 1968: 11; Grebler, et al. 1970: 131–135).

## OBJECT OF STUDY

In an attempt to explain the higher fertility of Mexican-American women Bradshaw and Bean, two sociologists, examined several abstracted empirical practices and circumstances which could differentially affect the fertility of 348 couples in Centex (a pseudonym), Texas. After looking at the influence of various demographic factors such as years of schooling, income, religion, age at marriage, marriage and presence of spouse, birth spacing, contraceptive use, and values and beliefs supporting fertility, the authors concluded that "... the cultural context of childbearing seems at this time to offer the most powerful set of explanations of higher Mexican-American fertility" (1972: 43).

Subsequent anthropological research done in the same city at a Model Cities family planning and obstetrics clinic — where approximately 76 percent of the clients are Mexican-American, 22 percent are black and 2 percent are other — suggests that the frequent, but seldom-mentioned side effects of the "pill" and the lack of clients' awareness of available options, together with health care delivery, socioeconomic, and educational variables account for much of the higher fertility rate of this group.

The purposes of this study are to consider several of these variables, to focus on the pill's side effects, and to suggest that there is a strong element of self-fulfilling prophecy involved when crucial variables such as health care delivery and socioeconomic and educational level are not scrutinized. This omission has serious repercussions. Among them is the fact that such users of social-science findings as policy makers and other social scientists embrace these notions of cultural uniqueness and often utilize them to "explain" why American institutions fail to reach the Chicano population.

## SETTING

The great majority of Mexican-Americans in Texas cluster around the south and central portions of the state. Centex is located in central Texas and has a population of approximately 252,000. As the location of many governmental agencies and of a main branch of the state university, the city is considered one of the centers of governmental and educational activities in Texas. Its economy is highly oriented toward state government; i.e. in 1960 nearly 30 percent of those employed worked for some form of government including the state university and the public schools. This traditional dominance by government and education continues into the present, although attempts are being made to diversify the economy by encouraging light industry, particularly research and developmental operations, to locate in the area.

Two major ethnic or minority groups accounted for approximately one-fourth of the city's population in 1970. Blacks comprised 11.9 percent of the population; persons with Spanish surnames, 14.2 percent. These "minority" groups are concentrated in approximately one-ninth of the city's area in what has become — since 1968 — Centex's Model Cities area (U.S. Department of Commerce 1970).

Model Cities is one of the community development programs of the federal government to assist the poor, using grant-in-aid and matching funds from the Departments of Health, Education and Welfare and of Housing and Urban Development. Its approach is a process to reform local agencies' methods of providing services to the disadvantaged; to develop new procedures for providing, enhancing, and expanding services by new and existing agencies; and to enhance interagency co-operation by acting as a liaison agency.

The Centex Model Cities area is populated by low-income families. Of these 76 percent are Mexican-American, 22 percent are black and two percent are Anglo families (U.S. Department of Commerce 1970).

Data gathered in the 1970 census show that 75 percent of the employed Model Neighborhood Area (MNA) residents of Centex hold unskilled jobs compared to 20 percent for the rest of the city. The median school years completed by persons over age twenty in the MNA is six years. Only 1 percent of the MNA residents are college graduates as compared to 22 percent for the rest of the city.

In November of 1971 a comprehensive multipurpose family outpatient clinic was opened for service to all MNA residents. The health care staff operates, among others, a family-planning and obstetrics clinic. The purpose of this family-planning clinic is to provide information and services to Model Cities Area women of childbearing age so as to improve maternal health, and "ideally" to provide these women freedom of choice in determining the size of their families and the spacing of their children.

According to the 1970 Census there were 20,680 residents in the MCA. Of these 4,414 are females between the ages of fifteen and forty-four years; they constitute the total population potentially eligible for family planning services. Women participating in the program must be Model Neighborhood residents and at least 10 percent of the caseload must be welfare recipients. In twenty months of operation the clinic has seen over 1,200 women. The family planning clinic is located in a section of the family outpatient clinic building and is composed of a large waiting room, two examining rooms, three private offices and a small makeshift laboratory. The family planning and obstetrics clinic in this locale (there are two other agencies "servicing" the MCA women of Centex) is open Tuesdays from 4.30 to 6.30 p.m.; Wednesdays from 8.00 a.m. to 12.30 p.m. and Fridays from 12 noon to 2.30 p.m. Model Neighborhood women learn about these facilities through their peers.

Outreach is done also by the public health aides of the project and the public health nurses of Centex. The clinic is staffed by one gynecologist; two registered nurses, one of whom is the clinic coordinator; two clinic aides who also serve as outreach workers; an office clerk and an average of three neighborhood community volunteers. One of the volunteers and one of the clinic aides are Spanish-speaking Mexican-Americans. This facility is exceptional in the sense that its clinic coordinator is a registered nurse very much aware of socioeconomic, educational and cultural differences between clinic staff and clientele. It is unfortunate that strong institutional, economic, and political restrictions limit her effectiveness. Services are periodically reassessed and new ways for more accessible health care are frequently being explored.

## METHODOLOGY

Data for this study were gathered by the author while serving as a clinic volunteer. The author is a registered nurse who is a Spanish-speaking South American (Colombia) and a graduate student in anthropology. These data are part of a larger study that has been in progress for the past fourteen months. The research techniques employed are participant observation and individual informal interviewing of each client as she proceeds through the clinic. Some clients are also visited and interviewed in their own homes and admitted as patients in the City-County Hospital. The population studied includes 125 clinic clients.

The clinic clients are divided into 38 primiparas (women in their first pregnancy) and 87 multiparas (women who have borne more than one child).

Every client seeking the use of the family planning or obstetrical clinic services ineluctably goes through a standard admission procedure; on her first visit the new patient checks in with the front-desk receptionist at the family outpatient clinic who routes her to the social service office, where she is screened for eligibility — she must meet the Office of Economic Opportunity poverty guidelines. After this assessment she goes to the office of the family planning admissions clerk, where her obstetrical and gynecological history is obtained. The patient then is channeled to the laboratory section of the waiting room. Here blood and urine specimens are collected for multiple pertinent analyses by one of the clinic's registered nurses. This is one of several time intervals during the patient's clinic visit when client and nurse are alone and much information is exchanged.

If the client is seeking prepartum (before-delivery) care and is having any abnormal signs or symptoms, e.g. swelling of ankles, low hemoglobin etc., either the clerk, clinic aide or registered nurse will inform the nurse in charge and enter it in the patient's chart. If the client is seeking family planning counseling, it is at this point during the patient's clinic visit when the nurse counsels in private with the patient. During this private session information is provided to the patient on different types of contraceptives available, on the advantages and disadvantages of each method, and on their use. Drawings, pictures, and a sample kit containing actual-size contraceptives are shown to the client, i.e. packages of different name-brand birth-control pills, types of intrauterine devices (IUD), diaphragm, condom, types of vaginal foam, and injection.

During this conference the nurse discusses the most common problems encountered and the most common errors made when using contraceptives. At this point during the client's clinic visit, procedures that will take place in the examining room are also explained, i.e., placing the client in the lithotomy position, insertion of vaginal speculum, and obtaining a cervical specimen for cytological cancer test. The client is encouraged to ask questions and to discuss any problems or doubts. By this time, usually, the client has chosen the contraceptive method that best suits her particular situation — contrary to widespread impressions, not all women are able to PHYSIOLOGICALLY tolerate the two most effective and acceptable contraceptive methods, the pill, and the intrauterine device. After this conference, the patient is taken to one of the examining rooms. The nurse helps position the patient on the examining table and remains in the room in order to reassure the patient and to assist the doctor.

The gynecologist performs a physical examination which lasts approximately four minutes. The doctor's examination includes the vagina (for cervical cancer — Papanicolau smear), pelvis, and breasts and screening for venereal disease. After the physical examination, the gynecologist occasionally rejects on medical grounds the method of contraception chosen by the patient. In these cases an alternative method is suggested. Approximately 83 percent of the clinic clients choose the pill, 12 percent the IUD, and 5 percent choose other methods. Due to space limitations, this study will consider only those patients who have used or are using the pill.

If the patient has chosen the pill, a prescription for a three-month supply is written by the doctor. This prescription is filled free of charge by a nearby pharmacy that is under contract with the Model Cities. The patient is asked to return in three months. One month after the client has been on the pill she is visited at home by one of the outreach workers. The worker helps with any problems that may have arisen and answers any questions that the client may have. A week before the patient is due for a pill-supply visit, a reminder of her next clinic appointment is mailed to her. If the client does not meet her appointment the nurse or outreach worker calls or visits the patient to ascertain the reason and to encourage the patient. It should be noted here that this clinic has a dropout rate of only 8 to 10 percent while the other family planning agencies in Centex have a dropout rate of 45 to 50 percent.

During the second visit the patient is encouraged to assess the degree of satisfaction with the pill and to discuss any problems encountered with its use.

Patients in the program for the first year are given physical examinations every six months. Those in the program thereafter are examined annually if they have a "negative" cervical cancer test and/or are under thirty-five years of age. Patients thirty-five years old or older or with "positive" or questionable cervical cancer tests are examined every six months. Subsequent visits for refills of their contraceptive supplies require only a brief stopover: long enough to pick up a prescription and to confer with the nurse about any problems that may have surfaced in the interim.

If the patient comes to clinic for prepartum (before birth of baby) care she will have the same laboratory and physical examinations done that are done on a client who is to go on the pill. After the examinations are done and the medical history is obtained, the patient is informed about the estimated date of birth of her baby. She is also given a three-month supply of vitamins and iron tablets and asked to return monthly for a physical checkup. During each monthly visit, the patient is observed for any complications of pregnancy.

The clinic pays the City-County Hospital, the only nonprivate hospital in Centex, for obstetrical delivery services to those clients who are on welfare. An uncomplicated delivery costs a minimum of $325; a delivery by Caesarean section costs a minimum of $670. Those who are not on welfare make their own financial arrangements for these services with the hospital. A copy of the patient's prepartum and obstetrical history is sent from the clinic to the hospital via direct teletype. The patient is visited in the hospital by one of the clinic nurses a day or two following the birth of her infant. The Wednesday clinic is usually the largest, averaging forty clients per session. Other clinic sessions average an attendance of twenty-five clients. During each visit the client spends an average of two to three hours at the clinic.

## FINDINGS

Reference has already been made to the fact that clients from the Model Cities outpatient family clinic are at the bottom of Centex's socioeconomic ladder. Ninety-two out of 125 clients interviewed are Catholic. Of these none voiced objections to birth control on religious grounds. Data from this study support findings of Alvirez (1973) and O'Grady (1973) in which Catholic Mexican-Americans seem unfettered by Catholic legalistic dicta on the use of birth control. Religion appears to be primarily comforting and traditional rather than institutional and binding.

During the twenty months that the clinic has been in operation, approximately six Mexican-American clients have come to the clinic for PREMARITAL counseling and/or birth control. The overwhelming majority of primigravidas seen at the clinic are in their middle teens. All but two of these primigravidas were pregnant before their eighteenth birthday. Of thirty-eight primigravidas interviewed none had completed high school; and of these, the ones that were married had husbands who were engaged in low-skill, manual, low-paying occupations. Only one of the women in this group had used any form of contraception; for a period of eight months after marriage she had used, INTERMITTENTLY, contraceptive pills which she had acquired from her sister.

Our data suggest that most of these women had married or mated in profound ignorance of family-planning issues. Only three of the women in this group had had some classes in sex education while in school. Some had bits and pieces of information, but modesty, lack of skill and habit in verbal communication, and lack of awareness of opportunities to learn about contraception, rendered most of these primiparas ill-prepared for decisions and events about sex and its probable consequences. Thirty-three of the women in this group replied that their pregnancy was unplanned. When asked if they would be interested in learning about means available to help "time" or "space" their future pregnancies more than half of the primigravidas answered affirmatively.

Classes instituted by the nurses to instruct primiparas in the anatomy and physiology of human reproduction and obstetrics, and to counsel them on various methods of contraception reveal that there is a surprising lack of knowledge of sexuality on their part and a very real barrier in communication between clients and most of the health-care deliverers. The clients' lack of accurate knowledge on these topics differs little from that of age-group peers of higher socioeconomic groups such as high school and college students. Upon request by community groups (e.g. a community health clinic serving the collegiate clientele at Centex) the Model Cities clinic's nurse coordinator provides rap sessions and teaching in general sex education and family planning. These rap sessions show that similar myths and misconceptions are shared by both teen populations, i.e. a girl can get pregnant only when the moon is at a half crescent (a version of the rhythm method?); to keep her from getting pregnant the pill is placed in the vagina before intercourse; douching soon after intercourse prevents pregnancy; a girl cannot get pregnant unless both partners participate fully in the sex act; withdrawal of the penis before ejaculation is an effective contraceptive measure.

A marked difference in language skills and frequency of verbal participation, however, is noted between these two chronological peer groups. In contrast to the relatively elaborate language structure and extrovertedness of the collegiate group, Model Cities Mexican-American primiparas' language more frequently is characterized primarily by short, simple often unfinished sentences without nuances of meaning and a marked timidness. This fact presents a serious challenge to deliverers of health care, the majority of whom are impervious to these differences. Or, if aware, they are only now experimenting with ways to bridge the gap.

Interaction between clients and the typically Anglo middle-class clinic staff is greatly hampered:

1.  By the staff's inability to translate cryptic medical nomenclature into familiar, easily understood "public" language;

2.  By lack of Spanish-speaking medical and nursing personnel familiar with the local Spanish dialect and the barrio's ethnomedical taxonomy, e.g. *regló* [menstruated], *hacer las aguas* [urinate], *me usó* or *panochar* [have sexual intercourse], *aliviarse* [to give birth; literally, to be relieved of an affliction], *hacer encargo* [expecting; literally, to place an order], *ha dieta* [the forty-day period following delivery, a time of dietary and behavioral taboos; literally, to diet], *no puede alborotar* [cannot reach sexual climax], *paño* [irregular deposition of facial pigment, (one of the pill's side effects); literally, wool cloth or piece of cloth], *quedar gorda* [to become pregnant], *la purgación* [syphilis], *deshecho* [vaginal discharge];

3.  By lack of personnel's time to listen carefully and to probe in order to get at the meaning of the client's questions and answers; and

4.  By lack of visuals, handouts, and other materials that help explain these matters in a simple and meaningful fashion; pamphlets available are notoriously insensitive to these women's minimal language skills and educational level.

A notable difference between primiparas and multiparas is the readiness among multiparas to discuss marital and birth control issues. It appears as if the reality of parenthood and of daily problems to be handled and the personal conviction of her fecundity prompts the multipara to deal with issues that she still does not fully understand but which she can no longer ignore as she did prior to connubiality and parenthood. By this time in her life she knows that conception comes as a result of sexual intercourse and that there are ways of preventing pregnancy. Another related difference noted between these two groups is that by this time in her marital relationship, the multipara and her partner are communicating feelings and problems associated with sex and contraception. With a very few exceptions, multiparas interviewed had discussed the issue of contraception with their partners.

Data suggest that a large proportion of these women's mates appear to view contraception as a woman's problem and a woman's choice; i.e. if she wants protection, he will not oppose it, but she will have to be the one to take the necessary steps to procure it and she will be the one who uses it. Research findings reveal that by the time a Model Cities clinic client has borne more than two children 96 percent of them have used some type of contraceptive measure at one time or another. Furthermore, of these 87 percent have tried the pill, but its use has been haphazard, and understanding of how and why it works is nebulous. The most alarming statistic is that 51 percent of these women were first introduced to the pill's use by a RELATIVE or FRIEND. The fact that her first exposure to the use of this contraceptive device comes from ill-informed peers or socially distant, insensitive health care personnel has severe consequences. The combined effect of the inaccessibility of sound contraceptive guidance, the frequent and disconcerting side effects of the pill, and these women's economic and educational reality severely handicap their chances of becoming effective contraceptive users, hence the noted unrelenting Mexican-American fecundity.

It has only been thirteen years (1960) since the first pill for family planning became available (Searle Laboratories 1970: 16). For the first time, here was a preparation which could be taken orally, at a time disassociated from the sex act, to prevent conception. This represented a significant departure from both mechanical devices such as the condom and the diaphragm and chemical barriers such as creams, jellies, and foams which had to be applied locally and just prior to coitus. By the fall of 1970, more than twelve million prescriptions had been filled for women in the United States (1970: 20). The pill contains two synthetic hormones — estrogen and progesterone — which inhibit ovulation. If the female egg is absent during copulation, impregnation of it by the male sperm cannot occur. The pill is 100-percent effective when taken as instructed

(Cherniak and Feingold 1972: 16). Its use is relatively "safe," easily reversible, and in the control of the woman.

It is not widely known that there are two oral contraceptive pill methods: the combination method, which causes changes in the woman's body so that she does not ovulate, and the sequential method, which prevents a fertilized egg from becoming implanted in the wall of the uterus. Each method has pills of varying dosage of these synthetic hormones which affect patients differently. Because of its relation to endocrine balance and its effect on body physiology, the pill is available only on prescription from a medical doctor. Proper use requires initial examination and periodic supervision by a physician. Oral contraceptives should not be used and are not prescribed for women afflicted with certain ailments such as heart disease, endocrine disorders, and blood-clotting disturbances.

Use of the pill even under the best of circumstances does present certain difficulties — difficulties which in the United States today could be considered inversely related to its consumer's socioeconomic status. At Centex to become a user requires an initial investment of approximately $37.50, if going the private physician route — this includes doctor, laboratory, and pharmacy charges. Thereafter, it averages $2.50 a month, which is the retail price of an envelope containing a month's supply of tablets. Some physicians issue prescriptions for a twelve-month supply at a time. If the patient is poor and eligible for Model Cities family planning services it requires that she be aware of the option and an initial time investment of from three to six hours to negotiate the transaction. The initial investment cost does not include revisits for control of side effects.

Remembering to take one pill every day is a nuisance even for women who understand its effect, know what to do in case annoying side effects are present, and do not live in overcrowded homes with little privacy and few places to hide the pill container away from the reach of children. Annoying side effects are quite common though transient in the first three months of CONTINUOUS use while the body is adjusting to the new hormonal levels. Side effects usually disappear by the fourth month of continuous use. The most frequent complaints are mood changes, irritability, headaches, nausea, weight gain, tenderness of the breasts, and bleeding between menstrual periods. Most side effects induced by oral contraceptives are related to estrogen.

If the pill is too highly anti-estrogenic (more progesterone than usual) for a particular woman she will experience mood changes including depression and changes in sexual desire, fatigue, decrease in amount and duration of menstrual flow, and other annoying symptoms which can usually be eliminated by switching to an oral contraceptive with less progesterone. Nausea is the pill's most common side effect. If it occurs, it usually appears within two days after the first pill is taken. This side effect can be avoided by taking the daily pill after a full meal, or by taking the pill just before going to sleep, or by taking it with a glass of milk or a mild antacid. Fluid retention can occur as a result of estrogen's effects on the body's fluid retention of salts. A general "bloated feeling," and a rapid weight gain (which is mostly fluid retention) are symptoms of this side effect. This condition can be alleviated by a low salt diet, restricted water intake, and if necessary, a diuretic to draw fluid from the tissues into the renal system.

Bleeding between menstrual periods while on the pill is a side effect caused by progesterone deficiency. If it occurs, such bleeding episodes usually disappear by the fourth month of CONTINUOUS pill usage. If it persists, a pill with a higher dosage of progesterone can be prescribed.

The fact that such a large majority of Model Cities clients have attempted to use the pill, and yet a considerable number desist before the body has adjusted to the new hormonal levels led to a scrutiny of questions such as: Who introduced the client to its use? Was the client satisfied with the results? Were there any problems? If so, what were they?

Multiparas appeared to be divided into three groups; those who were introduced to its use by friend or relatives, 51 percent; those who were introduced to its use by hospital personnel i.e. residents, interns, and nurses, 38 percent; and those introduced to its use by private physicians, 11 percent.

Of those who were introduced to its use by their peers a small minority has used the pill continuously since then. To obtain new supplies the woman asks her pill mentor to buy them for her with the mentor's prescription; or the client goes to a private physician or one of the three family planning services at Centex to enter as a client. Multiparas who had used the pill or were using it but were dissatisfied or encountered problems using it gave the following comments:

I tried it for a few days but I felt awful. (Awful?) Yes. I would wake up with a real bad headache that made me want to throw up. It would get worse during the day.

Oh gosh, I used it for about two months but it got so that I cried easily; I was mad at the kids all the time and did not want my husband to "use me".

When I used the pill I stopped *reglando* [menstruating] and this got me real worried, you know.

After I started using it I began to bleed all the time. My mother told me to quit using it because that was what was causing it.

Oh nurse, that stuff is so strong that my husband does not want me to use it anymore. (What do you mean by strong?) After I started taking it ... Oh I really feel ashamed talking about this ... (Well at times the pill does make a woman feel differently and makes her change moods.) Oh I know, after I started taking it I wanted my husband "to use me" everyday. This was fine with him for a while and he used to tease me about it. But later on when he could not do it and two or three days would go by without him using me I wanted to hit him. So he talked real rough to me and asked me what kind of chippie was I. I told him, what did he prefer? For me to come to him, or go find some other man. This really has bothered me. I have never felt this way before nor talked to him that way.

I gained so much weight after I started taking it that my husband has told me if I get any fatter he is going to divorce me. He teases me, but I really have gained weight. My dresses are now too tight on me.

I stopped taking them after I read in a detective magazine [printed in Mexico] that a woman in Monterrey who has been taking the pill gave birth to a monster with his heart outside his chest, the monster lived for a few days after birth. I got scared because I was taking the pill and had not menstruated for several months.
I thought I was pregnant and something was wrong.

I want to get off the pill but I want some protection like the IUD or whatever you call that thing they put inside of my sister's *matris* [womb] (Why do you want to get off the pill?) Because it makes me feel just awful — all dizzy and nervous like any minute I am going to explode. I work in housekeeping at the hospital and the slightest smell or sight makes me want to vomit.

Those things made me so nervous ... I was fighting with my husband all the time and *pegandole a los kids por cualquier cosa* [hitting the kids for the slightest reason].

We go to the [Mexican] border to see our relatives during my husband's vacation and on long weekends. Sometimes I forget to take the pills with me. I bought some in Nuevo Laredo but they are not the same. Those made me feel real shaky and funny all over.

Multiparas who meet the City-County Hospital's poverty guidelines (these are more stringent than those of the Model Cities clinic) and thus qualify for staff (charity) services at time of parturition are attended by the hospital's obstetrical and gynecology resident and interns. A woman spends an average of three days in the hospital following delivery of her infant. During one of these three days the intern talks to the patient about contraceptives. If she is interested, he provides her with a month's supply of pills and instructs her to return either to the hospital's out-patient clinic or to the Model Cities clinic for a checkup and free refills.

Multiparas from the Model Cities clinic who have been introduced to the pill by the City-County Hospital personnel are for the most part unaware of what side effects to expect or what to do in case they experience them. Furthermore, it is left up to the patient to seek follow-up care. Hospital personnel perform under the assumption that psychological factors play a large part in the incidence of side effects; thus, if a client is sensitized to expect side effects, they may very well occur. The data suggest that this attitude is detrimental and keeps many women from becoming effective contraceptive users. The following was discreetly taped during a session between an intern and a nineteen-year-old Mexican-American woman, who the day before had given birth to her third child.

Dr.    How are you doing today?

Mrs.  Fine [Patient smiles and lowers head]

Dr.    You will be going home pretty soon, Mrs. X. Has anyone ever talked to you about contraception?

Mrs.  Counter what?

Dr.    About spacing your children so they won't be born so close together.

Mrs.  No.

Dr.    Well, would you like for me to tell you about it?

Mrs.  All right.

Dr.    Well, there are several methods. The most popular is the pill because it is the easiest to take. Are you allergic to any drugs or medications that you know of?

Mrs.  [Hesitation, no answer]

Dr.    Have you ever had any severe throbbing headaches or problems with your blood clotting?

Mrs.  No, I guess not.

Dr.    Good ... now then, this is how you take the pill. Jot down the first day of your menstruation. Five days afterward you take the first of these white pills, then continue taking one every day for twenty-one days. You don't have to take the orange-colored pills, those are sugar pills and not necessary. Take only the white ones. One week before you run out of them go to the clinic and they will give you some more free. If you have any problems come and see us. Do you have any questions?

Mrs.  [Hesitation; shakes head from side to side]

Dr.    You are just fine. I'll see you later.

This patient was discharged from the hospital. A month later she came to the clinic for refills. The client did not know the name of the particular pills she was using. The clinic physician issued a prescription for a three months' supply. Two and a half months later the client came back to the clinic complaining that she felt extremely nervous and nauseated and that she had not had any "period" since the birth of her baby.

After a long conversation between the patient and the nurse it was ascertained that the client had been inadvertently switched from the combination to the sequential pill method. The patient was taking only the white pills and none of the colored ones, part of which are an essential component of the sequential method and necessary for menstruation to occur.

Other similar cases have occurred; they differ only in the fact that when menstruation does not occur the client discontinues its use. Eventually, these clients are again gravid. Often the client does not understand much of the terminology used by health care personnel. Terms such as allergy, contraception, estrogen, fertilization, hormone, sexual intercourse, menstrual cycle, menstruation, ovary, sperm, uterus, and vagina are unknown to her. Personnel should be aware that when a new concept is introduced the patient does not know enough about what it entails in order to ask questions at THAT PARTICULAR TIME.

A multipara from the Model Cities Clinic who has been introduced to the pill by City-County Hospital or Planned Parenthood clinic personnel is for the most part, as we have previously stated, unaware of what side effects to expect or what to do in case she experiences them. Furthermore she lacks the crucial "public" language introduction to the pill AND emotional reassurance during the first three cycles of pill use, which the Model Cities family planning clinic is just now trying to provide. The data suggest that repeated discussions on the same topic, asking the client to state in her own words the information just received, listening to the questions the client is trying to verbalize, and home visits by perceptive bilingual clinic outreach personnel pay big dividends in helping the client to become an effective contraceptive user.

## SUMMARY AND CONCLUSIONS

Research done in a Model Cities family planning clinic in a Mexican-American barrio in Texas indicates that, contrary to widespread impressions, Chicanas of low socioeconomic status are active seekers of contraception. However limited alternatives due to their narrow economic and educational range and the inadequacies of a predominantly middle-class health care delivery system and personnel, critically inhibit their effectiveness as contraceptive users.

Findings of this study suggest that the above variables account for much of the higher fertility of this group. Furthermore, unless more health care personnel and policy makers make these services accessible to these people, the poor in America, among whom the Mexican-American is highly and disproportionately represented, will continue to exhibit a high fertility rate.

# REFERENCES

ALVIREZ, DANIEL
  1973 The effects of formal church affiliation and religiosity on the fertility patterns of Mexican American Catholics. *Demography* 10:19–36.
BRADSHAW, BENJAMIN S., FRANK D. BEAN
  1972 *Some aspects of the fertility of Mexican-Americans.* Report of the Commission on Population Growth and the American Future. Washington, D.C.: Government Printing Office.
CHERNIAK, DONNA, ALLAN FEINGOLD
  1972 *Birth control handbook.* Quebec: Handbook Collective Press.
GREBLER, LEO, J. W. MOORE, RALPH GUZMÁN
  1970 *The Mexican American people.* New York: Free Press.
O'GRADY, INGRID P.
  1973 "Childbearing behavior and attitudes of Mexican-American women in Tucson, Arizona." Paper presented at the annual meeting of the American Association of Applied Anthropology, Tucson, Arizona.
SEARLE LABORATORIES
  1970 *Family planning with the pill: a manual for nurses.* Chicago: G. D. Searle and Company, Special Services Department.
U. S. COMMISSION ON CIVIL RIGHTS
  1968 *The Mexican American.*
U. S. DEPARTMENT OF COMMERCE
  1970 *Census of population and housing.* Census tract 17.

# Beyond the Individual for the Practice of Social Medicine: Household Networks as Etiologic-Diagnostic Units

PHILLIP J. EPLING, SUSAN E. VANDALE, GUY W. STEUART

In the context of human social evolution, there has been a concurrent evolution of health and disease patterns. In the last century, and particularly among peoples of industrialized societies, there has been a shift from predominantly communicable disease episodes and causes of death to noncommunicable, long-term illness. Epidemiological data increasingly indicate the importance of daily behavior in the etiology and natural history of the chronic diseases. While daily behavior is also a factor in the incidence of the infectious diseases, immunization as well as broad environmental action have reduced the need to manage and control infectious diseases by means of changes in daily behavior. No such management modes are available for the noncommunicable diseases. Thus, understanding of and intervention directed toward health-related behavioral change have become indispensable aspects of the control of noncommunicable diseases. And because the behavior of the individual is the product of numerous interactions with others, the group nature of the etiology and course is apparent.

Unfortunately the fee-for-service, one-patient-one-healer model has worked against the necessary shift toward larger diagnostic and therapeutic social units. Only after long years of dialogue have public health professionals begun to persuade some physicians that "family," "neighborhood," and "community" medicine are respectable specialities. For the most part, the trend toward greater specialization in services has led to a situation where medical personnel are lacking adequate knowledge of the whole of the biologic unit, as well as an understanding of group interaction. While some may perceive the need for maximizing the biological welfare of the whole of society, as opposed to the welfare of the upper and middle social classes, the profit motive of the medical and drug industries maintains a strong conservative restraint, often preventing necessary changes.

Among public health and preventive medicine personnel in the United States there is a general conviction that "family-centered" practice is desirable because the family as a therapeutic unit has the greatest possibility to effect change in the behavior of patients. At the same time there is also the idea that every population is made up of various kinds of social networks. Knowledge of these interpersonal relationships and interactions is thought to be helpful for planning health services within "community medicine." Further investigation of social networks seems justified on three counts: (1) they have embedded within them the "families" and, of course, the individuals; (2) they appear to be a basic communication and learning structure; and (3) they may have important etiological and intervention potentialities. Unfortunately, there is, to our knowledge, very little concrete epidemiological evidence that supports these general notions.

Because there is a growing consensus that illness is not evenly distributed among individuals and groups within any society (the class nature of certain conditions being increasingly evident), epidemiological analysis is needed to shed light on important etiological mechanisms. The question which is before us is: what "naturally" occurring social unit should be the focus of our attention? We suggest that this unit meet certain criteria. It must be easily delimited and visible. It must be meaningful to those individuals within it, as well as biologically salient. It would be helpful if it were transculturally valid so that methods developed for its delineation in practice may be more or less universally useful. It is made up of a focal household, kin-related households, and friends of the family-related households. It builds on the established ethnographic observation that humans (except in the extraordinary situations) normally cluster themselves into "households," and that certain patterns of relationships based on frequent face-to-face interactions are established among households. If it can be shown that conditions and processes of illness, as well as the epidemiologically associated behaviors, tend to cluster or nest in these structures, then it should be possible to exploit them as explicit diagnostic-therapeutic units.

The diagnostic system outlined below is a tentative one, designed to illuminate some of the structural and dynamic properties of this unit of practice. Although single domestic residential groups are a ubiquitous structural feature of human populations, there is no case we know of where these units stand isolated and independent within a community.

Even in the most highly urbanized and industrialized communities (*Milbank Memorial Fund Quarterly* 1969), it is found that households are linked into networks such as we describe. We suspect that these kinds of social structures (although the composition of ours is arrived at arbitrarily) are among the basic ways that human communities are "tied together." Our household network might be considered as approximately isomorphic with the Primary Sampling Unit long ago suggested by Whiting for cross-cultural studies. Ethnologists have had before them, for some time, the notion that "culture" and behavior are themselves nonrandomly distributed among the individuals of an ethnic community group (Roberts 1951). While the behavioral sciences have been made aware of intraethnic diversity (Valentine 1968) as a general rule, services and programs have been developed and implemented as if these clusterings did not exist or were of minor importance.

The practitioner may well ask "So what?" The answer, although dependent upon detailed analysis in specific populations, is this: if we are to move toward preventive and social medicine we will need larger, more efficient units of diagnosis and therapy.

Household-kin-friend networks are likely to be influential educational and cooperative units. When the properties of the group are analyzed its communication properties will be helpful in planning for therapy. There is increasing evidence leading us to suspect that most illness/health conditions are nested within groups similar to our household net and that these are the salient "real" units for illness/health-related behavior and possibily also for the spread of "epidemics."

If our test of household-kin-friend nets should confirm our hypothesis of nesting, this, of course, would not exclude other units from consideration. The point is that the household network is a more efficient unit than the individual household, because it is a more extended communication unit. On the other hand, the household network avoids the confusion which is caused by the notions of neighborhood or community as a homogeneous whole. In many societies, the household network may well be a "natural" similarity unit for culture in general. If so, we may build upon the notion of cognitive similarity which implies that things thought of as similar will, generally, tend to be acted towards similarly.

"Ecological studies" conducted for the purpose of testing distributional hypotheses (Hinkle 1961) suggest that illness and disease processes and etiologically linked behaviors are, in general, not randomly distributed throughout populations, and that in many cases they appear to be "clustered" or nested in "family groups." Our first concern is to describe and analyze more carefully the clustering of illness and related behaviors in such groups. From our reading of the literature, the clustering at the family-group level is not well understood. In our opinion, one reason for this lack of analysis of the family group is the amount of variation in the structure of this unit.

Assuming that the random model does not hold, we need to explore the likelihood that the household network of kin and friends is a real epidemiological and behavioral unit. The hypothesis which we need to test is: there is more similarity in health/illness episodes and related behaviors within matched disjoint household networks than between them.

The definitions, concepts, and measures, which are the basis of the test of this hypothesis are as follows:

1.  Household: all coresident individuals, the basic sampling unit.
2.  Household network: an arbitrarily defined set comprised of one key household and two kin and 2 friend-related households.
3.  Kin: individuals nominated by one household respondent as "kin" or "relatives," consanguines and affines.
4.  Friends of the family: a relationship between household members and other nominated individuals in which there is frequent visiting back and forth between the houses.
5.  All kin networks are assumed to be composed of symmetric $[r(A,B) = r(B,A)]$ and dyadic relationships which are complete homogeneous graphs, that is to say completely connected (Figure 1).
6.  Within friendship networks the assumption of symmetric and dyadic relationships also holds. But there is no assumption about the density of the net. (Barnes 1969: 225–226). In Figure 2, while individuals D, E, and F each, respectively, are in a relationship with A, they do not necessarily have any sort of relationship with each other.
7.  As a crude index, the size of the intersection between kin and friends nets, the degree of shared persons, tells how "closely knit" the population is. The intersection of the sets of kin and friends is the ratio of the actual number of joint members to the total possible number of shared individuals with a possible range of 0.0 to 1.0 (Figure 3). A measure of both intersection and density of the networks appears to be necessary as a gauge of the expected communications and behavior learning patterns (Barnes 1968).

In traditional and pre-literate and pre-industrial societies the kin and friends sets will often intersect. Within these types of societies, disjoint household networks within a single village may not be found. If a survey such as this were to be done among horticultural peoples, it might be necessary to combine several villages to arrive at a sample of twenty disjoint household networks.

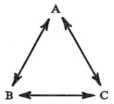

Figure 1. Kin are composed of dyadic relationships. Individual A is household informant and individuals B and C are relatives of A.

Figure 2. Determining the density ratio

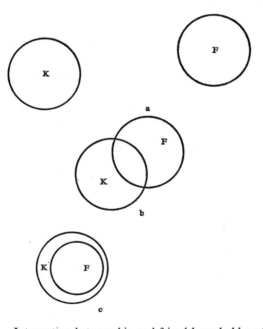

Figure 3 (a, b, c). Intersection between kin and friend household-centered nets:
(a) Joint membership equals 0 percent; (b) Joint membership equals 25 percent;
(c) Joint membership equals 100 percent.

It is likely that for some target populations, for example in urban-industrial areas, a significant number of key households will not have any kin-related households in the area of service. Thus, by our definition of household network, they do not qualify for inclusion in our system. The practical way to handle such situations from the service point of view is to create a separate category of these households in order to measure this phenomenon.

Below we outline the research steps which we are implementing in a rural North Carolina community with a patient/client population of approximately 1,000 people. With an average of five people per house-hold, or roughly 200 households, a sample of forty key households is drawn in a block design. Each block includes 200/40 or five household units, based on geographic proximity. For each key household, a list of two kin and two friend-related households is elicited. From this pool of forty households, at least twenty disjoint networks are located with controls for socioeconomic, ethnic, and educational level. Then a standard medical history questionnaire (Abramson 1966) and standardized questions concerning health-related behaviors are administered for each member (six years and older) of the key household and the related households. (Fanshel and Bush 1970; Goldsmith 1972). A register of health and related behaviors based on the responses to the interviews is compiled for each household network. Table 1 is an abbreviated example of such a register.

Pairwise comparisons among individuals in the health/behavior matrix yields a mean similarity score $\left[\dfrac{\text{matches}}{\text{matches and nonmatches}}\right]$ for each pair of persons within the network (Table 2).

Next, an overall mean similarity score is computed for each network matrix as a whole:

$$\text{similarity score} = \sum_{i=1}^{c} \text{individual similarity scores c,}$$

where $c =$ number of cells compared or $\dfrac{n(n-1)}{2}$

and $n =$ the number of individuals.

Then the mean similarity scores of the different nets are compared using analysis of variance techniques.

Similarly, comparisons are made between the matrices of the different networks to test the hypothesis that: there is greater similarity of health/disease episodes and behaviors within disjoint social networks than between them.

Table 1. Abbreviated example of health and behavior register: medical history and list of behaviors for individuals A, B, C, D, E, and F

| Medical data | A | B | C | D | E | F |
|---|---|---|---|---|---|---|
| Influenza | − | − | − | − | + | − |
| Heart disease | + | − | − | − | − | − |
| Diabetes | − | + | − | − | − | − |
| Hypertension | + | − | − | − | + | + |
| Kidney disease | − | − | − | + | − | − |
| TB | − | − | − | − | − | − |
| Behavioral data | | | | | | |
| Smokes tobacco | + | + | − | − | + | + |
| Drinks alcohol | + | + | + | − | + | + |
| Obese | − | + | − | − | − | − |
| Moderate exercise | − | − | + | − | + | − |
| Use of nonprescription drugs | + | + | + | + | + | + |

Table 2. Example of matrix of similarity scores for pairs of individuals

| | A | B | C | D | E | F |
|---|---|---|---|---|---|---|
| A | − | .6 | .5 | .4 | .2 | .4 |
| B | | − | .7 | .5 | .3 | .6 |
| C | | | − | .7 | .8 | .7 |
| D | | | | − | .5 | .4 |
| E | | | | | − | .6 |
| F | | | | | | − |

The results of these procedures provide a reasonably firm basis for accepting or rejecting the hypothesis in question. A positive result of this test gives support for the assumption that in the service population household networks are etiological and hence diagnostic and therapeutic units of some significance. Although our own studies are as yet in the preliminary stage, the procedures for this study are given here, because they are generally applicable.

Aside from providing information for testing the hypothesis of nesting, the health behavior register could serve as a preliminary screening and diagnostic tool. For example, it provides a rapid and continuous picture of health states, episodes, and behaviors within a unit of practice. At a glance, the health professional can see beyond the individual profile to that of the whole unit, as well as the similarity and difference within the unit.

Consider the following diagrams which are multidimensional representations of the similarity matrices of the two household networks, 1 and 2 (Figure 4). Such elementary information may yield great returns in intervention efforts. Take for example, the well-documented case of "Many Farms" in Arizona (McDermott, et al. 1972). Individual Navajo house-

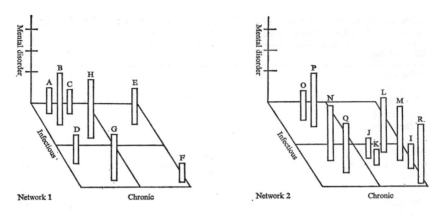

Figure 4.   A three-dimensional pictograph of clustering of illness in two household networks

holds were the unit of enumeration, diagnosis, and intervention in the Navajo-Cornell Field Health Project, in spite of the overwhelming data that the Navajos live in clusters of kin-related households (Roberts 1951). Perhaps some of the disappointing lack of effectiveness in meeting the goals of this lengthy research and service project was based on the use of the separate domicile group as the unit of practice. If Networks 1 and 2 in Figure 4 were two Navajo "camps," the planned intervention would be considerably different, on the basis of the biosocial condition suggested by the clusters. At the same time, the psychological, behavioral, and communication properties of the two units might be exploited for medical intervention.

For additional evidence of the predictive power of the clusterings, a further test may be considered. One year following the initial data collection, another health survey can be administered to the key households of the sample. A check of the second-year data is made against the first-year data to establish any differences in health and behavior status. Using stepwise multiple regression procedures, it is possible to test the hypothesis that the changes in illness episodes among individuals of the key household can be predicted by the pattern of the household network. If this hypothesis is true, then the amount of variance accounted for by successively employing information from kin- and friend-related households is nontrivial. The results of these procedures would yield information such as in Table 3. The prediction of conditions/episodes occurring among individuals in the focal household is significantly enhanced by knowledge of the pattern of these events in the related households of the net.

Table 3.   A greater proportion of the variance within household 1 is explained with the addition of information from successive households 2, 3, 4, and 5

| Step 1 | $R^2$ 1·2 | .25 |
|---|---|---|
| 2 | $R^2$ 1·23 | .32 |
| 3 | $R^2$ 1·234 | .56 |
| 4 | $R^2$ 1·2345 | .61 |

$R^2 = 1.0$, maximum

Having tested the clustering of disease conditions and related behaviors within household networks, the next step is to design a data-record system which would enable practitioners at all levels to make a rapid and reliable analysis of these networks for the purpose of diagnosis and therapeutic intervention. Figure 5 is a quasi-flow chart of a data system, which is capable of being automated and continuously updated. This system delineates and analyzes structurally the household networks of a whole population, beginning from a 20 percent sample.

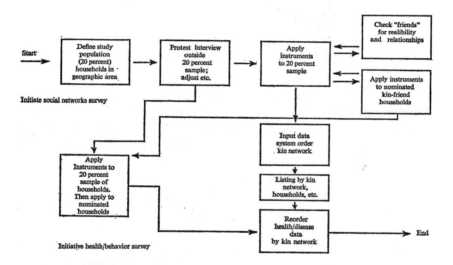

Figure 5.   Quasi-flow chart of a data system

Table 4.   Household 1 is a focal node and opinion leader of the household network

|   | 1 | 2 | 3 | 4 | 5 |
|---|---|---|---|---|---|
| 1 | − | + | + | + | + |
| 2 |   | − | + | O | O |
| 3 |   |   | − | O | + |
| 4 |   |   |   | − | O |
| 5 |   |   |   |   | − |

In conclusion, we turn to the practical application of the types of data and information we have been discussing. The matrix in Table 4 represents a household network reminiscent of those discussed by Loomis and Beagle (1950) with respect to the introduction of new agricultural practices (see also Figure 6).

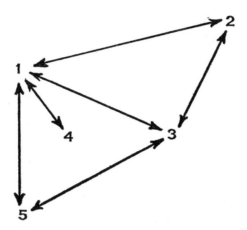

Figure 6.   Household 1 is a focal node and opinion leader of the household network

From the viewpoint of agriculture, as well as of public health and medical care, household 1 is clearly indicated as the household of entree to the network as a whole. It also appears to be the most likely primary partner for the continuing interpersonal relationship between agency and household network. The cooperation of household 1 can ensure continuity of care for the network as a unit of practice.

At least three interlocking dimensions are necessary as part of the initial entree process itself and in planning for long-term provision of care.

First, there is the dimension of interpersonal dynamics within the household network which influences significant social and behavioral components in the health and disease states of the network members. The matrix in fact reflects channels of communication and influence that play a formative or maintenance role in shaping the health-related habits of network members. For example, household 1 may be a source of influence upon the child rearing, care, and/or service-use patterns of the relative isolate household 4.

Second the clinical appraisal, including both previous history and present health status, may indicate behavioral components of a like or complementary nature characteristic of the network as a whole. Certain health and disease syndromes are likely to distinguish this network as a system in contrast to other networks.

For example, one network may show a history of frequent intestinal infection associated with personal habits. Another household network may show a high rate of alcoholism in the adult members. Care priorities may be set in treating the network as a whole. Existing behavioral change determinants, trends, or blocks, which characterize the interpersonal relations in the network might provide the foundations for attempts to influence behavioral components of health status in the member households or indicate the obstacles to be overcome. Thus, while household 1 may constitute a major source of influence on other households in the network, it may also represent a conservative, restraining influence retarding positive health-related change. Moreover, if shared needs felt by network members are sufficiently articulated, pressing, and feasible of solution, they may provide the initial motivations onto which the agency helping role can be grafted.

There is of course, the general expectation of an overall health-disease pattern characteristic of the household network and dinstinguishing it from other such networks. But even where this is not found, the matrix does represent at least one kind of communication network with potential for influencing the behavior of its members and, therefore, their health. More particularly for rural, less technologically developed areas with limited social life-space and mobility, the network may also be a potential action unit to deal with more immediate environmental hazards and for combating such problems. Formal action by the group may be the indicated mode of solution in the control of fly-breeding, malarial vectors, or animal-borne diseases.

With the positive finding that conditions of similar, related, or complementary etiology do characterize the network household members, the network as the unit of practice has considerable reinforcement. Influence attempts channeled through the focal household would be directly germane to the health status of the focal household itself, and, at the same time, would be a vehicle for change in other households in the network.

We have suggested that the household network is a biologically meaningful and behaviorally salient unit of practice intermediate between the individual and the community. A set of procedures is outlined for the testing and validation of the ideas for practice based on this notion.

There are certain major constraints on the emergence of units of practice such as we have described. These include the individual fee-for-service pattern of private practice, the almost exclusively biological emphasis of medical education, and the hegemony of the physician in health services.

All are, however, if somewhat slowly, being eroded in the United States and elsewhere as the need and demand for social medicine is confronted.

There are discernible trends toward universal medical insurance, comprehensive health planning primarily by nonphysicians, consumer participation in health service design and delivery, and the employment of social scientists and the establishment of departments of "community," "social," and "family" medicine in medical schools. If these and allied trends continue, this would suggest an increasingly favorable climate for the development of alternative units of practice.

## REFERENCES

ABRAMSON, J. H.
1966   The Cornell Medical Index as an epidemiological tool. *American Journal of Public Health* 56:287–298.
BARNES, J. A.
1966   "Networks and political process," in *Local level politics*. Edited by M. J. Schwartz, 107–130. Chicago: Aldine.
1969   Graph theory and social networks: a technical comment on connectedness and connectivity. *Sociology* 3:215–232.
BARNETT, G. O.
1968   Computers in patient care. *New England Journal of Medicine* 279: 1313–1318.
COLEMAN, J., K. ELIHU, H. MENZEL
1957   The diffusion of an innovation among physicians. *Sociometry* 20: 253–270.
FLAMENT, C.
1963   Applications of graph theory to group structure. Englewood Cliffs, New Jersey: Prentice-Hall.
FANSHEL, S., J. W. BUSH
1970   A health-status index and its application to health-services outcomes. *Operations Research* 18:1021–1066.
GOLDSMITH, S. B.
1972   The status of health status indicators. *Health Services Reports* 87: 212–220.
HACKENBERG, R. A.
1961   Papago population study, research methods and preliminary results. Tucson: University of Arizona Press.
HARARY, F., I. C. ROSS
1957   A procedure for clique detection using the group matrix. *Sociometry* 20:205–215.
HINKLE, L. E.
1961   Ecological observations of the relation of physical illness, mental illness, and social environment. *Psychosomatic Medicine* 23:289–296.
HUMAN ORGANIZATION
1972   Entire issue 31(2).

KATZ, E.
  1957   The two-step flow of communications; an up to date report on a
         hypothesis. *Public Opinion Quarterly* 21:61–78.
LOOMIS, C. P., J. A. BEAGLE
  1950   *Rural social systems*. New York: Prentice-Hall.
MCDERMOTT, W., K. W. DEUSCHLE, C. R. BARNETT
  1972   Health care experiment at Many Farms. *Science* 125:21–31.
MELTZER, J. W., J. R. HOCHSTIM
  1970   Reliability and validity of survey data on physical health. *Public Health
         Reports* 85:1075–1086.
MERTON, R. K.
  1949   "A study of interpersonal influence and of communications behavior
         in a local community" in *Communications research*. Edited by Paul
         Lazarsfeld and Frank N. Stanton. New York: Harper and Brothers.
*Milbank Memorial Fund Quarterly*
  1969   Entire issue 47(1).
NEWCOMBE, H. B., J. M. KENNEDY, *et al.*
  1957   Automatic linkage of vital records. *Science* 130:954.
SHANAS, E., G. E. STREIB
  1965   Social structure and the family. Englewood Cliffs, New Jersey:
         Prentice Hall.
ROBERTS, J. M.
  1951   *Three Navajo households*. Cambridge: Peabody Museum.
VALENTINE, C.
  1968   *Culture and poverty*. Chicago: University of Chicago Press.
ZOLA, I. K.
  1966   Culture and symptoms, an analysis of patients presenting complaints.
         *American Sociological Review* 21:615–630

# Human Relations versus Social Relations in Medical Care

BROOKE GRUNDFEST SCHOEPF

American medicine is in crisis today, and not only in the area of rising costs. Another significant area of crisis is the doctor-patient relationship. For many poor people in rural areas and in the inner cities, this relationship does not exist. Yet even when care is accessible, patient complaints and social science research reveal serious problems in communication. Spokesmen for the profession are asking us to help train physicians who can treat people as well as diseases. Some physician-educators and social scientists press for deeper understanding of the patient's cultural and psychological needs (Simmons and Wolff 1966; Bloom 1965; Blum 1960; Balint 1957). They also stress the need for greater sensitivity on the part of physicians (Redlich 1968) with which to overcome difficulties of "patient management." These authors apparently hope that greater knowledge and understanding will "remotivate" doctors to communicate more effectively with patients.

Concern for doctor-patient communication is relatively new and represents an about-face similar to that which occurred in industrial relations toward the end of the 1930's following a period of bitter labor strife. In 1951 Arensberg (1965) contrasted the human relations approach with the social structural approach in studies of industrial organization. The first approach searches for means of conflict resolution through opening channels of communication among the occupants of various statuses within a hierarchically structured social system based on discovering mutual understanding and respect.

Chapple (1953) writes that those who attempt to change values in the factory "ignore the very troublesome fact that susceptibility to conversion is generally very rare." Changes secured by these methods are short-lived.

Social structuralists explain this from their findings that the basic interests of persons and groups in hierarchically structured organizations are not only different, but often inherently opposed. This second analytical framework does not hold out much hope regarding the prospects for fundamental change in these institutional subsystems because it views interpersonal relations as an expression of the social structure and particularly the power relations in the organization. While the statuses of doctor and patient draw their specific definitions from the medical subculture, they are rooted in the wider social system of which medical care is one of several institutions devoted to system maintenance (Merton, et al. 1957; Parsons 1951a, b). Thus, consideration of the doctor-patient relationship must take into account not only the subsystem but the wider context as well.

Some aspects of that interrelationship are explored here. More recently another form of the human relations approach, organization development, has been suggested as a way of bringing lasting change to systems of medical care delivery (Barnes 1970). Drawing upon structural analysis and recognizing the positive functions of social conflict, proponents of this approach hope to alter power relationships within the system by drawing upon expanding resources and thereby transforming a zero-sum game into a "we-win" situation. An anthropological perspective on organization development in medical services will be offered in a later paper.

The discussion of findings reported here is normatively based. Social science is inherently a value-laden science, for although we strive for accurate description of events and objective explanation of causal processes, "By its very nature the exercise of critical thought implies a discrimination between what is merely given and what ought to exist" (Lichtheim 1966: 2).

I shall report here on a study of communication between doctors and patients in a surgical specialty facility of a large urban university medical center and its affiliated hospitals (Schoepf 1969). A variety of people come together in institutionalized interpersonal relationships directed toward the performance of instrumental tasks: surgical repair of the damage wrought by illness, trauma, and infection.

I interviewed disfigured patients to find out what the surgeons had told them to expect in the way of treatment and results. The initial aim of the research was to see if patients who were given explicit, realistic information could make a better adjustment to the actual outcome of surgery than patients who were told, "Yes, we can help you," and left to fantasize about what that might entail. We planned to see if the first group of patients got on with the business of adjusting to residual handicap faster than the second group who were encouraged to develop unrealistic expectations.

The research was suggested by an anthropologist who had helped the Center obtain funds for demonstrating the feasibility of surgical, social, and psychological rehabilitation of patients with particular types of visible handicapping and socially stigmatized conditions. Because so many of the patients returned for further surgery over a period of years (only fourteen who entered while I was there had completed their treatment two years later) an outcome study was infeasible. Instead I decided to concentrate on the process of treatment, for the problems that arise in patient care, stemming from the structure of the treatment institution, stand out here in sharp relief. The types of diseases treated at the Center cause many patients to develop deep-seated emotional complications that hamper their social functioning even when they are physically able to carry out many social roles. Furthermore, they are also punished by other people in their social environment who often withdraw from interaction with them or assault them verbally (MacGregor 1963). Some patients were also threatened by impending death from cancer, making them more emotional still.

Several authors (among them F. Davis 1960, Fox 1959, Glaser and Strauss 1965, Quint 1965) have described the difficulties experienced by medical personnel in dealing with similar situations of severe chronic, handicapping, or life-threatening illness. All but one researcher found physicians withdrawing from many of the patients and their families. The exception is the Metabolic Research Ward, described by Fox (1959) where the doctors to some extent made the patients partners in treatment. Yet disease and psychological threat do not fully account for difficulties in doctor-patient communication. M. Davis (1971) reports a study of interaction in a general medical clinic where disease is not a significant factor in communication difficulties. He finds that the interaction process is the key determinant in patients' compliance with doctors' orders but does not account for all the variance. My study suggests that both the interaction process and the structure of medical care facilities as social structural variables related to the wider social system interfere with therapeutic communication.

Some of the Center patients were poor, most were of middle income, and a few were extremely wealthy. Located in a new hospital used primarily for faculty practice and tertiary care, the same modern facilities were used by clinic and private patients. The surgeons were hardworking and offered expert service regardless of the patients' ability to pay. Nurses, aides, and receptionists were thoughtful and concerned. One of the

Center's chief difficulties lay in securing funds to pay for prolonged or repeated hospitalization for uninsured, medically indigent working people, or for patients who had come from other states and countries. A philanthropic society raised money for the Center and a social worker was employed to find funds and make aftercare arrangements as well as to consult about psychosocial problems during treatment. While money was a significant problem it was not responsible for the major difficulties that arose.

## AN ETHNOGRAPHY OF TREATMENT TRANSACTIONS

One hundred patients were interviewed and more were observed, while nine attending surgeons and twelve residents were observed in the examining rooms at clinical conferences and in the minor operating room and on hospital rounds. Staff members and visiting surgeons as well were interviewed, for the most part informally. The most important aspect of this study, however, consists in the recording of "backstage" expressions of attitudes and values in the conference room along with treatment-room behavior, in order to discover group norms and "rules for breaking rules" (Becker, et al. 1961).

Participant observation was the method of choice, not merely because of its congeniality to the anthropologist, but because the study hoped to get beyond what medical practitioners would say for publication, either to a social scientist or to the world at large, through formal interviews or their responses to attitude questionnaires, regarding their values or the purposes of their actions. The raw data are behavior-stream notations from treatment rooms, waiting rooms, clinical conferences, interviews, and conversational gatherings. In addition to verbal messages are notes of spatial arrangements; of rooms, furniture, and people; the passage of time; presentation rituals; paralinguistic utterances such as body postures, gestures, and facial expressions; and tones of voice and rapidity of speaking.

I have attempted to discover the social arrangements which exist apart from the conscious models of the actors and the motives and evaluative statements they apply to their acts, and to "analyze an institution as a concrete event, rather than ... to explore it in general terms as a functional equivalent for doing what is done ....." (Arensberg 1957: 105). This type of analysis of the structure of interpersonal relationships, of small groups as they occur within events and institutions derives in part from the tradition of the applied anthropologists (Arensberg 1965: 317).

Studying the treatment interactions as one would the ceremony of an exotic people, the non-technical aspects of the doctor's communications emerged as a ritual which translates for the patient a socially authorized versions of his or her place in the transaction. Furthermore, the GOOD "bedside manner" and the BAD "communications gap" were found to be two polar modes of interaction in a single system which allows the physician to "turn off" in potentially emotionally-charged situations.

The two transactional styles, however, result in different consequences for the respective patients. Recipients of the bedside manner find their claims to deference upheld; their claims to personal worth and dignity are reinforced by the much-in-demand, high-status physician. On the other hand, recipients of "impersonal care" are demeaned, for when the doctor withholds deference the "constant dialectic between presentational rituals and avoidance rituals" (Goffman 1961: 488) of social interaction is violated unilaterally. In the case of these low-status patients the behavioral language of the status ritual contradicts the verbal message conveyed by representatives of the treatment center when they emphasize the importance of helping patients to achieve a new self-image as normal human beings. Thus although the turnoff ritual does not necessarily violate professional norms, it may hamper the patient's achievement of "weller" psychosocial functioning. This is particularly apparent in illnesses where social rehabilitation is the stipulated goal of treatment.

Patients' questions were not generally welcomed by the surgeons. Those who persisted in asking questions despite the surgeons' attempts to discourage them were sometimes described as stupid, neurotic, troublesome, or hysterical. They frequently found these patients "difficult to manage." Sometimes the doctors shouted at them and treated them brusquely, driving them to tears. Several observers suggested that the surgeons were insensitive or overworked, and sometimes this was indeed the case. On the other hand, the doctors were highly sensitive to the plight of some patients whom they treated with tact and delicacy. With some other patients they apparently turned off their sensitivity. I began to explore possible sociocultural as well as psychological dimensions of this turnoff.

The psychological effects upon physicians of therapeutic impotence are described by other social scientists (Fox 1959). Many of the Center's patients were incurable and sometimes the surgeons thought about how little they could do. For example, one day a doctor turned the pages of a young boy's voluminous hospital record and slumped in his chair saying "Jeeze, will you look at the size of this chart! That means we never CURE them" At a conference where a young woman of eighteen with a grossly disfiguring disease was presented, the senior surgeons lowered their voices as they discussed alternative courses of action. Looking down at the floor while they spoke, instead of at each other, they detailed the disadvantages of each treatment. The boldest approach might very well kill her, while more conservative surgery would not do much to improve her condition. They were clearly discouraged. However, the two surgeons who had actually examined the patient were eager to proceed with radical surgery. One denied the patient's intelligence, the other denied her emotional sensitivity.

This discounting of the patient's social worth was found again and again in difficult cases. Apparently the doctors turned off their awareness of how little they could actually do for some patients and concentrated on the surgery. Therapeutic impotence as a medical student told Fox, "threatens the essence of physicianhood." In our culture, physicianhood signifies actual remediation rather than merely helping a patient to accept and live more comfortably with a medically incurable condition. Stereotyping and devaluing a patient's human worth make the turnoff easier to effect. Another surgeon described his feelings about incurable patients:

You can usually do something to improve their condition. But, of course, any improvement may be minimal. It's harder with the kids .... But with the others, well, you say to yourself, "This guy'll never make any great important contribution to society. He's not a poet or an artist or anything. It's unfortunate, but what the hell.

I asked him if he meant by this that he made an assessment of the patient's social value. He replied:

Exactly, you do just that. And then for the poor buggers you have to say, "That's the Lord's justice" and that's it. But I enjoy the work [and] some of the patients.

In one way, avoidance is functional for it allows the doctor to continue performing his or her professional tasks. Similarly Glaser and Strauss (1966: 178, Note 2) suggest that consigning the terminally ill to separate wards or nursing homes, although it constitutes rejection of these patients, contributes to staff morale and helps motivate them to work hard for those who are expected to recover. Ethical problems aside, it seems likely that errors of judgment become compounded in such situations.

The medical model of disease and treatment can lead to a lack of consensus between physician and patient as to what constitutes a successful outcome. The physician looks at symptoms and procedures while the patient looks for relief of the discomfort in his or her life that occasioned the visit to the physician. One patient who had been treated for five years and would always remain deformed described himself as a walking textbook. "If more surgery won't help me all that much, I don't think I want it," he told me. The surgeons continued to offer further operations which the patient accepted. Yet the chief surgeon had second thoughts. One day, after examining this man, he  whispered to me, "Sometimes I think we make surgical cripples of them." Still, there was no evaluation conference called to consider the patient's problems in their totality.

A doctor's medical judgment can also be influenced in subtle ways by stereotyping. At one of the Center's weekly teaching conferences, Dr. U. presented a very light-skinned black boy with a large brown birthmark on his cheek. He said that the child's mother wanted him to go on with the treatment even though lumpy scar tissue had begun to form. He planned to do a still deeper dermabrasion and then, if a keloid scar formed, he would excise and overgraft the area. Two of the senior men demurred because of the risk of causing a large unsightly scar. Dr. L. turned to Dr. U. and said, "You are treating this patient, not experimenting!" Dr. U. justified his treatment plan. In a loud voice, he said of the child's mother, "Dr. F. and I talked to her .... How can we know what's in her head? We explained, but with people of low intelligence it's very hard to get across the idea that the result might be more disfiguring."

Interviewing the child's parents following the conference, I discovered that they were middle class and college educated. They lived in an affluent, predominantly white suburb and the father, an attorney, practiced in the city. Normally a family in their income bracket would have been referred to a surgeon in private practice. Nobody had asked about their income when they came to the clinic. I asked if the boy's older sister was as light as he, and his father said "Oh, no. She's even lighter. She's blond." It turned out that the mother had indeed understood about the high risk of keloids in black people. But because her family was light-complexioned, she had hoped her son would be safe. She had been delighted when the resident said that he could do something, and her son was overjoyed. The family had decided to trust the surgeons and continue with the treatment even after a disfiguring scar developed.

The incident illustrates the complexity of medical decision making. What Langston Hughes (1953: 85) called "that powerful drop" of color apparently clouded the surgeon's perception of the mother, whom he dismissed as one of "those people." Armed with this, he let his profession-al self-interest influence his medical judgment. Dr. T. elaborated on that interest when he commented, "I know I'd want to have tried a lot of different ways of doing it [removing the birthmark] before I decided on one for a [private] patient of my own." Dr. P., another resident, agreed that they never had enough "clinical material" upon which to learn surgery. In this instance the intervention of the senior surgeons at the teaching conference prevented the resident, Dr. U , from proceeding with his treatment plan.

The ethics of the medical profession which Freidson (1970b) terms a "publicly waved banner of good intentions" place patients' interests ahead of doctors' private interests. Comments made by the senior men at case conferences demonstrate their efforts to enforce the medical service norms. These included: "What would you do if she were YOUR wife?" and "I know you don't want to leave the operating room, but we have a clinic to run," and so forth. On the other hand, there was also tolerance for the residents' interests as evidenced by remarks such as "You need another one of these [operations] for your boards don't you?" However, my observations suggest that colleague control, the mechanism which Freidson (1960) identifies as the most likely guarantee of the quality of medical practice in hospitals, is more likely to work from the top down than it is up or across the status ladder. It is difficult to challenge someone upon whom you depend for professional advancement and clientele, and still more difficult to change his behavior. Moreover, in our society, unless a person is explicitly designated in a teaching or supervisory role, it is considered extremely bad form to criticize another adult openly.

Comments by the residents when senior surgeons put their own interests ahead of patients' needs were murmured among themselves rather than addressed to their superiors  Among those that I recorded were: "He wants another one for his series. You know he's made a film of this operation." "Dr. A. gets a kick out of doing operations that other surgeons are afraid to try." "Look at how this place is turned upside down for Mrs. Chase [a society matron]! Everybody's walking on eggs. Nothing can get done." "He's going to risk that boy's life for a result that nobody else can even see, but it will be an historic operation." Criticism which cannot be offered openly and in a constructive spirit reinforced by the expectation of change, festers until it gives rise to alienation and cynicism. Patient care is likely to suffer in the process.

As several studies show (Merton, et al. 1957; Becker, et al. 1961; Schoepf 1969) the opportunity to exercise medical responsibility is highly valued and sought after by physicians-in-training. Resident surgeons at the Center liked to work at the affiliated City Hospital despite the dilapidated physical plant, antiquated "lab and record" room, chronic understaffing, and shortages of material that led to poor patient care. They cited the fact that they had far more medical responsibility at City than at College Hospital. They enjoyed more autonomy in making decisions and less interference from supervisors. The physicians' need for responsibility and practice sometimes conflicts with patient's needs for expert care. Several surgeons were explicit about using City Hospital patients because they were "the dregs," derelicts, and "social problems." Social and moral judgments derived from the wider society influence medical treatment, independently of patients' ability to pay in many types of settings.

Sudnow (1967) studied a hospital emergency room. He found that the ambulance sirens howled more stridently for well-dressed patients and children than for old people, derelicts, alcoholics, or addicts. Subsequent care in the emergency room was cued by the siren and more energy was expended on patients who were considered more socially worthy. The second group is stigmatized by the society and by doctors as unworthy persons (Becker, et al. 1961) and when the staff is overworked and has other interests, people are treated according to their social status rather than their medical needs. In our society low social status carries with it an implicit devaluation of personal and moral worth. The actual workings of the medical social system make this very clear. Using external social criteria provides a means for avoiding conscious conflict or cognitive dissonance between educational or research needs and professional ethics.

Physicians are not penalized for carrying social judgments over into the actual treatment of patients. In fact, the social structure of the organizations in which treatment occurs makes this a natural, normal, almost imperative state of affairs. In effect the stereotypes serve as turnoff mechanisms which allow doctors to avoid dealing with their use of patients for teaching and research, sometimes without seeking the patient's fully informed consent.

Pigeonholing also helps to excuse poor care delivered by other doctors. Many of the most seriously ill patients are working-class people with low incomes. Dr. F. stated that he almost never found patients with invasive skin cancers in his private practice. When I asked him why, he said, "These cancer patients are usually lower class. Anybody with half a brain would have these things taken care of before they reached that stage." Of two such patients who were being treated at the Center, one had consulted a neighborhood dermatologist without success, and the other had been treated by the neighborhood "compensation doctor" with a salve for over a year. Both patients had expected that the physicians would advise them where to go for further help if they did not have the expertise necessary to treat their illnesses. Both were working-class people who had received poor care at the hands of poor doctors. Dr. F., however, laid the responsibility for their poor care upon the patients by criticizing them rather than the practitioners. The medical fraternity, while claiming the right to self-regulation, in many instances fails to scrutinize the work of its members, either in the institutional network or among physicians practicing in the community. In neither case are the practitioners truly client-centered.

Discussing the subject of poor neighborhood medical care, the chief surgeon said, "That's the tragedy of giving these people Medicaid. The local physicians [in poor and working-class areas] give them care that is far inferior to that they were receiving in well-organized clinics." While well-organized clinics are difficult to find in the inner city this one certainly was way ahead of most. The Center was comparatively well-organized and attractive. For the most part the care was technically excellent; when poor medicine was offered it was not related to fees but to the social structure of the treatment organization and the patients' inferior place in the wider society.

Let us now return to the original problem of patients' questions and communication. Questions about the outcome of treatment are not merely an inconvenience in terms of time or emotional wear and tear on the doctors. It is not due only to the uncertainty inherent in treatment that makes results difficult to predict, nor to the assumption that patients are incapable of understanding doctors' replies. Two studies have found that patients comprehend more medical matters than doctors think they do (Pratt, et al. 1957; Korsch, et al. 1968). Surgeons at the Center and elsewhere have expressed the fear that if patients are given sufficient information to form a clear picture of the expected results, they might decide not to subject themselves to the physical and psychological discomforts of surgery. "If we told patients the truth they'd never show up for surgery," one resident said. Others agreed. Indeed, it sometimes happened that a surgeon let slip discrepant information and the patient grew wary and hesitated to consent to surgery.

Better-informed patients were sometimes observed to bargain for more conservative treatment. This ran counter to the surgeons' expectation that they alone would and should make the major treatment decisions. The doctors' description of patients as unintelligent, unsocialized, unwilling to keep appointments and unconcerned about their health appeared related to efforts by patients to inform themselves and to act in their own behalf, as well as to physicians' efforts to avoid ethical dilemmas. Recent discussions about the ethics of radical surgery which may prolong life at the cost of severe mutilation hinge on the issue of who shall make the final decision. Surgeons at the Center were critical of those in other specialities who "butchered those poor guys who only have a few miserable years ahead of them" as one man put it. They were less likely to cooperate with a patient of their own who sought to gather the information necessary to make his or her own choice.

At each level of the status hierarchy, the surgeons had interests which often entered into their judgment. The residents valued experience in the types of surgical procedures they would encounter most frequently in private practice; the senior men were eager to try new techniques that would contribute to the frontiers of surgical knowledge and further their careers; all sought to avoid emotional "scenes" and difficult patients. Management of the social and psychological aspects of patient care was supposed to be delegated to lower-status women in the treatment center. In actual practice, however, their recommendations were sought only when convenient or when they facilitated carrying out surgery. They also used the women to help them identify patients whom they should avoid treating because they might prove troublesome if displeased with the outcome of surgery. Because direct intervention by the women on the patients' behalf was resented and rebuffed, they employed manipulative stratagems to circumvent their lack of power. This sometimes worked to the patients' advantage in preventing outright disasters, but it did not make for consistent, high-quality effort. Among the women, a social psychologist, social worker, and three registered nurses, "the team approach" was a standing joke, particularly because one of them had designed research which demonstrated its importance in patient rehabilitation. The two masters-level workers felt their jobs to be threatened by their efforts, and their fears were not without justification. When one of them left the Center she was replaced by a woman with lesser professional qualifications. In their private offices the surgeons used nonprofessional women to screen patients. The issue of physician dominance explored by Freidson (1970a) was clearly at stake here. Thus the surgeons neither took responsibility for whole-patient care nor systematically assured this care by others. As some of the above examples show their behavior at times was antitherapeutic.

The data of this study indicate that the doctor-patient relationship can profitably be explored in the context of unequal status and power. While the rules in our society governing interaction between people of different classes are informal, they are nonetheless regular and tyrannical. Superiors initiate action for inferiors. Superiors speak first, except to pose questions. The most frequent type of initiation by inferiors is information-seeking (Chapple and Arensberg 1940). Hence requests for information often imply the lower social status of the questioner.

Physicians are high-status actors who must seek a great deal of information from persons of lower status. A good clinician is a good investigator and the information he or she gleans during the interview is an essential part of the data base. In order to gain information the doctor must develop rapport with patients. This involves conveying to the patient the doctor's concern with the patient as a valuable person. Although this is supposed to be standard medical practice it also places the high-status person in an ambiguous position with respect to the rules governing interaction in the wider society. Patients often attempt to "take advantage" of this situation by inserting unsolicited information which the physician may then discount, ignore, or otherwise discourage. Like executives in industry and administrators in other institutions, many physicians strive to control the information-seeking interview by directing it according to their own agendas. A patient who adds unsought-after information or asks for a response which the doctor is not prepared to give is acting in a participatory rather than a subordinate role.

Relationships of mutual participation between persons of unequal status involve turning around the normal flow of social interaction. They require the initiation of communication by subordinates and responses from superiors. Such a reversal is evidently the source of difficulties for the surgeons observed at the Center. In effect, once the patient has taken the first step by consulting the surgeon, the latter, a highly-trained and high-status person, expects to initiate actions for the patient, to which the patient is supposed to respond in order to get better. While the surgeon might prefer, in the interest of efficiency and his own comfort, to stabilize the situation with a unidirectional flow of communication, the transaction is a social, not merely a technical, event. When patients attempt to reverse the direction of communication the hierarchical relationship is often strained. One can then record the elements of a power struggle with bargaining, status forcing, retaliation, and withdrawal behavior following one another in rapid succession.

This is evidently what happened in the medical clinic studied by M. Davis (1971) where, primarily as a result of lack of consensus about control of interaction, 37 percent of the patients refused to comply with doctors' advice. Interaction process is also identified by Korsch and her co-workers (Korsch, et al. 1968) as the major source of difficulty in pediatric practice. The theoretical analysis presented here shows why we should expect this to be so even in cases of mild illness. Asking and responding to questions, offering opinions, and expecting positive response, the sphere of interaction process which Bales (1950) labels an affectively neutral task area are, in reality, political acts. According to Arensberg (1965: 322):

Often it is only when ... initiative from below is blocked that it is first apparent that such a basic relationship is failing, and it becomes clear that the blockage is having marked emotional consequences in the frustrated initiants-from-below.

Arensberg identifies three forms of up-the-line activity: "the successful examples in which communication from below is completed by a responsive action" from the superior; "the instances of blockage;" and diversion, that is, "all manner of informal 'pull,' indirect influence, protest, complaint grievance, etc." Both blockage and diversion can result in patients' noncompliance and sabotage of treatment, while diversion may result in physicians' withdrawal. These processes could be seen at work in transactions recorded at the Center (presented in detail in Schoepf 1969).

In some cases the patient had a special worth-conferring social status which the highest-status person in the treatment center validated at the outset. For example, in transactions with a young dentist patient, the chief received his communications with deference and attention. The senior surgeon not only accepted but solicited this patient's initiatives, responded encouragingly, and frequently acted in accordance with his views. The chief made sure the young man was treated as part of the medical fraternity. An up-the-line channel was opened for a female patient when the chief said to the resident, a European aristocrat: "Suppose this patient comes to you in [your country] and she's a relative of the king, or something .... This is a young, attractive woman. How would you treat her?" In another instance, a talented sculptor was introduced by the chief, who spoke respectfully of his art. In these examples the surgeons acted in terms of "latent" status of the patients which were higher or more valued than those of the general clinic population.

When patients attempt to bargain for participation on their own, without special socially desirable statuses such as youth, beauty, talent, or wealth and without legitimation from their doctor, they are on treacherous ground. The physician may employ overt action such as withdrawal or attack, or may give subtler cues such as avoiding eye contact, addressing other treatment personnel, and speaking of the patient in the third person, looking down at the chart except when absolutely necessary. Both the attacks and the more frequent avoidance behavior have "marked emotional consequences" for patients who attempt to initiate interaction and find their claims to participation rejected. In effect the subordinate finds the self he is trying to maintain disconfirmed by the transaction (Goffman 1956). Many simply suffer in silence so that they will be considered "good patients."

The data derived from daily recording of observations in the treatment rooms have thus been ordered in terms of concepts developed in a totally different institution of our society: the study of industrial organizations. The doctor-patient relationship has been shown to be more than an internally balanced and self-maintained dyadic social system. It emerges from this analysis as a dynamic interpersonal transaction, an open system related to the situation of disease, the organization of the treatment center, and the informal status system of the wider society in regular and definable ways. Throughout this analysis the concern has been with the structure of social relationships rather than with the specific content of the messages transmitted and received.

## DISCUSSION

The biggest criticism of the health services available to people who can pay for private care is that while physicians can treat many diseases, few can treat whole people, and still less can they affect the environment that keeps people well or makes them ill. Good medical care requires a partnership between client and skilled professional, which is rare in American life.

In the traditional model of the doctor-patient relationship the patient virtually abandons his or her adult status and places himself in the physician's hands. Indeed, we say, "You're the doctor," when we defer to someone else's judgment, perhaps without agreeing fully to the proposed course of action. Once a patient has decided to seek treatment, subsequent initiative lies with the doctor, unless the patient sabotages the treatment and ignores professional advice. However, many studies have shown that chronic diseases, convalescence and emotional disorders, and above all, preventive health care, require the patient's active participation. Szasz and Hollender (1956: 588) find that such participation occurs only when physician and patient are social equals. When this ideal situation is realized, the relationship is "characterized by a high degree of empathy [and] has elements often associated with friendship and the imparting of expert advice." However, they conclude that this crucial therapeutic model is "essentially foreign to medicine."

The model that does exist can undermine a patient's self-esteem in the process of excluding him from participation in his own care. Apparently doctors recognize the importance of such participation when they themselves are ill. A study of New Jersey physicians (Bynder 1967: 59) found that the majority did not choose the most experienced and highly trained practitioners to treat them. Instead, they chose doctors most like themselves in social and professional status. Social criteria overrode technical medical considerations when the doctors became patients.

CONCLUSIONS

Difficulties in the doctor-patient relationship extend beyond the dyadic interaction itself to the structure of the social system and subsystems in which treatment takes place. Duff and Hollingshead's study (1968) included wealthy patients who could afford "red carpet treatment" and their evidence of the inadequate care offered to all classes of patients in one of the nation's foremost hospitals is a devastating critique. While the sicker and poorer ward patients got less medical attention, incurred higher costs, and generally had poorer results than the other patients, all types of patients suffered from the social organization of medical care. Neither the technical proficiency of the academic physicians nor the private practitioners' smooth bedside manner can guarantee that treatment meets patients' needs. This five-year study found that *"The central purpose of the hospital — the care of patients, especially the personal aspects of that care — was not controlled directly or effectively by anyone."* (Duff and Hollingshead 1968: 375. Original emphasis.)

They conclude that all care proceeds from the impersonal, exploitative model learned by student physicians on the wards and note that researchers and private enterpreneurs have interests which limit their effectiveness in supervising the treatment of patients. To remedy this the authors suggest installing an ombudsman, *"a senior medical authority for each ward division to ensure that patient care is improved and the rights of patients protected."* (Duff and Hollingshead 1968: 381. Original emphasis.) As Duff (personal communication) recognizes, there is at present no way of ensuring that prestigious professors and wealthy private practitioners will follow the recommendations of such a person. Polgar (1963: 412) observes that "changes in behavior often precede changes in notions, but if notions remain the same only strong sanctions can maintain the new behaviors." One way to develop legitimacy for such an authority might be to admit openly that a conflict of interest often exists between research, teaching, careers, moneymaking, and institution-building, on the one hand, and service to patients on the other. Such recognition has not been widespread within the profession. Redlich, the Dean of the medical school where Duff and Hollingshead conducted their study wrote in his foreword to the book:

It is impossible for me to accept the fact that medical teaching and research are incompatible with good care. I do not believe that an inherent antagonism exists among physicians, hospital administrators and nurses or that hospitals are run for the benefit of the physician (1968: ix).

It is indeed curious to find a foreword which doubts the book's principa findings on the basis of prior belief. This writer is a proponent of the human relations approach who would have us make more sensitive phyᵗ sicians. Yet an open-systems approach to the study of doctor-patien communication and to systems of medical care show that the antagonisms are not due to personality conflicts, ill will, or dishonesty; they arise out of contradictions in the social structure. For this reason, attempts to induce physicians and surgeons to display greater sensitivity toward patients are unlikely to lead to changes in the system of medical care whose defects have been deplored for years by people inside the medical profession and out. The causes lie in the structures rather than in senti-ment, for it is the social structure of medicine and its place in the total social system that allows physicians to avoid many negative and stressful situations, difficult patients, and difficult cases.

This study has explored the complex interdependence of doctor-patient relationships in an organizational context, using a specialty facility in a teaching hospital where the need for comprehensive care is recognized in public statements but slighted in actual practice. The interplay of teach-ing, research, and private practice goals, along with patterns of deference and avoidance derived from the stratification system of the wider society, and the problems of coming to terms with severe pathology, lead to a situation in which the resistance to change in the direction of whole-patient care, or social medicine, is formidable indeed.

Although this study uses data from one surgical specialty, the prob-lems of communication described here are not unique and the analysis has wider implications. The other medical and surgical specialties have many similar organizational features and similar conflicting goals. Many patients have health problems which transcend the immediate organic difficulties while the model of disease employed by the healers neglects these broader aspects. Structural analysis of the doctor-patient trans-action suggests that a more inclusive disease model cannot take hold within the present system despite the good will of many medical practi-tioners. Indeed, the organic focus and turnoff go together: lack of em-pathy is fostered by the social structure of treatment, the training, and rewards; it helps the practitioner focus on things rather than persons, on narrow instrumental tasks. These in turn keep the practitioner from reflecting upon the consequences of episodic treatment, consideration of which might impede his or her ability to function within the present system of medical care.

The problem of narrow specificity extends beyond the bounds of medical specialty practice, and is potentially present wherever a body of persons with expert knowledge, professional enculturation, and career interests is called upon to act in behalf of uninitiated lay clients. It is particularly immanent whenever the goal of the application of expertise is eventual self-sustained activity by the client himself in a complex social milieu. These conflicts occur not only in medicine and in rehabilitation of the physically handicapped. They are also present in the schools and welfare centers of our central cities. Some students would have us believe that they exist in our universities as well.

My observations suggest that the lower the professional's estimate of his client's social worth, the more he expects to reserve to himself in the way of decision making, and the less he tends to allow the client to express his own estimate of his needs or to share in the helping process. With low-status clients particularly, the expert expects to do virtually all the decision making even when, in all likelihood, such unilateral action cannot achieve optimum results. When his method of helping fails, the expert may then either avoid recognizing the failure of therapy or blame the client or both.

Medicine is one of the core institutions of modern society, with the prescribed social function of furnishing a means of coping with illness, "a major threat to the effective operation of the economy and the society" (Merton, et al. 1957: 36). Not only is illness a threat to the labor power and morale of the citizenry, but medicine, as Parsons (1951b) informs us, is part of the maintenance system, one of the subsystems that ensures the reproduction of the ongoing system of social relations, affirming to the patient a socially authorized version of his or her place in society. In other words, medical care is a form of social control and medical practitioners are agents of the ruling strata whether or not they are actually employed by the state. The present stratified social system is well served by allowing the various powerful interest groups to further their own ends. Because of this social function an integrated system of health care delivery that meets human needs is not possible.

The implications of the social control function penetrate the very essence of the profession: its claims to autonomy and freedom from public scrutiny based upon highly specialized expertise. This is so because in the face of political sanction the profession jettisons its normative ideology. Sometimes capitulation to institutional goals of social control results in a situation where the goal of helping individual patients turns into its opposite, as in the case of the army psychiatrists studied by Daniels (1972). She describes the twists of ideology required to support and justify physicians sending patients to their deaths. For political purposes the men are defined as not in need of treatment. Medicine is not the only profession to act in opposition to its stated goals. However, the status of healing as the world's oldest and most respected specialty makes the utopian critique particularly salient.

Not only the ideology of the profession, but the tendency of critics to focus upon subsystem variables such as medical commercialism, corporate profit and institutional empire-building serve to mask this crucial structural imperative in the total social system. In seeking possibilities for change, however, we must not neglect the contradictions that arise from the service goals that many health workers, including physicians and aministrators, carry with them as part of their intellectual baggage. When physicians can openly admit, as so many do privately, that the present medical system cannot deliver high-quality care to all who need it and that this is because of political forces that are beyond their individual powers to control, we shall have one more potent force for change. As Parsons (1951b) notes, one of the prime threats to the established order derives from utopian critics who demand that those in power practice the preachments of their legitimating charter. The demand for health care as a human right is one such utopian critique, for the normative idealogy of service is potent inside the profession as well as out.

It comes as no surprise to the student of society to find that the theory and practice of medical care are related to the social structure of the society they develop in and help to maintain. Our perspective on the social foundations of knowledge had led us to expect that this should be the case. It is no accident that the chicken-egg paradox is understandable only in an transformative evolutionary framework. If the theoretical assumptions of the structural approach are correct then, under certain conditions, it should be possible to develop relationships of mutual participation between expert servers and persons who need help. The conditions would be a social structure which requires and facilitates the acting out of patterns, some of which are already present in the physician's behavioral and normative repertoire but which are in the main swamped by the press of other requirements.

Thus far, judging from the opportunities we have had to observe, health-care delivery systems that are in theory structured along different paths are not encouraging. Except in societies where widespread structural transformation is taking place the much-heralded changes in medical-care delivery turn out to be more of the same. Despite greater accessibility of services at lower cost, the problems generated by professional dominance and the organic model of disease continue. Their prevalence has predictable effects upon health care.

In effect, we are witnessing a curious convergence of problems in the American and Soviet health-care systems, with similar solutions being offered. Both Freidson and a Soviet critic, Dyagilev (quoted in the *New York Times*, September 8, 1968), advocate the private-practice route to ensure that patients can find physicians who are responsive to their needs for respectful, whole-person care. Freidson, who a decade ago criticized the quality of care in client-controlled private practice, now calls for producing sufficient numbers of physicians to develop a competitive market. Fully insured and able to pay fees for service, patients then would be able to withdraw from practitioners they dislike (1970a, b). Dyagilev calls for reinstituting private practice which was abandoned following the Soviet socialist revolution. This return to the marketplace sheds more light upon the hopelessness of critics than on creative solutions to the problems of delivering high quality medical care. Critical imagination, too, is apparently blocked by social structure.

Reports from China and Cuba indicate that models of health-care delivery that were devised many decades ago in the West (W. Schmidt, personal communication, May 1973) but never given widespread implementation or support in public policy are being adapted to the needs of poor rural nations. Here, in medicine as in the wider society, new contradictions are being solved by moving to higher levels rather than returning in despair to old models. In China the very theory of knowledge that gives rise to professional dominance in the West is being challenged. Its innermost essence, the concept of the professional expert who tells others what to do, is under attack through state intervention and widespread mobilization of popular energy and initiative. Other papers in this volume describe these developments. My purpose is simply to emphasize, by way of contrast, the connections between human relations, knowledge, and the structure of social relations in medical care and in society as a whole.

## REFERENCES

ARENSBERG, C. M.
    1957  "Anthropology as history," in *Trade and markets in the early empires: economics in history and theory*. Edited by K. Polanyi, C. M. Arensberg, and H. W. Pearson. Glencoe, Illinois: Free Press.
    1965  "Behavior and organization: industrial studies," in *Culture and community*. Edited by C. M. Arensberg, and S. T. Kimball, 301–324. New York: Harcourt, Brace and World. (First appeared 1951 in *Social psychology at the crossroads*. Edited by J. H. Rohrer and M. Sherif, 324–354. New York: Harper and Row.)

BALES, R. F.
 1950   *Interaction process analysis: a method for the study of small groups.*
        Cambridge, Massachusetts: Addison-Wesley Press.
BALINT, M.
 1957   *The doctor, his patient, and the illness.* New York: International Universities Press.
BARNES, L. B.
 1970   "Designing change in organizational systems and structures," in *Systems and medical care.* Edited by A. Sheldon, F. Baker, and C. P. McLaughlin, 314–348. Cambridge, Massachusetts: MIT Press.
BECKER, H. S., B. GEER, E. C. HUGHES, A. STRAUSS
 1961   *Boys in white: student culture in medical school.* Chicago: University of Chicago Press.
BLOOM, S. W.
 1965   *The doctor and his patient* (second edition). New York: Free Press.
BLUM, R.
 1960   *The management of the doctor-patient relationship.* New York: McGraw-Hill.
BYNDER, H.
 1967   Who is the doctor's doctor? *Medical World News,* November 24, 1967.
CHAPPLE, E.
 1953   "Applied anthropology in industry," in *Anthropology today.* Edited by A. L. Kroeber, 819–831. Chicago: University of Chicago Press.
CHAPPLE, E., C. M. ARENSBERG
 1940   *Measuring human relations: an introduction to the study of the interaction of individuals.* Genetic Psychology Monographs 22.
DANIELS, A. K.
 1972   "Military Psychiatry: the emergence of a subspeciality," in *Medical men and their work.* Edited by E. Freidson and J. Lorber, 145–162. Chicago: Aldine.
DAVIS, F.
 1960   Uncertainty in medical prognosis, clinical and functional. *American Journal of Sociology* 66:41–47.
DAVIS, M. S.
 1971   Variation in patients' compliance with doctors' orders: medical practice and doctor-patient interaction. *Psychiatry in Medicine* 2:31–54.
DUFF, R. S., A. B. HOLLINGSHEAD
 1968   *Sickness and society.* New York: Harper and Row.
FOX  R. C.
 1957   "Training for uncertainty," in *The student physician.* Edited by R. K. Merton, G. G. Reader, and P. L. Kendall, 207–241. Cambridge, Massachusetts: Harvard University Press.
 1959   *Experiment perilous.* Glencoe, Illinois: Free Press.
FREIDSON, E.
 1960   Client control and medical practice. *American Journal of Sociology* 65:374–382 (January).
 1970a  *Professional dominance: the social structure of medical care.* New York: Atherton.
 1970b  *Profession of medicine.* New York: Dodd, Mead.

GLASER, B. G., A. L. STRAUSS
  1965   *Awareness of dying.* Chicago: Aldine.
  1966   *The discovery of grounded theory: strategies for qualitative research.* Chicago: Aldine.

GOFFMAN, E.
  1956   The nature of deference and demeanor. *American Anthropologist* 58: 473–502.
  1961   *Asylums: essays on the social situation of mental patients and other inmates.* Garden City, New York: Doubleday Anchor.

HUGHES, L.
  1953   *Simple takes a wife.* New York: Simon and Schuster.

LICHTHEIM, G.
  1966   *Marxism in modern France.* New York: Columbia.

KORSCH, B. M., E. K. GOZZI, V. FRANCIS
  1968   Doctor-patient interaction and patient satisfaction. *Pediatrics* 42: 855–871.

MAC GREGOR, F. C.
  1963   "Facial disfigurement and problems of employment: some social and cultural considerations," in *Facial disfigurement: a rehabilitation problem.* Edited by B. O. Rogers, 123–133. Washington: U.S. Department of Health, Education and Welfare.

MAY, J. T.
  1973   A nineteenth-century, medical care program for blacks: a case of the Freedman's Bureau. *Anthropological Quarterly* 46(3):160–171.

MERTON, R. K., G. G. READER, P. L. KENDALL, *editors*
  1957   *The student physician.* Cambridge, Massachusetts: Harvard University Press.

PARSONS, T.
  1951a  Illness and the rate of the physician: a sociological perspective. *American Journal of Orthopsychiatry* 21:454–460.
  1951b  *The social system.* Glencoe, Illinois: Free Press.

POLGAR, S.
  1963   "Health action in cross-cultural perspective," in *Handbook of medical sociology.* Edited by H. E. Freeman, S. Levine, and L. G. Reeder. Englewood Cliffs, New Jersey: Prentice-Hall.

PRATT, L. S., A. SELIGMAN, G. READER
  1957   Physicians' views on the level of medical information among patients. *American Journal of Public Health* 47:1277–1283.

QUINT, J. C.
  1965   Institutionalized practices of information control. *Psychiatry* 28: 119–132.

REDLICH, F. C.
  1968   "Foreword," in *Sickness and society.* Edited by R. S. Duff and A. B. Hollingshead, ix–x. New York: Harper and Row.

SCHOEPF, B. G.
  1969   "Doctor-patient communications and the medical social systems." Unpublished doctoral dissertation, Department of Anthropology, Columbia University.

SIMMONS, L. W., H. G. WOLFF
  1966 "Hospital practice in social science perspective," in *Medical care.* Edited by R. W. Scott and E. H. Volkart.
SUDNOW, D.
  1967 *Passing on: the social organization of dying.* Englewood Cliffs, New Jersey: Prentice-Hall.
SZASZ, T., M. C. HOLLENDER
  1956 A contribution to the philosophy of medicine: basic modes of the doctor-patient relationship. *Archives of Internal Medicine* 97(5):585–592.

# Static Dynamics in Medical Care Organization

STANLEY R. INGMAN

The voluntary community hospital remains the dominant institution in the medical care arena with respect to controlling the organization of medical care manpower and resources. Physicians still dominate hospital policy formulation as well as community health policy. This situation prevails in most rural areas in the United States and must be analytically examined before medical care reorganization can be proposed.

I shall depict in broad terms how the multiplicity of social structural preconditions and societal ideologies determined medical care in one rural community hospital over a twenty-year period. Specifically, I shall attempt to describe both the external influences upon this rural community hospital as well as the internal dynamics that jointly determined the quality and quantity of medical care offered within this hospital. In addition, the health planning phenomenon of the 1960's will be examined and evaluated with respect to why it has had so small an impact upon the quality and quantity of rural medical care.

Among the formal agencies and groups that influenced the delivery of hospital services in this community, the most significant were: the county Medical Society, the Joint Commission on Accreditation of Hospitals, the State Hospital Board, the Regional Medical Program, the Comprehensive Health Planning "B-Agency," the State and National Medical Associations, and the School of Medicine. Informal pressure groups in the health arena, such as labor unions, corporations, and voluntary health and welfare agencies within and outside the region, roughly complete the social network of influences within which this community hospital evolved. The

An abbreviated version of this paper appeared in 1974 as "Health planning in Appalachia: conflict resolution in a community hospital." *Social Science and Medicine* 8: 135–142.

protagonists within this community hospital included the trustees, the physicians on the medical staff, and the hospital administrators whom the board had appointed.

Although this analysis is of one rural community hospital, a quick review of nearby hospitals suggests that it is not markedly atypical in terms of quality and basic organizational structure and purpose, i.e. division of labor, resource allocation, decision-making process, and legitimating goals and objectives.

The data were secured in part through careful review of files that had been collected for over a twenty-year period. Interviews with various health professionals, administrators, and community leaders served to clarify and expand upon the materials in the files. The local newspaper archives helped provide additional verification.

Essentially, it is a basic contention of this work that local leadership — including both health providers and lay persons — is unable to create the quality and quantity of health services that might be reasonably expected in such a region in the 1970's. A corollary is that external influences, such as those previously mentioned, are inadequate, either singly or in combination, for protecting the general welfare in rural community hospitals. I will try to provide an illustration to support these contentions.[1]

The "Dockston" Hospital[2] is a 200-bed, general acute-care hospital under voluntary sponsorship located in a semirural, economically depressed river town twenty miles north of the large urban center of "Metroville" within the Appalachian region. The hospital is characterized by a slightly atypical board of directors. For example, two members are politicians in the next town to the north. Otherwise, with few exceptions the board of directors represents the reputed leaders in the valley rather than formal political representatives.

In 1949, the board hired a young administrator who had no actual experience or formal training in hospital administration. However, this young man diligently pursued his work, read widely in the area of hospital administration, and soon became more knowledgeable about modern hospital patient care. He continually introduced innovations into the administrative structure of the hospital. As a representative of the new breed of what is called "clinical administrator," he also began to feel more and more that the medical care offered in his hospital ranked below the standards of a modern hospital. Consequently, he tried to encourage the physicians to reorganize themselves in order to improve care. The

---

[1]   Alford labels this coalition of interest groups as the "equal-health advocates" and shows how their efforts are likely to fail (Alford 1972: 145–146).

[2]   All names within quotes are fictitious.

hospital surveys conducted by the American College of Surgeons in 1945 and 1948 and later by the Joint Commission on Accreditation of Hospitals in 1955, 1958, 1961, 1964, 1965, and 1968 continually gave credibility to his prodding of both the boards and the staff to act. His strategy of persuasion won some minor success but basic reorganization was not accomplished during his stay at the hospital, which lasted eighteen years.

The medical staff must be given the major share of the responsibility for the medical care provided at the "Dockston" Hospital. The physical plant and administrative operation only indirectly affected the level of care offered at this hospital. On paper, the board held the official authority; yet I contend that in most rural hospitals in the United States this authority is typically confined to narrow limits for reasons that will be discussed (see Freidson 1970: 209–237).

At the "Dockston" Hospital the staff was controlled by an older group of general practitioners who over the years had become accustomed to having their own way without any interference from the board or the administrator. These general practitioners wanted the institution to remain limited in scope. They did not think it was desirable for the hospital to attract new specialists, nor was it thought feasible for the institution to enlarge its staff markedly. There was a small group of certified specialists on the staff who mostly disagreed with the general practitioners. Both the younger general practitioners and specialists who were of this persuasion found it hard to become involved in the policy-making of the medical staff. While national trends have been on the side of specialists, the general practitioners held the power in the "Dockston" Hospital.

Because there were no board-certified surgeons and gynecologists on the staff, general practitioners performed most of the work in surgery and gynecology in the hospital. In the 1950's there were no specific departments and, thus, most older general practitioners performed whatever tasks they felt qualified to perform.

In the late 1950's and early 1960's the older general practitioners began to resent the persistent agitation for change, especially by the administrator. In order to form a united front in their effort to obtain accreditation in 1958, the administrator was taken into the confidence of the staff. Later, a few physicians felt that the administrator was using this inside information to "brainwash" the board against them. The medical staff leader-ship also noticed that a small group of the younger staff members was more militant in their thrust for more prerogatives.

In late 1962 the "old guard" began to feel that the opposition had increased too rapidly over the preceding years, and they attempted to reestablish their authority once more. They focused their criticisms on the administrator, whom they envisioned as the leader of the "conspiracy." The staff felt that the board and the dissident members of the staff would lose their courage if and when the administrator were eliminated from the hospital. Without calling for a staff vote on the matter, a few officers went to the board and demanded that it fire the administrator, claiming that the administrator was meddling in their affairs and in general was very annoying. The board was somewhat shocked at this demand and indignantly refused to honor the staff's request. Instead a consultant was secured, and a major public dispute soon erupted into the courts and the public media.

## THE HOSPITAL: INADEQUACIES AND RECOMMENDATIONS

At the crux of the dilemma facing the hospital administrator, the staff, and the board was the quality of health care offered at the "Dockston" Hospital. The staff had been criticized as early as 1945, when the American College of Surgeons "seriously considered withdrawing their approval of the 'Dockston' Hospital because the staff was not meeting the minimum requirements for hospital standardization."[3] It was indicated that some problematic issues were not new to the board, e.g. "the poor condition of the medical records." It was also suggested by the associate director of the American College of Surgeons that monthly medical staff conferences with audits of clinical work were not being conducted, although these were required for accreditation.

The following needed changes were discussed: more consultations, a clinical laboratory facility, more autopsies, and the establishment of a department of surgery. The secretary of the board noted in 1945 that "a medical audit may from time to time deflate the ego of some of the staff, but if it saves a single life, is it not worth it?"[4]

In 1948, a surveyor arrived to determine whether the hospital deserved continued accreditation. The hospital scored 72 percent, 3 percent above the limit of the provisional approval level (60–69 percent). The hospital lost points primarily in relation to seven major areas: medical staff organization, medical record department, clinical laboratory, medical department, surgical department, obstetrical department, and medical social service department. Other comments dealt with the overcrowded facilities, the failure of some members to sign medical staff by-laws, the fact that

[3]   From a letter from the board chairman of the hospital to the medical staff, October 1945.
[4]   From the minutes of the board meeting.

there were no regularly appointed consultants, no regular presentations and discussions of hospital cases, no special clinico-pathological conferences, little improvement in medical records, an autopsy rate far below the minimum (2/185 in 1948), a need for more nursing supervisors, a general lack of qualified doctors[5] (fellows or diplomates) in the medical, surgical, and obstetrical departments, a high rate of infant mortality resulting from Caesarean sections, and, finally, the fact that there was no outpatient department. Full approval was given on the condition that steps be taken to correct the above-mentioned deficiencies.

It was not until 1955 that the hospital was again reviewed by an outsider. This time it was the Joint Commission on Accreditation of Hospitals (JCAH), which had been formed in 1952. There were sixteen different deficiencies outlined, and accreditation was denied. Many areas were labeled inadequate, e.g. medical staff committee meetings and minutes, the autopsy rate, medical records, the consultation rate, and the Caesarean section rate (twice the national average). Included in the review was the suggestion that they revise the staff by-laws and thereby its organization and that they appoint a joint conference committee in order to establish a liaison between staff and board (this last suggestion was quickly adopted).

After three years the board and the staff agreed to receive a new surveyor from the JCAH. Neat black books were prepared and a specific agenda was planned to "coordinate" the surveyor's visit. It proved to be a successful strategy and accreditation was granted. Some felt that accreditation was gained as a result of the neat black books rather than improved standards. The fact that the surveyor was a general practitioner was also thought to explain accreditation in 1958.

However, in 1961 the hospital attained a full three-year accreditation. It was again noted that the rate of autopsies should increase, obstetrical and medical records should contain more clinical information, and operative permission and procedures should be reviewed.

The normal JCAH survey cycle of every three years was interrupted in 1962 by a dispute between the staff and the board over the staff's desire to have the administrator fired. As a result, the board decided to hire a hospital consultant to settle the dispute and to restore harmony within the hospital. The executive director of the hospital council of the eastern part of the state recommended a nationally noted consultant, "Dr. Fargue." In November 1962, he and his associate began their survey.

[5] "Even today a vast bulk of the total surgical work in the United States is undertaken by doctors regarded as 'non-qualified' surgeons by the American College of Surgeons" (Mechanic 1967: 708).

In December 1962 the report was completed but was distributed first to only two board members on the executive committee, an attorney and a retired "Metroville" steel company executive. Later two other members were given copies to read. The report covered hospital utilization in "Coal Valley," board organization, hospital administration, and medical staff performance. The report was never made fully public, or even circulated among all board members.

According to the surveyors, hospital utilization was low (80 percent). Since 1955, the United Mine Workers (UMW) Welfare and Retirement Fund had eliminated the hospital from their approved list, and it was suggested that a new agreement be arranged between the hospital and the fund. A major stumbling block to negotiation was the fact that the hospital would not permit physicians in the "Circleville" UMW Medical Group to be on the staff. Before any agreement could be reached, this rule would have to be changed.

All three hospitals in the area showed a low occupancy rate in the maternity service. To achieve regional economic rationality it was suggested that some consolidation of the three maternity services would be advisable. It was also suggested that the hiring of a specialist in obstetrics would represent one way of increasing the occupancy of the maternity service. It would have required opening discussions with the two other hospitals in the area and the "Circleville" Medical Group.

Although the administration of the hospital received an excellent rating, the board was given some suggestions. First, the board was asked to modify its viewpoint with respect to "its rights and duties." A book on hospital trusteeship was handed to each board member to help transform his views. The report pointed out the need for extensive changes in the constitution and by-laws of the board, e.g. the consultant felt that the board had apparently delegated inappropriately certain "authority" to the staff. The surveyor rejected the claims voiced by some physicians that the administrator was incompetent and detrimental to the operation of the hospital. It was recommended that the board continue to support him.

According to the review, the staff organization looked good on paper, but did not seem to function according to the standards of hospital accreditation. It was recommended that new medical staff by-laws be adopted. It was also suggested that several new committees be added (a credentials committee, a medical audit committee, and others).

There were numerous charges of inadequacies. Surgery privileges were thought to be uncontrolled or left to the individual physician's discretion. Partly because "qualified" physicians and surgeons were lacking, complex cases in the area were often sent to "Metroville" hospitals. However, patients were referred to "Metroville" for other reasons as well. For example, although some physicians stated that local men were incompetent, others contended that they would be more assured of not having patients stolen by local colleagues if they sent patients to "Metroville" for specialty care. It was thought commendable for the hospital to refer complicated cases to "Metroville," but it was noted that such a procedure did result in a lower occupancy rate for the hospital as well as limiting the scope of the hospital.

The consultant suggested that the number of specialists be increased so that the scope of services at the institution could be expanded. It was also mentioned that although the hospital had adequate departments of radiology and pathology, they were functioning below 50 percent of their capacity. This could be explained partly by the staff's limited use of diagnostic and review procedures. To satisfy the need for physicians who were certified in obstetrics and gynecology, it was suggested that the specialists practicing at the "Circleville" Medical Group and at the "Blacksburg" Hospital be invited to head up departments at the "Dockston" Hospital. The consultant summarized his remarks about the staff in the following manner: "The physicians on the staff of the 'Dockston' Hospital are good family doctors and are practicing a brand of medicine which is adequate for family doctors but is not adequate for a modern hospital or medical center ...."

The consultant also illustrated the staff's inadequacies in his review of their committee work. The staff meeting had good attendance but failed to review the quality of medical work performed in the hospital. It was suspected that the tissue committee, although producing excellent minutes, never met, as was also the case with the infectious diseases committee. Therefore, the pathologist was never given the opportunity to attend the tissue committee meetings as required by the JCAH. It was indicated that the surveyor from this commission had been told otherwise. The low autopsy rate was again cited, as well as the slipshod means by which consent for operations was secured. The reviewer reported that the medical records committee and members of the department of surgery were holding meetings. In summary, he felt there was an overall need to revise the staff's by-laws, rules, and regulations.

The medical audit raised many serious questions about the quality of work performed at the hospital. As cited by the reviewer, the major problems lay in the inadequate review of clinical work done in the hospital, e.g. record keeping was incomplete for obstetrics and newborn cases, and review was lacking in cases of death. Preparatory tests and consent forms were thought to be underutilized, e.g. few pregnancy tests were recorded, and consent forms and consultations were lacking in some cases of hysterectomy, sterilization, and other surgical interventions. The medical audit, in general, showed a lack of supervision, control, review, and analysis of the surgery done in the hospital. The report did not claim that any generalized abuses of surgical privileges were occurring, but suggested that departmentalization might encourage better internal supervision.

In October and November of 1963, a special committee of the staff invited four prominent physicians from a nearby school of medicine to advise the staff on reorganization. Professors in internal medicine, surgery, pediatrics, and obstetrics and gynecology came (each on a separate occasion) to visit the medical staff. In brief, although all of the visitors were critical of the big city consultant for his coercive style, of the administrator for "practicing medicine," and of the board members for being unduly influenced, they emphasized the need for obtaining more specialists on the staff, for instituting limited departmentalization, for hiring a medical director, for instituting open staff policy, for utilizing more consultants, and for revising the medical staff by-laws. The professors based their recommendations on one afternoon's discussion with the leadership of the medical staff.

In the fall of 1963, the county medical staff became formally involved as a result of pressure from the American Medical Association and the state medical society. The chairman of the county medical society review committee wrote the hospital administrator: "considerable pressure has been brought to bear upon the committee ... to render a report ... we have heard complaints of the Medical Staff ... we want to meet the Board. This matter has caused great concern to organized medicine, both at the State and National level."

After its visit with the board, the committee made its recommendations. The report began by proposing that the staff should expand, improve, and supervise their own peers more closely; it also stated that the board had been justified in its actions. The medical society's committee felt that the choice of the consultant had been unfortunate and that the consultant had engaged in "dictatorial, abusive, and unjustified criticism." The real problem, they believed, was the loss of confidence, respect, and reasonableness on both sides. They called the board's action "revolutionary" and the staff's reaction "abusive and vindictive." They supported quality control and the introduction of more specialists, but they instructed the administrator to cease interfering in medical affairs. They also suggested that a medical director be appointed. Although they agreed that the staff by-laws needed revision, they suggested that the control of medical practice in the hospital should be returned to the staff. They felt that the key to the problem was the maintenance of proper communication channels.

In that same year the "big city" consultant returned to review the hospital. Although he noted certain improvements, he pointed out some of the same problems he had discussed earlier; e.g. the low autopsy rate, the board's failure to exert its legal authority ("have decided to settle for a mediocre hospital"), the failure to control surgical privileges, and the unresolved feud with the UMW clinic.

In 1964, the JCAH sent a specialist to review the hospital. The specialist granted accreditation for only one year. Twenty-four specific recommendations and comments were made in the survey, e.g. the tension between staff and administration was dysfunctional, there was a need for a written policy on the use of oxytocic drugs, there was a need for departmentalization, the autopsy rate should be increased, and surgery privileges should be checked. However, a general practitioner from the JCAH resurveyed the hospital in 1965 and gave the hospital a three-year accreditation. Accreditation was renewed for three more years in 1968.


INTERNAL DYNAMICS

In this section I shall present an abbreviated discussion of the social conflict between the board, the physicians, and the administrator. The genesis of the conflict can be traced back to the period when the administrator, who had become aware of the inadequacies at the hospital, attempted to indicate to the board its responsibility for improving the hospital. Although a few young specialists supported this new activist orientation, the medical staff leadership resisted passively at first and then later set out to destroy the reform movement by practically every means available to them.

However, both the reformers and the medical staff leaders became equally upset when the hospital board moved to appoint medical specialists from the nearby United Mine Workers clinic. The resistance from the hospital reformers at the hospital indicates that there were specific limits to the reform plans. They were unwilling to have the specialists from the so-called "socialist" UMW clinic help fill the specialist gap that had been pointed out by all the hospital reviewers. Therefore, although the board met with the UMW physician representatives to negotiate possible appointments, the resistance from the entire membership of the medical staff quickly discouraged any further negotiations.

Several months after the consultant's medical audit was completed, one staff member went so far as to steal the report from the administrator's office. When the board threatened legal action, the report was returned. Following this incident, other physicians covertly helped organize a citizen's group to apply pressure on the board to stop their plans to reorganize the medical staff. The theme of the group was that the board was going to run all of the physicians out of town. The medical staff leadership also sponsored advertisements in the local paper and some physicians attacked the board and the administrator on the local radio. As the board moved ahead with its plans to rewrite the hospital and medical staff by-laws, the staff secured two separate court injunctions to stop implementation. After recalling that the judge actually cross-examined the board members and openly supported the medical staff leadership, the rumor that the judge had been bribed seemed plausible.

Other pressures began to be applied. Prominent local entrepreneurs on the board were threatened with loss of business. With the court action and with apprehension about economic reprisals from both angry citizens and physicians, the board's activism dissipated markedly. Managers of absentee corporations in "Coal Valley" (some of the strongest reformers on the board) began to question the potential consequences of alienating local citizens in the name of improving the quality of medical care. Their reluctance to candidly tell the public "the whole story" was based on their fear of completely destroying public confidence in the hospital and their leadership. This fear of mass reaction kept citizens ill-informed throughout the ten or more years of the dispute.

The directors and owners of these absentee corporations began to discourage their local managerial representatives from remaining "responsible" and "involved," especially when it appeared that the hospital controversy might backlash (Pellgrin and Coates 1956). They feared that their own corporate operations in the valley might receive more careful attention by the citizens; for example, low corporate taxes might be questioned. With all supports backing down, the hospital atmosphere became so stressful for the administrator that he suffered two heart attacks and left the hospital. Although he vowed never to become involved in medical care administration again, two years later, a UMW clinic outside the immediate area managed to recruit him as their administrator.

The few physicians who had supported the board either left the area or accepted a partnership with one of the local physicians in the leadership group. Thus, the coalition between some board members, some specialists, and the administrator collapsed. The group legally responsible for ensuring the public welfare, namely the board, was unable to maintain its push for change.

## EXTERNAL INFLUENCES

### Hospital Accreditation

In the United States, where voluntarism reigns, medical and hospital professionals are very proud that they established the American College of Surgeons (1913) with a hospital review system, and later the Joint Commission on Accreditation of Hospitals. The first systematic review of hospitals took place in the United States in 1918 and 1919. Only eighty-nine out of 671 hospitals were approved as meeting the Minimum Standards for Hospitals drawn up in 1918. However, the list of hospitals approved and those disapproved was destroyed because too many important hospitals failed to pass inspection. The professional hierarchy worried about the terrific repercussions if this information were to be made public.

In 1952, the JCAH was formed from the American College of Surgeons (three votes), the American College of Physicians (three votes), the American Medical Association (seven votes), and the American Hospital Association (seven votes) (McEashern 1957). Although the new hospital reviewing board broadened the representation, it is essentially still a medically dominated body. However, it is the case that the American College of Surgeons and the American College of Physicians agree more often than not with the American Hospital Association.

In 1964, accreditation was almost denied to the "Dockston" Hospital, but after some pleading by the administrator, who warned the surveyor that the valley would explode if accreditation were to be denied, the JCAH granted a one-year accreditation. In 1965, a new surveyor essentially presented them with a "clean bill of health" and accreditation was granted for another three years. This was repeated in 1968 as well.

The past history of the "Dockston" Hospital was easily accessible to the new surveyor. The JCAH office, which makes the final decisions, was well informed about the history of the hospital, e.g. two staff members (from the leadership group) had visited the Chicago office in an attempt to explain the staff's side of the argument and had asked the JCAH to investigate the hospital. Although there were some observable changes in the character of the staff performance, it is hard to correlate improvement with accreditation at this hospital. In this instance, the JCAH seem to have avoided active involvement because of the controversy.

As a catalyst for change, the Joint Commission can be given some credit, but the voluntaristic ideology by which it is explicitly guided seemed to prevent it from serving as an effective advocate for hospital standards. The view of "let the locals decide their own affairs" or "we (JCAH) are not set up to punish but only to encourage" releases the commission from any responsibility for the medical care in the "Coal Valley." But if this is true, then who has the obligation to look out for the public welfare?

The incongruity between different surveyors' evaluations and the level of actual standards at the hospital raises serious doubts about the meaning of hospital accreditation as well as the efficacy of the Joint Commission to guard the public interest. Having professional colleagues judging and evaluating each other definitely has its limits with respect to public accountability.

*Big City Consultant*

Perhaps the consultant underestimated the potential of the staff hierarchy to resist reform. He did not correctly assess either the level or the types of value commitments of the staff or the board members. The extent of, or lack of, vested interests of all parties in the dispute was not evaluated. It is true that the consultant's confidence, knowledge, and convincing presentation as the expert incited the board members initially to act aggressively with little thought about staff reaction. Their boldness reflected a naive understanding of the emotional and ideological commitments of the staff as well as the economic interests that were threatened by their reform program. The consultant failed to prepare the board for the ensuing battle, which he should have been able to predict. If a consultant is truly concerned with having his suggestions adopted, he should devote considerable effort to informing the board of a hospital as to the possible consequences of their proposed reforms in realistic terms.

The majority of the staff was not motivated solely by economic considerations. Many expressed deep concern with their image as trustworthy physicians. Because of the lack of careful communication between each staff member and the board, some staff members became increasingly supportive of the status quo and violently upset with the board. Some physicians even retired. The circulation of false information by some staff members helped stimulate the wrath of men who otherwise might have remained cooperative with the board. However, because of the extreme personal attacks that were continuously inflicted upon the consultant and the board, their desire to find a harmonious resolution of the conflict dissipated rapidly.

## Courts

In the courtroom in "Branburry" the "big city consultant" was portrayed to the public by "Judge Parks" and by the staff hierarchy as an outsider attempting to interfere in local affairs. Under this public characterization, the consultant personified to the public the big city expert who had "brainwashed" the board to follow his every wish. The judge, especially in the second hearing, also attempted to discredit any physician who might agree with the board or with the consultant. For example, in the courtroom the judge asked whether one physician, who had agreed to the new by-laws, was related to the administrator. (In fact, he was the administrator's brother-in-law.) In another instance, he attacked the attorney of the board for conflict of interest because he was also a member of the board. By leading witnesses to divulge particular facts, he attempted to challenge the board's credibility.

The question must be raised as to why he behaved in this manner. Was the judge honestly hostile to an outsider pushing his fellow professionals and friends around? Was the judge truly antagonistic to a board of laymen trying to regulate and control physicians who were fellow professionals? Although there may be some reasons to reply in the affirmative, there exist other underlying facts that explain his overt support of the medical staff in the courtroom.

Several informants claimed that "Judge Parks" received $8,000 from several physicians on the staff for his support. One board member contended that certain physicians had such political influence in the county courthouse that it was quite unnecessary for money to change hands. Another informant claimed that two physicians on the hospital staff had boasted to him that they controlled "Judge Parks."

Nevertheless, it is evident that "Judge Parks" went out of his way to discredit the board and its allies. Recalling "Judge Parks'" connection with racketeers in the 1950's, this was not the first time that this judge had been rewarded for his cooperation. Naively, the attorney for the board, knowing of similar cases in which courts had ruled in favor of a hospital board, felt confident that the court would rule in its favor. He seemed unaware of what was awaiting him and the board in the county courthouse.

## Organized Medicine

As the dispute began to attract public attention, the American Medical Association became aware of the ongoing feud and notified the State

Medical Society to have it resolved. The officer of the state society in the "Metroville" area contacted the head of the County Medical Society. In December 1963, the county group contacted the hospital board, offering its help in resolving the dispute.

The Committee for the County Medical Society met separately with the medical staff and the board. Subsequently the committee presented its final report to the board. The committee agreed that the board was justified to act, but stressed that the consultant had been abusive and that the administrator should stop "practicing medicine." The members also stated that the staff had behaved poorly and had engaged in campaigns of personal vilification. Poor communication and misunderstanding were the major problems to be rectified. The committee essentially agreed with most of the recommendations of the consultant who was thought so vindictive. The employment of a medical director was considered wise.

After delivering its message, the committee disbanded and declined to make any public statement on the ground that it would hinder its future usefulness. Although the chairman of this committee stated that his hospital ("Coalton" Hospital) would not allow some of the "Dockston" medical staff members to practice medicine on his staff, neither he nor his colleagues felt any obligation to correct the situation.[6] It must be recalled that the chairman of the committee had firsthand knowledge about the performance of physicians on the "Dockston" medical staff, for he had been the former pathologist at the hospital. Reportedly, he had resigned because of the improper surgery that had been performed at the hospital.

Considering the quick retreat from the controversy on the part of the medical society, the board, even if it had wished to act, could not depend upon the support of the local medical society. The committee was against applying any pressure and diagnosed the situation as a problem of poor communication. Public disclosure of its findings was not allowed. However, whereas the medical societies in the region remained silent, the "Tri-County Association of General Practitioners" issued a statement attacking the administrator for "practicing" medicine. The bond uniting members of the medical profession is a strong force mitigating public intraprofessional conflict or meaningful peer accountability and review.

### Reluctant Participants

Labor unions, especially the United Mine Workers, had established various group-practice clinics in the region. Although they had struggled for

---

[6]   The two hospitals decided to merge boards and staffs as of 1972.

staff privileges elsewhere, they quickly dropped out of the "Dockston" Hospital controversy. When challenged about their public responsibility, the UMW chief of staff replied, "We can't save the whole world." The United Steel Workers proposed to take an activist role in the valley, but their plans were vetoed at the national level. The conflict between local leadership of the United Steel Workers and the United Mine Workers made consolidation of labor strength in the region difficult. Both leadership groups were critical of the medical care in the valley but were unwilling to act either together or singly.

The performance of the "Metroville" University group of experts was similar. They took a look, agreed that there were many underlying problems, but walked away saying that the locals must decide to institute change. Physician dominance seemed more important to the university professors than the actual level of medical care in the hospital. Likewise, the State Commission of Hospitals proposed a review but later declined to even visit the hospital in an apparent decision not to become involved. A "Metroville" hospital planner helped the board (1964) locate the "big city" consultant and then dropped out of the controversy.

## Regional and Subregional Health Planning

The most striking alternative medical care institutions were the two coal miners' clinics (UMW) in the region (see Weinerman 1971). The establishment of these clinics had caused many conflicts since their inception in the 1940's. In the first case, the miners marched in the streets and finally threatened to build their own hospital before their physicians were appointed to the local hospital medical staff. In the second case, the UMW threatened not to reimburse any patient care at the nearby "Blacksburg" Hospital, where 50 percent of their patients were either miners or their relatives. The board of this hospital quickly invited the physicians from the UMW clinic to join their medical staff. Both clinics introduced various medical care innovations in order to serve the people's needs better, e.g. nurses were trained to do tonometry examinations so that all older adults could be systematically screened for glaucoma every six months or so, while they waited to see a physician.

As in most parts of the country, this four-county region had the full range of voluntary health and welfare agencies and associations (Roemer and Wilson 1952). Some of these organizations had joined together to coordinate fund raising through the well-known community chest mechanism. This combined fund-raising mechanism is typically promoted and supported by the "corporate" rationalizers in the local towns. Historically and presently, these voluntary health associations have concentrated upon preventive education, medical research, and supportive services, and they have avoided any direct concern with delivery of "mainstream" medical care.

In the region of the "Dockston" Hospital some citizens and health professionals went a step further. They established the "Coal Valley" Health Services, Incorporated, which combined under one administration various formally autonomous agencies, i.e. homemakers service, visiting nurse's services, and medical loan closet. Later they added the council for exceptional children, a unit in the "Dockston" Hospital, and finally an outpatient mental health clinic. With one exception, namely the psychiatric unit, this agency did not attempt to create any programs that might influence the delivery of traditional medical and dental care in and outside the "Dockston" Hospital.

Thus, until the middle 1960's there had been essentially two main health-planning movements (McNerney and Riedel 1962: 149). First, there was the work of the miners, both in terms of developing two clinics in four-county regions and of gaining medical staff appointments at two of the fourteen hospitals in the region. Second, various communities and voluntary agencies started to combine funding efforts and in a few cases to combine administrations to increase efficiency and coordination. With the passage of numerous federal laws, 1965 was the benchmark for explicit federal entry into local health-planning affairs.

While public officials and voluntary agency people discussed regional health planning under the mandate of the Appalachia Regional Act, the medical care "establishment" (essentially composed of private physicians and hospital administrators) was getting organized to develop programs in response to the regional medical program (1965) which the school of medicine in "Metroville" was coordinating (see Clark 1966). Although regionalization of medical care delivery was a possible emphasis, this state subregional-RMP chose to concentrate its efforts on heart disease, cancer, and stroke. Therefore, the RMP typically focused on projects in one institution instead of broad planning to integrate or reorganize medical care delivery.

The program managed to link certain rural hospitals to large urban or suburban hospitals in or near "Metroville" in an attempt to rationalize referral patterns and to encourage more steady use of specialty backup in "Metroville." However, most of the rural-urban links were established between the more sophisticated rural hospital and the practitioners in the urban hospitals of "Metroville." The "Dockston" Hospital and other "problem" hospitals in the region remained outside the sphere of influence of RMP planning.

The Comprehensive Health Planning (CHP) legislation differed from RMP in that there was a requirement stipulating that 51 percent of its board members were to be consumers or nonproviders. After activists in the Appalachia regional program realized that there were no health funds available through this act, they shifted their attention to CHP. As the Appalachian program and the local "war on poverty" groups had attracted mainly Democratic Party leaders, so the CHP program attracted Democratic politicians rather than Republican corporation leaders (Schulze 1961). Some lower echelon health agency directors and professionals cooperated, but most hospital administrators, hospital board members, and physicians in the region chose to debunk or ignore any efforts to organize a four-county health planning agency.

Throughout the five or six years of planning that followed, few changes occurred as a result of CHP legislation. In addition to the failure to integrate the UMW leadership into the system, the local four-county CHP effort represented a basic cleavage between the local medical care "establishment" and Democratic county and town public officials.

In general, social planning and the bureaucratic organization of health services were not in harmony with either the social values or the dominant interests of this region. Any social movement to rationalize the delivery of medical services was associated with problems similar to those that occur when Western bureaucratic organizational models and social planning are introduced into non-Western cultures (see Presthus 1959). The introduction of concepts such as impersonality, technical supremacy, and loyalty to some abstraction such as the public interest (comprehensive health planning) was often blocked by traditional attitudes toward authority, social class rights and privileges, and professional autonomy, as well as by a strong dependency upon personal and family friendship.

Although most people in this area shared the notion that laymen and especially politicians should not interfere with medical practice, there was a small group in the population that was willing to question this assumption. Even though federal review bodies criticized the inadequate participation of consumers representing all socioeconomic groups in the CHP group, the lower classes with few exceptions were not yet aware of their new "rights" and were generally unwilling to demand a decisive role in health affairs.

Even if they were aware of the need to participate, lower class leaders often lacked the knowledge, interests, and skills to participate effectively. More importantly, the weak authority structure or mandate under which planning groups operated quickly discouraged serious participation. What continued to be lacking was the opportunity for lower and middle class participation in the establishment of medical care priorities. With the long history of struggles between the UMW and local hospitals, between the unions, between various hospital boards and their medical staffs, between medical staffs at different hospitals, and between different political jurisdictions, it is not surprising that working class and middle class citizens would not choose to expend a great amount of effort to rationalize medical care delivery over this four-county area.

## CONCLUSION

The following situations are hypothesized to be related to stagnation in rural health care systems: (a) weak self-perpetuating voluntary boards of community hospitals (Bellin 1971); (b) community willingness to accept a high degree of upper class paternalism in health affairs; (c) physician dominance in the delivery of medical and hospital services, as opposed to a balance between professional autonomy, administrative rationalization, and public accountability; (d) general acceptance of ideologies that emphasize consensus and better communication, as opposed to institutionalized conflict between vested interests (Balbus 1971); and finally, (e) distrust of lower middle class citizens to plan for their own medical care. As Freidson summarizes the situation: "professional dominance creates sufficient problems to require the development of a stronger countervailing administrative management and of a better organized clientele" (Freidson 1970: 168).

Social changes in rural health care are found within the following developments. The social organization of citizens to bargain with professionals is a necessary element to improve existing situations. The labor unions, who have organized for other purposes, provide the most powerful example in terms of financial resources and levels of sophistication. Coalitions between local dissidents (including providers and citizens) and government programs from outside the region have some chance of bringing about social change. The role of federal programs, e.g. the Comprehensive Health Planning Program and Regional Medical Program, are important to review and evaluate in this regard.

But as Bodenheimer points out, regional medical programs suffer from the same idealisms that have marked other private and public health programs (Bodenheimer 1969; see also Krause 1973). For one thing, the groups and individuals brought to the regional conference table are not markedly different from the existing influentials within a region. External (economic) incentives and "disincentives" are at present too diffusely administered to coerce or encourage community hospitals, health agencies, and health centers to create programs jointly for a region and to modify existing medical care delivery. Because of the lack of a strong articulate and informed consumer voice within decision-making processes, what will occur in the future will resemble what Alford calls "dynamics without change" (Alford 1972: 128).

The maldistribution of medical care in terms of quality and quantity in backward rural areas must be analyzed in relation to a profit-based economic system (Galbraith 1973). However, just as developing Third World nations cannot easily alter the distribution of goods and services between countries overnight and therefore must attempt to adopt institutional forms which meet their immediate problems (Gish 1973), so most backward rural areas in the United States resist suburban or upper class solutions to their medical care problems. To even begin to consider the issue of "who does what for what rewards," citizens must take control of their own institutions.

## REFERENCES

ALFORD, ROBERT R.
  1972   The political economy of health care: dynamics without change. *Politics and Society* (Winter).
BALBUS, I. D.
  1971   The concept of interest in pluralist and Marxian Analysis. *Politics and Society* 1:515–577.
BELLIN, L.
  1971   "Changing composition of voluntary hospital boards — inevitable prospect for the 1970's." New York: New York City Health Department.
BODENHEIMER, T. S.
  1969   Regional medical programs: no road to regionalization. *Medical Care Review* 26:1125–1166.
CLARK, H. T., JR.
  1966   The challenge of the regional medical programs legislation. *Journal of Medical Education* 41: 344–361.
FREIDSON, E.
  1970   *Professional dominance: the social structure of medical care.* New York: Atherton.
GALBRAITH, J. K.
  1973   *Economics and the public purpose.* Boston: Houghton Mifflin.
GISH, O.
  1973   Resource allocation, equality of access, and health. *International Journal of Health Services* 3:399–412.

KRAUSE, E. A.
  1973   Health planning as a managerial ideology. *International Journal of Health Services* 3:445–463.

MCEASHERN, M. T.
  1957   *Hospital organization and management.* Berwyn, Illinois: Physician Record.

MCNERNEY, W., D. C. RIEDEL
  1962   *Regionalization and rural health care.* Ann Arbor, Michigan: University of Michigan Press.

MECHANIC, D.
  1967   The changing structure of medical practice. *Law and Contemporary Problems* (Autumn): 708.

PELLGRIN, R. J., COLT COATES
  1956   Absentee-owned corporations and community power structure. *American Journal of Sociology* 61:413–419.

PRESTHUS, R. V.
  1959   The social basis of bureaucratic organization. *Social Forces* 38: 103–109.

ROEMER, M. I., E. A. WILSON
  1952   *Organized health services in a county of the United States.* Health Service Publication 197.

SCHULZE, ROBERT O.
  1961   "The bifurcation of power in a satellite city," in *Community political systems.* Edited by Morris Janowitz, 19–80. Glencoe, Illinois: Free Press.

WEINERMAN, E. R.
  1971   "Problems and perspectives of group practice," in *National health care.* Edited by Ray H. Elling, 206–220. New York: Aldine.

# Dialectical Materialism and Community Mental Health Programs: An Analysis of the Lincoln Hospital Department of Psychiatry

WILLIE KAI YEE

This paper is part of an ongoing process within the Department of Psychiatry of New York City's Lincoln Hospital. This process includes an attempt to make the Department a structure that can serve the needs of the community as well as an attempt to use the tools of dialectical materialist analysis to aid that process. Because the struggle is a continuing one and because there has been relatively little analysis of this type of situation, all the ideas presented here must be regarded as tentative. It is hoped that a presentation of them at this time will provide tools for future action, and stimulate others to make such an analysis in their own situation.

## BASIC PRINCIPLES OF MATERIALIST DIALECTICS

The following concepts are basic to this analysis (the reader is referred to Mao [1968], Lenin [1970], and Engels [1939] for further clarification):
1. The universality of contradiction: everything has two aspects which are mutually opposed. The struggle between these two opposites is what makes things move.
2. External and internal contradictions: internal contradictions are the basis of change, and external contradictions are the conditions of change.
3. The principal contradiction and the principal aspect of a contradiction: to understand the nature of a thing, it is necessary to understand which of its contradictions is primary and which is secondary. All contradictions are not equal, and to effect change it must be clear which

is the principal contradiction. Once this is understood, the principal aspect of this contradiction must be understood, and the contradiction under which the principal aspect becomes the secondary aspect, and vice versa.

4. The particularity of contradiction: although contradiction is universal, qualitatively different contradictions must be resolved by qualitatively different means. Contradictions can be antagonistic, requiring radical or violent means of resolution, or nonantagonistic, allowing peaceful, gradual methods of resolution.

5. The dialectical world view: the world is not composed of separate objects which can be understood by studying them in isolation. To understand a "thing," we must understand its relations to other "things," and begin to see it not as an object, but as a process which is intertwined with other processes. An object must be seen not only as what it IS, but what it is BECOMING.

6. The dialectical theory of knowledge: all knowledge comes from practice, and from it alone. Practice may be divided into (a) the struggle over nature (the struggle for production) from which derives natural science and (b) class struggle from which derives social science. From practice comes the material which is systematized by theory. This theory in turn is verified or discredited in practice in a never-ending "cognitive spiral" leading to greater knowledge and more effective practice.

7. The materialistic theory of society: the structure of society is determined by its material base, that is, the labor, technology, and materials available to that society (the forces of production) and the way these forces are organized (the modes or relations of production). The forces of production tend to outrun the relations of production, and this constitutes the principal contradiction in society. The secondary contradiction in society is between the material base of the society and the laws, government, ideology, and culture of the society (the superstructure). The superstructure is used by the ruling class of the society to justify and further its exploitation of the lower classes of the society. Thus dialectical materialism must subject everything to analysis in terms of whether it ultimately serves the ruling class or the exploited class.

## EXTERNAL RELATIONS OF COMMUNITY MENTAL HEALTH PROGRAMS

A community mental health center is a service agency and not a part of the productive base of the society, such as a factory or a farm.

There are also human activities or kinds of labour such as that of the artist or the teacher, which directly satisfy human needs without producing material objects or goods. Neither the labour involved in the distribution of goods nor activities which themselves directly satisfy human needs produce any material objects. For this reason they are usually called NONPRODUCTIVE LABOUR in contradiction to PRODUCTIVE LABOUR. All activities connected with the satisfaction, directly or indirectly, of human needs which do not result directly in the production of goods are called services. For the sake of brevity from now on we shall use the word labour only in the sense of productive labour, i.e., labour engaged in the production of material objects, and use the word SERVICES to cover all other operations connected with the satisfaction of human needs.

In order that services may be carried out, certain material objects like school buildings, films, musical instruments and so on are necessary. These we call THE MEANS OF PERFORMING SERVICES. Particularly important among these are THE MEANS OF DISTRIBUTION in the shape of facilities like shop-accommodation, shelves, cash-registers. Since the performance of services satisfies human needs without producing material objects the means of the performance of service must be classified as consumer goods. These means are employed and used up in the process of satisfying human needs (Lange 1963: 6–7).

Economically, it uses up capital rather than producing it. The economic support of the activities comes from above, from the government and from profits. Thus the mental health center is one of the superstructure institutions of our society and is supported by the ruling class in order to carry out its aims.

In order to make a complete analysis of the external relations of a mental health center, one would have to make an analysis of the United States society in general, and an analysis of the particular community in which the mental health center exists. This, of course, we cannot do here except in briefest outline. Basically, the United States is ruled by an elite of a few thousand people who include the boards of large corporations and banks, the trustees of foundations, universities, hospitals and public corporations, the upper levels of the military and the government and the major contributors to political campaigns. This highly influential group can make decisions affecting the entire remainder of American society from relatively wealthy management down to the poorest welfare recipients (Lundberg 1968; Domhoff 1967).

These decisions, however, must be made within the constraints of the monopoly capitalist system. In order for a corporation to survive, decisions must be made which will enable it to compete, even though at a rational and personal level those making the decisions find them distasteful.

Since the economics of this monopoly capitalist system contain contradictions which make it unstable (Baron and Sweezy 1968), the ruling class is constantly engaged in maneuvers to preserve its power, including foreign domination (imperialism) and domestic repression (fascism and racism). Because of the basic economic contradiction in capitalism, there is a contradiction within the ruling class, which may make this class's purposes in supporting community mental health programs contradictory and confusing.

Thus the politics of the mental health centers can be expected to be at least in part determined by class struggle. Political groups which have been opposed to the community mental health movement state that this movement is an instrument of the bourgeoisie, and that it functions through cooptation, tokenism, tranquilization, distraction, repression, and other means to diffuse the anger and the militancy of oppressed people living in the ghetto. At the very least, the program should label the victims of economic oppression and social decay as sick and remove them from sight. This prevents the common people from becoming aware of how the social system destroys people. This is relatively easy, whereas the process of involving political forces in the community in the interest of mental health is more complicated. One can expect that the outreach and community organizational aspects of the community mental health movement will be attacked first, but that the basic psychiatric services are likely to survive in one form or another.

The specific power structure through which superstructure policy is carried out at Lincoln Hospital is the Albert Einstein College of Medicine-Montefiore Hospital "empire":

To most observers the dynamics of Einstein-Montefiore economic expansionism are beyond economic law or organizational logic, and Einstein-Montefiore is written off as a case of medical liberalism run wild. Liberalism is part of the answer. The Einstein-Montefiore trusteeship network, centered in the Federation of Jewish Philanthropies, does not exactly correspond with the predominantly WASP banker-financier-internationalist world of the downtown medical school trusteeships. Liberalism however is only the permissive atmosphere in which an Einstein-Montefiore thrives — the motivating force surges out of the inner logic of the new government and philanthropic granting and funding system. Einstein-Montefiore has been riding the cycle of grants and demonstration projects. It sponsors medical demonstrations which advertise for and justify the next grant, hence the next project and so on .... The price of this reliance on public support is the continual fear of being upstaged by a yet-unconquered institution, or dethroned by an angry community. Einstein-Montefiore must always be one step ahead of the competition and the public — it must plan, erecting a vast framework of control and defense. Plans, in turn, are themselves marketable to the federal and foundation funding axis, which is increasingly nervous about the chaos of our national medical "non-system" (HPAC 1970: 67–68).

The trusteeship network mentioned above does not quite fit the definition of the American ruling class as determined by Domhoff (1967). However, within the setting of the Bronx, the concentration of wealth and power represented by this set of interests compared to the vast majority of the inhabitants of the South Bronx places them into the relationship of that of a ruling class. This set of interests determines the survival of the community mental health programs. It is interlocked into the federal government in a manner similar to the interlocking of the defense-related contract-dependent industries and the military establishment. Radicals working within the mental health center see their function in the area of class struggle but on the other side of this contradiction. They see their job as raising the class consciousness of the people whom they see, and intensifying the class struggle in the interest of the oppressed class. This is done through various methods of community organization, political education, and therapies designed to liberate people from their external and internal oppression. The degree to which this aspect of class struggle is allowed depends on the degree to which the liberal, reformist aspect of ruling class politics prevails and on the visibility of the threat of the ruling class caused by these activities.

Some of the contradictions within the ruling class are reflected in the structure of the mental health center. The most basic contradiction within the mental health center lies in the area of the social relations involved in doing the work of the mental health center.

The basic conflict is not the struggle between professionals and non-professionals. It is a conflict inherent in the attempt to introduce para-professionals into the delivery of services while trying to maintain the traditional conceptualizations of mental illness, which carry implicit ideas that non-professionals cannot heal (Kunnes 1973: 87–93).

What has developed is a situation in which the most progressive work in the mental health center is done by an indigenous person using a collective, democratic method (the drop-in room; multidisciplinary teams), but working within a traditional hierarchical structure. The work of the community mental health workers (CMHW) is done through horizontal structure, and the power and funding come through the vertical one. (In recent months the administration has gradually attacked the horizontal structure attempting to impose greater control over work through a vertical one.) This built-in contradiction has been termed "programmed failure" (Shaw and Eagle 1971), that is, it was a built-in mechanism to prevent the CMHW's from becoming too effective in their work, which would make them a threat to the stability of capitalist society.

This contradiction has underlain all of the issues, crises, and conflicts outlined above. There is a crucial distinction between this contradiction and the contradiction between the forces of production and the relations of production which exist in a factory. This is that the flow of wealth is in the opposite direction. Thus in a factory the workers produce the product and wealth, and the factory cannot survive without the workers. In a mental health center the wealth comes from public funds. If the workers stop working, wealth does not cease to be produced, but the lack of services increases public discontent. The ruling class pours money into this area to keep down social discontent. If it did not, more overtly forceful police methods would have to be employed. The forces that maintain the job of the mental health worker are therefore social, rather than economic, pressures.

A second contradiction exists within the process of therapy, and that is the basic alienation within the therapeutic process. This alienation is manifested in the concept of help as a commodity and in the unequal status of the patient and the professional helper (professional in the sense that the person is paid for his or her work). Help for personal and social problems is a constant activity of members of any society. In a decaying exploitative society, however, problems are created which cannot be dealt with by ordinary help. The superstructure thus develops more sophisticated ways of dealing with personal problems caused by the society. Professional helpers emerge, and help becomes a commodity which is purchased by the upper and middle classes, and is administered and dispensed to the lower classes. As help is delivered through public channels it comes to be conceived of as a right, not a privilege. When this happens some of the inequality of the therapeutic relationship is removed. This is progressive development, because communities in demanding certain helping services suited to their needs begin to alter the paternalistic and colonial relationships out of which mental health services were originally imposed.

The unequal status inherent in the therapeutic relationship varies according to the methods used (Halleck 1971). Medication, psychotherapy, and supportive psychiatric treatment administered by physicians foster dependency and continue this relationship. Group therapies in which clients are encouraged and developed to become autonomous human beings counter this.

In the drop-in room and in advanced therapeutic groups patients give help to other patients without the inequalities involved in the patient-therapist relationship. This contradiction in the actual therapeutic relationship builds a certain tension into the work methods of the mental health center. To the degree to which this contradiction is made conscious, new work methods will develop which will have effects on the entire mental health center.

The other major external relation of the mental health center which should be considered is the community.

Lincoln Hospital is wedged into a rapidly decaying ghetto community. More than a third of a million people live in the surrounding neighborhood of factories, congested traffic, and aging apartment houses. A large segment of the population is Puerto Rican, a smaller number is Black, and a decreasing number of aging White. The rate of unemployment in this South Bronx neighborhood is double that of the borough as a whole. Only the most acute health problems reach the hospital — a hospital which is the most physically deteriorated, ill equipped and understaffed of all the sparsely endowed New York Municipal Hospitals. Its totally inadequate ER — the second busiest in the nation and the family doctor of many in the South Bronx has helped earn Lincoln its reputation in the community as the "butchershop" (Health PAC 1970: 255).

Overpopulation, poor sanitation, unemployment, ethnic conflicts, poor education, and the results of these (drug addiction, broken families, and alienation) produce a weak, powerless, but relatively large class of poor, and much maneuvering between sometimes opportunistic and sometimes well-meaning community leadership.

The community is composed of many classes which interact with the mental health center at different levels. The poorest and most disorganized members come to the clinic as patients or clients. Some working class and *petit bourgeois* members of the community usually work in hospitals and mental health centers. More organized sectors may have contact through consultation or community organization efforts of the mental health center. The most bourgeois elements of the community will be represented on the board, the government, and other organizations which can influence and sometimes control the community mental health centers.

## INTERNAL RELATIONS OF COMMUNITY PSYCHIATRY PROGRAMS

The internal relations of the Lincoln Hospital Department of Psychiatry will be analyzed from three points of view. First, a series of discrete interest groups (subclasses) within the department will be defined and differentiated. These are groups of persons working within the program who have common interests in their relation to the program and in relation to the actual delivery of services provided by the program. They can be differentiated according to criteria of job description, salary, and educational level, where they live, and what organizations they belong to. Secondly, each may be viewed in relation to the other groups, that is, the contradiction between groups. Finally, and this is crucial knowledge if one is to be able to predict what will happen in a crisis, the contradiction within each group must be studied. In each group the primary contradiction must be defined, and the primary aspect analyzed. Contradictions that arise out of the nature of the work done by the people in any of these groups are studied to see how they affect the political interests of the group.

Table 1.   Subclasses in the Lincoln Hospital Department of Psychiatry

| Interest group | Job title | Education | Income | Affiliation |
|---|---|---|---|---|
| Supportive workers | Housekeeper<br>Security guard<br>Clerk<br>Receptionist<br>Secretary | High school or trade school | Less than $10,000 | Union 1199, or DC 37 |
| Patient-care workers | Nurses<br>Community mental health worker<br>Social worker<br>Nurse's Aide | Nursing school or some college | | ANA, nuses' union<br><br>Social workers' org. |
| Professionals | Psychologist<br>Resident<br>Psychiatrist | Medical or graduate school Residency | Less than $30,000 | Professional org.<br>AMA, APA<br>AECOM faculty |
| Administrators | Unit head<br>Department chairman<br>Administrator | As above institute | Less than $50,000 | Psychoanalytic inst.<br><br>AECOM faculty |
| Ruling class | Department chairman<br>Member, board of trustees<br>Dean | | More than $50,000 | Boards of corporation<br>Federation of Jewish Philanthropies |

The groups in the Lincoln Hospital Department of Psychiatry are listed and characterized in Table 1. Although they are listed as distinct, there is some overlap between them. Those whose jobs are in the overlapping areas have the most intense contradiction. In particular, those workers whose functions (i.e. patient care) overlap those of the professionals, and those administrators who must answer to both the ruling class above and the workers below, constitute pivotal areas in a mental health center.

The workers constitute the base of the mental health center. They constitute the numerically largest group in the mental health center. Among the workers, there are groups which must be distinguished. The first group includes janitors, security guards, receptionists, secretaries, and other job categories which are not unique to the mental health center. The second includes those who have direct "therapeutic" contact with the patients. This includes community mental health workers, nurses, nurse's aides, and social workers. In the Lincoln Hospital Department of Psychiatry these job categories in the second group can all be treated together, because they have the same function and similar salaries.

The first group of workers, who have supportive functions in the mental health center, usually live in the community. The nature of their job is routine, frequently boring, and usually offers little or no opportunity for career advancement. Their educational level is the lowest of all the groups. Because of this, and because of the general level of unemployment at the present time, they are the most vulnerable group of workers. They tend to rely a great deal on the union to defend them, although their involvement in the union varies greatly. They seldom meet together outside of the union structure. They often will stand aside from community worker struggles, although they can be involved under certain circumstances. Because of their continuity with the community they can be viewed politically as community members. Thus, if an action is intended to involve the community, its effectiveness can be estimated by how it is received by the group of workers. Although they may seem unwilling to take action against their employer (except under instructions from the union), their attitudes and opinions must be respected as being close to those of many workers in the community.

The Psychiatry Department uses a progressive team work approach. Within the teams there is no functional difference between social workers, psychiatrists or mental health workers. However, the clerical workers have not been included in the breakdown of job distinctions.

In the Fall of 1971, a Manpower Career Development Administration (MCDA) program for training community people to become mental health workers was introduced into the department. The clerical workers were again excluded despite earlier promise of upgrading.

Many of the clericals had been stuck in the same dead end position for years. Angry at being once again excluded and at the lack of support from Local 1199, they organized a worker's committee (including mental health workers) and called a work stoppage. They were supported by house staff and other professionals who not only agreed with their demands but had grievances of their own (HPAC 1972: 8).

The patient-care workers, like the first group, come from the community. However, their situation is quite different for a number of reasons. When the job of mental health worker paraprofessional was conceived by the National Institute of Mental Health, a certain amount of career escalation was built into the concept. Because of this, and because their job functions overlap those of professionals, there is a considerable amount of *petit bourgeois* thinking. That is, one of the trends in this group is to have a high interest in personal advancement, job security, status, and many of the advantages possessed by the professionals. This can take the form of rivalry with the professionals in terms of attacking their elitism, privileges, and colonialist mentality. In many cases, employment at the mental health center gives them the opportunity to move out of the community, which they sometimes do, depriving the community of needed leadership. At present they have achieved a considerable amount of job security through the union. At Lincoln, unions, as well as paraprofessionals' organizations have been used to divide workers, thus preventing them from becoming too powerful a group (Ehrenreich and Ehrenreich 1973: 23–24).

At Lincoln, community mental health workers, social workers and psychiatric nurses, have essentially the same function, and the divisions that frequently occur between para-professionals' organizations for each job category have not occurred. However, following the crisis of 1969, the program was split into two divisions, the Lincoln Community Mental Health Center, and the Lincoln Hospital Department of Psychiatry [all the data in this paper refer to the latter] and the workers in these two programs have drifted further and further apart. Further, in July 1972, many workers were transferred from the Einstein payroll to the newly formed Health and Hospital Corporation. This placed some of the workers into a separate union. Finally, the teams were ordered to appoint permanent team leaders, and these team leaders were put into a separate administrator's union. This has provided the administration with an excellent set of conditions for instituting departmental changes.

Early in 1972 the administration began to require that all workers in the department, including residents and professionals, fill out a Daily Activity Log stating how their time was being used each day. It was stated that this information was needed for statistical purposes, so that the department could justify its funding. Many workers and residents balked and procrastinated because of the increasing amount of paperwork to which they were being subjected, but also because they felt that this was the beginning of increasing surveillance and interference in their work. The administration denied that this was the case, and made a rather good case of needing the information for statistical purposes. The workers then stated that if this was the case, that they would be willing to fill in the sheets anonymously. The administration said that this was not acceptable, without giving any clear reasons why. After almost a year of haggling, the director admitted that the information on the sheets would be used for evaluation purposes, and that workers might be least shuffled around on the basis of the data on the sheets. At this point documents were produced from the budgeting sources stating that the information of Daily Activity Logs had to be submitted by name. A few of the workers continued to refuse to sign the sheets although they did fill them out. Finally, the director stated that disciplinary proceedings would be instituted against one of the workers who was not signing the sheets, not, coincidentally, the one who had been most outspoken about not signing them. Up until this point the workers and the residents and professionals had not managed to maintain a united action as far as signing the sheets. At times a whole team would decide collectively not to sign. At one time all the workers including professionals had agreed not to sign. The residents stated they would follow whatever was agreed on by the team, that if not, they would sign. Usually the refusal lasted for a few days to a few weeks, but the professionals and the workers who were now permanent team leaders gave in first, followed by others. When a worker was threatened by firing, however, a job action seemed imminent.

Workers and residents finally began to act in unity and it was clear that no one would tolerate a worker being fired. Meetings were held, and the matter was resolved when the director agreed in writing that the Daily Activity Logs would not be used for evaluation purposes.

The other aspect of patient-care workers is their relation to the community. Again, the National Institute of Mental Health conception of such workers is that they are "indigenous," that is, they come from the community. Furthermore, they are in the position of confronting on a day-to-day basis the problems of the community which the mental health center is supposed to serve. Thus, although the supportive workers most resemble the average community inhabitant, the patient-care workers are the ones that have the direct contact with inhabitant problems. This group of workers is therefore the one that will respond most immediately to issues which involve the real work of the community mental health center.

Thus, this group of workers is critical. The primary contradiction is between their individualistic, professionalistic aspirations, which take them away from the community, and their background and work functions which give them knowledge of and sympathy with the community. This contradiction must be kept in mind if the political direction of community mental health workers and similar workers is to be understood.

July 1, 1972 was the date set for transferring Einstein employees to the Health and Hospital Corporation payroll. This involved transferring the workers from one union to the other, and would have meant a cut in pay of workers within the same union working side by side at different pay scales. As July approached, it seemed that a city-wide strike was imminent, and the residents discussed what their role should be if a strike broke out. They drew up a proposal which involved setting up an emergency mental health service in the community outside of the hospital auspices, and approached the mental health workers to see if they would support such an action. It was felt by the residents that such an action was the only way to maintain some service to patients without scabbing on the workers. The workers stated that they would abide by whatever the union said. A clarification was sought, and the union stated that they were opposed to the workers participating in any service, because the lack of services would put more pressure on the Corporation to reach a settlement. The workers stated that they felt it would be permissible for residents to continue to see patients at their homes if they wished, but that they could not participate in working in any kind of service during the strike.

The psychiatrists, psychologists, residents, and other physicians comprise the second major category in the mental health center. The principal contradiction in this class comes from their dual status as workers, that is, their service function to patients, and members of an elite with special education, salary prestige, and opportunities. The primary aspect of this contradiction is the elite status of the professionals, because as workers they have a great deal more security and influence over their own working conditions than workers do. There are, however, conditions which enable the opposite aspect to become primary, that is, situations in which some professionals will act in the interest of the workers or the community. This can be clarified by examining the reasons why professionals come to work at Lincoln Hospital. Professionals come for two sets of reasons. The first set are individualistic reasons. For some, especially those with inferior qualifications or disadvantages such as foreign training, they come because there is no other place they can find work. Because of the working conditions of a ghetto hospital it may be difficult to find a competent professional staff. Thus some will come because this is the best that they can obtain for themselves. For others with better qualifications, Lincoln is an opportunity for professional advancement. Faculty appointments, research and publication opportunities, and openings at higher levels are attractions for this group of professionals.

The other set of reasons for which professionals come to Lincoln come from the service orientation of the professional and the educational opportunities which they have had. Most professionals maintain some degree of the humanistic ideals which are the stated traditions of the professionals. The degree to which a professional will honestly attempt to serve his clients varies considerably from one individual to the next. In a crisis situation this does not provide any clear guide to action, and professionals cannot be relied on to act in a consistent manner according to this ethic. Some may interpret it to mean the services should be maintained at all times (and administration will attempt to exploit this feeling) whereas others will feel that patients are best served by supporting the struggle. Furthermore, for some professionals, their decision to be at Lincoln may have been made on political grounds. Their actions may be along the same lines as the progressive workers, but their basis is different.

Most residents who are now at Lincoln were in college and medical school during the late 1960's, a time of rising political awareness on American campuses manifested by the Civil Rights Movement, the anti-war movement, and militant direct action on or near the campuses. Lincoln was similarly in the headlines at this time and therefore attracted a number of politically aware residents. Thus, their reasons for coming to Lincoln in the first place is different from that of the workers. Although the political awareness is there, this in itself is not sufficient to determine the reliability of the professionals in workers' and community causes because of the class and educational background of professionals.

EXAMPLE 1
In the Winter of 1973 the residents raised the complaint, which they had often done in the past, that they were working in the ER without adequate supervision. In the past, it had been arranged that an attending psychiatrist in the department would be available by phone to give advice to difficult cases. The residents stated that that was unacceptable because:
1. what was needed was on-the-job supervision to adequately transfer the skills involved in this critical area of work and,
2. the attending psychiatrists usually were not in practice available by phone.

Meetings were held with the director of the department and with the newly appointed acting chairman of the Einstein Department of Psychiatry. The third year residents were given responsibility to do some of the supervision and the faculty were approached to see if they would be willing to do some supervision in the evenings. As a group they stated that they would not all agree to participate in this because of their private practices. Several stated that they were interested in doing this sort of teaching and were willing to do it on a volunteer basis. Enough volunteered to make enough coverage available to satisfy the residents, but some implied that they would resign if forced to do this.

Administration shares the elite status and individual aspirations of professionals but differs in that they have little or no direct contact with patients.

Those factors which can unify workers and professionals are absent. Hierarchically, administrators always stand in an employer/employee relationship to workers.

The administrators of the mental health center function to maintain and coordinate the operations within the mental health center, but also to deal with the relation of the mental health center to the superstructure. Administrators have authority within the mental health center and must deal with the demands of workers and professionals. Externally, they must answer to the organized sector of the community and to the ruling class and its agencies, which dispense the money to maintain the program. The handling of the contradictions between the ruling class, the workers, the professionals, and the community is impossible if the administrators are not aware of the political basis of those contradictions.

There are two forces which struggle against the elite and individualistic tendencies of professionals. The first is that at Lincoln many of the professionals work on teams in the clinic, emergency room, or acute-inpatient psychiatric unit, and have a measure of unity with the workers. This unity comes from working closely with workers in a generally non-hierarchical atmosphere and from experiencing some of the same difficulties as workers (e.g. increased paperwork, increased workload, lack of influence in decision making). A professional's unity with workers can therefore be judged by how closely he is integrated with workers on an everyday working basis. The second force which combats individualism is involvement in a group. If professionals are acting as a group, their position can be relied on much more than if they are acting as individuals. Because of the political experience of the present residents at Lincoln, they have been the most able to achieve political collectivity. In this situation they have a great deal of power because of their privileged position, and because they are needed. An alliance of workers and collectively functioning professionals is especially powerful and should be sought on any issue in which the working power of the mental health center is needed.

EXAMPLE 2

In October 1972 the director of training went on a six month's sabbatical. During the two years in which he had occupied this post, he had actively engaged in creating a structure in which the residents took an active role in administering and setting policy for the residency training program. Decisions were made democratically and attempts were made to get workers involved in the training activities. After the director of training left, the director of the department stated that he was taking the function of acting director of training on himself, and that as such, he was appointing himself to be the chairman of the training committee. The residents stated that this violated the entire tradition of the committee and withdrew their representation on the committee. They stated that they would return to the committee only if democracy was re-instituted and if there was a clear commitment to an integrated training program for workers and residents. They appealed to the workers for their support, stating that such an integrated program was not only in the workers' interest but in their own, because the presence of workers in the training and planning activities made a qualitative difference in the residents' own training. A restructured training committee was proposed by the residents which contained an increased representation of workers. This was accepted by the administration, but another committee was added, called the Residency Curriculum Committee, to deal with the special needs of residency training. The residents stated that they would not serve on this committee until the function of the overall training committee was made clear. They feared that the major decisions regarding training would be made with the RCC and the rest of the training committee would be undermined.

After a few weeks it became apparent that this indeed was the case, and the RCC in fact was restructuring the entire residency program along traditional elitist, and conceptually traditional lines. The residents began to attend this committee in an attempt to preserve the progressive aspects of the program but as of this date it seemed that the program would be restructured over their opposition. In the meantime, the training committee concerned itself with only worker training, and received no information regarding the residency program and obviously had no authority over it.

Too often administrators see their job as maintenance internally and public relations externally. Dialectically, the administrators in both situations are serving as mediators in the community/workers and ruling class/bureaucracy contradictions. Essentially, they must convince the ruling class that their aims are being carried out so that the money will continue to be available to allow the aims of the community and workers to be carried out. During a crisis, administrators are often forced by circumstances and competing power blocs. Alone, they have relatively little power. One of the reasons for their inability to deal with crisis is the lack of dialectical thinking. Specifically, the contradiction between the ruling class and the worker of the mental health center and the community can only be resolved effectively if the contradictions within each of these groups are understood as well as the contradictions between them.

The present director of the department was installed following a crisis which was publicized nationally. Following that crisis several directors were appointed and removed. In December 1971, he stated "these first months were difficult indeed. It soon became obvious, that the events of 1969 had been so traumatic for many staff members, that they appeared to me to be "fixated" at that level. In other words, they could not get over the passion and the conflict of the strike, and continued to attempt to revive and relive the same situation, and to measure everything and everyone against their positions as they had been at that time. In this atmosphere work and progress was not possible. For the sake of the department, and its ability to serve patients, as well as for the sake of particular members of staff who had been so deeply scarred, it was better all around, that fresh blood be brought in (Koz 1971).

In the summer of 1972, he stated it somewhat differently, reflecting perhaps both the law-and-order orientation of the Nixon era and his separation from a psychoanalytic institute. "We have to take a close look at this hospital and learn from it, because community involvement is important. But the extreme it's been carried to, and the lack of definition of community control, are terrigying, and the lack of spirit and discipline this administration has shown has led to this sort of anarchy" (Koz 1972).

As should be apparent from the data already presented here, crises, not conflicts, continued to erupt in the department of psychiatry. A turning point appeared to have taken place in 1972 when a new acting chairman of the Einstein Department of Psychiatry was appointed, and when the Health and Hospital's Corporate mandate to restructure the municipal hospital system along corporation lines began to affect the department directly. This took place in the setting of increasing awareness of the Nixon Administration's blatant subservience to corporate interest and ideology.

In 1969, the present acting chairman called "anyone who disagreed with the medical model [and the prescribed approach] revolutionaries who don't have a program — they would rather talk than get down to work; as for sub-professionals, I don't know a person who comes in here who would like to be treated by an indigenous person — they want to see doctors!" (HPAC 1972: 10).[1]

A management consultant was placed on the payroll; residents who had become enthusiastic about involving the department in outreach, prevention and innovative therapeutically modalities felt increasingly frustrated about the lack of departmental support for those endeavors (Bartlett, et al. 1973). Meetings of administrative bodies which were formerly open to anyone to attend were now closed. An increasing concern with statistics accompanied a seeming unconcern for the quality and type of care being given. Threats made to workers and residents were over administrative matters and not over the quality of their patient-care work. The administration began acting with increased confidence knowing that it had backings for its conservative stand within the Einstein empire, the municipal hospital bureaucracy, and the Federal Government.

## CONCLUSIONS

Listed below are strategies, priorities and specific recommendations that arise out of the analysis made above. Their derivation from the analysis should be fairly obvious.

1.   Because the primary contradiction exists at all levels in the mental health center, it can be used as a guide to strategy, priorities, and alliances. All programs and changes should be analyzed according to this basic contradiction. Because the contradiction extends to the ruling class, alliances may be made at times between all classes, including liberal members of the bourgeoisie.

---

[1]   In a personal communication to the author, Dr. Wilder, Acting Chairman of the Einstein Department of Psychiatry, stated that the "comments in Health PAC article were distorted."

2.   The basic power alliance which will promote progressive development of the mental health center is the patient-care workers allied with the politically conscious supportive workers and the collectively oriented professionals. This alliance must always be steered toward unity with the community as far as possible.

3.   Professionals should be encouraged to engage in collective work with workers, and collective political study among themselves.

4.   The general orientation of the program should be along the theoretical lines of socioadaptive, political, dialectical, and systems models. Priorities should be set on prevention with emphasis on community consultation, education and organization, pediatric and family interventions, and outreach.

5.   Continued dialectial materialist analysis must be carried on. Some specific areas include:

a.   Translation of the idea of this paper into a form accessible to workers. This has been the purpose of Workshop IV, an ongoing group within the Department of Psychiatry.

b.   Dialectical models for individuals, group, family, and network therapy.

c.   A more thorough analysis of classes in the South Bronx community.

6.   An emphasis on residency training to the exclusion of staff is detrimental to the residents as well as the staff. It represents not a choice of residents over staff, but a choice of the reactionary aspect of the primary contradiction.

7.   Political leadership from the class of patient-care workers should be determined by a worker's ability to do his or her patient-care work in the mental health center.

## REFERENCES

BARON, P., P. SWEEZY
   1968   *Monopoly capital.* New York: Modern Reader Paperbacks.
BARTLETT, J., *et al.*
   1973   "A report of the residency training program at Lincoln Hospital." Paper presented to the Executive Committee of the Albert Einstein College of Medicine Department of Psychiatry, March 7, 1973.
DOMHOFF, W.
   1967   *Who rules America?* Englewood Cliffs, N.J.: Prentice-Hall.
EHRENREICH, J., B. EHRENREICH
   1973   Hospital workers: a case study in the new working class. *Monthly-Review* (January).

ENGELS, F.

1939   *AntiDühring: Herr Dühring's revolution in science*, chapters twelve and thirteen. New York: International Publishers.

HALLECK, S.

1971   *The politics of therapy*. New York: Science House.

HEALTH POLICY ADVISORY COMMITTEE (HPAC)

1968   *Bulletin* (June).

1969   *Bulletin* (May).

1970   *The American health empire: power, profits, and politics*. New York: Vintage Books.

1972   *Bulletin* (January).

KOZ, G.

1971   *Report on the department of psychiatry at Lincoln Hospital* (December). Albert Einstein College of Medicine.

1972   Quoted in *Medical World News* (July 21).

KUNNES, R.

1973   "*De-therapizing society*": *rough times*. New York: Ballantine Books.

LANGE, O.

1963   *Political economy*, volume one. Warsaw: Polish Scientific Publishers.

LENIN, V. I.

1970   *Karl Marx*. Peking: Foreign Languages Press.

LUNDBERG, F.

1968   *The rich and the super-rich*. New York: Bantam Books.

MAO TSE-TUNG

1968   *Four essays on philosophy*. Peking: Foreign Languages Press.

MINUCHIN, S.

1964   The professional and the use of confrontation in the mental health field. *American Journal of Orthopsychiatry* 39: 722–729.

SHAW, R., C. J. EAGLE

1971   Programmed failure: the Lincoln Hospital story. *Community Mental Health Journal* 7: 255–263.

# Medical Education in Transition: Tanzania

A. M. RAIKES

## INTRODUCTION

Tanzania is one of the poorest countries in the world, as well as in Africa. Her estimated Gross Domestic Product per capita is about $97.20,[1] derived mainly from primary production. The raw materials that she sells on the world market are produced by a peasant population living in the rural areas and comprising 94 percent of the total population (only 6 percent of Tanzanians live in urban areas). Primary education is not yet available for all Tanzanian children; it is estimated that 50 percent receive a primary education, while only 2.8 percent continue on to secondary school.

In Tanzania the annual expenditure on health per capita is about $1.43, and the doctor:population ratio is 1:21,000. About one-third of all children born in Tanzania die before the age of five years (Segal 1972).

That Tanzania is one of the poorest countries in the world is easy to document; however, by documenting this alone the dynamics behind this poverty are lost. It is only by looking at the poverty within the context of underdevelopment that an adequate comprehension of any sector can be made. Underdevelopment here refers to the situation of an exploitative relationship between Europe, Africa, and America that began in the sixteenth century with the slave trade and under which Europe

---

[1] All figures have been converted from Tanzanian shillings into United States dollars at the rate of 7/– Tanzanian to United States $1.00.

developed and industrialized at the expense of Africa. This situation was later perpetuated during the period of colonization.[2]

With this analysis of her past, Tanzania today has defined her goals of rapid development through socialism and self-reliance. Since the Arusha Declaration of 1967, plans and progress have been made.[3]

In documenting the existing situation in any sector today, as, for example, the medical training programs, paradoxes and inconsistencies are inevitable, given an understanding of Tanzania's poverty and under-development and her stated goals of socialist development. In the ten years since independence, the country has made enormous progress in many areas, but ten years is clearly insufficient time to undo the colonial structure of dependence — economic, political, and psychological dependence — that was built into the system (see Raikes and Meynon 1972). As President Nyerere said recently, "We don't pretend that we have a socialist society; we simply say that we have stated the objective and that Tanzania is at present experiencing the 'birth pangs of socialism'" (Martin 1973).


## EDUCATION, THE WIDER CONTEXT

If the medical training programs in Tanzania are to be understood, they must be seen within the context of the entire racially biased and elitist educational system set up under colonialism and of more recent changes in that system.

With the exception of a few early mission schools, the main thrust of German educational policy from 1890 to 1914 was to provide primary school education for the training of lower level functionaries of government, because direct rule provided no scope for the training of even a small African elite. The primary school education provided was marked by brutality and the inculcation of the racialist attitudes of the colonialists, but was reportedly more thorough and extensive than the education provided later by the British in the inter-war period.

The guiding principle of British colonial education was elitism, and it reflected the class and racial structure of the country. Primary and secondary education were provided for all children of the white population, although many of the children of the upper level civil servants avoided contact with lower class British pupils by attending private

[2]   Walter Rodney's book, *How Europe underdeveloped Africa*, gives the detailed background for the use of the term "underdevelopment".
[3]   A fuller account of the Arusha Declaration is given later in this paper.

schools in Britain. Again, primary and secondary schooling was provided for a high proportion of the Asian population, although at a lower cost. For the African population, on the other hand, only 50 percent of the relevant age group entered the first grade of primary school, even in 1959, by which time the numbers had been increased considerably in anticipation of independence. But the pyramid narrowed very sharply and in that year there were under 300 students who passed the final exam in the African secondary schools.

The secondary schools were the stage for intensive indoctrination into the attitudes of the colonial power. Though this socialization process was never taken to quite the extent that it was in the French African colonies, it was nevertheless certainly powerful. The earliest secondary schools had been mission schools and seminaries, but in the late 1920's, with the introduction of "indirect rule," a government secondary school for the sons of chiefs was set up at Tabora, in conscious imitation of a British public school. "Character training" played an important part in educating the elite, and religion, cold baths, and beatings were seen to be essential elements of this. This school was the model for other secondary schools, and, because all were boarding schools, "character training" remained an important aspect of secondary education for a long time.

At independence, the initial reaction of the new African government was to note the differences between European and African education and to try to reduce them. Enrollment in the primary schools has increased by about 60 percent since independence, but there has not been a similar increase in secondary school enrollment because admittance to these schools is strictly planned in accordance with the estimated manpower needs of the country. This has meant that the expansion in secondary schools has been far less than in many other independent African countries. This was a conscious political decision, to avoid the growth of unemployment among secondary school graduates and the consequent pressures for the provision of more higher education and more bureaucratic jobs. However, it has still left the problem of the primary school graduates, for only 10 percent of those who finish primary school gain entrance to the secondary schools.

The president's paper "Education for Self-Reliance" addressed itself largely to this remaining 90 percent, who had been taught that academic study was superior to manual work, and that they were therefore failures for not getting into secondary school. Agriculture and some manual skills, as well as political education and defense training, were made part of the school curriculum. The purpose of the new curriculum was to integrate this training into the teaching pattern, rather than making it simple drudgery and insurance for the failures, and many aspects of it are now also included in post-secondary school education — hence the field projects and political education that are part of the curriculum of the present-day medical students.

The extent to which the new policy has been successful in changing the elitist attitudes engendered by the colonial system is hard to gauge, but it is certain that these attitudes are not dissipated overnight, especially when those who hold them are the school teachers.

It is within this context of the elitist and racist education system set up under colonialism that the programs developed for the training of medical workers will be examined.

At independence the number of Tanzanian medical workers[4] was minute and most of them were paramedics. There were only fourteen Western-trained Tanzanian doctors and 388 equivalent nurses in 1962. A skeleton curative health care system existed and its manpower reflected both the elitist and racist structure of the overall educational system as well as the distinct hierarchy that is found in Western medical systems. That this hierarchy in the health services is inappropriate and inefficient is being discussed[5] in Britain and the United States today and questions of its appropriateness in Tanzania have also been raised. To see how this hierarchy of medical workers developed it is necessary to look in more detail at how the training programs evolved historically.


## THE COLONIAL LEGACY — THE GERMAN PERIOD

In the first fifteen years of German rule in Tanganyika there was little change in the basic structure of the economy inasmuch as all the imports and exports were handled and organized through Zanzibar; it was only later, with the tightening of controls, that the Germans managed to re-route the country's trading through Dar es Salaam to Europe. The German administration was organized through a tight centralized bureaucracy, for which the Germans trained a cadre of African subordinate administrators, the Akidas. In order to facilitate this training the government opened a few government primary schools.

The missionaries were the earliest Europeans to establish Western

---

[4] The term "medical worker" in this paper is used in the widest sense and includes paramedics, nurses, and physicians.
[5] For a recent study on the hierarchy in the United States medical system, see Ehrenreich and Ehrenreich (1973); for a discussion along similar lines for the British system, see King, et al. (1972).

curative medicine in any form, but their contribution was minimal and it was the German administration that first organized a curative medical service.[6] The Germans built, during their twenty-six years in Tanganyika, twelve general hospitals. In addition to establishing a hospital network, they started public health work by initiating research into endemic diseases and by conducting vaccination programs. The medical services that were established were on a very small scale, and as far as the training of African medical workers was concerned, there is no mention of this in the literature.

## THE EARLY BRITISH PERIOD 1918–1938

During World War I, public health services in the towns deteriorated, but these were revived and increased in the wake of growing urbanization following the war.

It was mainly in the towns that the European population had settled, and it was therefore for the safety of these people that a sanitation branch was set up to improve water supplies and waste disposal services and to attack the mosquito breeding grounds and the problem of communicable diseases. As the cholera epidemics in the nineteenth and early twentieth century in Britain had shown, epidemic diseases have no respect for class (or here one could read "racial groups"), and it was the deaths of the urban rich that led to the introduction of modern sanitation measures, for self-protection.

It was in the 1920's that the first programs for training African medical workers were started. There were three reasons for starting the programs at this time. First, there was a pressing need, the Medical Department felt, to expand the public health services, and there were not enough people to do this. Secondly, the department wanted to expand the health services to include curative work for Africans outside of government employment, and there were not enough European staff members available to do so. And thirdly, it was during the 1920's that it first became possible to recruit a sufficient number of literate candidates for training, because there had been a continuous expansion of the primary schools.

Three categories of African medical workers — sanitary inspectors, dispensers, and tribal dressers — were established, and recruitment procedures and training programs were planned for them.

[6] Much of the material about the development of the health services during the colonial period comes from a report to the government that was done in 1963; see Titmuss, et al. 1964.

The sanitary inspectors were recruited on the basis of literacy in Swahili, but, because of the educative nature of the work it was planned they would do, an attempt was made to choose people with some standing in the community. Their training program was to consist of three months of practical instruction in the Health Offices in Dar es Salaam, Tanga, and Tabora.

The African dispensers were planned to be more senior medical workers, and a higher educational standard, including English, was required of them. They were to get training that would equip them to work in the hospitals and dispensaries doing curative work. Their instruction included elementary anatomy and physiology, elements of medicine, minor surgery, and first aid, as well as other subjects. It was an eighteen-month course when it started and was conducted at the Medical Training School in Dar es Salaam.

The tribal dressers were recruited differently. Very often they were selected by their chiefs, who had been requesting the government to set up medical treatment services; therefore the amount of formal education did not matter, for it was the chief's decision as to who was the brightest or most competent to send for training. The training was carried out by the medical staff and lasted for about three months. It included the use of drugs and equipment and also practical sanitation and first aid.

The depression in the thirties affected mainly staffing, research, and public health work, but the training programs continued to function. It was during this time that the increasing numbers of African pupils who gained admission into secondary school caused higher entrance requirements for the medical training programs to be set. It was also the time when selected candidates were sent abroad for medical and nursing training for the first time.

By World War II the foundations of a medical service had been established and included both European and African medical workers and served both the European and African populations. But the Europeans obviously got the best of the medical services that they had designed for their own safety, and they were also, of course, in the influential administrative and decision-making positions in the system.

## THE FORTIES AND FIFTIES

Figures from a government medical report of 1946 show that the system was still racist and urban-based and the total medical establishment still tiny. Table 1 shows how the beds were divided according to racial

Table 1.  Hospital bed distribution 1944

| Racial grouping | Beds, government, mission, private, and industry | Rate per 100,000* |
|---|---|---|
| European | 126 | 2,086 |
| Asian | 102 | 224 |
| African | 3,343 | 117 |
| Not stated | 3,017 | |
| Total | 6,588 | 120 |

* Based on the estimated populations: European 6,040
Asian 46,558
African 5,489,069
Total 5,541,667

Table 2.  Medical workers as of April 15, 1946

| Category of medical worker | Urban-based | | Total strength | |
|---|---|---|---|---|
| | European | Non-European | European | Non-European |
| Medical administrators | 3 | 0 | 11 | 0 |
| Medical officers and compounders | 5 | 8 | 36 | 69 |
| Hospital assistants | 0 | 8 | 0 | 100 |
| Laboratory assistants and medical stores | 8 | 13 | 9 | 24 |
| Health inspectors | 4 | 0 | 15 | 0 |
| Health visitors | 2 | 0 | 5 | 0 |
| Junior health staff | 0 | 13 | 0 | 126 |
| Hospital matrons | 2 | 0 | 3 | 0 |

categories, in favor of the Europeans. Table 2 shows both how small the total size of the medical establishment was and also how urban-based it was (Uzaramo District is the coastal area in which the capital city was and still is.) It also gives an indication of the racial structure of the medical worker teams.

The 1950's in Tanganyika was a period of increasing British government investment and budgetary control, and it was also a time of policy decisions by the British on implementation of rapid development of the Tanganyikan economy. To facilitate the planned rapid economic development, Tanganyika was allocated $5\frac{1}{2}$M pounds sterling at a time when her total revenue was only 2M pounds sterling. With this allocation came a number of schemes and plans for agricultural development and, during the same period, there were also plans for expanding and developing both the medical services and the training facilities for medical workers.

Most of the government memoranda from the Medical Department at this time discussed the limitations of the department in terms of service and recommended an increase in services together with an increase in the training facilities for medical workers. The training of "B" nurses, the first basic nursing training program, was planned and started during the fifties, and it was further planned that this category would later be upgraded or developed into a higher category of the same standard as the British S.R.N. nurse.

There are three major points that must be noted here in terms of the types of training programs that were drawn up and expanded. First, the programs of the various training schools showed that the "curative" nature of the health services influenced directly the types of training that the medical workers were given. They were trained as "curative" health workers with curricula often based on those in use in Britain. For example, the rural medical aids, who formed a paramedical category and did not have an exact parallel in Britain but were nevertheless diagnostic (and treatment) workers, were taught anatomy, physiology, and microbiology as the essential basic training for diagnostic work, as were diagnostic workers in Britain. As the value and place of anatomy, physiology, and microbiology are now being questioned in Western medical schools, there is some justification for asking if this was in fact the most appropriate training for rural medical workers in Tanganyika.

Second, because the training programs were organized and taught by Europeans in the colonial service to African students, no allowance or accommodation could be made between the formal organized health service and the larger, by far, traditional health system. Some attempts were made to make the course more "relevant" to Tanganyika by including topics such as "customs and taboos," "traditional foods," and "the extended family," but these attempts must have been largely mystifying as the students knew far more about their own customs, values, and habits than the European instructors could ever hope to know. In addition, given the racist nature of most of the anthropology that was used, it could not have given the students any insight into the nature of their country's poverty in terms of underdevelopment, as mentioned earlier, which is the only way their poverty could be rationally explained. In other words, their culture and customs were used as the explanation of their poverty.

Third, the training programs, with their differences in entrance requirements, course contents, and length of training, created a hierarchy of medical workers that related directly to expected and actual salary differences in employment on completion of the training. This hierarchy was based on pay and status differences between diagnosis and treatment workers, nursing and caring workers, and the unskilled category of cleaners, cooks, and other hospital workers, and mimicked exactly the hierarchical ladder found in the British medical services. That this ladder must have seemed rational to the colonial administrators can be surmised in that there was no mention whatever in the memoranda concerning the appropriateness of this hierarchy either in Britain or in Tanganyika. Diagnosis and treatment workers were more skilled and were to be paid more than care workers, and male workers were to be paid more than female workers.

It is now a well-known fact that the medical system in Britain developed historically into a hierarchical class-based and sexist system that was still influenced considerably, in the fifties, by Victorian ideas and morality. The career structures were rigid, with a diagnostic and treatment ladder of licensed medical practitioners at the top of which were the members of the Royal Colleges of Physicians and Surgeons, who had to be graduates of Oxford or Cambridge University and were, therefore, men who were drawn exclusively from the ruling class. Then there were the apothecaries, skilled craftsmen whose training was very different, who served the poor and later became the general practitioners. There was a nursing care ladder, open to women, that was influenced largely by Florence Nightingale's model of a gentle, obedient serving-lady. There were also other technician ladders as well as a pool of unskilled workers who did the dirty work in the hospitals and who were at the bottom of the hierarchy.

In Tanganyika these ideas influenced the way the medical career structures were set up, and the case of the development of the nursing cadre of health workers is one that perhaps documents this best.

There was tremendous concern in the fifties over the backwardness of female education because this resulted in the situation that only males could and did volunteer for nursing training, for only they had achieved a sufficient level of elementary schooling. In an attempt to reverse this trend by training more female nurses, entrance qualifications to the nursing courses were lowered for females, with Standard VIII required for male students and Standards VII or VI accepted for female students (*Report on the training of nurses* n.d.). In addition to this, recruitment for girls was done directly through the schools, in order to reduce the chances that girls would be lost to marriage or other possibilities, whereas the male students were usually recruited from within the hospitals or dispensaries where they were already working. These policies did succeed, as can be seen from Table 3 below, in changing the sex pattern of ad-

Table 3.   Estimate of annual recruitment and output of male and female pupil nurses, 1950–1960

| Year | Total | Admissions | | Graduations | |
|------|-------|------|---------|------|---------|
| | | Males | Females | Males | Females |
| 1950 | — | — | — | 15 | 3 |
| 1951 | 45 | 20 | 25 | 18 | 8 |
| 1952 | 50 | 20 | 30 | 18 | 8 |
| 1953 | 60 | 20 | 40 | 18 | 8 |
| 1954 | 75 | 25 | 50 | 18 | 20 |
| 1955 | 90 | 25 | 65 | 18 | 24 |
| 1956 | 100 | 25 | 75 | 18 | 32 |
| 1957 | 100 | 25 | 75 | 18 | 40 |
| 1958 | 100 | 25 | 75 | 18 | 52 |
| 1959 | 100 | 25 | 75 | 18 | 60 |
| 1960 | 100 | 25 | 75 | 18 | 60 |

missions and graduations of trainee nurses to fit in with the British Nightingale stereotype mentioned above.

By the end of the British period in Tanganyika a number of training programs for medical workers had been established to provide African medical personnel for the skeleton health services that existed. These training programs were based on the British system, and from them the values and hierarchy that existed in the British medical service were assimilated. The rural medical aids and the medical assistants were not physicians but were, nevertheless, trained as diagnostic and treatment workers and seen as a totally different category from the nursing and care workers. The returning Makerere graduate physicians were seen to fit in at the top of the diagnostic and treatment ladder and took their places there to practice curative medicine.

## INDEPENDENCE AND THE HEALTH SECTOR

The new government at independence was faced with the task of counting and assessing the resources of all sectors of the economy and of planning the future. In terms of health, it was a period of counting heads, both of the total population and of medical workers, assessing resources and expenditures, and evaluating and planning. No longer could hospital beds be "white" beds, although grades have remained. In terms of manpower, foreign personnel would be there only on a short-term basis, and there was a sense of urgency for Africanization and for increasing the trained medical manpower as soon as possible to be as effective as possible for TANZANIANS. In terms of assessing and planning medical manpower, this period can be divided into two: the pre-Arusha period and the post-Arusha period.

The Titmuss Report was a product of the pre-Arusha Declaration period, when the government requested a committee to be set up to study the health services and to make recommendations on:

1. Ways and means of extending the curative services over the next five years in order to achieve maximum even coverage territorially;
2. How preventive medicine and other means of health education may best be promoted;
3. The staff which will be necessary to put expansion plans into operation;
4. How this staff may be trained locally, bearing in mind that it may not in every case be either necessary or desirable to insist upon United Kingdom qualifications, but that reasonable standards must be maintained; and
5. What proportion of available finance should be devoted to each activity of the health services (Titmuss, et al. 1964).

The outcome of the Titmuss Committee's work was a very detailed report and assessment of the existing health resources in the country. It detailed the curative and urban nature of the existing medical facilities and recommended that priority should be given to preventive health care over curative medicine.

In terms of manpower, the report, assuming a preventive health priority, recommended increasing the enrollment in all the training programs, but with a more rapid increase in the training of the rural medical aid cadre. It also recommended that a training program similar to that of the "Makerere-trained practitioner," based on school certificate entry for a four-year course, be started in Dar es Salaam. The report stated that this person should be regarded as "doctor" by the nursing and technical staff and should be seen as a full professional colleague by Makerere- or United Kingdom-trained practitioners; but at the same time he was to be trained as a general practitioner for rural services.

The other document that is crucial in the pre-Arusha period is the Tanzanian first Five Year Development Plan of 1964–1969. This plan did not advocate any radical changes in the health services, but advocated expansion of the physical medical facilities, located mostly in the urban areas, with the aim of one hospital bed for every 1,000 people.

The Arusha Declaration of 1966 altered the course of development in Tanzania. The declaration charted a course of development based on self-reliance and the building of socialism to attain the most rapid economic development of an equal and just society. Self-reliance, as set out in the declaration, is based on the premise that the only government primarily interested in the development of Tanzania in the interest of Tanzanians is the people of Tanzania. Foreign resources and skills would be used to complement and strengthen Tanzania's own efforts and must be within the framework of Tanzanian policies.[7]

In the health sector the country's new guidelines directly influenced the choice of priorities and the second Five Year Plan set a target of increasing the preventive and rural health services, mainly through the agency of rural health centers. The government was to construct new health centers that were to become the focal point of an effective rural health service, and they were planned to serve a population of around 50,000. They were to supervise the dispensaries and to organize preventive campaigns such as nutrition education, environmental sanitation, maternal and child health services, and immunizations.

The most important influence of the Arusha Declaration in terms of the training of medical workers has been its effect on manpower planning. The manpower planners, in line with the guidelines of the second Five Year Plan, have recognized that the implementation of the proposals to develop preventive care facilities through rural health centers will involve training more medical workers for preventive rural work, rather than expanding the cadre of curative physicians. The training of a rural medical aid at the moment takes three years at a cost of $400.00, whereas the training of a physician at the new medical school in Dar es Salaam takes five years at a cost of $7,142.90 per annum. The number of students accepted at the medical school has been frozen at fifty a year while the rural medical aid and the medical assistant cadres are scheduled to have increased admissions annually.[8]

The manpower experts, like many other experts, however, suffer from certain limitations of perception that are often inherent in their own very specialized training. Cost-benefit analysis is always a limited tool, and in this case its usage leaves out the questions of the relationship of the medical workers to class formation and of the development of an appropriate hierarchy. In terms of recruitment and training there has been no fundamental change in the pattern inherited from the colonial period, with the exception that there is now a regular enrollment of secondary school graduates into the new medical school. The training programs and syllabi still mirror the training for curative medicine. They involve long periods of instruction and are based on the teaching of skills required

[7]   The Arusha Declaration is printed up as a government pamphlet and can also be found in Nyerere (1968).
[8]   This information and also other figures on manpower were obtained from Oscar Gish, who was employed at the Ministry of Health in Dar es Salaam.

to diagnose and treat illnesses in the hospital and dispensaries. The new course at the Faculty of Medicine, as with the earlier training programs, was designed by men who were concerned with "Western" standards and much of it imitates courses found in Britain. There are hours and hours of anatomy and most of the first three years are spent in the classroom and laboratory. There is an "elective" period in the fifth year when, as in Britain or other schools in Europe, students are encouraged to go abroad to work or study something that appeals to them, however irrelevant this may be to Tanzania's health priorities. The innovations in the courses in community medicine have not yet transformed the medical training in any meaningful way.

In terms of the existing hierarchy of medical workers mentioned earlier, there has been little change and the programs still reinforce the belief that diagnostic and treatment work is superior to nursing care work and that the former is mostly a male occupation whereas the latter is a female one. There have been several attitudinal studies done with rural medical aid students and also with the interns that show that the medical officer or physician is always ranked at the top of the hierarchy, often followed by the medical assistant, the rural medical aid, and the nurse at the bottom.[9]

However, although there have been no radical changes in the training of medical workers in Tanzania since the Arusha Declaration, nevertheless, there have BEEN SOME CHANGES IN ALL OF THE PROGRAMS. All of the training programs are committed to including politics in their curricula. Also, there has been considerable debate on the inappropriateness of the separation of theory from practice and most of the schools now have a commitment to carry out part of their training in the villages instead of all of it being done in the classroom.

In addition to this there has been considerable discussion on how best to provide the new Ujamaa villages with preventive health coverage and medical services and new cadres; first-aid village helpers, as well as day-care center workers, are being trained. In the expansion of the day-care center program, it is planned that children of working mothers will be cared for and given a balanced diet while their mothers are at work.

An additional, and major, achievement has been documented recently in what is probably the largest health education campaign ever. This campaign was a radio education campaign covering major illnesses in Tanzania that are preventable: malaria, hookworm, dysentery, Bilharzia, and tuberculosis (water too was discussed). Seventy thousand group

---

[9]  Both G. M. Van Etten and Dr. J. Holmes have been working in these areas but as yet the material is unpublished.

leaders all over the country were trained in a period of four months to work within small study groups and then to participate in an action campaign against these diseases. It has been estimated that this campaign has reached 2,000,000 people and evaluation teams have reported that there has been considerable activity following the program (see Hall 1973).

The health sector, as with the other sectors of the Tanzanian economy, is in a period of transition and reflects aspects of her poverty and under-development and her policies of socialist development. The transition from a curative, urban-based health service to a primarily preventive service is a radical change. Such a change will necessarily involve the medical workers, who will be responsible for offering preventive health education, treatment, and care on a much wider scale than has been done so far. It would seem that in the next few years there will be some funda-mental changes that will emerge in the existing training programs.

## REFERENCES

EHRENREICH, JOHN, BARBARA EHRENREICH
  1973   Hospital workers: a case study in the "new working class." *Monthly Review* 24:8 (January).
HALL, BUDD L.
  1973   "Revolution in rural education: health education in Tanzania." Paper presented at the Ethiopia African Adult Education Association Conference, Addis Ababa, September 1973.
KING, A., N. RICHMAN. C. TUPLING,  C. WEBB, P. ZINKEN
  1972   Efficient management at large. *Needle* 12. London.
MARTIN, DAVID
  1973   Interview with President Nyerere. *New Internationalist* (May).
NYERERE, JULIUS K.
  1968   *Ujamaa, essays on socialism.* Oxford: Oxford University Press.
RAIKES, P. L., W. MEYNON
  1972   "Dependency, differentiation and diffusion of innovation: a critique of extension theory and practice." Paper presented at the Eighth Annual East African Universities Social Science Conference, Nairobi, 19–23 December 1972.
*Report on the training of nurses*
  n.d.   *Report of the Committee on the Training of African Nurses and Mid-wives.* Memorandum number 1334/45, 13/11/50, archives material held at Medical-School Library, East African Section, University of Dar es Salaam.
RODNEY, WALTER
  1972   *How Europe underdeveloped Africa.* Dar es Salaam: Tanzania Publishing House.

SEGAL, MALCOLM

1972 "The politics of health in Tanzania," in *Towards socialist planning.* Edited by the Uchumi Editorial Board: J. Rweyemamu, et al., 149–165. Dar es Salaam: Tanzania Publishing House.

TITMUSS, R. M., *et al.*

1964 *The health services of Tanganyika: a report to the Government.* London: Pitman.

# Regionalization of Health Services: Sociological Blocks to Realization of an Ideal

RAY H. ELLING

The idea of regionalization of health services has been the topic of thought, writing, and discussion in health administration, medical care, medical education, and health planning circles for many years. Its origins are found in the Dawson Report of 1920 (see Consultative Council on Medical and Allied Services 1920). In this crisply worded but far-reaching statement three general characteristics were highlighted: (1) a graded hierarchy of interdependent services with a two-way flow of patients, information, etc. between the periphery and the center of the system to cover economically a geographically defined population large enough to justify a relatively complete health care system (thus, several regions were recommended for Great Britain); (2) heavy emphasis on continuing education and on-the-job training to keep people up-to-date in relation to their jobs; and (3) education of the recipient public in health matters so as to spread the efforts of the necessarily small cadre of specially prepared health personnel.

These ideas remain as fresh and promising today as they were when first presented. Other characteristics have been added and refinements suggested, including comprehensiveness of services (both curative and preventive) and adaptation of the system of services to the economic, social, cultural, and political life of the people in the geographic area (Grant 1955; also, Organization of Local and Intermediate Health

I am particularly grateful to M. R. Pibouleau, Technical Officer, Division of Strengthening of Health Services, World Health Organization, and to Henry Clark, Visiting Professor, Department of Community Medicine, University of Connecticut Health Center, for their comments and suggestions.

Administrations 1972). More recently, as part of this latter concern, some attention has been given to involvement of consumers in health policy and decision-making at the regional as well as the most local level (see Elling 1971b; Silver 1971; Ingman, Goldfrank, and Greenwald 1971).

But there have been problems in realizing the ideals of regionalization. As Seipp wrote in justifying a promising experiment in Puerto Rico, "Although Lord Dawson's conception has won many adherents over the years, nowhere has the ideal of regionalization been realized completely" (Seipp 1963: 1364). A more recent assessment of this experiment records continuing difficulties as well as successes (see Arbona and Curt 1971).

Problems in regionalizing health services have been especially evident in the United States, where a pluralistic system allows full reign to conflicting interests.[1] But even in Eastern Europe, where lines of authority are more pyramidal, there are problems, for example, between cities as regions and rural regions (Weinerman and Weinerman 1969). An excellent inventory of problems experienced suggests that conflicting interests of different types are found to some degree in a wide range of settings and make the full realization of regionalization problematic (Cohen 1971).

These experiences suggest the value of analyzing the sociopolitical, economic, and cultural bases of conflicting interests which often prevent the fuller realization of regionalization. This task is important because, in spite of problems, the concept of regionalization is "one of the richest in present content and future potentiality" (Bridgman and Roemer 1972)[2] for organizing health services at the subnational level. By analyzing the sociological bases of these problems we may be in a better position to suggest new, more successful approaches to developing health services in relation to their socioeconomic and political contexts.

I shall describe some of the most essential goals and other organizational elements in an ideal conception of regional systems, identify and illustrate some of the problems which have been observed in different settings, and analyze major sociological constraints which prevent the realization of regionalization in its fullest sense.

---

[1]  See Bodenheimer (1969); Snoke and Glasgow (1970). A recent attempt of HIP (Health Insurance Plan of Greater New York) to regionalize its service program met such resistance that the long-time director of HIP resigned his position. For a summary description of the plan, see HIP (1972).

[2]  Bridgman and Roemer also record problems in realizing regionalization in thirteen countries covering nine types made up by the intersection of two dimensions: level of socioeconomic development and degree of centralization of hospital authority patterns.

## REGIONALIZATION, AN IDEAL

While general characteristics of an ideal regionalized system are identified in the introduction, in this section I will offer more detail as to goals and then provide a set of "should" statements concerning components and relationships among components hypothesized as necessary if the goals are to be achieved. It is recognized and emphasized that local conditions will require important alterations in any actual attempt to implement this model. In the next section reality problems will be described and illustrated and sociological constraints analyzed.

*Goals*

If the health system is economically organized to distribute health services resources so as to cover all the population of a region and is functioning adequately, we would expect it to have as an ULTIMATE OUTCOME a beneficial impact on the health status of the population in the region.[3]

There are links between the functioning of the health services delivery system and the maintenance and improvement of health — as when measles vaccine is administered and rates of occurrence of this disease are diminished, or when a "hot" appendix is removed and peritonitis and death are avoided.[4] But the forging of these links depends upon meeting a set of intervening or associated conditions, such as proper utilization of the service system, etc. These I will call INTERVENING OUTCOMES in the sense that their achievement is somehow between the functioning of the service delivery structure and the improvement of health status. However, health impacts on the environment (see below) may not be the result of health services at all, at least as these are traditionally organized.

It will be one of my concluding arguments that the acceptance and pursuit of such a broader mandate may be one of the conditions necessary for improving the impact of health services on health. Further, the system may not provide adequately for the achievement of the other intervening outcomes in the following list. Reorganization of regional

---

[3]   It cannot be a primary concern of this paper to deal with the need for improved health status indicators. But this need is great, especially for measures of human functioning which go beyond the usual measures of mortality and specific disease morbidity (see, for example, Nishi 1971: 68–77).
[4]   It should be clear that the health services system is not the only societal element, or even the most potent one bearing upon health status. For a discussion of health service systems in the context of health systems, see Elling (f.c.).

systems to better achieve these ends in ways appropriate to given local economic, political, social, cultural, geographic, and epidemiologic circumstances may be necessary for success.

If health systems are to maintain and improve health status, it is hypothesized that they must beneficially affect the following "intervening outcomes":

1.  The environment and conditions and ways of life of the people that are pathogenic;

2.  Sophistication of the consumers of the services as well as the providers, with regard to health problems and what to do about them, both in preventive and curative ways;

3.  Satisfaction with care on the parts of the providers as well as the consumers;

4.  The patient's timely entry into care (not too often, seldom, late, or soon);

5.  The logic of the care process, once a person or other treatment unit (family, community) has entered into care.[5] In this connection, the regional system and individuals providing service in it should merge in practice the knowledge of (a) pathophysiology, (b) the health care system, and (c) the patients and potential patients as persons in a socioeconomic, political, and cultural as well as physico-biological environment. Of these three, knowledge of health care systems and patients as social beings have been the least adequately incorporated in medical and public health education and practice. Without the merger of these different types of knowledge, the treatment will often not be logical, will not "make sense." For example, to prescribe a weaning supplement which is nutritionally adequate but not culturally acceptable to a mother will not prevent an incipient case of kwashiorkor with marasmus.

It is hypothesized that a fully developed, well-functioning regional system of care would beneficially affect these intermediate goals and thereby achieve an improvement in health status. It is not assumed here that current, so-called modern organization and technology are necessarily good. It is important to recognize that there are often iatrogenic and other undesirable effects of health services. This problem is partly taken care of by the logic of care. In part, there simply are such effects and we must hope that the good available in the health care system will out-

---

[5]   A concern for the logic of care may seem to carry with it a bias toward "developed" societies where orientations to "scientific" medicine may be stronger. I would argue against this impression by suggesting that a major part of the problem of logical care in some settings may be to accomplish a certain melding of folk and scientific medicine.

weigh the bad if available knowledge can be brought to bear appropriately.[6]

There are problems in achieving these goals. We hypothesize that an ideal regional system structured and functioning along lines we will now describe would offer a better chance of realizing these goals.

## Structure and Functions

SIZE OF POPULATION AND CHARACTERISTICS OF THE REGION  Depending on density of settlement and ease of travel and communication, the population should be roughly in the range from 500,000 to 3,000,000.[7] The area should be a functional one in the sense of a trading market concept and it should also represent historical, ethnic and political continuity and identity (Reiner 1968).[8] The essentials are, "a functional geographic area with sufficient population to support the full range of health facilities and services ..." (Rosenfeld 1972).

A GRADED HIERARCHY OF SERVICES  Generally, three tiers of service are desired within a region: the most local or peripheral unit, which may be variously conceived;[9] the intermediate unit offering special care to back up the general care of several peripheral units; and the regional center offering more specialized care. Extremely expensive and specialized components may be located nationally or so as to serve more than one

[6] Without attributing cause and effect, it is at least provocative to consider that during a recent physicians strike in Israel, the death rate declined. Also, many of the desirable effects of modern medicine probably occur not for medical technological reasons, but because the supporting culture allows patients to believe in the efficacy of such measures (Powles 1973).

[7] I would caution here against "magic numbers," which become enshrined and used as automatically accepted bases for planning.

[8] Note that a small country may be a single region. Note also that homogeneity of ethnic or other stratificational elements is not absolutely necessary, as the system should be capable of handling or referring whatever health problems a complex population may produce. However, it is necessary that health personnel know and understand the ethnic groups and other social differentiations. In this connection, it may be desirable that the most local service units have as homogeneous a population as possible, but this leads into arguments of segregation versus integration which we cannot take up here.

[9] Some of the possibilities are: local resident health worker(s) linked with physician and other back-up personnel by modern communication network; visiting health worker operating out of an intermediate center and covering a certain subsection of the region, a special variant being the flying doctor, and another being the circuit riding team; involvement of local consumers in various ways in solving their own health problems.

region; examples may be a medical school, a reference laboratory, etc.

AN INTEGRATED AUTHORITY SYSTEM    If there is one most important factor for achieving the ideals of regionalization, this is it. In pluralistic political structures one may be limited to aspiring to a coordinated authority system. The point is to achieve "a system of cooperative relationships and communications among interdependent facilities and services."[10] In the most basic terms, this implies control over the flow of all funds from nonlocal sources (public and private) for capital expenditures, operating expenses, and training and research by the central health care planning and decision body of the region.

The need for an integrated authority system does not discount the need for local involvement and sharing of control as emphasized below. Further, the regional authority should have both local and at-large elected representatives. With regard to local village and community funding, regional health authorities should be aware of such local initiatives without discouraging them, except when unnecessary duplication or poor conception are involved.

PROPER TWO-WAY FLOW BETWEEN THE PERIPHERY AND CENTER    Elements of exchange between the levels of the system include patients, information, personnel, and technology. The point is not to have a lot of activity, but to have a two-way flow which appropriately backs up the general care at the periphery with ready supplies, information, personnel, and technology, and utilizes the more expensive, specialized services at the intermediate and central levels as "sharpened instruments of prevention and care" brought to bear only when necessary.

PRIMARY THRUST TOWARD PREVENTIVE AND GENERAL CARE AT THE PERIPHERY    In a way this point repeats an aspect of the previous one — the use of intermediate and central facilities and services only when necessary. But the general direction of the system requires special emphasis. The regional system should function in service of the highest priority problems, namely the main preventive and general care problems found among the people. In turn, the most peripheral units should serve a triage, filter, and referral function which allows the more expensive and specialized central facilities and services to come into play only when needed. This thrust will be facilitated by the prepayment system, by the appropriate conception of peripheral units, by local citizens sharing con-

[10]    This is the second element identified by Rosenfeld as making up the regionalization concept (Rosenfeld 1972: 1).

trol, and by priorities, standards, targets, and regulations which reflect this concern.

PREPAYMENT ON A CAPITATION BASIS FOR TOTAL CARE FOR ALL MEMBERS OF THE POPULATION With funds allocated to an integrated regional authority to cover all elements of care (preventive, curative, and rehabilitative) for all persons for some future period of time (say, the coming year) the system should be motivated toward prevention and general care at the periphery. It may be that experience in different settings will show that a small deductible should be paid by the patient or the patient's family to avoid overutilization. But this is a complex socioeconomic matter, not to be determined by any single variable such as operating cost.

Except for such minor exceptions, knowing there is just so much for the total package, all concerned will benefit from efforts to bring preventive knowledge to bear, thereby avoiding expensive treatments. The danger may be that so much emphasis is placed on saving money that people are kept from needed expensive care.[11]

EMPHASIS ON CONTINUING EDUCATION AND ON-THE-JOB TRAINING The application of knowledge in a locally relevant way should be served by this emphasis. The problem implied by the saying, "He was well-educated but not prepared to go to work" can be avoided by on-the-job training. In addition, this function allows flexibility, providing a means whereby interested and able persons can shift from performing one set of tasks to another as needs and knowledge change. Further, it allows the up-dating of persons who continue in the same position.[12]

HEAVY EMPHASIS ON CITIZEN INVOLVEMENT The range of patterns of involvement runs from citizens seen as "consumers" of what is offered or "targets" of programs, through solicitation of opinions in a survey, to advisory bodies, to full citizen control in the sense of power to hire and fire health personnel. Although the most complete form of citizen involvement is ideal, it is fraught with problems. The extent, depth, and complexity of problems would seem in large part to result from the support or opposition to local community involvement stemming from the broader political structures. In some settings there is an authentic developmental thrust in this direction sponsored and encouraged by the highest

[11] The charge has been made that Kaiser Permanente and some of the other prepaid plans have had this effect. See Ehrenreich and Ehrenreich (1970); see also Garfield (1970).

[12] For a discussion of these functions of on-the-job and in-service training and the relations of schools of public health to such training (by extension one could add other schools for health personnel), see Fry, Shepard, and Elling (1967: 99–100).

political authorities.[13] In other places there is only uncertain lip service or frank opposition to local community involvement. In some settings even regionalization, in the limited sense of centralizing decision making within a region, may be an attack on localism (Ingman 1971). Without encouragement of local involvement, regionalization as here intended would not be authentic.[14]

Here we will emphasize the positive aspects to be attained through the realization of such participation. The rationale can be offered for citizen involvement bearing positively upon each of the goals identified above. But it seems especially important for increasing satisfaction with care, for improving the popular understanding of health problems and health care, and for timely entry into care. It also bears on the logic of care, for health personnel are bound to learn better who the patients are as persons in a particular sociocultural, political, and economic setting if they owe their livelihood to them. As already noted, such knowledge is important for making relevant care recommendations.

A GEOGRAPHICALLY ORIENTED PERIPHERAL UNIT WITH WELL-DEFINED GOALS. In order to achieve a merger of preventive, curative, and rehabilitative care in practical terms, the combination of personnel at the periphery, which includes the person or persons responsible for coordinating the care of patients throughout their "careers" in the health services system and back to home,[15] should have responsibility for providing total care for all persons who wish such care in some delineated, manageable geographic area.[16] As a set of specific targets, the peripheral team should seek to set up and pursue a complete health plan (preventive, curative, ameliorative and rehabilitative) for each member of each household in its area of responsibility.[17]

[13]   In Tanzania, for example, official policy is highly supportive of local community involvement. See the *Arusha declaration* and *TANU's policy on socialism socialism . . .* (Suchman 1967). The cases of China, Cuba, Niger, and Togo are also interesting in this regard.
[14]   For a discussion of authenticity in social participation, see Etzioni (1968).
[15]   The peripheral "team composition" is phrased this way as it is not at all certain, depending on local circumstances, that a physician in any usual sense will be included. The first physician one may find in some regional systems may be in the intermediate centers. For a good discussion of the four-month training and the functioning of "barefoot doctors," "worker doctors," and "Red Guard doctors," see Sidel (1972).
[16]   Two qualifications are necessary. First, some persons may continue to seek more impersonal care in an emergency room or otherwise seek care outside of the local system. There can be many reasons for this, among them the wish to avoid care which integrates aspects of the person's life he would rather keep separate. Second, some mass preventive efforts may be offered at the local level by mobile teams operating out of an intermediate level center.
[17]   For a discussion of such plans, see Wise (1968). A helpful consideration of issues and alternative forms of peripheral organization is given in the Hastings report (1972).

Such plans, accomplishments, remaining tasks, and reasons for remaining tasks (unavailable services or equipment, intractable disease, patient's lack of or different understanding, etc.) could serve as the basis for a useful information system for health planning and management. It is at this most local level that those responsible for care will be best able to improve the logic of care by merging in practice the three kinds of knowledge referred to earlier — pathophysiology, the structure and functioning of the medical care system and its technology, and the patient as a social being in a particular environment.

## SOCIOLOGICAL PROBLEMS IN REALIZING THE IDEALS OF REGIONALIZATION

*Contexts — The Organization of Authority and Level of Resources*

In many ways, the extreme problem case is represented by a country such as the United States,[18] which is highly developed economically, has a pluralistic or fractionated authority system, and is in a state of flux or rapid change. This kind of organizational environment at times seems to approximate what has been termed a "turbulent field" and frequently suggests the "disturbed-reactive" kind of environment (Emery and Trist 1965).[19]

We do not know how best to characterize organizational environments for different purposes. But for regionalization, two clusters of variables seem especially important. The first is the organization of authority in the society along two dimensions: highly centralized versus decentralized, and concerted versus pluralistic. The organization of authority within the health sector usually parallels that of the society, though the fit may be loose. In Britain, for example, local government plays an important role in most community affairs, but not in health. Regionalization has largely kept health concerns out of the hands of local governmental officials.

Our general working hypothesis is that regionalization can be most easily and completely realized in a society with a concerted, decentralized authority structure. Yugoslavia and Tanzania may be examples. "Noncommunist" examples might be found in Niger and Togo. Possibly China and Cuba are other examples. The difficulty is that data are lacking

[18] An especially helpful inventory and consideration of problems in the United States is given in Bodenheimer (1969).
[19] For an elaboration of these ideas, see Terreberry (1968); on medical organizations and environments, see Glaser (1970).

whereby such a typology could be filled out without becoming confused by popular labels such as "democratic," "communist," "capitalist," etc. Also, if we discuss cases as if they fit squarely in one category or another, it is a matter of convenience for the writer as well as a lack of data; cases should be placed along the two continua in a two-dimensional space.

In spite of this rather serious difficulty, we can continue to relate theoretically the different types implied by the two dimensions (concerted-pluralistic and centralized-decentralized) to the likelihood of achieving regionalization. In these terms, the next most supportive political environment would be the concerted, centralized authority structure. The Soviet Union and some of the Eastern European countries would seem to fit this pattern. The pluralistic, centralized structure may be next most supportive of regionalization. Iran, some Western European countries, and a number of Latin American countries seem to fit this pattern. The pluralistic, decentralized system would be least likely to support a full realization of regionalization. The United States seems to be the most obvious example.

The second cluster of contextual variables bearing importantly on the chances of achieving regionalization is the level of socioeconomic development, including the level of development of health services. Whether there is a "crowded" institutional environment versus a vacuum would seem to be especially important. In a "stuffed-up" environment, the level of competition and institutional jealousies is likely to be higher and commitments to previous courses of action stronger, thus making a coordinated, graded hierarchy of service more difficult to achieve. The so-called developed countries suffer more in this regard than do the underdeveloped countries. Richer countries have the counterbalancing advantage of resources to bring to bear on the health problems, but from a strictly organizational point of view, regionalization should be easier to achieve in an "open," uncluttered environment.

In the following analysis we will generally make reference to these two clusters of contextual variables in relation to each of the structural-functional elements of regionalization named above. It should be clear that the two clusters are not entirely independent. For example, the more crowded institutional environment is likely to occur either in the centralized-concerted or the decentralized-pluralistic environment. If the two authority dimensions and the "crowdedness" of the institutional environment could be thought of as independent, we would have a typology of environments for regionalization somewhat as shown in Table 1.

Table 1. A typology of environments for regionalization and hypothetical examples (data for placement lacking)

| Organization of authority in the society | | Level of development, especially "crowdedness" of the institutional environment in health | |
|---|---|---|---|
| | | *"Developed," crowded* | *"Underdeveloped," open* |
| Centralized | Concerted | Union of Soviet Socialist Republics, certain Eastern European countries | Certain Eastern European countries |
| | Pluralistic | Certain Western European countries | Iran, certain Latin American countries |
| Decentralized | Concerted | Yugoslavia | Tanzania, China, Niger, Togo |
| | Pluralistic | United States of America | Indonesia |

*Vested Interests and Misconceptions within the Health Sector*

Other problematic aspects of regionalization may be seen as internal to medicine and public health, although these internal problems reflect the contexts within which they occur. Among the "internal" problems we will discuss the definition of priorities and the interest groups and prestige-reward structures of medicine and public health. In this connection, the willingness of prestigious university health centers to play a broader leadership role vis-à-vis practicing physicians and other health workers, as well as health agencies and the public, could be a key element in defining and researching the problems of achieving regionalization, especially in decentralized-pluralistic settings where the concept is less widely understood and accepted (Clark 1966).

*Contextual and Internal Problems as Related to the Elements of Regionalization*

In this section we will describe and analyze problems in relation to each of the components of structure and function named above, as we suppose these components to be important for achieving the identified goals.

SIZE OF POPULATION AND CHARACTERISTICS OF THE REGION    In a decentralized, pluralistic, and crowded setting such as the United States, local autonomy is often so great and the units so small (as in the New England town concept) that functional regional areas with continuity and identity are psychologically and politically difficult to identify. In this case, "a region" may be arbitrarily drawn on a map by health planners, but it is essentially meaningless except as a statement of intent. Even in this limited regard there are difficulties, for the nature of environmental control problems (the course of rivers, sewage catchment areas, air flow patterns) usually suggests a different set of regional boundaries to the environmental health authorities than those chosen by health authorities concerned with hospitals and other personal health services. Thus a planner for one set of health problems may define regions differently from those defined by a health planner dealing with another cut of the health problem pie.

Quite aside from problem definition (but always involving problem definition as a point of ideological legitimacy), different health authorities, even within a single state health department, often appear to set up deliberately new regional boundaries for each program so as to avoid being coordinated by other programs and to assert an authority over the other programs (Seipp, et al. 1969).[20] Sometimes health authorities seek to protect themselves from loss of authority and integration into broader socioeconomic planning entities by having a different set of regional boundaries from those of the general plan organization.

In the developed society with a highly centralized and concerted authority structure, regions may be made to coincide for different purposes, but may be less meaningful than would be ideal for reasons opposite to those of local autonomy mentioned above. There may be serious problems of national authorities granting the necessary autonomy for planning and implementation within national standards, adapting these to local demographic, epidemiological, economic, cultural, and political conditions.

Again, in developed societies with highly centralized and concerted authority structures, although national authorities may be forced to recognize local ethnic and other political identities to some extent, regions may be structured so as to mix and blur identities, thereby avoiding too great a local organizational potential. This may be done in part to avoid too great a homogeneity within and disparity between regions. But it may also be done primarily to reinforce the role of central authorities.

The large metropolitan center presents special problems, regardless of the type of authority system of the country. Several regions may have to be formed in a single metropolis, but medical care utilization patterns

[20]   In one state, the human services agencies and the various programs within them had defined no less than twelve different sets of regions. A number of programs operated without any regional concept.

may not match well with regions and local residence. Within the city, hospitals may fail to form a division of labor of superspeciality services and thereby duplicate and misuse especially expensive services, such as open heart surgery, cobalt therapy, etc. The city's relation to its hinterland may be problematic, especially if more than one city is in a region or more than one region surrounds a major city. Also, transport facilities and traffic patterns may make access to central city services difficult, and suburban and outlying towns may seek to develop their own hospitals in ways that duplicate more central facilities (Navarro 1971).

The definition of meaningful regional areas is probably easiest in the developing rural society with some decentralization and concertedness of authority. (In such settings other problems arise, such as staffing all the necessary components of the system; these problems are more appropriately dealt with below in relation to other components.) But in some developing as well as developed areas there are problems of correspondence between political regions and natural geographic and trade areas. Sometimes nomadic tribes, who may be difficult in any case to reach with modern health services, move across regional boundaries. Or the population may be so dispersed or geographically isolated as to make the coverage of all persons difficult. Even though there may be problems, the developing rural society with some centralization and concertedness of authority would appear to be the easiest environment in which to achieve this component of regionalization — a well-defined, functional regional area.

A GRADED HIERARCHY OF SERVICES    In the developed society with relatively many resources and a decentralized, pluralistic authority structure, local community pride, jealousy, occupational group striving, and entrepreneurial activities all combine to encourage a more and more elaborate development of expensive facilities and services in more and more localities (Elling 1963). To cite only one bit of evidence of the problem of rationalizing the construction and proper use of expensive facilities in such an environment, one study showed that 777 hospitals in the United States were equipped to do heart surgery, but nearly 30 percent had not treated a single case in the year before the study. Of those hospitals treating some cases, 77 percent averaged fewer than one operation per week, 41 percent fewer than one per month. In underutilized hospitals, the mortality rate was "far higher ... than in institutions with a full work load" (Somers and Somers 1967, as cited by Navarro 1971: 878).

Even in countries with highly centralized policies and authority structures, there are facilities inherited from the past which are not logically placed in relation to current regional concepts. Also, facilities which have more or less filled their function, such as special tuberculosis hospitals, may be difficult to close down or reorient toward other functions because people have their identities and futures very much attached to these institutions. Even in the Soviet Union, there is "the pride of a local surgeon who wishes to do an operation in a small rural hospital when it ought properly to be referred to a higher echelon hospital" (Bridgman and Roemer 1972: 179). In the case of unwanted, low-prestige tasks or "dirty work," these may be pushed up the line until there is an overload at the center of the system accompanied by ineffectual functions. As one restricted report describes the matter in a particular case:

The laboratory is overwhelmed by thousands of requests for examinations which ought to be performed locally. Although everybody knows that stools must be examined within four hours in order to find living amebae, every day the laboratory receives specimens brought by special couriers from outlying areas after 24 hours delay. Every year, 7,000 to 10,000 specimens of stools are sent to no purpose.

Developing countries with more or less of a vacuum as regards hospital and other modern health facilities are in a better position to develop a rationally graded hierarchy of services. The problem in these countries is lack of resources for construction of hospitals and other facilities and for training of personnel. But even in these settings considerable local pressure may develop, leading to a proliferation of facilities beyond what would be most economical and necessary. Professor Kesić has indicated to the writer that in Yugoslavia, where there is regionalization along with highly developed local determination, each town may clamor for its own hospital when a small number could economically and effectively serve the whole region.

AN INTEGRATED AUTHORITY STRUCTURE AND REGIONAL MECHANISM FOR CHANNELING THE FLOW OF SUPPORT   In the developed, decentralized, pluralistic setting, the absence of an integrated authority structure may constitute the cardinal problem of regionalization. Each hospital board and the literally hundreds of relevant but autonomous voluntary and other health and welfare agencies tend to establish their own clientele, functional and geographic territory, and sources of support.[21] Efforts to achieve coordination in these circumstances are often limited to "umbrella committees" for "comprehensive planning," etc., which accomplish little

[21]   On the multiplicity of agencies involved, see Roemer and Wilson (1952). Some 150 agencies were identified as directly relevant to health care in a semiurban county twenty years ago.

more than the appearance of goodwill and intent.[22] Such committees and meetings may even serve as forums in which to plant false information, allowing the planter to compete better for scarce resources and public recognition (Ingman 1971).

The problem of separate authorities and parallel vertical structures may exist even within the Ministry of Health. Programs to attack and control malaria have been set up in such a manner in most countries of the world. Often, family health and planning programs have been developed in this separate manner. Sometimes these are not even coordinated at the local service level with maternal and child health programs. This appears to happen largely because well-financed outside interests have a special concern with a segmental problem and underemployed or poorly paid health personnel on the local scene are eager to respond.[23] These outside sources offer support on condition that a clear and separate chain of command is established for the program.

During a field trip to an area conceived as a health services region in a country with an absolute central authority, a visit was paid to an urban neighborhood health center. The first thing observed on arrival was a knock-down-drag-out fight between two young male patients. They may have been fighting for any number of reasons, but among them was certainly the frustration they experienced waiting in a crowd of some 150 to 200 patients jamming toward a corner where an aide was handing out tickets admitting persons to see the doctor after payment of the local equivalent of fifty cents. The doctor worked just two hours each morning in the clinic and otherwise devoted his time to his private office and hospital practice. If there were some 175 patients to see him and his actual time for seeing patients was 110 minutes (allowing ten minutes for getting settled, having tea, etc.) the average time per patient was thirty-eight seconds.

Naturally, the logic of care suffered. In fact, quite routinely, seemingly regardless of presenting complaint, patients were sent next door for an injection of vitamin $B_{12}$ and to the pharmacy for aspirin and vitamin C. During the course of the morning an observer noted that the physician used his stethoscope only twice. One of these times was shortly after the observer's arrival and seemed to be done to impress the observer. The

[22]  Even when the problem is rather well-defined, such as in tuberculosis control in a United States community, but several agencies are involved, the achievements may be poor (Wysong and Eichhorn 1971).
[23]  This in spite of mounting evidence that all kinds of health conditions vary together according to broad socioeconomic conditions such as poverty-nonpoverty (See Payne 1965).

second time involved a case of heavy and difficult breathing and seemed to urgently require this kind of assessment.

Just down the hall was the office of a female physician whom informants said was a person of high status, as her language suggested she was a member of one of the better families. This physician was in charge of the local family planning program, also within the Ministry of Health, but with a separate authority structure from the most local level up through the region to the deputy minister, who was personally appointed by the highest national authorities. At the time of our visit, this physician was in the garden chatting with the nurse-midwife of this program. Later, in conversation, we learned that she sees three to four patients in an hour. She did not use any kind of family health record, nor were her services available for the general health care demands faced by the physician down the hall.

Almost by definition the problem of multiple health authorities operating within a single region is ameliorated by a unified authority structure within a country. But there are problems in these settings as well. The illustration just offered suggests that multiple authorities can, in fact, grow or be set up within what is, to outward appearances, a single authority. Also, the unified authority structure may tend to be highly centralized to such an extent that regions are not able to plan and make decisions relevant to the local setting.[24] In short, there may be a unified authority within the region, but the seat of all effective power is national. In this case, the region means very little.

The question of divided authority extends beyond the health sector to other spheres. "Health has to be seen not only internally as an integrated whole, but also externally as an integral component of overall socio-economic development."[25] The whole United Nations strategy for the second development decade is based on "a unified approach." But this is a broader perspective than we can take up here in any detail.[26]

[24] In one such country, regional directors of health services are not only required to attempt to follow national priorities, guidelines, and standards set with little effective input from the region, they must even submit names to the central ministry for approval before employing drivers, laboratory assistants, and many other lower-level as well as upper-echelon employees. But there are promising instances in which a unified national authority has deliberately decentralized on a regional basis. See Waterston (1962). (However, the recent upsurge of Serbian nationalism underlines the dilemma faced in decentralization versus centralization.)

[25] From notes prepared for an address by Dr. H. Mahler, on behalf of the Director-General of the World Health Organization, to the VIIIth International Conference on Health Education, Versailles, page 1, July 8, 1973.

[26] The unified approach involves not only the coordination of different sectors, but a commitment to equity as well as growth. See "Report of the Secretary-General on the

TWO-WAY FLOW BETWEEN THE PERIPHERY AND THE CENTER   There are a host of potential sociological and social psychological blocks to effective two-way flow. Several of these blocks may differentially affect all the elements of exchange between the periphery and center and back: communications; referral of patients; back-up with special equipment and personnel, such as circuit-riding consultants; supply of drugs and other materials so as to reach peripheral units on time and in good order. We do not deal with obvious physical problems, such as poor transportation or communications equipment.

Local jealousies may operate preventing referral or provision of information; or the local persons may be uncertain of their competence and refer too often. Some illustrations were given in the section above dealing with a graded hierarchy of services. In addition the back-up services may be divided in location and function and referred patients may not find the way, or information may not get out of one channel or may get into the wrong one. Special service personnel may be oriented toward big city conditions and only reluctantly go out from behind their comfortable desks to follow footpaths to isolated village health centers.

The problem of improper two-way flow will be more difficult when the health authority system is divided, when there is poor citizen — as well as provider — understanding of the health system, when payment mechanisms do not encourage coordinated use of the system, and when the information system is not integrated. These are all alterable social conditions, perhaps related to, but also independent of, factors of geographic isolation, low level technology, etc.

If one major factor can be identified as interrupting proper two-way flow, it is the lack in most systems in all types of environments of an adequate approach to patient care coordination at or close to the periphery of the system (Walker 1966: 1315). Some person or combination of persons should be responsible for the overall logic of the patient care process (and possibly family care process or even a broader social unit). As it is now, in most systems, the only one who integrates all aspects of his health problems and health care is the patient. And the patient usually lacks the understanding to coordinate all the elements properly. In addition, there is the problem of patients wishing to go to the bigger centers because of their allure and presumed excellence, by-passing local centers where care could be most easily coordinated. Of course, the patient may be justified in this behavior if peripheral units are poorly supported.

---

expert group meeting on a unified approach to development analysis and planning" (1973).

PRIMARY THRUST TOWARD PREVENTIVE AND GENERAL CARE AT THE PERIPH-
ERY   This is a subtle, but very important, deep-running, and difficult
problem. It seems to be primarily attributable to (if not synonymous
with) the system of prestige and rewards in medicine itself. Even in a
medical school department devoted to general patient care coordination
and community health care, one can hear otherwise well-motivated and
able clinicians refer to patients presenting relatively simple, familiar
problems (U.R.I. or gastrointestinal infections) or difficult but familiar
problems (arthritis, drug addiction, alcoholism) as "junk" or "garbage."[27]

There seem to be few psychic or other rewards the physician can receive
from treating such patients well. Instead, because specialization pays and
is increasing at an ever faster rate in developed countries (Fahs and
Peterson 1968), it is the exotic special problem which is "a good case,"
"a real case," etc. Commercialism attached to the production and sale of
high-powered, high-priced medical gadgetry backs up this trend (Ehrenreich and Ehrenreich 1970).

There is an intellectual as well as a humanistic failing in this condition.
What could be more intellectually challenging than to piece together the
complex of personal, family, neighborhood, economic, and patho-phy-
siological conditions related to the person and any illness condition and
bring the armamentarium of modern medicine appropriately to bear on
the problem? Yet the microcosm of biochemistry and other highly specialized spheres of knowledge draw the attention.

Certainly, the patient does not wish to regard himself or his problem in
a disparaging way.[28] This suggests that the correction of this problem of
misdirected thrust lies in the direction of another of the dimensions —
full citizen participation in health policy and decision making. Indeed, in
countries where a social revolution has reoriented the system toward
service to all the people, the problem is less evident (Quinn 1972; Myrdal
and Kessle 1970; Orris 1970). But even in such settings there are incidents
of medical and other professional arrogance and detachment with which
to contend. It is for this reason that one must look within medicine at the
prestige-reward system as well as toward the environment.

PREPAYMENT ON A CAPITATION BASIS FOR TOTAL CARE FOR ALL MEMBERS OF
THE POPULATION   This component is frequently misunderstood. Capitation is usually understood as a method of paying individual physicians

[27]   It is likely that social class characteristics are mixed up in the use of such terms
(see Duff and Hollingshead 1968).
[28]   For a study of the effect of negative and positive self-concepts on participation in
a preventive care program, see Elling, Whittemore, and Green (1960).

and other health workers so much per person for a period of time regardless of the number of services rendered. This method of paying personnel has been used mainly with general practitioners in the British system, with the weaknesses of inflated lists and excessive referrals to allow a maximum number of patients with a minimum workload. The intended emphasis on prevention thus remains theoretical (Roemer 1971: 126–129). As to payment of personnel, a salary to cover their complete full-time labor is probably preferable. But there is conflicting evidence on this score, although it stems from the very special circumstances of a welfare clinic in Baltimore (Alexander 1967).

Prepayment is often equated simply with following the insurance principles of (1) payment ahead of time and (2) sharing of risks. Although these are important ideas, more is intended here. The idea of prepayment on a capitation basis as used here is that so much money is paid to cover all persons in a region for their total health needs for some period of time, usually a year at a minimum. The importance of local contributions and initiatives is not discounted by this principle. Local financing can be a stimulus to desired new emphases and can, in any case, be made known to regional health planners and administrators so that the total package can be estimated and taken into account. Possibly it should be termed a collective capitation system. In any case, the distinguishing characteristics are that it is relatively closed-ended and health workers, whatever the method of payment, are rewarded more if the most exotic, expensive, curative care is held to a minimum and emphasis is placed on effective preventive care, including mass preventive efforts as well as development of health knowledge in and among the people.[29]

These ideas will be more difficult to put in practice in certain sociopolitical contexts than in others. The individualistic culture with a pluralistic authority system and the impoverished setting where people are preoccupied with the immediate present are the most obvious examples of contexts inimical to the realization of these ideals. Another example of contextual resistance can be seen in the strong tendencies of "middle" and "upper" class patients in many societies to remain outside of any collective care system. With special funding for a "private" system, the better health risks are not shared with the poorer ones and prestige factors enter to undermine the quality of care in the public system (Strauss 1972; see also Suchman 1972). In addition, physicians who are

---

[29] In the Kaiser Permanente plan there has been lowered hospital utilization with equally good morbidity and mortality results compared with other systems. But it should be noted that the higher risk welfare and unemployed population has not been included (see Garfield 1970).

supposed to be on salary full-time for the public system often take large portions of their time and devote much of their attention to making extra money. Also, holding physicians and recruiting them to the public system becomes a problem (Maloney, Trussell, and Elinson 1960).

Internal to the health services system we find resistance primarily in the form of organized occupational groups concerned for their private gain. For example, physicians in the United States have been found to resist insurance mechanisms, especially public ones such as Medicare and Medicaid, and then to embrace them when they realize in practice that the funds were more or less open-ended, being limited mainly by patient demand (Colombotos 1969).

If there are two systems, one private and one public, there may be still something to achieve through deliberate change in the prestige-reward system. For example, in one socialist country where private forces are powerful enough to guard a mixed "market-command" economy (Ruderman 1972), full-time government service, including service in public clinics and hospitals, is required in addition to stringent selection criteria if one is to be a professor on the medical faculty. Great prestige is attached to such positions and patients value care in these institutions more highly than in private institutions. Consequently, the undercutting power of private services is lessened.

HEAVY EMPHASIS ON TRAINING ON THE JOB AND IN SERVICE   The major blocks to achieving this emphasis have to do with the educational institutions and with the ideas of education held by practitioners in the system. These conditions vary with the broad contextual characteristics of the society. In general, the more socially oriented the society, the less this aspect of regionalization is a problem.

But even in socially oriented societies, there are problems internal to medicine itself in the form of "professional" conceptions of education and inadequate provision for continuing education. With regard to this last, knowledge once imparted is not forever adequate because (1) it may remain valid but be forgotten,[30] and (2) if improved understandings are achieved, still practitioners themselves and practice institutions have not found effective ways to keep up-to-date.[31] Possibly the essential problem is one of rewards and motivation. If the practitioner can continue to get along and earn a livelihood without refresher education, he often does so.

---

[30]   This aspect is emphasized in Peterson, et al. (1956).

[31]   The rapid change and growth in scientific knowledge makes this a real problem, but the techniques of continuing education have not evolved to keep apace (Storey, Williamson, and Castle 1968).

But it is also a problem of health system administration. There may not be an adequate conception among administrators of in-service and on-the-job education to fulfill the functions of introducing people to their work, allowing a change between jobs, and updating one's knowledge, perspectives, and skills.

As to "professional" conceptions of education, educational institutions, reinforced by the struggles of occupational groups to improve their standing in society, develop yawning gaps between what is taught and what is required on the job to solve the health problems of the people (Elling 1971a). Even in China, a significant part of the cultural revolution was devoted to engaging university people directly with the problems of the people (Myrdal and Kessle 1970: 114). Faculty and other "educationists" tend to discount practically oriented education with the rationale that they are preparing the students in a more general way to cope with the future. This is valid. But it can be used to establish the autonomy of an institution to an extreme degree.

On the other hand, practitioners may call for "relevance" without appreciating logic and other general thought tools, the history and general context of a discipline, its content and internal consistency, or techniques of knowledge development and transmittal. But because of the prestige of the educational institutions, practice institutions do not usually make an effort to set up and emphasize their own training efforts.

Close, mutually supportive connections should be built between otherwise well-structured and functioning regional systems and the educational institutions in or serving the area. One can even hypothesize that the system of practice itself is a more potent teacher than the schools, through the social psychological mechanism of anticipatory socialization. If students look forward to practice in a system emphasizing preventive, coordinated care, they can be expected to learn things relevant to such an emphasis.

HEAVY EMPHASIS ON CITIZEN INVOLVEMENT    The resistances to this component are many, but some systems are fundamentally based upon and oriented toward the local citizen.[32] If we are most concerned with citizens at the periphery who have been excluded from participation in and enjoyment of adequate health care and other social goods, there may be resistive class and ethnic attitudes on the parts of more privileged citizens, as well as on the parts of providers and planners who will have to relinquish some of their power. If there is an elected, representative gov-

[32]    On China: Quinn (1972); also, Liang, et al. (1973). On Cuba: Orris (1970); also, Navarro (1972); also, Danielson (1973).

ernment, legislators may resist direct modes of citizen involvement with the worry that their power and mandate may be weakened in a general way and their control of the institutions in question undercut.

Similarly, if the form of government involves a single party, the local party organization may resist direct involvement of citizens except through the party. But, in some countries with a single party, the keystone of development may be seen in local community involvement.[33]

Finally, there are the mystiques of "professionalism" and "scientism" which operate in different ways on the sides of both the providers and the "lay" citizens. On the one hand, a citizen may lack confidence in his understanding of health problems and what to do about them, and may regard it as a hopeless task to learn. On the other hand, the health worker may support this set of beliefs, fearing loss of power but also being quite reasonably concerned with interference and loss of time when some decisive technical action is required.

But the boundaries are really unclear. A clinical colleague once asserted that if a patient is rushed to the emergency unit and cannot breathe, he has to do a tracheotomy before too many brain cells become deoxygenated. He said he does not have time to stand around talking to relatives in such a case. But if a relative would inform the physician that the patient has epilepsy, he could simply pull out the swallowed tongue and avoid making an opening in the throat.

In China the effective involvement of citizens with their own health affairs and with determination of the work of local health workers seems to depend upon three essential elements. First, the labor brigade pays the "barefoot physician" by assigning work credits to this person for work both as a physician and as a worker in the field when there are no patients in need of care.[34] Second, the People's Commune elects the person according to his or her interest and their perception of his or her ability, so that the element of trust is established (Myrdal and Kessle 1970: 113–114). Third, competence is assured by the combination of citizen determinations and training-school instructors.

[33] "The guiding principles of rural development — self-help, self-reliance — have already been laid down in the Arusha Declaration. The organizational structure, therefore, has to be one which will further the aims of community development based on self-help and self-reliance. The fundamental aim of community development has to be that people in the villages are enabled, through their efforts and in cooperation with one another, to bring about improvements in all aspects of rural life and the rapid betterment of their standards of living, with the government assisting by providing the technical assistance" (United Republic of Tanzania 1967: 67).
[34] "When I'm not receiving my patients, I work in the fields. I get paid just as much by the labor brigade for my day's work, whether I'm plowing or receiving patients" (Myrdal and Kessle 1970: 113). See also the paper by Heller (1972).

With this kind of integral involvement, sophistication develops as to the real economic and other value of preventive and curative care in the commune's life:

It is very important that health care shall be developed in the brigades and labor groups. Take Wang Fu-ying at Wangchiakou, for example. He was suffering from pains in the small of his back. They tormented him, and in 1967 and 1968 he visited a doctor in town. Altogether he lost thirty working days waiting in line for the doctor in town. Besides losing income from work, he had to pay out altogether 200 Y for treatment and his medicines. Now we have treated him. After three acupuncture treatments he feels well and has no pains. And if he needs help he comes to us. He no longer has to lose one or more working days getting into town and waiting his turn at the doctor's. And the medicine costs him nothing.[35]

For this realization at the local level to affect plans and decisions at the regional and national level, there must be local citizen representation provided for on the central decision body of the region, and the region and its plans must in turn be connected to national decision-making.

A PERIPHERAL UNIT WITH RESPONSIBILITY TO COVER THE POPULATION IN A DELIMITED GEOGRAPHIC AREA AND HAVING WELL-DEFINED GOALS  The major resistances to this component stem from (1) an otherwise poorly organized health care system which lacks the appropriate thrust toward prevention and solution of problems as close to the periphery as possible; and (2) certain contextual variables, especially selected characteristics of the population to be served.

The first-mentioned source of resistance comes into play in the process of establishing an ideal local services center. The ideal is a peripheral unit well connected with back-up facilities of the region, which has the objective of developing and following a health plan for each member of each household in its area. If such a local center is to be established, then other health workers, including many different types of indigenous practitioners, may resist the establishment of a center with such inclusive intentions. Often, means must be found of co-opting and supporting native practitioners.

An important sphere of work is to find ways of "bringing in" indigenous practitioners by "retraining" and "upgrading" them. Again the experience in China can be cited.[36] There are other settings where "bringing in" may

---

[35]  A quotation from Wang You-nan, a doctor in the village of Lui Ling (Myrdal and Kessle 1970: 114).
[36]  Horn (1969). One article connects the political ideology of Mao specifically with the use of indigenous medicines and approaches (Gibson 1972). For examples of

not be the appropriate term because indigenous practitioners far outnumber physicians and have a certain standing in the society. In Ceylon, for example, there are only some 3,500 physicians but there are about 12,000 certified Ayurvedic practitioners and an estimated 8,000 additional practitioners who are not certified.

The main problems in establishing an ideal peripheral unit will stem from the population itself, although for most people in most settings there should be no problem. Two difficulties are worth special mention.

First, some individuals in the population may resist the kind of coordinated, comprehensive care which requires an understanding of the person in his home and community setting. Some persons may seek more impersonal care in other or in more specialized settings. Many examples could be offered. To take only one, a drug addict or person with another disease carrying a social stigma may prefer treatment in a center unassociated with family and neighborhood. Such treatment may not be the most effective, but it may be the only kind the patient will accept at a certain stage of the illness.

Second, there is the problem of population movements. There is movement of persons and families and migration of whole nomadic groups. Nomadic populations require special mobile solutions. Health information systems must be devised to pick up and provide continuity to those who move temporarily or permanently (Haraldson 1973; also "Health services among scattered populations" 1972).

## SUMMARY AND CONCLUSIONS

The merit of regionalization as a general concept for organizing health services was considered in relation to the disappointments in achieving it. As a way of elucidating this problem, the ideal was spelled out further in terms of goals and structural-functional components of regionalization. Then sociological conditions facilitating or inhibiting the realization of this ideal were illustrated and analyzed. One set of these conditions was dealt with in two clusters of contextual variables. First, the authority structure of the society was considered in two dimensions: centralized-decentralized and concerted-pluralistic. Second, the level of development was considered, especially the "crowdedness" of the institutional environment in health. The second set of variables offering resistance to realiza-

merger of folk and modern medicine in other settings, see Simmons (1955), Newell (1957), Shiloh (1958), and McGregor (1973). For helpful reviews covering more than this aspect of cross-cultural health action, see Polgar (1963) and Foster (1958).

tion were found within medicine and public health, primarily in the form of prestige-reward structures which give an inappropriate thrust to the system.

In spite of difficulties, the regional concept remains the most promising for organizing health services.[37] If experiments to carry out regionalization could take into account the sociological conditions dealt with in this paper, the ideal might be more fully realized. University health centers could play an important leadership role in working toward more ideal regional health services systems by assisting in defining and researching the problems sketched out here.

## REFERENCES

ALEXANDER, C. A.
   1967   The effects of change in method of paying physicians: the Baltimore experience. *American Journal of Public Health* 57:1278–1289.

ARBONA, A., J. N. CURT
   1971   "A progress report on regionalization of comprehensive health services in Puerto Rico." Working paper for the Expert Committee on Organization of Local and Intermediate Health Administrations (World Health Organization/Community Health Services) Geneva; October 26–November 2.

ARUSHA DECLARATION
   n.d.   Dar es Salaam, Tanzania.

BRIDGMAN, R. F., M. I. ROEMER
   1972   *Hospital legislation and hospital systems, Geneva.* WHO Public Health Paper 50.

BODENHEIMER, T. S.
   1969   Regional medical programs: no road to regionalization. *Medical Care Review* 26:1125–1166.

CLARK, H. T., JR.
   1966   The challenge of the regional medical programs legislation. *Journal of Medical Education* 41:344–361.

COHEN, J.
   1971   "Regionalization of personal and community health services." Working paper for the Expert Committee on Organization of Local and Intermediate Health Administrations. World Health Organization Geneva, October 26–November 2.

COLOMBOTOS, J.
   1969   Physicians and Medicare: a before–after study of the effects of legislation on attitudes. *American Social Review* 34:318–334.

[37] In a renewed attack on Canada's health services problems following universal hospital and medical insurance coverage, one long-term student of the field offers regionalization combined with progressive patient care in "district health systems" (Tulchinsky 1973). In the case of Sweden, see Schicke (1972).

CONSULTATIVE COUNCIL ON MEDICAL AND ALLIED SERVICES
1920   *Interim report on the future provision of medical and allied services.* Ministry of Health of Great Britain. London: H.M. Stationery Office.
DANIELSON, R. S.
1973   "Cuban health organization: history and development." Unpublished Ph.D. thesis, University of Pittsburgh.
DUFF, R., A. B. HOLLINGSHEAD
1968   *Sickness and society.* New York: Wiley.
EHRENREICH, B., J. EHRENREICH
1970   *The American health empire.* New York: Health PAC.
ELLING, R. H.
1963   "The hospital support game in urban center," in *The hospital in modern society.* Edited by E. Freidson. New York: Macmillan.
1971a   "Occupational group striving in public health," in *Administering health systems.* Edited by M. Arnold, L. V. Blankenship, and J. Hess, 70–86. Chicago, New York: Aldine/Atherton.
1971b   "The local health center and the regional board," in *National health care, issues and problems in socialized medicine.* Edited by R. H. Elling, 245–262. New York: Lieber-Atherton.
1974   Case studies of contrasting approaches to organizing for health: an introduction to a framework. *Social Science and Medicine* (special issue devoted to social science research in World Health Organization).
ELLING, R. H., R. WHITTEMORE, M. GREEN
1960   Patient participation in a pediatric program. *Journal of Health and Human Behavior* 1:183–191.
EMERY, F. E., E. L. TRIST
1965   The Causal texture of organizational environments. *Human Relations* (February): 21–32.
ETZIONI, A.
1968   *The active society.* New York: The Free Press.
FAHS, I. J., O. PETERSON
1968   The decline of general practice. *Public Health Reports* 83:267–270.
FOSTER, G. M.
1958   *Problems in intercultural health programs.* Social Science Research Council, Pamphlet 12. New York.
FRY, H. G., W. P. SHEPARD, R. H. ELLING
1967   *Education and manpower for community health.* Pittsburgh: University of Pittsburgh Press.
GARFIELD, S. R.
1970   The delivery of medical care. *Scientific American* 222:15–23.
1970   Multiphasic health testing and medical care as a right. *New England Journal of Medicine* 283:1087–1089.
GIBSON, G.
1972   Chinese medical practice and the thoughts of Chairman Mao. *Social Science and Medicine* 6:67–93.
GLASER, W. A.
1970   *Social settings and medical organization, a cross-national study of the hospital.* New York: Atherton.

GRANT, J. B.
  1955   Medical regionalization and education. *Journal of Medical Education* 30:73–80.
HARALDSON, S. R.
  1973   "Socio-medical problems of nomad peoples," in *Theory and practice of public health*. Edited by W. Hobson. Oxford: Oxford University Press.
*Hastings report*
  1972   *Canadian Medical Association Journal* 107:361–380.

──────────

  1972   Health services among scattered populations. *Acta Socio-medica Scandinavica*, supplement 6:50–56.
HELLER, P. S.
  1972   *The strategy of health-sector planning in the People's Republic of China*. University of Michigan Discussion Paper 24.
HIP (HEALTH INSURANCE PLAN OF GREATER NEW YORK)
  1972   *Medical Care Review* 29:251–254.
HORN, J. S.
  1969   *Away with all pests*. New York, London: Monthly Review Press.
INGMAN, S.
  1971   "Politics of health planning." Unpublished Ph. D. thesis, University of Pittsburgh.
INGMAN, S., S. GOLDFRANK, L. GREENWALD
  1971   "Regional mental health councils: dynamics of effective citizen participation." Mimeographed manuscript, Department of Community Medicine and Health Care, University of Connecticut Medical School, Hartford, July 1971.
LIANG, M. H., *et al.*
  1973   Chinese health care: determinants of the system. *American Journal of Public Health* 63:102–116.
MALONEY, M. C., R. E. TRUSSELL, J. ELINSON
  1960   Physicians choose medical care: a sociometric approach to quality appraisal. *American Journal of Public Health* 50:1678–1686.
MC GREGOR, D.
  1973   Traditional beliefs, health, and Christianity, a study of change among the Wape people of Papua New Guinea. *Contact* 14. Geneva: World Council of Churches, Christian Medical Commission.
MYRDAL, J., G. KESSLE
  1970   *China: the revolution continued*. New York: Random House.
NAVARRO, V.
  1971   The city and the region, a critical relationship in the distribution of health resources. *American Behavioral Scientist*, 865–892.
  1972   Health services in Cuba, an initial appraisal. *New England Journal of Medicine* 287:954–959.
NEWELL, K. W.
  1957   Medical development within a Maori community. *Health Education Journal* 15:83–90.

NISHI, S.
   1971   The development of health status indicators in Japan for health plan-
          ning. *Bulletin of the Institute of Public Health, Tokyo* 20:68–77.
ORRIS, P.
   1970   "The role of the consumer in the Cuban national health system."
          Unpublished Master in Public Health thesis, Yale University.
ORGANIZATION OF LOCAL AND INTERMEDIATE HEALTH ADMINISTRATIONS
   1972   *World Health Organization Technical Report Series 499.* Geneva.
PAYNE, A. M. M.
   1965   Innovation out of unity. *The Milbank Memorial Fund Quarterly* 43:
          17–30.
PETERSON, O. L., *et al.*
   1956   An analytical study of North Carolina general practice. *Journal of
          Medical Education* 31(2).
POLGAR, S.
   1963   "Health action in cross-cultural perspective," in *Handbook of medical
          sociology.* Edited by H. Freeman, S. Levine, and L. G. Reeder, 397–
          419. Englewood Cliffs, New Jersey: Prentice-Hall.
POWLES, V.
   1973   On the limitations of modern medicine. *Science, Medicine and Man*
          1:1–30.
QUINN, J. R., *editor*
   1972   *Medicine and public health in the People's Republic of China.* Wash-
          ington, D.C.: Department of Health, Education and Welfare Publica-
          tion (Fogarty Institute National Institutes of Health).
   1972   "Report of the Secretary-General on the expert group meeting on a
          unified approach to development analysis and planning." Held at
          Stockholm, November 6–10, 1972 (E/CN.5/490, January 23, 1973).
REINER, T. A.
   1968   "Regional science," in *International encyclopedia of the social sciences*
          13:382–390. New York: Macmillan.
ROEMER, M. I.
   1971   "On paying the doctor," in *National health care, issues and problems
          in socialized medicine.* Edited by R. H. Elling. New York: Lieber-
          Atherton.
ROEMER, M. I., E. A. WILSON
   1952   *Organized health services in a county of the United States.* United
          States Public Health Service Publication 197. Washington, D.C.
ROSENFELD, L. S.
   1972   "Regional organization of health services in the United States: an
          international perspective." Paper presented at the Third International
          Conference on Social Science and Medicine, Elsinore, Denmark,
          August 14–18.
RUDERMAN, P.
   1972   "General economic considerations," in *Health planning, qualitative
          aspects and quantitative techniques.* Edited by William Reinke and
          Kathleen N. Williams. Baltimore: Johns Hopkins University Press.

SCHICKE, R. K.
1972 Die regionalisierte Gesundheitsversorgung Schwedens. *Krankenhausarzt* 7:402–410.

SEIPP, C.
1963 Puerto Rico, a social laboratory. *The Lancet* 1(1295):1364–1368. June 22, 1963.

SEIPP, C., *et al.*
1969 "Coordination, planning and society; cases in coordination: six studies of state mental retardation planning." Mimeographed manuscript, Graduate School of Public Health, University of Pittsburgh.

SHILOH, A.
1958 Middle East culture and health. *Health Education Journal* 16:232–244.

SIDEL, V. W.
1972 "Medical personnel and their training," in *Medicine and public health in the People's Republic of China.* Edited by J. R. Quinn, 151–171. Washington, D.C.: Department of Health, Education and Welfare Publication (Fogarty Institute, National Institutes of Health).

SILVER, G.
1971 "Community participation and health resource allocation." Paper presented at the International Epidemiological Association meetings, Primøsten, Yugoslavia.

SIMMONS, O. G.
1955 Popular and modern medicine in Mestizo communities of coastal Peru and Chile. *Journal of American Folklore* 68:57–71.

SNOKE, A. W., J. M. GLASGOW
1970 Regional planning: pious platitude or practical implementation. *Inquiry* 7:3 17–25.

SOMERS, H. M., A. R. SOMERS
1967 *Medicare and the hospital: issues and prospects.* Washington D.C.: Brookings Institution.

STOREY, P. B., J. W. WILLIAMSON C. H. CASTLE
1968 *Continuing medical education a new emphasis.* Chicago: American Medical Association.

STRAUSS, A. L.
1972 "Medical ghettos" in *Patients, physicians and illness* (second edition). Edited by E. G. Jaco, 381–388. New York: The Free Press.

SUCHMAN, E. A.
1972 "Social patterns of illness and medical care," in *Patients, physicians and illness* (second edition). Edited by E. G. Jaco, 262–279. New York: The Free Press.
1967 *TANU's policy on socialism and self-reliance.* Dar es Salaam: TANU Publicity Section.

TERREBERRY, S.
1968 The evolution of organizational environments. *Administrative Science Quarterly* 12:590–613.

TULCHINSKY, T. H.
1973 "Regionalization — The Manitoba experience." Paper presented to the Canadian Public Health Association, Annual Meeting, April 25.

UNITED REPUBLIC OF TANZANIA
  1967  Government paper number 4–1967. Dar es Salaam: Government
        Printer.
WALKER, J. E. C.
  1966  Prospects of ambulatory medicine in the teaching hospital. *Annals of
        Internal Medicine* 64:1315.
WATERSTON, A.
  1962  *Planning in Yugoslavia*. Baltimore: Johns Hopkins Press.
WEINERMAN, E. R., S. B. WEINERMAN
  1969  *Social medicine in Eastern Europe*. Cambridge, Massachusetts: Har-
        vard University Press.
WISE, H.
  1968  The family health worker. *American Journal of Public Health* 58:
        1828–1838.
WYSONG, J. A., R. L. EICHHORN
  1971  "The health services complex: Inter-agency relations in the delivery of
        health services," in *National health care, issues and problems in social-
        ized medicine*. Edited by R. H. Elling, 229–244, *op. cit.*
YOUNG, H. B., *et al.*
  1973  "Social and environmental factors accompanying malnutrition."
        Paper presented at the International Association of Behavioural
        Sciences, Biannual meeting, Ann Arbor, Michigan.

# Uses and Abuses of Innovations in the Delivery of Dental Care

MAX H. SCHOEN

During the past few decades, largely since the end of World War II, there have been three major developments in the organization and financing of dental care:
1. Third-party payment for services
2. Greater use of auxiliary personnel, both in numbers and in delegation of functions
3. Growth of group practice.

## THIRD-PARTY PAYMENT

The movement for change in the method of paying for health care services in this country, despite small earlier beginnings, received major impetus during the great depression of the thirties, with the start of Blue Cross and Blue Shield, whose primary goal was to save the hospitals and the physicians from financial disaster. Another spurt took place during and immediately after World War II to circumvent the restrictions of wartime wage controls. In this case, organized labor's bargaining strength provided a viable substitute for direct money benefits (Davis 1955).

More recently, as the cost of health care has escalated at a more rapid rate than that of other goods and services, and as workers have become more sophisticated about such care, certain gaps in coverage have become obvious. One major loophole was the lack of financial protection against the costs of treatment for dental disease. As a result dental coverage has become an important collective bargaining issue, and latest reports indicate that at least 15 million persons, or about 7 percent of the population, have some form of dental benefit (Mueller 1973). In addition, Title XIX of the Social Security Act has permitted states to include dental care under Medicaid. In California, for example, about two million persons are eligible for limited dental benefits under this system (California 1970).

## INCREASED USE OF PERSONNEL

As more dental care has been demanded by persons with funds available to pay for it, and as the proportion of dentists to populations has not increased along with this "effective demand," the use of ancillary personnel has grown. Table 1 compares the use of ancillary personnel in 1950 with that of 1970 (Cole and Cohen 1971; American Dental Association 1971):

Table 1.   Use of ancillary personnel

|  | 1950 | 1970 | Increase (in percent) |
|---|---|---|---|
| Dental hygienists per dentist | 0.09 | 0.16 | 78 |
| Dental assistants per dentist | 0.73 | 1.02 | 40 |
| Dental technicians per dentist | 0.10 | 0.28 | — |
| Total* | 1.10 | 1.46 | 32 |

This increase in personnel, together with technological innovation, can be presumed to have increased the productivity of the dentist. One estimate is that the change from 1952 to 1970 has been 80 percent as measured in constant dollars (Schoen and Doherty i.p.).

Within the past few years a number of pilot projects have demonstrated conclusively that paradental personnel can perform numerous functions currently limited to the dentist. Estimates of the increased amount of dentistry produced per dentist have varied but conservatively indicate a possible doubling of output (Lotzkar, et al. 1971; Soricelli 1972).

## GROUP PRACTICE

As in the case of third-party payment, the movement toward dental group practice has lagged behind the same trends in medical care. Dentistry involves less specialization and has almost no dependence on the hospital. Even though modern dental practice requires a considerable amount of

* The studies used as the sources did not include secretary/receptionists who also have increased at a rapid rate.

complex equipment, it is possible for this machinery to be contained within the office of a solo practitioner. There are few true "emergencies" and life or death is rarely involved, so the practitioner can maintain relatively regular hours, take vacations and, in most instances, can provide competent care for his patients without communicating with another dentist.

This picture is changing, however, as dental practice becomes even more complex and involves even greater numbers of auxiliary personnel and larger facilities. Apparently, the burdens of solo practice are increasing. The Triennial Surveys of Dental Practice conducted by the American Dental Association show that multiple-dentist offices not only produce larger gross incomes per practitioner, but also increase the net return to the dentist, as compared with solo practice (American Dental Association 1971). A recent study conducted by the Public Health Service identified over 700 dental group practices with three or more dentists (Brusseau, et al. 1972). Over 3,000 dentists were involved. Over half the groups were organized in 1965 or later, indicating a definite trend toward this form of practice.

## POTENTIAL EFFECTS OF THESE CHANGES

Before discussing the expected effects of the practice changes just enumerated, it is important to note that great strides have been made in the ability to prevent dental disease. Water fluoridation can eliminate about 60 percent of dental decay and is being used in an ever-increasing number of communities. Topical fluorides can reduce caries further. Periodontal disease and possibly caries can be minimized by reducing bacterial plaque on the teeth. This control can be achieved by a combination of office procedures, home care and diet control. However, this paper is concerned with the organization and financing of dental delivery and therefore will not consider the effects of these changes in knowledge even though probably they are greater than practice changes.

If dental care were considered in a vacuum, the combination of the three innovations would be expected to reduce the cost of care, increase its availability to the population by eliminating financial barriers, and provide enough personnel to deliver services to all who need them. Dentists' incomes would not suffer because productivity would have increased.

The magnitude of the effect of change should be great. For example, the current ratio of dentists to population is about 1:2,000, roughly the same for a number of years. Somewhat less than half the people visit a dentist in a given year (National Health Survey 1973) and only a portion of those receive relatively comprehensive care. Assuming that almost everyone should see a dentist at least once a year, productivity would have to be more than doubled to care for the total population. It is not known whether continuous maintenance care decreases the number of man-hours required over a lifetime as opposed to sporadic or episodic care necessitating major restorative efforts every so often. It even is likely that hardly any dental treatment at all, except for extractions and dentures, requires less time and cost than routine care. There is no question, however, that regular care can result in most people retaining most of their teeth for their lifetimes.

In any event increased use of auxiliaries, with the effect of at least doubling productivity would seem to come close to solving the manpower problem, without increasing the supply of dentists more than enough to maintain equilibrium with the population. The various third-party programs, by removing financial barriers should ease blocks to visiting the dentist and also reduce maldistribution by providing funds to communities normally without them. Dentists should have more areas where practice would be financially and professionally rewarding. Third-party payment, particularly when combined with group practice should aid in increasing utilitization by providing identification of population to be served. Eligible persons would be known and money would be available, therefore linkage with the providers should be easier than where no organization exists. Lastly, group practice should provide more care for less money by increased efficiency through better use of manpower and better control of services, both as to appropriateness and technical quality.

In sum, even without considering the effects of applications of new knowledge to prevent and limit dental disease, the major practice changes should be expected to produce equally major changes in the population. The results reported to date, however, appear to be relatively minor or sometimes even negative. In the remainder of this paper we shall try to provide some clues to this apparent paradox.

## DISCUSSION OF ACTUAL EFFECTS

With few exceptions, in the United States, dentists are private entrepreneurs. While they are not engaged in commodity production, certain analogies with this system can be drawn. Any improvements in the ability to produce dental care will be used primarily for the benefit of the dentist. There may be population benefits, but the lion's share goes to the practitioner. The lack of any true competition and restricted supply creates a monopoly effect which artificially pegs prices above real value. It is hypothesized that regardless of the method of payment or organization of practice, the same situation will prevail. Reforms as described earlier in this chapter, will result in improvement of the general population's oral health, but at great and unreasonable cost.

Does the dialectical materialist theory of the primacy of social relations to production, that has been applied to dental care, fit the available data? If not, is there any other relevant explanation? Unfortunately, few good data are available to determine exactly what has been happening, but enough information has been collected to give some clues.

## THE COST OF DENTAL CARE

Despite the various innovations which have increased the dentist's ability to produce more care per chair hour, the cost of services has risen more rapidly than the cost of living, except for the recent period of price control. From 1952 to 1970 the cost/price index rose 46 percent while dental fees rose 76 percent, according to Bureau of Labor Statistics figures. If American Dental Association data are used, the price increase is even greater. While the salaries of dental assistants, who are the most numerous auxiliaries, have risen quite a bit, the average of less than $5,000 per year is still lower than that for all full-time employed women. The dentist, however, has increased his average income at one and one-half times the rate of all employed males. His income is greater both absolutely and relatively in 1970 as compared with 1952. The level is within the top one or two percent of all incomes.

In addition, even within the confines of restrictive state dental practice acts, dentists have not employed ancillary personnel to the degree that they could. Many appear to be satisfied with their method of practice and their incomes and make no attempt to become more productive in order to lower fees, while retaining the same income. Some dentists who would like more patients still do not lower their fees.

In California, a number of dental offices have agreed to provide service to patients covered by third-party plans at the level of indemnity payment received from the fiscal intermediary. These tables of allowances are usually lower, often by a considerable amount, than the prevailing level of fees. Because the dentists in these offices can be presumed to make either average or above-average incomes, the question arises as to whether there really is a cost saving and, if not, what the "gimmick" is. There are several possibilities.

The obvious one is that technical quality of care is set at a lower-than-average level. Hastily performed procedures which save chair time and consequently cost less are not an appropriate way of reducing fees. Less obvious is the performance of inappropriate services. Certain types of care are more remunerative per hour than others, so emphasis on the higher-paying services, even though at a lower than average cost, can generate enough gross revenue to support a high dentist income. Coupled with inappropriate services is overtreatment. Even if one restoration is all that is needed, several may be provided. When multiple procedures are performed at one time, the cost per unit is decreased. Finally, if no attempt to recall patients is made, persons come for treatment with a greater accumulation of needs which, as stated previously, cost less per unit to provide than when only a single service is needed.

The apparent cost saving from this type of activity turns out to be either a cost increase or a dental health detriment. Overtreatment and inappropriate treatment at a low fee may not cost the patient any out-of-pocket money, but the increased bill to the intermediary eventually raises the premium, which is an increase in cost. Poor care may be harmful, certainly is not beneficial, and therefore represents wasted cost.

All in all, the various innovations have been abused so that they contribute to increased cost to the consumer rather than to the savings which could be achieved.


## ELIMINATION OF FINANCIAL BARRIERS

The advent of third party payment should lead to increased use of dental care by lowering financial barriers. Also, programs such as Medicaid should improve the distribution of dentists by making it financially possible for them to locate in poor communities.

The intervention of the fiscal intermediary has produced a concept called USUAL, CUSTOMARY, AND REASONABLE FEES (UCR). In the case of a service corporation each member dentist submits his schedule and if it is below a given percentile for the area, he is paid on the basis of his fee. Insurance companies select a specific fee schedule, which they assume to be UCR for the community and pay each dentist accordingly. Despite claims that UCR results in lowered costs, no hard evidence has been presented to this effect. On the other hand, application of UCR to small geographic areas can have untoward results. For example, dentists located in a poor community must charge their self-paying patients lower fees than those whose offices are in a wealthier area. Otherwise these patients will be unable to pay for services. Therefore the UCR fee in the poor community will be lower than in the more affluent area. This situation may be unrelated to the technical quality of any given procedure or the gross cost of providing that procedure. The UCR concept perpetuates this inequality despite the fact that the third-party payer is not "poor" and all services should be renumerated at their value — not above or below it.

Medicaid, as exemplified by Medi-Cal, provides a limited spectrum of dental care at a lower than average fee. In addition, numerous processing policies make it "obnoxious" to both patient and dentist. Also, because persons eligible for Medi-Cal have many problems of living, everything adds up to low use of dentistry. If a dentist doesn't have to practice in a poor community, he probably won't, and the patient who is poor, faced with inconveniently located services as well as all of the other problems, will tend to delay treatment until a crisis arises.

Even capitation programs which pay the provider, usually a group practice, on the basis of number of persons or families signed up in a particular program, generate more money for the provider if under-treatment occurs. The fewer people seen and the less time spent on treatment, the greater the profit.

While figures are hard to come by, those available show that the percentage of eligible persons using a third-party program, regardless of mechanism, is not very much higher than where no such program exists (Schoen 1969). In some instances it is lower. Use rates in Medi-Cal have been under 20 percent (Department of Health Care Services 1968) while the national average is over 40 percent. The disparity in fees and inability to practice comprehensive dentistry does not offer much inducement to dentists to work in poor communities, so maldistribution continues and care is inaccessible to many persons. Pumping more money into the existing system is not enough.

## SUFFICIENT RESOURCES TO PROVIDE CARE

It is not known exactly what the dentist/population ratio should be in this country in order to maximize oral health. It will vary from area to area based on the incidence and prevalence of disease. It also will vary depending on the method of work of dentists, on how many auxiliaries are used and on the way in which they are used.

It is the author's hypothesis that in dentistry, as in medicine, a large component of "need" is determined by the dentist and that the amount and type of this need can be expanded and contracted by the dentist in accordance with his "needs." Gross figures, covering a period of over a decade, show that the number of persons treated has increased at a much slower rate, 1.7 percent per year, than the growth in dental production, 4.4 percent per year (American Dental Association 1971). In other words, more dentistry is being performed on those people who do go to the dentist but the number going has expanded to a lesser degree.

A recent study illustrated the disparity in distribution of dental care services (Newman and Anderson 1972). While its figures are for 1964, the more recent, but less detailed, National Health Survey reports indicate that changes probably would be small. Families with no expenditures for dental care amounted to 38 percent of the total. But 16 percent accounted for three fourths of all expenditures while 2 percent spent one fourth of all dental monies. Similarly, 35 percent of families had no dental visits, 26 percent had three-fourths of all visits and only 3 percent accounted for one-fourth of the total number of visits.

The data for individuals was skewed to an even greater degree. 59 percent had no expenditure, while 0.8 percent spent one-fourth of all dental monies. Fifty-five percent had no dental visits in 1964 while 1.8 percent accounted for one-fourth of total visits. Socioeconomic status was correlated with patterns of use in the expected direction.

We don't know yet how much the extra dental care has slowed down the loss of teeth and resulting edentulism. Some studies have shown an improvement, but they are either of very small selected samples or show a small change (Schoen 1969; Moen and Poetsch 1970).

The temptation is to treat, particularly if that is the way one earns one's living. In many cases it may be better to observe, but then that creates less income.

There probably are enough dentists in the country today to treat the annual incidence of disease and to slowly catch up on the backlog, if services were provided rationally. In fact, there may be too many of some types of dentists — orthodontists, for example.

Assuming that orthodontic treatment is needed only once in a lifetime and that currently an orthodontist can start 100 full cases per year, the following figures may apply:

1.   There are about four million children in each age group. If one million need, seek, and get care, for "full" cases, 10,000 orthodontists would be required.

2.   Currently there are about 5,000 such practioners. However, expanding the duties of auxiliary personnel would increase their productivity at least fourfold. Except for diagnosis, treatment planning, and training and supervision of personnel all other duties can be delegated.

3. A fourfold increase in production would decrease the number of orthodontists needed to 2,500.

Will orthodontists willingly bring about this change? It is extremely
doubtful. Some who have done so as individuals have experienced great
problems. Fees remain high and continue to escalate and obvious esthetic
problems remain untreated. Little is known about the effect of malocclu-
sion on the incidence of dental disease. Effect on appearance is obvious
and is a good reason for treatment, but which other deviations from the
norm really require intervention? Even if there are benefits beyond esthet-
ics what is the relative weight of improvement in relation to harmful
sequelae of treatment?

## DISCUSSION AND CONCLUSIONS

While recent changes in practice have resulted in some improvement in
the oral health of the American people, it appears that the major beneficiaries have been the dentists. The rate of improvement is slow, and many
decades would be required to change the dental neglect that affects large
portions of our population. The technology and methods of both practice
and payment are available today which can alter this situation in the space
of a few years. However, there is no reason to assume this will occur.
Each advance, whether in payment, organization, or use of personnel
probably will be internalized as long as the dentist remains a private
entrepreneur subject to few controls.

The recent furor over a proposal to develop "dental nurses" similar to
those used in the New Zealand school system probably can be attributed
more to the suggestion that they be employed only in the public sector
than to the idea that they may not practice properly (Ingle 1972; Redig,
et al. 1973). It would be interesting to see whether a similar proposal,
allowing use by the private dental practitioner would be greeted with
nearly as much hostility.

The guild-like nature of the profession permits it to act like a typical
monopoly — establishing both prices and quantity, with much conversation but little action on quality. A last example should suffice. Every so
often legislation is introduced in one state or another to permit "denturists" to make dentures for patients without the use of a dentist. This idea
has always been opposed by dentists with great vigor on the basis that it
would result in a loss of quality. No proof is offered. Orthopedic technicians make many complex prosthetic appliances for other parts of the
body. Dentures are good business, however, bringing in high hourly

remuneration. Even more significant is the fact that the need for dentures can be eliminated almost completely by conservative dental care. If dentists were to treat dental needs early enough, edentulism would vanish almost completely and denturists would pose no problem (if they do anyway).

The general situation is not without hope, however. Dentistry is not central to the operation of our economic system — in fact, it is very peripheral. In response to greater and greater pressure for change from the bulk of the population, benefits can be made available on a more equitable basis (as part of modification of our entire health-care system). A national health security system can be instituted which would result in positive changes in practice without affecting the basic economy of the country.

## REFERENCES

AMERICAN DENTAL ASSOCIATION
   1971   *Dentistry in national health programs.* Task Force on National Health Programs, Report of special committees. Chicago: American Dental Association.
   n.d.   *The 1971 survey of dental practice.* Bureau of Economic Research and Statistics. Chicago: American Dental Association.
BRUSSEAU, LOUISE S., FERRIS M. HOGGARD, JERRY L. GRIBBLE
   1972   *Group dental practice in the United States, 1971: a survey.* Department of Health, Education, and Welfare Publication (National Institute of Health) 72–189. Washington, D.C.: U.S. Government Printing Office.
DEPARTMENT OF HEALTH CARE SERVICES
   1968   *One percent medical history study-utilization rates of persons eligible for Medi-Cal services.* State of California Medi-Cal Report 68–7.
   1970   "Annual statistical report, medical assistance program 1968–1969." Mimeographed manuscript. State of California, Sacramento.
COLE, ROGER B., LOIS K. COHEN
   1971   Dental manpower-estimating resources and requirements. *Millbank Memorial Fund Quarterly* 49:29–62.
DAVIS, MICHAEL M.
   1955   *Medical care for tomorrow,* part three: Evolution in economics. New York: Harper.
INGLE, JOHN I.
   1972   "American dental care 1972: a plan designed to deliver preventive and therapeutic dental care to the children of America." Paper presented at the Conference of Dental Examiners and Dental Educators, February 11–12, 1972.
LOTZKAR, STANLEY, D. W. JOHNSON, M. E. THOMPSON
   1971   Experimental program in expanded functions for dental assistants: phase three experiment with dental teams. *Journal of the American Dental Association* 82:1067–1081.

MOEN, B. D., W. E. POETSCH
1970   More preventive care, less tooth repair. *Journal of the American Dental Association* 81:25–36.

MUELLER, MARJORIE SMITH
1973   Private health insurance in 1971: health care services, enrollment and finances. *Social Security Bulletin* 36:3–22.

NATIONAL HEALTH SURVEY
1973   *Current estimates from the health interview survey, United States 1971.* DHEW Publication (HSM) 73–1505, series 10, number 79 (February 1973). Washington, D.C.: U.S. Government Printing Office.

NEWMAN, JOHN F., ODIN W. ANDERSON
1972   *Patterns of dental service utilization in the United States: a nationwide social survey.* Chicago: University of Chicago, Center for Health Administration Studies.

REDIG, DALE, *et al.*
1973   Delivery of dental services in New Zealand and California. *Journal Southern California Dental Association* 41:318–350.

SCHOEN, MAX H.
1969   "Observation of selected dental services under two prepayment mechanisms." Unpublished doctoral dissertation.

SCHOEN, MAX H., NEVILLE DOHERTY
i.p.   Dental fees, productivity and income. *Journal of the American Dental Association.*

SORICELLI, DAVID A.
1972   Implementation of the delivery of dental services by auxiliaries - the Philadelphia experience. *American Journal of Public Health* 62:1077–1087.

PART TWO


*Topias, Utopias and Counter-Utopias in Health Care*

# Capitalism and Public Health: A Neglected Theme in the Medical Anthropology of Africa

OMAFUME F. ONOGE

> In a non-colonial society, the attitude of a sick man in the presence of a medical practitioner is one of confidence. The patient trusts the doctor; he puts himself in his hands. He yields his body to him. He accepts the fact that pain may be awakened or exacerbated by the physician, for the patient realizes that the intensifying of suffering in the course of examination may pave the way to peace in his body.
> FRANTZ FANON[1]

> The bourgeoisie has stripped of its halo every occupation hitherto honored and looked up to with reverent awe. It has converted the physician, the lawyer, the priest, the poet, the man of science, into its paid wage laborers.
> KARL MARX and FRIEDRICH ENGELS, *The Communist manifesto*

Public health constitutes an area of enthusiastic research in contemporary Africa. Because the problems of health and disease are considered "safe" topics of research, Africanist medical anthropologists and sociologists are freed from the difficulties that their counterparts working on more explicitly political subjects encounter. They enjoy the charisma conventionally accorded to workers in community development and the early phases of the Peace Corps movements. African governments, as well as international bodies such as the World Health Organization, have readily placed their facilities at the disposal of these medical anthropologists and sociologists.

---

[1] In "Medicine and colonialism," *A dying colonialism*.

In short, there is today the sense of a veritable crusade strategically organized around the slogan of "preventive medicine."

A consequence of this holy crusade is the ready collaboration between medical and social scientists. On the evidence of Nigeria's experience, this collaboration has placed a heavy premium on the conclusions and directives proffered by social scientists. This in turn means that a sociological orientation about health and disease is now widely shared by research workers and policy-makers regardless of their disciplinary backgrounds. The central assumption of this orientation can be summarized, at random, with the words of an American anthropologist:

Public health is a social and cultural activity. Both its practitioners and the human targets of its services are, in their various interactions and transactions, fulfilling socially-defined roles in CULTURALLY DETERMINED WAYS, and a good deal of their behaviour is motivated, oriented and constrained by the social and cultural contexts in which it occurs (Lyle Saunders, cited in Read 1966:XIV–XV; emphasis added).

## TRADITIONAL AFRICAN HEALTH CONCEPTS

Man did not have to await the institutional consolidation of scientific activity before assigning importance to social and cultural factors in the etiology of sickness and health therapy. In traditional African theory and practice, there was always a sharp recognition that the genesis of sickness could be influenced by tensions or disturbances in social relationships. Indeed, some have argued that the well-known African invocation of the "aggressive" actions of witches and the "punitive" actions of ancestors as explanations of sickness is, in fact, a method of drawing attention to the objective disarray in the prevailing network of social relations in which the sick individual is implicated.

This is why the traditional healing process took on the character of a psychosocial drama. A major concern of therapy in precapitalist societies is the restoration of the patient to a THERAPEUTIC community. The invocation of witches and ancestors — fantastic as these phenomena are in terms of objective reality — is an occasion for publicly restating the moral norms which should unite the patient and his neighbors in a web of communitas.

## "SOCIOCULTURALISM" AND BLAMING THE VICTIM

However, despite the common recognition of the role of sociocultural factors in the maintenance of health shown by medical anthropologists and our "traditional" ancestors, there is little congruence at the level of interpretation. Medical anthropologists and sociologists have tended to elevate the cultural component into an omnibus explanation. The emphasis is on cultural determination. Even when social relations receive more than reflexive recognition, medical social scientists restrict the social relations to small "primary" group settings, such as the family, and factions at the micro unit of the village. Little or no attempt is made to encompass the totality of the larger society's social structure. Professor George Foster's remarks exemplify this exclusive cultural orientation:

It appears as if the MOST IMPORTANT categories of culture that should be more or less completely understood to carry out successful health and hygiene programs are LOCAL IDEAS about health, welfare, illness, their causes and treatment. (Cited in Batalla 1970:248; original emphasis).

Given the systemic, "holistic" claim of the purveyors of structural-functionalism, this persistent failure to incorporate small-scale networks into the larger vascular system of societal relationships is a major contradiction in theoretical terms. It is a truncated sociology. In practice, this restricted perspective, which in this essay I shall refer to as "socioculturalism," logically produces conclusions of the BLAMING-THE-VICTIM variety.[2] Let us illustrate some of the conclusions of "socioculturalism" in medical anthropology.

Typically, there is the covert attribution of irrationality to African health beliefs. Overtly, the assumed irrationality is phrased in terms of the African's supposed antiscientific cultural tradition. If only the African ceased to be a prisoner of his irrational cultural taboos, so that argument goes, public health problems in the continent would be vastly reduced. Africanist nutritionists are particularly preoccupied with this kind of exercise. If only the African masses were educated, they would eat balanced diets. If only they were emancipated from their beliefs, they would visit modern clinics and hospitals and follow the doctor's prescriptions, instead of consulting with *obos, babalawos,* and other traditional healers.

Courses in the medical sociology of Africa are overburdened with this cataloging of "inhibitory" taboos. Research follows a predictable hoarse refrain as the scientists investigate an endless stream of "sociocultural factors" affecting all manner of public health problems. In most of this research, the African masses, in whose behalf the studies are supposedly carried out, are themselves regarded as the primary obstacles to an improved public health because of their baggage of antiscientific beliefs.

In line with the scientists, state authorities have themselves singled out

[2]  See Ryan (1972). For a full exposition of the blaming-the-victim consequences of liberal cultural sociologies, see especially Chapter 1.

the scientific "ignorance" of the masses as the chief enemy of progress in the national effort to wipe out disease and even hunger from the body politic. Education — literacy — is advanced as the crucial solution. Consequently, uniformed paramedical functionaries (public health sisters and sanitary inspectors) are dispatched to the field, like an army, to educate the masses on hygiene and the falsity of their superstitious taboos.

It would be foolish, to put it mildly, to discount all of this educational activity as irrelevant to the resolution of Africa's public health problems. Surely the institutionalization of scientific activity has yielded rich dividends in the stock of precise and sophisticated medical knowledge from which our peasant-proletariat majorities are fully entitled to benefit. It would also be foolish to dismiss the necessity for understanding the cultural context into which medical innovations — and indeed all innovations — are to be introduced.

However, despite these caveats we maintain that "socioculturalism" leads to several distortions. First, the charge of a nonrational orientation to the problems of health and disease in the African cultural tradition is largely untenable. In contemporary Africa, the general cleanliness of our villages forms a striking contrast to the squalor of the cities. It is also significant that, in the area of nutrition, the basic ingredients of our national diets are still those discovered by our illiterate, "ignorant" forebears.

Consider our food vegetables. Surely it must have required an exploratory scientific attitude toward the ecology to select out what was edible from the billions of weeds. It required an experimental attitude to achieve the feat of processing vegetables and tubers that are poisonous in their natural state into safe items for the palate. The global charge of an antiscientific orientation is, in this context, particularly ironic because modern nutritionists in Africa — like their class colleagues — have themselves not made any further discoveries from the surrounding milieu to expand the range of food items. Their incremental "discoveries" have been wholesale borrowings of Irish potatoes, cabbages, broccoli, and the like. To be sure, our ancestors did borrow, but they also DISCOVERED![3]

The scientific temper of our forebears in the area of health and disease is further attested to in the way some of the societies contained epidemics like smallpox. Among the Yoruba, for example, although smallpox was represented as a deity, only persons who had survived an attack of the

---

[3] The uncritical elitist attribution of "ignorance" to the masses is largely a rationalization of class privileges in exploiting societies. Its continued manifestation in European socialist societies is one reason why socialist democracy has not yet included workers' self-management. The Peoples' Republic of China appears to be the exception.

disease could belong to the cult (Ajose 1957).[4] And it was they only, with their acquired immunity, who were permitted to come into physical contact with anyone afflicted with the disease. When a case of smallpox was suspected, the patient and his belongings were immediately quarantined until the members of the cult could be summoned to remove him for treatment. Under the circumstances, the representation of the disease in religious terms was a mechanism for ensuring strict conformity with the preventive medicine codes.

In other areas, pharmacologists are beginning to discover that the choice of traditional medicinal herbs was not accidental. In several instances laboratory analyses have revealed the striking medical attributes of the herbs. The abundance of effective bonesetters in African villages is also an indication of careful explorations of the human anatomy.

In the light of the foregoing, it is clear that the limitations in the fund of medical knowledge in traditional Africa were not strictly a function of an antiscientific temper. A more plausible explanation will have to be predicated on the level of sophistication of the technological base. A community without microscopes cannot be expected to formulate a germ theory of disease, when germs are invisible to the naked eye. Socioculturalism ignores the possibility that in such a community a germ theory is an even more fantastic hypothesis than a witchcraft theory of disease causation.

In addition to the mystification of the African past, a second and more serious fallacy of socioculturalism is the mystification of contemporary reality. The label of "modernity" with which socioculturalism presents the contemporary epoch in Africa hides more than it reveals. It fails to name the concrete social formations that now exist. African progress in various fields is interpreted through the prism of acculturation theory. And given the negative characterization of African cultures, the practical consequence of acculturation theory is the advocacy of development by the diffusion of "modernizing" European items.

This establishes the theoretical affinity, if not a direct filiation, that socioculturalism shares with the ideological rationalizations of the colonial epoch. In the colonial era, as is well known, the European presence, in its totality, was celebrated as a civilizing mission. Education, public health, and agriculture were the critical pillars of the colonizer's assumption of his civilizing mission on behalf of his "benighted native."

In fact, in recent years, colonial apologists of a liberal persuasion, who now admit to the political and economic exploitation consequent upon

[4] Ajose's is a significant paper attesting to the scientific orientation of Yoruba peasants' health beliefs and practices. But it is ignored by subsequent writers on the subject!

colonialism, still cling to the notion of colonial benefits by invoking innovations in the domains of education, public health, and agriculture. The continued veneration of the late Albert Schweitzer for his Lambarene "hospital," in spite of his well-known robust racism, is a dramatic case in point.

What is even more surprising however, is that many Africans themselves have come to make these allowances for colonialism. Typically, their anticolonialism is mollified with a "balance" of appreciation for the missionaries who "brought" education, the missionaries who "saved" the Africans from disease, and the like. In a classic replay of identification with the aggressor, many Africans have internalized the colonizer's contempt for their past. In a sense, therefore, their contemporary public health campaigns are merely a continuation, on a grander scale, of the "beneficial" health programs initiated by colonial authorities a few years back. This conception of the African transition is logically implied in socioculturalism.

It is for this reason that the colonial experience must be thoroughly demystified. Elsewhere we have argued that this demystification is a necessary first step toward a correct sociology of African economic development (see Onoge i.p.; see also Onoge 1973). In what follows, we shall illustrate the relevance of this demystification to the formulation of a valid medical anthropological perspective on public health problems in the contemporary situation. In our analysis, we call attention to the STRUCTURAL transformation of the continent, that is, the transition to capitalism, rather than CULTURAL resistances, as the more fruitful thrust in the apprehension of problems of public health in contemporary Africa.

## CAPITALISM AND PUBLIC HEALTH, THE COLONIAL PHASE

Contrary to the celebrants, we maintain that the colonial experience is best summarized in the words of Walter Rodney (1972) as, "how Europe underdeveloped Africa."[5] As with the domains of politics and economics, colonialism actually DEGRADED the health status of Africans. In view of the facts, it is indeed surprising that the deleterious impact of colonialism on African public health has been ignored for so long.

We are not here concerned with the importation of new diseases into the African milieu consequent upon the mere fact of contact with

[5]   Rodney's path-breaking book, which advances the methodology of a materialist historiography, contains brilliant replies to colonial apologists on the so-called "beneficial" presence of colonialism on African agriculture, education, and nutrition.

Europe. On the contrary, we link the degradation of African health to the very innards of the exploitative character of the colonial social system. The most vivid area of immediate adverse impact was that of nutrition. The needs of the colonial economy produced gross malnutrition. This occurred in several ways.

First, the alienation of large tracts of fertile agricultural and grazing land from the African population for the use of European farmers, who created plantations devoted to the production of export crops such as rubber, cocoa, coffee, and sisal, ushered in the era of regular famine into the continent. This alienation occurred without a corresponding techno- logical revolution to allow for increased productivity on the small, infer- tile plots left to the subject population. The hungry faces of Kikuyu pea- sants in Kenya and the African population of South Africa remain a cruel testimony.

Secondly, in addition to land theft, the needs of the colonial economy for African labor also aggravated malnutrition. In the many instances in which Africans refused to volunteer for work in the mines and plantations they were either forcibly conscripted (as in the Congo, Angola, or Mozambique) or coerced into emigration by the requirement that colonial taxes be paid in cash. With forced labor and the migrant system, the phenomenon of starving "manless villages" became a permanent feature of the rural landscape of colonial Africa.[6]

Third, wages paid to laborers in the mines and plantations were delib- erately kept low to ensure the superexploitation of the African popula- tion. Thus, because the African laborer could not survive on his wages, he was forced to depend on his kinswomen in the villages for agricultural staples, the supply of which was already precarious because of the enforced erosion of manpower. Even Bronislaw Malinowski, the vener- ated founder of the reactionary school of British "practical anthropolo- gy," was forced to testify to the adverse consequences of the migrant labor system.

In his 1938 paper, "Modern Anthropology and European rule in Africa," Malinowski, after romanticizing the enforced "pilgrimage to mine, plantation, or factory ... [as] ... a substitute for the glamour of lost

[6] This phenomenon was noticed but mystified by many anthropologists. One of the first and most famous studies is that of Richards (1939). This "classic" blames the annual famines consequent upon the coerced migration of male labor from Bemba villages on Bemba culture itself!

This mystification of the migrant system was intensified by some later anthropologists. One of the most remarkable was Van Velsen, who celebrated the system as a masculine RITE OF PASSAGE, necessary for the functional cohesion of African society! See Van Velsen (1961).

wars, cattle raids, elephant hunting and similar heroic exploits," conceded that:

family-budgets show that the expenditure necessary for the maintenance of the new standard very often, almost invariably, exceeds the regular earnings of the father of the family. This means that malnutrition, insufficient training for the children, and over-work in additional pursuits, often illegal, by wife and children, create conditions incompatible with the standard of expectations with health, and with all the advantages implied in the charter of transition (Malinowski 1938:19–20).

Malinowski's favorite solution, which he advanced in a number of papers celebrating the potential utility of anthropology for the consolidation of colonial rule, was that European employers should control the way in which the African laborer expended his earnings.

Fourth, the incorporation of the African into the colonial capitalist economy was not limited to the production process. The African was to be a consumer as well. Malinowski approved this double incorporation in the following memorable passage: "It is the African who has to be converted or contracted for labour; who has to be educated, or BE MADE INTO A consumer of imported goods; who has to be pacified and submitted to law, or trained into a USEFUL DOMESTIC servant" (Malinowski 1938: 5; emphasis added).

To assure the "partnership," as he called the subordination, the African has to be "weaned" from his "tribalism" and to "develop in him new needs and ambitions."

Malinowski acknowledges the priestly arm of the colonial establishment as an effective agent in the "weaning" process. For not only was the African Christian "the most loyal" to the colonial polity, but also, at the level of the economy, the "missionary has induced him to dress, and to use and appreciate the European goods, with which the trader supplies him for ready cash or credit" (Malinowski 1938: 9). The upshot of this socialization was that a large part of the African laborer's earnings, meager as they were, was spent on items that bore no intrinsic relation to his nutritional needs. If we may appropriate Herbert Marcuse's terminology, the colonial effort was geared to disorienting the African laborer-consumer into the pursuit of FALSE needs rather than REAL needs (see Marcuse 1964).

## FRANTZ FANON'S INSIGHT

The adverse impact of the colonial transition on public health is not exhausted by a consideration of the demands of the capitalist economy.

Whereas the economy worked directly against the precolonial nutritional profile, the racial hierarchy of colonial society ensured that the African could not fully benefit from the new stock of Western medical knowledge for which colonialism has conventionally been praised. This insight, which further allows us to clarify the limitations of socioculturalism, we owe to Fanon.

In fact, the deficiencies of the partial sociology of "socioculturalism" was a central concern of Fanon's essay on medicine and colonialism.[7] Observers have long drawn attention to the hesitation of Africans to visit Western hospitals introduced into the colonial societies. The proverbial anthropological interpretation, as we have pointed out, was phrased solely in cultural terms. But Fanon, who observed African behavior before and during the revolutionary phase of Algerian society, offered a different interpretation.

He pointed out that the ambivalent response of Algerians to French hospitals was primarily a function of their POLITICAL views rather than a CULTURAL definition of the Algerian colony. They perceived Western medicine as part of the oppressive system of colonialism erected in the wake of their military conquest by the French. From that historic and political vision, an enthusiastic acceptance of Western medical science represents an act of capitulation to the conquerors, a capitulation to the colonizer's boast that "were it not for us, there would be no country!"

This political definition of medicine also had a REAL premise in the concrete behavior of the colonial authorities:

The compulsory visit by the doctor to the *douar* is preceded by the assembling of the population through the agency of the police authorities. The doctor who arrives in this atmosphere of general constraint is never a native doctor but always a doctor belonging to the dominant society and very often to the army (Fanon 1965: 121).

As many Africans can recall, this official politicization of Western medicine had become such an ingrained part of colonial health services that even the African functionaries began to exhibit it at lower levels. An atmosphere of "siege" prevailed in the village whenever the uniformed sanitary inspector was expected. He was perceived as a POLITICAL rather than a health officer. Thus, in the villages, preparations for the inspector's visit had nothing to do with cleaning the houses, compounds, or streets. This was not necessary, because general cleaning was an established daily tradition. Instead, preparations involved taking a collection for cash and

[7] This exposé of the theoretical vacuity of bourgeois sociology for oppressed classes is the central theme of the entire collection of essays in his book, *A dying colonialism*. In this, Fanon was enriching the tradition of Cesaire's *Discourse on colonialism*.

livestock "gifts" to the inspector. Any community that failed to raise sub-stantial "gifts," let alone ignore the exercise, was sure to receive an adverse sanitation report and the consequent displeasure of the district officer.

The colonial doctor signified his politics by an overt participation in the economic pillage. His accumulated property and his affluent standard of living were concrete evidence of his collusion with the authorities in the eyes of the colonized. In the light of these factors, the doctor-patient relationship which, traditionally, is characterized by confidence, is, in the colonial milieu, one of deep mistrust. It becomes an encounter between enemies. The doctor's diagnostic questions become an "interrogation" from which the patient must protect himself with uninformative tele-graphic answers.

Again, this is not a question of culture, for as Fanon took care to point out, the same kind of distrust always emerged during World War II in the relationships between doctors and prisoner-of-war patients among the French and the Germans. "The German prisoner who was to be operated on by a French surgeon would very often, just before being given an anaesthetic, beseech the doctor not to kill him" (Fanon 1965: 123).[8] The same plea was made when the nationality of the characters in the dyadic transaction was reversed. The "state of war," which, in Europe, was a temporary irruption into the existing social relationships, was, in the Manichean world of the colony, the defining feature of the social order.

## CAPITALISM AND PUBLIC HEALTH, THE NEOCOLONIAL PHASE

The elimination of the racial factor from the social structure of the "post-colonial" societies of contemporary Africa has not fundamentally altered the pattern of structural constraints on public health. For capitalism, which in the colonial period was still a NASCENT phenomenon, has become institutionalized in the majority of the new nations. Capitalist penetration of our village systems has advanced beyond the forays of the colonial

---

[8]   Fanon also offered this tentative reason for the Algerian's distrust of the French hospitals: "It needs to be said, too, although it is not the rule, that in certain hospital services experimentation on living patients is practiced to an extent that cannot be considered negligible" (Fanon 1965: 124).

The recent scandals on the PRESERVATION, for "experimental" purposes, of the syphilitic condition of black patients, as well as the illegal sterilization of black women in certain hospitals in the United States' South, are instructive. If these experimenta-tions are possible in the liberal milieu of the United States, we can only imagine the fate of African patients in a colonial world where there was no independent investigative press. For accounts of the American scandals, see the *New York Times*, July 26, 1973, and August 1, 1973.

period. Class cleavages have been exacerbated. An indigenous bourgeois class, preoccupied with its self-perpetuation, has emerged. "Naked self-interest ... callous cash payment" is daily becoming the sole solvent of the "nexus between man and man" in capitalist Africa.

In this capitalist milieu, where "money talks," the benefits that should accrue to our peasant-proletariat majorities from the phenomenal increase in medical personnel and facilities remain, essentially, paper benefits. In spite of the high sentiments of the state constitutions and presidential manifestos, health is no longer a fundamental human right. In practice, public health is now fully implicated as a commodity in the market place. Health is simply for sale. Only those who can afford medical care can get it.

This is a major departure from the medical culture of precapitalist Africa. In the precolonial societies, a sick person was sure to have access to the available fund of medical knowledge, limited as this knowledge may have been. Although it was usual for the patient to pay for these services in those societies in which occupational specialization was advanced, it was unthinkable to ignore a patient on the grounds of his poverty. The appropriate tradition was that the poor patient and his kinsmen would be indebted to the healer. A healer who refused to supply his services on the grounds of cash ran the grave risk of being ostracized.

In many of the new nations, there is class segregation of medical facilities along the lines of the racial segregation of the colonial period. In colonial times, the best-equipped hospitals were restricted to Europeans. Today, these European hospitals and clubs have simply been taken over by the national bourgeoisie. The rationalizing argument of the national bourgeoisie that, unlike the colonial past, this segregation is based on the ability to pay rather than on race merely underscores the salience of the capitalist structure for public health. To argue, as they do, that there is a "freedom of choice" of health care is insidious. For they know only too well that the masses are in no position to exercise that freedom, in view of the price discrimination.

It is significant that in institutions in which labor contracts call for the provision of free medical services, two separate clinics are maintained. One for the "junior" staff and the other for the "senior" staff. The supporting argument is couched in terms of efficiency. It is necessary, so the argument goes, that senior staff receive speedy attention so that they can quickly return to their jobs, because the contributions of the senior staff are "more important" than those of their junior colleagues. It is but a short step from this argument — controversial as it is — to consider "senior" staff a superior breed of humanity.

This segregation is reinforced at the highest political levels. Many African leaders, despite their pious statements about their public health programs, abandon the national medical services whenever they themselves are sick. It is to Europe that they flee whenever they are in need of medical attention. This class distrust of the national services has begun to permeate the entire system even at lower levels. In public hospitals, where the majority of the patient population is lower class, nurses are becoming more preoccupied with emphasizing the boundaries between their petty-bourgeois class and those of their patients. In such settings, we can presume that hospitalization induces anxieties in the patient beyond those of cultural difference or those consequent on the mere fact of sickness.

Medical facilities in capitalist Africa follow faithfully the residential patterns of the classes. The villages, the home of the peasantry, have few clinics. In fact, in many instances, the few that exist are the result of the self-help of the villagers who volunteered their labor and financial resources to erect the buildings. Faced with this *fait accompli*, it became difficult for the state authorities to ignore the provision of drugs and medical personnel. Often, the political class deforms this mass enthusiasm for clinics into a crass political deal for getting votes. In Nigeria, at least, the rise and fall of modern health services in the villages is often intelligible only in terms of the voting behavior of the rural population.

And periodically, when the government's threat of a withdrawal of services is not enough to guarantee the votes, health officers, like sanitary inspectors, are converted into a repressive para-police force with powers to arrest and detain villagers for "endangering" public health. This practice was a daily occurrence in the Western Region of Nigeria during the crisis preceeding the crash of the first republic.

It is in the cities where the bourgeois classes live that we find the health facilities. But even here, as we have pointed out, the facilities are segregated so that the ruling circles will not be contaminated by the diseases of the proletarian class. The inferior facilities of the public hospitals reserved for the working class vitiate the efforts of a dedicated corps of medical and paramedical officers. From time to time this overworked, dedicated corps stage strikes to protest the national neglect. They are, however, in a minority. Their efforts are countered by the majority who, recognizing the capitalist logic of the African transition, stage strikes for the right to establish private clinics and private drugstores.[9] Their efforts

---

[9]   The unregulated sale of drugs in African markets dramatizes the capitalist profit ethic as well as the neocolonial status of African nations. There is evidence that foreign capitalist drug manufacturers consider African societies a dumping ground for dangerous drugs which have been banned from the market in their own countries.

are rendered meaningless by the poor housing and poor nutrition of the masses which capitalist economic exploitation has forced on them. Their efforts are countered by the pollution of our environment by foreign monopoly capitalist industries.

## THE RESPONSIBILITY OF PUBLIC HEALTH STUDENTS

In view of these tendencies, it is unfortunate that medical anthropologists and sociologists concentrate their attention on the search for "cultural resistances" to medical innovation rather than on the political economy of health. We for our part already have previews of the ultimate character of public health in capitalist society. The poor condition of health of black people, migrant workers, and poor whites in the affluent, super-stition-free milieu of capitalist America is now an open subject of discus-sion.[10] In the same way, the "miracles" of socialist societies like China in the area of public health, in spite of their relative technological and eco-nomic backwardness, are now widely known (see, for example, Horn 1969).

In the light of these contrasts, medical anthropologists and sociologists who are truly concerned with the health of African peoples, rather than with the temporary advancement of their personal professional careers, can no longer maintain an amnesia on the necessity of socialist revolution in Africa. The minority of dedicated medical personnel must realize the limits of an apolitical dedication. "To be a revolutionary doctor, or to be a revolutionary at all," wrote Guevara, "there must first be a revolution. The isolated effort of one man, regardless of the purity of his ideals is worthless" (Guevara 1969: 258). Fortunately, there are increasing signs that the African peasants and proletariats (who are the "objects" of sociocultural analysis) are beginning to realize that the amelioration of their health problems is tied to the struggle for socialism. They are becom-ing aware that in the contemporary chaotic milieu, the best "preventive medicine" is the SOCIALIST REVOLUTION.

## REFERENCES

AJOSE, OLADELE A.
  1957   Preventive medicine and superstitions in Nigeria. *Africa* 27:268–274.
BATALLA, GUILLERMO BONFIL
  1970   "Conservative thought in applied anthropology: a critique," in

[10]   For instructive bibliographic sources on the impact of capitalist values and rela-tionships on American health care systems, see Rosenberg and Schiff (n.d.).

*Applied anthropology.* Edited by James A. Clifton. Boston: Houghton Mifflin.

CESAIRE, AIME

1972    *Discourse on colonialism.* New York: Monthly Review Press.

FANON, FRANTZ

1965    "Medicine and colonialism," in *A dying colonialism.* By Frantz Fanon. New York: Grove.

GUEVARA, ERNESTO CHE

1969    "The duty of a revolutionary doctor," in *The Selected Speeches of Ernesto Guevara.* Edited by Ronaldo E. Bonachea and Nelson P. Valdés. Cambridge, Massachusetts: M.I.T. Press.

HORN, JOSHUA S.

1969    *Away with all pests, an English surgeon in People's China: 1954–1969.* New York: Monthly Review Press.

MALINOWSKI, BRONISLAW

1938    Modern anthropology and European rule in Africa. *Reale Accademia D'Italia,* Rome, 16:19–20.

MARCUSE, HERBERT

1964    *One-dimensional man.* Boston: Beacon.

MARX, KARL, FRIEDRICH ENGELS

1948    *The communist manifesto.* New York: International Publishers.

NEW YORK TIMES

1973    Articles on "experimentation" on black patients in the South. July 26 and August 1.

ONOGE, OMAFUME F.

1973    "The counter-revolutionary tradition in African studies: a critique of theories of the African transition." Paper presented to the African Heritage Studies Association conference, Baltimore.

i.p.    "Revolutionary imperatives in African sociology," in *Proceedings of the Nigerian Anthropological and Sociological Association.*

READ, MARGARET

1966    Culture, health and disease. London: Tavistock.

RICHARDS, AUDREY I.

1939    *Land, labour and diet in Northern Rhodesia.* London: Oxford University Press.

RODNEY, WALTER

1972    *How Europe underdeveloped Africa.* Dar es Salaam: Tanzania Publishing House.

ROSENBERG, KEN, GORDON SCHIFF, *editors*

n.d.    *The politics of health care, a bibliography.* Boston Medical Committee for Human Rights. Boston, Massachusetts: New England Free Press.

RYAN, WILLIAM

1972    *Blaming the victim.* New York: Random House, Vintage Books.

VAN VELSEN, J.

1961    "Labour migration as a positive factor in the continuity of Tonga tribal society," in *Social change in modern Africa.* Edited by Aidan Southall, 230–241. London: Oxford University Press.

# Implicit versus Explicit Goals: Medical Care in Argentina

JORGE SEGOVIA, OMAR J. GÓMEZ

To attempt to describe a country in a few paragraphs is not only difficult, but presumptuous. Nevertheless, this is precisely what we should try to do in order to give the reader an idea of the general frame in which the health system of Argentina is working.

Argentina is the second largest country by area and the third by population among the Latin American countries. A careful study of Tables 1, 2, and 3 will show that it also enjoys a somewhat privileged position; only Uruguay is consistently better according to social and economic indicators. Sometimes, one has the impression that the expression "developing countries" was coined precisely for these countries in the southern tip of the continent; but the fact is that Argentina, despite certain persistent conditions that show that it is still not a fully developed country, whatever that means, is located in the seventeenth place in a development rank constructed in 1960, using twenty variables among sixty-six countries of the world.

It is important to note some features of the demographic, social, and economic conditions of the country, some of which are easy to find in the tables mentioned. First, Argentina is a highly urbanized country, even for a region like Latin America that is far more urbanized than European countries were, for example, when they had similar socioeconomic conditions. In Argentina the population is extremely concentrated; nearly one-third of the population lives in the metropolitan region of the capital city, Buenos Aires (eight million out of twenty-three million); 72 percent of the total population lives within four of the twenty-two provinces. These provinces are located in a region of temperate climate, an important distinction to make, in view of the general idea that all Latin American countries are "tropical."

Table 1.   Area and selected demographic indicators of eight Latin American countries in recent years

| Country | Area, Square kilometers | Population — midyear estimate 1968 | Population — Density 1969 | Population — Percent of annual increase 1963–1968 | Population — Percent under 15 years 1968 |
|---|---|---|---|---|---|
| Argentina | 2,776,889 | 23,617,000 | 9 | 1.5 | 29.7 |
| Brazil | 8,511,965 | 88,209,000 | 4 | 3.0 | 42.8 |
| Chile | 756,945 | 9,351,000 | 13 | 2.4 | 40.0 |
| Colombia | 1,138,914 | 19,825,000 | 18 | 3.2 | 46.6 |
| Cuba | 114,524 | 8,074,000 | 72 | 2.2 | 37.3 |
| Guatemala | 108,889 | 4,864,000 | 46 | 3.1 | 46.6 |
| Mexico | 1,972,546 | 47,267,000 | 25 | 3.5 | 46.3 |
| Peru | 1,285,216 | 12,772,000 | 6 | 3.1 | 43.3 |

Table 2.   Indicators of age composition, urbanization, ethnicity, and literacy in the populations of eight Latin American countries in recent years (in percent)

| Country | Under 15 years 1968 | Rural 1970 | American Indian | Literate |
|---|---|---|---|---|
| Argentina | 29.7 | 22.4 | 0.6 | 91 |
| Brazil | 42.8 | 52.2 | 1.5 | 60.5 |
| Chile | 40.0 | 29.4 | 3.2 | 83.6 |
| Colombia | 46.6 | 44.1 | 1.6 | 72.9 |
| Cuba | 37.3 | 38.7 | — | 78 |
| Guatemala | 46.6 | 69.9 | 53.6 | 53.6 |
| Mexico | 46.3 | 38.2 | 8.8 | 62.2 |
| Peru | 43.3 | 50.8 | 46.7 | 61.1 |

Table 3.   Selected economic Indicators of eight Latin American countries in recent years

| Country | Gross national product (GNP) per capita (in dollars) 1968 | Gross agricultural product as percentage of GNP 1963–1965 average | Economic active population (in percent) |
|---|---|---|---|
| Argentina | 600 | 16.5 | 37.6 (1960) |
| Brazil | 291 (1967) | 29.0 | 32.3 (1960) |
| Chile | 518 | 11.1 | 32.4 (1960) |
| Colombia | 301 | 46.6 | 29.4 (1964) |
| Cuba | 518 | — | 33.8 (1953) |
| Guatemala | 297 | 31.2 | 33.1 (1964) |
| Mexico | 553 | 16.1 | 26.9 (1970) |
| Peru | 268 | 23.0 | 31.5 (1961) |

The population of Argentina is almost entirely of European extraction, and migrations are very important in the composition of the population;

in that sense, in Latin America maybe only Brazil and Chile are as cosmopolitan as Argentina. Of course, the matter of the ethnicity of the population is subject to a wide range of opinions. Undoubtedly there is a lot of Indian blood in the country, but the Indians' living conditions are more those of a poor rural population than of an Indian people; just a few thousand Indians are living in reservations in the north and in the south of the country. In terms of population, two important things distinguish Argentina from other Latin American countries: the rate of growth, which is comparable to the United States and European countries, and the age composition of the population — the percentage of population under fifteen years of age is 29.7, and although this is higher than in fully developed countries, it is one of the lowest in the region. These two things are very important factors in economic and health matters.

From the point of view of socioeconomic indicators, again we have an intermediate type: the gross national product (GNP) is high for the area, but not in comparison with the United States or other developed countries; the rate of literacy (91 percent) seems to be high also, but it hides the actual fact that only a fraction of Argentina's children finish the seven grades of mandatory school. The economy, although still relying on agriculture and cattle, is becoming increasingly diversified, and industrialization is high, although it is characterized as import substitution, meaning that the industries are dependent on imports such as raw materials and heavy machinery. There is no doubt that there is an important middle class; professionals, high-level bureaucrats, executives, military officers, intermediate industrialists, and businessmen are the components of this middle strata, which is highly visible, especially in the cities.

## HEALTH CONDITIONS

In describing the health conditions of Argentina in comparison with other countries, we face two major problems. First, the quality of the available information is poor; only a handful of countries are producing vital and health statistics with reasonable accuracy. Second, what we will be using as indicators of health are, in fact, the opposite; that is, we will be using indicators of mortality and, sometimes, morbidity. We know that the absence of death or disease is not synonymous with health, but we do not have any way of solving this conceptual problem.

A careful search of Tables 4 through 6 will give the reader a reasonable idea of the health conditions of Argentina in comparison with other Latin

Table 4.   Selected health indicators of eight Latin American countries and the United
States in recent years

| Country | General mortality | | Infant mortality | Death rates 1-4 years of age | Percentage of deaths under 5 years 1968 (approximately) | Percentage of total deaths by communicable parasitic diseases |
| | Crude death | Age adjusted death rates* 1968 | 1969 | | | |
|---|---|---|---|---|---|---|
| Argentina | 8.3 | 6.8 (1967) | 60 | 2.6 | 15.8 | 3.3 |
| Brazil | — | — | — | — | — | — |
| Chile | 9.0 | 8.7 (1968) | 86 | 3.2 | 31.2 | 6.2 |
| Colombia | 9.4 | 9.5 (1967) | 78 | 11.7 | 46.7 | 10.7 |
| Cuba | 6.6 | 5.6 (1965) | 40 | 1.6 | 20.7 | 4.3 |
| Guatemala | 16.6 | 15.7 (1966) | 93 | 27.6 | 49.2 | 22.1 |
| Mexico | 9.6 | 9.1 (1968) | 64 | 99.8 | 43.9 | 8.4 |
| Peru | 7.8 | 7.4 (1967) | 75 | 9.0 | 46.4 | 14.6 |
| U.S.A. | 9.4 | 5.0 (1967) | 21.5 | 1.1 | 4.6 | 0.0 |

*   Standard population: estimate age distribution for Latin America

Table 5.   First principal causes of mortality in selected Latin American countries and
the United States in recent years*

| Order of causes | United States | Argentina | Chile | Mexico | Guatemala |
|---|---|---|---|---|---|
| 1 | Diseases of the heart | Diseases of the heart | Influenza and pneumonia | Influenza and pneumonia | Influenza and pneumonia |
| 2 | Neoplasms, etc. | Neoplasms, etc. | Certain diseases of early infancy | Certain diseases of early infancy | Gastritis, enteritis |
| 3 | Vascular lesions affecting CNS | Vascular lesions affecting CNS | Neoplasms, etc. | Gastritis, enteritis, etc. | Certain diseases of early infancy |
| 4 | Accidents | Certain diseases of early infancy | Diseases of the heart | Accidents | Whooping cough |
| 5 | Influenza and pneumonia | Accidents | Accidents | Neoplasms, etc. | Measles |

*   Format from an idea in Project DISABO (Feld 1965) with some modifications and
actualized information.

Table 6. First five principal causes of mortality in selected Argentine provinces and federal capital

| Order of causes | Federal capital | San Juan | Catamarca | Jujuy |
|---|---|---|---|---|
| 1 | Diseases of the heart | Other forms of heart disease (A 84) | Other pneumonies (A 92) | Other pneumonies (A 92) |
| 2 | Vascular lesions affecting CNS | Vascular lesions affecting the CNS (A 85) | Vascular diseases (A 86) | Heart diseases, other forms (A 84) |
| 3 | Neoplasms, etc. | Isquemic disease of the heart (A 83) | Gastritis, enteritis (A 5) | Respiratory TBC (A 6) |
| 4 | Other forms of heart disease | Other pneumonies (A 92) | Isquemic disease of the heart (A 83) | Gastritis, enteritis (A 5) |
| 5 | Vascular diseases | Gastritis, enteritis (A 5) | Neoplasms (A 65) | Nutritional diseases (A 65) |

American countries and the United States. Again, Argentina is just in the middle of the road. One statistical device, which we think is useful and easy to construct from mortality tables, is the proportionally-grouped mortality (PGM), a further refinement of the Swaroop-Uemura index. The PGM shows the percentages of deaths in selected age groups from all deaths that are occurring; of course, most of the deaths should happen

Table 7. Approximate percentage of mortality in various age groups in selected countries in 1965

| Country | −1 year | 1–4 years | 5–49 years | 50 or more years |
|---|---|---|---|---|
| Sweden | 1.9 | 0.3 | 7.3 | 90.5 |
| Finland | 2.6 | 0.6 | 12.2 | 84.6 |
| France | 2.6 | 0.5 | 9.3 | 87.6 |
| United States | 4.2 | 0.7 | 12.7 | 82.6 |
| Japan | 4.2 | 1.1 | 15.7 | 82.4 |
| Argentina | 13.4 | 2.6 | 18.4 | 65.6 |
| Cuba | 20.2 | 2.8 | 15.6 | 61.4 |
| Chile | 29.8 | 4.7 | 20.7 | 45.4 |
| Mexico | 29.7 | 13.8 | 21.7 | 34.8 |
| Peru | 30.5 | 17.5 | 24.9 | 24.2 |
| Guatemala | 24.8 | 26.7 | 27.3 | 21.2 |
| Colombia | 30.0 | 17.5 | 21.2 | 32.0 |

Table 8.  Percentage of mortality in various age groups in the federal capital and selected provinces of Argentina in 1965/1967

| Political Division | –1 year | 1–4 years | 5–49 years | 50 or more years |
|---|---|---|---|---|
| Federal capital | 4.0 | 0.5 | 13.2 | 82.3 |
| San Juan | 22.1 | 3.8 | 18.5 | 55.6 |
| Chaco | 29.0 | 7.2 | 21.5 | 42.3 |
| Salta | 31.4 | 10.3 | 21.2 | 37.1 |
| Jujuy | 32.7 | 16.9 | 21.4 | 29.0 |

late in the life spans of individuals, as happens in Sweden, for example. In Tables 7 and 8 we show the PGM for different countries as well as for different political divisions of Argentina; the conclusions are obvious.

## HEALTH RESOURCES

Before going into the organization of the health system in Argentina, it is useful to look quickly at some common data about health resources. Table 9 speaks for itself in many respects; a good example is the incongruity of having more physicians in a country than nurses (even when the latter group includes all types of auxiliaries and empirical assistants with little or no formal training). Again, Argentina seems to be in a privileged position in terms of health resources, especially in relation to the number of physicians (fifth place in the whole world). Table 10 shows the differences between political divisions (federal capital and provinces) with the proportion of the total population in each of them. For example, the worst province in terms of the ratio of the population to physician (Santiago de Estero, with 2,714 people to one physician) is almost exactly equivalent to the average for nineteen Latin American countries (2,713). In terms of hospital beds, only two provinces are under the Latin American countries' average of 3.1 beds per 1,000 population, and they have 2.7 percent of the population of the country. On the other hand, only four provinces have more than the United States' rate of 8.3, and they account for the 2.2 percent of the total population; 31.5 percent of the population has a rate of more than six beds per 1,000 population.

There are many more elements in a medical care system than physicians or hospital beds, but it is difficult to get and evaluate figures about clinics, health centers, and other outpatient facilities; here we have a very important point, and it is that in the outpatient sector we lack figures and rates, such as beds per population, which may be deceptively easy to use, but nevertheless, are a useful tool for comparative purposes.

Table 9.  Health resources of eight Latin American countries and the United States in recent years

| Country | Population per physician | Nurses per 10,000 population | Hospital beds per 1,000 population | Percent of urban population with water supply, house connections |
|---|---|---|---|---|
| | 1968 | 1968* | 1968 (approximately) | 1969 |
| Argentina | 520 | 15.9 | 6.3 | 65.2 |
| Brazil | 2,800 | 4.5 | 2.2 | 30.2 |
| Chile | 1,800 | 20.6 | 4.0 | 56.7 |
| Colombia | 2,200 | 11.0 | 2.4 | 65.0 |
| Cuba | 1,130 | 14.9 | 4.8 | 76.5 |
| Guatemala | 4,550 | 7.4 | 2.3 | 39.7 |
| Mexico | 1,850 | 10.8 | 2.0 | 67.2 |
| Peru | 1,950 | 10.9 | 2.4 | 48.5 |
| U.S.A. | 658 | 88.1 | 8.3 | — |

* Graduates and auxiliaries

Table 10.  Health resources and proportion of the total population in Argentina, by political division, in recent years

| Political division | Percentage of total population | Hospital beds per 1,000 pop. | Population per physician | Per capita health expenditures public sectors, 1960 pesos |
|---|---|---|---|---|
| | 1968 | 1969 | 1969 | 1968 |
| Federal capital | 14.2 | 7.8 | 193 | 898 |
| Buenos Aires | 36.3 | 4.9 | 683 | 293 |
| Catamarca | 0.7 | 3.7 | 1,421 | 490 |
| Córdoba | 8.7 | 7.2 | 450 | 347 |
| Corrientes | 2.4 | 3.5 | 1,556 | 310 |
| Chaco | 2.4 | 3.6 | 1,858 | 320 |
| Chubut | 0.7 | 9.0 | 874 | 686 |
| Entre Ríos | 3.5 | 6.6 | 1,145 | 295 |
| Formosa | 0.9 | 2.9 | 1,824 | 302 |
| Jujuy | 1.2 | 8.8 | 1,272 | 936 |
| La Pampa | 0.7 | 7.1 | 1,101 | 86 |
| La Rioja | 0.7 | 4.5 | 1,234 | 550 |
| Mendoza | 4.1 | 4.7 | 666 | 678 |
| Misiones | 1.8 | 2.4 | 1,992 | 249 |
| Neuquen | 0.6 | 5.2 | 985 | 499 |
| Río Negro | 1.0 | 5.4 | 1,026 | 356 |
| Salta | 2.1 | 6.1 | 1,163 | 608 |
| San Juan | 1.6 | 3.5 | 855 | 666 |
| San Luís | 0.7 | 4.5 | 1,164 | 514 |
| Santa Cruz | 0.3 | 9.0 | 750 | 1,279 |
| Santa Fe | 9.0 | 5.9 | 638 | 246 |
| Santiago del Estero | 2.1 | 3.3 | 2,174 | 238 |
| Tucumán | 3.3 | 4.3 | 970 | 449 |
| Tierra del Fuego | 0.05 | 10.2 | 643 | 922 |
| Argentina as a whole | 100.0 | 5.6 | 529 | 2,187 |

## ORGANIZATION OF HEALTH SERVICES

Numbers and ratios about health resources convey very little information until they are fully framed in the organizational context in which they are used. Argentina is as good an example as any of a pluralistic system; it may be extremely easy to describe it because there is a strong temptation to say that there is no such a thing as a system; rather what we have is just plain chaos, just an aggregate of organizations without any pattern, coordination, or defined purposes and goals. One might say that the Argentine system has grown just by apposition, one new layer on top of the old ones without any serious intent of relating them for a harmonic functioning.

Adrian Abel-Smith (1965) has pointed out that any medical care system is a consequence of the general historical development of a given country. In Argentina this is very easy to verify because it is possible to find examples of almost any of the formats of medical care that have been used in the country; as a matter of fact, the observer will find them still functioning in many cases.

There are four major subsystems within the general system of medical care in Argentina; we will attempt only rough definitions of each of them. The reason for this is that there are only partial definitions of the subsystems in the literature and there are no clear-cut criteria for differentiating them.

1.  GOVERNMENTAL SUBSYSTEM: composed of a variety of health organizations owned and operated by the three levels of government: National (federal); Provincial (state); and Municipal or Departmental (local). Most of these facilities are theoretically free and open to the whole population. There is no coordination between the three levels, and a high degree of overlapping of facilities and services exists, especially in urban areas.

2.  SOCIAL SECURITY SUBSYSTEM (S.S): here we have quite a number of organizations which are united in the same group because their funds are raised through mandatory payroll deductions from employer and employee and because they have a directory, composed of employees, employers, and, in some cases, government officers. They are created and regulated by special and specific federal or provincial laws. Their total number is, believe it or not, unknown; a good estimate is sixty institutions.

3.  MUTUAL ORGANIZATIONS SUBSYSTEM: these are private organizations, most of them organized by unions or ethnic communities. They are financed through voluntary contributions by the membership (this is not entirely true in the case of union mutuals). Their number, again an educated guess, is 1,445.

4.  PRIVATE SUBSYSTEM: here we have, again, manifold institutions; the

major ones fall into two subdivisions: nonprofit (voluntary associations, small private neighborhood associations, etc.) and profit-making (the private offices of physicians and dentists, and proprietary hospitals).

A useful diagram of an overview of the systems and subsystems is presented in Figure 1.

Figure 1. Subsystems within the general system of medical care in Argentina

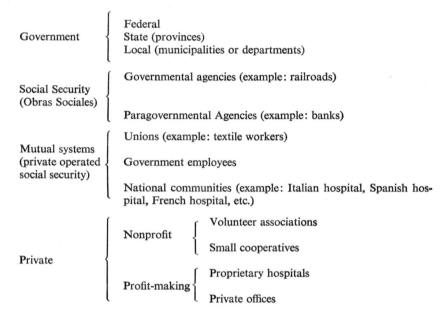

Of course, this description is a static one; it does not say anything about the performance of the system, which is, in our criteria, the most important point. The number of subsystems, the lack of coordination between them, and the fact that even the correct number of institutions within each subsystem is unknown, are good indications that such a system cannot be properly managed, but we think that more than this feeling is necessary to prove our point.

Unfortunately, there is very little information about the actual performance of the system. Only partial data are available; we will attempt to use them to convey a general picture of the functioning of the system.

It is important to weight the relative importance of the subsystem. The best way to do this is, again, a comparison between the number of hospital beds within subsystems; there is no way to have a similar figure about outpatient facilities and services. Table 11 shows the relative proportion of beds in the different systems, and shows that no subsystem can claim control over a sufficient proportion of hospital beds to be able to handle by itself a major change in the structure of medical care services. The governmental services have an accumulated percentage of 75.8 of the total beds, but this fact must be weighed against the fact that the control of these beds is, in fact, subdivided into four different parts: federal government (National Secretary of Health); other federal agencies (military hospitals, etc.); provincial government (twenty-two provinces and one territory); and municipalities (only nine provinces actually have municipal hospitals).

Table 11.   Health resources, using the number of hospital beds as indicator, in the different subsystems of medical care in Argentina in 1968

| By agencies | Number of beds | Percent | By subsystems | Percent |
|---|---|---|---|---|
| Federal secretary of health | 32,625 | 23.0 | | |
| Other federal agencies[a] | 10,424 | 7.3 | Government | 75.8 |
| Provincial agencies[b] | 43,342 | 30.5 | | |
| Municipalities[c] | 21,336 | 15.0 | | |
| Social Security[d] | 3,080 | 2.2 | Social Security | 2.2 |
| Mutuals[e] | 1,889 | 1.3 | Mutuals | 1.3 |
| Private[f] | 29,173 | 20.5 | Private | 20.5 |

[a]   More than 5 agencies.
[b]   21 provinces.
[c]   9 municipalities have hospitals; but the number with health services may be larger (only OP facilities).
[d]   Around 60 agencies.
[e]   More than 1,400 agencies.
[f]   Private offices of physicians, proprietary hospitals, voluntary agencies.

Although theoretically it would be easy to assume that the government should be able to gain control of all these resources, in practice this is very difficult to do, not only because of constitutional problems related to the federal organization of the country, but also because of the fact that each system has completely different patterns of salaries and wages, fringe benefits, and unions for their staffs. It has proven to be enormously difficult to convince union leaders to agree to standardize these different patterns of benefits, and for political reasons it is very unlikely that it will be done by governmental officers who are very concerned about the power of unions.

Another way of determining the relative importance of the subsystems is to look at the proportion of the population receiving coverage from each of them. It is doubtful, however, that the data available on this subject are accurate; we have only estimates. Table 12 shows them. As we can see, we are making important assumptions here. First, the governmental services are covering the entire population of the country; this is theoretically true, but it is wise to suspect that it is not happening. Second, the population covered by Social Security is, in fact, receiving all the services it needs, but there are important indications that they are not capable of providing these services. In fact, they collect dues and offer a certain level of medical care, but a study of the facilities (Abadie 1969) shows that they can serve only a fraction of the membership (50 percent in the case of railroad social security).

Table 12. Population covered by and utilization of medical services in Argentina and greater Buenos Aires in 1968 (by subsystem*)

|  | Government | Social security | Mutuals | Private |
|---|---|---|---|---|
| Population covered (estimates for the country) | 23 million | 3 million | 1.7 million | ? |
| Utilization of services in greater Buenos Aires in percent |  |  |  |  |
| Hospitalization | 29 | 6 | 23 | 42 |
| Outpatient | 16 | 9 | 6 | 69 |

* Utilization of services; data from Morbidity Survey, CIASP, 1967 (sample of population living in the greater Buenos Aires area, encompassing the city of Buenos Aires (federal capital) and 18 municipalities of the province of Buenos Aires).

Of course, this happens because almost everybody is shopping around for medical care and because, very often, on a family basis, there is a curious phenomenon of multiple coverage. This can happen if a given family has two or three working members, each of whom is covered by a different system, e.g. SS or mutual, as well as by government services, which, in theory, cover everyone. It is not unusual for such a family to pay also for some private coverage.

Many more things can be said and discussed about a system of such complexity. The selection of some specific points, as we are doing here, is only a reflection of the particular set of values that we have; the reader must be aware of this. But even through a biased analysis — if there is such a thing as an objective analysis — the reader will have an idea of how a pluralistic system fosters inequality in the medical care services provided to the population. The existence of many systems means more than just many different buildings; it also means different patterns of coverage, different services provided, and different fees or dues charged. To all these, we must add the factor of geographical maldistribution of facilities. These inequalities do not happen just by chance. As is the case throughout Latin America, almost independently of the modality of medical care, certain groups have more benefits and coverage. They usually are the white-collar workers, security and armed forces, high-level government bureaucrats, and also certain highly skilled blue-collar workers in certain important areas such as railroads and petroleum. So, the best paid employees and workers are the ones with the most benefits. But the important thing is that the costs of these services are not borne by them; in a good number of cases, these services have a huge deficit due to a combination of factors, not the least important of which is that they have a tendency to pay on a fee-for-service basis. These deficits are covered by grants, either by the government or by enterprises; the cost of these grants is passed on to the general population through a regressive tax system or through an increase in prices for services and goods.

But maybe the most astonishing consequence of the pluralistic system, as it is in Argentina, is that it fosters the practice of private medicine and encourages a pattern of differential quality. This is not a simple matter to explain, but we will attempt to do it because it is one of the most fascinating things about the system and it proves how a system can be distorted by a few powerful groups with vested interests.

1.   Although SS/mutuals are, at first glance, a strong competing force to private medicine, the fact is that they are also introducing to what we can call "pay medicine" a good number of people previously served by the free governmental services, so there is no way to know if the number of people paying, either by fees or prepayments, is increasing or decreasing. Another very important fact is that many SS/mutuals do not have their own services; they make contact with physicians for ambulatory care in their private offices, and they rent a given number of beds, or even entire floors, in the proprietary hospitals. This pattern is providing physicians and especially private hospitals with a fixed income which the hospitals then use to cover overhead expenses and to cope with periods of very few private clients.

2.   The modality of physicians' work is crucial to understanding how this operates:

a.   In government services the physician works for nothing or for a very nominal salary; only after long years of hospital work does the physician's remuneration become, to some degree, important. The government service physician works a couple of hours in the morning.

b.   In SS/mutuals the physicians work either under salary again, or, much more significantly, by capitation or by a fee for service, with the member bringing a voucher that the SS/mutual will redeem afterward. In the latter case, the physician can — and does in many cases — increase the number of consultations per disease episode, or resorting to a more direct unlawful approach, ask for more than one voucher for each visit or consultation. In both cases, it is very difficult to prove misconduct, and the patient rarely complains. But in both cases — salary or fee-for-service — the important point is that the physician is working on a part-time basis, often in his own private office. It is very important to note that physicians try very hard to obtain part-time work. In another context, the reader must remember that in the Chilean system, there is a rule forbidding physicians to work with the National Health Service for more than a maximum of six hours a day.

3. This pattern of part-time salaried or capitation work for SS/mutuals and government has the effect of allowing the physicians to have some fixed income, while they try to increase their private clientele. In Argentina, the competition for this is extremely high; just remember that in the city of Buenos Aires, there is one physician for every 193 people. For young physicians the acquisition of a private practice is the result of many years of hard work. When the clientele begins to grow, it is not difficult to imagine what services will suffer first from the problems of a very busy physician: free hospital, salaried jobs, capitation jobs, fee-for-service for SS/mutuals (usually lower fees than for private patients), in that order. Some years ago somebody coined the expression "taxi physicians" for this type of professional.

4. Of course, if our prototypical physician is working in an area with a medical school, it is very likely that he will have an honorary appointment on the faculty or in a teaching hospital. That helps in several ways: it is a source of clients (patients learn very quickly to differentiate between "qualities" of medical care without any sophistication in research techniques); it is a source of prestige; and also, it is a source of self-consolation because with this appointment, a physician can view himself as a practitioner of "scientific medicine" and not as the assembly line worker that in fact he is. That this picture is not out of touch with reality is not easy to prove, but we have some data to support our point (see Table 13).

Table 13. Modality of physicians' income in three areas of Argentina in 1970 (in percent)

| Modality | Buenos Aires | Tres de Febrero | Rural Buenos Aires |
|---|---|---|---|
| Fee for service | 20 | 26 | 23 |
| Fee for service and salary | 71 | 67 | 77 |
| Salary | 9 | 7 | — |
| N | 556[a] | 189[b] | 161[b] |

[a]  Sample of physicians living in the City of Buenos Aires.
[b]  All physicians living in these two areas.

5.   This particular system has another effect, which is that the patient soon discovers how to sort out the different kinds of expenses in medical care. The result is that outpatients' visits are, in the vast majority of the cases, handled by the private sector of medicine; the most simple cases requiring hospitalization will be handled by private hospitals (almost all of them proprietary hospitals) or SS/mutual hospitals. If the hospitalization is very long or expensive, it will be handled by SS/mutual and also by public hospitals. In some cases, the most complicated cases (as determined both by cost and the need of equipment) may be handled by the public subsystem. So, the public subsystem acts very much as a sort of buffer for the private sector; many physicians even advise their patients to get free clinical analysis and prescriptions from public hospitals to which the physicians have access because they probably work there; the patient saves, and then he is still able to pay the fee to the doctor. And everybody else pays ....

## CONCLUSION

We think that we have shown some of the special characteristics of a pluralistic system, and how it seems to be exactly the opposite of everything that is expected from a system of medical care. In this particular case, we have a country without a health policy, without planning, with a distorted distribution of resources, and with what seems to be an unavoidable inequality that is giving more and more to the ones that do not need it.

Two things come to mind in such a situation. First, has some kind of reaction toward the system arisen at some point in history? Here, we have a very important shortcoming: we cannot claim an exhaustive search of the literature and of all the documents produced since the beginning of this century in medicine and public health. But we can say that, despite the fact that some people and health administrations did produce a lot of documents and even books about public health, hospitals, communicable diseases, and also about the connection between disease and certain social conditions, one is justified in thinking that these documents and monographs have had very little effect on the system. The fact is that new systems, like social security, have been created to achieve more equality, to destroy financial barriers, and the like. But they have been twisted into just a little more than servants of a subsystem of private medicine, that is limping, but still moving with the aid of crutches like SS/mutuals and public hospitals.[1]

This should not be a surprise for anybody; most of the high ranking officers at governmental health services, social security, mutuals, and private proprietary hospitals are themselves part-time physicians, striving for a private clientele in their "spare time." It will be extremely interesting to try to note the potential conflicts of interest arising from such manifold positions. Of course, the situation is even more complicated because the power is not just in the hands of the physicians; they are also pawns in a more elaborate game that involves international drug and hospital supply companies. We cannot go into this topic in the present paper, but it is something to keep in mind.

The second point is the almost unbelievable prestige with which the traditional practice of medicine is regarded by the population and even by political leaders, whom one would expect to have a more critical view of the medical drama. In this sense, and only as a cue, it is very interesting to note that the Socialist Party in Argentina was founded by a physician and that up to one-third of the leadership of the party was in the hands of physicians. Perusing the two main books of one of these leaders, we found that the description of surgical procedures covers a good proportion of the books, but the description of the system of medical care in which he professes to believe only takes a handful of pages, without substance, platitudes incapable of translation into action. Another good example is the medical advisers of unions and mutuals, who again are physicians with good private clienteles, with "scientific" prestige, and good political connections. On the other hand, the public health movement, so energetic at the beginning of the sixties, has diluted itself in a fratricidal fight for the few available positions with pay and prestige, and we take our part of the blame for this.

How is it possible to change the system? Here we run into a matter of very strong ideological principles. Some people think that only revolution, a general social revolution, can achieve the necessary changes. We confess to be out of tune with the prevailing mode of the times; we prefer some sort of evolutionary movement, with very clear social objectives, within a basic philosophy of humanism in a just society. However, the components may be very similar, and we would like to mention just some of them:

[1] It is important for the reader to note that we are not including in this analysis some late developments in 1972 toward an increase in coordination in Social Security organizations. Also, we are not including here the last statements by the new health administration of the recently inaugurated constitutional government (see La Nación 1973).

1.   A very strong policy for the training of medical and paramedical personnel, encompassing not only changes in curricula, but also in the distribution and allocation of responsibilities and areas of domain with respect to the patient and the community. A sort of uniform public health career will encompass all health workers and allow for mobility between different levels; on-the-job training should replace a substantive part of academic training. The principle of an open university should be reconciled with the fact that we are producing far more physicians than we need. A process of continuing education should be adopted, with the universities going to the field.

2.   A carefully staged process to achieve at least a minimum of equality in the services; for that, several steps are needed:

a.   To put all health institutions under a set of regulations for achieving a minimum level of quality of medical care; this should encompass manpower, procedures, and equipment.

b.   To create some sort of corporation for the management of all hospitals and health institutions providing services to the public. The corporation will have a centralized normative system and a decentralized operation, with several regions in connection with the following item.

c.   To regionalize all health services on the basis of several criteria, e.g. urban-rural composition; social, economic, and geographical condition; cultural patterns; etc. Each region should have a good deal of independence in management of resources, budget, planning, and manpower policies. Different levels of health centers and hospitals should be planned with a careful, two-way flow of patients, manpower, and information.

3.   To adopt a strong philosophy toward preventive medicine in all the levels of the health system and to adopt the family as the unit of prevention and care.

4.   To foster the full-time appointment of physicians on the Health System network; this will discourage the double standard practice.

5.   We do not think that it is necessary to take measures against private medicine; only to establish controls so that physicians comply with certain rules for a minimum of quality and that they offer at least the same basic preventive medicine for certain groups. But the private subsystem should be self-supported, and the physicians in it should not be allowed to have positions at certain levels in the governmental system. Group practice within government institutions with fees and prepayment dues going into pools and no difference between paying patients and social security patients may be a dream, but we do not think that this is impossible to achieve.

6.   All of the population should be under a system of social security for

health with some differences in the collections and administration of dues, but with no differences in the services provided. The nonworking population should be covered either under unemployment benefits or disability insurance. Certain groups which are very difficult to cover, such as domestic workers and rural workers, may need special arrangements; nevertheless, the trend should be toward equality of services.

7.   Special arrangements would have to be provided for extremely dispersed rural population; even with a good regionalization program, certain people will be outside the reach of a "regular" system. For this case, the use of community health workers and visiting nurses probably would be, at least, a solution. The training for these types of health workers should be on a local basis with periodical on-the-job updating at rural hospitals. All these things are not new at all; we know perfectly well that they are just procedures and techniques. The most important thing is to put them in the context of a general plan for achieving a given level of well-being and social security for the population. This plan should have a good balance between techniques and politics. A basic philosophy of equality should underlie the health services offered, which should aim at making the most important difference between the national system and private medicine aspects of certain types of luxury accomodations, without relation to the quality of medical care. A very important point is to reassess the position and role of the physician in the context of genuine teamwork, which should stress responsibility for all members. The issue of consumer control should be advanced with meaningful and working mechanisms, which we must confess we do not know about. Perhaps the most difficult thing would be to have a system extremely critical of itself, through a complex overlapping of evaluation procedures that would stress adaptation and innovation to new conditions and needs. We do not think that all these ideas are out of place in a volume about utopias.

## REFERENCES

ABADIE, J. P.
   1969   Problemas cruciales en el desenvolvimiento de una obra social. *Medicina Administrativa* 3:5.
ABADIE, J. P., C. H. CANITROT, *et al.*
   1967   *Encuesta de morbilidad, resultados principales*, Informe 5. Buenos Aires: CIASP.
ABEL-SMITH, A.
   1965   The major pattern of financing and organization of medical services that have emerged in other countries. *Medical Care* 3(1).

BLANCO, J., A. GARCÍA BATES
1968   Analisis de los Recursos de Enfermeria para Atencion Médica. *Medicina Administrativa* 2(1). Buenos Aires: CIASP.

CANITROT, C. H.
1970   Un panorama poco alentador. *Medicina Administrativa* 4 (5–6).

CANITROT, C. H., J. P. ABADIE, J. A. MERA
1968–1969   Bases para la formulación de una política de atención medica (in two parts). *Medicina Administrativa* 2(5), 3(1–2).

CAPLOW, T., K. FINSTERBUSCH
n.d.   "*Development rank: a new method of rating national development.*" Unpublished manuscript.

CASTRO, J. O.
1962   *Los maestros: Emilio R. Coni.* Revista de Salud Pública 2. La Plata.

CENTRO LATINOAMERICANO DE ADMINISTRACIÓN MÉDICA
1971   "*How physicians use medical care: first and second preliminary reports.*" Unpublished manuscript.

ESCARDO, F.
1959   *Eduardo Wilde.* Buenos Aires: S. Rueda.

FELD, SIMON, *editor*
1965   *Project DISABO.* Buenos Aires: Ministry of Health.

FELD, S., C. H. RIZZI
1971   *Modelos de mortalidad proporcional agrupada.* Buenos Aires: Ministerio de Bienestar Social.

FERNÁNDEZ DE BUSSO, N. P.
1968   Disponibilidad y requerimiento de recursos médicos. *Medicina Administrativa* 2(1). Buenos Aires: CIASP.

FURTADO, C.
1970   *Economic development of Latin America.* London: Cambridge University Press.

GRANA, D. O., R. H. PISTORIO
1968   Capacidad de camas para atención médica. *Medicina Administrativa* 2(1). Buenos Aires: CIASP.

LA NACIÓN
1973   "La reforma sanitaria para todo el país." *La Nación,* June 23. Buenos Aires.

MERA, J. A.
1968   Características de la organización de la atención médica. *Medicina Administrativa* 2(1). Buenos Aires: CIASP.
1971   *Problemas y Perspectivas de la Atencion Médica en la Argentina.* Criterio 1624. Buenos Aires.

MINISTERIO DE BIENESTAR SOCIAL
1972   *Las obras sociales en la argentina* (second edition). Buenos Aires: Instituto Nacional de Obras Sociales.

MORSE, R. M.
1965   Urbanization in Latin America. *Latin American Research Review* 1(1).

PAN AMERICAN HEALTH ORGANIZATION
1970   *Health Conditions in the Americas.* Scientific Publication 207. Washington, D.C.

POLÉMICA
1970  El número de médicos en el País: problema o solución? *Medicina Administrativa* 4(3). Buenos Aires: CIASP.

PROVENZANO, S. D.
1968  Sistemas de financiación de la atención médica en el país. *Medicina Administrativa* 2(1). Buenos Aires: CIASP.

REPETTO, N.
1955  *Mi paso por la política.* Buenos Aires: S. Rueda.
1956  *Mi paso por la medicina.* Buenos Aires: S. Rueda.

ROEMER, M. I.
1963  *Medical care in Latin America.* Washington, D.C.: Pan American Union.
1964  Medical care and social class in Latin America. *Milbank Memorial Fund Quarterly* 47.

SBARRA, N.
1963  *Realidad sanitaria nacional.* Boletín de la Asociación Argentina de la Salud Pública 1.
1963  *Los maestros: Eduardo Wilde.* Revista de Salud Pública, No. 5. La Plata.

SECRETARÍA DE SALUD PÚBLICA
1971  *Indicadores de salud y de nivel de vida.* Departamento de Estadísticas de Salud, Serie 8, No. 2, Buenos Aires.

SEGOVIA, J.
1969  La salud como sistema social. *Medicina Administrativa* 3.

VERONELLI, J. C., N. RODRÍGUEZ CAMPOAMOR
1971  *La politica sanitaria nacional.* Cuaderno de Salud Pública, No. 6/7. (Escuela de Salud Pública de la Universidad de Buenos Aires.)

UNITED NATIONS
1970  *Social change and development policy in Latin America.* Economic Commission for Latin America. New York.
1971  *U.N. Yearbook, 1970.* 22nd edition. New York.

WORLD HEALTH ORGANIZATION
1968–1969  *World health statistics annual,* volumes 1 and 3.

# Environmental Health: Hong Kong Squatters and Engels' Remarks on the Housing Question

FRANK KEHL

In 1872 Engels wrote three articles attacking bourgeois solutions to the extremely severe housing problem of industrializing Western Europe. Recent discussion on how to deal with urban squatters in Third World cities has tended, almost point for point, to recapitulate the bourgeois "solutions" proposed a century ago. If they did not work for Europe when it was industrializing, can their fate be any better for the industrializing Third World today?

Taken at its face value, capitalist, colonial Hong Kong's resettlement policy would seem to give the lie to Engels: about 40 percent of the urban population lives in public housing, one and one half million squatters and their offspring have been resettled in the postwar period. Yet the absolute number of squatters in Hong Kong has remained constant for about the last two decades; resettled squatters are living at median densities of less than 20 square feet per person — 15 square feet per person below the Hong Kong government's own legal minimum of 35 square feet per person — and while it bankrolls budget-surpluses in London every year, the Hong Kong government says it has no intentions of ever resettling all squatters.

Whom does the Hong Kong bourgeoisie prove right: Engels or his bourgeois opponents? And what are the implications for theories of squatting and urbanization under capitalism or neocolonialism?

Let us begin to answer these questions by seeing how the nineteenth century European bourgeoisie proposed to solve their contemporary urban "housing question." (Recall that the scene that they were dealing with was rather like the squalid London of Dickens' descriptions and the smoke-belching, overcrowded, dilapidated Manchester of Engels' own

*Condition of the working class in England*).

In his articles published in English as *The housing question*, Engels ([1872]: 50–75) lists seven bourgeois solutions:

1. Transfer property in dwellings to the hands of the workers, i.e. make the worker into a capitalist;
2. Introduce the cottage system into the countryside;
3. Make the workers' barracks in the towns as tolerable as possible; (By "barracks" Engels seems to mean high density urban tenements.)
4. Establish working class colonies *near* the towns;
5. Have employers or factory owners build workers' housing; or have them assist workers to build their *own* housing by providing land and advancing building capital;
6. Establish cooperative building societies of a self-help, philanthropic, or speculative nature;
7. Have the state intervene in various ways:
a. by eliminating legislation and administration that accentuate the housing shortage, e.g. restrictions over the building trades;
b. by preventing narrow-minded individualism from reproducing the evil or causing it anew, e.g. by inspecting and closing down buildings which are unsanitary or dilapidated;
c. by using positive intervention to remedy the shortage to the most comprehensive extent, e.g. by granting loans or building "barracks."

After analyzing in turn each of these "solutions" to the housing problem Engels concludes: "In reality the bourgeoisie has only one method... This method is called Haussmann" ([1872]: 74).

He describes what he means by the term, which is the name of a Parisian city-planner of the time: "...scandalous alleys and lanes disappear ... but they appear immediately somewhere else and often in the immediate neighborhood" ([1872]: 75). In other words, all the "solutions" really come down to one solution: continually producing the problem anew. (In our own experience in the United States we might think of "urban renewal by urban removal.")

Now let's turn to the postwar Hong Kong scene and see how the Hong Kong bourgeoisie and the Hong Kong government recapitulated these century-old solutions in dealing with squatters and shantytowns in Hong Kong. We will see that all but one of the solutions obviously failed.

But first I shall give a few statistics to help the reader get oriented on Hong Kong. Upon the defeat of Japan in 1945, Hong Kong's population was about 600,000. It rapidly grew, attaining its prewar level of about 1.8 million by 1948–1949. It went over the two-million mark in 1950 with the influx of still more labor migrants from the countryside as well as landlords, capitalists, and KMT elements fleeing China because of Chiang Kai-shek's defeat in the civil war. Between 1950 and 1951 there was a net outflow from Hong Kong back to China AND THE BORDER WAS EFFECTIVELY CLOSED BY THE BRITISH TO FURTHER IMMIGRATION FROM CHINA. From 1951 onward, the population curve has risen fairly steadily, owing overwhelmingly to natural increase — not to illegal immigration, as the purple press would have us believe. Hong Kong's current population is about four million.

The squatters referred to in this paper are usually occupiers of wooden and tin shacks on land that doesn't belong to them, mainly in the urban areas. There is no intrinsic connection between squatters, postwar immigrants into Hong Kong from its rural hinterland, and what have been called "refugees from Communism."

The Hong Kong dollar is pegged at one-sixth of a United States dollar.

I shall take Engels' solutions in turn and see how they apply to Hong Kong.

1. People familiar with Hong Kong society would be rather surprised at the use of this solution because housing and resettlement, squatter control and government intervention have usually been couched by the Hong Kong government in the terminology of a neutral, classless, urban planner's necessity, rather than as bourgeois ideology. For example, it was said that squatters had to be cleared from Hong Kong if there was to be growth and economic development because the land they were occupying was a choking ring strangling the city. But some squatter perches would never be needed for urban development, therefore it was uneconomical and unnecessary to try to set out to clear all squatters as such. The *absence* of any government rhetoric about "the sacred inviolability of property," or the "rape of trespass" has led some to believe that completely rational, non-ideological, neutral, non-bourgeois considerations motivated the Hong Kong government's decisions in dealing with the housing question.

In the government publication, *Hong Kong annual report* (1948: 7) we read:

Thousands of people who in more settled times would have a house, flat or cubicle are living in small, overcrowded spaces or even in crude squatter's huts and shacks without water or sanitation. Such squatters' colonies are gradually being eliminated and displaced squatters are being permitted to build for themselves on several prepared sites a hut of standard design. Furthermore, arrangements have been made for the alienation by private treaty of land to persons for the purpose of building on it their own homes.

What the government was referring to were the original Cottage Areas or Cottage Resettlement Areas.

2.   I will take up solution 2 with solution 4.

3.   Ameliorating "barracks" in the towns. Because of the rapidity of migration into Hong Kong after the war, tenements that had not been bombed out were very quickly packed beyond capacity, and bourgeoning shantytowns quickly became the focus of any attempts at amelioration.

The topmost concerns on the government's part were ameliorating the problems of bad hygiene and endemic fires in shantytowns. In January 1950, 20,000 persons were made homeless in one squatter fire in the Kowloon City area:

This fire drew the attention of the public in a dramatic fashion to the fact that these large squatter areas were becoming a menace to the Colony as a whole. They not only presented a serious and increasing fire hazard, but the sanitary conditions in them were so appalling that they were also a threat to the health of a large part of the urban areas of Hong Kong and Kowloon. Moreover, every squatter fire was a costly business to the taxpayer since it resulted in considerable Government expenditure on the necessary emergency relief measures including the free feeding of thousands of persons for several months [with hindsight] (*Annual departmental report* [Commissioner for Resettlement] 1955–1956:1).

What were the attempts to ameliorate living conditions in existing shantytowns? One possible method of amelioration was for government to cut fire breaks or fire lanes through the densest part of some shantytowns. Another method was to cement the sides and boardwalk the top of the *nullahs* [steams or sewers] that oozed and gurgled through squatter areas. In fact, latrines were installed in squatter areas, as well as water standpipes. For instance, as of 1971 in the squatter area where I did research, there were two and one-half standpipes and a dozen and one-half latrines for a population of approximately 2100 people. The *nullah* was neither cemented nor covered over by the government.

2.   and 4.   Establish working-class colonies in the nonurban areas or *near* the urban areas. Because of its particular configuration and its "city-state" political economy, Hong Kong has no countryside hinterland as we usually understand it. Insofar as this is the case, the second and fourth solutions could never have been a live alternative. The Cottage Resettlement Estates of the early 1950's were again the Hong Kong Government solution.

The *Hong Kong annual report* (1951:82) voiced intentions:

A plan was prepared for the resettlement of these [300,000 squatters] by degrees in a number of areas, of which 16 are permanent [cement and stone] bungalow towns and three were designed as semi-permanent [wood] hut settlements the inhabitants of which would gradually move out into workers housing schemes (or back to China when conditions there permit).

[In] both types of settlement planned lay-outs are being followed in the construction of dwellings, each row of which is being separated by fire lanes. Water and sanitation are provided and arrangements made for policing and administration.

All these "bungalow towns" — Cottage Resettlement Areas — were planned for varying distances beyond the urban periphery. The closest was Homantin on an unused wedge of hills between both built-up coasts of the Kowloon peninsula. Chuk Yuen was to be built up the side of Lion Rock hill, the crest line of which is today the urban limit of Kowloon. There was Chai Wan on a hill slope in the eastern most extremity of Hong Kong island.

In these early years of dealing with the squatter housing problem, there was much loud heralding of this solution. A Chinese language newspaper headline of the period breathlessly exclaimed: "Urban Services Department Chairman Barnett reports rough outlines of various resettlement areas; residents will have the feeling of living peacefully and working happily" (*Wah Kiuh Yat Bo*, February 11, 1952). In the *Hong Kong annual report* (1953:114) a picture caption of one of these areas waxed elegiac: "The resettlement areas are miniature villages equipped with schools... as well as other essential services."

One of the things these areas were not equipped with, however, was employment. Newspapers of the period served up a steady fare of government attempts to entice small factories into these out-of-the-way, often roadless "miniature villages."

The *Ta Kung Pao* (May 23, 1952) voiced peoples' complaints that Ngau Tau Kok was remote and inaccessible, in addition to which getting water was a severe problem. The cottage areas almost by definition were beyond the existing urban network of mains and sewers.

It seems that [contractor's] speculation had become a problem, as evidenced by an article in *Chen Pao Yeh Kan*, June 15, 1954:

Government decides to investigate corruption in [Cottage] Resettlement Areas to eliminate black market for selling and buying houses. Officials are kind and easily approachable. Total reforms to improve workability.

But it was the earlier cited *Ta Kung Pao* article of May 23, 1952, that noted what was the real capper: "There are new buildings in the [Cottage] Resettlement Areas but if you have no money, it's still very difficult to have a room." (The going rate as of the year 1954 seemed to be 1600 Hong Kong dollars to buy or 20 to 40 Hong Kong dollars to rent a Cottage Resettlement unit, a price beyond the reach of the vast majority of working-class families [*Sing Toa Yat Po*, April 19, 1954, "Problem of Resettlement"].)

I have dwelt at relative length on this "solution" because it is the solution currently utilized by the ruling class of many Third World countries: to export squatters back, out of the city, part way in suburban or semirural colonies. But since there is no water, transportation, or employment there, the "solution" must be solved. ITS solution is: entice factories out with low tax or permit fees; install a road or two. If this does not come to be, ex-shantytown dwellers will probably drift back into the city again; if it does come to be, a black market and corruption in buildings (and land, in places other than Hong Kong) is likely to develop; speculators or wealthier non-squatters will buy out the cottage of the ex-squatter; the former squatter will return to squatting back in the city.

But what percentage of the urban shantytown population can take advantage of such a scheme in the first place?

5.　Employers build workers' housing or assist workers to build their own housing by providing land and advancing building capital. It is Chinese commercial tradition that small factory workers eat and sleep in the shop: on the floor, on benches, on work tables, on cots. This applies only to men however, not their families. Also, it is not universally practiced. In a way similar to that followed to entice factories to the Cottage Resettlement Areas by tax rake-offs, government attempted to get already existing factories to build workers' housing in the areas around them.

Government is prepared to sell land by private treaty at concessionary rates to factory proprietors and other employers for the erection of living quarters for their employees. Over the years, many industrial firms with large numbers of workers have taken advantage of this concession to build staff quarters and dormitories (*Annual departmental report* [Commissioner of Labor] 1966–1967: 39).

In fact, the only employers who ever took up the offer even to a certain extent were the very largest, usually foreign owned and operated enterprises: Taikoo Dockyard, Hong Kong Electric, Kowloon Wharf and Godown, etc.

At a late date in the period that interests us, the 1970 Labor Department annual report lists seventeen firms as providing accommodation to their workers. Though it is not actually stated, we get from the context that these firms are to be considered the front runners. They range from the British-owned Taikoo Dockyard, "pioneer of low cost housing for employees," which houses 9416 persons, to the British American Tobacco company with 322 persons. The median for the seventeen firms falls between one and two thousand. Taken together, they total approximately 30,000 employees and their families. In comparison, the same year Lo Fu Ngam, one of the smaller of Hong Kong's resettlement estates, had a population of 35,536 (*Annual departmental report* [Commissioner for Resettlement] 1970–71:41).

Perhaps no more than 1 percent of Hong Kong's manufacturing firms ever embarked on ANY sort of workers' housing schemes. The numbers housed probably never exceeded 2 to 3 percent of Hong Kong's total population, if that, and they were certainly fewer when the housing crisis was most severe.

6. Cooperative building societies, based on self-help, philanthropy, or speculation.

In the *Annual departmental report* of the Commissioner for Resettlement (1955–1956:3) we read:

In September 1952, another solution [sic] was tried when a non-profit making organization was formed to build cottages in resettlement areas. This Hong Kong Settlers Housing Corporation, the board of which consisted of public-spirited business and professional men, was partially financed by Government and partly from funds subscribed by the public. It eventually built over 1,555 cottages which will become the property of their occupants after monthly hire-purchase [installment] payments have been made for seven years.

In addition to this undertaking, there were also the nonprofit-making Hong Kong Model Housing Society, which was to build 400 units (*Hong Kong annual report* 1951:76), and the Hong Kong Housing Society, which was set up expressly for better-off workers and petty-bourgeois families.

Philanthropy came in with the contribution of a hundred cottages at Tung Tau in 1954 by Wu Man-Fu, the creator of the Tiger Balm financial empire (*Sing Toa Yat Po*, March 19, 1954) and with the chipping in of various foreign Christian groups (e.g. Catholics and Methodists). Needless to say, all these contributions combined made a dent on the housing problem that ran from small to minuscule — though they too were loudly heralded at the time.

From at least the mid-fifties there have existed "building management committees" in high-rise buildings, each unit of which is separately owned by members of the lower strata of the petty bourgeoisie. Some of the owners are occupiers, others are not and use the unit for speculative purposes. These "middle class" management committees only take over the affairs of the high-rise after it has been built by a big-time developer.

They are financially too limited to undertake the construction of buildings. Commenting on the housing problems of the petty bourgeoisie, the government-appointed Finance of Home Ownership Committee warned: "There is a pressing need for an Agency to be instituted to provide loan facilities for members of the middle income groups [incomes in the range of 900 to 2,000 Hong Kong dollars a month] to purchase their own homes" (*Report of the finance of home ownership committee* 1964). The Hong Kong bourgeoisie had enough problems figuring out how to make owner-occupiers out of the petty bourgeoisie in an anarchic real estate context. It further admitted the insolubility by these solutions of the much vaster working class housing problem.

7. Direct state intervention: eliminating legislation and administration that accentuate the housing shortage; preventing narrow-minded individualism reproducing the evil, e.g. closing down buildings which are unsanitary or dilapidated; using positive intervention to remedy the shortages to the most comprehensive extent, e.g. granting loans or building high-density urban tenements.

What did the Hong Kong bourgeoisie do to validate Engels' analysis? First and foremost, they tolerated squatting, in spite of the fact that squatting trespassed on Crown Land, or violated certain tenancy leases on agricultural land, or contravened innumerable terms of the building code. This toleration has been institutionalized and reinstitutionalized at several points in the two-decade period we are concerned with. It took the form of setting up a Squatter Control Unit that surveyed all huts existing in the urban area at a certain time and having that unit paint the dimension of each hut beside the doorway. This procedure was meant to "freeze" the number and size of urban squatter huts. If anything was added after the paint went on, it could be summarily demolished. The fact that this "freezing" had to be done more than once, and *more* structures tolerated, indicates that this "solution" had a perennial quality to it.

The building code standard of 35 square feet per person has rarely if ever been enforced in the private sector tenements. As we shall see, it is also honored in the breach in public housing. To the best of my knowledge no tenement building in postwar Hong Kong has ever been closed down for lack of sanitation. There have been, however, innumerable demolitions for reasons of dilapidation and imminent danger of collapse. However, rather than "preventing" narrow-minded individualism — i.e. slumlordism — as Engels suggests, the demolitions seem tightly linked with a steady move by Hong Kong's "broad-minded" real estate developers to turn prewar tenements and tenement districts into office buildings, luxury hotels, and other kinds of extensions of the central business district (CBD). Elliot (1971:9) caustically comments: "When the building boom ceased in 1956, the buildings also ceased to become dangerous, no doubt out of consideration to landlords."

On Christmas Eve 1953, Hong Kong's biggest squatter fire ever burned down the homes of 53,000 persons in Shek Kip Mei. In earlier years there had also been similar squatter fires of considerable size.

The contradictions of dawdling on the housing question had become too great for the bourgeoisie. Emergency relief alone for such fires ran into millions of dollars. And emergency relief pays neither rent nor interest: it is pure expense. Realizations such as this galvanized the bourgeoisie to take action. They set about tackling the squatter housing problem with a degree of seriousness previously unmatched. The speed with which they had multistory resettlements blocks built surprised even themselves (*Annual departmental report* [Commissioner for Resettlement] 1955–1956:6). Their alacrity was due to the realization that the old "solutions" were empty, and that a massive capital outlay of government funds had to be made to provide SOME form of high-density, fire-proof, low-rent, close-to-places-of-work housing for large numbers of Hong Kong's workers then living in the streets or in shantytowns. If the government did not get into housing in a big way, its treasury would roll down the hill like the rock of Sisyphus every time there was a major squatter fire.

The government DID move into high-density, low-rent housing for Hong Kong's working people. But did this do the trick? Did it solve the housing question? The answer is no. It neither resettled all the people living in shantytowns or in huts on rooftops, nor did it provide viable housing conditions for the majority of those living in the high-rise resettlement blocks or in other government aided housing. A look at the most current statistics tells the story. In April 1971 the total authorized population of resettlement estates was 1,156,102 (*Annual departmental report* [Commissioner for Resettlement] 1971:41).

This represents basically ex-squatters and their offspring. As for squatters under the jurisdiction of the Resettlement Department (excluding squatters in the semi-rural areas under the jurisdiction of the New Territories Administration), the figure was 329,700 (*Annual departmental report* [Commissioner for Resettlement] 1971:6). Recall that after a government survey in March of 1951, it was estimated that there were "about 300,000 squatters living in 47,000 huts" (*Hong Kong annual report* 1951:82).

A staunch defender of the Hong Kong bourgeoisie might immediately raise three objections. First he would be quick to point out that the

392,000 figure has been steadily dropping from the peak year of 1964 when squatters in the urban area numbered "over 600,000... in surveyed squatter areas or rooftops" (*Annual departmental report* [Commissioner for Resettlement] 1963–64:2). This was during the building boom when tenements were so prone just to "fall down."

Considerable evidence has now accumulated that shows a direct relation between overcrowding in tenements or their demolition, and an increase in squatting (Hopkins 1971; Kehl 1969; *Report of the 1963 working party on government policies and practices with regard to squatters, resettlement, and government low cost housing*).

While attention quite justifiably had been focused on the poor conditions of shanytown housing, the overcrowding of tenements, especially rent-controlled prewar tenements, was of such magnitude that even without a "building boom" in the CBD, young families were being squeezed out of the tenements and into squatter shacks. This high density (crowding) and high rents in tenements continue to operate in creating squatters since the building boom was shown in 1967, when 20,000 people invaded a site and squatted at Tai Wo Hau. Over 70 percent of them came from tenements, in adjacent Tsuen Wan and Shum Po.

The second defense that our defender of the Hong Kong bourgeoisie might make is that all this may be true for the past but the March 1971 decennial census shows that the picture is not so bleak at least where squatting is concerned. Instead of the 392,000 squatters in the urban areas estimated by the Resettlement Department, the census showed only 188,000 persons living in "roof shacks," "temporary structures," and "derelict boats," i.e. in various forms of squatter shacks (*South China Morning Post*, June 9, 1971, "Shocks for Government in analysis of census data").

"You see," the defender would say, "the housing problem IS being solved! That's the lowest number of squatters since the immigration influx of the late 1940's." However if you analyze the population figures of people living in shacks in BOTH the urban areas AND the rural New Territories, the Hong-Kong-wide total of shantytown dwellers in 1971 is not appreciably different from the figures given for squatters exactly two decades earlier: approximately 375,000 (based on extrapolation of the partial data given in Table 17, *Hong Kong Population and Housing Census* 1971). What IS the key difference is that the squatter shantytown "geographical center of gravity" has shifted farther and farther outward from the CBD in the course of time. Whereas two decades ago the squatter population of the semi-rural New Territories was miniscule, now it is the equal, or almost, of the urban area.

This too is the function of how the Hong Kong bourgeoisie solves the housing problem — mainly by exerting greater squatter control the closer a shantytown is to the CBD; or, conversely, using "permits" to encourage squatters to set up on land not currently needed by the bourgeoisie in the New Territories. As the capitalist-based city expands, it constantly meets its old albatrosses that it had thrown ahead. And when there is no more frontier...? Finally, our bourgeoisie defender might say, perhaps with less gusto than before: "But no matter what you say, there are still 1,156,102 persons living in resettlement estates that didn't have low-rent, fireproof houses in 1951. The problem may not be solved yet, but there's progress!"

Wrong again. We need only to look at the records of "decantation" in resettlement estates to see that the housing question, rather than pressing toward solution, is being created anew ("decantation" is an Orwellian technical term used by the Resettlement Department to describe the program to relieve overcrowding in resettlement estates). The table "Relief of Overcrowding in Resettlement Estates (for the year 1970–1971)" indicates that in 1971 there were 47,839 families in densities below 24 square feet per person.

This is about one-third of all resettlement estate families. It means that each adult in the family (children are counted as half an adult) has the equivalent of less than 4 feet by 6 feet of space in which to live his or her life.

It is not at all surprising to find that the resettlement estates where there is the greatest crowding are those that were built in the mid-1950's at the start of the multistory resettlement block solution. Those with relatively least crowding are the more recently built estates. However, the allotted space on entry — 24 square feet per person — has remained substantially unchanged for all estates, no matter when they were built. The cause for the difference in crowding is to be found in the natural effects of the family cycle over a period of fifteen years, when the bulk of the income residents were still-fertile families already with young children.

Like the dwellers of the superdense tenements before them, these crowded resettlement estate families are given three alternatives: breathe deeply and bear it; rent a cubicle in a private tenement and place part of the family there; or go out and build or buy a squatter shack on a hillside. Those eligible for "decantation" are a minority.

And thus the cycle of crowded and poor housing begins again.

The Hong Kong bourgeoisie has indeed vindicated Engels' century-old analysis that the only solution the bourgeoisie has for the housing of workers is to create the problem anew.

In summation, every bourgeois solution that Engels excoriated a hundred years ago was tried by the Hong Kong bourgeoisie in the postwar period: from band-aid type amelioration efforts and attempts to entice factory owners to build workers' housing to housing societies and grander attempts at establishing workers' cottage colonies. Initially, it was even thought that workers could be made to acquire their own houses in the Cottage Resettlement Estates. Subsequently, only "middle class" families were urged toward the solution of individual home ownership. Simultaneously and in tandem, the solutions were proposed and implemented. Some, like philanthropic donation of housing, were embraced as soon as a would-be donor popped up. Others, like Cottage Resettlement Areas, were rather slowly and minimally implemented over a period of years. None of them made any significant dent in the problem except for high-rise large scale Resettlement Estates, where now possibly one-third of all households are living at densities below 24 square feet per person — and WELL below the government's own legal minimum of 35 square feet per person. It would seem that resettlement estates have become the new tenements; alike in crowding, but lower in rent. The cycle of overcrowding leading to new squatting seems on its second spiral, with squatting and wood-and-tin-shack living in the once rural New Territories now almost the equal of squatting in the more urban parts of Hong Kong.

The significance of the postwar Hong Kong experience with urban squatting is this: it not only proves Engels' Marxist analysis uncannily correct as to how the capitalist mode of production is incapable of solving the need of working people for decent housing, it also proves another whole theory of urban development to be wrong.

The ruling classes and governments of capitalist Third World countries — not to mention their various imported economic and urban planners — have invariably explained their inability to deal with the existence and growth of squalid urban shantytowns by throwing up their hands in soulful despair and saying: "To build decent housing for urban squatters would mean both diverting funds from more productive economic development projects, and adding a further 'pull' on rural out-migration. There is nothing we can do."

But Hong Kong has had:

1.   what in effect amounted to an impermeable border against the rural hinterland — and thus rural immigration — for two decades;

2.   an economy which has had, during those two decades, one of the highest growth rates of any city or country in the world;

3.   about a million-plus squatters and their offspring who, during these two decades, have been moved into government built and owned multi-

story resettlement estates. AND STILL SQUATTER SHANTYTOWNS PERSIST.

Some people might conclude that the "squatter problem," the contemporary form of the nineteenth century "housing question," is for reasons still obscure, insoluble: if even Hong Kong couldn't solve it, that must mean it can't be solved.

Such a conclusion would be wrong. The Hong Kong example shows that "rural push-urban pull" explanations of urban squatting are inadequate. Hong Kong, for all intents and purposes, has been freed from the "debilities" of a backward rural hinterland for two decades and more. It still has squatters and will continue to have them into the foreseeable future. The reason why it still has them is suggested by Engels' analysis of a century ago: bourgeoisie, capitalist "solutions" to the housing problem, no matter their variety or content, all boil down to this — creating the problem anew.

But let us conclude on a note of optimism.

Squatting in the People's Republic of China is beyond the scope of this particular paper. But on the basis of brief observation of eight cities in China in 1971 — as large as Shanghai and as small as Yenan — I can say this: there are no shantytowns in or around Chinese cities. Yet, we know that in 1949 shantytown dwellers formed a significant proportion of the population of China's coastal cities. Accounts about Shanghai are especially explicit on this.

The People's Republic and the Chinese people have managed this feat in urban housing in spite of the devastation bequeathed them by eight years of war, followed by four more years of similarly disruptive civil war, a United States trade blockade, and a Soviet withdrawal of economic aid. These are added burdens that the people of India and Brazil have not had to bear — to mention just two of the biggest Third World countries with severe urban squatter problems. The explanation for this, it seems to me, lies not in the differences of national character of the Brazilian, Indian, or Chinese people, but rather in the fact that the ruling classes of Brazil and India are applying bourgeois "solutions" to those countries' housing problems (and not just to housing problems). In China, following the tradition started by Marx and Engels, the people and their leaders have long since seen through these "solutions" and struggled, with initial success, to work out proletarian solutions to the problems of providing decent housing for workers.

# REFERENCES

*Books*

ELLIOT, ELSIE
  1971   *The avarice, bureaucracy and corruption of Hong Kong*. Hong Kong: Friends Commercial Printing Factory.
ENGELS, FRIEDRICH
n.d. [1872]   *The housing question*. New York: International Publishers. (Originally published as three articles in German for the *Leipzig Volkstaat*, 1872.)
HOPKINS, KEITH, *editor*
  1971   *Hong Kong: the industrial colony*. Kuala Lumpur: Oxford University Press.
KEHL, FRANK
  1969   "Hong Kong squatters: interim report." Unpublished manuscript.

*Other Publications*

*Chen Pao Yeh Kan*, 1954.
*Hong Kong annual report*, 1948, 1951, 1953.
*Hong Kong annual departmental report*, 1966–1967, 1970.
  Commissioner of Labor.
*Hong Kong annual departmental report*, 1955–1956, 1963–1964, 1970–1971.
  Commissioner for Resettlement.
*Hong Kong population and housing census*, 1971.
  Hong Kong: Government Printer.
*Report of the finance of home ownership committee*, 1964.
  Hong Kong: Government Printer.
*Report of the 1963 working party on government policies and practices with regard to squatters, resettlement and government low cost housing.*
*Sing Toa Yat Po*, 1954.
*South China Morning Post*, 1971.
*Ta Kung Pao*, 1952.
*Wah Kiuh Yat Bo*, 1952.

# Health Care in Ukambani *Kenya:* A Socialist Critique

ANTHONY E. THOMAS

Indirect rule, so closely associated with British colonialism in Africa, is not dead in contemporary Kenya. A decade after political independence the political, legal, educational, and health systems have retained the structure of colonial rule — even in the presence of radical changes in the façade. The key personnel have changed: Africans have replaced Europeans in practically all of the important positions in politics, administration, justice, education, and health. Consequently, the ministries appear radically changed, but for most rural Kenyan Africans, encounters with courts and dispensaries have not changed very much. The ordinary African citizen has very little political participation in these institutions (Thomas 1971).

Many dispensaries are now called health centers, but the health care experience for most rural Africans in Kenya is largely the same as it was during the colonial era: waiting for long periods in crowded waiting areas to see clinicians for usually about one minute of diagnosis and often less time for treatment. Also it is rare that a patient has the opportunity of referral to clinicians who are more specialized in their knowledge and technology for dealing with ailments exhibiting puzzling symptoms, or for those chronic illnesses which do not yield to medicines provided at the rural dispensaries and health centers.

I conducted research in the Northern and Central divisions of the Machakos district between November 1968 and October 1969. The Kamba comprise approximately 10 percent of the total Kenyan population of 8,636,263 (Morgan and Shaffer 1966). The citizenry who are the concern of this study are the Kamba people, living in *Ukambani*, which is administratively included in the Machakos district.

Kenya gained full political independence on December 12, 1963, after seventy-five years of British colonial hegemony. Conferences for planning African independence were begun in 1960.

# PLURALISTIC RULE AND THE HEALTH CARE SITUATION IN RURAL KENYA

The medical dispensary system, like the native tribunal system, was designed according to the ideology of indirect rule, a form of pluralistic rule (see Kuper 1969: 1–65).[1] These sets of "native" institutions — the African dispensaries and the African courts — were undersupported, closed systems during colonial rule in Kenya. The colonial administration wanted to keep to a minimum its allocation of resources to African health care and to encourage rural Africans to continue to rely on their indigenous healers and midwives. The "natives" were expected to keep their medical and legal problems to themselves, that is, to deal with these problems at the African courts and dispensaries in the reserves.

This colonial system of rural medical care has been reformed only very partially. ON PAPER rural peasants can seek health care beyond the dispensary. However, for the ordinary person who has neither wealth nor political connections, seeking health care beyond the rural dispensary usually means going to a larger treatment center (e.g. a district hospital), and getting the same kind of treatment. In fact, the diagnosis and treatment at a hospital outpatient clinic is sometimes more cursory than that provided at the rural health centers. Furthermore, the waiting period at the district hospital outpatient clinic in *Ukambani* is usually much longer than at the rural dispensaries and health centers — not infrequently as long as six hours.

Of course, there are specialized clinics at the district hospitals at which an ordinary patient can be seen by medical specialists, e.g. an ophthalmologist. And in the district hospital general outpatient clinic, a minority of cases are referred to on-duty government physicians for consultation. Nevertheless, it is very clear from my own observations and research experience in 1968 and 1969 (Thomas 1971) and from other experts' reports (Vogel et al. 1968: 13) that government officers can avoid delayed

---

[1]   Pluralistic Rule is capitalized to subsume the Kenyan colonial era's indirect rule and the postcolonial era's pluralist rule: "... societies with sharp cleavages between different population groups brought together within the same political unit" (Leo Kuper 1969:3).

"The characteristic expressions of pluralism, in this context, take the form of dissensus, and of conflict between racial, tribal, religious, and regional groups; and the system is maintained by domination, regulation, and force" (1969:3).

"*In their colonial phase, all recently independent African states were plural societies; and despite independence, most of these ex-colonies retain their plural character with marginal alteration* (emphasis added). Thus pluralism and colonialism are not homologous. Colonialism is merely one mode of pluralism, characteristically instituted in the form of a plural society" (Smith 1969:29; see also van den Berghe 1969:67–81; Barth 1969; Hechter 1971).

and inadequate care by being privileged to go directly to a government physician for diagnosis and treatment. And the economically well-off African people who do not enjoy the perquisites of government service can contract with private doctors so as to get quicker and more adequate medical care.

## THE NEO-COLONIAL POLITICAL ECONOMY OF HEALTH CARE PRACTICE IN RURAL KENYA

The colonially created health care sectors in rural postcolonial Kenya have essentially remained unchanged during the decade following political independence (1963–1973). These sectors can be defined in terms of congeries of so-called "traditional" and "modern" practitioners. The traditional sector includes midwives, herbalists, and diviners. The modern sector includes (1) "legal" government-trained practitioners (medical assistants, health assistants, enrolled nurses, midwives, and "dressers");[2] (2) "illegal" government-trained practitioners who have left government service: ex-medical assistants, ex-enrolled nurses, and ex-dressers; and (3) the shop dispensers, located in the central market concentrations and in the scattered isolated shops.

Practitioners in both of these sectors are flourishing, particularly the diviners and the "illegal" ex-government practitioners. These practices are generally much more lucrative than farming and other forms of rural enterprise. The homesteads (*misyi*) with successful diviners and/or higher-level government officials are the emerging economic elite among a rural people which, prior to colonial rule, was economically and politically unstratified.

### The "Traditional" Health Care Sector

Selection of preventive and curative home medicine alternatives, other than use of commercial shop-dispensed medicines in which a specialist is not consulted, plays a very minor part in the medical behavior of Kamba populations. This general absence of consciously employed home medicine alternatives may be partially explained by the abundance of traditional specialists (Thomas 1971: 28–32) and by the widespread belief that use of herbs requires highly specialized knowledge of preparation and administration.

---

[2] The medical assistants, health assistants, enrolled nurses, dressers, and ungraded assistants are practically always men; the "midwives" or enrolled nurse "obstetricians" are invariably women.

The characteristic which differentiates the diviner, or religious-medical specialist (*mundumue*) from the other specialists, i.e. the herbalist and the midwife, is the *mundumue*'s privileged use of *ue* [supernatural power] for solving problems of sickness or other misfortune. In contrast, the role of the herbalist (*mukimi wa miti*) is more narrowly limited to that of a traditional pharmacist who administers individual herbs and mixtures of herbs for specific illnesses such as stomach-ache or rheumatism. In the process of diagnosis and treatment, he does not claim to utilize supernatural power. For example, unlike the religious-medical specialist, the herbalist does not usually transform *miti* [herbs] into *ng'ondu* [magical substance] for treatment. Rather, his expertise is considered to lie in the administration of herbs as medicines in their natural state.

Traveling herbalists are beginning to appear occasionally in the remote areas that I surveyed in lowland Machakos. In 1969, these outsider herbalists, who follow a market-day circuit to spread out their wares among other sellers in an open-air market, accounted for a very small share of the total choices of therapies among these remote Kamba populations of Masii and Mbiuni. On one market day in Mbiuni I observed a traveling herbalist from a tribe in western Kenya display his herbal cures on the tailgate of his Peugeot station wagon. The names of the diseases for which the herbs and herbal mixtures were intended were written in English. The herbalist proudly showed us a document signed by an official in his district that gave him the right to practice herbalism in Kenya. Nevertheless this enterprising herbalist did not sell very many of his products in this community, which had at least thirty-eight local herbalists (Thomas 1971: 32).

The definitive task associated with the role of the midwife (*mwiskya*) is the delivery of babies. However, in the cases of renowned midwives, the assuagement of perinatal problems is included in the midwife role, and the administration of relevant herbs may attend this expanded role.

Except for the minority of one or two very famous midwives in each Kamba community who also perform other health-related or religious-medical services, midwives are considered to be very unspecialized people. This lack of perceived specialization and importance of the midwife role results in very meager payment for birth delivery service. Kamba women are not very dependent on midwives. Any woman can assume this role if she is needed. And some women who have already delivered children will choose solo delivery for subsequent births (Thomas 1971: 68). In contrast to midwives, diviners and herbalists of note earn high incomes. A midwife of high reputation usually cannot approach the level of income that herbalists or diviners of medium reputation are able to maintain.

It is generally believed that a religious-medical specialist's abilities expand as the ancestor spirits bestow more power on him. A minimum demonstration of power is the ability to perform at least one type of *ng'ondu* [magical substance] ceremony, e.g. treatment of a sick person who has transgressed an incest tabu. When the power of divining is bestowed on a religious-medical specialist he is able to communicate directly with his supernatural benefactors, the ancestor spirits, for purposes of solving people's problems such as chronic illness or other misfortune. When this qualification of divining is recognized by the community, the religious-medical specialist may attain a very high position of prestige and considerable income. The religious-medical specialist sometimes performs midwife and circumcision services, but his principal activities and services of high prestige and income are divining, performing anti-sorcery ceremonies, and leading ancestor appeasement rituals — usually appealing to the ancestors for absolution of transgressions which involve some kind of ritual impurity.

The British colonialists' policy of indirect rule was designed to protect indigenous practices and practitioners. This policy was rationalized as being humanitarian. This romantic ideology of cultural pluralism championed the anthropologists' principal article of faith, "let the exotic peoples remain relatively undisturbed" (Mead 1943: 193–197). The irony in this doctrine is that tribal peoples in eastern Africa and in other parts of colonial Africa were not left undisturbed. In fact, quite the contrary. For example, Kamba and Kikuyu men were lured and coerced into the European-controlled labor force, and both tribes suffered from a shortage of land as a result of white settler incursions. To argue for letting the "natives" deal with their OWN legal and medical problems in their OWN way was, of course, a cruel hoax, considering that the conditions of their existence were being changed radically by the colonialists.

Diviners, herbalists, and midwives were tacitly supported by the colonial regime because the colonialists did not want to allocate resources for better medical care. Better medical care would have been costly for the white-settler-dominated colonial regime. The colonial policy throughout eastern and central Africa was to draw labor from the tribal reserves but to arrest the natives' acculturation as much as possible (Magubane and O'Brien 1972). With the influence of the colonially imposed monetized economy and the policy of arresting the acculturation of the Kamba people in *Ukambani*, diviners and religious-medical specialists have been able to manipulate the traditional obscurantist belief system so as to accrue fortunes through their divining and treatment ceremonies.

## The "Modern" Health Care Sector

Rural health clinical practitioners of the Kenyan government (see Figure 1) are the district medical officer, the medical assistants, and the enrolled

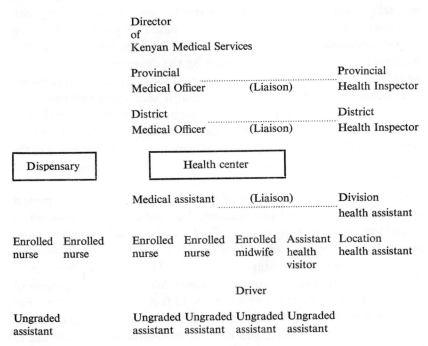

Figure 1.   Organization of rural medical and health personnel (1971)

nurses (male clinicians and female midwives). Additional practitioners in the modern health sector are the ex-government paraprofessionals or auxiliaries who illegally administer injections and other government-controlled medications in their homes. A room is set aside for this purpose and referred to by the client population as *hospitali* — the same term used for government dispensaries, health centers, and hospitals. The owners of the shops which dispense the uncontrolled medicines are, of course, also members of the modern health sector.

Government preventive and promotive medicine practitioners are the district health inspector, the division health assistants, and the location health assistants. According to the definitions inherited from the British colonialists, the district medical officer and the district health inspector are the only professional positions. All the remainder of the personnel who IN FACT do practically all of the rural health work are defined as auxiliaries — a rather contradictory term for categories of health workers who are actually working independently. This schism of professionals and auxiliaries is inherited from colonial rule wherein African "dressers" would man the outlying dispensaries, and the other three categories of health workers would ASSIST European nurses and doctors in the town and city hospitals.

In the 1960's when self-rule by Africans was imminent, the government began to make plans for expanding some dispensaries into "health centers." Rex Fendall, then Director of Medical Services, hoped that these health centers would not merely serve as overgrown dispensaries but would provide comprehensive health services to the rural community. His hope was clearly not fulfilled in *Ukambani*; in fact, his vision of new kinds of rural health units was not even approached. A decade after Fendall published his ideas, health care in *Ukambani* is still caught up in the colonial pattern. The only significant change following independence in 1963 was President Kenyatta's decree which made all rural outpatient services free. This decree resulted in very steep increases in the number of outpatients, which in turn resulted in even less adequate medical care for the average outpatient (see Vogel, et al. 1968: 2).

Substantial additions of personnel and space were made to a few of the already existing dispensaries in the district during the 1960's. The dispensaries prior to 1960 were usually one-room buildings manned by a dresser — a person with some primary school education and practical training in dressing wounds. In the 1960's some *Ukambani* dispensaries were enlarged to two or three rooms and staffed by personnel with more training — usually two male enrolled nurses. An enrolled nurse usually has eight years of primary school and sometimes two years of middle school or high school. The enrolled nurse grade in the health system is usually required to have a three-year, on-the-job training course at a district hospital. The enrolled nurse's duties in the rural treatment unit includes combinations of the following tasks: diagnosis and prescription of treatment, administration of injections, minor surgery, application of dressings to wounds and ulcers, and dispensing pharmaceutical mixtures.

To acquire the title of health center, a dispensary needed to add a nurse-midwife and a maternity section to the rural health unit. In these health centers, a medical assistant was also often added if available as the onsite senior clinician. The medical assistant has approximately the same level of general education as the enrolled nurses, i.e. eight to ten years. However, in addition to the three years of practical training in basic curative services, the medical assistant has had one year of additional training in diagnosing specialized cases and education in promotive and preventive medicine practices.

The guidebook role expectation (see King 1966: Chapter 3, Section 5) for the health center medical assistant is that he act as supervisor of the curative, promotive, and preventive services of the health center. However, my field study in *Ukambani* clearly showed that the major responsibility of the medical assistant was the diagnosis and prescription of treatment for adults in the health center under observation in 1968 and 1969 (Thomas 1971: 90–91). The medical assistant did very little supervision, and he completely stayed out of any involvement with promotive or preventive medicine. The medical assistant devoted all of his work time and some of his leisure to meeting the heavy demand for primary outpatient care.

In summary, an *Ukambani* health center in the 1960's was a collection of paraprofessional personnel assisted by several ungraded workers. These paraprofessional personnel were IN THEORY being supervised by the district medical officer, but IN PRACTICE they were rarely overseen and generally left to do their tasks with only the minimum of supervision by the senior paraprofessional in the health center — the medical assistant. There was no operative structural arrangement for the medical assistant to act as local manager of the health center. In fact, there was practically no coordination between the work of the outpatient clinicians, the midwife, and the health assistant. Consequently, these rural health centers were extremely inefficient health care facilities.

I cannot provide a very detailed analysis of the part played by the ex-government health workers who carried on illegal medical practice in their homes. To avoid jeopardizing any of the people in the communities that I studied, I was careful not to probe for information on these controversial *kitali* [doctors] who were trafficking in the controlled drugs and giving injections without legal authority. However, a certain amount of information was volunteered, so I am able to sketch the rough outlines of the situation of the illegal "modern" practitioners.

Most Kamba people use the same term of reference for the dispensary clinicians as for the ex-government auxiliaries who are dispensing "modern" controlled medicines in their home treatment centers. The term applied to both is *kitali*. In fact, all male practitioners associated with the modern medical system are referred to as *kitali* regardless of ethnicity, status, or legality. *Kitali* is a shortened form of *ndakitali*, an adaptation of the Swahili term, *daktari*. The district medical officer (an M.D.) is called *kitali*, and so are the dispensary's male enrolled nurse and the health center's medical assistant.

As in colonial times, the traditional and illegal practitioners are doing very well financially. Healing for profit is much more lucrative than growing crops and raising livestock. In fact, this profitable "fee-for-service" medical business makes it difficult to keep trained personnel in legal government practice. The factors which probably make these fee-charging "modern" practitioners attractive are tribal and kinship ties, proximity to a patient's homestead, availability when the health center or dispensary is closed, and the prestige accrued from showing that one can afford the services of a private practitioner. These ex-government workers usually make more money than their counterparts who have remained in government service. And there is considerable theft of dispensary drugs — sometimes with the cooperation of dispensary employees. Radical reform of the rural health system is needed to deal with this problem.

There have been no efforts in Kenya, or in *Ukambani* in particular, to co-opt the services of traditional personnel for providing health care. For example, there is an obvious shortage of government midwives on the basis of ratios of modern-trained midwives to the annual number of women bearing children. Yet there have been no projects to upgrade the services of traditional midwives. And it is not difficult to predict, on the basis of what has happened to more medically acculturated groups such as the Kikuyu, that in the next few decades the production of traditional midwives will diminish at a faster rate than the production of modern midwives.

## TOWARD A SOCIALIST SYSTEM OF HEALTH CARE IN UKAMBANI

Democratic centralism would be the foundation on which to build a socialist system of health care in the provinces and districts of Kenya. *Ukambani,* or that part called the Machakos district, can serve as a point of focus for discussing the reorganization of rural health care throughout the Kenyan nation. And we can also use this Kenyan rural health situation and its potential as points of departure for discussing socialist redesigns of health care in other African nations which have POLITICALLY extricated themselves from foreign control.

Socialist democratic centralism for Kenya would be the kind of social order that Julius Nyerere (1969) and compatriots have been building in Tanzania and what Oginga Odinga (1967) dreamed of and struggled for in Kenya. Both of these African leaders have been influenced by European and Asian socialist thought and action. Yet they reject the importation of any forms of socialist doctrinairism.

Julius Nyerere's efforts at decentralization in a socialist framework — at least his ideological efforts — are similar to those of Mao Tse Tung (1968). First, both leaders hold similar visions of the future: local communities or communes taking on more and more socialist initiative and gaining more control over their lives. Second, both Nyerere and Mao recognize the paradox of creating decentralization through a dynamic and powerful political center which puts equal stress on educational change and structural change. Both Nyerere and Mao are disdainful of bureaucratic socialism and have worked to prevent the ossification of government bureaucracies.

Another similarity in political ideology between Nyerere and Mao is their distrust of the Marxian vision of the rich socialist industrial nation and its transcendance as the exclusive measure of progress for all backward nations. Perhaps both Mao and Nyerere have independently recognized two things: (1) rich industrial status is an unattainable goal for either of these "proletarian" or "Third World" nations; (2) rich industrial status is antisocialist in a global sense. That is, the planet cannot bear the burden in terms of resource input or in terms of pollutant output of all the world's nations attaining a per capita affluence equal to the United States or Russia.

Probably the formation of a unified health service will be the most important step in the process of creating a socialist system of health care in Kenya. This will mean unifying the so-called modern and traditional sectors and instituting much closer coordination between the promotive, preventive, and curative practitioners in a unified system. For example, this will require structuring a health system which will coordinate and manage the activities of a midwife, the preventive activities of a health assistant, and the curative activities of a medical assistant or herbalist.

The old system, which maintains separate lines of authority for medical services and for public health, would be anachronistic in a socialist system designed to serve the citizenry. The dual system's design functions to perpetuate the dominance of physicians and serves their interests (Freidson 1970). At the upper levels in the Kenyan health system, the dual lines of authority result in lack of coordination between the research projects authorized by the provincial and district medical officers and those health projects authorized by the provincial and district health inspectors. This lack of coordination results in inadequate health care and in poor environmental health for the rural citizenry.

These dual lines of authority also hinder the efficiency of the day-to-day running of the rural health centers. The medical assistant and the enrolled nurses usually put in a full day's work because of the heavy burden of outpatients waiting for free diagnosis and treatment. To some extent these clinicians are accountable to each other as a result of the process of dividing the outpatient work load. However, the midwife and her assistant often are idle because of the small number of women using modern midwife services for prenatal, natal, or postnatal care.

The medical assistant who is usually the senior resident person in the health center has difficulty exerting authority over the midwife who is defined as under the authority of the district medical officer who infrequently visits and inspects the health center. Consequently I observed, on many occasions in *Ukambani*, patients waiting for two to four hours for simple outpatient care which a midwife could provide; yet the midwife and her assistant sat idle in their wing of the health center while the overworked medical assistant and the distressed patients bore the burden of this inefficiency.

The health assistant, who represents what Rex Fendall calls promotive and preventive medicine (King 1966), is not even housed in the health center — let alone responsible to any figure of authority in that organization. The health assistant — given the previously described dual lines of authority — is responsible to the district health inspector who, like the district medical officer, seldom visits the rural areas.

The midwife and the medical assistant at least have the same boss, and therefore could be required to share their workload. However, the health assistant is not tied to the health center in any way other than by the fact that his work does involve health. His job is generally a sinecure. He is expected to inspect meat shops for rotten meat and generally keep an eye out for major threats to public health. There are none of the natural constraints in his job such as lines of outpatients; consequently he spends most of his time doing trivial inspection tasks and idly chatting with local shopkeepers.

Usually the health assistant is fairly well trained in family and personal health. With the proper kind of health-center organization, his training would allow him to carry out effective health education work with patients in the health center. Furthermore, a Kenyan health assistant could head a team for eradicating certain local diseases, e.g. venereal disease and schistosomiasis. But given the present inadequate health center organization, the health assistant's abilities are largely wasted.

Then there are the practitioners in the traditional sector, the midwives, the herbalists, and the diviners. What is their proper role in a socialist system of health care? Can they be brought inside the modern system with relative equality, like the acupuncturists who are brought inside the modern surgical theatres in China? Or must they be patronizingly co-opted like the diviners in Dr. Adeoye Lambo's community psychiatry projects in postcolonial Nigeria? (Lambo 1964; also see Asuni 1972).

It is my contention that the services traditional midwives provide can be upgraded and incorporated in a socialist system; and the services of the herbalists can be regulated if not incorporated in a publicly supported system of rural health care. It may be possible that herbalists can be made clinical associates in *Ukambani* health centers as are traditional pharmacists in China and North Vietnam.

In regard to diviners, the only acceptable socialist solutions are to create legislation which makes divining for money illegal or keeps fees at fair levels for a poor peasantry.[3] The diviners' present exalted economic status has been largely created by the imposed monetized economy of the colonial and neocolonial situations. My field research has shown that such practices as divination and ordeals, though "functional" in precolonial times as mechanisms of social control, are in colonial and postcolonial times counter-productive for the Kenyan citizenry (Thomas 1974). The sorcery complex, on which divining depends, is a social system of thought maintained by the diviners for their own advancement. Their curing powers cannot transcend the very pathologies which they perpetuate — the pathologies associated with the obscurantism of sorcery and ritual impurity.

However, the diviners probably need to be phased out rather than instantly abolished. This probably can be done, partially at least, by preventing their fees from reaching excessive levels. Then, as people are educated in the principles of scientific and humanistic socialism, the beliefs in magic will become attenuated and diviners will no longer be sought after. Patience will be needed to phase out diviners so as not to drive them underground into nefarious activities. Amilcar Cabral, the socialist leader in Guinea Bissao, maintained an anti-obscurantist vision for African peasants but recognized that a scientific socialist understanding of social reality could not be forced on people (1971: 160):

We are proud of not having forbidden our people to use fetishes, amulets, and things of this sort .... It would have been absurd, completely wrong to have forbidden these. We let our people find out for themselves, through the struggle, that their fetishes are of no use.

[3] Specifically for populations from the Central and Northern divisions of Machakos district, I collected the following data on the economic level of Kamba peasants. In the Northern Division a community of 331 homesteads exhibited 18 percent with any concrete floors, 14 percent with any kind of motorized vehicles, and 14 percent with any radios. In the Central Division a community of 501 homesteads exhibited 23 percent with any concrete floors, 0 percent with any kind of motorized vehicles, and only 10 percent with any radios.

## DISCUSSION

What is needed in rural Kenya is decentralization of the health service wherein onsite practitioners will be given responsibility. This must be implemented in conjunction with firm socialist central guidance so that public accountability can be fostered and maintained in the total system. To accomplish this difficult goal of attaining decentralization of authority will require intelligent theory in designing the new system, but above all it will require the creation of feedback mechanisms so that practice can be regularly utilized to reformulate theory.

An effective feedback system in which positive coercion does not become negative repression will depend on an intelligent, dynamic, and antibureaucratic political center. Julius Nyerere (1972) has recently outlined a theoretical plan for provincial decentralization to be monitored by a powerful center. It will certainly be important to observe how well this theory works in practice in the next few years in rural Tanzania.

To make a new rural health system work, it will be very important to identify and train community leaders who will educate the people regarding the new health service. To accomplish this task, it will be essential to form structures which will ally these community leaders with the health service personnel. Self-criticism sessions will be needed to galvanize the solidarity of health workers, community leaders, and the peasant farmers.

In a socialist system of health care, promotive and preventive medicine will be given an equal footing with curative medicine in both theory and in practice. Health-service personnel will formulate and reformulate methods for educating patients about important health matters. And health-service personnel will work closely with community leaders in educating people regarding the practice of environmental health.

Everyone will be encouraged and helped to become a health specialist. However only specially selected and trained cadres of workers will be given the full responsibility of transforming health conditions in the community (e.g. disposal of wastes and use of public water sources), as well as the mandate for radically changing the health beliefs and practices of the community members. The key concepts here are expertise, sensitivity, and accountability. Effective health workers must be expert in the processes of health and social change, sensitive to protecting people's dignity, and accountable to both their supervisors and to the people they serve.

CRITICISM — STRUGGLE — CRITICISM must be woven into the fabric of a new socialist health system. Three practices of criticism will need to be fostered: (1) self-criticism, (2) supervisor-supervisee mutual criticism, and (3) group criticism. Without this kind of dynamic socialist praxis a public system of health care will probably function with many of the inefficiencies and "impersonalisms" of a rigid bureaucratic national health service.

## REFERENCES

ASUNI, TOLANI
1972 "Socio-psychiatric problems in transitional Nigeria," in *Rural Africana*. Edited by S. D. Messing. East Lansing, Michigan.

BARTH, FREDERIK
1969 "Introduction" in *Ethnic groups and boundaries*. Boston: Little, Brown.

CABRAL, AMILCAR
1971 *Revolution in Guinea*. New York: Monthly Review Press.

FREIDSON, ELIOT
1970 *Professional dominance: the social structure of medical care*. New York: Atherton.

HECHTER, MICHAEL
1971 Towards a theory of ethnic change. *Politics and Society* 2:21–56.

KING, MAURICE, editor
1966 *Medical care in developing countries: a primer on the medicine of poverty and a symposium from Makerere*. Nairobi: Oxford University Press.

KUPER, LEO
1969 "Plural societies: perspectives and problems," in *Pluralism in Africa*. Edited by Leo Kuper and M. G. Smith. Berkeley: University of California Press.

KUPER, LEO, M. G. SMITH, editors
1969 *Pluralism in Africa*. Berkeley: University of California Press.

LAMBO, T. ADEOYE
1964 "Patterns of psychiatric care in developing African countries," in *Magic, faith, and healing: studies in primitive psychiatry today*. Edited by Ari Kiev. New York: Free Press.

MAGUBANE, B., J. O'BRIEN
1972 The political economy of migrant labor: a critique of conventional wisdom; a case study in the functions of functionalism. *Critical Anthropology* 2 (2).

MAO TSE TUNG
1968 *Four essays on philosophy*. Peking: Foreign Languages Press.

MEAD, MARGARET
1943 The role of small South Sea cultures in the postwar world. *American Anthropologist* 45:193–197.

MORGAN, W. E. W., N. M. SHAFFER
1966 *Population of Kenya — density and distribution*. London: Oxford University Press.

NYERERE, JULIUS K.
1969 *Nyerere on socialism*. Dar es Salaam, Tanzania: Oxford University Press.

1972 "Decentralization: the people's role in planning." President J. K. Nyerere's Statement at the National Executive Committee of the Tanganyika African National Union. Iringa, Tanzania, May 1972.

ODINGA, OGINGA
1967 *Not yet Uhuru.* London: Heinemann.

SMITH, M. G.
1969 "Institutional and political conditions in pluralism," in *Pluralism in Africa.* Edited by Leo Kuper and M. G. Smith. Berkeley: University of California Press.

THOMAS, ANTHONY E.
1971 "Adaptation to modern medicine in lowland Machakos, Kenya: A controlled comparison of of two Kamba communities." Unpublished doctoral dissertation, Stanford University.
1974 Oaths, ordeals, and the Kenyan courts: a policy analysis. *Human Organization* 33:59–70.

VAN DEN BERGHE, PIERRE L.
1969 "Pluralism and the Polity: theoretical exploration," in *Pluralism in Africa.* Edited by Leo Kuper and M. G. Smith. Berkeley: University of California Press.

VOGEL, L. C., A. G. DISSEVELT, C. F. QUADROS
1968 A work study in the outpatient department of Machakos Hospital. Research Protocol. October 20, 1968. Nairobi: Medical Research Center.

# Contemporary Health Planning Trends in Tanzania

JANAKI N. TSCHANNERL

> Finally attention must be drawn to one of
> the most important consequences of colo-
> nialism on African development, and that is
> the stunting effect on Africans as a physical
> species. Colonialism created conditions
> which led not only to famine, but to a
> chronic undernourishment, malnutrition,
> and deterioration of the physique of the
> African people. If such a statement sounds
> intellectually extravagant, it is only because
> bourgeois propaganda has conditioned even
> Africans to believe that malnutrition and
> starvation were the NATURAL lot of Africans
> from time immemorial.
>
> WALTER RODNEY[1]

## THE AIM

Tanzania has inherited a structure built for the systematic underdevelopment of its society. Since independence it has progressively committed
itself to socialist development. For the individual this has meant focusing
on values of self-reliance, increased skill, material well-being, and
cooperation. On the level of the nation, as Julius Nyerere has put it,
"self-reliance means that they will use the resources and the skills they

[1] In *How Europe underdeveloped Africa*, pages 259–260. (See also Josue de Castro,
*The geography of hunger*.)
I am indebted to Dr. Oscar Gish, until recently with the Ministry of Health, Republic
of Tanzania, who provided information and interpretation.

jointly possess for their own welfare and their own development" (1968: 390 ff.).

## THE LEGACY

There are two major categories of obstacles to such development. The first is the problem of inherited COLONIAL STRUCTURES. The primary function of the colonial system was to use the resources of the colonized for the benefit of the mother country. A minimum number of socio-economic services, such as education, health, and transportation, had to be maintained to carry out more efficiently this purpose. Rodney (1972: 259) points out and cites evidence from Josue de Castro's studies to show that in the health dimension

the African diet was previously more varied, being based on a more diversified agriculture than was possible under colonialism. In terms of specific nutritional deficiencies (and hence disease), those Africans who suffered most under colonialism were those who were brought most fully into the colonial economy: namely the urban workers.

He goes on to cite several specific examples. The purpose of the health structure was not so much to develop services for the people as to maintain sufficient health and sanitation standards at the lower tier so as not to cause epidemics, and to provide excellent care for the higher tier.

Given this aim of the inherited structure, the bureaucracy was centralized and hierarchical; the government (or the missionary or religious voluntary agencies which can be considered to have the same characteristics as the ruling body) provided CURATIVE SERVICES IN THE FORM OF HOSPITALS, and a minimum of sporadic preventive measures, often in an emergency, as for instance the "Mosquito Brigade" during World War I.

The curative services were based entirely on the belief that only the doctor, with his professional expertise, was considered able to offer the necessary therapy. It is characteristic that an authoritative book considering the past and present health services in Tanganyika (Titmuss, et al. 1964: 1–2), states that medical services began "in 1888 with the period of German administration," with the institution of a "medical department and a hospital system." Before this, any early voluntary endeavors "made little impression on the health practices of the African population." Nowhere in the book is there a detailed analysis of the causes of the poor health situation among the African people, under colonialism or at independence. Precolonial Africa was not a health utopia, but it certainly did not anticipate the process of deterioration from occasional famine in precolonial times to chronic hunger, from protein-rich foods to mealy-meal [maize], from a varied diet to beri-beri and rickets.

Even when describing the development of the hospital system under colonialism, *The health services of Tanganyika* gives no clear description of whom the hospital and sanitation were meant to serve. Given the colonial governmental system, the structure was hierarchical and there was obviously no talk of people's participation in determining their own well-being. A prerequisite of such well-being, of course, would have been the removal of colonialism and capitalism.

Second, the legacy of colonial structures incorporated within it values which did not automatically change when structural changes were made. Just as a centralized, hierarchical bureaucracy was passed on to the independent government, so too were the values. Many of the people who occupied the middle and lower echelons of the health services, as well as some of the higher-level officers, were inherited from the colonial government. Many subsequently were trained in a system such as the British, which taught an ethical framework inimical to socialist development. There was a high, elite professional commitment; medical practitioners thought in terms of filtering downward medical services from a high competence directed toward the individual patient to public health measures for the lowly masses. The focus was the individual patient to be cured at great cost rather than preventing disease for large numbers and providing at least minimum care for a maximum number. It followed that because the government was unable to pay the high cost of hospital care for everyone, such care was available only for those who could pay. This health care for the upper tier moreover siphoned off precious health services in the form of initial government expenditure on hospital equipment and services and specialized training.

The commitment to a high professional competence combined with the mystique surrounding doctors bred elitism in medical training which seems to have become an abiding value.

## THE TRANSITION

Valuing a high degree of professionalism, termed "competence," often served to make sure that the new medical practitioners who began taking over the medical system would remain in the hospitals and in the cities. There was a basic pro-urban, anti-rural bias, which was reinforced by the idea that a sophisticated level of facilities was indispensable for proper health practice.

Tanzania in particular was faced with the problem of withdrawal of medical personnel, first the colonial staff and then gradually the Asian doctors. In 1961 there were 549 registered medical practitioners in the country, seventeen of whom were African. Ten years later, in 1971, there were 100 fewer.

One year ago a major private hospital in Dar es Salaam was functioning at only 70 percent capacity. The reason given was the lack of personnel, but a legitimate question was raised as to whether this shortage was not due to a set of criteria which led to choosing people suited to a more affluent situation and not applicable here.

The problem of the inherited structure, with its consequence of an inherited ethos suited to a dependent, colonial system, brings in its train the question of models of change. Much of the technical help in the form of advisers, and much of the money came from British and American sources, carrying with them a commitment to the model of the country's medical system, notwithstanding their contradictions.

Part of the negative baggage that penetrates and makes it more difficult to transform an underdeveloped system is the entry of the commercial drug producer. Evidence is accumulating to show that the market for Western pharmaceutical firms is being established at any cost, from dumping of drugs to direct bribery to ensure initial ordering of drugs from particular manufacturers, sometimes at a price much higher than a competitor's product. It must not be forgotten that the intense competition among these manufacturers, often supported by their respective governments, leads to a dangerous and dehumanizing situation.

One contradiction which has been allowed to penetrate Tanzania is the reliance on curative services. In 1970–71, as Malcolm Segall (1972) has pointed out, the "curative services received 75 percent of the current health budget while the preventative services receive about 5 percent." He also points out that the curative budget overspent its allocation, while the preventative actually underspent it, the former having spent seventeen times the latter.

A second major contradiction derived from using the Western model is that of overdevelopment of large hospitals, the largest being in Dar es Salaam, the capital, serving 2 percent of the country's population, and receiving 16 percent of the curative expenditure. Similar attention is given to the two large hospitals in the towns of Moshi and Mwanza.

A third contradiction is in the training given to doctors which is aligned to "that of a Western medical school, and the content is often unsuitable to the needs of the country...." This situation, where the doctors of the country are not being trained singlemindedly with the urgent health needs of the people in view, is only possible because it is taking place within the protected environment of the University. It is not exposed to, and does not have to be defended before the mass of the population" (Segall 1972). There is a strong preoccupation with "international" standards, meaning "Western" standards.

In the light of the framework of technical help offered in changing the Tanzanian health picture, it is not without significance that the recommendations contained in *The health services of Tanganyika* (Titmuss, et al. 1964) pay a great deal of attention to the exact place of the different categories of medical personnel from auxiliary staff to practitioners and supervisors. It lays out what should be the methods of referral among the different grades (A and B) of hospitals. It talks about the nature of duties which should fall upon the personnel at different levels in the hierarchy, and how these must be carefully regulated. The major preoccupation is with reforms within the structure, where the hope is that somehow, with closer cooperation among the various rural sectors, a new dynamic may be "infused." Apart from this somewhat mechanistic approach and wishful thinking, however, there certainly are some useful suggestions contained in the report, such as those dealing with additional facilities and the strengthening of rural health units.

But the central point is that this report does not attack the problem at its root. It backs into the solution, finally suggesting a more broadly based rural health care by recognizing that, given the present situation, Tanzania cannot maintain a sophisticated curative upper tier of health care. Nor can Tanzania "hope [for] ... extensive recruitment from abroad." So the report finds itself calling for a broadening of medical personnel and a shortening of training. But there is a major preoccupation about how such a program — especially for the medical practitioners — should be acceptable according to the World Health Organization (WHO) report, "Internationally Acceptable Minimum Standards of Medical Education." This preoccupation is all the more interesting because in the beginning of the report the new training is described as aimed at producing doctors trained to a high standard "to meet the health needs of Tanganyika, equipped with a philosophy of preventative medicine, and qualified to assume the roles of leader, teacher, and clinician in the health centre team" (Titmuss, et al. 1964: 184–185). Why then this apparent fear of an "international standard"?

## NEW TRENDS

The current budget (Tanzania: 1973a, b) in its allocation shows a shift of emphasis which seems to indicate a recognition that new priorities need to be set. In 1970–71 and 1971–72, 52 percent of the health budget was allocated to hospitals, two-thirds of which was concentrated in Dar es Salaam. In 1972–73 there was a sharp reduction to 27 percent of the allocation to hospital services, 10 percent of which was for Dar es Salaam. For the current year 1973–74 the amount is further lessened to 15 percent of the budget, 5 percent of which is earmarked for the Dar es Salaam hospital facilities. The capital budget this year is larger than in the previous four years.

The shift in allocation to hospital services implies a reordering of priorities. There is now a structural commitment in the statement that the "Second Plan will increase emphasis on the development of preventative and rural health services." First importance has been given to the RURAL HEALTH CENTERS: It is hoped that these will number 300 by 1980. There were twenty-two in 1962. There are 100 now, eight of which were completed in the past year, while fifty more are being constructed to be completed by the end of the current plan. The aim is to have one center to every seven or eight dispensaries for every 50,000 of rural population. Each center has fourteen beds — eight holding and six maternity.

DISPENSARIES are second in the order of priority. There were 990 in 1962, increased to 1,560 in 1972, ten years later. The target is 2,300 by 1980. It has been decided this year that regional imbalances should be rectified: of the sixty or so districts twenty-five have been selected for building dispensaries. Three major criteria were considered in making the allocations:

1. high population density,
2. easy access to the people, and
3. the population living in *Ujamaa* villages.

Attached to the dispensaries are the NUTRITION HEALTH CLINICS, which in 1970–71 numbered 119 units operating in twelve districts, and increasing to eighteen districts (out of sixty) in 1971–72. During the current year it is expected that work will begin on 300 units.

Next in importance are the TRAINING PROGRAMS, the most expensive, of course, being that of the doctor (about a quarter million Tanzanian shillings). A new program for training maternal and child-health aides to work out of the health centers has begun. Table 1, taken from the Economic Survey 1972–73 (Tanzania 1973b) and supplemented with current figures, gives some further idea of the shift in emphasis.

Table 1. Training programs

| Output | 1970/71 | 1971/72 | Intake 1972/73 | 1973/74 |
|---|---|---|---|---|
| 1. Medical officers[a] | 37 | 43 | 21[b] | 64 |
| 2. Assistant medical officers[c] | 20 | 22 | 20 | 24 |
| 3. Medical assistants | 4 | 48 | 66 | 72 |
| 4. Rural medical Aides | 40 | 34 | 43 | 338 |
| 5. "A" nurses | 76 | 47 | 57 | 53(?) |
| 6. "B" nurses | 241 | 267 | 331 | (Not available) |
| 7. Health auxiliaries | 64 | 31 | 28 | 35 |

[a] Graduates of the Faculty of Medicine, University of Dar es Salaam.
[b] The sharp decrease is due to those who left to practice abroad.
[c] Do not have the full medical training by the Faculty, but are licensed medical practitioners, usually trained in South Asia; can be upgraded after further training.

Table 2. Medical practitioners

| | 1971 | | | 1972 | | |
|---|---|---|---|---|---|---|
| | Citizen | Noncitizen | Total | Citizen | Noncitizen | Total |
| Public | 146 | 127 | 273 | 186 | 121 | 307 |
| Voluntary agencies | 4 | 106 | 110 | 4 | 111 | 115 |
| Private | 5 | 91 | 96 | 5 | 67 | 72 |
| Grand total | | | 479 | | | 494 |

The table shows that while there is still a substantial intake in the Faculty of Medicine at the University of Dar es Salaam in this academic year, partly to offset the high loss of trained doctors last year, the dramatic emphasis is on the training of rural medical aides necessary for both the Health Centers and the dispensaries. The number rises from forty in 1970–72 to 338 beginning training currently. There are five Rural Medical Aide Schools in existence, five under construction, and six planned. All except two are under government auspices.

Last on the list of priorities are HOSPITALS. As indicated earlier, there hase been a drastic cut over the past two years in the proportion of the budget allocated to hospitals. It was decided, however, that the number of beds should not be allowed to decrease, but grow at the rate of population increase, by about 300 beds per year. There is an increasing awareness of differences in distribution, and a demand upcountry for an increasing share in the number of beds. The problem, of course, is not only the high initial cost, but the high recurrent expenditures which are not written into aid agreements.

Table 2 may further clarify the availability of medical practitioners, and their distribution.

It is encouraging to note that there has been, in fact, an increase in the number of doctors in the country, as well as a small increase in the amount of public service. The figures, while including voluntary agencies, do not include doctors from the People's Republic of China, who number about 100, working primarily in rural areas.

## CONCLUSIONS

There is a change of emphasis in the current budget in Tanzania which is unique among Third World countries. A brief look at neighboring Kenya will illustrate this. In the last Five-Year Plan 40 percent of all health expenditure was on National Kenyatta Hospital. Rural health centers in their turn received 1.4 percent of the health budget. Thirty health centers are being built over a five-year period. In Tanzania, twenty-five are being built and planned every year. In Kenya, seventy-six dispensaries are built over a five-year period, compared to the 100 each year in Tanzania.

The budgetary allocation can influence structural changes, but the actual social implications of these changes are still to be assessed. One problem will be the possibility of urban restiveness, especially among the petty bourgeoisie if the rural emphasis in fact predominates. They cannot afford to pay for the few private medical facilities available, and they may find that the better health facilities formerly available to them are being modified to become accessible to more people.

As the rural medical aides begin to function, they may find that they are performing a number of services considered to be only a doctor's prerogative, and working extremely hard in the rural context, yet getting neither the pay nor the status accorded the doctor. As they grow in numbers their wishes may have to be acknowledged by the medical bureaucracy.

Both these problems, and others of similar nature which can be cited, are those of status differences which will sharpen as the contradictions are more clearly seen. Here, basically, is a class seeking new advantages and seeing itself threatened by an attempt to shift services to a broader mass of people. There may be a postponement of the problem by accepting larger amounts of help from aid-giving agencies and voluntary institutions. These may provide as temporary relief, some doctors or loans. The latter seem to be offered primarily for rural health, but does this also mean release of funds for maintaining hospital facilities in towns? At some point the contradiction is going to surface because foreign assistance cannot indefinitely uphold and maintain health services.

On the other side of the coin, the rural population is being exposed to health education in a mass campaign which differs from programs in other countries, notably India, in that it is organized through existing active adult education centers. The *Mtu ni Afya* (Man is Health) programs have spread over the country, making people aware also of health services. There has been a recent suggestion by the Youth League of TANU (the party of the country) to organize the closing of schools for a period so that students may teach literacy and health, along the lines of the Cuban experience.

Further heightening the awareness of the people, in this case particularly the urban population, though not exclusively, there has been an intensifying debate on family planning and population control. Through newspaper articles and public debates there is increasing rejection of population control theories especially in their racist and capitalist manifestations. The discussions are, however, still largely male chauvinist, denying the woman's role in deciding on family planning. The recent scandal about the contraceptive pill Depro-Provera, which has proved harmful to women taking it (and which may have been discontinued in Tanzania following its partial ban in the West) provides a lesson in making people realize that decisions about health services and what goes into them have to be carefully examined, because the use of drugs and population theories, among others, have neocolonial ramifications. Health planning (including demographic considerations) must be a part of the planning of the entire society for its development; its process cannot be piecemeal.

These are but two examples of an increasing awareness in different sectors of the population about the system of health services. The government seems to be currently affirming, explicitly in the budget, that it proposes to lay structural emphasis on serving the rural and urban working class. The question is going to be whether the inherited ethos of elitism and professionalism from the colonial past, now becoming entrenched in a newly forming class, can be changed, or at least be adapted to serve working-class interests. Meanwhile, with increasing skills and awareness, the population can steadfastly oppose vested interests which would deprive them of legitimate services. The new health trends in structures, training programs and mass campaigns in Tanzania are beginning to be committed to providing such services.

## REFERENCES

DE CASTRO, JOSUE
  1952   *The geography of hunger.* Boston: Little, Brown.
NYERERE, JULIUS K.
  1968   "After the Arusha Declaration," in *Freedom and socialism: a selection from writings and speeches, 1965–1967.* New York: Oxford University Press.
RODNEY, WALTER
  1972   *How Europe underdeveloped Africa.* Dar es Salaam: Tanzania Publishing House.
SEGALL, MALCOLM
  1972   "The politics of health in Tanzania," in *Towards socialist planning.* Edited by the Uchumi Editorial Board: J. Rweyemamu, et al., 149–165. Dar es Salaam: Tanzania Publishing House.
TANZANIA
  1973a  *Budget speech.* Dar es Salaam: Government Printer.
  1973b  *The economic survey.* Dar es Salaam: Government Printer.
TITMUSS, R. M., *et al.*
  1964   *The health services of Tanganyika: a report to the Government.* London: Pitman.

# A Critical Description of Medical Services in Canada

HERMAN JAMES

In his award winning book, Anderson (1968) describes private and public financing of health services in the United States as being in an "uneasy equilibrium." On the other hand the descriptions of private and public financing of health services in Canada depict a fairly stable equilibrium. If the frequently stated observations that the medical care delivery systems in the United States and Canada are similar in their methods of operating are reasonably valid, then the descriptions of the financing situations in the two countries are additionally interesting. However, one of the major points of this paper is that a stable equilibrium in the area of financing medical care does not necessarily equilibrate the rest of the system. It is on this operating principle that Canadian medical care administrators have begun to embark. Can we learn from the Canadians' experience?

On a grand scale, the medical care systems in the United States and Canada can be characterized as "loose" systems. Medical care systems are characterized as "loose" if there is a low degree of formalization and centralization (Anderson 1972a). Although the various components and their units within the system may operate in concert, the decisions that affect the interrelationships, the networks, tend to be more informal and decentralized. There are certain benefits and certain disadvantages associated with any arrangement. Anderson stated that a "loose" system is inherently untidy — that is, some people are left out, and some services are inadequately covered — but there is room to maneuver in a service where new technology is being improved constantly, and cost patterns are changing (Anderson 1972a: 293).

It is my contention that for Canadian society, the disadvantages of such an "inherently untidy" system far outweigh the benefits. In American society, the cost factors have been, historically, minimized by other factors; two such factors are higher per capita incomes and larger philanthropic contributions to health care expenditures. Consequently, in Canada, the attempt to retain the benefits of a "loose" system at minimal costs, or at least to redistribute the cost equally, has resulted in a constantly expanding role of the governments — federal and provincial — in the area of financing medical services. It should be noted that similar forces — the skyrocketing cost of medical care and significant reductions in philanthropic contributions — underlie the movement toward a national health insurance scheme in the United States.

Governmental involvement in the financing of personal medical care in Canada is not a recent activity. The direct involvement of some provincial governments in the creation and supervision of their respective Blue Cross insurance plans is one example of the active participation by the governments in the financing of personal health services (Royal Commission on Health Services 1964: 386–392). In contrast, Blue Cross and other voluntary health insurance plans in the United States were not given any direction by the government, except for the usual insurance licensing and rate setting procedures. Around 1953, voluntary health insurance was given the unannounced backing of the Republican administration and the blessings of the American Medical Association (Anderson 1968: 130–141). It should be noted that by 1953, four of the provinces in Canada had enacted some form of government-sponsored hospital insurance program (Royal Commission on Health Services 1964: 406–410).

On the federal level, at least two major legislative enactments pertinent to medical services should be mentioned. In 1948, the Dominion Government introduced the National Health Grants Programme. As the staff of the Royal Commission stated, "It was the hope of the government that the health grants would provide firmer foundations on which the edifice of health insurance might later be erected" (Royal Commission on Health Services 1964: 405). Basically, the health grants were designed to strengthen existing programs and expand certain facilities.

The Health Grants Programme consisted of direct grants and matching funds. It is similar to the Hill-Burton Program enacted by the United States Congress in 1964. Of the several categorical areas earmarked for funds, hospital construction was allocated the largest proportion. That is, of the 52.2 million dollars allocated, 17.9 were earmarked for hospital construction — 30 percent of the total. Like the Hill-Burton Bill, the funds of the National Health Grants Programme of 1948 for hospital construction and expansion were provided on a matching-grant basis.

Another major enactment by the federal government was the Hospital Insurance and Diagnostic Services Act. Passed in 1957, this legislation, based on the success of many of the provincial hospital insurance programs, provided Canada with a national hospital insurance scheme. Some of the factors that led to the creation of the 1957 Act can be found in the following statement:

Despite the achievements of the methods of voluntary prepayment and commercial insurance, the hard realities could not be overlooked: that demands on provincial governments and municipalities for increased hospital grants were large and persistent; that even in Ontario with the highest proportion of the population accessible through pay-roll deduction, only two thirds of the population had any degree of insurance protection, and much of this was inadequate; that most of the rest of the population could not afford the rising hospital charges; and that hospitals were by and large in serious financial difficulty (Royal Commission on Health Services 1964:410–411).

The main principles of the Act are reasonable in terms of implementation, and extremely admirable in respect to humanitarianism. Some brief summary statements of the main principles are presented.

1. It is a joint federal-provincial program, with the provinces having the responsibility for administering it.
2. The services covered by the Act are all inpatient and outpatient services normally provided at the standard ward level in active treatment hospitals, hospitals for convalescent, and the chronically ill; but not in mental hospitals, tuberculosis sanatoria, or nursing homes. Hospital benefits are available as long as deemed medically necessary.
3. The program is based on universal coverage of all citizens on uniform terms, irrespective of age, sex, physical, or economic condition.
4. The federal share of the program is 50 percent, i.e. the Federal Government pays one half the cost of approved services to insured persons. However, the contribution to a specific province is proportionately higher in low-cost (i.e. in terms of the prices for the approved services) provinces than in high-cost provinces (Royal Commission on Health Services 1964:411–412).

The statements in the main principles of the 1957 Act that referred to the organizational aspects of medical care delivery tended to favor the status quo. For example, the following summary statements are given:

1. The Act assumes no change in the status of ownership of hospitals; moreover, it also assumes no change in the responsibility of management to direct and control the affairs of hospitals.
2. The Act requires that each province indicate in its Agreement the means whereby it proposes to "License, inspect and supervise the standards of hospitals" (Royal Commission on Health Services 1964:412).

The last two statements from the main principles of the Act reflect the minor emphasis on reorganization. Whereas one statement called for no change, the other called mainly for supervision, not reorganization or control. This is of interest since one of the main principles of the 1957 Act stated that "the legislation is not concerned solely with 'insurance' or financing mechanisms" (Royal Commission on Health Services 1964: 412). I shall return to some of the consequences that the lack of control has had on the cost of hospital care.

The act became effective on July 1, 1958, and initially, only five provinces participated. Quebec was the last province to join the program. The methods of financing somewhat reflect the federal-provincial approach to government in Canada. There are basically three methods used by the provinces for financing their share of the cost of the hospital insurance; they rely upon premiums (generally through payroll reduction), other earmarked taxes, or provincial general revenues.

As of 1964, two provinces relied on a singular method. Newfoundland used provincial general revenues, while Ontario relied on premiums. The other eight provinces employed various combinations of the three methods, with the exception of the province of Alberta, which employed a per diem charge for hospital services along with provincial general revenues, and the province of British Columbia, which relied on a retail sales tax, provincial general revenue, and a per diem charge of one dollar a day for hospital services.[1] The province of Quebec employed two methods, a retail sales tax and provincial general revenues (Royal Commission on Health Services 1964: 415; Minister of National Health and Welfare 1967).

By the end of the fiscal year of 1966–1967, 99.1 percent of the Canadian population was insured under the Hospital Insurance and Diagnostic Services Act. Seven provinces and two northern territories (Yukon and the Northwest Territories) had 100 percent of their population covered. The three provinces with less than 100 percent were Saskatchewan, Manitoba, and Ontario; the respective percentages of insured persons in their populations were 99.5, 99.5, and 97.5 percent. This accomplishment should not be minimized. After all, hospital care does consume the largest proportion of personal health-care expenditures. Note that in the United States, there is a sizable segment of the population that has no hospital insurance coverage. Moreover, if the proportion of the population without coverage is added to the proportion of the population whose coverage

[1] It is more likely the case that the per diem charges of 1.50 to 2.00 dollars per day in Alberta and the 1.00 dollar per diem in British Columbia are attempts to reduce possible overuse of the hospital services than to help meet the provincial share of the cost of the program.

is considered inadequate, the result indicates a serious problem — perhaps a crisis — particularly if one reflects on the economic consequences that a catastrophic illness would have on the average American family. The costs of medical services alone would be enormous.

Nevertheless, a strategy that initially and primarily focuses on inpatient care rather than ambulatory, outpatient, primary care is open to criticism. In order to help stabilize the financial untidiness of the "loose" system, the Canadian government opted for a universal hospital insurance scheme. The effects of such a scheme on the delivery of medical services, often, are either insignificant or counterproductive. The use of primary, preventive medical care services will not be radically affected. However, the use of secondary, episodic care, i.e. hospitalized services, is likely to be exaggerated since reimbursement is certain. In other words, the hospital and diagnostic act is "sickness" insurance, in which the costs are redistributed somewhat equally through payroll taxes, general and/or sales taxes.

There are significant differences among the provinces in respect to medical care services — the delivery and financing of them. Some of the provincial differences in respect to the hospital insurance program have been presented; therefore the discussion on the role played by the provincial governments in the health field will be centered on outpatient services. The earliest provincial legislative enactments for the financing of outpatient services on a province-wide basis occurred in the western provinces of British Columbia, Alberta, and Saskatchewan. The first province-wide, and probably the most well known provincial medical care program is the one enacted by the provincial government of Saskatchewan in 1962.[2] Alberta followed this lead and enacted its program in 1963. The eastern provinces, particularly Ontario and Quebec, the two most populated provinces in Canada, did not enact province-wide medical service programs until much later. In fact, when the province of Quebec enacted its program in 1970, it was one of the last of the Canadian provinces to institute such a plan. The province of Ontario implemented its medical services insurance plan in 1966.

A less diversified and industrial economy, a lower per capita income, and a more sparsely distributed population are probably the dominant factors in the regional differences in the stages of development of the provincial governments' implementation of province-wide medical service programs. Indeed, Badgley and Wolfe in presenting a background picture

[2]   This enactment received international attention, probably because of the strike by the physicians of the province following the passage of the bill. For a thorough account of the Saskatchewan story, see Badgley and Wolfe (1967).

of the doctors' strike in Saskatchewan stated:

Because of harsh climate, rural isolation, and a mixed population, the people of Saskatchewan — the settlers of the "last best west" — from early on became used to helping each other through collective and co-operative action. The boom-or-bust grain economy forced people to look to government for assistance to solve their health and welfare problems (Badgley and Wolfe 1967:3).

The general basis of the province-wide medical care programs is the arrangement of payments for physician services through medical insurance plans. The insurance plans are generally financed through governmental subsidies from provincial general revenues and premiums. Compulsory payroll tax deduction is the general method for collecting the premiums. Fee-for-service remains the dominant form of remuneration. The physicians are paid by either the provincial government or an intermediary on a per unit of service basis. "Out-of-pocket" payments are reimbursable (Blishen 1969).

Again, an earlier observation is evident. The emphasis of most of the provincial medical services program is on financing. Most of the schemes do not even provide mechanisms for checking on the quality of care. Therefore, the fee-for-service arrangement, without control mechanisms, basically leaves the delivery systems intact. Even though some communities have implemented prepayment plans (i.e. service-on-demand) and the physicians are remunerated on a capitation basis (Badgley and Wolfe 1967), they are the exceptions, not the rule (Blishen 1969).

Undoubtedly, the various provincial medical care programs have resulted in an increase in the utilization of physicians' services. According to Blishen, from 1966 to 1968 the volume of care increased about 4.4 percent per year (1969: 139). However, there have been corresponding increases in the physicians' fees and salaries. Between 1965 and 1967, the appropriate professional body in every province updated the physicians' fee schedule (Blishen 1969: 138). Under the universal medical insurance schemes, physicians were able to "reap substantial benefits ... in Newfoundland the payment under universal medical care is $52,911 compared with an average gross income in 1961 of $22,412; in Prince Edward Island the comparison is between $32,503 and $20,229 ..." (Blishen 1969: 137). Some of this increase in earnings can be accounted for by an increase in the volume of care. But some of the increase in the volume of care may be due to unnecessary medical services (Blishen 1969: 139).

According to Blishen, the medical profession's ability to minimize any attempts by the various governments to encroach upon the organizational and technical domains of medical services and practices is due to the pervasive influence of the provincial medical associations and the statutory powers of the provincial colleges of physicians and surgeons (1969: 85–103). Some degree of uniformity among the various provincial medical associations and colleges is brought about through the corresponding national organizations: the Canadian Medical Association and the Royal College of Physicians and Surgeons.

The overriding issue that concerns the Canadian Medical Association and the provincial associations about government participation in the medical care field appears to be the degree of interference in certain areas of medical care practice for which the profession of medicine claims exclusive control (e.g. utilization reviews and evaluation of quality of care). The issue of control over certain medical domains of the profession permeated the earlier strike by physicians in Saskatchewan and the more recent strike in Quebec. Of course, as Blishen (1969) and Friedson (1970) have argued, the claims to domain exclusiveness can often serve as an ideological subterfuge for other basic beliefs (e.g. fee-for-service). Nevertheless, the ideological statements of the medical profession in Canada appear to be less pecuniary, capitalistic, and entrepreneurial than the statements of the profession in the United States (Blishen 1969; Freidson 1970).

Based on the data collected by the Royal Commission on Health Services, Blishen shows that regardless of several factors such as length of time of practice, type of remuneration, type of specialty, approximately two-thirds of the physicians surveyed preferred that the financial sponsorship of medical services be retained by the medical profession; approximately one-fifth preferred voluntary insurance companies; and fewer than one-tenth preferred governmental agencies (1969: 165–175). However, an examination of the contents of the ideology of the medical profession found that public (collectivistic) responsibility for medical care ranked above private (individualistic) responsibility. Professional control ranked first and freedom of choice was second (Blishen 1969: 151).

The interpretation of these statements is clear. The medical profession in Canada feels that if necessary the financing of medical services should be a public rather than a private responsibility, but the agencies responsible for remunerating the physicians should be voluntary rather than public. The major role of the governments should be subsidization and disbursement of funds to the voluntary agencies. In fact, the evidence indicates that this is the case. In 1967, in Saskatchewan, a breakdown of the sources from which claims for reimbursement came to the Saskatchewan Medical Insurance Commission showed that 36.4 percent came directly from physicians, 59.4 percent from voluntary agencies, and 4.2 percent from patients (Blishen 1969: 129). As Blishen points out, however, more and more physicians are beginning to forward their claims directly to the commission; in 1963, 21.1 percent of the physicians submitted their claims directly to the commission.

Obviously, the medical profession can compromise on this issue. The change does not mean a loss of professional control or of freedom of choice. One of the major potential consequences that freedom of choice has on the delivery of medical services is the maldistribution of medical manpower. Without control mechanisms, sponsorship of the cost of medical care is unlikely to affect positively the supply and the distribution of medical manpower. In fact, the effects are likely to be negative.

Between 1951 and 1962, the proportion of physicians practicing in the urban centers of Canada rose from 73 percent to 86 percent, while during the same period there was only a 10 percent increase in the general population of these centers (Royal Commission on Health Services 1964). Moreover, the rural-urban differences were even more pronounced in the larger metropolitan areas. In the province of British Columbia, in 1961 the population of the Vancouver metropolitan area made up 49 percent of the total population of the province, but 63 percent of the physicians in the province practiced there. The population-physician ratio for the area was 584, but for the entire province it was 758. In Ontario, the Toronto area accounted for 29 percent of the practicing physicians of the province. The population-physician ratio was 776 for the province, but it was 578 for Toronto. Similarly, whereas the metropolitan area of Montreal had a ratio of 568, the ratio for the entire province of Quebec was 853. Forty percent of the population of the province resided in the Montreal area but 61 percent of the physicians of the province had practices there (Royal Commission on Health Services 1964).

From 1944 to 1962, Canadian medical schools produced 14,146 graduates, or an annual average output of 786 physicians. Of the total 14,146, four medical schools — the Universities of Laval, Montreal, McGill, and Toronto — accounted for almost 60 percent of Canada's graduates (Royal Commission on Health Services 1964). It is interesting to note that from the years 1946 to 1961, Canada experienced a net loss of 1,842 physicians to the United States; in 1961 alone there was a net loss of 229 physicians to the United States. However, the loss in physician manpower to the United States has been regained by the immigration of physicians from other countries to Canada. During this period, 4,181 physicians immigrated to Canada (Royal Commission on Health Services 1964).

Since medical education is under the control of the provincial Colleges of Physicians and Surgeons, the supply of medical manpower is regulated by the profession and not by the dictates of the market place or by the provincial government. Needless to say, the powers of the College of Physicians and Surgeons are enormous:

It has the power to recognize specialties: to determine educational content of graduate specialty training programmes in hospitals and elsewhere; to decide which hospitals shall be accredited for graduate training; to specify the type and content of specialty examinations; to assess the moral and ethical acceptability of candidates for fellowships; and to judge the subsequent behavior of the specialist, but through the standards it lays down for specialty training it effectively controls standards in hospitals, which it accredits for graduate training (Blishen 1969:96).

Even more significantly, this enormous power of the colleges does not rest on some de facto arrangement: it is statutory. And it is not as simple as "those who gave it, can take it away," even though such a possibility is realizable.

The specialists are in full control. Even their medical brethren — the general practitioners — have not been able to halt the "deterioration of their own professional status" (Blishen 1969). And that is stating the problem mildly, because the very survival of general practice is at stake. In 1954, the College of General Practice was established. However it does not have the statutory powers at the federal or the provincial level that are equivalent to the powers of the College of Physicians and Surgeons. If the general practitioners are fortunate enough to establish a department of general medicine in a hospital, such a department is limited by law to the functions of administration and education. It can not provide clinical services and no patients can be admitted to the department (Blishen 1969: 98).

In an exploratory study of a small sample of general practitioners in Canada, Wolfe (1963) found that 40 percent of his respondents expressed doubts about the future of general practice, and of the 60 percent that expressed positive attitudes about the future of general practice, 56 percent had two or more years of training and had redefined their roles as general practitioners. Only 33 percent of those expressing doubts had extended their training and had redefined their roles (Wolfe 1963). It is interesting to note that some of the suggestions to remedy the problem that Clute (1963) received from the general practitioners he interviewed were strikingly similar to some of the suggestions frequently offered in the United States. The most popular, of course, was changing the name of the general practitioner and extending the residency requirements. It was also suggested that the number of general practitioners on medical faculties be increased and general practitioners be appointed to head certain departments in the hospitals (Clute 1963: 115–141).

The disappearance of the general practitioner and the consequence of such a condition has been repeatedly dramatized. Two important consequences are the loss of an integral part in any attempt to provide comprehensive and continuous care, and the exacerbation of the problems of "under-doctored" geographical areas. More often than otherwise, the physicians who practice in such areas are general practitioners.

In fact, as Clute (1963) demonstrated in his study, the situation has already become critical in some of the rural areas of Ontario and Nova Scotia. When the problem hits the rural areas, it is more critical simply because the residents of the urban centers can at least receive medical care from the specialists — particularly internists, obstetrician/gynecologists, and pediatricians — whose practices generally are dependent on volume and therefore tend to be urban-based. But the problem can become a general one. It can reverberate on the other components in the medical care delivery system. The most immediate and obvious component to be affected is the emergency room. As Snell has observed:

The rapid increase in the number of patients attending the emergency unit has created a load beyond the capacity of the attending staff or the house staff to handle on the traditional part-time basis. As a result, an increasing number of Canadian hospitals employ full-time physicians to treat emergency patients who have no doctors or whose doctors are unavailable ... (1969:45).

The evidence clearly shows that the Canadian society continues to be seriously plagued with the problem of the supply and the distribution of physician services. The expanding role of the governments in the financing of medical care has not had a positive effect on the problem. And, so long as the medical profession retains the controls that it presently has, it is unlikely that any major changes will occur. In the area of hospital services, the picture is somewhat different. The problem is the skyrocketing cost of hospital services. Again, this problem can be related to the attempts by the Canadian governments to equally redistribute the cost of medical services without attempting to gain control over the way the services are delivered.

The Royal Commission on Health Services grouped the hospital facilities in Canada into three categories: General and Allied Specialty, Mental Hospitals, and Tuberculosis Sanatoria. Using these categories, the Royal Commission reported that as of 1960 Canada had a total of 192,162 hospital beds, or 10.8 beds per 1,000 population. Of the total beds, 112,649 or 58.6 percent were in general or speciality hospitals. There were 6.3 beds per 1,000 population in these facilities. For the province of Quebec, the comparable figures as of 1960 were 52,494 total hospital beds, or 10.2

beds per 1,000, of which 29,369 or 55.9 percent of the total were in general or speciality hospitals, with a ratio of 5.7 beds per 1,000 population in these facilities (Royal Commission on Health Services 1964: 299). The comparable figures for the United States for 1961 were 729,000 beds, or 30.2 beds per 1,000 population in non-federal short- and long-term facilities (Reed 1965). However, 362,000 or slightly more than 50 percent of the total beds in the United States in 1961 were for chronic, convalescent, and nursing home care. Therefore, the ratio in the United States, in 1961 was 5.4 beds per 1,000 population in general or speciality hospitals (Reed 1965).

Using a slightly different definition of general and speciality hospitals, McCracken shows that from 1958 to 1966 the ratio had changed in Canada from 6.7 beds per 1,000 to 6.8 per 1,000. In the United States, during the same period, the ratio changed from 4.6 to 4.9 per 1,000 (1969: 24–25). A ratio of somewhere between 6.7 and 7.3 general hospital beds per 1,000 is considered among Canadian health authorities to be a desirable level. But, as McCracken points out, such a ratio at the national level does not reflect regional differences (1969: 24–25). And the differences exist.

In 1965, the ratios for the two northern territories were extremely high. The Northwest Territories had a ratio of 19 beds per 1,000 and the ratio for Yukon was 10.7 per 1,000. The western provinces had the second largest set of ratios. In Saskatchewan and Alberta, the ratios were the same, 8.3 per 1,000. In Manitoba, the ratio was 7.3 per 1,000. Newfoundland and Prince Edward Island had the lowest ratios. They were the same: 5.8 per 1,000. The ratios for British Columbia, Nova Scotia, Ontario, and Quebec were 6.8, 6.2, 6.9, and 6.3 respectively (Minister of Health and Welfare 1967: 43).

An examination of 1965 data on hospital admissions for the provinces and territories in Canada substantiates the earlier observations by Milton Roemer. That is, hospital admission rates correlate positively with the supply of hospital beds (Roemer 1961). It was found that the number of admissions per 1,000 population was higher in the two territories. The rates for the western provinces were generally lower than the rates for the territories, but they were higher than the eastern provinces (Minister of Health and Welfare 1967: 38). The correlation between the ranks of the provinces and the territories on the two variables (bed-population ratio and hospital admission-population ratio) was very strong (RHO = 0.88).

Obviously, it can be argued that this relationship simply reflects effective and efficient utilization of hospital facilities and services. However, data on the per capita cost for inpatient services in 1964 do not fully support such an explanation (Minister of Health and Welfare 1967: 27). A strong positive rank-order correlation was found between the bed-population ratios and per capita costs (RHO = 0.66). However, the average length of hospital stay was negatively correlated with the supply of beds (RHO = —0.75). The provinces that have the higher average length of hospital stay tend to rank lower on the number of beds per 1,000. The availability of hospital beds may result in higher admission rates and higher per capita costs, but the average length of hospitalization is shorter.

The involvement of the governments in Canada has done little to control this situation. If anything, the effect of their involvement may have been an exacerbation of the problem. The Hospital Insurance and Diagnostic Act of 1958 provides for federal contributions to the cost of inpatient services. However, the administration of the program rests with the provincial governments. This authority in some provinces has been granted to specifically created Provincial Hospital Commissions. Other provinces have granted this authority to the Provincial Ministry of Health.

Organizational and fiscal control of the provincial hospital programs are the responsibility of these provincial authorities. However, the means and areas in which the provincial authorities have selected to exercise their authority are extremely narrow. In the organizational area, they have tended to confine their activities to planning for the construction and expansion of hospital facilities. But since most of the health administrators believe that the current bed-population ratio is reasonably adequate, the planning activities of the provincial authorities often mean granting approval for the construction of new bed facilities. There is minor evidence of any involvement in reorganizational efforts among these provincial authorities (Snell 1969; Law 1969).

Even though the provincial hospital authorities have the power to control the fiscal activities of the hospital, the evidence suggests that they do not exercise their authority effectively. Virtually all of the hospitals in Canada participate in the Hospital Insurance and Diagnostic Program (Minister of Health and Welfare 1967; Wallace 1969). The various provincial authorities responsible for the hospital program disburse the operating funds to the hospitals on the prospective budgeting basis. The prospective budgets are based on the operating cost of the previous year and one year projections of anticipated demands for services. Some provinces require a line-by-line budget. Other provinces employ a global budgeting scheme, with certain allowable annual percentage increases (Wallace 1969).

Have the more direct budgeting schemes in Canada been more effective in controlling hospital cost? The answer by Andersen and Hull is no. In their attempt to account for the rapid rise in medical expenditures in the United States and Canada they stated that

by far the most important factor is the price increase in hospital care independent of the rest of the economy. It appears that since 1950 and up to the current time such increases have been more rapid in Canada than in the United States. This took place despite the more direct controls utilized in the Canadian system (Andersen and Hull 1969:19).

Andersen and Hull reported that although from 1950 to 1967 both per diem costs and per discharge costs were higher for hospitals in the United States, the annual increases were higher for Canadian hospitals. In fact, by 1967, the differences between the hospitals in the two countries on these two cost factors were minimal (1969: 17–19). In his attempt to account for the 1968 17 percent increase over the 1967 per capita cost for inpatient services, Simms presented the following figures: 14.9 percent was related to new beds and facilities, 44.1 percent was for increased salary rates, and 17.5 percent was for increased staffing (Simms 1969: 69).

The evidence indicates that even with the direct budgeting control schemes that the Canadian Governments employ, the organizational and fiscal activities of the hospital administrations are relatively free from controls. In summarizing his remarks to the Canadian-American Conference on Hospital Programs, Wallace observed:

... We have come a long way in Canada in the first ten years of our national hospital insurance program. We have provided our citizens with hospital care of better quality in greater quantity. [However] we still maintain the splendid luxury of large numbers of autonomous institutions planning and operating in relative isolation from the communities they serve. Nor have we succeeded in organizing the professional artisan ... It now appears that we have realized that this is not good enough, and we are about to embark on the development of an effective, well organized health care system in Canada. We can no longer afford the luxury of an inefficient uncoordinated health care system (1969: 82–83).

With the title of his book, published in 1972, Anderson raises the question: *Health care: can there be equity?* Perhaps not. But as one section of the book, "The Endless Search for the Dream," indicates, the answers to the question are sought through degrees of actions. In Canada the search continues because the realization of the dream is still some distance away.

# REFERENCES

ANDERSEN, RONALD, JOHN T. HULL
  1969   Hospital utilization and cost trends in Canada and the United States. *Medical Care* (supplement) 7(6):4-22.

ANDERSON, ODIN W.
 1968    *The uneasy equilibrium.* New Haven, Connecticut: Yale University Press.
 1972a   "Health-services systems in the United States and other countries: critical comparison," in *Patients, physicians and illness* (second edition). Edited by E. Gartly Jaco. New York: Free Press.
 1972b   *Health care: can there be equity?* New York: John Wiley and Sons.

BADGLEY, ROBIN F., SAMUEL WOLFE
 1967    *Doctors' strike.* New York: Atherton.

BLISHEN, BERNARD R.
 1969    *Doctors' and doctrines.* Toronto: University of Toronto Press.

CLUTE, KENNETH F.
 1963    *The general practitioner.* Toronto: University of Toronto Press.

FREIDSON, ELIOT
 1970    *The profession of medicine.* New York: Dodd, Mead.

LAW, JOHN T.
 1969    Impact of the Canadian federal-provincial program on the voluntary hospital. *Medical Care* (supplement) 7(6):34–42.

MCCRACKEN, GEORGE
 1969    Trends in facilities, personnel and capital funds in Canada and the United States. *Medical Care* (supplement) 7(6):23–28.

MINISTER OF HEALTH AND WELFARE
 1967    *The annual report on the hospital insurance and diagnostic services act: March, 1967.* Ottawa: The Queen's Printer.

REED, LOUIS
 1965    Hospital utilization under the Canadian National Hospital Insurance Program. *American Journal of Public Health* 55(3):435–445.

ROEMER, MILTON
 1961    Bed supply and hospital utilization: a natural experiment. *Hospitals* 35(36).

ROYAL COMMISSION ON HEALTH SERVICES
 1964    *The report of the Royal Commission on Health Services,* volume one. Ottawa: The Queen's Printer.

SIMMS, G. GRAHAM
 1969    Critical review of fiscal and administrative controls on costs and use in Canada from the point of view of a provincial hospital authority. *Medical Care* (supplement) 7(6):57–74.

SNELL, BERNARD
 1969    The changing position of the physician in Canadian hospitals. *Medical Care* (supplement) 7(6):43–49.

WALLACE, J. D.
 1969    Critical review of fiscal and administrative controls of cost and use in Canada. *Medical Care* (supplement) 7(6):75–83.

WOLFE, SAMUEL
 1963    Talking with doctors in Urbanville: an exploratory study of Canadian general practitioners. *American Journal of Public Health* 53:631–644.

# Cuban Health Care in Process: Models and Morality in the Early Revolution

ROSS DANIELSON

## METHODOLOGY

Toward the end of my ten-week visit to Cuba in the autumn of 1968, assisted by many interviews and a briefcase weighted by statistics, I became increasingly aware of a gaping hole in my understanding of the "Cuban health system" and in my ability to describe the system to others, especially to a cynical North American audience. What I had seen in Cuba had seemed real enough, but the words I had for friends and colleagues back home had the unconvincing sound of new jargon and new formulas. I was prepared to describe the Cuban system, but I could not explain it. My description thus had a kind of hollowness, and the "new physician," for example, who went "wherever the Revolution called," could easily have been mistaken for a socialist robot. I was told that I could gain credibility by "toning down my comments." The point, I realized, was that rhetoric, formulas, and new values sounded and looked real in Cuba because they were nestled within a specific historical context. To communicate that reality I would have to communicate that context. But this context was ineffectively communicated by a simple introductory digression on the history of the Cuban Revolution; to speak of the Cuban Revolution as external to the health system, which I had seen as a very dynamic sphere of social activity, turned the evolving health sector into a passive, albeit important, by-product of the political and economic order. Nothing less would suffice than a history of revolution IN the health sector.

In the following pages I shall sketch the outlines that I have uncovered of early development under the Revolution, organizing my discussion by institutional subdivisions of the health sector. Somewhat arbitrarily,

I consider the early transformations as the period from 1959 to 1964 and interpret the years after 1964 as the period of consolidation. In the first period, with its own turning point in 1962–1963, I shall discuss separately the transformation of the rural health service, the university medical school, the ministry of public health, and the institution of mutualism. A discussion of the second period, with its turning point in 1968, is beyond the scope of this paper,[1] it would focus on the Cuban polyclinic (or health center), which has become the key unit of the evolving new health enterprise, with secondary attention to the university and mutualism.

A principal finding of historical investigation is that the foremost problems of the health system in the 1950's — analyzed, in fact, in a 1957 Havana conference on the "medical crisis" — were essentially the features that had predominated since the 1930's and that had been clearly enunciated in a 1934 report of the International Labor Office and in other studies. Both the conference of 1957 and the report of 1934 pointed out the "plethora of physicians in Havana," a phrase that immediately suggests the underlying urban-rural contradiction and the antagonism within the medical profession between a privileged minority and the marginal majority. Here it is especially interesting to note the degree to which the first directions and values under the Revolution have their origins, first, in the frustrated prerevolutionary consciousness of health advocates and, second, in the conflicts and antagonisms that are intensified within the process of the Revolution. (Examining the period of consolidation, however, one discovers that as early changes produced their own contradictions within the Revolution, new directions were increasingly signaled by concepts and norms that do not antedate the Revolution itself.)


## EARLY TRANSFORMATIONS

The most important health effort of the new government in 1959 was clearly the building of a rural health service. This was followed in 1961 by the expulsion of old leadership from the medical school and in 1962 by the reorganization of the ministry of health. Nonetheless, it must be understood that while the rural service and other new Cuban departures were being established, the institutions of mutualism, the mainstream of previous health care development in Cuba, were omnipresent as ever

---

[1] The present work is partially excerpted from Danielson (1973). The larger work rather ambitiously examines the changes in organization of health services from early colonial times to the present.

in Havana — and growing in the early revolutionary environment. In a sense, the predominant developments in health services ENCIRCLED mutualism, with the Revolution striking more directly at rural Cuba, major public institutions, and the medical school. Therefore the account of changes in mutualism will follow an account of changes external to mutualism that were the central developments of the new Cuban health system. Yet by trying to keep in mind an uninterrupted role of mutualism, one is more likely to avoid too extreme an emphasis on the break with the past.

## The Rural Health Service

At the turn of this century, when rural Cuba lay devastated by years of cruel warfare with Spain, the meaning of the urban-rural dichotomy was suddenly and profoundly altered by metropolitan sanitary improvements and the end of the great urban epidemics. In earlier times, it was commonplace for the rich to flee Havana for the healthier environment of rural Cuba. But a new perspective on rural Cuba was probably retarded by the impression that rural problems were a passing circumstance of war, and the reality of rural life was hidden, throughout the presocialist period, by the inadequacy of rural morbidity statistics, itself a consequence of the lack of services. While the reach of a considerable and well-intentioned sanitary movement among physicians was restrained by ineffective and disinterested government, the majority of physicians were blind to rural needs because of a predominantly curative and individualistic, not to say capitalistic, medical orientation and their own urban middle-class origins.

As with sanitary services, the always increasing value of clinical medicine was withheld from the rural population for two principal reasons: the variable poverty of rural Cuba generated insufficient and irregular "real" demand for the physician's services, and the small rural towns seldom offered the conditions for middle-class life that were regarded as essential for a physician and his family. Unable to effect changes in these conditions and without the means to transcend such difficulties, the International Labor Office clearly, but ineffectually, stated in 1934 that one way to resolve the "plethora" of physicians in Havana was to move them to the interior. In 1935, the Commission of Cuban Affairs of the Foreign Policy Association stated the problem most succinctly (Smillie, et al. 1935: 117–118, 122):

Cuba is training more physicians than the island can possibly utilize UNDER THE
PRESENT PLAN OF PRIVATE PRACTICE OF MEDICINE and the probable course of
economic development of the country ....

But there exists relative scarcity of physicians in the interior where the need is
greatest, and a great overabundance of physicians in the capital. With each
annual increase of young medical graduates, conditions will continue to grow
worse .... The difficulty is that no system has been devised whereby the great
mass of Cuban people who live in the interior and really need good medical and
hospital service can secure it.

While these words lost some of their force as Cuba slowly climbed out
of the depression years, they lost none of their validity. They were underscored in 1953 by the national census and again in 1957 by a survey of
rural Cuba that was conducted by the Agrupación Católica Universitaria.
Finally, at the end of the Batista years, a situation emerged that was
similar to the situation at the end of the Machado tyranny. Medical
students and some physicians were once again engaged in militant opposition, while the number of physicians had doubled after 1940, and the
medical school was again closed in 1957. In 1959, however, the outcome
of rebellion promised a direction for the energies inspired by the period
of violent struggle.

It is significant that during the preceding years a special concern for
rural health had been maintained among a small minority of physicians
who developed the speciality of tropical medicine and parasitology, as
the two were customarily combined. Many health problems treated
under this heading were most critical among the rural population and
the urban slums. Here the advances of treatment methodologies were
frustrated by the nonpayment by patients and by the greater probability
of reinfestation or reinfection. The nature of the field therefore caused
its students to be sensitive to the need for an integration of sanitary and
preventive measures with inexpensive or free curative services. Their
medical ideology became, so to speak, that of "social medicine."

The combined importance of rural health services and previous development of tropical and social medicine in giving an orientation to the
new Cuban health system is suggested by the many features of the contemporary Cuban "model" that appeared in the very first plans for the
rural health service. An example is the plan authored by Rafael Calvó
Fonseca and the Finlay Institute (1959). The plan was apparently semi-
official, as it carried the name of a research arm of the ministry of health.
Central to the plan was the concept of a rural health center which would
integrate prevention and cure, medicine and sanitation, physician and
health team, and professional and lay participation in health work. The

centers would replace or supplement the long-degraded system of municipal sanitary chiefs. They would establish — in the military terms that have since lent an epic spirit to the Cuban battle against disease — beachheads of modern services in the rural environment. Thus in unmistakable terms, the plan of rural services emphasized the PERIPHERY of services (Calvó Fonseca 1959: 9): "Here we are working in reverse; instead of carrying health from the center to the periphery, we intend to begin with the periphery establishing these modern services of health."

Minimally, the center would employ a physician who would serve as director, a visiting nurse, a midwife, and a laboratory technician who would also serve as sanitary inspector. The first task of the new physician was to carry out a sociomedical survey of the area. Officials, teachers, and important farmers were to be visited and a census made of midwives and folk healers. Earlier data on births, deaths, and morbidity were to be gathered from every possible source, and, the proposal suggested, a large map of the area could be constructed and posted on a prominent wall of the new facility. The next step for the new physician-director was to initiate a program of meetings with specific groups, such as parent and teacher associations, making sure that other revolutionary officials of the area also attended the meetings in order to indicate convincingly the social importance of the new center and of the meetings themselves. Thus an idea emerged that would later yield results beyond any original expectation. The purpose of social relations between health center and community was not simply to gain passive acceptance or to alter beliefs; the larger aim was to ORGANIZE THE COMMUNITY FOR ACTIVE PARTICIPATION IN HEALTH PROMOTION:

It will turn out convenient, after a certain time has passed and the neighbors of the zone are impressed by the work carried out, to build Health Councils ... or whatever they may be called, formed by representative persons of the zone (and with these Committees we have magnificent personal experience), thus obtaining citizen cooperation and erasing the incomprehension and indifference — when not the hostility — with which such efforts are received in many places where illiteracy and absurd beliefs stand in the way of sanitary measures. This social action would help neighbors cooperate in the protection and development of their own health and that of the community (Calvó Fonseca 1959: 10).

If one may judge from reports published by the first rural physicians, it seems that the elements of the plan presented above correspond closely to the practice that in fact developed.

The rapid construction of rural facilities indicates the strength of government commitment and its impact on physicians who were drawn to rural service. By 1963, 122 rural centers and 42 rural hospitals, with a combined total of 1,155 beds, were established, employing in that year some 322 physicians and 49 dentists. Considering variation in the time spent in rural service, which was first programmed for one-year periods, the number of physicians who by 1963 had performed rural service was much larger than the 322 positions budgeted in 1963. Law 723 of 1960 obligated medical graduates to spend one year in rural service, and by 1963, 1,500 physicians and 50 dentists were estimated to have experienced rural service (Font Pupo 1963: 57). In addition, hospitals, medical associations, and the medical school were asked to develop programs that would support the rural effort.

On the one hand, the rural service effectively constituted a national experiment in "tropical" and "social" medicine. On the other hand — because the context was a snowballing program of agrarian reform, mass mobilization, and the preoccupations of a popular movement threatened from abroad — many physicians effectively became medical CADRE, in the sense that their work became a part of a POLITICALLY DEFINED organization, life style, and personal identity. The revolutionary integration of the health enterprise was not a mere formality. After all, many of the rural facilities were actually built by INRA, the politically conscious umbrella organization that implemented the program of agrarian reform. Often the supplies of rural facilities came from INRA, and where there were no pharmacies, or inadequate pharmacies, the new People's Stores served this purpose. When the health center sought community cooperation, the center was logically directed toward the organizations created by the Revolution that were effecting such participation. Thus the stint of the rural physician could not help but be, in addition to a course in tropical and social medicine, a course in political economy and social dynamics.

A turning point — where this "revolutionary," "tropical," or "social" medicine became CUBAN medicine, or at least a self-conscious VANGUARD of Cuban medicine — is marked by the Tenth National Medical Congress held in Havana, February 17–24, 1963, and attended by some 2,000 physicians. Prominent among the approximately 600 papers presented at the congress were reports by physicians of the rural health service. Here the rural pathologies, whose broad features had been sketched before 1959 but which had to be rediscovered, with difficulty, by each medical generation, now appeared in the intimate terms of the community case study and direct experience serving rural health needs. One report, by a physician of the Rural Dispensary of Bernardo, Baracoa, Oriente, offered a conclusion that has become a basic principle of contemporary health practice (Amador Garcia 1963: 34, 43):

The local mass organizations are our best aid in the arduous task of elevating the sanitary level of the zone ....

The physician, faced by the magnitude of these tasks, can only be coordinator, orientor of this mass.

## The Medical School

Medical education was profoundly changed in the first years of the Cuban Revolution. Its principal features by 1963 reflected the new general features of the university:

1. a change in the social origin of students, inspired by free tuition, residential scholarships, and political incentives;
2. the implementation of the contract system in faculty employment, thus terminating the much-abused and unwieldy system of *concurso-oposición* and fifth-year evaluation;
3. student and national government authority in university administration, thus ending the formal hegemony of the faculty in university affairs and also the formal autonomy of the university;
4. a great expansion of the university budget, designed to favor practical human resource needs of the society;
5. the frequent employment of foreign and young Cuban professors to replace the large number of prerevolutionary professors who ended their work during the first years of educational reorganization; and
6. the constant visible presence of the Revolution in the university, manifested in new organizations: the student and faculty militia, the new Federation of University Students, and others.

Specifically, medical education changed in the following directions:

1. an increase in the number of teaching hospitals from four to seven, and the establishment of a medical school in the University of Las Villas and Santiago de Cuba;
2. the incorporation of hospital internship as a prerequisite for graduation;
3. the creation of a new school of preclinical sciences for the first two years of medical education;
4. an early curriculum emphasis, consistent with compulsory rural service, on epidemiology, statistics, social medicine, including health services administration, and rural or tropical medicine; and
5. a crash program to greatly increase the number of Cuban physicians.

To the outside observer, the changes that were effected by 1963 — in curriculum, departmental organization, and student careers — may not seem extreme. But the rapid and impatient changes overstepped cumbersome procedural regulations and thus raised conflicts with professional associations and their privileged immobility, while government involvement violated the grand ideal of university autonomy. That is, the Revolution assaulted the very ideals that were considered in the prerevolutionary period to be victories of the Cuban professional and medical class.

The new goals of the health sector, the rural service in particular, pressured changes in medical training. The number of rural physicians could hardly be increased by graduating medical students who were, almost without exception, from the urban middle class. New physicians could hardly be expected to perform in the isolated conditions of rural service if their training remained highly verbalistic and theoretical, sometimes without clinical contacts until the fourth year. And few students could emerge as effective general physicians if their clinical training in the last years of medical school was heavily concentrated in a single specialty, under the tutelage of a single professor. If there were so few internships (fewer than 30 for an average class of nearly 200), students would continue to be ill-prepared for modern hospital work that rests on collaboration among various health workers, specialists, and professionals; new physicians would fail to acquire the diagnostic familiarity that was essential in rural service. Important branches of medical science, such as biochemistry, totally absent in the prerevolutionary school, needed to be added to the curriculum, but in which of the jealous departments should they be included, if new departments and institutes were opposed?

The problem faced by reform in medical education is suggested by the despair with which the previous social democratic governments of Grau San Martín and Prío Socarrás had regarded medical education. As a highly positioned official of those years, now in the United States, remarked in an interview in 1969, within the old system the only feasible way to change education was to build an entirely new school.

Before 1959, university and professional autonomy had served different interests, uniting all who feared the vicissitudes of government and valued the role of the university as a somewhat detached critic of government and society. But it is also true that by 1959 the concept of autonomy had lost much of its intrinsic appeal through years of abuse by the Cuban government and by the professors and professionals themselves. The always insufficient financial support and indirect intervention by government reinforced the islands of authoritarian self-sufficiency of some faculty and the network of favoritism that linked them to a mass of part-time appointments. In the lumbering giant that the university had become, autonomy no longer suggested the positive or dynamic quality it may once have promised; autonomy was correctly confused with the negative concept of immobility, Moreover, the great popularity of the Revolution undermined fundamental preconditions for such ideals: fear of government, perceived discontinuity between government and public interests, the social alienation of intellectuals. Thus, by mid-1960 ACTIVE support for the old system was bound to be concentrated in an easily isolated group: independently powerful faculty, strict proceduralists, and anti-communists. In large measure the old ideals simply disappeared, and a new concept of the university integrated into the Revolution emerged, with new ideals.

The threatened end of autonomy and of *concurso-oposición* (the much-abused method of verbal contests, held for aspirants to vacant positions on the faculty) and other proposals for university reform divided the medical faculty and also the active members of the Cuban Medical Federation, some of whom were already taken aback by the purge of the prestigious administrative committees in Calixto García and other public hospitals. Thus, when the medical faculty was convened on the evening of July 29, 1960, to decide its posture vis-à-vis a newly formed (revolutionary) Superior Governing Board for the university, the faculty was evenly divided on the issue. A few days later, the Superior Governing Board was provisionally recognized by the revolutionary government; some professors were fired, others left the university in protest, and new professors were appointed. Finally, in laws enacted in 1961, numerous structural reforms and the direct participation in university affairs by the Ministry of Education, alongside evenly weighted student and faculty representation, were instituted.

The indignant response by some Cuban faculty cannot surprise anyone who has witnessed the anxieties of faculties disrupted by student protests of the last decade in the United States. Where these and other efforts have been directed toward university reforms — open admission, special programs for disadvantaged students, curricular innovation, changes in grading methods, departmental reorganization, student and junior faculty power in governance, the increased employment of women and Third-World minorities — senior faculty has everywhere formed the strongest opposition.

The situation was not so different in Cuba. Large numbers of scholarship students entered the university, most of them not from Havana. The number of poor, rural, black and mulatto, and women students greatly increased. For many reasons, including the fact that the best pre-university high schools were in Havana, the new students were necessarily less prepared academically than the traditional middle-class students of Havana, thus raising the specter among faculty and middle-class students of declining quality of education and lowered standards. The new students were, however, IDEOLOGICALLY superior and conscious of their role as the youth of the Revolution. To some, the new students were feared as "red thugs." And, without doubt, many of the new students — and not a few "old" students — must soon have become as vigilant in detecting "reactionary" and "counterrevolutionary" ideas as militant black students are vigilant in detecting "racist" ideas and practices in many North American universities, often to the distress of their professors and fellow students. As one middle-class former medical student, now in the United States, said in an interview in 1973, "We knew who each other were, and they were always suspicious of us."

From these comments that suggest a clear class conflict within the university, one may correctly anticipate that on one level the conflict between university professionals and the Revolution took the form of a CULTURAL conflict. The nostalgic DECORUM of a "bicentennial" university was shattered by the new revolutionaries. Thus, in reference to the armed occupation of the university by students in January and February of 1959, a senior member of the medical faculty wrote, with the characteristic note of injured dignity and pride:

Professorial authority was left seriously stained and many professors who for their experience and executive ability should have been the directors of University Reform were left on the side, separated by an abyss of unresolvable incomprehension, on being confronted by a student mob, whose passions had been demogogically exalted (Portuondo de Castro n.d.: 19).

The University Council was appalled as much by the disrespectful tone of student manifestoes as by the demands presented therein. Indeed, a way of life was threatened, it seemed, and "culture was offended." Of the new university, the same professor added:

Even the gallant and suggestive whistle has been quieted. How could one whistle at the [woman] militia comrade who boasts of hate, of absence of every feminine sentiment and, on top of all this, of filth, with her pride diverted by consuming no more than one bar of soap per month, by not using deodorant, perfume, or other articles which, disrespectfully called bourgeois, contribute so much to achieve the enchantment of femininity (Portuondo de Castro n.d.: 54).

Such pedestrian concerns suggest that the departure of faculty and middle-class students or, more correctly in my view the ROUT of Cuban physicians into emigration, is not to be explained simply by reference to new policies of curriculum, organization, and governance. (After all, there was no great emigration of faculty when, in fact, the university was CLOSED by Batista.) Rather, the rout of Cuban physicians, like the rout of the middle class as a whole, is explained by the escalating social turmoil and speed of the larger Revolution. In a country whose fate had turned for the previous 100 years on the approval and disapproval of the United States, only the most imaginative of the older middle class could suppose that hostility with the United States would not end in the demise of the Revolution.

My conclusion, at any rate, is that many *émigrés* were less reactionary than naively opportunistic and, if they had had more time and been less pressured by the escalation of events, could have found a useful niche and reconciliation with the Revolution.

While the period of turbulent polarization peaked in 1961 with the defeated Bay of Pigs invasion and continued through the great missile crisis of October, 1962, physicians who stayed or who joined the faculty of the university in this period found a remarkably different university. The departure of professors and many middle class students created an impact well beyond the effects of their number. Perhaps two-thirds of the old medical faculty and one-third of Cuba's physicians had left the country by 1963. But the loss of faculty had one profound effect — aside from reducing the "plethora" of physicians — it created a profound sense of solidarity amid an embattled university within an embattled and righteous society. In this solidarity, the exaggerated social distance between students and faculty was reduced out of necessity, out of the milieu of new social contacts — militia, voluntary labor, membership on committees and political groups — and endless meetings. The sense of equality of comrades in arms was imperceptibly merged in the title of *compañero* with the ideology of equality among men and women under socialism. As the university adopted the identity of a socialist university (another term in an already rich vocabulary of revolution), the departure of physicians left an unmistakable image of the prerevolutionary physician that would be recalled to future generations of medical students: HIS PRIVATE SELF INTEREST WAS PLACED ABOVE THE EXERCISE OF HIS ART; HE ABANDONED HIS COUNTRY IN ITS HOUR OF NEED.

Thus, the flight of physicians and great polarization gave substance to a developing counterconcept of the "new" physician. Unlike the old physician, the new physician would be formed according to the needs of the society, interpreted by the Revolution, and would practice where the need, not the profit, was the greatest — or, as many students were by then saying, "wherever the Revolution sends me." Considering that *émigré* physicians included prominent figures in private practice who seemed to have left their country in pursuit of economic gain, it was not inconsistent that the new physician also renounced private practice, suddenly the symbol of medicine "before the Revolution."

The changing social origins of students, already noted, was greatly intensified, first, as a direct consequence of the departure of many middle-class students, and second, as a consequence of the dramatic response of the revolutionary government to the departure of physicians. In a celebrated speech of 1962, Fidel Castro analyzed the "shameful" flight of physicians and called on revolutionary youth — workers and students — to volunteer for medical training. The call found an enthusiastic response in the university, in the high schools, and among working youth. Students in law, humanities, and social studies transferred to medicine, while many high school students decided on a medical career. But almost half the students in the first-year class in the autumn of 1963 were working youths, many of whom were given special preuniversity courses before entering the medical program proper.

New students, then, had not simply chosen a medical career; they had been called by the Revolution. The new class of more than 1,000 students consciously perceived itself as different from earlier classes and was born amid the pains of a new society, WITH A SENSE OF MISSION THAT DERIVED DIRECTLY FROM ANTAGONISMS IN THE OLD MEDICAL CLASS. The new students of 1963 were destined to celebrate the tenth anniversary of the triumph of the rebellion with their entrance to internship programs. In the ensuing years, their presence in the university would set the tone of student life and medical education. Moreover, after 1962, the medical program would itself be CONSCIOUSLY preparing students for a new political and social role. For the moment, this meant that seminars on Marxist social analysis and guerrilla warfare would be part of premedical training; lectures might lapse into political discussions; and technical visits to new facilities would always include a nontechnical reminder of how things were before the Revolution. And someday, the 1963 Cuban report to the World Health Organization announced, Cuba would offer medical assistance to other countries "in process of liberation."

Other responses by the university to the flight of physicians included a reduction of the preinternship period from six to four years and in dentistry from four to three years. Where emigration seriously affected specialties, medical students were recruited to "vertical" internships that offered early specialty certification. These changes were reversed in 1965, the year which definitively ends the first period of transition; preinternship curriculum was extended to five years and the escalated vertical internship was abandoned in favor of the rotating internship for generalists that was already compulsory for other students. The improved internship and clinical years were made possible by the greatly expanded organization of teaching functions in Havana hospitals and by the sharpened definition of preclinical studies in the new preclinical center. It is also true, however, that the first few years (perhaps through 1963) were marked by a somewhat cavalier disregard, probably impossible to avoid in these circumstances, of certain scientific concerns, methodology of scientific research, and research itself. One might also say that, with the exception of increased attention to the various topics of social medicine, the curriculum itself was not greatly changed, and the work of different departments, on the concrete level, continued to be performed in relative isolation. This characteristic, not uncommon to other medical schools, probably continued to be influenced by the organization and facilities of the principal university hospital, "Calixto García," which was actually a cluster of separate little hospitals. Moreover, the improvisation required to keep each department functioning and staffed with competent personnel gave little opportunity to develop a perspective — much less a really new perspective — of the whole enterprise of medical education.

## The Emerging National Health System

In 1959, when the Ministry of Public Health was given broad powers in matters relating to health services, few could have anticipated how far this authority would be used to create a new health system. Except for the new services to rural Cuba, no new organizational direction was apparent for health services as a system. Quite in line with normal expectations, the power of the ministry was first used to purge *batistianos* and sinecures, while the administration of some important hospitals — and the ministry itself — was turned over to physicians who had served in the rebel army and to other trusted physicians. Meanwhile, the social bias, if not the precise direction, of changes to come was suggested by legislation to lower the price of medicines and medical accessories and, of course, by the rural program, whose broad implications were not immediately visible.

In 1961, at a turning point in Cuban history, the first plan for a comprehensive national system of health services began to take form. This plan, implemented in 1962 and significantly revised in 1965, included many of the formal structural features of the contemporary Cuban system. It created decentralized provincial and regional levels, responsible for concrete administration and planning, and a national level, responsible for norms and orientation. All levels integrated the functions of public health: treatment, health protection, long- and short-range planning, and scientific improvement of health workers.

Although the first plan appears as a close adaptation of the Czech variant of East European and Soviet models, it is clear that some form of national health planning was in any case called for by the Cuban experience of 1959–1961. The increased mobilization and military organization of Cuban society, the socialist declaration, the open role of aid from socialist countries, and the high tide of internal political polarization all favored the introduction of the most comprehensively nationalized system at a time when the health system itself was already leaning in this direction. Assuming continuity of power by the Revolutionary government, I believe that the initial phase of great quantitative change was bound to give way to a phase of qualitative change involving organization and planning on the level of the whole system.

Naturally, the commitment by national administration to organization, procedure, and rational, systematic planning as the *sine qua non* of modern and socialist health promotion created conflict between those whose immediate concern was the construction of a new system and those whose immediate concern was the direct delivery of services and administration of specific facilities.

This conflict between unit and system was resolved by 1965 in a decidedly Cuban form. To see this process, it is yet necessary to bring into focus the concrete circumstance of public services, for the new system was launched on the crest of a great surge of public health expansion in 1959–1961. This suggests, therefore, that the implementation of the new system is a process of antagonism with both prerevolutionary and NEW-revolutionary organization.

Aside from the familiar rural deficiency, the principal contradiction within the prerevolutionary government sector of health services had been the disparity between great formal centralization of authority, reaching directly from the national to the municipal level, and the separate and semi-autonomous organization of operational units — dispensaries, first-aid stations, general hospitals, and specialty facilities. The latter category included several lines of services (e.g. for tuberculosis, venereal disease, leprosy, maternity, and pediatrics) which were administered by separate vertical agencies roughly under the direction of the Ministry but often with appointment of officials directly by the President of the Republic. Added to this inefficient structure (the more inefficient as optimal medical care became more expensive and complex) was a second contradiction, partly a product of the first: the constant insufficiency of government funds, lost in graft and redundant administration, was surpassed by the even greater insufficiency of services provided. Because funds were always regarded as inadequate, administrators were said to have had few qualms about their misdirection; because accountability was variable and distant from operations, few public servants experienced the constraints of personal accountability. For both reasons, the working conditions within the public sector were without the *esprit de corps* of internal cohesion and self-esteem, having neither social incentive nor social recognition.

It was into this structure that the new government poured investments after 1958, and here the expansion of rural services began as yet another independently administered sector. Not surprisingly, one consequence of the burst of investment was to make old structural inefficiencies more costly and more apparent, while inexperienced administration and social disruption added new inefficiencies. To these rather simple difficulties of transition, one must add the similarly unsurprising inadequate planning of much rapid expansion in the absence of a clear methodology for rationalizing services or for the weighing of various needs. In this respect, it is extremely fortunate that the investments were GENERALLY directed by the rural priority. Here, as we have seen, there was a good plan for the organization of individual facilities, even if the notion of a rural NETWORK of services was yet immature. The rural focus meant, for the most part, the building of primary facilities where the risk, for poor planning, was less than in the conspicuous urban investments which had been the mark of the past (when the wife of each president had felt compelled to build yet another maternity hospital, and each president a new plan or hospital for tuberculosis). In the delivery of a long-needed rural service, nobody could quarrel with the first work of the Revolution. By late 1961, however, shrinking resources and greatly expanded services meant that a simple approach to planning would no longer do. Great inefficiencies, over the long run, were possible. Isolated facilities were sometimes too elaborate for the low patient load and in relation to referral options; sometimes locations were ill-chosen and, on occasion, too luxurious. It was soon realized, for example, that too many small general hospitals were being built in rural areas. In some cases, the linkage of smaller, predominantly outpatient rural facilities with larger hospitals located in cities and large towns would have been far more efficient than a rural hospital. That meant more and improved services for small urban centers.

One way or another, the expansion of rural services was destined to place greater demands on the URBAN centers of rural regions. In this way the rural emphasis on primary care, within a concept of comprehensive service, created its own politically influential pressure for a rationalized network of regional services. And just as more preventive services lead, not to less, but to greater demand for curative services, and more primary services raise demands for more secondary services, so the expansion of rural services sharpened the previous contradiction between the simple level of rural and provincial services and the concentration of sophisticated services in the capital. That is, rural service also pressured for a NATIONAL network of services. By building a BASE, attention was directed ultimately toward the SYSTEM.

A sharp eye, dedicated to a complete view of the system under study here, would probably find very substantial informal and extra-institutional developments that constituted real change in the health system that preceded (and also superseded) the formal structure reform of 1962. One would hypothesize that increased size in the absence of greater effective controls would lead to greater independence of far-flung units. New social programs and political mobilization would mean new relations between health facilities and the environment, and new patterns of social interaction that were not prescribed by the medical system proper. Clusters of services and personnel with similar experiences, as in rural service, would likely lead to self-conscious interest groups.

Thus, in the Cuban case, a mechanical implementation of an external master plan borrowed from the Czech model was impossible. The plan, rather, would have to adapt to a vigorous mass of social activity, especially to the clusters of rural services, with their own pressures for system rationalization from the bottom up. This would not have been the case if, for example, a new comprehensive state structure had been promulgated in early 1959.

If the Cuban rebellion had been an ordinary seizure of power, if external threats had been less extreme, if the pace of social change had not accelerated, and, in the case of the health system, if the emigration of physicians had not been so pronounced, the period of the "aftermath" might soon have disappeared in a newly stabilized administration. As it was, however, the health system was kept in a state of flux. To the disruption of the period were added the effects of the United States blockade, the nationalization of the large pharmaceutical firms in 1961, and the ban on the sale of many medicinal products that were redundant or without medical quality. Meetings necessarily turned into explanatory, pedagogical sessions, as much dedicated to external conditions as to the immediate internal problems of health organization. Threats of counter-revolution and sabotage led to the creation of hospital vigilance committees, akin to the Committees for the Defense of the Revolution, in 1960 and to the Vigilance and Public Health Committee of the Cuban Medical College in 1961. The organization of the militia, the threat of invasion, and finally, in 1962, the threat of nuclear war, involved physicians in emergency planning in collaboration with the army and other defense organizations. No one could have been more conscious than Cuban physicians and health workers of the grim implications of an invasion by the United States.

Such conditions magnified not only pressures for consensus and solidarity but also, as in the university, the social isolation of some. The high tide of this polarization in 1962 was marked, on the one hand, by the new plan for health organization and the antipolio campaign and, on the other hand, by the rather far-fetched claims by disgruntled *émigré* physicians of deteriorating health and medical conditions.[2]

One may suppose that in such an arena of activity the simple declaration of new structural definitions, rules, and procedures would produce few substantial changes, the more so because personnel were accustomed to working out of channels. But this was not how the substance of the new system was affected. The course of the new organization of services was set by the relationship of the ministry to practical matters. This relationship began in a flourish of technical activity under the initiative of the new Scientific Council of the ministry and the action programs in preventive medicine under the Subministry of Hygiene and Epidemiology. Technical conferences were held on the regional, provincial, and national levels to establish norms or guidelines for many practical matters of health work and organization, and specific campaigns were planned. The 1962 polio vaccination campaign was prototypical (and was repeated, with improvements, every year thereafter). Both norms and campaigns involved the formation of interspecialty and interorganizational task forces which were loosely attached to the vertical hierarchy established in 1962. Other practical directions included the organization in 1962 of a national chain of hospital libraries, guidelines and regulations for hospital administration, a plan for the evaluation of medical work, and, along with the creation of residency specialization, the review by examination of all

[2] For example, a prominent Cuban pediatrician announced at the Minneapolis Meetings of the Panamerican Sanitary Organization in 1962 that an epidemic of polio was sweeping Cuba and, over the "Voice of America," the same physician claimed that more than 2,000 children had died in one week in the Hospital Municipal de Infancia. See Gómez Wangüemert (1962). But in the same year, Dr. Albert B. Sabin had already confirmed the successful immunization of most of Cuba's youth (Sabin 1962).

specialty credentials, thus finally ending the self-determination of specialists.

It seems to me that the creative role of this activity with respect to the internal organization of public health rests on the ability of these programs to follow informal networks in order to bring together the efforts of people from different institutions. This was facilitated because it was the cooperation of individuals rather than institutions that was initially involved, although, in the execution of consequent programs, institutional cooperation became the focus. Moreover, as activities that were functionally or professionally (rather than regionally or politically) defined, there was little conflict of hierarchy; yet at the same time, it was easy to organize and channel such activities within the hierarchy defined by the new plan. Together these observations lend support to another, i.e. that the technical and scientific activities of the ministry served to create, through specific recruitment or cooptation (in the sociological sense), a vertically linked technical cadre under an increasingly prestigious national technical direction. Indirectly these activities also served to broaden the influence and practical exposure of university professors, who inevitably were drawn into this activity.

This process is at once lubricant and cement; it raises the accessibility of vital information to all parts of a system while it creates extra-institutional vertical bonds in an otherwise decentralized structure. It helped to establish channels for a new system and, as a special consequence of public health campaigns, established channels for an active interface between health structures, other sectors, and community organizations. Ties were formed between the new system and the conglomeration of informal networks that had already emerged in the first three or four years of public health work under the Revolution.

*Mutualism*

The most distinctive and characteristically Cuban feature of prerevolutionary health organization was the institution of mutualism — a wide range of prepaid schemes that offered varying ranges of comprehensive services in exchange for a few dollars each month. Their origin dates to the earliest colonial times but especially to the practice of housing the paying quarantine ill in large country houses (or *quintas*) outside Havana. This development took a very special turn in the second half of the nineteenth century when a rising tide of Spanish immigrants, always susceptible to endemic yellow fever, were also made subject to forcible return to Spain if their condition became a burden on the state. As a result, a variety of immigrant clubs, based on Spanish ethnicity (Catalonian, Andalusian, Basque, etc.) and on occupational categories, formed to provide basic social services to their members.

The large hospitals thus built were in a position to dominate much of medical practice when, at the turn of the century, the medical revolution made curative medicine increasingly dependent upon a hospital or other institutional base, and the end of the great urban epidemics opened the hospitals for broader functions. Moreover, Spanish immigration burgeoned after 1900, not to decline until the 1930's. As employees of institutions under lay control, physicians reacted against the large institutions, on the one hand, by demanding higher wages and improved conditions of employment and, on the other hand, by forcing limitations on prepaid plans in order to favor private practice and by organizing a variety of alternate, physician-controlled, prepaid programs, many of them organized for profit and dominated by a single physician.

In the course of the years, the essential antagonism within mutualism lay in the differences between large programs, of which there were fewer than ten in Havana in the 1950's, and small programs, which numbered more than twenty-five. The former might have contained between 10,000 and 30,000 members each, the latter between 500 and 10,000. Large mutualism tended to pay higher salaries to physicians and provided more than adequate hospital services, while small mutualism — run by physicians — tended to pay lower salaries and enjoyed less than adequate hospital resources. Small mutualism, in a sense, made wasteful use of physicians, with an average of one physician per 200 members in 1933, whereas large programs employed one physician for every 1,000 members (Dechamp and Poblete Troncoso 1934: 17–18). Large mutualism was historically settled in Old Havana, while small (and new) mutualist clinics arose in the suburbs, especially in the wealthy sections. It is thus suggested that one consequence of mutualist organization was to INCREASE the concentration of physicians in wealthy Havana, for without the magnetic facility of mutualism, marginal physicians would more likely have tried their profession in the small towns of Cuba.

In addition, mutualism at once created an identity among physicians as LABORERS and instituted the "exploitation of the physician by the physician." In two important ways, mutualism paved the way for the new socialist system: it created a tradition of corporate rather than individual responsibility toward the patient, situating care in a clinic or hospital, and it inhibited the development of private practice. While an analysis shows that mutualism was, by the standards of a comparable society, in many ways MISDEVELOPED, private practice remained UNDER-DEVELOPED. (Nonetheless, it should be noted that private practice was everywhere present as an enclave in other institutions: prestigious physicians built their private practices — and sometimes their private mini-hospitals — through mutualism, and hospitals of all kinds made special provisions for private patients.)

As one might anticipate, the new Ministry of Health began with an ambivalent attitude toward mutualism, and although the Ministry was given the authority to demand the cooperation of all health-related institutions, it was slow to pressure drastic changes. A dual system emerged, then, with little public attention directed toward mutualist institutions. (But most of the few completely private nonmutualist clinics or mini-hospitals of ten to forty-five beds were nationalized by 1963; the most exclusive, a private hospital serving the wealthy Miramar suburb, became a special clinic for the many young scholarship students who soon occupied the abandoned mansions of the area.)

Given the overburdened and second-class character of public facilities in prerevolutionary Cuba, the goal of most people who had to use public services was to achieve the economic status necessary to join a mutuality. But many overextended their means, especially when they were pressured by salesmen (representatives) who were retained by most mutualities. (Some representatives also collected the monthly fees, keeping an 8 to 10 percent commission.) If the economy did not decline, such units would tend to grow.

Thus, one of the first consequences of the Revolution for urban health services was a sharp increase in mutualist membership. A substantial increase in disposable personal income was the immediate effect of the first measures of the Revolution, notably the halving of urban rents and the expansion of employment opportunities. While some poor persons now joined the religious sects of "*Santería*," paying upward of $1,000 per initiation, many others thronged to the membership rolls of mutualism. By 1966 mutualism may have included somewhat more than half of Havana's population and some 400,000 in other parts of Cuba.[3] The latter figure was especially the product of the income redistribution policy and the flow of resources to the countryside, although this membership continued to be concentrated in a handful of interior cities (Santiago, Camagüey, Santa Clara, Matanzas, and Pinar del Río).

What were the effects of this increase? First, it helped to mitigate whatever effect the emigration of private physicians might have had on

[3]   These are rough estimates of López Valdés (1966: 81).

the general urban population. Second, it lessened certain pressures on public services as they underwent periods of reorganization. Third, the expansion increased the intensity of contradictions within mutualism, the increased numbers making more acute the consequences of "anarchy" among various services. The latter effect was strengthened by the limitation on physical and personnel expansion of mutualism that derived from two new external conditions: (1) the aim of the new government to expand and improve public facilities with priority to new services in rural areas and (2) a general shortage of essential resources for health services that developed in Cuba, at least after 1962 and 1963. Working together, these two conditions placed strong constraints on mutualism. The general condition was not altogether unlike, for example, the transformation of the Health Insurance Plan (HIP) of New York City, which underwent a rapid increase in membership at a time of skyrocketing medical costs. On the whole, these developments tended to reduce the disparities between mutualism and the public sector (the latter could expand, the former could not), but the intensification of problems within mutualism threatened to produce an antagonism between mutualism and the revolutionary government which seemed to be responsible for the painful constraints. A great achievement of the Revolution was that it helped mutualism to resolve the internal contradictions that were intensified, though not created, by the Revolution itself.

The internal problems of mutualism took the form described above. The inability of small mutualism to provide comprehensive services, often guaranteed on paper, was a more severe problem as membership increased. Under previous circumstances, this influx would have prompted a chaotic growth of duplicated services and facilities, an increase in the price of care, and a tendency to encourage — in one way or another — more treatment under private arrangements within mutualism. Prohibited by government directives and by concrete circumstances from moving in these directions, the directors and physicians of mutualism must have been frustrated indeed, restrained for the first time from acting in old ways. Not surprisingly, some private figures of preeminence in mutualism retired from the country.

To consider such problems, a task force on mutualism was formed from mutualist physicians. Their report, presented in a national assembly of mutualism, provided the basis for an official plan to consolidate and to rationalize mutualism. The point of departure was the goal of achieving direct cooperation between large and small units. To this end, under the principles of regionalization that were developing within the Czech model in the public sector, five mutualist districts were created in Greater

Havana, in each case assigning to the largest or most capable institution the role of "base clinic." Each district collectively carried the obligation to arrange comprehensive health services for all its members, establishing necessary referral privileges, closing redundant or inefficient facilities, regrouping personnel, and expanding some services and facilities according to newly defined needs.

These measures eliminated the most glaringly speculative aspects of the pseudo-mutualities and financial irregularities that existed even among the truly cooperative centers. Some private facilities, interestingly, were nationalized and incorporated into mutualist districts.

Psychiatric services provide an example of the process of regional integration. Although most mutualist plans included mention of psychiatric care, in reality only five large mutualities provided hospitalization (all elements, in fact, of "old" or ethnic mutualism). With the exception of the women's quarters of "Covadonga," no provision was made to separate the acute from the much larger number of chronic cases, and thus, in the words of one writer, the hospitals "were converted into true warehouses of chronics" (López Valdés 1966: 62). Hospitalization for men generally predominated, although some care for women was contracted to a number of very small private clinics. Seven clinics provided irregular outpatient psychiatric consultations, but they did not employ more than a few hours of labor of one psychiatrist. Twenty-one clinics provided no psychiatric attention of any kind. By 1965, however, regionalization provided a system that extended to all mutualist members hospitalization for all acute cases by referral and left the provision of outpatient services unresolved in only seven of Havana's mutualities. In this fashion, optimum use of scarce facilities and psychiatrists was achieved, and psychiatric care was extended, with limitations, to half of Havana's population and by referral to 400,000 *mutualizados* of other areas. Furthermore, because chronic care was greatly improved during the same period in the National Psychiatric Hospital, it was reasonably intended that more hospitals would soon give greater attention to acute and chronic cases with potential for rehabilitation. Thus was built the basis for badly needed improvement in the quality of care. Medical care to mental patients was generally improved and a closer integration with general hospital services was urged; work therapy (known as "ergotherapy" in Belgium, Holland, England, and the United States) was systematically begun, perhaps for the first time in Latin America. Statistical work, archives, and case review were systematized. In addition to making more efficient use of resources, the regionalized structure of mutualism made clear the overall deficiencies and projected resource needs in psychiatric care, signaling the obligation of the medical school to train more and improved psychiatrists, psychiatric nurses, social workers, and auxiliary personnel. The absence of health education measures and preventive orientations was also made apparent.

It may be concluded that, far from experiencing deterioration in the quality of care, the population of Havana that was used to the irregular facilities of prerevolutionary mutualism benefited in important ways from the early changes introduced under the Revolution. The revolutionary Ministry of Health benefited in turn by the experience and expertise that developed within mutualism in the course of regionalization, and, more directly, by the growing cooperation between public and mutualist facilities.

## TOWARD CONSOLIDATION OF A COMPREHENSIVE NATIONAL SYSTEM

The interested reader may supplement the present discussion with several sources that analyze the contemporary Cuban health system.[4] Here I shall conclude by suggesting some of the ways whereby the early processes gave form to the emerging model.

The growth of hospital services, which by 1965 were better distributed throughout the country, and the simultaneous diminution of private practice (the consequence of emigration, public employment, social incentives, and the renunciation of such practice by new graduates after 1965) were also two sides to a greatly increasing demand for outpatient services; while more services were rendered, a new bottleneck in follow-up and continuity of care threatened to weaken the contribution of new hospital investment. This dilemma of services paralleled the tension between the mass of activities begun before 1962 and the rationalization of services within the Czech model. The former had emphasized the extension of small units in the rural periphery and the consolidation of prerevolutionary services; the latter increased the concentrated organization, from the top down, of hospital and specialist services.

The resolution of these tensions was moderated by two commitments: (1) a commitment AGAINST the substitution of services by professionals of less training for primary care by physicians and (2) a commitment to the eventual integration of all primary services with the most sophisticated hospital care. The emigration of physicians made the first commitment a matter of national pride. The second, given the level of prerevolutionary

---

[4] The best-informed and most complete analysis is Navarro (1972: 397–432).

services in Havana, was supported by the overall commitment of the Revolution to egalitarian values. And both commitments were strongly supported by the great influence of physicians in the determination of technical orientations.

The concrete development was a decision in 1965 by the Ministry of Public Health to establish and emphasize the polyclinic and its "health area" as the basic Cuban unit of health services delivery and administration. The polyclinic is designed to provide, integrate, or otherwise be responsible for four health functions — clinical services, environmental services, community health services, and social services — in a defined area and population. Under the leadership of a physician-director, these functions are served, respectively, by four health teams. With an average population of 25,000 to 35,000 in urban areas and sometimes as few as 7,500 in rural areas, the health area is small enough to be accessible and large enough to provide efficiently a substantial range of primary services. Close to the concrete tasks of sanitary control and community health work, these functions can be organized and directed by the same organization that provides clinical and social services.

The polyclinic was not invented in 1965, but its form and expanded future were decided. While its development was PRESSURED by practical problems that arose in the first five years of revolution, the roots of INVENTION and the Cuban predisposition for the polyclinic lay in the rural health center, mutualist organization, dispensaries of the prerevolutionary Ministry of Health, and Czechoslovakian experience.[5] When to these preconditions were added the POLITICAL disdain for private practice as a vestige of capitalism and the TECHNICAL disdain for the solo office practitioner as an archaic source of health services, the new Cuban polyclinic seems to follow as if by logic.

Like the polyclinic, the rural health center was administratively independent of the hospital; in the rural center the public health responsibilities for a specific area were integrated and liaison with organized popular participation in health promotion was emphasized. The People's Health Councils of the rural centers were clearly precursors to the Area Health Commission.

---

[5]   After almost complete destruction of many medical facilities and loss of half of all physicians in World War II, by 1960 Czechoslovakia had constructed a system that linked even the most remote village to a highly sophisticated regionalized structure of public medical and sanitary services. (See Weinerman (1969). In 1961–1962, Czech professionals provided the technical support for the first mass campaign of polio immunization in Cuba, based on their own experience with a similar campaign in 1959–1960, and gave technical input for the regional plan of public services that evolved in the same year.

Thus, if one envisions an organizational and political conflict between the 1959–1961 development (small dispensaries and rural hospitals) and the 1961–1963 rationalization of hospital services (provincial and regional administrations and service levels), one might argue that the 1965–1968 emphasis on the polyclinic and the health area represent a victory of the first tendencies in the context of the second.

Like the polyclinic, the precursory mutualist programs offered comprehensive medical responsibilities and, regardless of many inadequacies, set important traditions of physician EMPLOYMENT and corporate rather than individual responsibility. Unlike the polyclinic, however, mutualist clinics were removed from sanitary and many preventive functions, were inadequately linked to hospital and specialty services, made ineffective use of auxiliary personnel and extravagant use of physicians, and were disconnected from a geographically defined base. But the rationalization of mutualism under REGIONALIZATION in 1961–1964 transformed many mutualist clinics into a form that strikingly approximates the modern polyclinic. Some clinics, in fact, were converted directly into public polyclinics before 1965. Increasingly, mutualist clinics, like the well-known Clínica Reína in Havana, were made to serve the dual function of area polyclinic and mutualist program, offering identical services to both categories of patients.

The completion of the polyclinic and health area represents a final stage in the integration of mutualist and public services, for by creating a public outpatient service that is similar in most respects to the evolving mutualist clinic, the *raison d'être* of mutualism — the consumer's need to avoid both the second-class care of public institutions and the high cost and insecurities of private medical care — disappears. A "withering away of mutualism" was thus expected and, as a sign of this anticipation, the budget function of mutualism was included after 1967 within the budget of the Ministry of Public Health. Although the membership programs of mutualism continue to exist, the "withering" process is such that mutualism is increasingly invisible as a health institution in Cuba today.

All these developments have been reflected in medical education. The rationalization and regionalization of hospitals included, of course, all teaching facilities. The effect of this was to enhance the sense of responsibility of a teaching unit toward a given population (as opposed to the passive attitude of the prerevolutionary hospital), to provide opportunities for the student to see the process of interrelation between hospital and community, and to make clear the greatly expanded new role of health auxiliaries who were being trained especially for the community component of services. The organization of the health area and the poly-clinic increased these tendencies. Like all other physicians, teachers and students were required to give services in the area polyclinics, and some polyclinics near teaching hospitals have developed specialized teaching functions. The consequence has been to give Cuban medical education a very strong "community orientation." One highly respected specialist in international health services research concluded, for example, that Cuban medical education was the most community oriented of any system known to him.

Such are the bare outlines of early transformations and their con-tribution to the contemporary Cuban model of health care organization. Perhaps it is unnecessary to add that were it not for the imposing unity and profound social commitment of the Revolution as a whole, such simultaneous developments would have been impossible or mutually antagonistic and characterized by destructive conflict. The Revolution not only propelled simultaneous developments but moderated their contradictions into creative resolutions. Political cadres, norms, and procedures of the new ministry (as well as working outside of channels) created a framework for the whole system together with its social ob-jectives which enabled the creative resolution of old and new antagonisms.

In contrast to the narrowly economic and political perspective with which the outsider commonly views the Revolution, the insider sees the development of the health sector as integrated within the heart of the Revolution. By presenting the elements of this history, I hope to contribute to a more complete image of Cuban reality. Such a focus has and will support the tendency to keep foremost the goals that are essential to the humanist nature of the Revolution. The success of a revolution is not measured in production quotas alone, but in actual increments in the quality of human existence. The aim is to build a healthy, sane society which liberates the positive potentials of humankind. Broadly conceived, the goals of health promotion are the goals of the Revolution itself.

## REFERENCES

AMADOR GARCÍA, MANUEL
    1963   Enfermedad y condiciones de vida. *Revista Cubana de Medicina* 2(1): 34–45.
CALVÓ FONSECA, RAFAEL
    1959   Servicio de salud en el medio rural: proyecto de organización sanitaria-asistencial. *Revista KUBA de Medicina Tropical y de Parasitología* 15 (1–6). (Written with the aid of the "Finlay" Institute.)

DANIELSON, ROSS
   1973   "Cuban health organization: history and development." Unpublished
          doctoral dissertation, University of Pittsburgh.
DECHAMP, CYRILLE, MOISÉS POBLETE TRONCOSO
   1934   *El problema médico y la asistencia mutualista en Cuba.* Report of the
          International Labor Office. Translated into Spanish by Rafael de la
          Torre. Havana.
FONT PUPO, CARLOS
   1963   La salud del pueblo, preocupación básica de la Revolución. *Cuba
          Socialista* 3(20):41–60.
GÓMEZ WANGÜEMERT, LUÍS
   1962   Falsedad desmentida. (Reproduced from the editorial page of the
          Havana newspaper *El Mundo*). *Revista Cubana de Pediatría* 34(5):1–2.
LÓPEZ VALDÉS, JORGE
   1966   Organización de la asistencia psiquiátrica en el mutualismo. *Revista
          Cubana de Medicina* 5(1):62–81.
NAVARRO, VICENTE
   1972   Health, health services, and health planning in Cuba. *International
          Journal of Health Services* 2(3):397–432.
PORTUONDO DE CASTRO, JUAN M.
   n.d.   *Como se apoderaron los comunistas de la Universidad de La Habana.*
          Miami: Ediciones del Directorio Magisterial Cubano (Exilio).
*Revista cubana de medicina*
   1964   Informe del Ministerio de Salud Pública a la XVII Asamblea Mundial
          de la Organización Mundial de Salud sobre el desarrollo del Plan de
          Salud durante el año 1963. *Revista Cubana de Medicina* 3: 283–292.
SABIN, ALBERT B.
   1962   La erradicación de la poliomielitis. *Revista Cubana de Pediatría* 34(4):
          28–33.
SMILLIE, WILSON GEORGE, *et al.*
   1935   Section on public health in *Problems of the new Cuba.* New York:
          Foreign Policy Association, Commission on Cuban Affairs.
WEINERMAN, RICHARD E.
   1969   *Socialist medicine in Eastern Europe.* Cambridge: Harvard University
          Press.

# Thesis: Cultural Anthropology and Community Psychiatry
# Antithesis: World Health Organization and Basic Health Services
# Synthesis: Community Development

PHILIP SINGER, ENRIQUE ARANETA

It has been shown that predominant problems and attitudes as well as acculturation patterns that prevail in different communities are reflected in the type of psychiatric disturbance or maladaptation syndromes that exist in those communities (Institute of Social and Economic Research of the University of West Indies 1967: 221–236).

The relationship between community characteristics and psychiatric disorders has been further discussed by Amiel (1965). He emphasized that adjustment difficulties can be properly evaluated and remedied only in the context of the culture in which they manifest themselves. If this is so, then it follows that the solutions that are devised to meet the community's problems are simultaneously potential remedies for relieving the strained adjustment and attendant emotional stress that may be imposed on the members of the community. To the extent that community problems and attitudes are reflected in the adjustment difficulties and emotional demands imposed on its members, the problem of community development is very much a problem of community mental health.

## THE HEALTH TEAM: A PREFERRED SOURCE OF ASSISTANCE

Although it seems illogical that persons who have problems in coping with economic and social stresses and in developing the social skills and judgement required to secure personal gratifications through social relationships should seek help from a physician or hospital or clinic, the fact is that most of them do. This is true not only when frustrations find expression in psychosomatic symptoms such as headaches, sleeplessness, impotence, etc., but even when feelings of rejection, helplessness, isolation, and irritability beset the individual. It may be that the confidentiality attributed to the "doctor-patient relationship" fosters this trend, or it may be that the traditional concept of "the healer," and not just the "technician," still prevails in the image of the physician. In any event, the physician is often sought after for help in failures at making adequate adjustments.

Whether or not this outlook or tendency is reasonable is not of immediate importance. The fact is that the physician is accorded an image of competency in solving failures in personal fulfillment of whatever cause and this image grants him the potential for developing effective community leadership. However, in what manner that leadership is to be exercised and by what means are questions that demand close scrutiny.

## THE FUNCTIONS OF PSYCHIATRY:
## MEDICAL COMMITMENT AND SOCIAL RESPONSIBILITY

For psychiatry to be relevant to community development efforts, its functions need to be clarified. Because psychiatry is the only medical specialty which did not originate in response to the demands of the patients, but rather from the demands of society for its own protection, much ambiguity has plagued the definition of psychiatry's function. Whereas psychiatry is committed, in accordance with medical tradition, to the amelioration of the patient's suffering, it is also bound to meeting the demands of the society. In reconciling this dual responsibility psychiatry attempts a resolution by acquiring a better understanding of the major factors that produce behavioral disturbances. These include:
1. disturbance in the functioning of the central nervous system, and
2. disturbances in relationships that develop between the patient and his environment in its various aspects.

Viewed from this perspective, the functions of psychiatry can be visualized as the promotion of social reorientation and integration through medical and psychosocial intervention. Toward these ends the functions of the psychiatrist-physician may be specified.
1. The recognition or discrimination between organic and functional

causes of behavioral changes and the medical treatment of the organic causes. (We have still to bear in mind that despite the sophistication in diagnostic methods in the United States, there is a much greater incidence of intracranial mass lesions, particularly tumors, in the autopsy materials from mental hospitals as compared with those from general hospitals, where most people go for neurological and neurosurgical assistance.)

2. The second function would be the amelioration of physiological (autonomic and metabolic changes or symptoms wrought by the functional disorder) disorders. Recent experience has shown that tranquilizers and electro-convulsive therapy, although not capable of changing the patient's ability to adapt to his environment, nonetheless help to reduce the physiological changes that heighten the patient's propensity for disintegration, thus rendering him more accessible to psychosocial intervention.

3. Because the emotional autonomic responses have been shown by the physiologist Pavlov and his students to be modifiable through "conditioning," yet another medical function has to be served by the psychiatrist, and that is study and dissemination of the procedures (facilitation of psychotherapy) that facilitate or reinforce and extinguish or modify emotional or behavioral patterns of response (habits) to particular situations.

4. In line with the task of psychosocial intervention, the psychiatrist-physician also has the task of identifying the cultural values and the culture definers of the community or society to which the patient belongs, and promoting activities or organizations that would enhance the relationship between the patient and these agents of cultural definition and reality. In several studies comparing the results of psychotherapy of the psychoanalytic type with simple clinic "check-up", it has been found that the incidence of recovery among comparable cases of both groups is about the same, and that the common factor found among those who recovered in the latter group is the development of companionship or of an interested friend. Thus it would seem evident that the social reorientation through psychosocial intervention can be as effectively accomplished by lay members of the community as by professionals.

5. In a study on Long Island in the United States, in which the disturbed children of a school were referred to management by the mothers of the healthy children of the same school, it was found that the recovery rate was superior to that of those who were referred to psychologists or child guidance clinics. In Guyana, referral of patients for therapy by the indigenous healers produced equally impressive results. So we see that

still another function of the psychiatrist-physician is the promotion of increased understanding among the leaders of a given culture about the patient's sufferings and the direction of efforts at adjustment with the goal of increasing the community's capacity for accommodation. This activity could very well lead to a re-examination of the values that may no longer be congruous with the developing social and technological changes and may thus promote the adaptive compensatory actions in the community that may serve to offset the potentially disruptive effects or influences that these changes may bring.

As for promoting social reorientation and reintegration, it will be noted that we propose the use of culturally accepted agents or mediators for promoting personal development values, i.e. we propose that disturbed children be placed under the care of effective mother surrogates, disturbed adolescents under appropriate "ego-ideals," and disturbed family relationships be mediated by accepted culture representatives. In the development of community "assumptive systems," the "assumptive world" of the therapist should not be far removed from that of the sufferers. Indeed, the most fundamental assumption for effective community mental health work should be that the community components of any community mental health program must derive from the particular community culture.

## SOCIOCULTURAL ENVIRONMENT: DEVIANCE AND COMMUNITY DISRUPTION

By suggesting that community psychiatry could be a new frontier for community development, we are saying that widespread problems and concerns with DEVIANCE, the ABNORMAL, and NONCONFORMITY exist in every community. We are also suggesting that every community expends considerable resources in controlling and socializing the persons who manifest these tendencies. Further, if we extend the concept of psychiatry to include communities, not necessarily just individual pathological states, it is possible to harness an important community strength with significance for other aspects of community development. Whether the incidence of mental disorder is 50 percent, or one out of five, or one out of ten is NOT our concern.

With Leighton (1961: 24–31) we find that the best approach to an understanding of the relationship between sociocultural environment and psychological experience is that of the COMMUNITY. This is because there is hardly any mental illness which can be identified with a specific agent. Thus, the community model, or even wider, the ecological medical model, embracing the traditional public health notion of host, agent, and environment, is most appropriate. Our concern, however, is not with the adequacy or inadequacy of the community as a social system according to any set of criteria.[1] Rather, we would take as our operational definition ANY community in which there is a community development program already in existence or in the planning stages. It would, of course, be interesting to know how such communities are selected. On the other hand, if it is the desire of a community development program to tackle the most disintegrated communities in terms of the criteria noted above, then the community psychiatric approach offers the possibility of a direct attack upon the regressive forces of the community.

In this connection, it is significant that Leighton's work shows that a disintegrated area will have about 59 percent impaired individuals[2] as contrasted to 29 percent in a community that is not disintegrated.

Again, we would emphasize that the prevalence of psychiatric disorder need NOT be the basis for a community psychiatry program, which in turn can provide the thrust for a wider community development program.

Our concern is with the POINT OF ENTRY into the community. Obviously, there can be many points of entry, including agricultural extension, "food for peace," maternal and child health center, *panchayat* (village council), etc. Although each of these could enhance any community program if it were initially concerned in a SUFFICIENTLY COMPREHENSIVE WAY, none of them possesses the degree of interrelatedness between environmental factors and biological factors that community psychiatry possesses. Also, while a community psychiatric approach can touch all other factors, it is rare that a new community developmental approach will touch upon the problems and opportunities that a psychiatric approach, most widely understood as BEHAVIOR, encompasses.

---

[1]  For example, in the Leighton's Sterling Study, ten indices were developed against which to determine the degree of "integrated" or "disintegrated" state of the community. The ten were: (1) Poverty-instability of income as well as low level. (2) Cultural confusion, i.e. confused and conflicting values. (3) Secularization, i.e. absence of religious values. (4) Frequency of broken homes. (5) Few and weak associations in the group, both formal and informal. (6) Few and weak leaders. (7) Few patterns of recreation. (8) High frequency of hostile acts and expressions. (9) High frequency of crime and delinquency. (10) Fragmented network of communication (1961:28).
[2]  "Impaired" refers to definite psychiatrically disordered persons whose disorder interfered with their work, plus those with psycho-physiological or sociopathic symptoms (Leighton 1961:28).

# THE ANTHROPOLOGICAL APPROACH TO
# COMMUNITY PSYCHIATRY

## Interrelatedness of Personality Organization and Cultural Institutions and Processes

Community psychiatry is conceived of and approached in a variety of ways. Those that emphasize the treatment of "illness" lean toward the medical model approach, and those that emphasize prevention lean toward what may be described as applied social psychiatry (Goldston 1965).

We suggest the cultural or anthropological view, predicated on the interrelatedness between the existing and developing cultural institutions of the community and the modal personality organization. This approach deals with the system of mutually qualifying and prescribing relationships between the individual and his culture, not with the patient and the various social factors independently. There is no need in this conceptualization for the creation of a "therapeutic community." The system itself is the therapeutic community into which psychiatric services and activities are to be integrated. The degree of integration of the cultural institutions within the system is reflected by the degree of integration of the personalities, and the intensity of the relationship between the institutions and personalities determines the therapeutic and developmental potential of the communities. The task of development and the task of therapy become identical and consist of promoting new concepts, services, and goals to be incorporated, integrated, and institutionalized into the ongoing system.

The assumption in this approach is that therapy, like mental health and, for that matter, development, are ongoing processes that have no meaning and cannot exist independently of the system.

## Community Psychiatry and Conceptualization of Psychiatric Disorders

Psychiatric disorders involve a problem of adjustment. It is in relation to this problem of adjustment that physicians differentiate psychiatric disorders from the rest of the medical disorders. Yet the concept of "illness" is promoted. This conceptualization poses incongruities in the management of these disorders and serves to isolate patients from the community despite the fact that the basic aim is one of readjustment and resocialization. This concept also interferes with the proper understanding of behavioral problems, which have meaning only in the cultural context in the community in which they manifest themselves and involve belief systems and life-styles. The concept of "illness" exonerates the "patient" from responsibility for his maladaptive or deviant behavior and precludes the concepts of "self-help and mutual help" from operating effectively in the treatment process. Further, the concept of "illness" implies a physical or organic substrate to the dysfunction with potential for genetic transmission, and often leads to the elaboration of ideas of family stigma — an assumption that not only is unwarranted, but raises more social difficulties and alienation problems.

Because functional psychiatric disorders become unacceptable only to the degree that they cannot be accommodated in a particular culture, "mental illness" is really a cultural construct involving social issues rather than a discrete disease process. As such it would be more appropriate to deal with these disorders as social phenomena, whose degree of acceptability or unacceptability will vary as community social values vary; also because the potential for their causation and modification inheres in social processes and changes, they are amenable to a community development approach. To a large extent, community psychiatry has been held back from truly entering the community as a developmental force just because of this persistence of the medical model.

In order best to utilize a community development approach to community psychiatry, it will be necessary to move away from the disease concept of mental illness, or even from the notion of chronicity (because most functional "illnesses" are reversible), toward a cultural-operational definition in relationship to concepts of normality or abnormality. This approach demands that the worker deal with the entire community and its values, attitudes, beliefs, and norms as they are behaviorally demonstrated in institutions and technology.

### Diagnosis versus Social Problems: Problem of Mediation

Deviant behavior or "mental illness" in the community context, in which it is perceived and usually treated, is in most developing countries very often "an occasion for social judgement." So, what is diagnosis to medicine is a moral issue to society; and, as a moral issue, its management depends on the belief systems and culturally defined mediating processes of the community (Firth 1959).

Inasmuch as psychiatrists are not likely to represent the culturally appropriate mediator for the promotion of the emotional and social development of a particular patient of a particular age, religion, and socioeconomic status, one cannot expect such a therapist to perform directly the task of cultural mediation in a developing country. Indeed, even at the Veterans Administration and state mental hospitals in the United States, the aides and attendants are often more likely to develop a more meaningful relationship with most patients than do the psychiatrists or psychologists, whose cultural backgrounds are far removed from those of the patients.

We suggest, therefore, that social reorientation through psychosocial intervention has greater chances of success in the hands of the culturally accepted mediators of a particular society or subculture, for in the ensuing relationship, there is greater hope for permanence, and the patient's reactions are most meaningful in the community context.

This cultural, functional approach to the understanding of personality organization and behavioral deviance and its redirection through social cultural processes is unfortunately still missing from the usual conceptualization of "community psychiatry." Indeed, at the PAHO/WHO Seminar on Mental Health in Kingston, Jamaica, in September 1965, it was unanimously agreed that the psychoanalytic type of psychotherapy has proved ineffectual among mental patients of the Caribbean area.

Yet another consideration in having the community involved in the psychosocial reorientation of the patient, or "psychotherapy," is the fact that an interview lasting one hour per week with the psychiatrist is far less effective than the influence exerted by community pressures and attitudes. In the social process that we call psychotherapy, the importance of the "support system" of the community in influencing the "assumptive system" of the patient cannot be overestimated (Linton 1945: 94).

*The Therapeutic Tradition and Psychiatric Healing*

Traditionally, therapists in a society constitute an elite that mediates between the sufferer and the conflictual social processes, the supposed magical powers or gods, or, as in modern society, between the sufferer and the so-called "psychodynamic" processes. With increasing understanding of, and emphasis on, natural processes, modern medicine has veered toward becoming a technology and has become a dyadic rather than a community process. This has had the effect of making the modern therapist the sole definer of therapeutic procedures and goals — a situation which has made the role of the sufferer a purely passive one. Efforts by psychiatrists to depart from this trend meet with resistance from patients who find this departure incongruous with the medical model.

However, some societies clearly perceive that "doctor work" refers to organic illness responsive to the special armamentarium of the scientific healer, and they make a distinction between "doctor work" and what may be called functional disorders or "mental illness" of nonorganic origin (Singer and Araneta 1967). As Western medicine takes a firmer hold on the developing countries, concepts of sickness and health that were perceived as part of and closely linked to the sociocultural systems, seem to be breaking down. But the concepts of mental illness and health have for the most part resisted the Western disease-technology approach in favor of the social problems approach. Mental health is still, for the developing countries, very much a reflection of the state of social well-being defined by the World Health Organization (WHO).

In most developing countries and societies, "therapy" as applied to "mental illness" has retained for the most part its traditional meaning: "to worship, to attend." This utilizes the social elements of community support of the relationship of healer and sufferer based on mutually held belief systems and shared rites and ceremonies.

In psychiatric therapy, in which "assumptive systems" rather than specific pathogens are involved, "treatment can only be undertaken in the general context of beliefs..." (Loden 1965: 139).

In discussing the popularity of the indigenous healer, Firth notes that

... they are in intimate contact with the members of the community and are often in a position to find the network of social relationship factors related to psychosomatic illness ... (Firth 1959: 152–153).

Again, not merely illness but also problems of a moral order may be referred to them.

## Psychiatry as Therapy and Community as Milieu

Despite all the claims for psychopharmacology in the treatment of mental illness,[3] the fact remains that talking and listening remain the primary therapeutic methods of psychiatry.

Recognition of this fact has led some psychiatrists into simultaneous treatment of groups of patients, to which the name "group therapy" has

[3] The conclusion drawn in 1964 on the effects of drugs seems just as valid today. In reviewing the field, Dr. Wortis (1965:648) evaluated the usefulness of the pharmacological armamentarium for mental illness as follows: "Hospitalization is often delayed or averted, the behaviour of hospitalized cases is improved and discharge rates increase; but there is a distressingly high readmission rate, and in the ambulatory case sooner or later the hospitalization rate matches that of patients on placebos."

been given. Indeed, some psychiatrists who talk with groups of fifty and more hospitalized patients at a time call what they do "mob therapy." Of course, this simultaneous approach to therapy is unthinkable to any physician, even those who have overflowing waiting rooms. Indeed, it is this group approach to therapy, perhaps more than anything else, which illustrates the qualitative difference between mental illness and organic illness. The fact that diagnostic evaluations have also been made systematically in the group setting is a further example of basic, important differences (Snell 1966: 880–885).

We have been arguing that to the extent that most mental illness is a functional disorder, it should be conceived as a community problem and should be handled in the community through community development efforts. We should not allow the developing countries to follow the model of the West and to independently discover for themselves the expensive truth about the "social breakdown" syndrome or "environmental oppression" and the fact that the hospital is a very expensive social system.

## WORLD HEALTH ORGANIZATION AND
## COMMUNITY APPROACHES TO MENTAL HEALTH

The World Health Organization has long recognized the important role of the community and community development in making provisions for the mentally ill (World Health Organization 1959).[4]

However, it has preferred to use the term "social psychiatry" and has comprehensively defined it as

all areas where mental illness and the functioning of society come into contact, including the details of administrative and forensic practice AND THE TECHNIQUES OF COMMUNITY DEVELOPMENT (World Health Organization 1959: 5).

Most important, perhaps, is the recognition by the Expert Committee that "in whatever way a society may be organized, it is not so much the type of mental disorder that varies as the community's reaction to abnormal behavior" (World Health Organization 1959: 6).

Thus, there is explicit recognition that hospitalization of "psychiatric casualties" may not be realistic "in relatively unchanged agrarian socie-

---

[4]    This report is the work of a WHO Expert Committee on Mental Health. It is pertinent to quote here the official attitude of the WHO toward the reports of expert committees. The WHO notes that such reports "are of basic importance to WHO. While not necessarily expressing the views of the Organization, they are taken into consideration in developing policies and programmes." This comment appears with every publication of the Technical Report Series.

ties," where there may not only be an absence of hospitals, but where the patient will eventually have to be "reintegrated in the joint family system at a later stage." Under such conditions the report urges bringing skilled help to the patient within the family milieu.

However, it notes that in rapidly changing societies, reintegration may be more difficult. Although deploring the "creation of enormous mental hospitals ... in which patients and staff [live] cut off from the community," the report nevertheless leaves the impression that such hospitals are necessary, because the mentally sick person has "been excluded from the community for the duration of his illness."

Thus, the report suggests that the crucial variable in getting the former mental patient back into the community, is the "attitude of the ordinary man and woman to psychiatric illness and psychiatric practice." However, this emphasis on "attitudes," as representing the essence of community, and the exclusive reliance on the mental hospital, are precisely where the real difficulties lie in coming to grips with the community approach to mental illness. Communities are not primarily "attitudes," but social structures within which a variety of attitudes may be held and which are made up of relationships with persisting patterns of interaction, and in which norms exist in terms of role definitions, opportunities, and expectations. There are leisure relationships, work relationships, neighborhood relationships, etc., even in the shantytowns of the most contemporary and rapidly changing societies. Reliance upon idiosyncratic "attitudes" to be determined through some sort of "attitude research" as recommended by the report (World Health Organization 1959: 38) as well as reliance upon "community leaders," defined as "politicians, administrators, employers, trade union chiefs, religious leaders, teachers as well as journalists, and other writers," to change attitudes, may be appropriate for marketing soap, but has little relevance to community involvement with the mentally ill.

Of course, a good part of this reliance upon "attitude change" in order to bring about "acceptance" for the discharged mental patient is due to the insistence that mental illness is a "disease" and must be treated by appropriate medical personnel. But given that basic assumption, it is understandable that there will then result an emphasis on passive "attitude" change in the community instead of active community involvement. The social devices noted by WHO that have been developed by psychiatrists to reintegrate patients into the social community, such as the open-door principle, day hospitals, night hospitals, and therapeutic social clubs are laudable in themselves; however, they remain institutions grafted onto the community and not basic to the community. The WHO

Report's insistence that "specialized activities in the field of mental health should be integrated, or at least closely coordinated, with other general health services" again reveals the basic assumption that mental illness is a disease which must be treated by specialists. Indeed, the report specifically states that "mental illness is just as susceptible to treatment and cure as is physical illness" (World Health Organization 1959: 29). Such an attitude can only result in widening the gap between the community and those who are "mentally ill."

Also, such an assumption makes the report's suggestion that the psychiatrist be called upon more frequently to advise, for example, in schemes for community development (World Health Organization 1959: 33) more a reflection of optimism than a realistic assessment. The fact is that most psychiatrists are ill-equipped to participate in community development just because they operate under the disease model frame of reference.[5]

The psychiatric disease model basically enables the psychiatrist in a relatively brief time, less than an hour at best, to make an evaluation of such social factors as the patient's motivation, ego strength, and relationship to reality, and then decide "whether to prescribe further evaluation, medication or other organic treatments, hospitalization, deep or supportive psychotherapy, short-term treatment, group therapy, or referral" (Anonymous 1968).

However, neither the evaluation nor the prescription have very much to do with the community or with the patients' problems in relation to such factors of reality as employment, racial integration, housing, physical illness, nutrition, recreation, and indeed all those relationships and involvements that make an individual a fully participating member of his community and culture.

Obviously, the difference between working with one person (or a group as in group therapy) and working with one person in the community and the institutions of the community itself is large and real. Neither the Basic Health Services of developing countries nor the general hospital has devised, or is in a position to develop, community strategies other than the notion of changing attitudes. The psychopathological label and the psychodynamic formulation are too restrictive to cope with community complexity.

The change in public attitude recommended by the WHO report is in reality a desire to exchange an already existing set of attitudes held by the individual and the community about the "status" of deviant behavior, which involves the individual, the healer, and numerous aspects of the

---

[5] For a discussion of the failure of psychiatrists to work successfully in the community, see DeSole and Singer (1968).

community, for another set, which primarily involves the "patient" and the "physician." The older attitude, which the report would change, provides an entire way of life; the "new" attitude fragments the individual and isolates him even further from a culture undergoing rapid change.

### Prospects for Mental Health Services and the WHO Concept of Basic Health Services

It does not appear at all likely in the foreseeable future that either the WHO, or the governments themselves, will be prepared to adopt and implement medical plans involving major capital outlays for hospital construction and expensive psychiatric manpower training programs demanded by the "disease entity" approach to mental health. Indeed, a review of the WHO's projections in the health field for the second Development Decade, indicates a virtual absence of any regional objectives for mental health (World Health Organization 1969). The only exception is to be found in the Regional Committee for the African Region, which noted that although problems arising from mental illness do not constitute a major priority, they are nevertheless "likely to receive increasing attention because of the growth of urbanization and industrialization." The committee further notes that "it will be necessary to undertake extensive staff training to meet both existing deficiencies and increasing demands" (World Health Organization 1969: 37).

On the other hand, WHO does recognize the existence of mental conditions and the need to do something about them within the framework of Basic Health Services, which should be one of the programs in any national health plan. Among the functions of the Basic Health Services they note the category of "services of a personal kind" which

... include first aid, the detection and disposal of acute medical, surgical and mental conditions, and immunization. They are the major channel for personal and communal health education (World Health Organization 1969: 62).

Although WHO is fully conscious of the importance of community effort in relationship to the Basic Health Services, nevertheless the structuring of the establishment and maintenance of the Basic Health Services has little in common with popular participation and community involvement and motivation as understood and practiced in community development programs. It is still basically a static, service-oriented institution. Although this model can serve medical conditions admirably, it is questionable how effective it can be in terms of mental illness as defined here. There surely is an important area for joint program development and thinking between WHO and the community development project designed to assist the medical personnel staffing the Basic Health Services — the physician, nurse, midwife, sanitarian — in understanding and treating patients within the community milieu and not just the Basic Health Services Unit.

### The Basic Health Services and the Community

The problem with the present form of the Basic Health Services in relationship to such a complex problem as mental illness is that the unit is still basically conceived in terms of the classical medical dyadic-helping relationship. Such a medical, dyadic-helping relationship is the very opposite of a community social relationship, in which the dyadic episode is viewed primarily as a BREAK in a complex and continuous network of social relationships. There is little reciprocity in a Basic Health Services Unit, and reciprocity is the very essence of a community development approach. But then again, reciprocity is not a major component in the dyadic medical relationship in which the helper does something to or upon the person of the other, regardless of the other and his social boundaries. Indeed, the very idea that Basic Health Services "may serve a population of 20,000 to 25,000 through a group of small health posts *whose number would be determined by the size of the area, and its geographical features*" is the very opposite of the concept of social boundaries which is so central to the community within which people relate to each other and to the concept of mental illness as "status" (World Health Organization 1969: 62).

## INTEGRATING A PSYCHIATRIC SERVICE INTO A COMMUNITY IN GUYANA

### Community Problems and Mental Hospital Admission rates

Social changes wrought by technological change resulted in a multiplicity of pressing problems... . The problems are rooted in economics, technology, social organization and government, but, the severe stresses they engender are psychological stresses with behavioural consequences, that, within themselves constitute new problems (Yolles 1965).

In Guyana at the time that the following observations were made, ongoing racial and political polarization had created many uncertainties which accompanied the displacement of families and increasing unemployment. A heightened state of suspiciousness increasingly infused itself into the population; rioting became more frequent and more intense. To what degree these factors influenced the admission rates at the mental hospital is difficult to verify because statistics on the population size in the age group susceptible to "mental illness" were inadequate. The fact is that there was an increasing rate of admissions: from 229 in 1960, to 281 in 1961, to 301 in 1962, to 307 in 1963, to 350 in 1964, and finally to 490 in 1965. It was evident that discharge rates comparable, if not exceeding the admission rates, were imperative in order to maintain a constant standard of care in the facility, which, in fact, was in dire need of improvement. Discharging patients into the community was a problem that had to be studied because it depended on the conceptualization of "mental disorders" and on how capable the patient's social milieu was of accommodating to the situation.

Of over 550 patients who were at the mental hospital in August of 1995, 100 were considered to be sufficiently recovered to be able to return to the community. In letters and interviews with relatives who visited these patients, most of whom were from the city, two major difficulties were expressed — one was financial and the other was the fear that the families would be identified as having a "madman" among them and that this would spoil the opportunities of their female members to get married.

Another interesting observation was that most of the relatives who visited patients were East Indians or Negroes from the RURAL areas. It became evident, therefore, that there was greater chance of discharging patients, especially East Indians, from the rural areas. Interviews with both patients and their relatives brought forth some understanding of the general concepts of "mental illness" held by the different ethnocultural groups:

1. Most rural East Indians considered "mental illness" either as an act of superior forces or gods or as the bad influence of "wicked" persons. Therefore, they did not consider the patient culpable.

2. Most urban dwellers, especially the "creolized" Negroes and East Indians, regarded mental illness as something shameful, probably hereditary, reflecting "wickedness" (probably because most of the early admissions to the hospital were due to CNS syphilis).

The implication for the expectations of the various groups regarding the mental hospital became obvious.

*Developing Mental Hospital Services and Policies to Meet Community Expectations*

On the basis of the concepts of "mental illness" and of the role of the mental hospital expressed by the major groups, the policies and services of the hospital were modified. Because the rural East Indian communities near the hospital were eager to have their patients back and were more willing to accommodate and rehabilitate them, the admission wards were converted into intensive treatment units and modified electroconvulsive therapy (ECT) was reintroduced. Patients whose families were eager to get them home, or who showed adequate premorbid adjustment, or whose illnesses were of recent onset, were given priority in treatment with ECT.

Meanwhile, increased participation in the "tasks" of living in the hospital was encouraged. As patients started to integrate, they were assigned to the various groups that participated in the daily maintenance activities of the hospital. These groups included laundry details, sanitation details, ground maintenance crew, farm workers, library workers, recreational therapy assistants, pharmacist assistants, clerical assistants, kitchen assistants, assistants at the press, carpenters' apprentices, occupational therapy assistants, messengers, assistants to the supply officers, and various other ESSENTIAL activities groups, some of which were engaged in services for the other hospitals in the district. "Living therapy" was emphasized more than "talking therapy": goal-directed efforts more than self-contemplation. The underlying principle was "one is what one does"; self-definition is an ongoing process related to functional effectiveness and social acceptability rather than to introspective formulations.

*Socialization: A Process of Mutual Help*

Unlike other fields in medicine in which the doctor assumes a total responsibility for the treatment of the patient, in psychiatric therapy the responsibility for most of the treatment, which is the adequate functioning in society, is channeled back to the patient. This is obvious, because in personality development, as in community development, the process that is being encouraged is increasing self-determination and self-responsibility.

To encourage socially acceptable behavior at the mental hospital, patients participating in the various work details previously enumerated were not only given grounds privileges, but were further encouraged to organize picnics on the mental hospital grounds and farm, as well as at various other popular places in the vicinity. Within a short time even the chronic patients asked to join the various groups. The rate at which psychotic patients integrated was quite impressive. In time, most of the patients and staff spent the greater part of the day out of doors, and the problem of behavior regulation shifted from the staff's concern to the patients' as well. A freer communication developed as patients became co-workers with the staff. The hospital farm became the showcase of the district; the cricket team was one of the most powerful in the country. As patients learned to help each other, they learned to understand and regulate their relationships more effectively. Personal and social growth became an ongoing process through mutual help.

## Integrating Mental Hospital Activities into Community Life

As the general hospital atmosphere improved, more visitors came. Through the efforts of the hospital administrator, a group of civic-minded citizens, who called themselves "The League of Friends," was encouraged to meet weekly at the mental hospital with the patients to discuss their problems with them and even to share some of the patients' projects. This group also helped organize fund-raising fairs, bazaars, dances, and athletic competitions with the patients for the needed improvements at the hospital. The members of "The League of Friends" gradually became less apprehensive about the "patients," and started to take them out to their homes on weekends and to invite them to participate in and help at various social functions. There developed a free interchange between the population of the neighboring communities and the mental hospital, and quite a few patients spent most of their days in the neighboring communities as part-time help and contract workers. Gradually, more and more organizations came to visit and share in the activities of the mental hospital. Indeed most of the social activities of the neighboring communities either took place at the hospital grounds or involved the participation of the hospital personnel and patients.

## Psychiatric Rehabilitation and Community Needs

Occupational therapies, as they are frequently administered in psychiatric hospitals, often have little or no bearing on the needs of the community or on the preparation of the patient to become a more valuable member of the community. The fact that patients are not integrated into the road improvement programs or agricultural projects and the like, and that instead they are trained to make bird cages and fancy baskets, reflects the persistence of the alienating attitude toward these "deviants" that accompanied the development of psychiatry.

In the community approach that we have been describing, the mental hospital farm became an experimental station for agriculture and animal husbandry for the community. The carpenters and other trades-men among the recovered patients were sought out by the community. Indeed, the community development workers and consultants used the mental hospital facilities to demonstrate their efforts at introducing the new techniques in agriculture and other cottage industries that they were promoting.

An assumption inherent in the concept of the "therapeutic community" is that lessons learned in the structured environment are automatically transferrable and relevant to relationships in the greater community. That this is, however, often incorrect is reflected in the increasing re-admission rates and frequency of re-admission notable on most reports concerning such programs. The fact is that if we want the structured community to be relevant to the greater community, the hospital com-munity must be made a part of the greater community's life. The hospital within the community then becomes one of the social institutions con-cerned with personality and social development and integration. The greater community itself becomes the "therapeutic community" into whose various social, cultural, and technological institutions the hospital programs must be integrated.

*Mental Health Education Through Experience and Social Growth*

Requests for "lectures on mental health" were answered by having the requesting group come, observe, and even participate in the activities of the hospital. The goal was to conduct the mental health education of the public by experience, by providing the public with an opportunity to gain a direct understanding of patients in the course of their rehabilitation. The result was a rapid change in the attitude toward the "mentally ill" and greater community accommodation.

It has been observed that lectures often served to threaten the listener with the possibility that he might have some psychological weaknesses or to strengthen his sense of separateness from those he considers "afflicted." Indeed, it is difficult for people to realize that "mental health" is an ongoing endeavor that is dependent upon the quality of the continuing interactions between the individual and his environment; that it is, in fact, a social process in every sense of the word although its deterioration is experienced very personally.

### The Out-Patient Clinics: A Barometer for the "Felt Needs" of the Community

As a health team attempts to work with community psychiatry concepts as tools in community development, it is dealing not only with the usual psychiatric population, but indeed with the entire community.

In Guyana, the out-patient clinics were not attended so much by persons who were aware that they were mentally disturbed, but by a wide variety of persons who came from different communities seeking different kinds of help and reflecting a variety of attitudes toward deviance, family interactions, finances, education, etc. This made possible not only the identification of the modal personalities of the various ethnocultural groups, but also an understanding of their conceptualization of "mental illness," their choice of symptoms, and the "felt needs" of the patient's particular sociocultural milieu. Thus, in considering the kind of "patient" population likely to be involved in a variety of psychiatric facilities in a developing country, one must be prepared to broaden considerably the concept of "patient" and the concept of "therapy" to include the concept of "client" and the concept of "development." The fact is that both the selection and the exclusion factor are far more flexible in developing countries than they are in the developed countries.

### Integration of the Psychiatric Services into the Cultural System of Healing

In Guyana, a system of cross-referral was established between the local "Kali Healer" and the psychiatrist; in this system the management of a Hindu patient's adjustment was handled by the "healer" while it was the psychiatrist's task to render the patient amenable to participation in the healing ritual. In time, the healer would bring patients for "electric shock treatments" and "calming pills" or for "physical check-ups" to the mental hospital as part of his therapeutic efforts. What happened was that "doctor work" became a phase of the continuous process of social integration and adjustment, for which the healer was the accepted mediator for his community (Singer and Araneta 1967b).

## ASSESSMENT OF RESULTS

Table 1.   Admission and discharges and hospital population

| Year | Total admissions | Discharges and paroles | Population at year end |
|------|------------------|------------------------|------------------------|
| 1963 | 307 | 354 | 543 |
| 1964 | 350 | 368 | 525 |
| 1965 | 490 | 545 | 460 |

Table 1 shows that the rate of admissions rose steadily while the rate of discharges rose at an even higher rate resulting in a progressive decrease in the total in-patient population.

Table 2.   Admission and re-admission rates for 1964–1965 (by race)

| | New admissions | | | Re-admissions | | |
|------|---------|-------------|-------|---------|-------------|-------|
| Year | African | East Indian | Other | African | East Indian | Other |
| 1964 | 129 | 121 | 35 | 33 | 20 | 12 |
| 1965 | 120 | 140 | 35 | 88 | 67 | 40 |

Here we find that there is a general increase in the re-admission rate for all ethnic groups, but the increase in new admissions is mainly among the East Indian group.

Table 3.   Admissions by race and by county

| | Essequibo | | | Demerara | | | Berbice | | |
|------|---------|---------------|-------|---------|---------------|-------|---------|---------------|-------|
| Year | African | East Indian | Other | African | East Indian | Other | African | East Indian | Other |
| 1964 | 3 | 2 | 5 | 108 | 60 | 35 | 51 | 79 | 7 |
| 1965 | 7 | 10 | 3 | 150 | 77 | 52 | 51 | 120 | 20 |

Here we find that the increase in admission rate is accounted for by a large increase in the East Indian admissions from Berbice. When we relate this to Table 2, we find that the rise in African admissions is mainly due to re-admissions from Demerara whereas the rise in East Indian admissions is accounted for by both new admissions as well as re-admissions.

Table 4.   Admission and re-admission rates by counties

|      | Esquibo | | Demerara | | Berbice | |
|------|----------------|------------------|----------------|------------------|----------------|------------------|
| Year | New admissions | Re-admissions | New admissions | Re-admissions | New admissions | Re-admissions |
| 1964 | 7 | 3 | 169 | 24 | 108 | 19 |
| 1965 | 14 | 6 | 150 | 129 | 131 | 60 |

Here we note that the increase in the re-admission rate is highest from the Demerara area. Comparison with other tables show that this high rate comes from both Africans and East Indians. In Berbice, where the greatest rise in East Indian admission is noted, we find the increase to be mainly due to new admissions, and the hospital records show that these are mainly "involutional depressions."

These findings suggest that the population of Berbice used the mental hospital facilities more and usually voluntarily, and that that population fared better in community reintegration, as indicated by the lower re-admission figure.

Table 5.   Comparison of out-patient clinic attendance

| Year | Mental Hospital Clinic | Port Mourant Clinic | Skeldon OPD | Georgetown OPD |
|------|------------------------|---------------------|-------------|----------------|
| 1963 | 764 | 48 | 87 | 2038 |
| 1965 | 1832 | 426 | 349 | 2636 |

These figures indicate a greater acceptance and utilization of the out-patient facilities by the population of Berbice, as reflected by the marked increase in the attendance of these clinics.

Indeed, even more important than these figures, is the integration into the community of the mental health services not only as a medical, but also as a social and educational resource of the community.

## REFERENCES

AMIEL, J. L.
   1965   "Prospective psychiatry." Paper presented at the PAHO-WHO Caribbean Seminar on Mental Health, Kingston, Jamaica, September.
ANONYMOUS
   1968   The computer now aids private practice. Frontiers of Clinical Psychiatry 5:1.
DE SOLE, D. E., P. SINGER
   1968   Cultural anthropology of community psychiatry. Medical Opinion and Review (1968): 76–84.

FIRTH, R.
 1959 "Acculturation in relation to concepts of health and disease," in *Medicine and anthropology*. Edited by I. Galdston. New York: International University Press.
GOLDSTON, STEPHAN E., *editor*
 1965 *Concepts of community psychiatry: a framework for training*. Washington D.C.: U.S. Department of Health, Education, and Welfare.
INSTITUTE OF SOCIAL AND ECONOMIC RESEARCH OF THE UNIVERSITY OF WEST INDIES
 1967 Hinduization and creolization in Guiana: the plural society and basic personality. *Social Economic Studies* 16:221–236.
LEIGHTON, A. H.
 1961 "The Stirling County study: some notes on concepts and methods," in *Comparative epidemiology of the mental disorders*. Edited by P. H. Hoch and J. Zubin, 24–31. New York: Grune and Stratton.
LINTON, RALPH
 1945 *The cultural background of personality*. New York: Appleton Century-Crofts.
LODEN, J. B.
 1965 "Social aspects of ideas about treatment," in the Ciba Foundation's *Symposium on transcultural psychiatry*. Edited by A. V. DeReudk and Ruth Porter. Boston: Little, Brown.
SINGER, P., E. ARANETA
 1967 Integration of indigenous healing practices of the Kali cult with western psychiatric modalities in British Guiana. *Revista Interamericana de Psicologia* I.
SNELL, J. E.
 1966 Psychiatric evaluation in open biracial groups. *American Journal of Psychiatry* 122:880–885.
WORLD HEALTH ORGANIZATION
 1959 *Social psychiatry and community attitudes*. World Health Organization Technical Report Series 177.
 1969 *Comments by member states and organizations concerning international development strategy for the 1970s*. E/AC.56/L.1/Add.5; E/AC.54/L.32/Add.5.
WORTIS
 1965 Psychopharmacology and physiological treatment. *American Journal of Psychiatry* 121:648.
YOLLES, S.
 1965 "The integration of the mental health programs into public health planning." Paper presented at the PAHO-WHO Caribbean Seminar on Mental Health, Kingston, Jamaica, September.

# The Regional Approach to Health in the Republic of Slovenia

ROBERT G. DYCK

Two of the most important current dimensions of health planning and administration in the Republic of Slovenia are the regionalization of its health services and the recent amalgamation of its health insurance programs for workers and farmers. Slovenian health services and health insurance programs were first organized in the postwar government on a regional basis in 1951. Separate health insurance programs for workers and farmers existed, however, until the referendum of 1972 which led to the first combined health insurance system in Yugoslavia, initiated in 1973.

Although Slovenia's population of 1.8 million is relatively small in comparison with larger republics such as Croatia and Serbia, Slovenia is the most socioeconomically advanced of all the Yugoslav republics. It often plays a pivotal role in the development of new policy approaches elsewhere in Yugoslavia, in health as in other fields. Thus the Slovenian developments considered in this paper are not only important in their own right but also in terms of their implications for health policy in other parts of Yugoslavia.

For example, the Autonomous Region of Vojvodina recently also has adopted a regional approach for its Institute of Health Protection, located at Novi Sad. Regional and local health services are integrated on a regional basis with the activities of the Institute of Health Protection and

The project presented here was performed pursuant to a grant from the United States Office of Education, Department of Health, Education, and Welfare. However, the opinions expressed here do not necessarily reflect the position or policy of the United States Office of Education, and no official endorsement by this Office should be inferred.

also with the social insurance program.[1] The Institute of Health Protection for the Banja Luka area (northern Bosnia) operates in much the same way as the Slovenian institutes of health protection, although insurance for workers and farmers is not combined.[2] The Republics of Croatia and Serbia have been interested in the regional approach developed in Slovenia and also in combined health insurance. Neither has yet been able to develop analogous approaches, although for health purposes Croatia is divided into several large but essentially independent regions. Both republics have sent political and professional representatives to review Slovene practices, but have farming populations too large to switch easily to a combined insurance system.[3]

The implications of regionalization and combined health insurance in Slovenia will be here examined with reference to likely future developments in Yugoslavia, as well as their applicability to other countries. Particular attention will be given to implications for preventive health programming, which is historically important in Yugoslavia because of the revolutionary organizational work of Andrija Štampar. Attention will also be given to implications for functional integration of health, environmental protection, and regional development programs, and to the evolution of a more generally federalistic approach to governance in Yugoslavia.

## GENERAL BACKGROUND

Since the major federal constitutional changes of 1971, each of the six republics and two autonomous regions of Yugoslavia have had their own individualized health services and health insurance programs. Prior to this time, it was possible to speak of Yugoslav health services, as in an article by C. Vukmanovic, Director of the Federal Institute of Public Health (1972). Since 1971, the republics have become increasingly autonomous and individualistic in the organization and administration of all their internal affairs. The new constitutions, which are expected to be adopted at federal and republic levels in the fall of 1973, will continue

[1] Telephone interview with Professor Dušan Savić, Vojvodina Institute of Health Protection, August 28, 1973.
[2] Telephone interview with Diplomate Economist Sabahudin Osmančević, Banja Luka Institute of Health Protection, August 29, 1973.
[3] Interview with Saša Cvahte, Director, Institute of Health Protection SR Slovenia, August 21, 1973.

this pattern of decentralization, and may provide for the first time Presidia at the republic level.[4]

The new federal constitution is expected to provide continued assurance of the right of everyone to live in a healthy environment, but the future organizational structure and role of the Federal Institute of Public Health was still problematic in August 1973. The Federal Health Council was dissolved in 1971, and in the meanwhile the Federal Institute of Health only rarely called meetings involving all the directors of Republic Institutes of Health Protection, or otherwise attempted to coordinate republic health operations.[5]

It is necessary to understand two fundamental dimensions of the entire current social organization in Yugoslavia, in order to grasp the significance of regionalism in Slovenia. One is that the principle of "workers self-management," first inaugurated in industry in 1951, is operative in the entire social organization. This means that workers in all types of organizations freely determine organizational objectives, methods of carrying them out, and dimensions of cooperation or competition with other self-managing organizations. Federal and republic constitutions set only general standards, even for local government (communes). There is no hierarchical vertical integration among enterprises or among levels of government. Each unit is essentially autonomous.

The other principle is "self-financing," which means that the level of income for an organization is determined by the amount and quality of its work, and in turn by the amount and quality of work of individual workers in the organization. This principle was also first applied to production enterprises. As applied to social services organizations, it means that they contract for services according to work to be performed, usually on the basis of prior performance. Direct budgetary allocations from any given level of government to its line agencies are thus substantially reduced in favor of transfers contracted among organizations, which buy and sell services to one another.

When establishing prices for services, health institutions act in accordance with general regulations and agreements among all concerned parties at various levels. These determine criteria, guidelines, and the starting points for specific social agreements or contracts.

The Assemblies are the highest bodies of authority and self-management for the territories in which they are elected, from the communal to

[4] Interview with Professors Peter Jambrek, Matjaž Maček, and Albin Igličar, Law Faculty, University of Ljubljana, Aug. 23, 1973.
[5] Interview with Djordje Kozarević, Director, Department of Chronic Diseases, Federal Institute of Public Health, Belgrade, August 15, 1973.

the federal level. Currently the Federal Assembly is comprised of six chambers, as follows:
1. Federal Chamber (general franchise)
2. Chamber of Nations (elected by Republic Assemblies)
3. United Chamber of Working Organizations, which itself is comprised of the following three chambers:
a. Economic Chamber
b. Education and Culture Chamber
c. Health and Social Welfare Chamber.

Assemblies for other levels of government are analogous. The Assembly of the Republic of Slovenia has no Chamber of Nations but does have an advisory Conference of Communal Delegates. It has a Republic Chamber and a United Chamber of Working Organizations, which is subdivided in the same manner as the Federal Assembly.

Under the provisions of the proposed new constitution for the Republic of Slovenia, the Republic Chamber will be replaced by a Chamber of Communal Delegates. Each of the four other chambers will be retained, but will not have permanent representatives — membership will be chosen on an *ad hoc* basis from the membership pool comprised by the Chamber of Communal Delegates. Selections will be made by the respective communal delegations, on the basis of expertise or other qualifications of their members to work in various issue areas.

At the federal level, it is expected that the new constitution will provide for a Federal Chamber elected by communal assemblies, together with a Chamber of Republics and Regions. The members of this chamber must also be members of Republic or Autonomous Region Assemblies, elected by those bodies (see Note 4).

Historically, the work of the Yugoslav health leader Andrija Štampar had a tremendous impact on the organization of public health services in Yugoslavia, in Europe, and throughout the world. Štampar became head of the Department of Hygiene and Social Medicine at the Yugoslav Ministry of Health in 1919, when the new Kingdom of Serbs, Croats, and Slovenes was still suffering the ravages of World War I. The new nation had infectious disease and other health problems of almost unimaginable magnitude.

Štampar's work from 1919 to 1931 in the Ministry of Health was revolutionary in at least six major areas:
1. REGIONALIZATION. Public health planning, programming, and administration was organized through nine Banovinal (provincial) Institutes of Hygiene. Each of these had its own regional subunits which included infectious disease control dispensaries, infant and maternity care

dispensaries, sanitary engineering services, etc. The Central Institute of Hygiene in Belgrade served as the technical and methodological center.

2. FEDERALIZATION. Although the health system was nationalized and hierarchical to a degree, it was essentially uncentralized. Štampar consciously developed a federalist framework allowing each unit in the system to adjust its activities to local needs.

3. CITIZEN INVOLVEMENT AND EDUCATION. Health centers, wells, water-works, privies, and other sanitary facilities were at first provided with public funds, but often later were built by voluntary labor, while the government provided only materials. Health became the work of all the people. The main initial purpose of the School of Public Health, establish-ed in Zagreb in 1927, was to provide health education to the Yugoslav peasantry.

4. PROGRAM INTEGRATION. Outpatient health care and environmental health functions were administered jointly. In addition, the health institutions deliberately tended to link their work with the promotion of agriculture, veterinary medicine, education, and the general welfare.

5. PREVENTIVE CARE. Prevention of disease and disability was the hall-mark of the Štampar program. This was evident not only in the infectious disease control and sanitary engineering programs, but also in the institutional innovation of the *Zdravstveni Dom* (Slovene) or *Dom Naradnog Zdravlja* (Serbo-Croatian) [literally 'Home of the Population's Health' or 'Health Home']. This new institution provided free outpatient medical care, with emphasis on preventive care. Thus a dual medical-care system was established, since outpatient and inpatient services continued to be offered privately. The health homes were attached administratively to the Banovinal Institutes of Hygiene.

6. INTEGRATION OF PLANNING AND IMPLEMENTATION. The organizational arrangements mentioned above facilitated the integration of research, analysis, and planning with programs of direct implementation. On the one hand, outpatient care was provided to serve the objective needs of the population; on the other, sanitary facilities were also provided on the basis of community and regional analysis and plans (Dyck 1973a and 1973b).

Štampar's approach was too revolutionary for Yugoslavia's medical societies and for King Alexander, who fired Štampar for alleged in-competence in 1931. However, Štampar's basic organization plan con-tinued in effect until World War II. After World War II, the health services were reorganized by the new government, but Štampar continued to have influence at the federal level through his affiliation with the

School of Public Health at University of Zagreb and through his seminal role in the World Health Organization, which he helped found in the years immediately following World War II.

Currently, Štampar's ideas enjoy their strongest support in Slovenia, Croatia, Vojvodina, and Belgrade. In Slovenia, the Director of the Republic Institute of Health Protection is a strong advocate of Štampar's ideas, especially his ideas concerning "positive health."[6] Regional integration of health services was established in Slovenia in 1951, the *Zdravstveni Domovi* still exist, and public education plays an increasingly important role in the programs of the Institute of Health Protection of the Republic of Slovenia and its affiliated units. A federalist approach to health organization still exists in health services and health insurance, though it is probably more decentralized than in Štampar's time. Almost all health services are socialized. However, in citizen involvement (particularly in the rural areas), integration of health care and environmental health programs, and in integration of planning and implementation programs, current Slovene health programs do not appear to reach the levels advocated in the original Štampar model.

Of course, health conditions have changed markedly in the intervening years. Acute infectious diseases, such as tuberculosis, malaria, endemic syphilis, typhus, and trachoma were critical during the early Štampar years. Now instead the critical problems are respiratory diseases, injuries, gastrointestinal diseases, diseases of the central nervous system and sensory organs, etc. At least the first three reflect environmental conditions. Currently, the most frequent causes of death are chronic diseases, among which the most important are cardiovascular diseases, neoplasms, diseases of the central nervous system, and respiratory diseases. Accidents and suicides rank next in importance. Disability is also an increasingly serious problem (Dyck 1973c).

Standard indicators of health show that substantial improvements have been made in recent years. Infant mortality, 25.3 per 1,000 live born in 1969, is decreasing. It was 80.6 per 1,000 in 1950. (Cvahte, Kastelic, and Odar 1966: 1). Life expectancy for females is increasing slightly and was sixty-seven years during the 1960's. Life expectancy for males is showing its first signs of decrease, and was approximately sixty years during the corresponding period. Overall, life expectancy did not increase during the period 1961–1969, and the report from which the above data are obtained concludes that the health situation in Slovenia is not im-

---

[6] "Positive Health" is defined in the Preamble to the World Health Organization Charter as "... a state of complete physical, mental and social well-being and not merely the absence of disease or infirmity."

proving and that the need for health protection expenditures is growing (Cvahte, Kastelic, Neubauer, and Odar 1971: 11, 27).

However, expenditures for health protection increased faster in Yugoslavia than did gross national product during the period 1956–1969. Health expenditures increased an average of 23.4 percent, whereas gross national product was increasing at an 18 percent average per year. Whereas health protection outlays were 6.05 percent of gross national product in 1969, they were 3.35 percent in 1956 (Cvahte, et al. 1971: 25, 28. No adjustments for inflation).

In 1961, there were approximately 1,500 physicians in Slovenia, or one for every 1,074 persons. In 1972, there were 2,350 physicians, or one for every 735 persons. Numbers of nursing, dental, and other medical and paramedical personnel also showed impressive growth during the period (Health Services 1972: 59).

Hospital beds increased in number only slightly, from 7.4 per 1,000 population in 1961 to 7.42 in 1972. This increase is calculated on the basis of actual beds (it would be only 6.46 on the basis of standard beds), just barely keeping up with population increases. However, a fine new central hospital was constructed in Ljubljana, designed as a model for all of central Europe. Substantial centralization both of hospitals and health homes occurred during this period, reflecting efficiencies that could be achieved on a regional basis. Whereas there were previously thirty-two hospitals, there were only twenty-four in 1972; whereas there were 170 health homes, there were only nineteen in 1972. The range of services provided at these facilities grew impressively during the period, just as did the numbers of personnel staffing them (Health Services 1972: 38, 39, 48, 54).

## REGIONAL HEALTH SERVICES IN SLOVENIA

Slovenia is unique among all the Republics in that it has adopted a regional administration format for all its health services.[7] Following the approach developed originally by Štampar, in 1951 health care and environmental health and preventive health institutions in several designated regions in Slovenia began to cooperate with one another through the formation of regional councils. The membership of these was representative of all health institutions in the region except health insurance organs. The member institutions included hospitals, health homes, and regional

[7] The initial descriptive material in this section is drawn from Dyck (1973a: 9–12).

hygiene institutes. Their functions included a broad range of environmental planning and action programs as well as the other social medicine, health planning, and epidemiological activities which present-day Institutes of Health Protection perform. The regional approach was especially appropriate in Slovenia because of the dispersed distribution of its population, its long-standing experience with social insurance (well over 100 years), and recognition of efficiencies in use of social insurance which could be realized through consolidation of health services.

A serious problem developed, however, in connection with this original regional council approach. Distribution of regional health insurance monies was being made on the recommendation of the regional council, which had a large preponderance of its representation from hospital and health home personnel (approximately 70 percent and 25 percent, respectively). As a consequence, most of the available support for regional health activities was captured by the hospitals. The regional health homes and regional hygiene programs got even less than their proportionate share.[8]

Subsequently, in 1962, regional health functions were reorganized in Slovenia. The regional health councils were reestablished on the basis of the new federal legislation mentioned above, and new budgeting procedures were introduced. These were meant to assure that allocations from health insurance were based on evaluation of program plans submitted to a given regional health insurance organ by each regional health service institution. Health insurance organs thus became the most powerful members of the regional health councils. The regional hygiene institutes were renamed "Institutes of Health Protection," and most of their original environmental protection functions were delegated to communal "Sanitary Inspection" organs. Evident reasons were the general decentralist tendencies of that time and related concerns that too much power was otherwise allocated to one institution.

Currently, each regional health institution operates on the basis of self-management and self-financing principles, with about 75 percent of the budgets of all health-care institutions coming from social insurance, and about 90 percent of the budgets of the regional Institutes of Health Protection coming directly from health insurance.[9] Only one and one-half percent of the total Slovene health insurance budget is labelled "preven-

---

[8] Interview with Saša Cvahte, Director, Slovenian Institute of Health Protection, Ljubljana, July 7, 1973.
[9] Interview with Marica Eltrin, Economist, Union of Health Insurance Associations SR Slovenia, Ljubljana, August 17, 1973.

tive," but it is stated by certain authorities in Yugoslavia that 30 to 35 percent of all health expenditures throughout the country goes for preventive purposes (Dyck 1973d).

The health insurance program is organized on a federalist basis involving a more-or-less "theoretical" federal government role. Strong basic policy guideline powers are exercised by the Union of Health Insurance Associations of the Republic of Slovenia; specific policy-making powers are exercised within those guidelines by regional health insurance associations and health working organizations; and administration is by local health insurance associations.[10] The republic and regional level health insurance associations provide coordination of health plans and programs through their financial control.

In 1962 there were nine health regions in use, embracing the entire territory of Slovenia. At the present time, the sixty Slovenian communes, which are units of local government similar to U.S. counties, are still organized into the same nine regional configurations for health purposes. Health is the only social function thus organized.

The region is not a level of government in Slovenia, although there is some current interest in establishing such a level. In Ljubljana there is, however, a quasi-metropolitan Central Committee with representative members from each of the five communes which comprise Ljubljana.

Each health region in the Republic of Slovenia has its own regional Institute of Health Protection, although two are as yet unstaffed. The Institute of Health Protection of the Republic of Slovenia coordinates its work on a republic-wide basis, although of course each Institute operates under the same self-management and self-financing principles which apply to all working organizations.

The regional institutes conduct programs in health statistics, health planning, social medicine, hygiene (including community hygiene) and epidemiology, and laboratory analysis that are similar to and related to those of the parent body. Some of the regional institutes are better staffed and carry out more complete programs than the others, depending on local needs, financing capabilities, and urbanization factors.

The preventive health battle against infectious diseases, initiated during the Štampar period and ending after World War II, has been largely won. Currently the public health services are faced with chronic disease problems related to the impact of industrialization and urbanization,

---

[10] Interviews with Joze Piano, General Secretary, Union of Health Insurance Associations SR Slovenia, Ljubljana, July 23, 1973, and with M. Eltrin and Arne Mavčič of that organization on July 31, 1973.

together with related problems of environmental health and environmental protection.

As pointed out above, many of the former functions of the republic and regional level health institutions in the environmental area have been delegated to local government. Partly as a consequence of local inability to cope adequately with these problems, a number of environmentally oriented research and political action groups have sprung up in Slovenia in recent years. Their outlook tends to be republic level or regional, and their approach is multidisciplinary. The health professions are not excluded, but all the groups seem to recognize the necessity for a more functionally integrated approach to solving environmental problems than the health professions up to this time have been able to mount.

One such group is the voluntary *Skupnost za Varstvo Okalja Slovenija* (Slovene) or "Community for Protection of the Environment of Slovenia." After two years of existence, it has six chapters in Slovenia. It has also initiated similar organizations in all other republics, the two autonomous regions, and at the federal level. It is a political action group with evident influence, particularly at the level of the Slovenia Assembly. It currently is pressing for a Republic Secretariat for the Environment as well as substantially reorganized local Sanitary Inspection organs.

Partly through its efforts, a fifteen member Commission for Protection of the Environment has been established in the Assembly. This legislative review and advisory commission is heavily burdened by a very large workload of sensitive republic and regional environmental protection issues ranging from river pollution control to the scenic impact of new highways. Many of the regional issues could be handled more appropriately at the regional level, if appropriate regional authority existed. The problems are too big to be handled well by local communes, but too small to be handled efficiently or effectively by republic bodies. These factors, plus the inevitable political liabilities incurred by the Assembly members working on these issues, suggest that the Assembly will find a way to delegate some of its authorities to the regional level.

Dissatisfaction with the limits of a solely biological approach to solving the problems of the environment led to the formation of a new Commission for Protection of the Environment in the Slovenian Research Council in 1972. This scientific research body now has a strongly multidisciplinary approach to problems of the environment, and includes some health professionals among its broadly ranging research affiliations.

Slovenia's Institute for Regional Spatial Planning was established in 1968, and was the first such body in Yugoslavia. It is related somewhat indirectly to the Slovenia Institute for Socioeconomic Planning. It has a mandate to develop republic-wide urban development plans and has certain environmental protection responsibilities in this connection.

At the federal level, a potentially far-reaching "white paper" embracing the need for functionally integrated, intergovernmental, long-term urban development policy plans was adopted by the Federal Assembly in 1971.[11]

All of the above-mentioned new organizations maintain ties with existing health organizations and professionals. Yet their very existence is evidence of the institutional and professional lags in existing organizations; they make the new organizations necessary, despite the best intentions and the often close personal relationships that exist between counterpart professionals in, for example, public health and urban planning organizations.

Of course it is difficult to switch rapidly to a functionally integrated regional approach to urban-environmental-health problems, especially in the context of governmental decentralization which prevails throughout Yugoslavia. It is clear, however, that the regionalization of preventive health, including environmental protection, is not yet as well developed in Slovenia as regionalization of health care. Now that environmental problems are perceived to exist in the regional context, it should not be too difficult to federalize upwards planning and implementation of environmental protection programs during the course of the next several years. The health-care programs provide a prototype (Dyck 1973a: 37).

## UNIFIED REGIONAL HEALTH INSURANCE IN SLOVENIA

Slovenia has a long tradition of experience with health insurance, going back to 1858 when it was introduced both as an inducement to working people to remain in Slovenia and to prolong the working years of those who did remain. At the time there was a large emigration to the United States and other countries. Because of this long tradition, the idea that health insurance is a basic right belonging to everyone is well established. This undoubtedly contributed in an important way to the outcome of the 1972 referendum in which it was decided by 90 percent of the voters that there should be a single, unitary insurance system for both farmers and workers in Slovenia. Up to that time there were separate systems, based largely on the distinction that farmers were self-employed and had relatively lower cash incomes than workers (Dyck 1973b).

[11] More detailed description of the various multidisciplinary approaches cited above may be found in Dyck (1973a: 16–30).

Slovenia has a dispersed population settlement pattern, but some 60 percent of the farmers live in villages. Workers and their families also show a strong preference for living in villages and smaller towns. As a consequence, the classic antagonism between rural and urban populations is not as strong in Slovenia as elsewhere in Europe. This also eased the way for the success of the referendum.

In addition, the life-style preferences of Slovenes mean that health services, like other public services, are highly dispersed and accordingly more expensive. Consolidation of health services and supportive insurance programs on a regional basis has been one way of realizing efficiencies and reducing costs inherent in such a system.

As a consequence of the 1972 referendum, workers and farmers now have the same rights, except that farmers do not yet have compensation for income loss due to illness or disability. By 1980, farmers will also have income loss compensation.[12] Only 12 percent of all the inhabitants of Slovenia are farmers. However, many are over fifty years of age and are not able to finance their own health insurance. At the present time workers contribute 25 percent of the total resources required for their insurance. In other areas of Yugoslavia, where the proportion of farmers is higher, it is not yet feasible to distribute the additional costs of unified insurance in such a manner.

In fact, it probably would not have been possible to integrate health services and health insurance organizations on a regional basis, as was done in Slovenia in 1962, except for the fact that the workers' regional health insurance organizations already insured the bulk of the population. If workers' and farmers' regional insurance associations had had more equal numbers of insurees, it would have been difficult for either of them to arbitrate the budgetary requests of a single set of health care institutions.

However, the amalgamation of the two insurance plans simplified the allocation problem in both political and professional terms, and provided more equal protection for all members of society.

The regions utilized for health insurance programs, beginning in 1962, were the same as those already in use by the Institutes of Health protection and the various health care institutions. Their centers are at Celje, Gorica, Koper, Kranj, Ljubljana, Maribor, Murska Sobota, Novo Mesto, and Ravne. These regions continue in use.

In 1966, the *Zveza Skupnosti Zdravstvenega Zavonovanja SRS* (Slovene) or "Union of Health Insurance Associations" played a major role in

[12] Interview with Joze Piano, General Secretary, Union of Health Insurance Associations, Ljubljana, July 20, 1973.

reducing the total number of regional health institutions. Working through an order issued by the Republic Secretary of Health and Welfare, it was able to reduce the number of Health Homes from eighty to twenty. One hundred and fifty separate ambulatory dispensaries and fifty separate dental-care units were also consolidated into the twenty remaining Health Homes. The number of hospitals was reduced from about thirty to twenty-four. These changes had to be accomplished quickly, because of the distastefulness of such a move in a nation priding itself on decentralization. But the changes were necessary from an efficiency point of view.

Generally, the Union of Health Insurance Associations does not operate in such an apparently hierarchical manner. It is comprised of four delegates from each of the nine regional health insurance associations. Each year it prepares, negotiates, and enters into, a so-called social agreement dealing only with the starting points for financing and execution of regional health services for that year. It provides the basis of regional contracts worked out by the regional health insurance associations, regional insured workers' associations, and regional health services institutions. In practice, however, the principal negotiators are the regional health insurance and health services organs only. This practice is expected to be legitimized by the republic constitutional changes proposed for adoption in October 1973.[13]

Thus BASIC social agreements are developed at the republic level, while more SPECIFIC social agreements are negotiated at the regional level. Each regional health insurance association is further subdivided into local health insurance associations, but the latter are administrative rather than decisionmaking bodies. This pattern stands in sharp contrast to the larger decisionmaking and implementing powers delegated to local government in almost every other sphere of governmental activity. The reader is reminded, for example, of the contrast with respect to land use control and environmental protection powers described above. It seems likely that the social agreement format may in a few years find similar usage in these functional areas, in order to bridge the intergovernmental gaps between policymaking and implementation that exist in those areas.

Health insurance, because of its powerful financial influence, is in a strong theoretical position to influence the distribution of funds between curative and preventive health programs. Although the total amount distributed to preventive care may approach 30 to 35 percent, less than 1.5

[13]    Interview with Joze Piano, July 23, 1973.

percent is actually EARMARKED for preventive work at the present time. These monies provide nearly all the support of the regional institutes of health protection (Dyck 1973a). It will be interesting to watch how quickly Slovenia is able to increase allocations to the preventive health sector: it is a relatively wealthy nation, and the Union of Health Insurance Associations is in a good strategic position to research and implement worthwhile tradeoffs vis-à-vis expenditures in the health-care area. If this were to happen, there would be a major new force directing the functional integration of health with other environmental protection activities and urban and regional development policy.

## ANALYSIS AND CONCLUSIONS

According to the measures of effectiveness mentioned earlier in this paper, it appears that there has been considerable progress in health conditions in Slovenia during the last twenty years or so, despite the disclaimer issued by the ZZVSRS in 1966 (Cvahte, Kastelic, Neubauer and Odar 1971). While it is true that life expectancy was levelling off at that time, socioeconomic conditions in Yugoslavia have been steadily improving, and it is hard to imagine that the general level of life quality has not improved during the last twenty-year period. We need, however, more accurate indicators of positive health to make a more definitive statement.

We cannot judge with certainty whether or how much the regional framework adopted in 1951 has contributed to the effectiveness of the overall health program, on the basis of the material reviewed here. However, there seems to be no evidence suggesting that the regional approach has harmed program effectiveness or that it has had negative side effects on other programs. The range of health services available has increased.

As far as efficiency is concerned, we have only presumptive evidence that the regional approach is more efficient in use of limited resources than an alternative approach. Health costs were indicated to be rising more rapidly than gross national product. However, we do not know that health costs would not have risen even more sharply in the absence of a regional approach. It appears, in fact, that regional management has made possible a number of economies with respect to the distribution of health facilities.

Nevertheless, we need to look elsewhere to appreciate fully the apparent general satisfaction with the regional approach in Slovenia. Its potential to accommodate to future needs is, ultimately, a more critical consideration. It is entirely consistent, for example, with future anticipated urban growth patterns. Regional growth will be managed in a polycentric pattern resulting in population dispersion, with urban centers linked in the most efficient time-distance relationships. The regional approach in health provides intergovernmental flexibility to accommodate to the health-services needs of such a population distribution. In addition, the regional approach is better adapted to environmental protection requirements than local government, since many of the problemsheds are regional in scope.

Add to these considerations the fact that the regional approach is the only way to accommodate the needs of workers and farmers simultaneously. It provides simultaneously a vehicle for greater equity in provision of services, political workability, and simplicity in administration.

Similar observations can be made concerning the integrated health insurance program recently adopted. We cannot be sure that such a program is necessarily more effective or efficient than an alternative, including the possibility of no health insurance at all, as we have no base of comparison. However, it is clear that more people will have better insurance coverage than under the dual system existing until 1973. It also stands to reason that there will be administrative efficiencies in operating one, as opposed to two, separate insurance systems. Again, considerations of equity, political workability, and simplicity in administration are equally or even more important. The administrative separation of financial support of health services from actual provision of health services provides an additional opportunity: the objective evaluation of whether monies are best spent in curative health care or in other categories of expenditure contributing more effectively or efficiently to overall levels of health. In other words, there is the opportunity to consider tradeoffs between curative and preventive expenditures. Ultimately, one might expect a higher level of support for environmental protection activities from health insurance. This could help finance a more functionally integrated approach to life quality.

For the various reasons given above, it can be anticipated that regional organization of health services in Yugoslavia will spread from Slovenia into other parts of the country, as in Vojvodina and northern Bosnia. Regionalization is a natural solution to the accommodation of both general and specialized health services. It also lends itself to the accommodation of environmental protection and urban development strategies. Perhaps most importantly, it provides a vehicle for resolution of intergovernmental problems in a federalist manner, balancing extreme forms of decentralization without abrogating local self-management principles. For the latter reason, it may be expected that the popularity of the regional approach will also increase for other social functions as well as health.

Development of regional planning and administrative mechanisms for health can also be expected to lead to regional health insurance, and initially in the more industrialized areas with relatively small farming populations, to integrated health insurance for farmers and workers. There are too many advantages in terms of equity, political workability, and administrative simplicity for the outcome to be otherwise.

Finally, social agreements developed at Republic and regional levels in Yugoslavia for the planning and budgeting of combined health care and environmental health programs, provide a model potentially useful in other countries for general regional services administration. The social agreement format provides appropriate decisionmaking and allocation responsibilities to each involved level of government, and obliges intergovernmental cooperation through mutually negotiated terms under the force of law. It is a very useful vehicle for functional integration of services, and for this reason it also points the way towards realization of Štampar's elusive concept of positive health.

# REFERENCES

CVAHTE, S., I. KASTELIC, Z. ODAR
  1966   *The state of health of the population of Slovenia 1956–1964.* Ljubljana: ZZVSRS, Slovene.
CVAHTE, S., I. KASTELIC, R. NEUBAUER, Z. ODAR
  1971   *Health conditions of the population of the Republic of Slovenia.* Ljubljana: ZZVSRS, Slovene.
DYCK, ROBERT G.
  1973a   "A critical examination of the Slovenian federalist model for joint administration of health care and environmental health." Paper given at the annual meeting of the American Public Health Association, San Francisco, November 8, 1943.
  1973b   "A futuristic review of health services innovations pioneered by Andrija Štampar." Unpublished manuscript.
  1973c   "Overview of health conditions in the Republic of Slovenia." Unpublished manuscript.
  1973d   "A review of health insurance arrangements in Slovenia: 1973." Unpublished manuscript.
HEALTH SERVICES
  1972   Statistical report on the work of the health service for the year 1972. Slovenia.
VUKMANOVIĆ, C.
  1972   Decentralized socialism: medical care in Yugoslavia. *International Journal of Health Services* 2(1).

# Community-Based Medical Care
# in Three Settings

IAN R. LAWSON

This paper is an account of patient care in three countries. The care in two of them, northeastern Scotland and Connecticut, was concerned with the elderly and chronically disabled. In the third, Punjab, it was concerned with village populations.

These patient-care areas show common problems with regard to medical services. It is difficult for the prevailing care system to reach them. Qualified professionals, especially physicians, tend to avoid them. Yet the morbidities they present are frequently complex and severe, inextricably bound to social milieu and environment. So, in order to meet their needs, quite an elaborate range of resources is required, strongly organized and coordinated, and capable of sustained effort over a long period of time.

Somers (1968: 15) describes the situation well as regards the elderly in Western society:

The influences of the growing numbers of the elderly on the quantitative aspects of demand are too well known to need further proof. The irony of the declining mortality rates has frequently been noted: the fact that a large proportion of the population survives into middle and old age means more illness and disability per capita. It also involves a marked change in the nature of illness and disability. Morbidity studies confirm that in a youthful population acute illness predominates, whereas, in an aging population, chronic and mental illness inevitably become more prevalent.

The corollary of that shift is increasing need for long-term preventive, rehabilitative, semicustodial, and medical-social health services. Most chronic diseases take months or years to develop and require early diagnosis to be treated effectively. The period of treatment is, by definition, extensive. If cure is achieved, a long period of subsequent rehabilitation often is required. Generally, the most optimistic solution is stabilization — for example, in diabetes or glaucoma — under continuous lifetime medical supervision. With such changes in morbidity and disability patterns, the distinction between health and illness becomes blurred, and the actual medical need increasingly difficult to pinpoint in space or time. Rather, a continuous spectrum is seen with varying degrees of emphasis. It begins before actual illness; it does not cease with a hospital discharge. Continuity and comprehensiveness have become indispensable aspects of effective medical care.

Nevertheless, despite such complex needs, these patient-care areas correspond to what the economist would call "marginal land": land not worked if there is easier and more productive soil to work, so far as professional livelihood goes. In that they represent, however, a very major segment of the morbidity of those societies, they assume particular importance so far as the design of care systems is concerned. If the "marginal" land is being tended, the rest is probably being adequately cared for.

One of the myths about these areas, and crippling if propagated in public policy, is that a simple, or even an inferior order of professional expertise will suffice for them. On the contrary, from the above specifications, they appear to require highly developed "management" systems, as well as specialized resources and skills, which systems in turn depend on a supportive fiscal-administrative apparatus. Altogether, therefore, they demonstrate the stage of sophistication that the care system has reached.

## SCOTLAND

The first phase was a period of five years as a consultant physician, with principal duties in the Regional Geriatric Service of the Scottish North Eastern Regional Hospital Board — a full-time salaried appointment, as were the others I shall describe.

The financial context for the patient was a prepaid, free-of-access care system. Remuneration of medical institutions was based on an annual budget (not bed-occupancy) with regional boards and management boards having some discretion as to the proportionate expenditure of funds, whether on inpatient care, outpatient care, or day care, for example. Professional senior staff opinion was formally involved in the allocating of resources by the regional hospital authorities.

The geographic context was a highly regionalized one: one large center, Aberdeen, functioned in the combined role of teaching hospital and district general hospital on a comprehensive basis to about one-half million people, geographically defined.

The professional structure was clearly demarcated between the hospital services supervised by salaried specialists, the primary care system provided by general practitioners, and the home care supportive services provided by local government.

Within the hospital system, responsibility for patient management lay with the consultant physician under whose care the patient was admitted. House staff acted in delegating that responsibility. Outside the hospital, the patient was the responsibility of the general practitioner, and access to hospital care was possible only through referral initiated by him.

The quality control systems were informal and unwritten. There was a complete absence of "utilization review," i.e. formal committee review of patient records with regard to the physician's fulfillment of certain basic criteria. "Peer review," i.e. formal review of one physician's work by others, was also absent. There was no "third-party" fiscal scrutiny, i.e. evaluation by the financing party of even the fact of services rendered, far less their necessity or "eligibility" for financing.

Complete autonomy was exercised by the consultant physician with regard to the use of beds under his direction (some 250 in my own case), admission, length of stay, and deployment of his team. Nevertheless, this autonomy was counterbalanced by the responsibility of the geriatric unit and its consultant physicians to the community: any general practitioner in the region had the right to present his elderly problem cases directly to the consultant for solution or admission. Access to the general practitioner in his turn was not only free, but on a long-term contractual basis (through a capitation payment system) for twenty-four-hour responsibility.

All this had an important effect on the direction of "pressure" from problem patients (in the case of our own unit, the elderly and chronically disabled). First the pressure was palpably directed at the medical profession. The greater the morbid-social tangle in the individual case, the greater the expectancy by patient, or relatives, or community local government agencies that the medical services, the general practitioner, and eventually the hospital services, could and would "do something about it." By the nature of the referral process, the decisionmaking of what that "something" should be, in the case of the elderly disabled, fell ultimately on the consultant geriatric physician. If difficult problem solving on referral is the essential nature of consultant role and hospital team expertise in the United Kingdom, then this particular responsibility with regard to the extreme morbid complexity of the elderly is entirely in keeping with it.

Those familiar with American care systems must already note differences in function, role, authority, and responsibility, that make it very difficult to use terms such as "specialist" or "consultant" or "chief" without further qualification, and it may be questioned as to what extent, therefore, the resultant types of patient services, beyond the technicalities of drugs or procedure, are really comparable.

So much for the basic structure and principles. The operational consequences in terms of consultant and ward (floor) activities were as follows: the responsibility of the geriatric service was for the elderly and chronically disabled of the northeastern Scotland community, when the chronicity, or severity, of disease and entanglements thereof had reached intolerance level. The intolerance point one may define in terms of what patient and/or relatives and/or general practitioner (whose referral was invariably necessary) thought or felt (and feelings were often strong) that they could no longer put up with. Multifactorial complexes were typical of such problem cases, and a statistical description of the multiple pathologies involved was published some years ago (Wilson, et al. 1962).

The prevalence of morbidity in the elderly on the one hand, and the shortage of hospital accommodation for long-stay care on the other, led to an important functional development in the role of the geriatric consultant physician, which is now usually written into the contract. No patient was admitted to the geriatric service except by the prior assessment of the consultant physician in charge (with or without the assistance of the medical social worker). In three out of four cases, this involved a home visitation by the consultant — a strenuous practice when working on a radius of fifty or seventy miles and handling many hundreds of referrals during a year.

This home assessment visit was performed as a prerogative of the specialist but was operationally forced upon one as the means of "managing" strictly limited beds and services. If this is contrary to American views on the "economic" use of doctors' time, this is simply because doctor functioning there has been largely divorced from the management responsibility for resources. Indeed, there could be no more striking example of functional and semantic differences than the situation on one side of the Atlantic of private physicians rendering primary care almost exclusively from offices, and the situation on the other side of full-time hospital-based specialists spending up to half their time on home visitation. But the latter practice is replicated, I believe, by at least one major Connecticut bank, which keeps a register of its senior officers' visits to its industrial customers' places of work, although the latter no doubt are well able to visit the officers at the bank. In both roles, that of the Scottish geriatric physician and that of the Connecticut bankers, there is the common operational need to meter and manage defined resources accurately so as to fit in with complex, individual needs.

The geriatric physician's analysis by home-assessment visits was intended to match resources against needs. The arrangement of those resources was in the form of a spectrum of care on a basis of minimal adequacy. The full spectrum extended from general practitioner care and home care to the full range of hospital care. Hospital care in the geriatric service embraced general internist care with subspecialist backup, rehabilitative care, long-term nursing care, and outpatient and day-hospital care. (There are very few independent nursing homes in the United Kingdom.) The home-assessment visit therefore determined not only basic suitability for hospital care, but also provided a basic-care plan for the use of the spectrum of resources, and so was essential for the dynamic operation of maintaining the right patient in the right bed for the right length of time. By "minimal adequacy" of resources one means that they were slender enough to exact pretty constant strain on decisionmaking, and barely met the expectations of the public and general practitioners as to timely access even of suitable patients. However, while long-term-care beds were significantly fewer than in the United States, home-care services were notably better provided.

There was a team deployment of house staff, nursing staff, and social and rehabilitative workers around the managerial role of the consultant and his care plan based on the home visit. Formal designation of authority was probably less important in our role than initial analysis and strategy. The range of complex needs involved mutual decisionmaking and free information exchange, not least in discharge planning. Formal conferences, particularly in discharge planning, were held regularly, but only on selected cases, and then rarely more than once. (I shall discuss later the place of conferring when professional role and responsibility are ambiguous.)

There was a functional need also for close cooperation with the other two sectors of the tripartite system — the general-practitioner and local-authority services — and at an individual-case level it worked well providing there was scrupulous attention to communication. By "functional necessity," one means that the services for which one was responsible could hardly run without that particular course of action. (This is to be distinguished from "ideal" or "desirable" courses of action or cooperation, which seem excellent but carry no operational penalty if allowed to go by default; and it is also to be distinguished from "bureaucratic," whereby charts of organizations and written manuals mandate modes of cooperative action.)

Similarly, the need for anticipatory or "preventive" care became apparent from the operational pressures. Prevention of total, irredeemable breakdown of home care of the disabled (and extra demand, therefore, on limited beds) required timely and regular support of those relatives responsible for the care of the disabled at home. Clinical concern for the disabled member necessarily had to extend to those who supported him, and to their environment. This required an awareness of alternatives and amelioratives in care other than permanent institutionalization. So, short-term "holiday admissions" and day-hospital care (to give supporters a break and provide reassessment, or "top-up" rehabilitation, for the disabled person) were given high priority by geriatric physicians. Precisely because institutional beddage was in short supply and the community obligation "absolute," the overall operation of geriatric services had to be elastic and anticipatory to maintain viability. Problems of quantity and adequacy of services were obviously and always present, but because they were present as steady, predictable states, one's operations could take account of them.

I have used the terms "operational" and "management" and have so far not mentioned statistics. Figures were important but not in the manner in which they were ordinarily collected. The operational need was for "logistics," the mathematics required for strategic (as opposed to day-to-day) decisionmaking because the situation was very critical due to slender resources. Small changes in bed complement or changes in the population at risk could compound slowly to produce profound operational difficulties. Long-term care is an accumulative process, with latent periods between change of circumstances (e.g., an increasing proportion of elderly, or an increased skewing towards the over-eighty-year-olds), and the results of those changes. Unfortunately, once those changes begin to ensue, they can do so acutely and intractably, and have an accelerating effect by virtue of encroachment on beds devoted to short-term rehabilitation care and other bed-sparing operations.

The lack of necessary logistical information may be partly attributed to a failure to ally the available data collection system to the operation of clinical services. The available data largely concerned secondary phenomena or accessory information, among which one includes I.C.D. diagnoses, bed-utilization and turnover, costs of drugs, and, in general, those statistics most readily available.

A second organizational problem concerned new functions that could thrive only by joint agency involvement. I happened on at least two situations of this type: one was an anomalous situation of the hospital authority contracting for long-term, hospital-type care to be supplied by a local authority in a residential-type institution. Both authorities were functioning outside standard practice, and the going was difficult. The second was the matter of transport of frail patients over long distances — best done in winter in the comfort and convenience of rail car, compared to the arduous, prolonged "milk runs" of motor ambulances. Here again, there was a requirement of two authorities, rail and hospital, to cooperate outside standard practice; and the issue was not resolved fruitfully in my time.

Whatever the applicability of "game theory" to real life situations, this kind of nongame is common; that is, the steadfast nonhappening of a joint venture, which, on the face of it, seems desirable and feasible even to the agencies whose cooperation is necessary for it to come to pass. It may have to do with the number of agencies involved, and the number and kind of conditions which need to be satisfied on the part of each. Also each individual agency may have priorities of satisfaction incompatible with the others. Fougasse, the English cartoonist, illustrated this once by a cartoon of two secretaries who quite failed to establish telephonic communication between their bosses because each boss would agree to lift up his phone only if the other were already hanging on the line. The Aberfan disaster, in which a coal tip overwhelmed a school, was a tragic example of nongame between several authorities which could have taken preventive action. The concept had a bearing upon the expectancies of my later Connecticut efforts to arrange "spectrum care" by means of multi-agency involvement on a voluntary basis.

Finally, this consultant physician role described in geriatric care would probably be accepted as conventional by the majority of some 200 consultant physicians in the regional geriatric services in the United Kingdom (British Geriatrics Society 1963). It is interesting that few of the first generation of this specialty received special orientation or training, but derived from the conventional specialist-internist cadre. Much professional satisfaction has been found in developing these operational and clinical skills toward a group of patients that medicine generally has found so difficult to accommodate with enthusiasm, and the experience was a springboard for the author into the second and third geographic areas of "unpopular medicine." Nevertheless, a major component, lacking in the other two areas to be described, was that "geriatric medicine" was an acceptable career ladder, offering to impatient and ambitious young men an ascendancy to "consultant" posts not easily or early obtainable on the longer established ladders of hospital specialist careers.

## PUNJAB

The circumstances of my involvement in rural Punjab, I have related elsewhere (Lawson 1969). Of the three experiences, it was the one least complicated by organizational divisions or by external professional or regulative considerations.

There was a practical absence of professional work in the immediate area apart from what was provided from the rural health centers under my control. This left room for elasticity of action and directness of operation. The tone of the symposium on medical care in developing countries (King 1966) expresses this well. In the West, twice its bulk would have to be devoted to requirements for the preliminary negotiations with organized interests already in occupation of the field.

The rural Punjab communities were generally responsive to ideas of modern medical care, although villages were highly varied and required a very individual style of negotiation. The menfolk of the land-owning group were educated in the principles of anticipatory care from agricultural experience with irrigation, fertilizer, and pesticides. As regards immunization of children and the school health program, the problem was one of meeting demand rather than one of creating it. Maternity care and family planning were special problems because of the influence of older women, who were much below their male peers in education and worldly awareness.

Intrusion into the village to see selected domiciliary cases was crucial to my own role and overcame much of the somewhat justified former criticism of the work of the health centers: they comprised unhappy groups of introverted, isolated paraprofessionals, who, with the exception of one or two individuals, were ineffective in their respective communities. Directed into extroverted and highly mobile activity, they made loyal and imaginative teams. It was a practical endorsement of the World Health Organization doctrine (World Health Organization 1968) on the functioning of medical auxiliaries that they should be educated and supervised by the physician as direct extensions of his own functioning (and participants in his status).

While the physician was responsible in this situation for the construction of primary-care outworks, the role was still not unlike that of the British consultant — where one acted as a central focus for referred cases and service problems.

Here, however, the management of services was more complete in the control of ancillary facilities, especially clerical and transport. The personnel operated in diverse roles and were oriented much as professionally qualified members of the team. The team concentrated on the community or patient-service interface, as follow-my-leader to senior-physician thrust.

A start was undertaken to making data gathering logistically more oriented to elementary studies of patient derivation, seasonal patterns, and epidemiology. From such unitary administrative-clinical complexes in underdeveloped countries have issued the unique exposition of logistical principles as a main arm of medical effectiveness to disadvantaged communities (King 1966). It certainly contributed to our young interns-in-training having a heightened respect for the intellectual challenge of village India.

Nevertheless, the community was highly sensitized by numerous previous "surveys" performed by medical undergraduates in training. One recalls the example of Dube (1955) who "floated" his sociological enquiry of a southern Indian village in association with the medical and veterinary services of his university.

Using the diversity of a team operating in a care vacuum, a spectrum of services was rapidly improvised, ranging from primary clinic care (deliberately restricted, for the really ill tended to be found at home), to school health (hearing and vision), and tetanus immunization.

Of course, the spectrum was lacking in both extent and depth — a straightforward problem of quantities, however. Also, the spectrum was integral: so that various parts could be remodeled as need or strategy determined, and a patient could be placed in one or another segment with reasonable ease — without necessity for negotiating with another agency, or a reexamining insurance eligibility, for example.

Financing such limited services was on a relatively simple basis. Fee-for-service applied to those who could pay. Staff salaries were paid from central institutional funds, and drugs were subsidized from charitable sources. Health care was still at the cheap, productive end of the law of diminishing returns, so that small expenditures could result in large gains, such as tetanus immunization for two rupees. Indeed, the villages were sufficiently wealthy to support universal school immunization. Poor patients contributed a nominal sum, the well-to-do paid actual costs. Village or philanthropic support of the poor was mediated through professional recommendation and assessment, conjoining with village leadership.

Searching out the "marginal land" was a central part of the physician's role. The professional beggar population has conditioned the affluent to believe that all the poor are clamant for their attention; thus, "visiting" the sick and society's dropouts has been a classic paradox of Christian altruism. Yet, while village clinics produced numerous middle-class or well-to-do patients, again and again one's visits to the *harijan* quarters and domiciliary visits indicated the isolation or apathy of the poor and severely disabled in regard to a care system of conventional access by self-referral.

One was unable to separate preventive, or anticipatory, care from active, or curative, care, except with regard to emphasis. The professional team that could not, on the one hand, deliver individual care was popularly suspect, and failure to deliver anticipatory care, on the other hand, devalued the lasting worth of the curative enterprise. Decisionmaking in community care and in individual care has, in fact, many similarities. The problem of providing continuity of care seemed just as great in its preventive as in its curative aspects, with real success in the former confined to the "one-shot deals" of vaccination and immunization, whereas family planning, which required more prolonged and complex involvement, was in a less happy state.

It was necessary to negotiate about one's professional role and services directly with lay community leaders before one could act — a novel experience for one from the hierarchical British health services; on the other hand, services could be constructed extremely rapidly once agreement had been reached. This was not only a result of the elementary nature of the services supplied; equally important was the mobility of operation of a pyramidal team in a setting analogous to desert warfare — a health-care landscape uncomplicated by other regulative or professional interests.

It bears emphasis that this was a voluntary enterprise: a joint affair between a voluntary institution and Indian philanthropy of imaginative and generous proportions, both deployed in a highly responsive area.

## CONNECTICUT

It took the first two months of case sampling to verify that the clinical needs and character of the "problem people" (the elderly and young disabled) were the same as in Britain. It has taken several more years to understand why it is so difficult to meet those needs in a wealthy, idealistic society.

There is the problem of medical insurance eligibility at a patient-care level. I am involved with a patient of a familiar clinical type — a multiple sclerotic paraplegic, or an elderly disabled person. We are allowed to make use of resources whose limits neither he nor I can be fully aware of except by trial — say, by admission to hospital or to extended care — for the regulations of use are too complicated to anticipate completely. The conditions of "eligibility" may accommodate only a part of the requirements of care, and sometimes imply that one should choose a patient with a different configuration of needs.

In constructing a spectrum of services everyone agrees that the ideal design of services should represent "continuity" and "comprehensiveness." A site visit indicates a profusion of material compared to the scanty resources of Punjab and the lean, often elderly, structures of Britain in the 1960's. However, when one goes to put or use the resources together one finds that they are all pretty firmly cemented where they are.

One's first impression was of adequate institutional provision. There were in the area a large "continuing care unit" of another hospital, several hospital-based rehabilitation services, a voluntary rehabilitation center providing outpatient care, and, relative to British statistics, an abundance of general-hospital and convalescent-home beds, the latter providing long-term nursing care. Home-care agencies, on the other hand, were in very short supply and they complained of not being fully understood or utilized by physicians. The preference of the latter for hospital or office-based care is well known, and occurs in a context of a general retreat from primary care to a specialist role. The financial context is payment by fee-for-service, and institutions are remunerated on a bed-filled basis.

My first hospital facility was planned for temporary use only and was much behind the physical standards of our "competitors." The particular area to be devoted to "chronic sick" care was seriously lacking in both staff and resources. Nevertheless, in a field of obvious complexity and abundance, one was not anxious to duplicate what might well have been available elsewhere.

I therefore deliberately aimed at the "marginal land" for possible problem patients. On my visits to the "grass-roots" agencies which provided visiting (home) nursing and home care, I indicated interest in referral of patients to me under three conditions:

1. If a physician were already involved, my own involvement was conditional on his consent.

2. The problem should be such that the patient, agency, and physician had no obvious alternative in care.

3. The patient or relatives should be desperate enough to wish help under any circumstances (in view of my substandard resources).

What resulted was a referral over nine months of some fifty problem cases of familiar type: multiply disabled elderly and younger patients, with a predominance of locomotor and neuropsychiatric disorders, together with weighty social problems. Only three were on direct referral by physicians — a comment on the restricted role of the specialist even when set in a medical school. The remaining referrals were at the initiative of agencies, with physician involvement ranging from close to tenuous or nonexistent, the latter frequently with respect to the black ghetto population.

The total numbers are small and doubtless unrepresentative. Nevertheless, these patients provided not only complicated morbidity, but a test of the system of options in medical care, if followed carefully from pickup point through as far as circumstances permitted. They also provided a test of one's professional role in the context of multidisciplinary, multiagency involvement, with which aspects I shall mainly concern myself.

Problems of professional operation toward this group were consistently present:

1.   Problems of fiscal regulation.
2.   Fiduciary regulation and quality control.
3.   Fragmentation of the spectrum of care.
4.   In multi-agency involvement, problems of responsibility and authority, with "continual negotiation" of role.

The problems of fiscal regulation were and remain of a complexity that one can hardly exaggerate, and seem often of a more formidable nature than the clinical disabilities of the patients.

One is concerned to limit the description to fiscal conditions as they influenced professional operation, and not to extend into the general field of the financing of health care for the elderly. Nevertheless, as these fiscal conditions originated from the consequences of one kind of management and at present strictly limit what can be undertaken in alternatives, a brief general review is necessary.

Social Security provision under Public Law 89–97, or Medicare, was for the funding of items of services conventionally rendered, not for the direct provision or creation of new facilities or services. In the case of the provision of long-term care, it was an open-ended commitment, an obligation to finance patients who fulfilled certain criteria for occupying convalescent home beds. There was no limit set on the number of patients Social Security was liable to finance for this kind of care. The situation mushroomed.

Powerless to set a limit on beds or to limit institutional demands in a budgetary way, Medicare focused on the individual patient-care transaction, and by its insistence on proof of need introduced a radical change of principle in American medical insurance. The manner of its introduction may be a precedent for other forms of revolution in the American care system. Represented by the Social Security Administration as merely a strengthened administration of Medicare, it was in fact a complete upturning of medical insurance (Aetna Life and Casualty Insurance 1968). Hitherto, physicians and institutions had been arbiters, by and large, of the need for their own services; and the insurance agency supported that, verifying only that the services claimed for had in fact been rendered. Now, by this strengthened interpretation, the insurance carriers for Medicare have interposed themselves as arbiters of particular clinical needs. The question of whether they can employ the necessary professional expertise is secondary to the radical change of insurance principle, analogous to a change of criminal law from "innocent until proved guilty" to "guilty until proved innocent." The changing complexity of the regulations of eligibility has required a forensic rather than clinical skill on the part of the physician. Fitting the patient in is often a tedious, unhappy operation.

Problems of eligibility came particularly with the utilization of cheaper alternatives, especially nursing-home care and home care, and they hinged around the definition of need for "skilled care." If the service was performed for the patient by a registered nurse but the items of service did not fall under the definition of "skilled care," it was not remunerable by Medicare. If the care could have been provided by "the average nonmedical person" — even if such a person were not actually available in the patient's home and the patient had to remain under institutional care for the lack of it — THAT care was not allowable.

Furthermore, even when the elderly person required provable skilled care in a nursing home or from home care facilities, it was allowable as a charge to Medicare only for that particular condition which was documented as being the one that brought him into hospital care originally. (Hospital care is the Medicare condition of entry to other types.) If the patient has other coincidental or intercurrent conditions that keep him disabled and needing care, the situation is not covered (Tierney 1970).

In point of fact, multiple diseases and social circumstance are so inextricably interrelated in the elderly that only an uninformed or desperate logic could reason them to be separable.

The end effect has been to compound the increased need for clinical services by the elderly by an increased burden of documentary proof. The easiest segment of the care spectrum to use is the most expensive — the hospital. Some relaxation of definition of eligibility has since been made, but the principle remains: a rationing of services by intrusion of fiscal definitions of eligible care.

Quite different were the operations of Title XIX, or Medicaid, to the indigent (including many of the elderly) in Connecticut. Mediated by the State Welfare Department, Medicaid proved elastic at the individual patient-care level, doubtless because the premise for funding was the support of persons in continual, total need. But it only applied to individuals so impoverished by their circumstances (such as by paying privately for the long-term care that they already occupied) that alternatives were already restricted. Furthermore, while the program provides for the nursing-home care of many thousands, it appears to have little authority or competence to initiate the bed-sparing functions which the hospital authorities in Britain regarded as so critical to the viability of their overextended resources.

As constituted, there is generally a separation of the agencies that fund patient care from the agencies that provide patient care. This may represent a dichotomy inimical to the kind of unitary expertise required for an enterprising and economical management of public resources. The result has been a swing from possibly excess utilization of all services in the first years of Medicare to a decimation of the Extended Care and Home Care programs in recent years (See Social Security Administration n.d.).

Fiduciary regulation is a composite of conditions and criteria governing medical institutional function. Derived from statutory bodies such as state health departments, from accrediting professional organizations, and from third parties providing finance, it represents an attempt to establish standards of adequacy of structure and staffing. As such, it embraces not only the standard of facilities and the level of staffing, but professional functioning: defining, for example, the character and frequency of medical and nursing record-keeping, stipulating certain laboratory and clinical examinations in long-term care, and regulating professional staff meetings.

However, as well as establishing the levels of adequacy (and putting down illegality and faulty care) fiduciary regulation has also been cast in the role of agent for the sponsoring of excellence. For example, the committee process of utilization review was heavily endorsed by Social Security as the central, medical-professional operation of long-term care; the springboard, hopefully, of better innovative management.

One must question the likely efficacy of committee review as a means of using alternatives to institutional care after the event, when many of the principal determinants, such as family attitudes, are malleable only before admission. At any rate, utilization committees that meet to provide a fiscal justification for physicians' decisions in patient care have appeared to achieve no more than that.

Altogether, fiscal and fiduciary regulations appear to reinforce present practice rather than encourage alternatives. "Day hospital" care and what is glibly referred to as "maintenance care" — the delicate art of keeping difficult situations going — are hardly remunerable under present circumstances, although their operations are materially bed-sparing in effect. Day-hospital care consequently exists as a rarity, largely dependent on special funding.

However, these third party disabilities and reactions have to be set in the context of the necessity for controls in a fee-for-item system of remuneration applied to long-term care. And no alternatives to such controls are readily obvious in this setting. If really inseparable from their particular system of payment, they must be regarded as one of its chief professional costs. They are notable restrictions of the physician's freedom and the patient's options in situations where elasticity of wide-ranging care is particularly necessary. Indeed, if restrictive bureaucracy and form-filling are the hallmarks at patient-care level of "socialistic medicine," then, in the three geographic areas reviewed, they appeared only, and in an extravagant form, in the care of Connecticut "problem patients" and long-term care.

As already described, there was a separation of the segments of care, geographically, administratively, and professionally, particularly in regard to long-term nursing care, the hospital, and rehabilitation services. While cooperation was still possible, the operation of patient care was thereby laborious — and made more so by the pecularities of the fiscal system which, in the case of Medicare, regularly penalized or threatened efforts to utilize the cheaper segments.

Viewed as managerial systems, the situation was more complex than even the structural divisions implied. The name or classification of an institution described not only its functional nature, but its fiscal basis of remuneration which could vary markedly.

In hospitals, actual costs were met on a per diem cost basis. In long-term convalescent home care, the state welfare department mediating Medicaid determined an arbitrary figure based on state-wide averaging of costs, at about one-quarter or one-fifth of the rate of hospital care. Both hospital and long-term institutions were remunerated on a beds-filled basis, that is, only for patients actually occupying beds.

These fiscal arrangements profoundly affected institutional motivation and operated particularly against bed-sparing alternatives to the use of long-term institutional care. It worked like this: the better one's clinical selection, rehabilitation, and discharge planning, the sicker and more disabled were the residuum in long-term care. Because of this, staffing requirements became heavier, and the discrepancy between what bed-occupancy was funded for and what bed-occupancy really cost increased. For the "averaging" system encompassed at least two opposing selection processes: the one, clinical and social, selecting for greatest need; and the second, "actuarial," selecting for minimal needs compatible with Third-Party tolerance.

At the level of patient care, the physician's management consisted only in providing his knowledge and skill with regard to the varieties of fiscal apparatus, and was only as continuous as his ability to negotiate his patient through the segments and interfaces of a mosaic of care.

Problems of responsibility and authority must always be inherent in a care system where the contract is for items or periods of service rather than for a standing relationship. Such problems become more pronounced when a part of the patient's problem may consist in having exceeded the tolerance of the system by being too ill for too long — added to which was the physical difficulty of access (by virtue of locomotor disorder), poverty (or inadequate insurance coverage), and the disadvantageous behavior accompanying brain damage or of merely being old.

Within the general hospital patient care was a delicate arrangement of mutual responsibility between a number of physicians, the house staff and their supervisory "attending," the patient's personal physician, and consulting specialists. The care plan of the personal physician was accepted on a negotiated basis, to which a convincing rationale was an essential element. So the negotiation of role and influence was unique to each case. The nature of this medical staff system left nursing staff somewhat uncertain as to who was finally responsible, and they tended to pursue, with respect to physicians, an independent rather than team-oriented role.

Observation of several American units devoted to special care of the chronically disabled indicated a directed, structured, team approach with medical house staff infrequently involved, however. My own first operation of a single-doctor unit allowed fairly easy integration with nursing and other professional staff in a care team of familiar type. As team integration in these circumstances is functionally necessary rather than hierarchically ordained, the lack of an explicit designation was no great handicap, but would have been had our institutional operation of merely forty beds had the scale or elaborateness of Scotland.

Outside the hospital walls, in relation to home care and other agencies, there was also negotiation of role but for different reasons. First, there were the number of agencies involved. "Problem patients" usually had a sequence of involvements with various autonomous agencies, frequently in duplicative effort. It was not uncommon to have three or more social workers involved. So "who does what?" was an important aspect of patient conferences. There was also a tendency to recommit the issue to the melting pot when another agency's interest became known. Again, the complex of agencies or workers was usually unique to each case, so precedent contributed only slightly to what one's particular role would be in a future case.

A second element was the general withdrawal of physicians from domiciliary care. Home visits were therefore not only exclusive to other professionals (nurses, therapists, social workers), but left them in a substitute role, with the patient's expectations of them often exceeding their legal and professional bounds.

In convalescent homes, the larger part of nursing care is provided by semiskilled aides, with little or no training, supervised by registered (RN) or licensed practical nurses. Being hospital trained, the RN is often in unfamiliar territory when she has this responsibility.

The separation of long-term care of the elderly from general hospital care has had a further important effect, analogous to the substitutive role of the home-care agencies in the case of the physician. Lay concern, mostly faith related, has resulted in the construction of nonprofit institutions for the long-term care of the elderly under lay directorates. So the medical professional wishing to extend beyond the mere provision of technical skill into a determinative or "management" role must negotiate directly with the lay directorate, as in Punjab, for the establishment of his role and function. And his success is directly proportional to his "charisma" and educational ability. However, if the results of agreement between lay leadership and professionals are less speedily apparent in the United States than in Punjab, it may be attributed to the different context of health care. Professional willingness and informed lay support were adequate in Punjab on very slender resources. Paradoxically, it is the profusion to excess of such resources in Connecticut that makes these qualities no longer sufficient: the mopping up of available funding and the incurring of increasingly rigid fiscal and fiduciary conditions result in restricting the possibilities of introducing and engaging in alternatives, even when everyone agrees that they are ideal.

## SOME CONCLUSIONS

While concerned with clinical casework, this paper does not describe private or office-type physician care. In three different settings, the casework of the physician related to a variety of community resources, which included institutional care, using them if not always controlling them. Some obligation to meet large-scale volume need existed in two of the areas (Scotland and Punjab), and the character of need deliberately selected for was often little short of *ultimum moriens* in the individual case. Taken together with the populations concerned, the disabled elderly and villagers, the character of the need explains some of the unpopularity that such services have for professionals: they have a necessarily complicated nature; there is an apparently intractable morbidity, and a lot of it; there is geographic inconvenience; and community demands and patient needs consistently are liable to exceed the supply of resources.

Perhaps the first point to make is that while all of this makes for difficulties, none of it makes for impossibility. Most of it is susceptible in some degree to skill and interest on the part of professionals, given adequate control of the modicum of resources available.

Manifestly, being a professional in these situations is not primarily a matter of formal qualification or of social status, but one of a consciously adopted, continuously evaluated, public-service role. It involves risk-taking with very limited resources at an interface with many sharp challenges and potential impasses at the case and community level. With this type of problem solving there is really no substitute for field experience in order to develop requisite skills. Postgraduate education undertaken one mile or a thousand miles away from such interfaces and tensions may provide answers and training only for problems of narrow methodology, not always relevant to local requirements. J. B. S. Haldane (1965) noted precisely analogous problems in basic science research. Similarly, conventional management science tends to be disabled by its own orderliness and prior cost-benefit experience. To a management experience derived from wealthy industries that produce standard products and services to market demand, the biologic profusion and idiosyncratic needs of this type of health care present a frustrating and untidy perspective; oversimplification of the issues is often a first, and disastrous, reflexic response.

Yet, for similar reasons, even an involved professionalism is vulnerable to misunderstandings of its nature and priorities. It is easily criticized for its social profile as well as for its technical competence: inefficiency (always), idiosyncracy, authoritarianism, elitism. But how much are these the inseparable, if misunderstood, characteristics of relative success in running basic health services?

Local communities relate poorly to ambiguous leadership that cannot produce locally apposite answers. Between community resources, enough or scarce, and the need of the individual (person or group) lies a unique interface, made up of problem clusters both health and social. The matching of resources with need requires first a specificity of analysis by direct, skilful observation (which includes exquisite social sensitivity), and secondly, an authority over needed resources. This authority over resources must include the ability to make them malleable to the needs identified at the interface by molding and by rationing them. These are the minimum requirements for the effective operation of services under duress, and for the engendering of community confidence.

Overconcern with evaluation and cost benefit at the outset (often a systems expression of distrust in the professional) may so burden services as to make them unresponsive to public need and unattractive to professional enterprise, even though their bookkeeping and process compliance are impressive. On the other hand, overconcern with a corrective sociology of the professional team (especially with respect to physician dominance) can lead to vitiating effective authority, and to such intricate and absorbing intra-relationships that consumer and community needs lose the effectiveness and priority of effort due to them. A final problem is a rigid separation of professional decisionmaking in casework from managerial authority over resources. In this system, the clinical professional certifies eligibility but does not hold management responsibility for the resources he uses. Coordination and strategic development of services, nonduplication and cost effectiveness, are some of the reasons for this model's popularity, as well as physician disinclination to accept other than an entrepreneurial or solo role. However, finesse at case and community level becomes particularly difficult to sustain in this divided situation and social appropriateness and economy have yet to be demonstrated by it.

There are, it appears, always penalties for someone or some interest in every system of care delivery, particularly when it aims to embrace such disadvantaged groups of people. The question is where society wishes to tolerate or impose such penalties: in fiscal policy (and taxation), in professional sensibilities, in political-administrative control, or in the ultimate effectiveness of the services provided. Certainly, sensitive, dynamic services at delivery level are strenuous acts of professional commitment at all times. They are not among the natural laws of the universe for they are neither natural nor easy to put into effect. They are easily wilted by clumsy, intermediate mechanisms designed to favor other priorities.

## REFERENCES

AETNA LIFE AND CASUALTY INSURANCE
    1968   *Covered versus non-covered care.* Medicare Bulletin ECF-106 (August).
DRESSLER, F. G.. JR.
    1971   *Extended care facilities and patient-care review.* Connecticut Health Services Monograph 1. New Haven.

BRITISH GERIATRICS SOCIETY
   1963   Memorandum on "Medical staffing of geriatric departments."
DUBE, S. C.
   1955   *Indian village.* London: Routledge and Kegan Paul.
HALDANE, J. B. S.
   1965   "Biological research in developing countries." in *Man and Africa.*
          Edited by G. Wolstenholme and M. O'Conner, 222-238. London:
          J. and A. Churchill.
KING, MAURICE, *editor*
   1966   *Medical care in developing countries, a primer on the medicine of
          poverty and a symposium from Makerere.* Nairobi and London:
          Oxford University Press.
LAWSON, I. R.
   1969   Comparative clinical management in Punjab and the North-East:
          a personal view. *Health Bulletin* 27(4). Scotland.
SOCIAL SECURITY ADMINISTRATION
   n.d.   "Monthly benefit statistics." Extended Care Facilities.
SOMERS, ANNE R.
   1968   Some basic determinants of medical care and health policy. *Milbank
          Memorial Fund Quarterly* 46, 1(2):15.
TIERNEY, T. M.
   1970   What causes those "retroactive denials"? *Modern Nursing Home*
          (January) 9, 10.
WILSON, L. A., I. R. LAWSON, W. BRASS
   1962   Multiple disorders in the elderly; a clinical and statistical study.
          *Lancet* 2:841–843.
WORLD HEALTH ORGANIZATION
   1968   *Training of medical assistants and similar personnel.* World Health
          Organization Technical Report 385.

# Toward a Convergence of Modern Western and Traditional Chinese Medical Services in Hong Kong

RANCE P. L. LEE

Over the last several thousand years, the Chinese people have gradually built up their own tradition of medical care.[1] They were wholeheartedly dependent upon it until the introduction of Western scientific medicine into China in the late nineteenth century. Since then the efficacy of traditional medicine has been under critical challenge. Influenced by the scientific ideology and impressed by the remarkable advancement of Western technology, Chinese people have begun to abandon their traditional heritage in favor of Western medical science.[2] A major criticism against traditional medicine is that it is scientifically unverified and is therefore "backward," "superstitious," and "unreliable."

It cannot be denied that traditional medicine has no scientific basis. But its knowledge and skills are developed out of, and have been tested by, the empirical experience of billions of people over a very long period of time. As Croizier has claimed, although traditional Chinese medicine failed to establish a scientific method for observation of data and for verification of its theoretical principles, it has been naturalistic and rationalistic as opposed to magical and superstitious (Croizier 1968: 14–19). Hence it

This paper was written under the auspices of the Social Research Centre at the Chinese University of Hong Kong. I would like to acknowledge the valuable advice of S.L. Wong of the Chinese University of Hong Kong and L.K. Ding of the Chinese Medical Research Center in Hong Kong. The paper uses part of the data from my health systems study, which was financially supported by the Harvard-Yenching Institute, the Lotteries Fund of the Hong Kong government, and the Chinese University of Hong Kong.

[1] For a comprehensive description of the historical evolution of Chinese medicine, see Huard and Ming Wong (1968).

[2] This is not the occasion to describe in depth how Western medicine has come to replace Chinese traditional methods and what kinds of tensions or issues are involved. For a comprehensive and useful orientation to this subject, see Croizier (1968).

would be erroneous if we gave up the entire heritage outright merely on the ground of scientism. There is abundant evidence from the recent development of medicine in contemporary China to support this assertion.

Responding to Chairman Mao's call of "maintaining independence and keeping the initiative in our own hands and relying on our own efforts" and his assertion that "Chinese medicine and pharmacology are a great treasure-house; efforts should be made to explore them and raise them to a higher level," medical and health workers in China, since 1958, have been struggling hard to revive and refine their own medical tradition (Hou Chin-wen 1970).[3] They constantly seek to improve its quality, to widen its utilization by citizens, and to integrate it with the modern Western approach. Their devoted and persistent hard work over the past twenty years has made remarkable contributions not only to the advancement of medical knowledge and skills, but also to the increase in the quantity of medical care.[4] A larger volume and a greater variety of medical care services are now available for use by the 800,000,000 dwellers in the mainland.

In view of the medical movements and successes in Communist China, let us ask in what way traditional Chinese medicine is related to modern Western medical care in other Chinese societies, especially those which are not under the control of a Communist regime.

A small but prominent next-door neighbor to Communist China is the city of Hong Kong, which is located on the southern coast of the mainland. Its total area is about 400 square miles. As a British colony, Hong Kong has been politically dominated by the British government since the late nineteenth century. Its residential population is largely Chinese. According to the population census in March 1971, 98.3 percent of the 3,900,000 residents are Chinese in place of origin (Hong Kong, Census and Statistics Department 1972).

[3]    For an elaborated social-scientific analysis of the role of political ideology in the development of China's health care system, see Gibson (1971). Gibson argues that the thoughts of Mao serve as a guide to treatment priorities, a basis for diagnosis and therapy, and explanation of health care failures, a rationale for health delivery systems, a channel for patient gratitude, a justification for health, sensitivity training for health workers, the basis for health ethnocentrism, and also as motivational devices for health workers and patients. Chin, in his unpublished paper "Changing Health Conduct of the New Man in China" (1972), has also explicitly pointed out that health behavior in China is more accurately described as health "conduct," because it is moral and political.
[4]    It is not my intention here to engage in a comprehensive description of the dynamics of China's health care system. Nevertheless, let me suggest a few concise and relevant articles: Chien (1964); Health Policy Advisory Center (1972); Rifkin and Kaplinsky (1973).

The question arises, in that Hong Kong is populated by Chinese people but politically dominated by the British, to what extent is the Western culture integrated with, or separated from, the local Chinese way of life? We may also raise a related but value-loaded question: should we and how do we foster the integration of or the separation between the two cultural systems (Gould 1957)?[5] I shall attempt to shed light on these broad issues by concentrating on the area of health and medicine. To be more specific, I have two questions in mind: (1) In what ways is the traditional Chinese medical system related to the modern Western medical system? (2) Should we and how do we push toward a unification of the two seemingly divergent medical traditions? In other words, I shall examine the topias, i.e. the conventional patterns, in health and medicine for the purpose of suggesting a utopian plan, i.e. a radical yet realizable approach, for developing and integrating traditional Chinese and modern Western medicine in Hong Kong. It is not my intention to be value-free; as a social scientist and as an ordinary citizen, I intend to be critical of the existing order and to make suggestions for effecting changes.

## THE TOPIAN ORDER

The medical care sector in Hong Kong can be characterized as pluralistic and entrepreneurial. There exists a great variety of medical and health care services, both Chinese and Western, public and private (Fang 1970; see also *Hong Kong Year Book* 1973). The emphasis of the entire sector is on "individual responsibility of medical care," "fee-for-service solo practice," and "free choice of physician." Although the government has organized and supported a number of health programs (Choa 1972), the center of gravity of medical care remains in private practice. Medical practitioners have considerable control over the technical as well as the socioeconomic content of work.[6]

Within the sector, there coexist two systems with different orientations and approaches to medical care: traditional Chinese medicine and modern Western medicine. Instead of coexisting in a coordinated fashion, the two systems are competitive on an unequal basis. Because of its scientific base and its Western origin, Western medicine has been closely tied to the

---

[5]   On the basis of the data from a North Indian village, Gould has given a penetrating analysis of the interaction between folk medical practice developed in the indigenous culture and scientific medicine borrowed from the West.

[6]   For an excellent discussion on the mechanisms for, and the pitfalls of, professional autonomy in medicine and health, see Freidson (1972).

British-dominated power structure of Hong Kong. Being supported by the political power, the profession of Western medicine has been dominating the whole sector of health and medicine. On the other hand, the traditional Chinese medical practitioners, whose services are generally regarded as "nonscientific," have failed to be associated with the power structure and have been practicing in a subordinate and inferior status. Let me give some evidence.

The Medical Council of Hong Kong plays the most crucial role in the legitimation of medical practice and in the formation and implementation of social policies dealing with medical care. The council consists of representatives from the armed forces, government medical services, the university medical school, and medical associations in Hong Kong. However, all these representatives are Western-trained doctors; none of them represents the interests of traditional medical practice. Furthermore, only the Western-trained practitioners can be registered with the Medical Council and thus are recognized by law as qualified medical doctors. On the other hand, Chinese medical practitioners cannot be registered with the Medical Council and are not regarded by the legal authority as duly qualified doctors. Chinese practitioners, for instance, have no legitimate right to issue medical certificates of death and are not entitled to practice surgery.

The medical school of Hong Kong University, the only one of its kind in Hong Kong, concentrates on Western medical science, giving very little attention to traditional medicine. The government provides and subsidizes a number of medical and health care programs, but none of them is oriented toward Chinese medicine. There are a total of thirty-four nongovernment hospitals, but only one of them provides a very small outpatient clinic in Chinese medicine. Social workers in government or voluntary welfare agencies do not refer their clients to traditional practitioners.

All these facts clearly indicate that the traditional Chinese medical system is subordinate to its Western counterpart. Western medical dominance, however, has by no means wiped out the widespread existence of traditional services in Hong Kong. It was estimated that there were a total of 2,317 Western-trained doctors in 1970 (Hong Kong, Government Information Services 1970).[7] But according to the survey in 1969 by the Hong Kong Medical Association in cooperation with the Census and Statistics Department of the Hong Kong government, there were then

---

[7]   This total includes 1,844 doctors registered with the Medical Council of Hong Kong and 473 unregistrable but permitted doctors, who were mostly trained in China, with few trained in other countries such as Germany and France.

4,506 traditional Chinese medical practitioners of various kinds. There are thus considerably more traditional Chinese than Western-trained medical practitioners in Hong Kong. Why is this so?

The magnitude of medical demands is not the crucial reason. As will be reported later in this paper, most residents in Hong Kong tend to consult Western-trained doctors rather than Chinese medical practitioners. It seems that a more important reason for the large number of practitioners of traditional medicine is the lack of legal control over the practice of Chinese medicine. The Medical Ordinance in Hong Kong regulates Western medical practice only. There are no standard examinations or licensing procedures for qualifying as practitioners in traditional medicine. In fact, any person can practice Chinese medicine without interference. As a result, it is easy to have a situation in which there exist a very large number of traditional Chinese medical men.

In view of the general discussion above about the widespread, though unequal, coexistence of Chinese and Western medical practice, let us investigate and compare the two systems in some detail with regard to four dimensions: (1) locational distributions, (2) interorganizational connections, (3) evaluation of medical efficacy by medical practitioners themselves and by the public, and (4) patterns of utilization by local residents. In making these comparisons, I shall utilize part of the empirical data I gathered in 1971–1972 about medical organizations and health behavior in Kwun Tong, an industrial urban community of Hong Kong.

Kwun Tong is a newly developed industrial satellite town. It is located on the east coast of the Kowloon peninsula of Hong Kong, covering about 3,200 acres. Before 1956, the district was considered a remote region consisting of a few scattered villages. The total population of villagers was estimated at about 1,000. Since 1956 onward, the district has been rapidly developing into a large industrial and residential area. Its rates of population growth and industrial expansion are faster than those of any other district in Hong Kong. Currently there are more than 2,000 industrial undertakings and about a half million Chinese residents in the community. Most people reside in public housing of various kinds. About 14 percent live in private apartments and tenement buildings. The residents are therefore largely in the middle or lower income groups.[8]

I undertook three health surveys in Kwun Tong in 1971–1972. The first one was an enumeration of all the medical and health care units in various subdistricts of Kwun Tong. The second survey focused on the organiza-

[8] For a more comprehensive description of the Kwun Tong community, see "A Preliminary Ecological Analysis of the Development of Kwun Tong, 1954–1970" (Wong 1970).

tional structures of all the Western general outpatient clinics as well as the Chinese herbalist services. Health-related attitudes of their medical practitioners were also assessed. In the third survey, I studied a random sample of 702 household heads for the purpose of understanding their health concepts and behavior. The data collected in these three surveys will be used in the following discussion about the relationships between Chinese and Western medical care in Hong Kong.[9]

Let us first investigate the pattern of locational distribution. There were a total of 174 Chinese health care units and 101 Western units in the entire district of Kwun Tong in 1971–1972, but both types were unequally distributed in various subdistricts. Western services were more unevenly distributed than Chinese services. Nonetheless, the locational distributions of Chinese and Western services are strongly correlated. The larger the number of Chinese services in a particular area, the larger the number of Western units, and vice versa. Why? The data suggest that both types of medical service are greatly dependent upon two common factors: population size and socioeconomic status (as measured by the quality of residential housing) of particular subdistricts. The larger the population size and the higher the socioeconomic status, the more Western as well as Chinese medical services were available. Relatively speaking, the availability of Chinese services is more dependent on population size but less on socioeconomic status than that of Western services.

The above analysis suggests that Western and Chinese medical services tend to concentrate in the same areas. But to what extent are they connected to each other? Let us examine the pattern of connections between health services in terms of three criteria: (1) patient referrals, (2) membership in professional associations, and (3) friendship cohesion.

With regard to the referral of patients, I note that (1) Western-trained doctors are likely to refer patients to colleagues of their own kind, while Chinese practitioners are unlikely to do so, and (2) it is more likely for Chinese practitioners to refer patients to Western-trained doctors than the other way around. In terms of professional membership, Western-trained doctors are more likely than Chinese practitioners to be members of medical associations in Hong Kong. With respect to the friendship pattern, both Western-trained and Chinese practitioners are more likely to maintain close friendship with those who are practicing in the same, rather than a different, medical tradition. All these data suggest two possible conclusions. First, there is little interaction between the Western and

---

[9]  For a comprehensive description of the research procedures and statistical findings of the three health surveys, see my research reports and papers (1972a, 1972b, 1972c, 1972d).

Chinese medical care systems. Second, Western-trained doctors are a more cohesive group than Chinese practitioners. Then the question arises, does it mean that Western-trained and Chinese practitioners distrust each other?

I find that most Western-trained doctors believe that their own colleagues are medically more competent than those in Chinese medicine, while most Chinese medical practitioners feel that there is no significant difference in competence between the two groups. Hence, Western-trained doctors are in fact more distrustful of their counterparts than are Chinese medical practitioners. The distrust in traditional practitioners by Western-trained doctors could be a barrier to the interaction between the two groups of practitioners.

A more specific question arises: which type of traditional practitioners do Western-trained doctors distrust the most? Chinese medical practitioners can be classified into three major types: (1) herbalists, specializing in the use of herbs for internal medical care, (2) acupuncturists, treating illness by inserting needles into certain points of the body, and (3) bonesetters, specializing in the treatment of sprains and contusions. A great majority of the traditional practitioners in Hong Kong are herbalists (about 70 percent), followed by bonesetters (about 20 percent) and acupuncturists (about 10 percent).[10] The data in my health studies in Kwun Tong show that Western-trained doctors distrust acupuncturists the least and are most distrustful of herbalists.

The focus of the above analysis is on the quality of traditional PRACTITIONERS in Hong Kong. However, a distinction should be made between the competency of practitioners and the efficacy of medical KNOWLEDGE itself. It could be that Western-trained doctors have faith in traditional medicine but not in the training and qualification of the existing Chinese practitioners in Hong Kong. There is some evidence to support this hypothesis. Most Western-trained doctors agree that hospitals should set up a Chinese medical division and that a government-recognized Chinese medical college should be established for training qualified practitioners. Furthermore, both Chinese and Western-trained practitioners tend to believe that the convergence of Chinese and Western medical traditions could be realized.

I have presented some findings about the evaluation of medical quality by practitioners themselves. Let us now shift our attention to the evaluation by the lay population. The data show that Western-trained doctors are considered by local residents to be superior to traditional practitioners

---

[10] Percentages are roughly estimated on the basis of the survey results obtained by the Hong Kong Medical Association in 1969.

in terms of technical skills, but there is no difference with regard to professional ethics and service attitudes.

How do they compare the efficacy of Chinese and Western pharmacology? In general, they believe that Western medicines are more effective than Chinese medicinal herbs in preventive care, but less effective in tonic care. In respect to curative care, IN GENERAL they have more confidence in Western drugs than Chinese herbs. To be more specific, however, most of the local residents suggest that in the treatment of most diseases (1) Western drugs work faster than Chinese herbs, but (2) Chinese medicines are less likely to produce side-effects, and (3) Western medicines are good for the treatment of symptoms whereas Chinese herbs are more effective in curing the disease.

The local residents under study were also given a list of specific types of diseases to make comparisons between the two medical traditions in curing them. The list includes coughing, sprains and fractures, tuberculosis, measles, stomachaches, dysmenorrhea, skin diseases, mental illness, heart disease, rheumatism, fevers, throbbing, diarrhea, and anemia. The people in the sample prefer Western to Chinese medical care with regard to the treatment of most diseases, especially tuberculosis and fevers. Opinions are evenly split with respect to measles. Chinese medical care is regarded as more effective than Western medicine in dealing with rheumatism, sprains, and fractures.

All of the above evidence suggests that, in general, the lay population is more trustful of Western medicine than of the traditional approach. Nevertheless, Chinese medicine remains more trusted in some specific areas, such as tonic care, the avoidance of side effects, the curing of diseases rather than of symptoms, and the treatment of such illnesses as measles, rheumatism, and sprains and fractures. In light of these findings, we might expect that Western medical services are more widely utilized by local residents than Chinese services, and this, in fact, is the case. Most residents reported that they had consulted Western-trained doctors more often than Chinese practitioners. Moreover, Western-trained doctors reportedly have many more patient contacts per week (on the average, about 244 contacts) than Chinese practitioners (about 100 contacts).

Although Western services are more widely utilized, there exist combined uses of Chinese and Western medical care by the local population. A number of residents indicated that they attempted to shift between Western-trained doctors and traditional practitioners for the treatment of the same illness. In investigating the process of seeking medical help, I noted that most residents began with self-medication. If it failed, then they would consult Western-trained doctors. When Western-trained doctors

did not seem to be successful, they would shift to traditional practitioners. The process of seeking help suggests that most residents prefer to
consult Western-trained doctors, but it does not mean that they would
not contact Chinese practitioners.

In that most residents self-medicate in the initial stage of illness, it is
necessary to discover what kinds of medicines they use. I find that many
of them use Chinese medical pills and ointments. The use of Chinese
medicine, therefore, continues to be quite pervasive.


## A UTOPIAN PLAN FOR INTEGRATION

In the above analysis, we have observed that in many ways the traditional
medical system is indeed subordinate to the Western medical system and
that the two systems are rather separate. Let us in this section raise two
broad questions: (1) Should we, and how do we, facilitate the development of Chinese medicine in Hong Kong? (2) Should we, and how do we,
integrate and coordinate traditional Chinese and modern Western medical practices into a cohesive whole?

It is my opinion that Chinese medical services should be developed and
expanded. Why? As reported by the government in 1970, the ratio of
Western-trained doctors to the population in Hong Kong is about 1 to
1,720, whereas it is 1 to 870 in Britain and 1 to 670 in the United States
(Hong Kong, Government Information Services 1970). Although Hong
Kong has become rapidly industrialized in recent years, its doctor-pop-
ulation ratio is still considerably lower than that of its mother country
and of the United States. The inadequacy of the existing health services
in meeting medical and health needs has also been demonstrated by the
empirical findings in my health studies in Kwun Tong. Most of the medical practitioners (both Chinese and Western-trained) and local residents
under study reported that, in their views the existing medical facilities
were not yet sufficient. Moreover, it was noted that, on the average, each
Western-trained doctor has about 244 patient contacts per week, and that
most of them spend generally about five minutes or less for each consultation. In fact, many Western-trained doctors recognize that they are overloaded with patients.

The worst is that medical and health services are by no means equally
distributed. As reported, the existing services, especially those provided
by Western-trained doctors, tend to concentrate not only in more populated areas but also in economically wealthier areas. Although people

living in affluent areas may have greater DEMANDS for medical care, they do not have more medical NEEDS than those living in poverty areas.

In view of these deficiencies in the existing Western services, we should, of course, attempt to increase the supply of Western medical personnel and facilities. But meanwhile, the existing Chinese medical resources should also be mobilized and developed. As argued, Chinese medicine today is an historical product of several thousand years. Its potential value and contributions cannot be disregarded purely on the ground that its theoretical rationale and medical effects have no scientific basis. Instead of rejecting the entire tradition, we should draw on its rich fund of experience and resources so as to remedy the deficiencies of Western facilities and to make more services available for use by the local population.

So far my argument for the development of Chinese medicine is primarily a quantitative one. It should be underscored that its development will also contribute to the quality of medical care in general. Many clinical practices in China have proved that for some medical purposes, the traditional approach alone or its combination with modern Western techniques is more efficient than the Western approach alone. It is not only more effective, but it is also safe, simpler, and more economical. The effect of acupuncture anesthesia for surgical operations is a well-known example (Anonymous 1972). Others include the notable successes in treating extensive burns covering over 80 percent of the body surface, in rejoining severed limbs even ten or eighteen hours after injury, and in dealing with chronic diseases like neuralgia, arthritis, neurasthenia, and sequela from infantile paralysis (Revolutionary Committee of the Chinese Academy of Medical Science 1970). The successes in China clearly indicate that the efficacy of medical care will be improved if we push forward the growth of Chinese medicine and then systematically combine it with Western methods.

However, a major prerequisite to the utilization of Chinese medical resources in Hong Kong is the control and improvement of the technical quality of Chinese medical practice. Granted that the medical knowledge itself is sound, the most serious problem faced by traditional medicine in Hong Kong today is the lack of uniform control over the education and practice of its medical practitioners. Some practitioners are well qualified, but others are quacks.

To overcome this deficiency, I suggest that a government-recognized College of Chinese Medicine (preferably affiliated with the university) and a Chinese Medical Council of Hong Kong should be established. These two institutions would take the responsibility of providing and maintaining minimum technical standards of Chinese medical services. They would have control over the training of students, the registration and licensing of medical practitioners, and the ethics of medical practice. Chinese medical practitioners who were trained by the college or were registrable with the council should be recognized by law as duly qualified doctors.

It is expected that the vested economic interest of Western-trained doctors, however, will appear as a resistant force to the legitimization of Chinese medical practice. To legitimize their counterparts means an increase of "rivals" in the free market of medicine and health. Hence, it will be helpful if both the government and the university can play an active role in the process of legitimizing and developing Chinese medical practice. With its political power the government can enforce a legal recognition of Chinese medical care, while the university with its academic status can confer the technical competence of Chinese medical practice and thus contribute to its social legitimation.

In addition to the control function, the college and the Chinese Medical Council should also aim at systematizing and upgrading the knowledge and skills of Chinese medicine. Because the scientific method has been proven to be the most effective approach to the development of valid knowledge and to the betterment of social life, it should be introduced into the Chinese medical system for the purpose of testing and improving the medical effects of traditional herbs and techniques. New discoveries in Communist China should be reconfirmed and then made available for use by medical students and practitioners.

The introduction of uniform standards and scientific procedures into the profession of Chinese medicine should generate several advantages. First, the Western-trained doctors who are presently dominating the medical care system in Hong Kong will be less skeptical of the competence of their Chinese medical "subordinates," and will then become less resistant to the development of Chinese medical services. Second, those Chinese people who prefer to consult Chinese medical practitioners will be able to receive adequate care and will be protected from running into quacks. Third, the utilization of Chinese medical services by the local population will be increased. Let me elaborate on the last point.

It seems that many Chinese residents in Hong Kong continue to have a deep-rooted interest and belief in their own medical tradition. As I have found, most Chinese people normally keep certain Chinese medical drugs at home for possible self-medication; most of them also prefer the Chinese to Western medical approach in respect to tonic care, minimum side effects, and the treatment of disease rather than symptoms. Another indicator of the public's interest in the traditional approach is the fact that a number of Chinese newspapers and magazines in Hong Kong have special columns discussing and popularizing the nature and use of Chinese medicine.

All these facts suggest that many Chinese in Hong Kong have not yet entirely given up their trust and dependency on the knowledge and skills of traditional medicine. In fact, as I have found, although most residents more often consult Western-trained doctors, many of them make use of Chinese medical services at about the same time. Hence, given that the public is assured of the technical qualification of Chinese medical practitioners, the utilization of Chinese health resources would be increased.

In order to increase the utilization of qualified Chinese medical services by the public, we should also consider two major obstacles: (1) the rising cost of Chinese medical care, and (2) the inconvenience in taking Chinese medicines. Many residents as well as Chinese medical practitioners have made complaints about Chinese medical herbs becoming increasingly expensive. For the treatment of most diseases, it has become more expensive to use Chinese than Western medical care. Up to now, the government and a great majority of the voluntary agencies in Hong Kong have been providing and supporting only the Western medical and health services. In order to increase the availability of adequate medical care to the public, especially to the poor, both the government and the voluntary agencies should begin to offer or support accessible, low-cost, qualified Chinese medical services to the people. Otherwise, the use of traditional medicine will gradually become a privilege of the well-to-do, rather than of the people in the middle or the poor.

Another obstacle to the use of Chinese medicine is the amount of time and effort required for preparing medicinal herbs for consumption. Most herbs are in the form of preserved roots and brews. It takes special effort to prepare them for medical treatment. A solution to this problem is to transform the medical herbs into patent medicines.

In recent years, pharmaceutical workers in Communist China have already made a substantial contribution in this area. By means of scientific methods of extraction, they have succeeded in putting before the public a number of traditional medicines in the form of tincture tablets, medicated liquors, and capsules and condensed pills. To name a few examples, these drugs include those used in treating schistosomiasis, tumors, fulminating epidemics, and cerebrospinal meningitis, and for curing septic shock resulting from toxic dysentery.[11]

---

[11]   For a detailed list of the products and a description of their medical functions, see the bulletin "Chinese Patent Medicine" (Chinese Patent Medicine Exhibition 1972).

Many of the Chinese patent medicines are also available for purchase in the Hong Kong market. It is suggested that medical practitioners and local residents should be advised to make use of these medical products. I believe that the availability of patent medicines, together with the accessibility of qualified low-cost services, will greatly increase the utilization of Chinese medical care by the local population.

Up to this point, I have argued for increasing the utilization of Chinese medical resources in Hong Kong and controlling and improving the technical quality of Chinese medical practice and have also identified some possible ways to do this. In addition, I have suggested that both Western and Chinese medicine be combined and integrated into a cohesive whole. The integration, I believe, will upgrade the efficacy of medical care. However, in view of Western medical dominance in Hong Kong, would the Western-trained doctors accept the idea of integration with Chinese medicine? My answer is positive. Let me spell it out.

First, as I have reported and argued, most Western-trained doctors distrust the quality of Chinese medical practitioners in Hong Kong rather than the medical knowledge itself. If they become convinced that Chinese medical practice is under appropriate control and that its medical effects have been examined by scientific procedures, then they will be less resistant to Chinese medicine.

Second, under the impact of medical advancement in Communist China, there have recently appeared several movements within the Western medical profession in Hong Kong toward learning and adopting the Chinese medical skills. Let me give a few examples. University medical students who receive formal training only in Western medicine have organized a public exhibition of Chinese medical herbs and techniques. Several articles have been published in the official newspaper of the University Student Union's Medical Society criticizing the University Medical School for its exclusion of traditional medicine. Several renowned Western-trained doctors have been publicly advocating the unification of Chinese and Western medicine. More important is that they have taken the initiative to establish a small Chinese Medical Center as a beginning step toward integration. The center currently places its focus on acupuncture and has already given training to about 100 Western-trained doctors. The Hong Kong Medical Association is also planning to offer a series of lectures about acupuncture to its Western-trained members, while some faculty in the departments of physiology and anatomy at the

---

For a brief report of the development of the pharmaceutical industry in China, see "Developing China's Medical Science Independently and Self-Reliantly" (Revolutionary Committee of the Chinese Academy of Medical Science 1970).

University Medical School have been undertaking scientific research on the effects of acupuncture.

In light of the two aforementioned points, I tend to believe that when Chinese medicine is under appropriate control and is developed through the use of the scientific method, Western-oriented doctors and students in Hong Kong will become increasingly receptive to the idea of integration. Now the question arises, how do we facilitate the integration?

The long-term goal should be the integration of both Chinese and Western medical knowledge and skills into a single, cohesive system. The most fundamental approach to achieving this goal is joint research. The central question to be tackled is: which method is the best for dealing with which disease? Both Chinese and Western-trained medical and health workers should conduct research together and evaluate in a scientific manner the RELATIVE efficacy of Chinese medicine, Western medicine, and a combination of both for dealing with various kinds of medical and health problems. These research workers should preferably maintain close contact and frequently exchange findings with those doing similar research in Communist China. It is also suggested that local hospitals in coordination with medical schools play a crucial role. They normally have a rich amount of financial, intellectual, and technological resources for medical research. No less important is the fact that in hospitals we can find a great variety of patients and disease patterns.

Concomitant to the undertaking of joint research, we should encourage and assist students and practitioners in learning the basic logic of the other tradition. Intercommunication and mutual understanding will reduce the skepticism between the two groups and will subsequently contribute to the confluence of the Western and Chinese traditions.Many measures can be employed to facilitate the communication flow. For instance, medical schools and professional associations should regularly offer lectures and training programs about the other medical approach; joint conferences and seminars should be held so that medical workers of both traditions can exchange their theoretical insights, research results, and clinical experiences; journals and brochures about the similarities, differences, or relationships between the two medical approaches should be published and then widely disseminated to students and practitioners.

The third approach to achieve the goal of integrating medical knowledge is the coordination of existing Western and Chinese services. As I have reported, many residents in Hong Kong have attempted to make use of both Western and Chinese methods in the treatment of disease. It is these medical recipients who currently attempt to "coordinate" and "integrate" the two medical approaches. If we accept the proposition that laymen are technically incompetent to do the coordinating, then these recipients are indeed running a great risk. Hence I suggest that medical practitioners should take the initiative in coordinating treatment. It will protect the local population from miscombining the two approaches. An added virtue is that the experience of practicing in coordination with each other will subsequently contribute to the integration of knowledge and skills of the Chinese and Western practitioners. The question is, how do we make the coordination possible?

At least two conditions have to be met: medical practitioners of both traditions must be (1) willing and also (2) able to coordinate their medical practices. As I have argued, if intercommunication and mutual understanding are facilitated, practitioners of one medical tradition should be increasingly willing to cooperate with their counterparts. Willingness is necessary, but it is not sufficient. They must have the ability to work together, which depends on whether they know the conditions under which they should or should not coordinate. As I have suggested, a major contribution of joint medical research is the discovery of which method is the best for dealing with which disease. Hence if joint studies are in progress, I believe that a medical practitioner will be increasingly able to work with those of the other medical tradition. He can easily find the right answer to the crucial question of whom he should consult with or refer patients to in dealing with specific diseases.

When medical practitioners become increasingly willing and able to cooperate in medical practice, there will gradually emerge a colleague network between Western-trained and Chinese practitioners for mutual consultation and patient referrals. Although such a network may appear and function on an informal and voluntary basis among some practitioners, it would be desirable if hospitals and community health centers would foster the coordination by purposely designing and formulating medical teams composed of practitioners from both traditions. I do not intend to engage in a detailed discussion about the structure of the medical team here. Nevertheless, let me suggest a few rudiments of a possible scheme.

I think that the key member of the medical team ought to be a "generalist" who has received basic training in both the Western and Chinese traditions; other members should be specialists in some areas of Chinese or Western medicine. The generalist makes the initial diagnosis. He may then either refer the patient to the appropriate specialists in the team or provide treatment in consultation with some specialists. In either case, he should be responsible for coordinating the team members in the process of diagnosis and treatment. Whenever appropriate, the patient should be allowed to make his choice between Chinese and Western-trained specialists. From such a medical team, the patient will be able to receive the specialized yet comprehensive and coordinated care of both Chinese and Western medicine. One should remember that the distinction between Chinese and Western practice in the informal colleague network or medical team will steadily decline as Chinese and Western medical knowledge and skills are increasingly integrated into a unity.

In short, I have suggested three possible approaches to achieve the long-term goal of integrating both Chinese and Western medical traditions into a cohesive whole — joint research, intercommunication, and coordination of medical practices. If the integrated whole continues to be developed by incorporating the major medical traditions of other societies, such as those in India, the Middle East, and the African countries, then the ideal of forming "world medicine" will be gradually realized.

## SUMMARY AND DISCUSSION

I have examined the existing pattern of relationships between traditional Chinese and modern Western medical services in the British colony of Hong Kong for the purpose of identifying some realizable ways of unifying the two traditions.

The existing pattern of relationships between Chinese and Western services in Hong Kong's pluralistic health care sector can be characterized as "noninteractive" and "unequal." Although the locational distributions of Western and Chinese sevices are strongly associated and are both dependent on population size and socioeconomic status, there exists very little interaction and exchange between medical practitioners of the two traditions. Moreover, because of its ties to political power and scientific ideology, Western medicine has been dominating the entire sector of health and medicine.

There are more traditional practitioners than Western-trained doctors in Hong Kong, but these traditional practitioners are held in low esteem. Western medicine is legally recognized, but not Chinese medicine. Most local residents are generally in favor of Western medical care rather than Chinese medicine, although they continue to be dependent upon traditional methods in some specific ways. Western-trained doctors are, for the most part, skeptical of the technical competence of traditional practitioners, although they seem to have trust in the efficacy of Chinese medical knowledge itself. It is suggested that the major problem faced by Chinese medicine in Hong Kong today is the lack of uniform control over the training and practice of traditional practitioners.

I have proposed that Chinese medical resources in Hong Kong be revived and developed on the basis of two considerations. First, the existing Western medical facilities are inadequate in meeting the health needs of local residents. Second, the efficacy of traditional medicine cannot be rejected outright merely on the ground of scientism, as demonstrated by medical progress in China. In order to push toward an increase of utilization and an improvement of medical efficacy, we should introduce uniform standards and scientific methods into the profession of Chinese medicine and should also increase the availability of Chinese patent medicines and of low-cost Chinese medical care. Furthermore, the medical knowledge and skills of both traditions should be systematically combined into an integrated whole through the undertaking of joint medical research, the exchange of information, and the coordination of medical practice. The creation of a new medical science that incorporates the best of both the Chinese and Western approaches will upgrade the quality of medical care and will make greater contributions to humanity.

On the basis of the above analysis, some general statements may be suggested. Nowadays, modernity has become an important goal of most nations throughout the world. For most developing nations, however, modernization in effect means Westernization. It is the process of change toward those types of institutional and technological systems that have been developed in advanced Western societies such as the United States, England, and Germany. A typical example is the dominance of Western medicine in the health sector of most developing societies. Because of its Western origin and scientific technology, Western medicine has been stressed to the exclusion of traditional medicine. Is the policy of Western medical dominance an appropriate strategy for the development of medical and health care services?

The goal of a health care system is to provide the BEST care to the MOST people. This goal implies two basic elements, i.e. the quality as well as the quantity of medical care. Because of their low levels of economic development, developing societies usually have extensive needs for medical care but do not possess the necessary resources for provinding sufficient and high-quality Western medical services. As a result, the limited amount of high-quality Western medical facilities favors the relatively rich minority at the expense of the masses of people in poverty status. It may take many years before the total population can obtain accessible, high-quality Western medical care. To foster the development of both quantitatively and qualitatively adequate medical care to the people, we may follow Mao Tsetung's calling of "walking on two legs." In other words, concomitant with the development of Western medicine, medical and health workers in developing societies should also mobilize and refine, rather than exclude, their traditional medical resources.

Some traditional medical techniques may be magical and superstitious, but many of them have been used on an empirical basis. They should be functional in some ways, otherwise they cannot survive the test of centuries. Furthermore, it has been demonstrated by this paper and by many other studies that even if Western services were abundantly available, a number of people would remain dependent upon traditional methods in one way or another.[12] Hence, if the rich fund of empirical experience in traditional medicine is mobilized and refined, it will not only increase the quantity of qualified medical care, but also protect the people from unqualified traditional practitioners. In addition, as demonstrated by the notable successes in China, the incorporation of traditional skills into Western medical science will contribute to the advancement of medical theory and practice. The question is: how should traditional medicine be developed?

What is most important is to modernize both the TECHNICAL and the ORGANIZATIONAL content of traditional medical practice. The technical efficacy of traditional medicine should be modernized through the application of scientific methods. In other words, traditional techniques should be systematically classified and their medical effects should be tested and modified on the basis of logical reasoning and objective data. When appropriate, traditional medicines should be put into the form of medicated liquors, pills, or inoculations.

To modernize the organization of work, the most important task is to introduce into the traditional medical profession minimum technical and ethical standards for training and practice. Traditional knowledge and skills should be taught in university classrooms with standard textbooks, instead of being passed on through apprenticeship. Professional coordination in the form of mutual consultation or patient referrals should be encouraged. Traditional practice should be incorporated in hospitals and health centers. Voluntary agencies and the government should provide accessible, low-cost, high quality traditional services to the public.

To conclude the discussion, let me restate my central proposition. In order to provide the best medical care to the greatest number of people, medical and health workers should attempt to reexamine the knowledge and practice of traditional medicine, to modernize the technical as well as the organizational content of work, and to selectively incorporate the

---

[12]   For a good example, see Gould (1957). Gould reported that in a North Indian village, folk medicine tends to serve the chronic nonincapacitating dysfunctions while the scientific mode of healing serves critical incapacitating dysfunctions.

traditional approach into modern Western medicine. To discard outright the traditional medicine which has been accumulated for centuries is in fact "unscientific" behavior. Let us look forward to the creation of a single modern medical science which is built on the best of all medical traditions throughout the world.

# REFERENCES

ANONYMOUS
  1972  "Acupuncture anaesthesia." Peking: Foreign Languages Press.
CHIEN HSIN-CHUNG
  1964  Chinese medicine: progress and achievements. *Peking Review* (February):16–19.
CHIN, ROBERT
  1972  "Changing health conduct of the new man in China." Paper presented at a conference sponsored by the University of Michigan School of Public Health and the Macy Foundation, May 14–17.
CHINESE PATENT MEDICINE EXHIBITION
  1972  "Chinese patent medicine." Hong Kong: Chinese Patent Medicine and Medicated Liquor Exhibition in Hong Kong, June 1972.
CHOA, G. H.
  1972  *Hong Kong annual departmental report of medical and health services for the financial year 1971–1972.* Hong Kong: Hong Kong Government.
CROIZIER, RALPH C.
  1968  *Traditional medicine in modern China: science, nationalism, and the tensions of cultural change.* Cambridge, Massachusetts: Harvard University Press.
FANG, HARRY S. Y., *editor*
  1970  *Medical directory of Hong Kong.* Hong Kong: Federation of Medical Societies of Hong Kong.
FREIDSON, ELIOT
  1972  *Profession of medicine.* New York: Dodd, Mead.
GIBSON, GEOFFREY
  1971  Chinese medical practice and the thoughts of Chairman Mao. *Social Science and Medicine* (1971):1–25.
GOULD, HAROLD A.
  1957  The implications of technological change for folk and scientific medicine. *American Anthropologist* 59:507–516.
HEALTH POLICY ADVISORY CENTER
  1972  China: revolution and health. *The Health-PAC Bulletin* 47.
HONG KONG, CENSUS AND STATISTICS DEPARTMENT
  1972  "Hong Kong population and housing census in 1971: basic tables."
HONG KONG, GOVERNMENT INFORMATION SERVICES
  1970  "Hong Kong's medical and health services."

HONG KONG YEAR BOOK
   1973   "Medical Services." Hong Kong: Wah Kiu Yat Po.
HOU CHIN-WEN
   1970   Mao Tsetung thought lights up the way for the advance of China's
          medical science. *Peking Review* 13(25):23–27.
HUARD, PIERRE, MING WONG
   1968   *Chinese medicine*. New York: McGraw-Hill.
LEE, RANCE P. L.
   1972a  "Population, housing, and the availability of medical and health
          services in an industrializing Chinese community." Hong Kong: Social
          Research Centre, Chinese University of Hong Kong.
   1972b  "Spatial distributions of modern Western and traditional Chinese
          medical practitioners in an industrializing Chinese town." Hong Kong:
          Social Research Centre, Chinese University of Hong Kong.
   1972c  "Study of health systems in Kwun Tong: health attitudes and behavior
          of Chinese residents." Hong Kong: Social Research Centre, Chinese
          University of Hong Kong.
   1972d  "Study of health systems in Kwun Tong: organizations and attitudes
          of the Western-trained and the traditional Chinese personnel in an
          industrial community of Hong Kong." Hong Kong: Social Research
          Centre, Chinese University of Hong Kong.
REVOLUTIONARY COMMITTEE OF THE CHINESE ACADEMY OF MEDICAL SCIENCE
   1970   Developing China's medical science independently and self-reliantly.
          *Peking Review* 13(1):24–30.
RIFKIN, SUSAN B., RAPHAEL KAPLINSKY
   1973   Health strategy and development planning: lessons from the People's
          Republic of China. *The Journal of Developmental Studies* 9(2):213–232.
WONG, SIDNEY
   1970   "A preliminary ecological analysis of the development of Kwun Tong,
          1954–1970." Hong Kong: Social Research Centre, Chinese University
          of Hong Kong.

# Serve the People: What It Would Mean for Health Care in the United States

LESLIE A. FALK, JOHN N. HAWKINS

"Serve the people" (*wei renmin fu wu*) is a phrase widely used in China and now repeated in the United States in reports of visitors and scholars. The phrase was first used by Mao Tse-tung in a 1944 article written to commemorate the death of a Chinese People's Liberation Army soldier (Mao Tse-tung 1968: 3).[1] Since 1944 it has become a guiding concept for virtually every social activity in China. Party cadres are exhorted to serve the people and to develop "a good work style with the masses" as they carry out their duties. Teachers are encouraged to serve the people by providing a meaningful and participatory learning environment for their students. The Chinese are taught to care for each other, to love and help each other, to love workers, peasants, and soldiers, to love both physical and intellectual labor, and to keep the public good in mind. The Chinese attempt to create people who will put the needs of others before their own, who will be motivated by altruism, instead of by self-interest (R. Sidel 1972).[2]

Gratitude is expressed to our wives, Joy Hume Falk, who was born in China and has maintained a consistent interest in that country even during the days of the greatest United States — China communications blackout, and Judith Takata Hawkins, whose Hawaiian upbringing and Japanese ancestry give her great understanding of both East and West. Clerical assistance was provided by, and under the supervision of, Ms. Joyce Foley, Administrative Assistant, Department of Family and Community Health, Meharry Medical College. Victor and Ruth Sidel have been generous in sharing their experiences and views. We have also been influenced by the National Medical Association delegation, especially Doctors Ralph Cazort and Montague Cobb.

[1] For an extended discussion of the concept "serve the people" and Mao's role in education see Hawkins (i.p.).
[2] This is a recent, readily available source. See the selected reading list on pages 193–194.

But nowhere is the concept "serve the people" more evident than in China's health care delivery program. The changes have been most pronounced since the Cultural Revolution in 1967. Then, the Chinese dismantled an overspecialized, unbalanced, and elitist medical educational system, replacing it with an egalitarian one to "serve all the people of China." The medical curriculum was reformed, trimmed, and eventually rewritten. Organization of service provided a more functional health care system, and it emphasized interaction between Chinese and Western medicine. Admissions to medical school were based on consumers' choices of their best peoples, as well as on other principles[3].

The result today is that the Chinese are able to provide adequate health care to virtually all 800,000,000 of their people. Most important, the people themselves play an active role in performing and supporting public health efforts.[4] They participate in health education programs designed to train neighborhood health workers and personnel in the health care team. The "barefoot doctor" and the "lane doctor" are links between the people and the more highly trained personnel. The teams pool a variety of skills in a basic unit providing comprehensive health care for the areas in which they work. The Chinese have achieved a remarkable degree of success in prompt elimination of many major diseases; e.g. malnutrition, opium addiction, typhoid fever, cholera, syphilis, and gonorrhea. They have a network of health care organizations proving to be highly effective in disease prevention (V. Sidel 1972a, 1972b). In addition, unwanted children are a rarity.

## HEALTH CARE EDUCATION AND DELIVERY IN CHINA

As in other educational areas, medical students are selected on the basis of their class background, ideological soundness, and academic ability. The training period has been shortened from five to three years, and subject matter has been reduced by one-third (Dimond 1971). Still, the Chinese are convinced they can continue to turn out quality physicians by integrating Chinese traditional medicine (such as the use of acupuncture, pulse

[3]   See several articles in the Chinese press describing recent medical reforms: *New China News Service (NCNS)*, Nanning (July 19, 1972): 3; *NCNS*, Kuming (May 18, 1972): 11; *NCNS*, Shenyang (July 21, 1972): 40; *NCNS*, Sian (October 21, 1972): 9–10; *NCNS*, Peking (February 6, 1972): 22.

[4]   The astonishing success of China's health care program is documented and verified in several reports by foreign observers. In particular see Horn (1969, 1972) and the University of California report on the visit of the Medical School team to China (1973).

diagnosis, and the medicinal uses of various herbs) with modern medical practices (Beau 1965). They combine practical experience with theoretical training; concentration is on the training of general practitioners rather than specialists. Upon graduation, the new doctors are assigned to public health units, usually in the countryside, where they assist in the development and expansion of public health and the training of local medical practitioners. Thus, the new doctor is part of a new approach to the problem of providing health care for a heavily populated, basically agricultural society.

In establishing the new health care program, the initial problem was the organization of facilities and personnel. Thousands of physicians, nurses, and auxiliary medical assistants formed and joined medical teams which toured the adjacent rural areas to determine health needs and strategy. An integrated network of regional, city, and county hospitals, with commune clinics, was coordinated and oriented toward providing the peasantry with a comprehensive health care organization. Mobile medical teams were maintained to facilitate the education and care of the local inhabitants.

A primary goal has been to educate the local villagers to accept an increased responsibility for their own health needs, thus insuring a more effective preventive medicine program. Although the localities are encouraged to sustain a portion of the cost of such care, the major burden falls on the revenue of the cities, counties, and provinces, which are supplying in some cases close to 90 percent of medical care costs. Coordination of health care between the villages, counties, and cities is maintained by telegraph and telephone. When an emergency of potential epidemic proportion breaks out, health teams can be notified and dispatched quickly, thus facilitating the control of crisis situations.

Innovative training methods for health care practitioners are also followed. Short-term medical training classes have been established both in the urban and rural colleges and in informal village settings. These courses are providing the major means for expanding public health facilities and programs to China's countryside. The curriculum follows a practical course, and the teachers are guided by the general principles of lecturing more on common diseases, emphasizing major diseases, lecturing less on rare diseases, and omitting diseases never found in the locality.

Folk remedies which have proved successful are combined with modern medical techniques, a factor in reducing the cost of medical care and winning the confidence of the local inhabitants. In addition, the students receive instruction in the history and culture of the area in which they will work and, if dialect differences exist, they receive language instruction as well.[5]

Although the basic thrust of medical education is toward the rural areas and involves general and primary training, research projects have not been neglected. The medical teams are studying medical histories of individuals in the villages, and doing regional epidemiological research, as well as identifying and classifying herb medicines. In addition, studies are being conducted to develop more efficient and practical types of medical apparatus more suited to the scarce resources available in the country-side.[6]

The practical benefits of such a program are clear when one considers the vast needs of the Chinese countryside and the increase in medical and paramedical personnel such a program will create. This program will greatly expand public health facilities in the rural areas and provide increased medical care for more people than did the previous urban-oriented, overspecialized system of medical education.[7]

What will China's new educational alternatives mean as a model for other nations to emulate? The reforms have not been in operation long enough to give precise answers, but tentative judgments can be attempted.

[5] In the period 1968–1973 it is estimated that over 1,000,000 "barefoot doctors" have been trained in China specifically to work as members of health care teams in the rural areas. In areas previously lacking medical facilities (e.g. Kiangsu province in East China), clinics have been established in every commune. The frontier or border regions of China have always been characterized by inaccessibility and thus lacked even a minimum of health care. Since 1968 over 100 separate medical teams have been dispatched to China's vast frontiers, where they have permanent health care facilities with links to major medical centers in the provinces. For further information related to the efficiency and effectiveness of China's preventive medicine program, consult *New China News Agency (NCNA)*, Shanghai (August 15, 1973): 3–5; *NCNA* Nanking (August 5, 1973): 15–16; *NCNA*, Huhehot (June 12, 1973): 2; *NCNA*, Sining (July 31, 1973): 5–6.

[6] The Chinese have been particularly successful in opening new avenues of medical treatment by a rational combination of Western and Chinese medical practices; the political and social preparation of members of the health teams is an important ingredient in the application of this kind of medical care. For current reports of the endeavor see *NCNA*, Nanning (July 2, 1973): 4–5; *NCNA*, Peking (July 7, 1973): 2; *NCNA*, Lhasa (July 17, 1973): 2–3.

[7] Several provincial-wide medical conferences have recently been held in China to report on the numerous research efforts currently underway, particularly those focusing on the prevention and treatment of common and recurrent endemic diseases of working people. See *NCNA*, Changchun (May 16, 1973): 5–6; *NCNA*, Peking (July 16, 1973): 1–2; *NCNA*, Sining (July 24, 1973): 4–5.

## THE UNITED STATES — NOW

In the United States, health conditions are sacrificed when profit ("good business"; "the economy") is at stake. Health care is highly biased toward physician-dominance, hospitalization, and the prescribing of pharmaceuticals. "Scientific medicine" and specialization dominate. Availability is basically related to the ability of the individual or family to pay, and is modified, or mollified, only partially by social measures such as Medicare for persons over age sixty-five, Medicaid for welfare recipients, and the existence of a "second class" system of public hospitals. There are a few hopeful "comprehensive health centers" offering broad benefits, but even these are suffering under the current administration in Washington. As members of a black medical institution, we see such problems with particular poignancy.

There is a wide chasm between public health and medical care activities in the United States. Public health services tend to be limited, e.g. to public health nursing service for the poor and to certain environmental health activities. Policy-making authority lies in boards of health, presumably responsible to the public but almost always representing the medical society (private-practitioner dominated), and a few wealthy and/or politically prominent "leaders." The people are almost never represented directly. We could go on, but the diagnosis is rather well known.

## SERVE THE PEOPLE — UNITED STATES VERSION

In the American health care system, what would "serve the people" be like?[8] Let us try to apply some lessons.

First, it would almost certainly aim to protect those in greatest need; that is, those with the highest mortality, morbidity, and disability rates, and those with previous lack of care. These are the poor members of minority groups, the unemployed, disabled, less privileged workers, farmers, and lower middle class people. How might serving them start? Blacks, browns, reds, yellows, and poor whites might be asked to identify their "healers" (be they granny midwives, voodoo practitioners, *curanderos*, medicine men, root and herb doctors, or preachers). They would also be asked to identify their leadership persons, at home and at work. People's religious and philosophical views would be carefully studied, and their beliefs and health care practices made to interact with those of the "scien-

[8] We have been reminded since giving this paper that the Black Panther Party in the United States has used the expression "serve the people" extensively. Our discussion is not significantly in the context of their activities.

tific" stream. This would be done by offering continuing education opportunities to their healers and neghborhood health leaders in an atmosphere of THEIR culture, THEIR beliefs, and THEIR "home bases," in a two-way interchange of personnel and sometimes of mobile facilities.

New health care education schools would be founded as brown-, red-, poor white-, and yellow-led institutions. Meharry Medical College, Howard University, and the Charles Drew Postgraduate Medical School now represent this for black people, and they would be strengthened and enabled to serve entire regions of the United States.

Training of the primary care and preventive health teams would dominate, with efforts to unify preventive and curative medicine. Nurse practitioners and others with "expanded nurse" or "health worker" roles would be favored, and the number of medical students would be increased. Admission to medical schools would give preference at first to women, minority students, folk or native healers, and representatives of the poor, rural, and working class populations. Mountain and rural area recruitment and experience would be stressed.

Housing projects, neighborhoods, factories, and rural communities would all identify their "health workers" and encourage them to become PART-TIME professional persons on the health team. Equal emphasis would be placed on the part-time and AMATEUR health leaders and health associations. Health councils would be led by such people. They would have the authority and financing to wield great influence at the policy level, to delve into environmental hazards, and to influence the basic conditions of life of their members in jobs, housing, environment, food, recreation, education, and the political process, as well as in medical care.

Medical school admissions representatives would discard the Medical College Aptitude Test (MCAT) as a culture-bound, misleading, "objective" aptitude test. They would place great stress on service-mindedness, ethical sense, innovations, group leadership capacities, likelihood to practice in specific places, and in specific kinds of practice. The ability to acquire technical and practical competence would be maintained, but in better balance. Research and teaching would value the social sciences and the humanities equally with the natural or "basic" sciences. Values such as kindliness, cooperativeness, and self-sacrifice would replace stress on individual "success," with its superspecialty and guild protectionism practices at present. Medical and financial audit would be conducted for quality, comprehensiveness, honesty, and compliance with the stated health goals. Incompetence would not be tolerated, but habilitation and rehabilitation would be offered throughout the lifetimes of all health personnel.

Financial barriers to care would be removed, and an organized, but simple, health care system would be developed as a national health service, based on health care as a right (Falk 1971). Local control would be basic, but district and regional organization would also be strong, enabling access to care and health personnel from larger units, such as district and teaching hospitals.

Health education would become central. It would first grapple with the self-care or "self-reliance" dimensions. All people would be given the necessary basic understanding of the environment and healthy personal life styles (food, sex, exercise, avoidance of cigarettes, drugs, etc.). As a professional field, health education would have firm links with the poor, deprived, and mid-stream consumer groups, and would resist the technological seduction techniques of human manipulation by an elitist "in-group," for example, subliminal advertising. It would, thus, place priority on social investment to minimize the disturbing of nature by environmental exploitation (e.g. by strip mining). This would certainly focus on preventing pollution of air, water, food, and living and working environments.

Military expenditures would, of course, represent a low priority and this would enable social reimbursement to eliminate vested interests inimical to health, e.g. those of cigarette vendors, tobacco farmers, bartenders, prostitutes, pimps, drug addicts, drug pushers, and others. Such people would be helped to use their energies in developing better forms of living. Subsidy funds to enable production enterprises to concentrate on healthy products would lead to better food, housing, factories, and the like and to a decrease in unhealthy products or habits.

The television, radio, newspaper, movie, and billboard resources would be made fully available to the health goals and activities decided on. None would be available to "push" patent medicines, alcohol, cigarettes, or polluting or unsafe products onto the public.

Pure air, water, and food, adequate housing, transportation, education, and recreation would be put first, as would the personal medical care system used to detect their breakdown. Population control would be voluntary, but birth control information and devices would be universally available. Sex education would also be easily available, conducted by people's peers as much as possible, and with beliefs and values clearly stated, but with tolerance for differing views.

In summary, what would it take to get the people served? It would take changes in the political, economic, and social system so that the central authority and resources are focused on health values and actions, instead of on their opposites, which is the situation today.

Is it possible to effect such changes? Are we not doomed to fail? We should remember that the situation in China's health care prior to 1949 resembled in some ways the problems of the United States today, apart from technological differences. The Chinese suffered from an overspecialized, elitist, and in many ways dysfunctional medical care system during the 1930's and 1940's. The Chinese give as an example even the important "modernizing" medical care education efforts of the United States in China — the Rockefeller-sponsored Peking Union Medical College. Much well-meaning effort was spent on training high-quality physicians, mostly from the upper middle class, but many of them practiced in the cities, and primarily for those persons who could pay. There were some attempts to reach the rural regions of China, but the medical problems continued to worsen. It took a twenty-year period marked by war, civil war, and revolution before the entire Chinese people were able to have their needs humanely and effectively served. Even since the founding of the People's Republic of China, the country has had to continue to struggle to provide a medical care system which genuinely "serves the people."

As social conditions in the United States deteriorate on almost all fronts, we must assess the situation soberly. We must recognize the probability of having to go through many of the same kinds of struggles as did the Chinese and other people, who have had to suffer in order to create a better future.

## MODELS

The medical profession especially can, and should, play a progressive role in any such endeavors. We might adopt as one model (in the Chinese tradition) the best of our neighbor, Dr. Norman Bethune (Allan and Gordon 1968), now immortalized by the Chinese (Mao Tse-tung 1968: 7). Dr. Bethune arrived in China in 1938 to aid in the war of resistance against the Japanese and Chiang Kai-shek, then being fought primarily by the Chinese Eight Route Army in northwest China. Bethune died in 1939 of septicemia acquired from an infectious case he was treating. His perfection of medical skills, his selfless attitude in work, and his ability to identify with health care for all people made him a physician worthy of emulation. Mao's widely known tribute to Dr. Bethune includes these statements:

His utter devotion to others without any thought of self, was shown in his boundless sense of responsibility in his work and his boundless warmheartedness towards all comrades and the people ... We must all learn the spirit of absolute selflessness from him. With this spirit everyone can be useful to the people. A man's ability may be great or small, but if he has this spirit, he is already nobleminded and pure, a man of moral integrity and above vulgar interests, a man who is of value to the people (Mao Tse-tung 1966:171).

It is not too difficult to visualize similar things being said about health care leaders of the peace movement, such as Dr. Benjamin Spock, in an analogous leadership role in the United States. Dr. Martha Eliot, who has pioneered in women's rights, abortion, and birth control is another such model, as is Dr. Paul Cornely, a courageous black public health figure.

Under our present political and economic organization, the prospects for a health care delivery system that would truly "serve the people" may appear dim. But history does not stand still despite the efforts of those who try to make it do so. We would profit from the example of those "China experts" who predicted in the 1930's and 1940's that China was, and would remain for some time, the "sick man of Asia." History proved otherwise. With dedication and sacrifice, it will prove otherwise in the United States as well.

## REFERENCES

ALLAN, T., S. GORDON
   1968   *The scalpel, the sword; the story of Dr. Norman Bethune*. Oxford: Oxford University Press. (Originally published 1954. London: Hale.)
BEAU, GEORGES
   1972   *Chinese medicine*. New York: Avon. (Originally published 1965 in French. Paris: Editions du Seuil.)
DIMOND, E. GREY
   1971   Medical education and care in the People's Republic of China. *Journal of the American Medical Association* 218:1552–1557.
FALK, LESLIE A.
   1971   Functional group practice in a national health program; based on E. R. Weinerman's "Organization and quality of service in a national health program." *Yale Journal of Biology and Medicine* 44:153–158. (Reprinted 1971 in *Weinerman memorial volume*, Weinerman Memorial Committee, Yale University School of Epidemiology and Public Health, New Haven, Connecticut.)
   1973   "The potential role of the medical school in rural health care delivery," in *Rural and Appalachian health care*. Edited by Robert Nolan and Jerome Schwartz. Springfield, Illinois: Thomas.
HAWKINS, JOHN N.
   i.p.   *Mao Tse-tung and education: his thoughts and teachings*. Hamden, Connecticut: The Shoe String Press.
HORN, JOSHUA S.
   1969   *Away with all pests*. New York: Monthly Review Press.

1972   Building a rural health service in the People's Republic of China. *International Journal of Health Services* 2:377–383.

MAO TSE-TUNG

1966   "In memory of Norman Bethune," in *Quotations from Chairman Mao Tse-tung*. Peking: Foreign Language Press.

1968   *Five articles*. Peking: Foreign Language Press.

NEW CHINA NEWS AGENCY

1973   Articles on medical research and programs.

NEW CHINA NEWS SERVICE

1972   Articles on recent medical reforms.

SIDEL, RUTH

1972   *Women and child care in China; a firsthand report*. New York: Hill and Wang.

SIDEL, VICTOR

1972a   Health services in China. *International Journal of Health Services* 2:385–395.

1972b   Serve the people: medical education in the People's Republic of China. *The New Physician* 21:284–291.

UNIVERSITY OF CALIFORNIA

1973   "The great experiment." *Alumni News* (September):1–2, 4. University of California at Los Angeles, Medical Center.

1972   Changing concepts in comprehensive health care; comprehensive care in health programs – III. *Journal of the National Medical Association* 64:471–475.

## PART THREE

*Social Science in Health Research and Action*

# The Role of Applied Research in the Development of Health Services in a Chicano Community in Chicago

STEPHEN L. SCHENSUL, MARY BAKSZYSZ BYMEL

In 1963 Congress enacted legislation to establish "community" mental health programs in urban and rural sites throughout the country. One such program was established in September of 1967 in Chicago's West Side Medical Complex. Its objective was to provide mental health services to the adjacent black community and to a large area immediately to the south in which Mexicans were rapidly replacing long-term residents of middle-European origin. To accomplish the task, four outpatient "storefront" clinics were set up in each of the main communities of the catchment area and were linked to inpatient and specialized services available at the Medical Center. These outpost clinics were to extend psychiatric services to people who until then had had little access to such care. From a community base, these centers were to mobilize community forces to help in the care and rehabilitation of patients and to effect positive changes in community structure so that mental illness could be prevented as well as treated.

The first of these outpost clinics was established in El Barrio (a pseudonym), a predominantly Mexican community located on Chicago's Near West Side. The El Barrio Mental Health Clinic began its operations at a time when few service institutions in Chicago had come to terms with the fact that there was a large population of recently immigrated Mexicans requiring new programs, resources, and services.

For the residents of El Barrio, this situation was reflected particularly

While the major responsibility for writing this paper was ours, the development of the ideas was a collaborative process of community activists and members of our research staff. These include: Philip Ayala, Albert Vázquez, Juan Velázquez, Humberto Martínez, Émile Schepers, Pertti J. Pelto, Elias Sevilla-Casas, Santiago Boiton, Susan Stechnij and Kay Guzder.

in health care. A few local physicians and an overloaded county hospital were the main health resources for El Barrio residents. Differences in language, attitudes, and health practices among Mexicans were not understood by the medical establishment, creating additional barriers to effective uses of even these limited resources. The Community Mental Health Program had a difficult task in trying to establish a mental health service in a community with limited services and no experience with Anglo-American mental health concepts.

In the beginning of 1969, the director of the program hired the authors to establish an anthropologically oriented Community Research Unit for the purpose of providing information concerning the Mexican, middle-European, and black populations in the area. This research was seen as providing a base for planning new clinical programs designed specifically for Mexican residents and constructing preventive programs to integrate mental health services into community development. Our research unit was to collect information on the "natives" of the area so that plans, policies, and therapeutic methods could be developed by the program staff which would meet the special cultural and community needs of the area. This position closely parallels the traditional role of the applied anthropologist — that of a provider of information to dominant policy-making and power sectors on behalf of economically and politically marginal groups in a society.

Over the past five years a series of events, both in the community and in the program, changed this role drastically and created a situation in which our research unit collaborated directly with community groups in El Barrio in formulating independent health projects. In describing this collaborative process we will examine the events and actions that led to the establishment of community health programs and the strategies used by our community research team to facilitate these developments.


## COMMUNITY LIFE AND HEALTH ISSUES IN EL BARRIO

The El Barrio community is Chicago's "port of entry" for Mexican immigrants and its major residential enclave for Mexican-Americans. A great majority of the Mexican population has arrived in Chicago within the last ten years directly from Mexico. Approximately 20 percent are from Texas and only 5 percent of individuals in a recent survey are Chicago-born (Schensul 1970). These different origins in various segments of the population — "Tejanos," Mexican nationals, and Chicago-born Chicanos — produce differences in attitudes, life experience, and behavior.

The influx of Mexicans into this area continues a long history of a succession of immigrant groups. Prior to the 1880's Irish and German immigrants and native-born Americans came to work in the small industries that were located in the area. Poles, Czechs, Slavs and other middle-European groups began to enter the area in the mid-1880's and by 1900 were the predominant ethnic groups. For the succeeding fifty years the community maintained a strong middle-European ethnic character — one which has left a visible mark even now on the community.

With the construction of a university campus north of El Barrio, many displaced Mexicans began to move south into the houses vacated by the outgoing middle-Europeans. This movement, combined with a growing influx of people from Mexico and the American Southwest, resulted in a rapid increase in the Mexican component of the population. By the end of the 1960's, the Mexican-American sector had increased from 30 percent to almost 70 percent of El Barrio's population. Most of the migrants of this period came directly from Mexico from cities such as Monterrey, San Luís Potosí, Guadalajara, Michoacán and other urban areas in western and northern Mexico.

The El Barrio community has a total population of 44,660 people, including 35,750 Mexicans, 2,211 Puerto Ricans, 5,631 middle-Europeans and 1,068 blacks. Low rents (averaging $88 a month), a close proximity to places of potential employment, rapidly decreasing numbers of middle-European residents, and the availability of Mexican goods and services make El Barrio a highly appropriate area for settlement by in-migrating Mexicans.

The overwhelmingly Mexican character of El Barrio permits the recent migrant to interact in Spanish in most contexts. Ethnographic data indicate that in Chicago a number of job situations exist which do not require English language abilities. Contacts through relatives and friends can lead to relatively satisfactory incomes through employment in Spanish-speaking work crews.

Spanish is the major language in most of the commercial establishments in the area. Availability of Spanish-language newspapers, magazines, music, household items, and food such as large quantities of *carnitas, chicharon,* and *pan dulce* convey a strong feeling of old Mexico.

El Barrio is viewed by many in Chicago as a typical inner-city "ghetto." In a recent article on economic and social status in Chicago, one of the city's newspapers rated El Barrio as eighty-fourth in a ranking of eighty-five Chicago communities (*Chicago Sun-Times* 1972). This rank was based on such indicators as rent, average education, job level, home value, and family income. Figures like these are frequently used as justification for urban renewal and slum clearance. However, a different image from that conveyed by census data is created by walking through the area. It is true that in El Barrio the housing is old and that excessive subdividing has created crowded conditions in some sectors. However, most buildings are structurally sound and well maintained, which makes the area a more desirable place to live than one would expect from its low rank in the city. The median income is $8,000 per year and an extremely low 2.3 percent of the population are unemployed. During the time the 1970 census was given, only 1.3 percent of the residents of El Barrio were on welfare.

These figures are considerably lower than the national average and present a striking contrast to welfare and unemployment rates for other ghetto populations.

The situation in the El Barrio community is one common to many inner city areas that have gone through rapid sociocultural change. In order to accommodate El Barrio's new Mexican population, city and community institutions have been under some pressure to change the nature of their services. This change is usually resisted, and even when changes do occur they are agonizing and frequently unsuccessful. The response of Mexican residents has been to avoid contact with these institutions and seek alternate resources among friends and relatives to meet their needs. The political and economic powerlessness of this group has allowed these institutions to continue to resist significant changes in policy and operation. This situation is particularly evident in the area of health services where unique health needs are not being met by standard American health institutions.

The conclusions of our own and other research efforts point to clear differences between Mexican-American and general American populations in disease rates, health attitudes and practices, disease configurations, and psychopathology. These differences can be summarized as follows:

1.  Chicano death rates are higher than national averages as a consequence of the diseases of poverty including influenza, pneumonia, tuberculosis, neonatal death, and rheumatic fever. Alcoholism and drug addiction, traumatic injury, and infectious conditions exacerbated by malnutrition are also recognized as major problems.

2.  Unlike Anglo-American medical beliefs, the traditional Mexican view of disease causation and symptomatology does not reflect a distinction between the mental and physical aspects of healthy functioning; this interrelationship between physical and mental factors is a key to the lack of understanding of Mexicans toward the separation of medical and psychiatric services.

3. Mexican-American beliefs about disease causation and symptomatology include a large number of illnesses that are unique to Mexican-Americans as a group. These disease configurations, or "folk illnesses," include *el ojo malo* [the evil eye], *empacho* [stomach upset], *bilis* [the product of extreme anger] and *susto* [result of fright or shock].

4. The existence of *curanderas* or traditional Mexican medical practitioners is a very important health resource in the El Barrio community. From our research we can say with some confidence that more individuals utilize folk curers in El Barrio than use "standard" medical and psychiatric facilities. The *curanderas* provide low-cost care with an emphasis on a personalized and "sacred" approach. They use a large herbal inventory in addition to other techniques such as dietary restrictions, chiropractics and religious-magical curing.

5. Mexican psychiatric patients show pathology and personality structures that are clearly different from those reported for other ethnic groups. For example, visions and voices are a widely acceptable part of normal functioning and maintenance of health in the Chicano population. A member of our research team has demonstrated the potential for misinterpreting visions and voices as psychopathology by non-Latin psychiatric staff (Schepers 1972).

6. Our research in the El Barrio community indicates considerable ethnic and intraethnic diversity in other health-related problems. In drug addiction, for example, we find that patterns of drug use and life situations among Chicano addicts are quite different from what has been described by addicts of other ethnic groups. We have also observed differences in drug use and life situation that distinguish first-generation Mexican addicts from those who have come to Chicago from Texas and those that were born in Chicago (Schensul 1972). Other research currently being conducted in the El Barrio community on psychiatric difficulties, alcoholism, and old age is beginning to indicate a wide range of additional factors specific to this ethnic group.

The reluctance of Mexican-Americans to utilize medical and psychiatric facilities has been well documented. This underutilization involves a number of factors including: the existence of *curanderismo*, the tendency of American doctors to scoff at folk beliefs, as well as outright rudeness and racism on the part of health professionals. Madsen (1970), Clark (1959), and others, have made recommendations for professionals concerning possible changes in their behavior and procedures to bring them into closer fit with the standards of Chicano culture. These and other studies (e.g. Rubel 1966) document instances in which Chicano patients, or would-be patients, have been discouraged by what seems to them to be a rejecting or patronizing attitude on the part of medical personnel.

From the standpoint of first-generation immigrants, Chicago's El Barrio community may be among those most culturally and linguistically Mexican in the United States. A continuing flow of new migrants promises to maintain this strong Mexican orientation. As a consequence, we can expect that many of the health attitudes and practices described above will continue to be salient to this community, rather than diminish in importance as has been noted in other Mexican communities.

## THE COMMUNITY MENTAL HEALTH PROGRAM

The Community Mental Health Program, through the El Barrio Mental Health Clinic, represented the first publicly funded service to direct its attention to an aspect of health in the Mexican community. However, given El Barrio's broad health needs and the lack of information about the functions of the mental health outpost, the Mexican-American people did not consider the program to be relevant to their health needs. In addition, the program's narrow definition of mental health care precluded a broad attack on the community's health problems.

In its first several months, the clinic found itself devoting most of its time to serving older middle-European patients who had long histories of mental illness and hospitalizations. Few Mexican residents sought help at the clinic and on the whole its existence and services were largely ignored. The difficulties in establishing an effective mental health service in the El Barrio community were exacerbated by the fact that the clinic was staffed almost exclusively by non-Latins who lacked an understanding of Mexican culture and the necessary bilingual ability for communicating effectively with Spanish-speaking patients. In addition, the clinic was burdened by a series of bureaucratic and political contingencies in the Medical Center that made it difficult for the various components of the Community Mental Health Program to coordinate their services effectively.

Another problem faced by the program in this area was that of citizen participation. An important part of the community mental health movement was the involvement of citizens and consumers in the direction and formulation of program policies and objectives. Several attempts to form advisory boards for the clinic failed, and the idea of advisory boards was eventually abandoned. Thus, residents neither used the services nor were very interested in becoming involved in the clinic's operations. The clinic, and in turn the program, stood outside of the mainstream of community life and only tangentially related to the community's health needs.

There were great expectations on the part of the clinical staff that our Community Research Unit could quickly discover the key cultural and community factors that could solve their problems in communication, underutilization, and citizen participation. Because these problems were very real and immediate, the clinical staff felt that the anthropologists had to provide this information almost immediately even though we had not been brought on the staff until one and one-half years after the clinic had been established. It soon became apparent to the clinicians that we had not entered the situation with a prepackaged set of principles that would immediately help them out of the difficulties they faced in the community. They also communicated to us that they were not willing to give us the time we needed to learn about the community and its people. Their reaction was to "write us off" as an important component of the program; as a result, there were the inevitable clinician-researcher tensions in our relationship to the rest of the program. After this initial interaction with the clinical staff it became clear to us that information about the community and its various cultural and ethnic groups was producing little interest and only minimal changes in the program. While in retrospect we can see that both sides failed to appreciate the point of view and professional concern of one another, the effect at that time caused us to withdraw from intensive involvement in the clinical and policy aspects of the program. We turned to a search for new situations in which our research data could make useful contributions to positive social action. We found these action situations as a part of the process of community development that had already begun in El Barrio.

## COMMUNITY DEVELOPMENT AND HEALTH SERVICES

### The Rise of a Chicano Organization in El Barrio

In the initial stages of our involvement in El Barrio in 1969, one community organization dominated the scene. This organization, the Neighbors' Group, was established in 1954 and had its roots among the middle-Europeans in the community. The Neighbors' Group had developed a buying cooperative, housing and community-development committees, and a credit union. However, an increasing number of Mexican residents felt that the Neighbors' Group was not working effectively for Latin people though the group had made an effort to recruit Mexican members. The firing of several of the Mexican staff led to the development of a new group emphasizing its Mexican background and challenging the policies and programs of the older organization. The struggle between these organizations ended with the collapse of the Neighbors' Group, and the Chicano group began a broad-based attack on the problems of education, urban renewal, and a number of other major issues.

The strategy of our Community Research Unit in this period was to develop positive relationships with leaders and activists in all sectors of the community. Our newness to the situation allowed us to maintain these relationships without having to choose sides and view community events as neutral observers. However, this "objectiveness" as well as the lack of identity in the area of the Community Mental Health Program served to keep us on the periphery of community life.

## Organizing Residents' Groups

In June 1969 a significant breakthrough occurred in our relationships with community residents. The local settlement house developed a program in community organization in which clubs would be organized on scattered blocks throughout the neighborhood. Our decision to become intimately involved with this effort provided entree and rapport for our fieldworkers, and gave us the opportunity to demonstrate to an important sector of the population that the information we were able to collect and disseminate could make a significant contribution to the goals of their programs.

Throughout the following year our tactics were to seek out opportunities in which our research personnel could be useful to community groups that were involved in a broad range of problems and issues. In this period, general ethnographic data, the results of survey operations on the blocks and the schools, and information collected through the program provided a body of material that proved to be useful to these groups. For example, information we collected through surveys of public and parochial school students and their parents proved useful to a community group working on education.

## A Period of Organizational Decline

Toward the end of 1970, the Chicano group began to experience great difficulty in maintaining their objective of dealing with a wide variety of community problems. They had difficulty achieving success on individual issues, and were overcommitted in a number of areas of community action. As a consequence, attendance at meetings began to decline and the organization lost a number of members. Over a period of several months, organizational activity declined significantly and, soon after, the organization existed in name only. Other community organizations with broad mandates also experienced difficulties in maintaining their efforts during this time. The decline in organizational activity was made more severe by the fact that block residents' organizations, supported by settlement house staff during the summer, never seemed to maintain themselves during the nonsummer months.

In this period of scattered and inconsistent effort in which community action groups shifted from one issue to another, all we could do was hope that we had appropriate bodies of data to address immediate concerns, or that we could construct a "rough and ready" operation for quick feedback. In this fluid situation prior to 1971, community action objectives were often unclear and efforts were transitory, and as a result we were frequently caught with insufficient information to contribute. Our strategy up to this point was to:

1. Construct research operations in areas that we thought would have maximum benefit for community action research.

2. Seize opportunities in which community action groups, concerned residents, or agency staff could provide us with entree to data-gathering opportunities in the community.

3. Emphasize rapid feedback of research information to Chicano organizations and individuals in the El Barrio community.

4. Participate actively in community action organizations to the extent that such activity was approved by its members.

## The Rise of Specialized Action Groups

In the beginning of 1971 a new climate began developing both in the wider society and in the local community. The apparent success of César Chavez and the Farmworkers, the efforts of Tijerina in New Mexico and Corky Gonzáles in Colorado, the increasing demand for recognition of Chicanos in the Midwest, and the developing sense of Chicano identity, made people in the El Barrio community aware of the role they could play in a solution to community problems. At the same time a group of Chicanos who had gained organizing knowledge in past community efforts developed a number of voluntary groups, each of which focused on specific issues. These efforts centered around the creation of new youth facilities and greater availability of educational opportunities, and were linked to demands for significant bilingual and bicultural programs in area schools and equal opportunities in jobs.

A significant portion of these specialized activist groups began to direct their attention toward the health services situation in the community. For example, one group, with the help of some volunteer medical personnel, organized a free health clinic in a neighborhood settlement house to serve the El Barrio community. A group of Chicano ex-addicts developed a volunteer program in drug abuse, and a group of residents with experience and training in mental health sought ways to increase the number of Chicano mental health workers in the area. These efforts were organized for the most part by Chicano residents who had special experience, training, and talents for working on these health issues. Our applied research group was fortunate in this period to have established good working relationships with many of these groups. As they were getting organized we were asked to participate in a number of aspects of the groups' development and at the same time to contribute research results on some of these specific issues.

With the development in 1971 of this new stage in which community organizations established long-term and relatively concrete goals in specialized areas, we began to plan more long-term and specific operations that could have direct input into the efforts of these groups. The first goal of these specialized action groups was to make institutions both in the community and in the city more relevant to Chicano populations. For example, through the efforts of a group of community activists more bilingual and bicultural personnel were added to the staff of the El Barrio Mental Health Clinic.

However, attempts in other areas met with considerably less success. A group of Chicano ex-addicts sought help from the state drug program for the drug abuse situation in the El Barrio community but the state was unresponsive. A number of groups met the same reception from city, federal, and private agencies. As it became evident that existing agencies were not going to change to meet the needs of the El Barrio residents, these community action groups shifted from their initial institutional change objectives and began working toward the development of alternative community-run facilities. Several of these groups sought federal and private funding to establish such programs. The problem now became one of gaining funding and planning alternative programs. Community action strategy shifted to one of trying to take advantage of some of the money that was newly freed for "minority" community development.

## A Search for Funding

This search for outside funding was greatly enhanced by the effects of the Chicano movement in the wider society as well as in the community. The movement had put increasing pressure on federal agencies to provide funds to Chicano groups. Research in a number of fields had shown that there were special requirements in the areas of health, mental health, and social service programs for Chicano populations. The federal administration had begun to view Chicano groups as an increasingly potent force in determining the outcome of national and state elections. Therefore, there were political motives favoring the granting of funds to Chicano groups.

Community organizations and activists were well-prepared to take advantage of this opportunity. By 1972, they had gained experience in confronting institutions, had developed a good working knowledge in their special areas of concern, and had built effective organizations with considerable community support.

For the first time, we had a very specific context in which our research could be utilized: "grant proposals," i.e. documents for which we supplied extensive portrayals of community problems and their effect on residents as part of the background, rationale and justifications for requests for federal, state and private funds. The research data collected in our initial two years were reexamined in the light of the informational needs of each funding proposal. In addition, we were able to conduct interviews and examine archival data to help members of each group to express their ideas within the specific format of the proposals.

The procedure of submitting proposals involved a very close collaboration between members of our research team and community activists. The relationships established in the course of working on these proposals were to be extremely important for later and more extensive collaboration between our Community Research Unit and specific health programs.

Our data at this point were not yet extensive enough to provide community people involved in the situation with new information they did not already have. But our statistics and qualitative descriptions were good enough to give outside funding agencies a clear picture of the community and its needs. At the same time, as these new programs were being formulated, it was becoming clear to many of the community activists that effective information-gathering procedures needed to be built into the development of their programs. By the time the proposals were submitted, special research operations had been developed on a collaborative basis between researchers and activists in order to do a better job in getting accurate information for the planning of new programs in the future.

In the period between June 1971 and June 1972 proposals submitted by community groups in El Barrio for children's programs included a comprehensive youth program, a day-care center, an outdoor recreational facility and a vocational program directed toward dropouts in the community. Proposals in the area of education included a bilingual library, a bilingual reading program and a college recruitment program for Chicano youth. In the area of health, proposals were submitted for the support of a program to train Chicano residents in mental health, for the support of a free-health clinic, and for the development of a Chicano drug abuse program to serve El Barrio residents.

Of the ten major proposals that had been submitted, only one was denied funding. In the fiscal year 1971–1972 there was no community-controlled federal and private-agency money in the El Barrio area, whereas in the current fiscal year (1972–1973) there is over $600,000. Grants for succeeding years now total over two and a half million dollars.

*Establishment of Community Health Programs*

1.   The health services picture for the El Barrio community showed a considerable change as a result of this funding. There is now a free health clinic supported by volunteer help and federal funds, which provides health services to over 300 patients per week. This clinic has been able to establish a working and referral relationship which eases the problems of access and entree of community residents into the County Hospital and other facilities in the nearby medical center complex of West Side Chicago.

2.   The Chicano Drug Abuse Program was able to expand from a small volunteer staff providing methadone and minimal counseling of thirty Chicano clients, to a comprehensive drug program providing a wide range of services to a hundred clients. This program, operating with a bilingual and bicultural staff, is attempting to develop treatment modalities attuned to the culture and experience of Chicano clients and has been able to draw in clients who have never received treatment.

3.   The Chicano Training Program is training thirty Chicano residents to become mental health practitioners. It has established a mental health curriculum leading to an A.A. degree taught by Chicano faculty and accredited by a local university. In the process of finding jobs for trainees, this program has brought about significant changes in hiring policy among mental health institutions, has developed greater sensitivity to Chicano mental health needs on the part of mental health institutions, and is for-

mulating a new model of Chicano mental health services that will be more effective and culturally relevant for El Barrio residents.

4.   The El Barrio Mental Health Center has become, over the past two years, an increasingly valuable resource in the overall health service picture of the community. The change was due directly to the fact that a recent Chicano social work graduate with long experience in the community was hired as the director. He very quickly moved to recruit Spanish-speaking personnel, opened paraprofessional positions for residents knowledgeable about the community, and began to tie the clinic into other community-run service programs. The changes in policy are graphically reflected in the nature of the caseload at the Clinic. During the period that these changes were occurring, the caseload shifted from approximately 80 percent middle-European and 20 percent Mexican in 1969, to 80 percent Mexican and 20 percent middle-European in 1972, which is reflective of the current population ratio (Vázquez 1972).

There are close working relationships among the key staff people in each of these four programs. On many occasions, individual staff have been called upon to lend their expertise to mobilize community support, to use their contacts in both the local community and the wider society, and to provide other general support for each other's programs. The Chicano activist groups are now in constant communication with each other in developing new strategies, sharing information and consultation, and lobbying in the community's interest on a broad variety of issues. Because of this close collaboration, it became possible to coordinate services and referrals so that an effective health service system could be developed.

The building of this coordinated network has proceeded most effectively among those programs offering health and health related services. For example, in the area of services, the El Barrio Mental Health Clinic has detached a worker to the Free Health Clinic who can provide counseling to individuals whose difficulties have an emotional basis. The Drug Program utilizes both the Free Clinic and the Mental Health Clinic in dealing with the physical and emotional problems of drug addicts, and the Mental Health Clinic refers clients with drug problems to the Drug Program. The Chicano Training Program selected a number of its interns from the staffs of health and mental health agencies so that they could benefit from in-service training in a bicultural mental health program. In turn, Latin psychiatrists and psychiatric social workers on the staff of the Mental Health Clinic are part of the faculty of the Training Program, and have also provided specialized training to the staff of the Free Health Clinic and the Drug Program.

In addition to collaboration in the areas of education, training, and service there have been some meetings recently devoted to considering a coordinated research project that would satisfy much of the informational needs of all the social service programs. While such an effort has yet to be fully established, our unit has made every attempt to stimulate its development so that the expertise to conduct needed research would exist in El Barrio.

Apart from defining common research interests, each program is now actively concerned with producing information that is relevant to the provision of services and justifies renewed funding. Such information includes survey data on the population served, evaluation of success criteria, and operations which examine new aspects of the problem in the general community. We are working closely with the personnel of these programs to help them provide this kind of information. In those programs where there are no research personnel, we have played the role of being the primary collectors of information. Thus, we now find ourselves in a much more difficult phase of research — that of attempting to furnish information of immediate practical utility to people involved in service programs.

In defining the specific research operations, we have made the most progress with those programs connected with the health service network described above. In response to the need for success criteria for clients in the Chicano Drug Program, we had developed a detailed interview schedule for gathering information on language use, origin, family and household structure, drug use, prison record, copping procedures, and income. A record-keeping procedure has been set up which will allow consistent data collection. We have interviewed staff members extensively concerning program goals, organization and attitudes. We are also conducting participant observation among addicts in the program and will soon be developing procedures to assess the nonclient addict in the community. Among other uses, this information was particularly useful in determining whether or not the Drug Program was doing a good job in reaching all segments of the addict population in El Barrio. Finally, we want to compare the data collected on Chicano addicts with those of addicts from other ethnic groups to determine the unique features of Chicano addiction. These research and information collection procedures have been developed and are conducted in collaboration with staff of the Drug Program.

In the Chicano Training Program, our research team works closely with a part-time research assistant on the staff. Procedures have been developed for assessing the impact of the program on training skills, attitudes, behavior, and work performance, as well as in assessing the Training Program's impact in creating institutional changes. Within this program, work continues on an examination of *curanderismo* and its implications for the development of new Chicano mental health models.

In collaboration with the Free Health Clinic, a detailed survey instrument was developed to examine the health status, attitudes, and practices of residents in the El Barrio community. This instrument was seen as an important tool both in stating the case about health needs to outside groups and in providing information for the establishment of particular kinds of health programs at the free clinic. This survey will also be implemented by another free clinic in a Latin neighborhood to the west of El Barrio.

The developments over the past two years at the El Barrio Mental Health Clinic have resulted in closer cooperation between our unit and this component of the Community Mental Health Program. One result of this better relationship has been an increasing collaboration with psychiatric staff on research directed toward the role of social and cultural factors in mental and emotional difficulties in El Barrio. Currently, we are examining patient records and have drawn a sample of clients from the clinic for intensive interviewing with a battery of interview schedules and psychiatric questionnaires.

This article has dealt with the development of health services and research in the Chicano community of El Barrio. In considering both service and research, we feel that the information we have presented here supports the view that change-oriented programs need to fit within the cultural and social life of the community and must be primarily determined and developed by community residents sensitive to indigenous behavior and concerns.

The experiences of our unit in working with the Mental Health Clinic particularly brings out this point. The clinic began its activities with models derived from Anglo-American psychiatric practices and was staffed by non-Latins who were unfamiliar with Chicano culture and community life. It demanded that the unit answer questions posed in terms of that alien model of psychiatric treatment. We felt, as anthropologists, that questions derived from community residents and activists took priority in terms of the information required to make mental health services more effective in the community. Thus, we turned away from our original task and directed our research to the informational needs of the developing indigenous human service system. As for the clinic itself, it was only when more bilingual and bicultural staff were hired that it sought to fit into the indigenous system, rather than insisting that it began to do an effective job in picking up a part of the responsibility for the establishment of a comprehensive health care delivery system in the community. Thus, a service and a research unit, both supported by state and federal funds, found themselves to be considerably more effective when they began to support and facilitate indigenous community organizations in achieving increased community development and in transforming their ideas into concrete community programs for human service. It is only now that we have reached this point — each being articulated to similar pressures and community events — that we have begun to realize a series of effective anthropological-psychiatric collaborations based on problems of health-care delivery in the community context.

The establishment of this community health system, in our view, underscores two major generalizations. First, the development of adequate health services for "minority groups" and "economically disadvantaged" communities is a direct function of sociopolitical power. It is clear to us that had it not been for the Chicano movement and local successes in other types of programs, the El Barrio community would not have obtained the funds for the health programs that are currently operating. In turn, it is interesting to note that changes in health institutions and agencies serving El Barrio were impossible to effect until community groups were "legitimized" by receiving governmental and private funds. Now, at least in some sectors, these changes seem to come with relative ease and rapidity. We have learned, as a result, that information no matter how accurate, well-timed, and directed, always takes second place to political power in creating positive social change.

Secondly, the various health-related projects in El Barrio have established a coordinated effort in which organizations with different resources, expertise, and interests work together to create an optimal system from which to meet community needs. This coordination arises from close relationships among community activists and in turn their relationships with community residents. This collaborative arrangement contrasts strongly with the typical human services pattern in which a series of city, state and federal agencies compete with each other and duplicate services.

It is important to note that the health programs in the El Barrio community still fall far short of meeting the total health needs of its residents. Specialized programs for alcoholics and senior citizens are still lacking and the Free Health Clinic, even at full capacity, serves only a small segment of the community population. While indigenous programs in El Barrio are working toward full coordination and cooperation, there are still ways in which this system could be improved.

However, the most overwhelming deficiencies in the health service system come as a result of the failure of federal, state, and local agencies to make funds available to the El Barrio community. While some improvement has been made in health-care delivery, the medical establishment has a great many changes to make in staff and programs before they can claim that El Barrio residents have access to health care on a par with residents of other Chicago communities. Most community leaders and activists view the current situation as a beginning in the process of gaining their share of health resources for the community. They also clearly feel that unrelenting pressure must be applied if they are to make gains in the future.

## ACTION RESEARCH IN HEALTH

It should be apparent, by now, that in describing our own activities we are talking about a very different kind of social science research from that usually carried out by anthropologists in this kind of setting. Neither the traditional academic model (in which research questions are formulated in terms of the theoretical concern of colleagues), nor the typical applied research (responsive only to the questions constructed by alien change agents) is appropriate to this kind of health service development. What we are attempting to construct is an action-research model in which:

1.   The community is both the object of study and the most important recipient of the results of that study.
2.   Research priorities are constructed in terms of the kinds of information that will be most helpful to programs that create positive social change. In this way research is seen as one of the means for achieving community goals.
3.   Researchers also participate in other kinds of action when necessary to work for a commonly agreed upon goal of service and action.
4.   Researchers, service providers, and community activists collaborate with one another in basic research activities such as problem formulation, data collection, data analysis, and dissemination.

The action-research and community development models that we have presented here move toward producing a close match between the culture, behavior, and needs of residents, and the nature and type of health service programs that are developed.

We have frequently encountered, from the medical establishment and from social science researchers, the criticism that responding to the issues set forth by community organizations would produce results that were superficial and scattered in impact. We feel this is not true, particularly in terms of the information we have collected on Chicano health and related issues. The fact that we have worked in close conjunction with several health-related programs has provided us with information on health gained from a number of different perspectives. Close collaboration with these health programs has also insured that information we have produced on health issues would be of maximum benefit to those involved in developing solutions for health problems in the community.

As we continue to stay in close contact with community action in El Barrio, we find that programs and activities related to health problems are always in a constant state of change as new situations arise, new resources are made available, and new problems identified. In response to these pressures, we must constantly develop new information and new techniques on an ever-widening number of problems and issues. Thus, at any given point in time we may be evaluating an aspect of an already established health program, working on a proposal for the establishment of a new program, or doing preliminary work in problem identification and community involvement on a health-related issue that has never before received much attention.

We still feel we have a great deal more to learn about making research a useful part of community development and health service programs. We are currently struggling with the difficult task of evaluating program effectiveness and providing service staff with solid information on which to base important programatic decisions. Finding the staff and resources to do an effective job of information collection on a wide range of topics has always been a difficult task, but has been made more difficult by the quality and depth of information required by the large number of established community programs.

With all its difficulties, we feel that the kind of action-research in health that we have been involved in has been extremely productive in a number of ways. First, the demands for information by community residents call upon us to produce health data and theoretical models which are far more substantive and profound than those demanded by colleagues who have little information concerning the specifics of the El Barrio community. Second, our collaboration with action people and groups provides a continuous process of discovery, testing, and retesting of the efficacy of applied research methods and techniques. Third, interaction of research results and action provides a continuous process by which the reliability, validity, and accuracy of research results may be evaluated. And finally, the model of action research in health that has evolved in the last five years of our work did not develop as a pre-determined set of policy decisions in our initial phases of work. We came to our present position because we were closely articulated with the events and actions that developed in the El Barrio community and in our own Community Mental Health Program. We expect important, but unpredictable, changes in our action research model as we continue to articulate with events and issues in the community. Thus, rather than advocating a specific health research model, we are recommending that social science researchers collaborate with community residents to develop indigenously controlled and responsive health service systems.

# REFERENCES

*Chicago Sun-Times*
  1972    Section 1A, page 3. October 22.
CLARK, MARGARET
  1959    *Health in the Mexican-American culture: a community study.* Berkeley: University of California Press.
MADSEN, WILLIAM
  1970    "Society and health in the lower Río Grande Valley," in *Mexican-Americans in the United States.* Edited by J. Burma. Cambridge, Massachusetts: Schenkman.
RUBEL, A.
  1966    *Across the tracks: Mexican-Americans in a Texas city.* Austin: University of Texas Press.
SCHENSUL, STEPHEN
  1970    "Preliminary results from a pilot research project in an El Barrio elementary school." Unpublished manuscript.
  1972    "A new model for the understanding of drug addiction in a Chicano community." Paper presented at the American Anthropological Association meetings, Toronto, Canada.
SCHEPERS, ÉMILE
  1972    "Voices and visions in Chicano culture: some implications for psychiatry and anthropology." Paper presented at the American Anthropological Association meetings, Toronto, Canada.
VÁZQUEZ, ALBERT
  1972    "The effects of a change in the cultural orientation of a community mental health clinic." Paper presented at the American Anthropological Association meetings, Toronto, Canada.

# Policy-Evaluative Research: Some Methodological and Political Issues

EDMUND H. RICCI and JAMES E. NESBITT

## THE DOMAIN OF POLICY-EVALUATIVE RESEARCH

The social science disciplines have been profoundly affected by the significant changes initiated in the United States during the chaotic, violent, tragic yet hopeful sixth decade of the twentieth century. The most visible effect has been the interest in the applications of social science knowledge shown by increasing numbers of established and aspiring social scientists. Policy and evaluative research encompass much of the domain of applied social science. POLICY RESEARCH is research which has as its primary objective the development of information to be used in the formulation of policy and in the development of specific programs to implement policy. EVALUATIVE RESEARCH is activity which has as its major purpose the assessment of the effects of a specific program or organization. While policy and evaluative research have typically been conceived as two separate and distinct activities, we prefer to conceptualize them as highly interrelated activities. Here we will describe the dynamic interrelationship of both areas of research by identifying and critically examining the concepts and processes they employ.

Quotations from an article entitled "Annals of politics" by Daniel Moynihan suggest most, if not all, of the more serious and interesting issues and problems involved in the utilization of social science theory and methods in policy and evaluative research.

Arthur Burns, then Counselor to the President, who opposed the Family Assistance Plan, did so as a social scientist. What, he would ask repeatedly, was the

The authors acknowledge the contribution made by David Weiss in providing an extensive critique of an earlier draft of this paper.

evidence that a guaranteed income would contribute to family stability? There was none. To the contrary, the most reasonable proposition would have been that there was a welfare problem because there was a welfare program, and that anything that would make welfare more attractive would make dependency more attractive. The proponents of FAP did not deny this but argued that by providing support for families headed by males, the attractions of welfare as such were relatively diminished (Moynihan 1973b: 63).

As a social intervention, FAP was the quintessence of simplicity: people were to be given money and left to their own devices. The assertion that no one knew how to do anything better — if indeed, anything was better — did not deter the President. In truth, the assertion that there was no confident social science advice to be given probably encouraged the President to take the largest of his options on the judgments that small measures were not likely to have much effect (1973: 65).

The issues suggested in the quotations are: what is known about the causes and cures of societal problems which could form the basis for new policy? What methodologies are available to obtain additional information? What provisions can be made to evaluate the effects of the new policy and programs? How adequate can social planning and program evaluation be, given the current state of development of social science theory and methodology? What factors affect the utilization of policy and evaluative research?

Before we immerse ourselves in the issues stated above, a more fundamental question should be posed: "In what sense is policy-evaluative research a part of the domain of social science?" In some disciplines, e.g. economics and educational psychology, a strong concern with social policy has been embedded in a significant amount of research and writing. That is, representatives of these disciplines have shown a great concern for the policy relevance of their work. In certain other disciplines, notably anthropology and to a lesser extent sociology and political science, evaluative research and research designed to be used in the development of policy have been less of a concern.

It is our contention that the development of theory, concepts, and methodology relevant to any discipline can be facilitated by applied research. One could argue, in fact, that the involvement and concern with the applications of knowledge shown by economists and educational psychologists has been a major factor in accelerating the development of basic knowledge in these disciplines. We feel that the other social science disciplines could benefit greatly from the development of an active applied group, as this would quickly and powerfully put existing theory and methodology to test, would open the disciplines to comment and critique from outsiders, and would further the development of interdisciplinary exchange.

Having taken this stance, we may proceed to a related matter. Is policy-evaluative research fundamentally different from basic or discipline-oriented research? One point of view has been presented by Williams, who has stated that "... basic policy research differs from other basic research only in requiring that the researcher have an appreciation of policy issues and needs and thinks in terms of the research implications that flow from them" (Williams 1972b: 313). Williams would no doubt agree that this shift in perspective has profound significance for policy-evaluative research and possibly for the social sciences.

Whereas we agree with the position taken by Williams, it is of interest to note that Coleman views the matter somewhat differently.

It is important at the very outset to sharply distinguish a methodology that has as its philosophic base the testing and development of theories from a methodology that has as its philosophic base a guide to action. This is not to say that the methods developed as an aid in theory construction cannot be used as components of a methodology that constitutes guides to action. It is rather to say that at the most fundamental philosophical level, a difference exists: the goal is not to further develop theory about an area of activity, but the goal is to provide an information basis for social action .... However, it is important first to distinguish clearly the research that I am calling "policy research" from research which, though it studies the impact of public policy, is designed to implement knowledge in the discipline .... But this is not policy research, it is designed to aid the discipline. Its results are not intended to serve as a guide to action in specific policies; its audience is not an audience of political actors, but an audience of political scientists. In policy research, the audience is a set of political actors, ranging from a single client to a whole populace, and the research is designed as a guide to action (Coleman 1971: 2–4).

For reasons noted above, we feel Coleman's view, that discipline-oriented and applied research somehow should coexist but as separate domains of activity, will not be constructive in the further development of the basic disciplines.

The current popularity of policy and evaluative research is, in part, related to the proliferation of social action programs during the Johnson administration, in a general context of social unrest during the 1960's. Developing as part of this milieu were the War on Poverty programs, some of which attempted to change individual behavior directly and others more indirectly, through "planned" intervention at the institutional or organization level. Rossi and Williams have discussed the evolution of the involvement of social scientists in program development and evaluation during this period.

The behavioral sciences were invited into the War on Poverty in the enabling legislation, which called for mandatory evaluations and set aside earmarked funds for such research. Similar provisions were incorporated into the Elementary and Secondary Education Act (of 1965), into the legislation setting up the National Institute of Law Enforcement and Criminal Justice and into many other pieces of legislation .... As a consequence there has been a considerable flowering of applied social research. Social scientists were not merely to be the recipients of benefits in the 1960's round of social legislation but also to be participants in the policy-making process through the exercise of their special professional competences (Rossi and Williams 1972: 14).

The following example of a policy-related question and research effort provides a clear illustration of the manner in which social scientists have become involved in policy and evaluative activities.

*A Case Example: The Family Assistance Plan*

During the years of the Johnson administration, serious concern about the effectiveness of the welfare system, particularly the Aid to Families with Dependent Children program (AFDC), developed to the point that mere reform was no longer seen as an adequate corrective measure. Although no specific actions were taken before Johnson left office, a guaranteed income plan was proposed during this time but was ultimately rejected.

During the month of June 1968, the Subcommittee on Fiscal Policy of the Joint Economic Committee of Congress held hearings on income maintenance programs, which included the present welfare system with its categorical grants, the negative income tax, family allowances, children's allowances, etc. Similar conclusions were reached: mere reform or patch-work would not suffice (United States Congress 1968).

Then, late in 1968, a field experiment on income maintenance was begun by Mathematica, a New Jersey research firm, and the Institute for Research on Poverty at the University of Wisconsin, under contract to the Office of Economic Opportunity (Orr, et al. 1971; see also Watts 1969).

On August 8, 1969, less than seven months after taking office, President Nixon, in a nationally televised address, proposed a "Family Assistance Plan" as the Republican alternative to the welfare "crisis."

That there was a "crisis" no one of any political affiliation doubted; however, perceptions of the nature and causes of the situation varied along political lines. In addition to citing the growing number of dollars and recipients involved, the interpretation of the long-term effects of this situation was presented for strategic political reasons in a context of the subjective problem of dependence rather than in the more objective but related context of poverty *per se*. As Moynihan states:

Welfare arose not as a deadlock within the system but as a threat to it. Welfare evoked racial fears, perhaps, and became a vehicle for a good deal of racial animosity, but what was far more important, in an irretrievably interdependent society, was that it evoked the fear that one day a critical number of persons would cease to cooperate, having sensed that the society at large had by tiny gradations passed beyond that point where it would any longer impose serious sanctions for non-cooperation, and was defenseless against even mass defections from the norms of behavior on which the success of the society depended. The crisis in welfare — such was the term always — did not arouse an alarm about a politicized and vengeful proletariat or any comparable class-defined defection from the social order. It was, to the contrary, a singularly atomized response by millions of individuals all somehow acting in the same way but not for a common purpose. If it evoked fear, it was fear of a general strike by the unorganized and the unattached and the unaware (Moynihan 1973a: 35–36).

The dramatic example chosen by Moynihan to illustrate the problem and to support his interpretation came from the welfare situation in New York City.

In 1960, there had been 9.7 persons in private wage employment in the city for every welfare recipient. By 1972, the ratio was 2.3 to 1. Combining government employment with public assistance, Nicholas Kisburg, of the Teamsters Union, estimated that by 1972 there was one person living off tax money for every 1.5 persons in private employ. In the context of much general uncertainty — which precise condition led to which specific response? — the overriding reality was clear enough. Income from welfare had become "competitive" with income from work. Members of a family headed by a female would not be much worse off on welfare than members of a family headed by a male earning low-skill wages ... (Moynihan 1973a: 36).

Serious contradictions and powerful disincentives not to work were inherent in the current welfare system, again, specifically within the largest and most expensive of all welfare programs, AFDC.

The A.F.D.C. (Aid to Families of Dependent Children) system was character-ized by lunatic penalties against employment. Typically, any money the female head of a dependent family might earn was wholly deducted from her welfare payment; in a phrase then unfamiliar to Washington, this was a hundred-percent marginal rate of taxation. Without in the least intending anything of the sort, the welfare system had devised the most powerful incentive for families to become dependent, and to stay that way. That women went to work even so, and that the welfare rolls turned over at a considerable rate, was powerful evidence that families headed by females, as much as any other families, strove to escape dependency, but the system hardly helped them do so (Moynihan 1973a: 40).

Another pattern was emerging which made this situation even more serious and puzzling. The relationship between new AFDC cases and the unemployment rate was remarkably strong (a positive correlation) in the United States through the late 1940's and most of the 1950's. But then in the 1960's, with the gross national product rising by leaps and bounds and unemployment dropping, the number of AFDC cases was increasing dramatically. Fundamental questions were raised about the interface of social and economic policy (Moynihan 1973a: 39).

At this point Moynihan and others at the Department of Labor began to suspect that a government services-oriented strategy was no longer viable, and a form of direct income redistribution was called for — a strategy that would bring forth a market response rather than a bureaucratic response.

It was, then, in this general context that a Family Assistance Plan (FAP), a form of negative income tax, was presented to the President, and later to Congress.

It would replace the existing program of Aid to Families with Dependent Children (A.F.D.C.), under which welfare support is, for practical purposes, available to impoverished households headed by females. FAP was to cover the working poor and the dependent poor alike. Thirty-seven percent of the potential FAP recipients — heads of families with children — worked full time all year, and forty percent more had some work during the year. FAP payments would decrease as personal income rose, and strong work incentives were written into the program, which the President described as "workfare," contrasting this to welfare, in part to protect the program from political attack from the right and in part out of an expectation that the long-term impact of the program would be to decrease dependency and increase the number of families that were essentially self-sufficient (Moynihan 1973a: 60).

*The Single Case Study*

A negative income tax such as this focuses on an individual's income deficiencies (his income below some minimum level) and increases his income while allowing him to benefit from any additional earned income in the future. The negative tax rate, conceptualized as the DISINCENTIVE RATE, specifies how much an individual will have to give up of each additional dollar earned. Depending upon family size and structure and the amount of earned income, a guaranteed income furnishes a floor from which to begin the calculations.

This brief review gives the outlines of the problem with which the income maintenance experiment was to deal. Using the DISINCENTIVE RATE concept as a basis, the first specific objective of this policy-oriented experiment was to determine the relationship between an individual's willingness to work and the receipt of supplementary income. In other words, by varying the amount of the guaranteed floor and the negative tax, what will be the work-leisure trade-offs for the poor, in particular, for the working poor?

The definition of a family unit is important in this context, and the question as to whether family stability might be undermined so that individuals can qualify for higher negative tax payments becomes critical (Lefcowits 1971b: 105–110; see also Orr 1971: 64–66). The effects of this experiment on fertility rates and on community institutions, the interactional effects between this program and others such as Medicaid, Medicare, food stamps, etc., and the impact of a specific disincentive rate and a guaranteed income on retirement age are just a few of the additional policy research questions that are being studied in order to determine the value of an income maintenance strategy and the structure of an income maintenance program.

The nature of this experiment most closely resembles the pilot program concept with its emphasis in flexibility, innovation, redirection, and reorganization. This is research of an exploratory nature, designed explicitly to affect the relationships between varying participant and community characteristics (preconditioning variables), differing arrangements of program structure and content (independent variables), and the behavioral responses or desired effects (dependent variables). In evaluative research, a presumed "causal process" is set forth, and attempts are made to relate the impact of the program or organization to the effects; e.g. is the program attempting to change attitudes, behavior, or knowledge, or all of the above? Failure of the program to achieve desired results may occur for at least two principal reasons (Suchmann 1971: 46–47): (1) the program has failed to properly operationalize the theory, and (2) the theory itself is deficient.

This type of problem demonstrates the interrelationship among policy, evaluative, and basic research, and indicates that opportunities exist for policy-evaluative research efforts to make contributions to the theoretical and methodological development of the social sciences. Additional discussion on this point appears below under Social and Political Aspects of Policy-Evaluative Research.

Having presented the income maintenance problem as an example of policy-evaluative research, we may proceed to a consideration of certain aspects of the conduct of this type of applied research.

# METHODOLOGICAL AND CONCEPTUAL ASPECTS OF POLICY-EVALUATIVE RESEARCH

## Policy Research

The policy formulation process typically involves several steps. Initially, the need for a social program or policy becomes publicized, an assessment of what is being done to handle the problem is made (Who and how many people are involved? What resources are available? What is the extent of the problem or need?), and a review of the state of knowledge about the problem is started. On the basis of this information about needs, resources, and knowledge, policy and programs are formulated.[1] In its more sophisticated application, providers and consumers are surveyed to obtain suggestions about the content of the policy statement and the form which the program will take. Usually this phase does not involve systematic surveys of potential consumers and providers; rather it is commonly handled by establishing a variety of forums in which spokesmen for special interests express their points of view. In some cases those who prepare legislation or policy statements have invited national leaders representing differing points of view to discuss the policy issues with them informally or to testify before legislative committees. National conferences have also produced policy statements from which legislation and programs have been derived.

Policy research is a term used to refer to at least three different processes: (1) research on the process of policy formulation, this meaning being commonly employed by political scientists; (2) research to assess the state of knowledge in a particular subject area in order to provide background for the development of programs and/or policy; (3) research which is expressly designed for developing policy; this can be of two general types: (a) planning research, e.g. surveys of organizations, professionals, or consumers, to assess need, receptivity, awareness, and acceptability of the policy formulations being considered; and (b) evaluative research of social action programs which is used to further develop, evaluate, and modify policy.

---

[1]   This kind of planning has been criticized by some planners who claim that the matching of needs with resources and solutions usually never results in an evaluation of and ordering of societal priorities, and as a result, important societal needs remain unmet as resources are expended in a somewhat random fashion which has its basis in the operation of special interest groups.

## Evaluative Research

POLICY-EVALUATIVE RESEARCH AS AN INTERRELATED PROCESS    A comprehensive evaluation program is one which provides information concerning the extent to which major program (or organizational) objectives are being met. It indicates areas in which the program is working smoothly and areas in which it is not. The evaluation program should provide the basis for both short- and long-range planning and day-to-day program management, and as such, evaluation is an essential administrative tool.

Although evaluation is a vital administrative function, it is often neglected by administrators for several reasons. Sound evaluative designs are difficult to create, and few are totally adequate to accomplish complete evaluation. To obtain even minimally valid and reliable information concerning program activities requires a significant investment of organizational resources for the regular and systematic collection of information about major aspects of the program, as well as a commitment on the part of personnel to make this information system work.

This discussion of program/organization evaluation is based on a number of assumptions. FIRST, evaluation should be directed to the measurement of all major program goals and functions. This requires a comprehensive design in which all evaluation activities are related in a coordinated evaluation system. SECOND, evaluation is based upon research, and evaluation research should meet the standards and criteria of all scientific research. THIRD, evaluation activity should include individuals within the program or organization being evaluated and "outsiders" to the unit being evaluated. The inclusion of "outsiders" should increase the objectivity of the evaluation report while the "insiders" will assure that the evaluation report is enlightened by the in-depth knowledge of those who are members of the organization. FOURTH, the most adequate evaluation will incorporate both qualitative and quantitative data. Quantitative data systematically obtained for the major aspects of program operation should be assessed in the light of judgments gathered from those who are knowledgeable about the operation of the program. FINALLY, evaluation is viewed as a dynamic process which should be an integral part of the management of the program or organization and ultimately contribute to the continuing development of policy. The relationship of evaluation to other aspects of management and to the development of policy is graphically portrayed in Figure 1.

In this view, evaluation is thought of as a process which measures the extent to which program objectives are met and provides for meaningful feedback to management and policy makers. The evaluative information

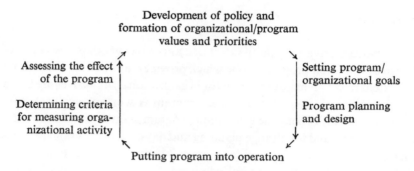

Figure 1.   Policy-evaluative process (adapted from Suchman 1967:39)

is used to determine how well each part of the program or organization is working and forms the basis for the modification of both program goals and social policy. Evaluation thus contributes to both short-term management and short- and long-range program and policy planning.

One additional comment about the purpose of evaluative research deserves emphasis. Program evaluation focuses upon the response of a program or organization to a problem which the organization, as a unit, is attempting to ameliorate. Program evaluation as we are using the term is therefore quite different from the efficiency rating of personnel, in which the focus is upon how well an individual is or is not performing.

For example, a review of computer data about a particular clinic may reveal that a great reduction in service has occurred. This reduction, although possibly related to the efficiency of the personnel who operate the clinic, could also be attributed, in part or totally, to certain unusually difficult environmental conditions under which the clinic operates or to the overall structure or location of the clinic. One use of program evaluation, then, should be the analysis of structural problems that the clinic personnel may be facing to determine ways in which structural changes may improve the operation of the program or organization.

LEVELS OF EVALUATIVE RESEARCH   Evaluative research may be conducted on a variety of levels of assessment. On the most elementary level, evaluative research is concerned with measurement of the output or activity of the program or organization. Here we are concerned with counting or assessing the extent to which the organization is producing some product, whether it be material goods or a service. Typical indicators on this level are the number of persons served, number of services by type delivered, number of client referrals, etc.

A SECOND level of research would require the specification and measurement of certain factors, usually program characteristics, which affect output and in some way employ these factors to explain the level of a program output. The attempt is to "explain" variations in program performance by understanding the manner in which the program structure is affecting the output level. Further refinements of this approach would include the identification and measurement of preconditioning and intervening events which could affect program activity.

A THIRD level of evaluation requires a somewhat broader perspective. Assessment on the first and second levels is done entirely within the context of the program or organization, using basically organizational factors. The questions asked are: To what extent is the organization achieving its goals? What organizational characteristics are impeding or facilitating goal achievement? The third level of evaluation seeks assessment of the appropriateness of the program goals. The question is: Are the objectives viable for the organization and/or useful for the larger social community of which the organization is a part? In asking this question the researcher is engaging in policy discussion and analysis.

On the FOURTH level of evaluation the researcher probes the unanticipated and less visible consequences of the program activity. In correcting one problem are others being created or solved? What are the more subtle functions and dysfunctions of the organizational activity for the larger society of which the program is a part?

THE EVALUATIVE RESEARCH PROCESS We can identify four steps in the actual conduct of evaluative research. FIRST of all, it is necessary to develop a clear statement of the research problem. This statement should imply a set of variables which can be sorted into the categories "dependent" and "independent." Generally, in evaluative research, the dependent variable (or variables) is the program goal (or goals) or desired effects and the independent variable (or variables) consists of characteristics of the program. A more involved network can be envisioned which can be thought of in terms of preconditions, independent, intervening, and dependent variables, and consequences.

This categorization of variables can serve as a plan for the researcher in that it is useful in identifying the relationships between environmental influences, program structure and operation, and the effects of the program activity. It also serves as a guide for data collection and analysis. A model of this process is shown in Figure 2.

This form of conceptualization is essential whether or not a strictly quantitative design is envisioned. Clear identification and sorting of variables in the categories outlined above will greatly facilitate the conduct

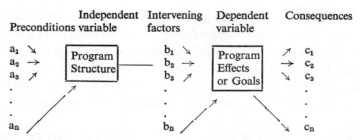

Figure 2.   The evaluative research process (adapted from Suchman 1967:89)

of both qualitative- or process-oriented research and studies which are more quantitative in nature.

The SECOND step in the conduct of evaluative research is an overall design strategy or approach. There are five basic variations in research design and these have been clearly described by Suchman (1967: 93–96).[2]

*The Single Case Study*

Observations or measurements are made of the individual or group only after exposure to the program being evaluated. This is probably the weakest and yet the most common evaluative research design. There is no baseline measurement of the study group with which to compare the post-program measure and no control group which has not been exposed to the program to assure that the observed effect was due to the experimental stimulus or program.

*The One-Group, Pre-test, Post-test Design*

In this evaluative design, the researcher introduces a base measure before the program is put into effect, to be followed by an "after" measure at the conclusion of the program. While this design does permit one to measure change objectively, it does not allow one to attribute this change to the program being evaluated. Five main sources of "error" are still possible: (1) other extraneous events may occur simultaneously as the experimental stimulus which influence the effect being measured; (2) the effect may be due to "unstimulated" change as a result of time alone, that is, some people improve with or without exposure to the program; (3) the "before" measure itself may constitute a stimulus to change regardless of the program itself; (4) the "after" measure may reflect time changes in measurement due to fatigue or instrument unreliability; and (5) unreliability may produce statistical regression with shifting values toward the mean.

*The Static Group Comparison*

Two groups are compared in this approach, one having been exposed to the program and the other not. If the exposed group shows a significantly higher

[2]   Suchman's classification was adapted from that presented by Campbell and Stanley (1963: 171–246).

incidence of the desired condition or behavior, it is assumed to be attributable to the program. This is really the basic logic of much epidemiological research. Two groups with varying frequency of a disease condition are compared and differences between the two are viewed as possible causes of the disease. However, this design affords no way of knowing that the two groups were equivalent BEFORE the program, although selective matching and retrospective measures of the two groups according to pre-program characteristics may help.

## Pre-test, Post-test, Control Group Design

In the classic experimental design we begin by setting up two equivalent groups which are as alike as possible before the program is put into effect. Such equivalence is best obtained by random assignment to experimental and control groups. Where this is not administratively feasible, one may have to resort to selective matching. Then, a "before" measure is made to determine the base line from which change is to be evaluated, and for providing a check on the equivalence of the two groups. One of the groups (the experimental group) is exposed to the program being evaluated while the other (the control group) is not, care being taken to keep the groups from coming into contact with each other. At the conclusion of the program (or at appropriate time intervals), an "after" measure is made which may be compared with the "before" measure for both experimental and control groups to indicate the changes produced by the experimental program.

The logic of this design is foolproof. Ideally, there is no element of fallibility. Whatever differences are observed between the experimental and control groups, once the above conditions are satisfied, must be attributable to the program being evaluated. One source of possible contamination exists if the process of making the "before" and "after" measures can conceivably interact with the experimental variable. For example, the mere act of making the "before" measure may sensitize the experimental group to the program that is to follow. Solomon suggests the following extension of the basic experimental design in such cases.

## The Solomon Four-Group Design

This design controls and measures both the experimental effect and the possible interaction effects of the measuring process itself. Where such interaction effects are highly important and one is not in a position to set up a four-group design, it is probably better to use a modified static group comparison (No. 3) in which equivalent experimental control groups are selected before the evaluation; the program is administered to the experimental group only but no measurements are made of either group until after the program is completed.

The THIRD step in an evaluative study is the selection of a set of indicators that are to be used in measuring the variables selected for study and the collection of data concerning program structure and operation. Often this becomes the most difficult aspect of the research process. Clear and precise conceptualization is often wasted because adequate measurement is not carried out. Once a basic research strategy has been decided upon, study variables identified, and indicators developed for each variable, the data collection may begin.

Data analysis and interpretation, the FOURTH step in evaluative research, requires considerable technical and creative ability. The analysis plan becomes implicit in the decisions made concerning the overall design strategy. Two levels of analysis are possible. On a descriptive level we identify variation in the dependent variables, i.e. we describe the program activities and/or effects. On an explanatory level other classes of variables are related to the dependent variable in an attempt to discover cause and effect relationships.

BROAD RANGE VERSUS NARROW RANGE OBJECTIVES    One of the major points of confusion in the design and use of evaluative research centers around the goals of the program being evaluated. While the experimental design is an ideal to which researchers should aspire, it can only be approached in programs which have narrow and precisely stated objectives. Many programs, however, have goals which are broad in scope, perhaps diffuse in definition, and which change over time. Examples of such goals are: (1) to increase the quality of life in a community; (2) to achieve more effective utilization of the existing institutions by citizens. Such goals are difficult to conceptualize in a fashion amenable to precise measurement. However, many objectives are more precisely stated, for example: (1) to increase the language facility of a group of individuals, (2) to rehabilitate substandard housing, and (3) to prepare untrained persons for jobs. For precisely defined objectives such as these, adequate measurement is much easier to accomplish.

In general, one finds programs which have diffuse objectives operating in changing environments in which the technology for accomplishing program objectives is unclear. Under these conditions the aim is often to maximize program creativity, flexibility, and adaptiveness. Where environmental conditions are relatively stable and technology is well-known, goals can be precisely stated and measured. Under these conditions the desire is to maximize rational decision-making and control in order to achieve efficiency in program operation.

In programs which have broad objectives it is quite likely that basic aspects of the program will change with the passage of time. Stated another way, we are likely to have, under unstable conditions, changes in the independent and dependent study variables. Changes of this type cannot be absorbed easily within the experimental design. Other technical problems related to the use of experimental design in evaluating programs that have broadly conceived objectives are: (1) random assignment becomes difficult; (2) controls are difficult to maintain; and (3) the use of comparison groups is usually pointless.

When the objectives for a program have been broadly designed, as pointed out above, the environmental conditions are likely to be unstable. Under these conditions any good administrator will modify the program as the need for change becomes apparent. In order to deal with these conditions an alternative methodology to the experimental one should be considered. This methodology, called process-oriented or historical research, is better able to accommodate the research complexities which develop when programs change rapidly. The approach is oriented toward: (1) understanding the nature of the system prior to the intervention program; (2) fully describing the nature of the intervention; (3) explaining the structure and operation of the new system which contains the intervention itself. In using this approach, clear conceptualization is just as important as for an experimental design; however, qualitative data rather than quantitative data provide the bases for evaluation.

EVALUATIVE AND ORGANIZATIONAL STRATEGIES    A recently published book by James Thompson, *Organizations in Action* (1967), is based upon the proposition that organizations strive to manage the uncertainty which can intervene in the conduct of organizational affairs. The nature and amount of uncertainty with which an organization must deal, however, varies not only by kind of organization, but also as to where within the organizational structure this may occur. In general, organizations, and particularly those of an instrumental nature which induce or coerce participation (Thompson 1967: preface), have as their highest priority the prevention, elimination, or amelioration of problematic intrusions into the technical core (1967: 11). Under norms of rationality, organizations will make the greatest efforts to complete both conceptual and operational closure, if possible, at the basic level of responsibility and control. Thompson calls this the "closed system strategy" (1967: 4–6, 10–13).

An "open system strategy" or a "natural system" model approach to organizations is most appropriate, as one example, in the study of the relations between an organization and its external environment:

Again, it is clear that in contrast to the rational-model approach, this research area focuses on variables not subject to complete control by the organization and hence not contained within a closed system of logic. It is also clear that students regard interdependence of organization and environment as inevitable or natural, and as adaptive or functional (Thompson 1967: 7).

We would suggest that the presence of these strategies in organizations may be related to the use of evaluative research, and two models are suggested in Figure 3.

Figure 3.  Organizational strategies under varying conditions

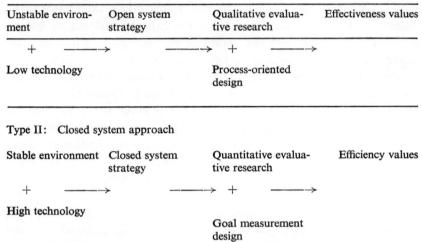

Type I:  Open system approach

| Unstable environment | Open system strategy | | Qualitative evaluative research | Effectiveness values |
|---|---|---|---|---|
| + ———→ | | ———→ | + ———→ | |
| Low technology | | | Process-oriented design | |

Type II:  Closed system approach

| Stable environment | Closed system strategy | | Quantitative evaluative research | Efficiency values |
|---|---|---|---|---|
| + ———→ | | ———→ | + ———→ | |
| High technology | | | Goal measurement design | |

In Figure 3 we have outlined two networks which permit us to begin identifying the conditions under which certain evaluative processes should take place. For example, under unstable environmental conditions in which knowledge about how the organization should operate is low (low technology), the organization will tend to develop an open system strategy (broad goals, extrinsic over intrinsic measures of fitness, maintaining or increasing alternatives). Under these conditions program effectiveness (performance) will be stressed over efficiency. A qualitative or a process-oriented approach will be more appropriate in this situation, and failure to use these methods could result in significant tension between the researcher and administrator. Extreme difficulty in aligning research results and recommendations with program accomplishments is likely to result in little if any use of the study findings.

Under stable environmental conditions in which knowledge about how the organization should operate is great (high technology), the organization will tend to develop a closed system strategy (narrow, precisely defined goals, time and place functions sharply delineated, intrinsic over extrinsic measures of fitness). Under these conditions program efficiency will be stressed. Quantitative research designs are more appropriate here, as they will provide the clearest documentation of program output.

## SOCIAL AND POLITICAL ASPECTS OF POLICY-EVALUATIVE RESEARCH

### *Organizations, Goals, and Research*

It is not so much the principles of research that make evaluation studies difficult, but rather the practical problems of adhering to these principles in the face of administrative considerations. To a far greater extent than the basic researcher, the evaluator loses control over the research situation (Suchman 1967: 21).

Perhaps the most salient feature that structures this contingency in addition to the end process involving the use of the findings, is the organizational context of evaluative research. Organizations are certainly concerned with activities other than the realization of "official goals" and objectives, the determination of which is usually a first step in any evaluative undertaking. But as Etzioni notes:

... organizational goals, particularly public ones, have an illusory quality in that they may never have been intended to be realized. When this is the case the program administrator will be troubled very little by the researcher's finding that his previously enumerated organization goals are not being achieved (Schulberg and Baker 1971: 75).

The previous statement should not simply mean that deceit is at work, though that is not uncommon. Evaluations, which become locked into a narrow goal-attainment model of research, fail to consider that organizations are multifunctional in their structural and functional dimensions. Weiss makes this point quite vividly:

Even rudimentary knowledge of organizational behavior indicates the salience of the drive for organizational perpetuation, personnel's needs for status and esteem and their attachment to the practice skills in which they have invested a professional lifetime, conservatism, inertia and fear of the unknown consequences of change, sensitivity to the reactions of various publics, costs, prevailing ideological doctrines, political feasibility, and the host of other considerations that affect the maintenance of the organization (Weiss 1967: 432).

Thus the politics of evaluative research begin long before goals and objectives of the activity to be examined are made explicit, before any research activity is undertaken, and most certainly before either recommendations are made or any attempt is made to implement them following the evaluation. Too often evaluative researchers are brought into the picture only after a decision has been made to carry out such an effort, and they may never know WHY the evaluation is "needed." The latter point is critical in that it bears directly not only on the nature of the research effort, but also upon the later question of effective utilization of the findings. An effort to undertake an "objective" evaluation of some organizational activity can (should?) lead to the evaluator questioning the very theoretical and value underpinnings of a program. In addition, an evaluation begun under the best of circumstances and intentions may be short-circuited in midstream as a program administrator discovers that the evaluator may be only too serious.

In many broad social action programs, such as the Model Cities and Community Action Programs, as well as in more narrowly conceived programs, one suspects that the only reason evaluations are undertaken in the first place is that they are required by the funding source. Needless to say, most of this activity is not evaluative research, but mere data-gathering and reporting. The internal and external politics of the situation generally swamp any potentially damaging material. In fact, one is able to make a strong case for the position that the quality of delivery capability and services is not high on the list of priorities for such programs, nor was it in the initial planning. If this is the actual case, almost any findings involving these areas become immediately irrelevant.

Whether to use "in-house" or "outside" evaluators is a common theme in the literature of evaluative research and will not be gone into in any detail here. There is no pat answer to this issue but one should probably revolve about the purposes of the evaluation. From the organizational viewpoint, a general working principle might be as follows:

When evaluation is conducted for the purpose of accounting to an outside body, utilization of external evaluators appears preferable. If, on the other hand, evaluation is conducted to assist an organization in its program development efforts, an internal evaluation unit may be able to contribute more effectively (Caro 1971: 17).

Other organizational structural conditions also bear not only on whether evaluations will be done, but also on the nature of the evaluative effort, e.g. exploratory, formal, in-house, outside, etc. For example, organizational interest in evaluative research, when considered in conjunction with organizational involvement in social change, describes the nature of an organization's participation in evaluative research (see Figure 4).

None of these broad categories are mutually exclusive. For example, change may be perceived as impossible or undesirable. Yet an evaluative study may be requested as a means to rationalize or postpone any such involvement. The scheme is flexible in that the data gathered from evaluative research are subject to probably greater political vicissitudes in the public sphere than data resulting from more basic research; i.e. one

Figure 4. Organizational participation in evaluative research (adapted from Caro 1971:7)

Organizational involvement in social change

| Interest in evaluative research | High | Low |
|---|---|---|
| High | rational, planned flexibility; anticipation of economic and social changes | interest in evaluative research primarily for legal or political reasons; conservative initiator of, and respondent to, change |
| Low | ideological, not empirical orientation | conceptual and empirical closure; rely on internal information and interpretation; emphasis on maintaining stability |

would question — at least in one's own mind — the uses to which any findings might be put in an organization noted for its rigid adherence to a status quo, regardless of its public stance. INTEREST in evaluative research, in this context, can mean many things to many people, and a wise evaluator will not readily accept any one definition of the situation, or of the problem.

Administrative-political considerations become quite important when an administrator must depend upon an evaluation to inform him of the effects of an activity, particularly when these are not directly and immediately evident. For example, Coleman states:

Education is a social institution in which the direct mechanisms of change through competition among alternative offerings is less frequent .... In part it is due to the fact that the results of education are not immediately apparent, and thus even if parents had a choice among competing alternative educational systems, the criteria for wise choice are not directly apparent, unless the differences between effectiveness of educational programs are extreme ... Thus in carrying out evaluation of a program, an educational researcher is bridging a gap which allows an evolutionary system to work more efficiently, by making apparent the educational effects of programs, to allow choice among them (Coleman 1969: 6–8).

Another structural situation occurs when formal evaluations are requested, and that is when either social and/or geographical distance exists among policy-makers, program administrators, and the recipients of services (Caro 1971: 7). When policy-makers are in some manner "closer" to service recipients, the tendency is probably to rely more on one's own informal, unsystematic knowledge of program operation. Recognition, either voluntarily or because of some requirement, of formal evaluation introduces an element of uncertainty for the administrator, particularly in those instances in which the use of outside consultants becomes necessary. One very common means of effecting closure about program operation is to retain sensitive information in-house. Most often this occurs in situations in which program activities are not really moving toward stated objectives, or in which certain actions should have been taken, but were not. Under these conditions, the introduction of an outside evaluator increases the likelihood of a negative evaluation, which threatens not only the administrator, but possibly the very existence of the program. The general principle of supposed greater objectivity from this kind of evaluation is itself an uncertainty to be dealt with, and often subtle hints to the consultant of other contracts leads him to the obvious conclusion that there are contingencies attached to these rewards.

## The Interpersonal Research Context

On an interpersonal level, an analogous situation with regard to the element of uncertainty can be said to exist for the researcher as well. In most instances of evaluative research, the context and control of the research process is considerably out of the control of the researcher. In this nonacademic setting, one has little, if any, control over one's audience, and behavior cannot be manipulated. The forces that impinge on the research process and context are not only myriad, but may fade in and out of the picture with such irregularity and rapidity that one is seldom able to get a firm grasp on these currents and their effects.

In addition, the researcher in this context often finds himself operating under constraints, which, given his prior training and academic experience, may put him in the very uncomfortable position of feeling that he is the one being controlled. Although this may be objectively true, the tendency to ascribe subjectively nonrational or irrational aspects to this process can lead one to completely miss what may be the most important part of the research.

The issue of service versus research is another common problem facing evaluative researchers. Working styles, value orientations, and status inconsistencies are just some of the areas of potential conflict between the researcher and managerial or practitioner roles.

Often a researcher, whether of the in-house or outside variety, is in a marginal position in this kind of setting. For example, although hired by management, he must not let himself become overly identified, either actually or perceptually, with this level, nor with any other. On the other hand, if the researcher does not derive his authority to do his work from the very top of the organization, it is questionable that access to records or to various levels of the entire operation will be forthcoming. Too, by reporting directly to the chief administrator, there is less possibility of a sanitizing affect occurring in his findings.

One other principal activity that most often generates political controversy is the researcher's making of recommendations based on his findings. Aside from the common defensive tactics used by those in disagreement, such as attacking the research design and methodology, many evaluative reports are written in a language which makes interpretation, and therefore utilization, extremely difficult. But even more fundamental is what Lazarsfeld calls "the great leap," the process of going from the data to recommendations. We are not suggesting that this process is purely arbitrary, but only that the "fit" between the data and recommendations is not always clear, particularly when the consequences of actually implementing any such statements is seriously considered.

In their interpretations and explanations researchers often tend to deal in generalities, and often with a more long-range time perspective, whereas administrators usually emphasize immediate or more short-run problem-solving requiring rather concrete answers. Explanations of problems differ between those who are immersed in dealing with them and those who study them.

When both administrators and evaluators acknowledge difficulties in implementing programs, administrators are likely to look for explanations that are idiosyncratic (incompetence or emotional instability) and moral (dishonesty or laziness) in contrast to social scientists, who emphasize amoral and structural factors (Caro 1971: 15).

Although Suchman describes evaluative research as those procedures which "... increase the possibility" (1967: 8), the act or art of "proving" is itself an inherently sociopolitical process, particularly in this context.

## Policy-Evaluative Research in Perspective

At this juncture, we would like to examine broadly the development of evaluative research from a more "macro" perspective, that is, from its historical development and in its relationship to its practitioners and the academic disciplines.

Very little systematic or comprehensive evaluative research was done by social scientists for, or in, government as recently as the New Deal era. Primarily involved during this period were economists, reflecting the differing historical involvement of direct policy research and analysis of this discipline. "Roosevelt's Brain Trust had several economists as members, but one notes in retrospect that sociologists, psychologists and anthropologists were conspicuous by their absence" (Rossi and Williams 1972: 12). Moynihan states that prior to the development of several War on Poverty programs, a search was made for studies of the effectiveness of New Deal programs; little but the grossest measures were found (Moynihan 1969).

So the early evaluative efforts of social scientists were sporadic and were generally limited to the accumulation of information, such as was available at the time. Even the monitoring of social trends such as unemployment rates, educational attainment, and fertility rates did not develop until the 1940's. As mentioned above, it was not until the early years of the Johnson administration that evaluation became an explicit and integral part of legislation and program planning.

Most of the War on Poverty programs were developed in an intensely political activist climate. The Model Cities requirement, for example, that programs begin almost immediately upon site selection, led to programs for which very few, if anyone, could offer systematic, rational, and realistic reasons for their being. In those few instances in which program need was demonstrable, programs were developed around the most idealistic goals and objectives, with little or no emphasis on strategies, problems of implementation, or practicalities. The focus that programs took in their delivery of services was related more to what existing facilities, personnel, and on-going programs were available than to any innovative or experimental strategies that might have resulted in greater effectiveness. The resulting confusion between means and ends, goals, objectives, outcomes, and consequences was practically paralyzing for any systematic application of evaluative research techniques. The expectation that any contributions to increased scientific knowledge and methodology for program administrators and policy makers might result from this opportunity to engage in field experimentation and testing was almost futile to say the very least.

The most identifying feature of evaluative research is the presence of some goal or objective whose measure of attainment constitutes the main focus of the research problem. Evaluation cannot exist in a vacuum. One must always ask evaluation "of what." Every action, every program has some value for some purpose — therefore it is meaningless to ask whether a program has any value without specifying value for what .... Given the basic importance of a clear statement of the program objectives to be evaluated, it is not difficult to understand why so many evaluation studies which fail to define these objectives prove unproductive. This is tantamount to undertaking a basic research project without first formulating one's hypotheses (Suchman 1967: 37–38).

A second major stumbling block to the development of evaluative research is that in many, if not most, instances, policy makers do not ask the right kinds of questions when soliciting research efforts from the scientific community, and all too often the decisions of what to study and how to go about it are left in the hands of the "experts." Williams, writing from the vantage point of Chief of the Research and Plans Division of the Office of Economic Opportunity, states:

And to close the circle (with social scientists), the vital link with that group, the central analytical office, left much to be desired in specifying relevant research to aid in policy-making for the disadvantaged. Central analysts made little headway in defining clearly the types of studies required and in selling these socially important and methodologically challenging studies to social science researchers. While the social science research community may have been wrong in believing that policy-relevant studies were inherently low-level, their perception that quick and dirty studies were what the agencies had in mind when they talked about relevance often was quite accurate (Williams 1972a: 8–9).

... What is surprising is that, for critical social policy areas, analytical offices have not in the past systematically assessed what is known, pointed out what is not known, assessed the relevance of the unknowns for policy-making, and from the set of policy-relevant questions tried to formulate in some detail the kinds of research (e.g., nonfield research vs. experimentation) that will most effectively get at the important issues (1972a: 152–153).

A third possible factor which inhibits the contributions of evaluative research lies with its practitioners. Until quite recently, most, if not all, evaluative research efforts have been bogged down in examining individual programs or projects without any attempts to generalize beyond those narrow confines.[3] While evaluations of this type are certainly legitimate and necessary, one is left with the feeling that these separate studies will never be meaningful beyond their present administrative boundaries, if then. Suchman discusses this problem by stating:

The concept is the primary variable of interest in basic research; it is translatable into observable units, but these data remain only operational indices of the underlying concept and their worth derives from their ability to represent this

---

[3] Some recent exceptions to this general statement are: Coleman, et al. (1966), Acirelli, et al. (1969), Orr, et al. (1971).

concept reliably and validly. In evaluative research, on the other hand, the observable and measurable indices are the phenomena of interest, the action program usually is aimed directly at changing the values of these specific measures, and only indirectly at the underlying concept .... Program evaluation refers to the test of a total product with the purely practical objective of determining whether exposure to the program was accompanied by certain desired effects. Variable testing, on the other hand, is concerned with singling out specific components of the program, AS INDICES OF SOME MORE GENERALIZABLE STIMULI; and testing the effectiveness of these variables. Program testing has almost no generalizability, being applicable solely to the specific program being evaluated. Generalizations (to other products, populations, times) "have the status of untested hypotheses." This is a major reason why so many evaluation studies appear repetitive — one can never be certain that a program which works in one situation will work in another (Suchman 1967: 76–77; see also Hovland, et al. 1949).

This brings us to a fourth, and perhaps the major point: the limitations of evaluative research in its present state for both the development of social science theory and methodology, and its usefulness to program administrators and policy makers. Very few efforts to undertake evaluative research of the explanatory type are noted in the literature, most of these being descriptive in nature and limited to a specific program or project. It is on the explanatory level that evaluative research must turn to social science theory for guides as to why a particular activity or program should be expected to, or actually did, work. This is also the context within which policy-evaluative researchers might make contributions to the development of theory, working in conjunction with their academic counterparts.

But even assuming that more explanatory designs and efforts are attempted, there still remains the ominous question of what positive contributions current social science theory can offer within this context. For example, Rossi and Williams raise this issue in the following manner:

A large part of the problem presented by broad aim programs lies in the absence of reasonable social science theories which could serve as a guide to the design of social action programs. There are very few social scientists of any repute who have strongly held ideas as to what sorts of social action programs ought to be undertaken to handle most social problems. For example, no social scientist has a clear idea of why the rates of serious crimes have been increasing steeply in the last decade. If social scientists have no clear ideas, then how much more at a loss are members of the Congress or presidential advisors? (Rossi and Williams 1972: 42–43).

Williams has described this problem in another manner. He characterizes information resulting from studies as being of two types: (1) macronegative; or (2) micropositive (1972a: 7). The former data demonstrate the dimensions of a problem in broad, negative terms — e.g. certain groups are not obtaining certain opportunities, and this fact is associated with other socioeconomic characteristics such as race, ethnic group, class, etc. The general content of this set of data revolves about what is not working, or is missing, in a program. The latter data — micropositive — specify what would work. And, according to Williams, it is precisely these latter data that are not available to program administrators or policy makers. He cites several reasons to support his thesis (1972a: 59).

(1)   The unknowns that now plague policy makers in the social agencies often require research studies employing techniques and approaches (e.g., Experimental and Developmental Projects) different from, and more difficult than, those predominating in the past within the social science research community.
(2)   The reward structure of the social science community (except in economics) militates against policy-oriented research resulting in a low state of the policy arts in the major social science disciplines except economics; but here the policy competence was (and primarily is) in traditional areas such as monetary and fiscal policy, not social policy.
(3)   The available data including those generated by the major federal statistical surveys are generally inadequate to support relevant policy work in the social areas; and policy-relevant data are difficult to develop because of severe conceptual, methodological, and logistical problems.
(4)   The combination of the established government/research community relationship which allows scholars great freedom in developing their studies with the failure of policy-makers (particularly the central analyst) to delineate those needs has left scholars relatively naive about what information actually is relevant for major social policy questions.

What factors indicate that a piece of research is of potential policy relevance (this being a matter of degree, of course)? Williams has suggested at least three interrelated questions that bear on this concept (1972a: 55–56):

(1)   Does the work investigate key factors amenable to agency policy manipulation?
(2)   Is the study of adequate quality to provide information that will increase the likelihood of better policy outcomes?
(3)   Will the information be available in time to affect major policy decisions?

Policy research, as defined here, can be closely aligned with basic research as conceived by the academician. The rigor required in conceptualization, data collection, methodology, and judgment is, or should be, no less than that of the academic researcher. Although there is less explicit emphasis on the development of theory in policy research, the apparent unavailability of requisite theory from the social sciences has created a serious problem which limits the growth and contributions of evaluative and policy research. Basic academic studies are critical, but they are not the only, nor always the best, means toward the kind of theory and understanding needed in policy research. The broadness of studies that may be incorporated under the rubric "basic policy research" suggests that the older differentiation between "basic" and "applied" research does not apply here; on the other hand, a policy perspective does not mean that a researcher should feel that whatever he does may someday result in a policy input. Williams states:

"What is being suggested is that the analyst may find that crucial gaps in policy knowledge can be answered only by basic studies the results of which will lead to more applied types of studies. Both the basic and applied work in this case would be policy-relevant" (1972a: 56).

A second major distinction which exists between basic research and policy (basic) research is that the latter tends to concentrate on variables which are amenable to policy manipulation. Depending upon the purpose of the research, this is a legitimate approach, and one which has heretofore been neglected, particularly by the behavioral sciences. But as Coleman warns:

A causal model is independent of the circumstances that some variables happen to be policy variables. Excluding from the analysis variables that are a part of the causal structure because they are not policy manipulable can easily lead to biased estimates of the effects of the policy variables (1972: 99).

A third and crucial distinction, oversimplified here, lies in the area of the value orientations of program administrators or organizational managers and those who do research, particularly of the "basic" kind. This sharp division of labor is usually characterized as involving "men of action" who are interested in answers, on the one hand, and "men of study" who try to separate the mixing of social observation from judgment, on the other. The evaluative researcher, or the policy researcher using evaluative methodology, inhabits a place somewhere between these two poles. While searching for "answers" by defining problems from a policy perspective, he also can contribute not only increased knowledge of social processes, but can help the policy maker toward sounder judgment by making assumptions, values, logical processes, and intuitive propositions more explicit.

The operator's normal impulse is to ask for the conclusions of a social science research project and to regard the argument as none of his concern. But the payoff for him will usually be precisely in the argument rather than in the conclusions .... Thus, the test of effectiveness will lie not in whether the research leads to a new and unfamiliar conclusion, but in whether it clarifies and makes explicit the logical basis for a conclusion already perceived or suspected (Millikan 1959: 167).

Policy research, in the prior-to-policy development field experiments we are discussing here, studies those areas of behavior in their social and institutional aspects about which little is known, at least in their particular aspects; a researcher is as often interested in just these qualities of his subject matter as in their more general relations. Social science theory may, in general, tell us what to expect as the outcome of a policy-oriented field experiment, but that is most often not sufficient. For example, psychological theory states that positive incentives are generally more powerful than negative ones; theory also indicates that aspiration levels are quite flexible, particularly upward (United States Congress 1968: 148). Any attempt to move from an income maintenance system that is characterized by negative and punitive incentives to one that encourages and rewards additional work by additional income must certainly take into account these principles in research and program design.

On the other hand, severe conceptual and methodological problems arise when one attempts to measure the impact of an income maintenance program on community structures in, for example, a saturation type experiment.

Substantial difficulties arise in the pursuit of potentially interesting issues in this broad area because there are neither measurements nor adequate theory with respect to community structures and dynamics .... In order to determine how many "saturation" sites one would need in order to actually estimate institutional change due to income maintenance reform, one must have some prior theory about what is "normal" institutional change and some proximate measures of the orders of magnitude of such change (Lefcowitz 1971a: 151).

Whether the development of such theory can come from policy research is not presently clear. The design and operation of a policy-oriented field experiment is somewhat different from that of a laboratory or nonfield social experiment principally because the purposes are different. For example, the selection of policy variables, in part, depends upon whether one intends to study these under the assumption that these constitute a valid replication of their form and content in a national program (Orr 1971: 50). If they cannot be studied under this assumption — i.e. they may not be subject to manipulation in either the experiment or in a national program, or conceptual problems are too severe — these variables may be discarded, at least for the moment.

Experimentation and data-gathering for the purposes of policy development generally do not fulfill the requirements for the development of theory. If the latter is to be the case, then a policy-oriented experiment must be intentionally designed to allow for this efforts as well. *Ex post facto* analysis of data gathered primarily for administrative purposes is often too narrow a base upon which to build concepts and theory. We need not be overly restrictive on this point though. Coleman's recent work on equal opportunity in education, while a policy-directed study, raises and contributes to critical theoretical, conceptual, and methodological issues (Coleman, et al. 1966; see also Mosteller and Moynihan 1972). Coleman raises a particularly interesting and challenging point in rebuttal to criticisms of his educational model by two econometricians.

... econometricians ordinarily deal with areas in which there are quite specific theoretical models. Consequently, the task in an empirical analysis becomes one of estimating values of parameters in this causal structure, and the policy results of the study lie in those parameter values. Sociologists ordinarily work in areas without such theoretical models, and the task of their empirical analysis is to gain more information about possibly relevant variables and about plausible causal structures. The policy results of their research lie in such things as uncovering important processes that had previously been unknown or ignored in policy (Coleman 1972: 99).

Whatever other issues may be raised by Coleman here, implicit in his comment is the interdisciplinary nature of policy research. Theoretical models peculiar to a particular discipline are usually not adequate for this kind of research.

There is another area within this context of policy research which has been neglected and to which evaluative research itself has not yet contributed. As the measurable indices are the point of interest themselves, the relationship between these and any underlying concept becomes of secondary interest. The problem here becomes one of establishing the "fit" between the data and interpretations, which are used for policy input, legislation, program development, and field implementation.

### Academic and Policy Research Perspectives

At the most general level, the policy researcher has made at least a tentative commitment to the values of intervention, whereas the academic researcher has traditionally avoided this orientation. But these two perspectives and modes of operation are not mutually exclusive, nor should they be. A basic policy research experiment may be structurally far removed from any eventual policy and program development, i.e. not tied to a budgetary or decision-making schedule. On the other hand, a particular piece of policy research may involve an issue more directly linked to such considerations, and the context therefore would be more politically flammable, thus increasing the likelihood of the researcher becoming more personally involved.

That there may be strong personal value conflicts among social scientists about undertaking policy research is to state the obvious. To believe that social problems in an action context can be conceived as essentially technical is to be naive. And to believe further that social science can bring to bear a totally disinterested perspective and understanding of these problems is to be something more than just innocent or naive. Whether a scientific identity is fundamentally incompatible with the purposes and *modus operandi* of policy-evaluative research is a question that each must answer for himself.[4]

# REFERENCES

ACIRELLI, V. G. *et al.*
  1969  *The impact of Head Start. An evaluation of the effects of Head Start on children's cognitive and affective development,* volume one. Report to the United States Office of Economic Opportunity by Westinghouse Learning Corporation and Ohio University.
CAMPBELL, D. T., J. C. STANLEY
  1963  "Experimental and quasi-experimental designs for research on teaching," in *Handbook of research on teaching.* Edited by N. L. Gage, 171–246. Chicago: Rand McNally.
CARO, FRANCIS G., *editor*
  1971  *Readings in evaluation research.* New York: Russell Sage Foundation.
COLEMAN, JAMES S.
  1969  Evaluating educational programs. *The Urban Review* 3:6–8. (Reprinted 1971 in *Readings in evaluation research.* Edited by Francis G. Caro. New York: Russell Sage Foundation.)
  1971  "Methods for policy research." Paper presented to the Conference on the Impact of Public Policies, St. Thomas, United States Virgin Islands, December 3–5.
  1972  "Reply to Cain and Watts," in *Evaluating social programs: theory, practice and politics.* Edited by Peter H. Rossi and Walter Williams. New York: Seminar Press.

[4]  A quite provocative article on this point is: "Notes on the 'Crisis of Sociology'" (Flacks 1972). See also *The Use and Abuse of Social Science* (Horowitz 1971).

COLEMAN, JAMES S., ERNEST Q. CAMPBELL, CAROL J. HOBSON, *et al.*
   1966   *Equality of educational opportunity.* Washington, D.C.: Government Printing Office, United States Office of Education.
FLACKS, RICHARD
   1972   Notes on the "crisis of sociology." *Social Policy* (March/April).
HOROWITZ, I. L., *editor*
   1971   *The use and abuse of social science.* Transaction Studies in Social Policy SP2. New York: Transaction Books, Dutton.
HOVLAND, CARL I., ARTHUR A. LUMSDAINE, FRED D. SHEFFIELD
   1949   *Experiments on mass communication.* Princeton: Princeton University Press.
LEFCOWITZ, MYRON J.
   1971a   "Introduction: community effects," in *Income maintenance: interdisciplinary approaches to research.* Edited by Larry L. Orr, Robinson G. Hollister, and Myron Lefcowitz. Institute for Research on Poverty Monograph. Chicago: Markham.
   1971b   "Marital stability," in *Income maintenance: interdisciplinary approaches to research.* Edited by Larry L. Orr, Robinson G. Hollister, and Myron Lefcowitz. Institute for Research on Poverty Monograph. Chicago: Markham.
MILLIKAN, MAX F.
   1959   "Inquiry and policy: the relation of knowledge to action," in *The human meaning of the social sciences.* Edited by Daniel Lerner. New York: Meridian Books.
MOSTELLER, FREDERICK, DANIEL P. MOYNIHAN, *editors*
   1972   *On equality of educational opportunity.* New York: Random House.
MOYNIHAN, DANIEL P.
   1969   *On understanding poverty.* New York: Basic Books.
   1973a   "Annals of politics (income by right — I)." *The New Yorker*, January 13.
   1973b   "Annals of politics (family assistance plan — II)." *The New Yorker*, January 20.
ORR, LARRY L.
   1971   "Introduction: strategy for a broad program of experimentation in income maintenance," in *Income maintenance: interdisciplinary approaches to research.* Edited by Larry L. Orr, Robinson G. Hollister, and Myron Lefcowitz. Institute for Research on Poverty Monograph. Chicago: Markham.
ORR, LARRY L., ROBINSON G. HOLLISTER, and MYRON LEFCOWITZ, *editors*
   1971   *Income maintenance: interdisciplinary approaches to research.* Institute for Research on Poverty Monograph. Chicago: Markham.
ROSSI, PETER H., WALTER WILLIAMS, *editors*
   1972   *Evaluating social programs: theory, practice and politics.* New York: Seminar Press.
SCHULBERG, HERBERT C., FRANK BAKER
   1971   "Program evaluation models and the implementation of research findings," in *Readings in evaluation research.* Edited by Francis G. Caro. New York: Russell Sage Foundation.

SUCHMAN, EDWARD A.

1967   *Evaluative research.* New York: Russell Sage Foundation.

1971   "Evaluating educational programs," in *Readings in evaluation research.* Edited by Francis G. Caro. New York: Russell Sage Foundation.

THOMPSON, JAMES D.

1967   *Organization in action.* New York: McGraw-Hill.

UNITED STATES CONGRESS

1968   *Hearings before the subcommittee on fiscal policy of the joint economic committee, Ninetieth Congress, Second Session,* volume one: *Proceedings.* Washington, D.C.: United States Government Printing Office.

WATTS, HAROLD W.

1969   Graduated work incentives: an experiment in negative taxation. *American Economic Review Proceedings* (May): 463–472.

WEISS, CAROL H.

1967   "Utilization of evaluation: toward comparative study," in *The use of social research in federal domestic programs,* part three: *The relation of private social scientists to federal programs on national social problems.* Washington, D.C.: United States Government Printing Office.

WILLIAMS, WALTER

1972a  *Social policy research and analysis: the experience in federal social agencies.* New York: American Elsevier.

1972b  "The capacity of social science organizations to perform large-scale evaluative research," in *Evaluating social programs: theory, practice and politics.* Edited by Peter H. Rossi and Walter Williams. New York: Seminar Press.

# Insinuating Social Science into Medical Thinking: Problems and Possibilities

DOROTHEA C. LEIGHTON

The progress of medical knowledge and techniques in this century and the preceding few decades has had the effect of radically altering the pattern of diseases that afflict the majority of U.S. citizens. Up until the time of World War II, it was hard to tell who was winning the struggle between man and microbe. With the advent first of the development of vaccines and anti-serums and then of sulfanilamide and the antibiotics, however, man rapidly gained ascendency over microbe — or so we all believed. Later it appeared that our destruction of microbes had cleared the way for ultramicroscopic organisms (generally classified as viruses) to flourish as previously unrecognized diseases (to some extent, because other organisms overshadowed them). Examples of the latter are poliomyelitis, influenza, and even, as current research seems to indicate, cancer. As traditional infectious diseases declined, moreover, there appeared to be a marked increase in psychiatric disorder, particularly of the milder varieties. While it is still not certain whether this was only an unveiling of problems that had always been present, it seems likely that there was an absolute increase related to the readjustments required by the circumstances discussed below.

Concomitantly many sociocultural changes affecting health were taking place: the replacement of muscular energy by steam, electrical, combustion, and mechanical energy; mass production; food processing; a change from widespread poverty to an ever-increasing affluence; industrialization at the expense of individual enterprise; urbanization with its pervasive alterations of life styles and social relationships, and so on. We have discovered only in looking backward the many interrelationships which existed between the changes in sociocultural patterns and the changes in health patterns.

Both medical science and social science were taken by surprise by these developments and their implications. It seems fair to say that the changes themselves contributed largely to a deepening and widening of thought in both fields. Man of the old verities appeared quite inadequate to explain the new events that were occurring. No one, it seemed, had had the necessary intellectual tools to foresee the consequences of most of these changes and were thus powerless to advise political or economic decision makers. As horizons widened, each of the many professional disciplines tended to set up boundaries, cutting out a piece of the action for its meticulous and private investigation, feeling less and less kinship with other territories, making little effort to see what was going on elsewhere that might be relevant to its interests, or trying to communicate its findings to other disciplines.

The many needs which arose during World War II for concerted national and international effort provided the impetus and motivation for a lowering of some of the interdisciplinary barriers a few notches. One such effort was the study eventually published as *The American soldier* (Stouffer et al. 1950) which was a product of sociologists, psychologists, psychiatrists, medical staff, and many others, done in the national interest. Other studies could be cited in which members of several disciplines worked together to solve a common problem. Perhaps it was mostly the participants in such joint efforts who furthered the new style of applying the multidisciplinary approach in several investigations as a way of making use of varied techniques and points of view in order to comprehend as fully as possible whatever question was being studied or discussed. For the most part, the medical profession tended to withdraw once more to its encapsulated position when the war was over. A slight recognition of the possible relevance of social science to problems of medicine was evident in the occasional employment of a sociologist or anthropologist by a medical school, but effective communication and collaboration between them and the doctors was rarely established.

To be sure, the medical profession was not alone in this disciplinary retreat. My own considerable experience with multidisciplinary work[1] leads me to see all such moves as a human proclivity to seek out others of congenial outlook, interest, appearance, income, sex, age, or various

---

[1]   My first interdisciplinary work was in the joint study done by the U.S. Indian Service and the Committee on Human Development of the University of Chicago, called the Indian Education Research Project, which occupied my time from 1942–1945. The next was the Stirling County Study of Psychiatric Disorder and Sociocultural Conditions conducted by the Cornell Program in Social Psychiatry, 1952–1965. In the midst of this, I worked on the Cornell-Aro (Nigeria) Project, similar to the Stirling County Study except for the setting. Since 1965, I have been at the multidisciplinary School of Public Health in Chapel Hill, North Carolina.

other characterstics. Such clumping together with one's peers (by some definition) serves to diminish anxiety and to promote comfort and a feeling of adequate orientation to the social scene. The lack of such social support was certainly a considerable factor in the usually short tenure of the lone social scientist in the medical school, and has also contributed to the difficulty of maintaining interdisciplinary research teams over time. While comforting and supportive, however, congenial segregation can also be stultifying and is all too likely to limit and narrow the people involved, interfering with the developments which might take place through melding knowledge gained by other types of experts with that of their own discipline.

Contributing to segregation in the professional world has also been the increased production of "experts" as disciplines defined their limits ever more precisely. Described as someone who "knows more and more about less and less," the expert soon had a turf to defend and a security system which depended upon a single-minded devotion to his subject. This naturally limited cross-disciplinary discourse. Further, it introduced a rivalry and a protectiveness of one's own knowledge which has been quite damaging to the promotion of interdisciplinary harmony and collaboration. It has also hindered the synthesis of knowledge and understanding from all sources which the modern world so badly needs. Currently, the necessity for getting along in an overpopulated world and for surviving our defilement of an overexploited environment is becoming a resurgent force towards such synthesis of knowledge. It may well prod us all towards more effective collaboration.

Both anthropology and medicine are good examples of overspecialization. It has become increasingly difficult to produce a generalist in either field, due to some extent to the information explosion, and further impeded by the unresolved conflict of interest between student and professors. The student wants to acquire a beginning level of knowledge, get his degree, and start to work, while the professors want to assure their own status by turning out a sort of universal expert who knows each of his professors' specialities. Fortunately there are indications that the students' wishes are beginning to be seen as legitimate. Many youth are now feeling a need to take part in the world's problems and to achieve relevant preparation for this. Other changes include a return to the notion that "anthropology" means "the study of man" in all his aspects; an awareness that quantification can be useful; a focusing on people under any cultural circumstances (even in the anthropologist's own society); a revival of willingness to apply knowledge to help people solve problems by providing anthropological insights which increase the ability to make choices.

Medical students are somewhat similarly influenced and further are disquieted by rumors that, in spite of undisputed excellence in medical knowledge and technical skill, the United States is far down the rank ordering of nations according to their health status.

Thus it appears that the time is approaching when these two disciplines, at least, should make an effort to communicate and to enrich each other by doing so. It is worth pointing out that there has been a gradual rapprochement developing since the fifties: physicians have taken part in research involving social science, sometimes directed by the social scientists. Anthropologists (and others) have worked in medical settings studying such matters as epidemiology of program acceptance, patient attitudes towards medical services, or the sociocultural reasons for the failure of technically well-planned health programs. It has been possible for both physicians and anthropologists to learn from these joint endeavors. Many of both the successes and the failures have been well described in such books as those of Benjamin Paul (1955) and Arthur Niehoff (1966). It is now abundantly clear to all who are willing to think about it that technology in medicine is not enough. Health is a much more complicated state of equilibrium than just not having too many germs on board, or exactly the right proportion of vitamins and hormones. The remarkable interlocking systems of balance and controls within the animal body, working (in the "normal" state) according to understandable laws of biology, physiology, chemistry, and physics, are easily affected and upset in various ways by sociocultural and psychological factors that the doctor needs to know about.

As they have become aware of this, some physicians have actually gone back to school to learn about social science, usually sociology or anthropology. It has not been easy for them to winnow out the kernels of knowledge that would be of greatest use in medical work, and many have spent valuable years satisfying their professors rather than being able to achieve the limited enlightenment they want and need more directly and economically. In short, for best results both the medical and the social science professions need to do considerable collaborative thinking and planning so that (1) fully trained social scientists will be able to learn enough about the structure and culture of the health care system, and (2) fully trained physicians will be able to learn enough about cultural and social factors in health; both will then be able to work together effectively. In such a utopian situation one could expect that health would be better preserved, patients and doctors would be better satisfied, and social science would have a testing ground for its skills and theories in a practical, real-life setting of a special sort.

It is very heartening indeed that the National Board of Medical Examiners now has a Behavioral Sciences Test Committee, and that the first trial of behavioral science questions has been judged a success which will be repeated. Nothing could serve as a stronger incentive to medical students to learn about social science, and for medical staff to also increase their knowledge. It behooves anthropology to pull together its experience, vis-à-vis medicine, in our society and elsewhere, and to determine its most telling contributions for this purpose. It needs to gear up also for research projects or demonstrations which would help medically oriented professionals become more sensitive to the causative sociocultural aspects of their clients and the potency of sociocultural treatment. In the long run it should be a rewarding undertaking for both sides, for each will learn new things and gain new insights into familiar matters.

What is required to realize this dream? First, we need a good many medical anthropologists who are well trained (1) in culture and health, (2) in educational techniques, and who are (3) familiar through personal participation with the U.S. medical system and profession, especially with its hierarchical aspects and its value systems, both overt and covert.

Second, we need specified opportunities to teach health professionals things they need to know. Exposure to social science in the pre-medical and nursing years is very important, as well as during the first year in medical school. Pre-medical students are extremely interested in anything pertaining to disease and treatment, and are quick to grasp implications of sociocultural factors. Some regular participation by social scientists in the first and second medical years would also be helpful, discussing entry into a community, determining leadership patterns, detecting ethnic or subcultural differences in beliefs and habits related to health, giving instruction in field methods of acquiring needed information, and so on.

Third, and most difficult, a medical anthropologist should be on hand as much as possible for case conferences, patient rounds, and other occasions when the cultural aspects of the disease under consideration could and should be pointed out, and probably will not be unless the anthropologist is present (at least at the start).

Before any of this, of course, the medical anthropologists and the medical and nursing staffs will have to talk to each other about the best way to fit the variety of subject matter together for its greatest coherence to medical and nursing students. This provides the first opportunity for bilateral education of the staff members and, for success, requires considerable tact as well as sensitivity to the interdisciplinary problems that have been discussed above.

The anthropological material related to health is intrinsically interesting to most people and even more so to people with a medical interest who soon become intrigued with such new information, if presented appropriately. Technical anthropological terminology and concepts should be shunned — after all, nearly anything concerned with human behavior can be explained in everyday English (or whatever the local language might be). Medical people will not be interested initially in kinship systems, linguistics, house types, ethnic myths, or other non-medical esoterica. On the other hand, they will commonly be fascinated by the kinds of diseases encountered in a given group, means that have been devised for treating disease, contributing factors from the environment, from usual activities, from beliefs about causes and cures, and so on. After they become familiar with a cultural group from their own point of interest, they may well want to know anything the instructor can tell them about the formerly inappropriate topics.

Pre-medical students are less insistent on medical relevance than those already in medical school, in my experience, but still pay more avid attention to such material, as do others with health careers in mind. They are easy prey to a course with "medicine" in the title and will often take such a one as the social science requirement. This seems to offer an excellent opportunity to start their education in social science as it relates to their chosen field. While the fact that I am myself a physician doubtless was an added attraction, it hardly seems as if it would be crucial to the success of the course I have taught. I have had nine classes of mixed pre-med and other undergraduate students, plus a number of graduate students from anthropology, public health and psychology. As an example, the description of the course (originally worked out by Prof. Charles C. Hughes) follows:

*Medicine and Anthropology* (one semester, three hours credit)

1. Introduction:
Health is a persistent and prevailing concern in all cultures. Modern diseases can mostly be traced back to earliest animal remains. Archaeological evidence shows very ancient attempts at treatments, social class differences, in types of diseases incurred. Relationships between healing and religion, healing and pragmatic techniques and medicines. Medico-religious system a mirror of the culture, its values and beliefs. Medical anthropology is a meeting ground for natural (hard) and social (soft) sciences. Students read Dubos, *Mirage of health*.
2. Medicine and health in two cultures:
a. In the far north – Eskimos of St. Lawrence Island, Alaska. Description of life and its hazards to health – climate, hunting, housing, clothing, food scarcity. Illnesses encountered, vital statistics, available native medicines, accidental and

intentional preventive practices, shamans, and séances. Introduction of modern medicine. Ideas of cause and cure. Factors influencing mental health. Modern changes. (From Hughes, *An Eskimo village in the modern world.*)

b.   In the southwest – Navajos in the high dry country. Contrasts to Eskimo life. Different ways of sustaining life. Climate, living patterns, farming, and herding. Illnesses encountered, vital statistics, remarkable population increase. Special diseases such as trachoma and congenital dislocation of the hip. Common factors (with Eskimos) of poverty and marginal existence in relation to health. Elaborate religio-medical system. Singers and other medicine men. Ideas of cause and cure. The Many Farms study of how to introduce modern medicine to the Navajo. Interrelationships between the two medical systems. Navajo medicine as psychotherapy. Extensive modern change. (Kluckhohn and Leighton, *The Navaho*, and Adair and Deuschle, *The people's health.*)

3.   The position of health concern in other cultures (briefly):

a.   The Cheyenne – more concerned with warfare than with health.

b.   The Dobu – everything caused and cured by spells and witchcraft.

c.   The Thonga – the ancestors hold the key.

4.   Intercultural health concerns:

Problems encountered when modern medical concepts and public health practices are introduced into other cultures. General findings from Foster, *Problems in intercultural health programs*, SSRC Pamphlet 12. Students read several cases from Niehoff, *Casebook of social change.* Class descriptions of several cases from Paul, *Health, culture and community.*

5.   Introduction to U.S. medicine and its problems:

A good many of the chapters of Jaco's *Patients, physicians and illness* are assigned to individual students to read and report to the class. Considerable personal experience and anecdotes are always part of the ensuing discussions. Students are required to condense the message of each chapter to a five minute talk. Other students are assigned a group report of Rutstein, *The coming revolution in medicine*, and Tunley, *The American health scandal.* Someone is tagged to read and report the first four chapters of Selye, *The stress of life.*

6.   Social psychiatry as the meeting ground of medicine and social science: There are lectures on the interrelationships between sociocultural stress factors and personality functioning and on some of findings of social psychiatric studies. The final exam consists of accounts of their own experience with adequate or inadequate supply of certain basic human needs.

A term paper of ten or more pages is required on a topic of interest to the student and related to the subject matter of the course.

*Assigned Reading*

DUBOS, RENÉ: *The mirage of health* (Harper, 1959).*

WILSON, ROBERT N.: *Sociology of health* (Random House, 1969).*

NIEHOFF, ARTHUR: *Casebook of social change* (Aldine, 1966).*

JACO, E. GARTLY (ed.): *Patients, physicians and illness* (Free Press, 1958).

RUTSTEIN, DAVID: *The coming revolution in medicine* (MIT Press, 1967).
   or
TUNLEY, ROUL: *The American health scandal* (Dell Books, 1966).*

LEIGHTON, ALEXANDER H.: *My name is legion,* Chapters 1–4 and 7 (Basic Books, 1959).

*Additional Bibliography*

ADAIR, JOHN, KURT DUESCHLE: *The people's health* (Appleton-Century-Croft, 1970).
APPLE, DORRIAN (ed.): *Sociological studies of health and sickness* (McGraw-Hill, 1960).
BURLING, TEMPLE, EDITH LENTZ, ROBERT N. WILSON: *The give and take in hospitals* (New York, 1956).
CAUDILL, WILLIAM: *The psychiatric hospital as a small society.*
FOSTER, GEO. A.: *Problems in intercultural health programs* (SSRC Pamphlet 12).
GLASSER, WM.: *Mental health or mental illness* (Harper and Rowe, 1960).
HUGHES, CHARLES C.: *An Eskimo village in the modern world* (Ithaca: Cornell Univ. Press, 1960).
KLUCKHOHN and LEIGHTON: *The Navaho* (Harvard University Press, 1946).*
LEIGHTON, CLAUSEN, WILSON (eds.): *Explorations in social psychiatry,* Chapts. IV, V, VI and XII (Basic Books, 1957).
MECHANIC, DAVID: *Medical sociology* (Free Press, 1968).
MERTON, ROBERT K., GEORGE READER, PATRICIA LAZARSFELD (ed.): *The student physician* (Harvard Univ. Press, 1957).
PAUL, BENJAMIN: *Health, culture and community* (Russell Sage, 1955).
SELYE, HANS: *The stress of life* (McGraw-Hill, 1956).*
SIGERIST, HENRY: *History of medicine,* vol. 1, *Civilization and disease* (Yale Medical Library, 1951).
WOLFF, HAROLD: *Stress and disease* (Thomas, 1953).

* Available in paperback.

A very different experience was teaching similar concepts to a required class of public health students — all graduates, many with extensive work in the health field in many different capacities. A difficult feature was the extreme variation in previous education, some students having graduate degrees in social science, others having had very little exposure. It was probably the intermedidate group between these two extremes who tolerated the course best and got the most out of it. Ideally, the offering should have been presented to groups at different levels separately, perhaps omitting entirely those who already were well-versed in social science and presumably had already made their own application of it to health work. To me the most curious reaction, and one that seemed impossible to overcome, was a pragmatic focus which made some students quite impervious to any subject that they did not see as of some immediate practical consequence to their future careers. They seemed unable to translate findings from an Indian tribe, for example, to black people, Chicanos, or other disadvantaged groups with whom they might expect to work.

At the medical school level, it is probably unrealistic to hope to teach medical anthropology as a discrete subject — rather it must form a part of other courses and, above all, the medical anthropologist must be on hand to bring up his set of topics whenever opportunity presents itself. This will be the most difficult task of all — how to insinuate and integrate subject matter not seen as very important by those in charge, and in competition with topics believed by staff and students to be of much greater significance. The medical anthropologist can only bide his time, persistently cultivating medical acquaintanceship and devising medical-anthropological exercises or researches which will catch the imagination of at least some of the students.

It seems doubtful that this would be a worthwhile expenditure of the anthropologists' time if the only outcome were to force some useful information on unwilling hearers. It is my hope and belief that, in becoming familiar with the medical setting from his background in anthropology, the medical anthropologist will see ways in which the whole health field can readjust itself and its values in order to cope more effectively with the health-related problems of citizens. Remembering other cultures' ways of coping, what is relevant to our own? How can the various facets of the picture in the U.S. be reconciled and altered so that runaway costs are reduced, health is maintained rather than lost and regained, doctors receive a reasonable compensation for their educational expenses and their responsibility, the work is shared by many levels of helpers and becomes thereby more accessible to all?

Why should anthropologists bother with this, why not leave it up to the sociologists? It seems to me that training in anthropology is more likely than sociology to sensitize a student to the important inner meaning of human phenomena which motivates people and either alienates them or enhances the social and interpersonal support systems which are so important in the illness and wellness of humanity. Ideally, the two disciplines should work together — the sociologist contributing the aspects he does best, like structure and quantity, and the anthropologist attending to his special concerns of meaning and quality. Such a combination of talents, brought to bear on the medical subculture and its problems, could go far toward improving the organization and delivery of help for the ill and of preservation of health for the rest of society.

## REFERENCES

NIEHOFF, ARTHUR
   1966   *Casebook of social change*. Chicago: Aldine.
PAUL, BENJAMIN
   1955   *Health, culture and community*. New York: Russell Sage.
STOUFFER, S. A., *et al.*
   1950   *The American soldier*, four volumes. New York: John Wiley and Sons.

# Use of Social Research in Population Programs: A Case Study of a Policy Debate Among Social Science Experts

JEFFREY G. REITZ

Social research can be an extremely useful aid to policy making, but it is becoming increasingly clear that it can seldom if ever provide a complete answer to particular policy questions. Even after extensive investigation and analysis, informed guesswork and intuitive hunches are still required (see Reitz 1973; Lazarsfeld and Reitz 1970; Lazarsfeld, et al. 1967). In the present article we probe the limits of relevance of social research to the formulation of policy. We analyze here a debate among social scientists about the policy implications of their knowledge in order to clarify some of the problems involved in using social research.

In recent years, sociologists have begun to debate policy issues in print more often. The published debates over the Moynihan Report (Rainwater and Yancey 1965) and the Coleman Report (Mosteller and Moynihan 1972) are well-known examples. Such debates make it possible to analyze in detail how social science knowledge is thought to be relevant to policy, and why presumed experts disagree on its implications.

The specific policy debate selected for analysis here concerns the implications of research on human fertility for programs to control "overpopulation" in India. There are two major schools of thought represented in the literature. One favors the widest possible dissemination of family planning propaganda and contraceptive devices, and the other urges that a major share of available resources be used as material incentives to limit reproduction, and to promote certain institutional changes.[1] The litera-

---

[1] There are related policy debates as to whether population control is the best way to achieve increased per capita income, and the relation between both of these goals and still other goals such as physical and mental health. Some might prefer to reserve the term "policy" for decisions involving broader issues of that kind. However, from the

ture on this debate is fairly extensive, though scattered, in journals such as *Demography, Population Studies, Studies in Family Planning,* and *Science*; in books arising from major conferences on population; and in other publications.

Policy debates among experts are of particular importance for understanding the relation between research-based knowledge and policy decision. In such debates, the limits of the policy relevance of research are tested by adversaries both of whom are competent in social science. This explicit testing of relevance usually does not occur in the rather more common disputes between experts and policy-makers. Typically, an expert/policy maker "debate" is really only a one-way affair. The expert presents a detailed critique of the policy maker's position, but the response, if any, and whatever its merits, is usually lacking in detail. Debates among outside experts are important because arguments on both sides receive informative elaboration.

First of all we can analyze the actual content of the expert debate. Do the policy disagreements relate primarily to differences in the goals that the participants wish policy to serve? Or, are there differences in the criteria of acceptable scientific knowledge? Perhaps there are crucial gaps in existing knowledge, which are filled according to different intuitions. In this case, we can ask about the prospects for a resolution of the debate in future research.

The relation between social science and the actual policy process may be clarified when expert debates are well understood. If government policy is favored by some experts and opposed by others, it is important to determine the basis for the disagreement. Social scientists, of course, have the obligation to make scientific judgments. However, a theory of the use of research in policy making must take account of whether policy disagreements arise from disagreements about scientific fact, or about matters which cannot be resolved in scientific discourse. As will become clear, these extrascientific matters may include not only goals and values, but also assumptions about human behavior which cannot be derived from research. The following discussion will deal primarily with policy debate among social science experts, but some implications of the debate for the analysis of research use in government policy making will be noted in conclusion.

---

point of view of the logic of decision making and research application, there is no fundamental difference among levels of decision because the distinction between means and ends is logically relative.

## EARLY KAP STUDIES: POLICY DEBATE

In India, the goal of reducing population growth to improve economic and medical health was officially established twenty years ago. Since then, the population has grown by some 50 percent to a present total of over 550 million persons. Concern with population growth has increased correspondingly. The budget for population control grew from 1.5 million rupees in the First Five-Year Plan to over 3 billion rupees in the Fourth Five-Year Plan just completed. The current official goal is to reduce the crude birth rate from over 40 births per 1,000 per year to 25 per 1,000 per year, nearly a 40 percent reduction by 1980.

The debate over which programs would achieve this goal most quickly has taken place in the context of research on the causes of high fertility in India, and research evaluating specific programs. The so-called KAP surveys (the letters stand for KNOWLEDGE, ATTITUDES, and PRACTICE with respect to fertility) show that the average size of completed families in India, as in most developing countries and unlike the developed countries, is greater than the size people say is "ideal."[2] Surveys find that almost half of the people say they want no more children, but few know much about contraceptive methods. When they are asked about family planning most people approve in principle and say they want to know more about it (cf. Bogue 1962: 505, 507; Mauldin 1965: 1–10; Berelson 1966: 659–660; Chandrasekaran 1966: 545–559). These data make it possible, at least in principle, to classify the population into two groups: one in which people have more children than they want because of ignorance of modern birth control methods, and another in which people have large families for various economic and cultural reasons.

The policy debate concerns which of these two groups should be the main target of a population control program. One school of thought holds that the first group should be the main target in the immediate future, and that family planning programs should be expanded to provide more birth control education and the necessary devices, sterilization, or

[2] Estimates of these two paramaters vary, but there is agreement on the direction of the discrepancy between the two. Bogue (1962: 504) presents data showing that the ideal ranges between 2.6 children in a sample of Calcutta workers to 4.7 among women in rural Mysore. This is compared with an "actual average of between 6 and 7 children ever born per married woman aged 45 in both rural and urban areas." Ridker (1969: 280) cites Kaur and Edlefsen (1968), and says that the ideal is "closer to three in urban areas and closer to four in rural areas." The actual number of children at the time of completion of family size is estimated to be 4.5 — by "applying mortality rates to a figure for completed fertility — (live births per woman at the completion of fertile period) of 7.4" (Ridker: 282). For figures on other countries, see Mauldin (1965) and Berelson (1966: 657–658).

abortion. A leading spokesman for this school, Berelson (1963: 179) states that the group "ready" for family planning is between one-fourth and one-third of the "typical traditional community of the underdeveloped countries" and that family planning programs would cause a substantial decline in the birth rate (Berelson 1966: 658). Agarwala (n.d.: 10) estimates that between 40 and 50 percent of the married Indian women of reproductive age will accept family planning advice.

At present, the advocates of family planning programs comprise an "establishment," in the sense that most of the budget allocations for population control in India are for family planning programs (see Simmons 1971; Nortman 1972). According to careful observers such as Hauser (1967: 405), the surveys have "helped to persuade prime ministers, parliaments, and the general population" to support family planning, and have provided "justification" for family planning administrators.

A growing number of critics reach very different policy conclusions. They argue that the more resistant group should also be the target of major social programs. Many Indians prefer very large families, by comparison with standards in industrialized countries. In India the family remains a major source of rewards, both economic and noneconomic. The critics recommend programs which go well beyond traditional family planning, and they attempt to alter the existing structure of incentives favoring large family size norms. The proposed measures include payment of material incentives for limiting reproduction (Enke 1960; Kangas 1970; Rogers 1972), bringing women into the labor force (Blake 1965), discouraging marriage, at least until a later age (Davis 1967), lowering the infant mortality rate (Heer and Smith 1968), and a host of other measures.[3]

Programs to provide incentives and promote institutional change obviously would be more expensive than family planning programs. Why should they receive high priority now? Davis (1967), one of the critics, suggests that there is a conflict over goals. He predicts from the KAP surveys that Indians who know modern methods of family planning will still plan to have a lot of children, and the population will continue to grow too rapidly. Clearly, the higher the goals one sets for a population program, the less likely one is to be content with reliance upon family planning, or with reliance upon any program which focuses only on a subgroup of the population. The logical goal, according to Davis, is zero population

[3]   An extensive classification of these proposals is presented by Berelson (1969a: 1–3). Note that a classification of debaters into only two camps is an approximation which helps to simplify discussion. Actually, the debate is more complex and not by any means completely polarized.

growth, "because ANY growth rate, if continued, will eventually use up the earth." It must be said, however, that the actual consequences of zero population growth in the near future are still obscure in the literature, and its advocacy is still a minority concern.

For many of the critics of family planning programs, goals do not seem to be the major issue. These critics are not vigorously challenging the more limited target set by the government of a 40 percent reduction in the birth rate by 1980. Their most explicit concern is whether family planning programs can achieve even the more limited government target.

The issue raised by these critics in an empirical one. It concerns THE SIZE OF THE GROUP WHICH IS POTENTIALLY RECEPTIVE TO FAMILY PLANNING PROGRAMS, i.e. the actual "market" for family planning. The smaller the estimated market, the less current efforts should be concentrated on family planning programs, and the more they should be concentrated on programs to create a market. Hauser suggests that family planning advocates make a crucial methodological error when they use the KAP surveys to estimate the potential market for family planning. He points out that the EXPRESSED PREFERENCES are not valid predictors of BEHAVIORAL RESPONSES to family planning programs. As he puts it,

The generally accepted [policy] interpretation [of KAP surveys] is methodologically naive in the sense that in an analogous situation it would be the equivalent of a market research organization concluding that a 70 percent affirmative response to a question of whether the respondent would like to have a jeep constituted a measurement of the market for jeeps (Hauser 1967: 404).

According to Hauser, the usual survey question on ideal family size may be meaningless in many cultures. Expressions of interest in family planning may reflect politeness rather than real concern. He says that the use of the survey results in family planning programs has been "uncritical," and recommends studies that would probe "intensity" of interest more deeply.

Actually, leading advocates of family planning do not appear to be ignorant of methodological objections to the research. Policy decisions, however, do not always await further research. Freedman, for example, says that he would

accept the responses on [KAP] surveys as valid initially until they are tested by a really effective, persistent, all-out service and information effort. Devious psychological explanations of why respondents really did not mean what they said may be too easy rationalization for a feeble or insufficiently thorough effort (Freedman 1966: 815, quoted in Raulet 1970: 228).

In other words, what the advocates of family planning are saying is that, for policy purposes, as opposed to scientific purposes, they are willing to risk taking interview responses at roughly face value as indicators of the existing potential market for family planning. They do not necessarily deny that actual interest in family planning may be lower than indicated in the early surveys. Instead, they may be guessing simply that it is not so low that family planning programs cannot make an effective contribution to lower birth rates. The assumption implicit in the literature advocating institutional change is that the potentially receptive group is much smaller; thus other programs would be needed before significant results could be achieved. But this, too, is guesswork.

The reasoning behind this guesswork is not always explicit. In the case of the family planning advocates, it appears possible that there is a belief that smaller families are in the immediate self-interest of Indian parents, as well as in the interest of Indian society as a whole. This belief is reflected, for example, in Bogue's (1962: 517) statement that "under the present changing conditions [Indians will accept arguments either that] the large family does not really give the result desired, or that the desired result can be obtained by the small family also." That is to say, the small family does make rational sense, or ought to make sense, and it is plausible that substantial motivation underlies the surprisingly widespread expressions of interest in limiting family size. Chandrasekhar (1972: 288) holds the same view that the economic advantage of small families "looks so simple and so commonsensical" that persuasion efforts should be continued. He adds that "perhaps incentives can play some part."

Advocates of institutional change, such as Blake (1965: 1184), appear to believe that the advantages of small families to individual Indian parents are not at all obvious under the present circumstances. There is no reason to expect that people are motivated by nonexistent advantages, however great the propaganda barrage which insists that advantages do exist. Beliefs concerning the "true interests" or "basic needs" of any social group are of a speculative kind, but they are certainly part of the whole debate over population programs.

## FURTHER MOTIVATIONAL RESEARCH: POLICY DEBATE

Can this unglamorous guesswork be reduced by the better research methodology that Hauser suggests? A reason can be easily given why, in principle, this research may not be able to resolve the debate. To use information on the intensity of interest in family planning to assess the size of the market, and therefore to decide the likely success of family planning programs, one must determine what intensity is sufficient for education and services to be effective. This determination must come from a source other than the motivation research. An additional uncertainty is introduced by the fact that the programs are themselves subject to innovation and possible improvement, so that increasingly less intense interest may be sufficient to produce a positive response.

Nevertheless, by now more detailed research on motivation has been completed and used to reach updated policy conclusions. A paper by Ridker (1969) is devoted to this. A main point is that existing motivation for small families is weakened by a preference for boys. Ridker cites the studies by Poffenberger (1968a, 1968c) showing that Indians tend to prefer boys to girls; in urban areas many may say they want three children, but they also say they want two boys. Obviously the two desires may conflict, and when asked about this, people often say that the desire for boys is the overriding consideration. In a rural survey, 83 percent of the respondents said they would have at least four girls before they stopped trying for a boy, and 50 percent said they would have at least six girls before giving up.

Ridker concludes from this that family planning programs are indeed based on erroneous assumptions. He says that "effective desire," which he defines as "a level of desire sufficiently intense so that the average couple's behavior is capable of being influenced by the provision of supplies and information," is for a family size larger than previous KAP surveys had indicated. He therefore concludes that Indians must be offered material incentives before they will begin to limit family size.

Ridker's guess in this instance is that the desire for at least two boys is as strong as people say it is, that is, stronger than the desire to have only three children in all. It would be interesting to know how many advocates of family planning have revised their expectations for such programs on the basis of Ridker's analysis. It should be noted, however, that the researcher who studied the preference for boys, Poffenberger, reaches policy conclusions somewhat different from Ridker's. In one study (Poffenberger 1968b) of a sample of urban and relatively well-educated Indians, he found that only half used birth control, despite the fact that almost every respondent (over 90 percent) had heard of family planning and thought it was good for India, and that almost all of those with two or more children wanted no more. Poffenberger attributes the low level of use of birth control to an ambivalence caused by the desire for boys. But then he goes a step further. He asked people about their greatest "hopes and fears" for themselves and for India in the future, and found that the greatest concerns were economic. People wanted a higher standard of living. Almost none mentioned population limitation as a national priority. Poffenberger suggests that the ambivalences of these people about family planning is caused by ignorance of the relation between population growth and economic prosperity. He therefore suggests that family planning propaganda could win these people over if proper stress is placed on the national economic importance of family planning.

Before turning to consider the impact of evaluation research on the debate, one further problem should be noted. The need for the policy maker to make guesses does not stop after the size of the potentially receptive group is decided. To decide on family planning programs, he must also estimate the indirect effect such a program might have on the resistant group. Bogue (1962) suggested that people who are converted to family planning could thereafter act as influential opinion leaders. Their visible presence might demonstrate to resistant people the merits of small family size, and the social acceptability of family planning. Family size norms would decline, and the resistant group would shrink. Berelson agrees, suggesting that "the best way to spread the market is to exploit the existing one" (1963: 170; see also Berelson 1966: 658–659; Raulet 1970: 227).

Simon (1968: 505) criticized this idea on the grounds that attempts to apply the opinion leader concept in marketing have been successful only when the product is highly visible. He cites experience marketing farm silos as an example indicating the degree of visibility necessary. To the extent that birth control is a taboo topic for public discussion, there would be no secondary effects of conversions. But the question of whether family planning is a taboo topic in India is also debated in the literature, and the kind of assumptions needed to draw policy conclusions is by now fairly clear.

## EVALUATION RESEARCH ON POPULATION PROGRAMS: POLICY DEBATE

Evaluation research on population programs has been a major topic of discussion in the debate. Evaluation research measures the results of actual programs. If the effectiveness of a particular program on a particular type of population is in dispute, the dispute can be resolved by an evaluation study. This relative simplicity is behind Moynihan's (1970: 193) general advice to restrict policy inputs from the social sciences to evaluation studies. Yet evaluation research on population programs has been used as ammunition on both sides of the debate.

In the first place, none of the family planning programs in India are shown in evaluation studies to be achieving government goals. The most optimistic reports, by Berelson (1969a) and Simmons (1971), have claimed significant achievements. Berelson states that in India, from 5 to 14 percent of the married women of reproductive ages have "accepted" some form of contraception as a result of the programs, when these are carried out with "some energy." Based on cost/effectiveness considerations, he concludes that "overall, it appears that a vigorous program can extend contraceptive practices by an economically worthwhile amount wherever conducted" (1969a: 9). Simmons (1971: 88) estimates that a 9 percent reduction in the birth rate has been achieved in fifteen years of the program. The methodological adequacy of these reports is controversial (see Nortman 1972; Lapham and Mauldin 1972). Overreporting in the government statistics is a possibility often mentioned.

Resolving such methodological controversies does not, however, decide the question of how to achieve the government targets, because even the most optimistic reports indicate that present programs will not do this. A policy alternative arises. How long should the policy maker support efforts to "debug" the family planning programs, and at what point should he begin to allocate a more significant share of his resources to programs based on other assumptions?

There have been many proposals for "debugging" the family planning programs. Disappointment with early programs in the 1950's led many to believe that improved birth control technology was the answer. In the 1960's, the IUD and sterilization were incorporated in the programs. An evaluation of one intensive IUD program in the impoverished town of Lulliani, near Lahore, West Pakistan, showed a reduction in the birth rate of only 4 percent during the first thirty months of operation (Coob, et al. 1965). The report indicates that in many cases, use of the IUD had been discontinued and many women complained of bleeding and other side effects of the IUD. Nonusers expressed fear of these side effects. The authors of the report suggest that additional improvements in IUD design and insertion techniques are needed, and that properly organized clinics might be able to reduce the birth rate in all the cities and towns of Pakistan by as much as 15 percent in ten years.

Advocates of incentives and institutional change disagree. For example, Wyon and Gordon (1971: 276–279), reviewing the Lulliani study and other studies, conclude that the reason for poor results is low motivation. In their words, "most couples see no good reason why they should control births much more than they do." Their own recommendations call for a variety of efforts to change the structure of incentives for reproduction, as well as efforts at persuasion. Other critics of family planning programs take the evaluation results as reasonable proof of the small potential market for family planning. Ridker (1969: 281) explicitly states that one might "judge the desired number of children by the parity of couples that accept a contraceptive method," that is, by the number of children they have before trying to stop. The guess here is that those who do not use contraception do not want to, because they have had an access to it that Ridker evidently feels is adequate (see also Hauser 1967: 404).

Note that the two alternative policy conclusions do not necessarily involve different views of the causes of disappointing program results. In a sense, it can always be argued that motivation was "inadequate." The question is whether success is more likely to be achieved by increasing the motivation or by making the technology so convenient that increased motivation is unnecessary. Thus, Berelson's status resport in 1969 includes the proposition that: "The contraceptive technology is a key element in the spread of effective family planning: almost certainly, over the short run, an acceptable innovation in method results in more family planning than change in attitude" (Berelson 1969b: 364). At the same time, Wyon and Gordon assert that: "Improved contraceptives are desirable, but experience has proved many times that they remain unused in the absence of a determined will by a majority to refrain from reproducing" (Wyon and Gordon 1971: 245).

These statements indicate how policy implications can be phrased in such a way that they sound almost tautological. In reality, evaluation studies do not decide this kind of policy question. The above conclusions can be reached only on the basis of other kinds of considerations, usually implicit.

Bogue provided the most extensive list of suggestions for debugging family planning programs. He acknowledged in 1962 that

the program of family planning in India has not produced the results its sponsors and friends hoped it would when it was launched. ... the number and percentage of couples who are availing themselves of family planning services and information is discouragingly low (1962: 503).

Pointing to the KAP survey data indicating receptivity to family planning, Bogue insisted that Indians are potentially receptive, though they may feel some ambivalences. His list of suggestions to counteract these ambivalences falls almost entirely within the context of traditional family planning. As examples, he recommends that

1.  Communication efforts should be intensified, and the channels diversified to include the use of the printed page (for those who are shy) and informal social networks.

2. The "pitch" should be more subtle, at first suggesting only postponement of pregnancy. This would enable people to learn techniques and then decide later to limit family size when there is less anxiety about the method itself. The welfare of existing children should be emphasized as a rationale.

3. An effort should be made to focus messages on the most receptive people. However, within the family unit, special efforts should be made to convert the men, who are less receptive than the wives, but who are less shy, more often literate, and are often the authority figure in the family.

Many of these suggestions have been criticized by Simon (1968) as also being inconsistent with previous marketing experience. Such criticisms do not necessarily imply the abandonment of family planning, because further debugging can always be suggested. In fact, Simon (1968: 505) does just that. For example, he suggests that instead of focusing repeated messages on the most receptive people, just the opposite should be done. According to him, repeated messages have been found to have sharply diminishing returns in advertising.

Other suggestions for improving family planning programs have focused on additional aspects, such as the ties to public health facilities. It is argued that the use of health professionals in family planning programs increases the cost of the program, and places unnecessary restrictions on the relation between disseminator and client (Stycos 1962; Linder 1971). Probably the possibilities of such "fine tuning" are limited only by the human imagination.

Among the proposals of the incentives and institutional change school, only the use of material incentives has been evaluated in studies. Rogers (1972: Chapter 2) calls the existing incentive programs expensive but "amazingly successful," and reports that the Indian government has expanded the incentive program considerably as a result. One objection is that acceptance of incentives does not necessarily involve attitude change, and an appearance of success might result from cheating.[4] Just as many types of family planning programs have been suggested, there is a bewildering variety of proposals for exactly how incentives should be paid. They differ according to WHAT should be paid (money or merchandise), HOW MUCH should be paid (20 rupees, 100 rupees, or what?) and WHO should be paid (possibly only low-parity women). Interestingly, research has given some clues. The research already cited suggests that people want sons to support them in their old age. Incentives might be paid in a way that compensates for this. But again there are contrary pro-

---

[4] Conflicting theories on the likely effect of incentives on attitudes are cited in the social psychology literature (compare Rogers [1972: 20] with Sprehe [1972]).

posals for how best to accomplish this. One suggestion is to pay incentives into a retirement fund, as in a program conducted at the South India Tea Plantations (Rogers 1972: Chapter 3). Another is for incentives to be paid into an educational fund for existing children, so people can feel that these children will have a bright financial future (Rogers 1972: Chapter 4; Finnigan and Sun 1972).

## SUMMARY AND DISCUSSION

From this brief review,[5] it is evident that knowledge from research leaves room for significant policy debate even among experts endorsing the same policy goals and norms. The underlying reason for this is easily summarized, and may have more general applicability. Research permits a tentative classification of the population into two or more groups according to the degree and type of resistance to some desired behavior. To decide how to allocate resources between programs designed to deal with each group, specific programs for each group have to be invented and some estimate made of how many people of each type are likely to respond favorably. Indirect effects of programs for one group on other groups must also be estimated. These elements enter into a complicated utility calculus. The decision cannot be derived from research, because no one can be sure how many people of a given type will respond to a novel change in their environment. Specific programs can be tested, but there will always remain untested variations.

The assumptions and ideas external to research which are used to estimate the likely response to specific programs and program modification are difficult to identify precisely. We have suggested that one assumption in the present case derives from beliefs about "true interests" or "basic needs" of a population, which place limits on the degree to which people can be manipulated by propaganda. This is mostly speculation, and other debates should be analyzed to see whether corresponding assumptions, or perhaps quite different ones, can be identified.

Beyond these beliefs about true interests, another essential ingredient in the decision is imagination which yields economically practical ways to do things. A main reason for hoping that family planning programs will work is that they promise to be cheaper and have fewer disruptive side

---

[5]   The literature review here has been only partial. We have, for example, omitted a discussion of research on the effects of infant mortality on the birth rate, although some of the debate focuses on this research (see, for example, Heer and Smith 1968; Chandrasekhar 1972).

effects. Berelson shies away from the expense of incentive and welfare programs, and notes the probable effect of increased female employment on male unemployment rates. However, if ways to improve the effectiveness of family planning programs without significant increases in costs cannot be devised, they would have to be supplemented by increased allocations for incentives and other programs aimed at reducing the motivation for large families. Some all-out family planning programs involving home visits have cost over $100 per acceptor, and if such costs could not be reduced, incentive programs and programs to promote institutional change would begin to look much more attractive.

The accumulation of research knowledge clearly has affected the course of the expert debate, even though no research ever can resolve it finally. Obstacles to a reduction in the birth rate come into sharper focus in the development from the early KAP studies to the more detailed motivational studies and finally to program evaluation studies. From any point of view the situation looks increasingly difficult for family planners. This does not mean that supporters of family planning as the most cost-effective approach have been forced into a scientifically untenable position. But their initial assumptions do become subject to critical review, and their specific program recommendations become subject to repeated revision.

Up to this point we have concentrated on the cognitive content of the debate among social science experts, as it appears in the published literature. What is the relation between this debate and actual policy decisions made in the Indian government? The expert debate reveals both uses and limitations inherent in social research as a tool for developing social policy. It therefore has implications for the analysis of how research is actually used.

Every social scientist participating in the policy debate agrees that research should be "used" in policy making. One concern is that policy makers may "resist" research findings because of a commitment to existing policy. However, the expert debate makes clear that the potential for research to affect policy does not depend only upon whether research findings are resisted or accepted by policy makers. To "use" research, assumptions and ideas external to research findings also are needed. How these additional elements are introduced into decision making is as important to the final decision as whether the research knowledge itself is accepted.

In the history of policy to achieve population control in India, there are a whole series of controversial decisions to be studied. Population control methods have been repeatedly reviewed and changed over the past two decades, within the context of increasing overall priority for population control. The earliest Family Planning Programmes involved only clinics where people could come for information and service, but later, propaganda campaigns were added. Originally, only the rhythm method of birth was emphasized, but later a number of other birth control methods, including sterilization, were advocated and abortion laws were liberalized. The use of incentives is now part of the Family Planning Programmes, and accounts for about one-fourth of the Programme budget. Allocations for other kinds of efforts so far have been small. According to one report on population policy, the Third Five-Year Plan (1961–1965) included "social policies like education of women, opening up new employment opportunities for them and raising the age of marriage" (Estimates Committee 1972: 5–6). No details were given, but it is clear that such measures have not received great emphasis.

Indian government reports indicate that the use of social research in population programs is a major priority. The government funds a substantial amount of social research on fertility. Its interest in research is reflected also in the detailed list of proposed research topics that the Department of Family Planning prepares, and in the familiarity with existing research demonstrated by top officials in that Department and at higher levels in the Ministry of Health and Family Planning (some of whom are themselves researchers). Overviews of research findings are prepared from time to time by organizations such as the Central Family Planning Institute for use by policy makers (see, for example, Rao 1968).

Among government policy makers and advisers who are aware of the research findings, how does the potential "policy debate" proceed and how is it resolved? One constraint on the debate may be the structure of the existing state bureaucracy in India. Policy makers most familiar with population research may be those responsible for the Family Planning Programme, and they may have little power to affect policy outside the Ministry of Health and Family Planning. They may not be in a position to decide how funds should be allocated between family planning and alternative programs dealing with employment for women, old age pensions, and so on. The most visible use of research in population policy making has been made by family planning officials. For example, the decision to increase the investment in family planning propaganda in the early 1960's was the result of a review of research and family planning experience by the Director of Family Planning (see Freyman 1965: 15; Pathak 1968: 60). Recently the Secretary of the Ministry of Health and Family Planning reviewed available research and concluded that "more motivational efforts are necessary" and that these might include the more effective use of community leaders in propaganda drives (Estimates Committee 1972: 162). However, policy papers do come out of the Ministry of Health and Family Planning which reflect an interest in policies for compulsory education, child labor regulations, and increasing the marriage age, from the point of view of their effects on the birth rate (see Raina 1965). It would be interesting to know how such proposals are channeled through the Indian state bureaucracy.

Reliance on family planning programs to reduce the Indian birth rate is sometimes attributed to various foreign and domestic political forces having little relation to relevant social science research. For example, the United States Agency for International Development, and other foreign agencies sympathetic to family planning, provide technical assistance and earmarked funds to the Indian Government (Estimates Committee 1972: Chapter 10), thus possibly exerting an influence on population policy. It is also suggested that some of those giving advice on population control have a vested interest in family planning programs (see Raulet 1970: 227; Hauser 1967: 408–409). However, the part played by research in this context cannot be prejudged. Research findings may be selectively ignored by some advocates of reliance on family planning, but this is not necessary to their position.

We have seen that it is possible to argue for or against reliance on family planning POLICY without violating any norms of scientific RESEARCH. There simply may be a greater willingness to give family planning programs the benefit of the doubt where the future is concerned, as a result of political factors. And, whatever the political context, Indian policy makers may still favor family planning programs on their merits. As a matter of fact, increased emphasis on incentives may develop not because it is seen as dictated by research findings, but because past shortcomings of family planning programs make them a political liability within India.

Some changes in the relations between researchers and policy makers in the Indian government may be occurring, with consequences for the way in which research findings are reviewed. For example, foreign experts have been blamed for some past failures, and reliance on them seems to be on the wane (Estimates Committee 1972: 163, 191; Banerji 1971). A new kind of population policy research group has been recommended, with the power not only to allocate research funds, but also to gather its results and formulate policy proposals (Estimates Committee 1972: 157).

There is no obviously ideal way to use research findings. One may consult the opinions of many different experts, but this really begs the question. Putting the matter in the hands of some autonomous advisory group may help, but there is no guarantee that their recommendations would be accepted, or for that matter that they would be in any way superior. The physicist Alvin Weinberg (1972) suggests the term "trans-scientific" for questions which "can be stated in scientific terms but are beyond the proficiency of science to answer." Weinberg wants the public to debate "trans-scientific" issues. In any case, it can perhaps be hoped that social scientists will increasingly feel obliged to state clearly where scientific considerations leave off, and nonscientific considerations enter in. In this way there may be a more explicit recognition of not only the uses but also the limitations of social science in policy making.

## REFERENCES

AGARWALA, S. N.
  n.d.   "Population control in India: progress and prospects." Unpublished manuscript (circa 1960).
BANERJI, D.
  1971   *Family planning in India: a critique and a perspective.* New Delhi: People's Publishing House.
BERELSON, B.
  1963   "Communication, communication research, and family planning," in *Emerging techniques of population research,* 159–171. Proceedings of a Round Table at the 39th Annual Conference of the Milbank Memorial Fund, September 18–19, 1962.
  1966   "KAP studies on fertility," in *Family planning and population programs.* Edited by B. Berelson, et al., 655–668. Chicago: University of Chicago Press.
  1969a  Beyond family planning. *Studies in family planning* 38:1–16.
  1969b  "National family planning programs: where we stand," in *Fertility and family planning.* Edited by S. J. Behrman, et al., 341–387. Ann Arbor: University of Michigan Press.
BLAKE, J.
  1965   Demographic science and the redirection of population policy. *Journal of Chronic Diseases* 18:1181–1200.
BOGUE, D.
  1962   "Some tentative recommendations for a Sociologically Correct Family Planning Communication and Motivation Program in India," in *Research in family planning.* Edited by C. V. Kiser, 503–538. Princeton, New Jersey: Princeton University Press.
CHANDRASEKARAN, C.
  1966   "Recent trends in family planning research in India," in *Family planning and population programs.* Edited by B. Berelson, et al., 549–559. Chicago: University of Chicago Press.
CHANDRASEKHAR, S.
  1972   *Infant mortality, population growth and family planning in India.* London: George Allen and Unwin.

COOB, J. C. *et al.*
1965 "Pakistan: the Medical Social Research Project at Lulliani." *Studies in Family Planning* 8:11–16.

DAVIS, K.
1967 Population policy: will current programs succeed? *Science* 158:730–739.

ENKE, S.
1960 The gains to India from population control: some money measures and incentive schemes. *Review of Economics and Statistics* 42:175–181.

ESTIMATES COMMITTEE FIFTH LOK SABHA
1972 *Family planning programme* (thirteenth report) New Delhi: Lok Sabha Secretariat.

FINNIGAN, O. D., T. H. SUN
1972 "Planning, starting, and operating an educational incentives project." *Studies in Family Planning* 3(1):1–7.

FREEDMAN, R.
1966 "Family planning programs today," in *Family planning and population programs.* Edited by B. Berelson, et al., 811–825. Chicago: University of Chicago Press.

FREYMAN, M.
1965 "India's family planning programs: some lessons learned," in *Population dynamics.* Edited by M. Muramatsu and P. Harper. Baltimore: Johns Hopkins Press.

HAUSER, P.
1967 Review of books on "Family planning and population programs." *Demography* 4:397–414.

HEER, D. M., D. O. SMITH
1968 Mortality level, desired family size, and population increase. *Demography* 6:104–121.

KANGAS, L. W.
1970 Integrated incentives for fertility control. *Science* 169:1278–1283.

KAUR, S., J. EDLEFSEN
1968 Some observations regarding KAP research in India. New Delhi: USAID Mission to India.

LAPHAM, R. J., W. P. MAULDIN
1972 National family planning programs: review and evaluation. *Studies in Family Planning* 3(3):29–52.

LAZARSFELD, P. F., *et al., editors*
1967 *The uses of sociology.* New York: Basic Books.

LAZARSFELD, P. F., J. G. REITZ
1970 *Toward a theory of applied sociology* (A progress report). New York: Bureau of Applied Social Research.

LINDER, F. E.
1971 Fertility and family planning in relation to public health. *Milbank Memorial Fund Quarterly* 49(4):192–207.

MAULDIN, W. P.
1965 Fertility studies: knowledge, attitude and practice. *Studies in Family Planning* 7:1–10.

MOSTELLER, F., D. P. MOYNIHAN
1972   *On equality of educational opportunity.* New York: Vintage.
MOYNIHAN, D. P.
1970   *Maximum feasible misunderstanding.* New York: Free Press.
NORTMAN, D. L.
1972   Status of national family planning programmes of developing countries in relation to demographic targets. *Population Studies* 26:5–18.
PATHAK, S. H.
1968   Implementation of family planning in India. *Population Review* 12 (1–2):60–68.
POFFENBERGER, T.
1968a   "Motivational aspects of family planning in an Indian village," chapter five. Draft report prepared for the Central Family Planning Institute, New Delhi.
1968b   Urban Indian attitudinal response and behavior related to family planning: possible implications for the mass communication program. *Journal of Family Welfare* 14:31–319.
1968c   "Urban Indian attitudinal response and behavior related to family planning: possible program implications." Draft report. New Delhi: Ford Foundation Mission to India.
RAINA, B. L.
1965   Possible effects of public policy measures on fertility in India," in: Papers Contributed by Indian Authors, World Population Conference, Belgrade, Yugoslavia.
RAINWATER, L., W. L. YANCEY
1965   *The Moynihan report and the politics of controversy.* Cambridge, Massachusetts: MIT Press.
RAO, K. G.
1968   "Studies in family planning in India, a review for program implications." Mimeographed manuscript, New Delhi: Central Family Planning Institute.
RAULET, H. M.
1970   Family planning and population control in developing countries. *Demography* 7:211–234.
REITZ, J. G.
1973   "The gap between knowledge and decision in the utilization of social research." New York: Bureau of Applied Social Research.
RIDKER, R. G.
1969   Desired family size and the efficacy of current family planning programmes. *Population Studies* 23:279–284.
ROGERS, E. H.
1972   "Field experiments on family planning incentives." East Lansing, Michigan: Michigan State University.
SIMMONS, G. B.
1971   *The Indian investment in family planning.* New York: Population Council.
SIMON, J.
1968   Some "marketing correct" recommendations for family planning campaigns. *Demography* 5:504–507.

SPREHE, J. T.

1972 "Incentives in family planning: time for a new look," in *Incentive approaches in population planning programs: readings and annotations.* Edited by O. D. Finnigan. Manila: USAID, Offices of Health and Public Services.

STYCOS, J. M.

1962 "A critique of the traditional planned parenthood approach in underdeveloped areas," in *Research in family planning.* Edited by G. V. Kiser, 447–501. Princeton: Princeton University Press.

UNITED NATIONS ADVISORY MISSION

1970 India: UN mission evaluation of the family planning program. *Studies in Family Planning* 56:4–18.

WEINBERG, A.

1972 Science and trans-science (editorial). *Science* 177:211.

WYON, J. B., J. E. GORDON

1971 *The Khanna study: population problems in the rural Punjab.* Cambridge: Harvard University Press.

# Social Science and Health in Cuba: Ideology, Planning, and Health

SALLY GUTTMACHER, LOURDES GARCÍA

It is our aim to examine here the role of social science in the health care of the Cuban people. As the development of all key Cuban institutions is now planned centrally, it is essential to discuss planning and principles of health services in the context of the major problems and organizing principles underlying development of the whole society. Moreover, the interplay between ideology and actual social structure is more explicit in socialist planning than in market-centered economies; so the organization of Cuba is directly guided by broad, basically Marxist ideological principles.

## PRESENT SETTING AND PREREVOLUTIONARY HEALTH

Cuba's population of eight and one-half million is racially heterogeneous, 27 percent being black. Although the deepest roots underlying Cuban nationality and culture may well lie in Spain and Africa, her more recent ties are with the Americas, especially with those countries bordering on the Caribbean Sea and Gulf of Mexico.

Today Cuba is in the relatively early stages of modern development which is being undertaken in the context of a colonial legacy and of persistent United States hostility, including a trade embargo in effect since the early sixties. This embargo was intended to put pressure on the Cuban economy and to isolate her. It is only in the last year or two that Latin American countries other than Mexico have begun to recognize and trade with socialist Cuba.

We are indebted to Eric Holtzman and Myra Jehlen for their thoughtful criticism and useful ideas.

At the time of the revolution, Cuba's standard of living was comparatively high by Latin American standards. But there were pronounced inequalities between the rural and urban populations and between middle and lower classes. The country was run by a dictatorship and its economy was dominated by United States enterprises, ranging from sugar production to tourism and gambling. Revolutionary Cuba has adopted the strategy of relying on its major economic resource, its agriculture, as a base for raising and equalizing the standard of living. From the outset, the stress has been on universal basic education, health care, and social security. In these areas, Cuba already compares favorably on a per capita basis with the most developed Latin American countries. But, although she is still underdeveloped,[1] Cuba's implicit models for standards of nutrition and health care derive from Western industrialized countries, and she has opted to lay particular emphasis on the introduction of modern techniques.

Cuba's major crop is sugar. Her agriculture is now more adequate than it was before the revolution to meet such domestic needs as food, fiber, and hide production. But, despite an increased emphasis on such export crops as oranges, sugar remains central to Cuba's economy and will be so for some time to come. About 40 percent of the work force is in agriculture, 40 percent in service and professional jobs and 20 percent in industrial production. The economy is emerging from a period of intensive capital accumulation; in this period heavy stress was laid on investments such as herds of cattle and flocks of poultry with concomitant rigorous rationing of consumption. The most pressing agricultural problems now relate to improvements in productivity. Mechanization will play an increasingly important role in this respect. Although important aspects of the cane harvest are already largely mechanized, this clearly represents a crucial area for future development. For example, only 10 percent of the initial cutting is done by machine. Agricultural research and the training of technicians are increasingly emphasized. The overall effort is to overcome shortages in expertise and equipment (resulting from historical factors such as the past dependence on United States technology and the flight of a section of the upper middle class) through extensive training of personnel in Cuba, coupled with technological advice and assistance from other countries.

Cuba maintains extensive trade relations with other socialist countries

---

[1] Cuba has virtually no proven domestic oil reserve and no alternative source of power, such as hydroelectric potential; she also lacks coal and other essentials for steel production, but she does produce nickel and some other minerals. Thus her industrial potential is restricted.

(as well as with Japan, England, and other nonsocialist nations) and she has received important amounts of direct economic aid, especially from the USSR. However, in her small size, her limited resources, and her history and social traditions, Cuba differs significantly from either European or Asian socialist countries, and the Cuban leadership has carefully sought to adapt its socialist program to the country's particular needs. Much stress has been laid for instance on maintaining a flexible policy relating to work incentives. The balance between material or economic incentives (salaries, bonuses, special access to scarce goods, etc.) and moral incentives (such as public acclaim and selection for positions of responsibility and status) is viewed as a crucial influence on the long-term possibilities for creating a developed, humane society. The general intention is to de-emphasize such economic incentives as income differentials, in pointed contrast to the development policies of other Western Hemisphere countries. But a balance is sought between moral and economic incentives. For example, there are wage differentials and some docking of wages for excessive absenteeism or lateness. Still, Cuba has consistently tried to minimize such methods and, where feasible, she rewards the surpassing of production norms through nonmaterial means.

The emphasis on balance is apparent, for example, in a recent statement of Prime Minister Fidel Castro warning against a too premature transfer to purely moral incentives, and arguing that Cuba has entered the phase in which rewards are to be distributed.

from each according to his abilities, to each according to his work... Together with moral incentives we must also use material incentives, without abusing one or the other because the first leads to idealism[2] and the second to the growth of individual egoism. We must act so that economic incentives do not become the exclusive motivations for man or moral incentives the pretext by which some live by the work of others (*Granma* 1972).

There is also an effort to balance incentives that operate at an individual level with some that operate at the collective work-group or local community level.[3]

Wage differentials among occupations requiring different skills, training, or hours are much less than in the prerevolutionary situation. The salary and wage range for those trained since the revolution is 85 to 450 pesos per month. Professionals or other workers who have remained in

[2] Idealism, in Marxist terms, relates to the failure to ground thoughts in concrete reality.
[3] For a clear analytical discussion of the interplay of individual, collective, moral and material incentives (see Riskin 1973).

their prerevolutionary occupations can earn higher salaries based upon their "historical" earnings, although recently this has begun to be modified toward a policy of the same pay for similar occupational status. However, the effect of wage differentials is offset by the high degree of job security, the rationing of basic commodities, and the fact that food, rent, education, health care, and other "social security" items are free or priced well within the means of all. Such factors at once reduce economic pressures and severely circumscribe purchasing power.

Restaurant meals, extra cigarettes (beyond those available as part of rationing), and a few other nonrationed luxury goods are priced quite high and thus do provide a type of economic incentive. But scarce items such as major appliances or new housing are allocated by elected workplace or community organizations whose decisions are based upon need and merit. Even though the price of appliances is high, a relatively large income still does not give one privileged access to such goods. Social and political honors, such as being selected as a vanguard worker, or being elected into the communist party, are major incentives for the more politicized segment of the population. In addition, although individual motivations may be mixed, Cuba remains in the stage where a sense of shared purpose is widespread.

Cuba is acutely aware that education is crucial to her development. Thus great care is expended in explaining current economic and social problems and their proposed solutions to all segments of the population. This is carried out by a variety of mechanisms ranging from the classroom to small group discussions on a local-community or work-place level. They all present Fidel Castro's elaborately detailed public speeches in which he summarizes and explains overall approaches, specific policies, and statistical information.

Finally, as will be clear when we discuss health programs specifically, mass participation is basic to Cuban development. Mass-based organizations provide a means for democratization of important phases of local decisionmaking (e.g. concerning allocation of scarce goods and aspects of the administration of justice). Work-place and block-level associations such as the trade-union organizations, the Federation of Cuban Women, and the community Committees for the Defense of the Revolution are centrally involved in encouraging such participation and in providing mechanisms for widespread discussions and airing of problems.

Prerevolutionary Cuba had no national health system and only rudimentary coordination of services. (It is true, however, as Danielson (1975) points out, that the mutualism system, based on group health plans, ran and coordinated health services for a limited segment of the working population on a private basis.) The United States was heavily influential in medical care since North American drugs and medical equipment dominated the market, and North American journals and texts, expressing the values and patterns of the United States system, were the most commonly read. Prerevolutionary medical training was largely isolated from social needs. Students trained for private practice and the emphasis was on the curative rather than preventive medicine. Since 63 percent of physicians practiced in Havana, which contains slightly under a quarter of the population, much of the most advanced medicine was focused there or in other large urban centers where the Cuban upper-middle class could afford to pay for private services. The state services, insufficient in quantity, of poor quality, and unevenly distributed, were virtually unavailable to the rural population, which relied heavily on folk practitioners (*curanderos*).

The health status of the rural population was typical of an underdeveloped, agricultural Latin American nation. Although the statistical data on birth and death rates collected prior to the revolution were of poor quality, particularly for the rural areas, we can roughly sketch the health profile of prerevolutionary Cuba. The 1957 statistics, for example, revealed that infectious diseases, largely controlled in developed countries, took a large toll of the population, especially among infants. Diarrheal diseases, including gastroenteritis, were the highest cause of death in 1957 and the number one cause of infant mortality until 1962 (Navarro 1972a:397–432). Other infectious diseases, such as tuberculosis, poliomyelitis, diphtheria, whooping cough, tetanus, and malaria were the major health problems immediately facing the revolutionary government.

## FOCUSING ON PREVENTION

The most serious health problems of underdeveloped countries are not those of chronic morbidity requiring an advanced technology, but rather relate to diseases of infectious and parasitic origin. These can readily yield to relatively simple medicine, but what is necessary for their solution is a social apparatus capable of distributing and administering fairly elementary techniques of hygiene and treatment. Another way of expressing this is to say that the medical priority of an underdeveloped country ought to be preventive rather than curative.

This priority is, in fact, the one Cuba has chosen. The focusing of resources on prevention has ideological implications, because it necessarily means a mass orientation to health problems. A preventive focus necessitates dealing with the social issue of health care and delivery services. The curative focus, on the other hand, prevails in the United States, and has placed more emphasis on the technological aspects of health care than on the social. It also has allowed a dual medical system to flourish and has emphasized the individual relationship between the patient and his personal physician.

Since it is not our purpose to describe and analyze the organization of Cuban health care but rather to discuss the place of social science in its delivery and assessment, our summary of some of the major changes in the system is brief.[4] We will focus on the roles of social science and on aspects of the system of particular interest to social scientists.

To develop a national health system and a unified and coherent health policy, all health institutions have been integrated into the state system, including the private sector and the drug and medical equipment industries. Since 1964, medical school graduates have pledged not to be involved in the private practice of medicine. Some private practitioners do remain from the older generation but they are few and their numbers are declining. Physicians who maintain autonomous practices are employed by the state and paid on a scale from 225 to 615 pesos per month, depending upon their training. The rise in service offered by the increasing number of polyclinics has also contributed to the decline of private practice.[5]

Equalization of the quantity and quality of health services available throughout the country is being effected first by a reorganization of existing services to maximize efficiency, and second by injecting new resources into the system. Policy and programs are evaluated by the national Ministry of Public Health and most of the input at this level is made by physicians and other professionals. Hospital services are centralized in each province. Facilities are integrated into a network with a hierarchy of services; from the most sophisticated province-level teaching hospital, which provides specialized care for one to one and one-half million people, down to the regional hospital centers, with limited capacity for specialty treatment but good secondary facilities for about one-quarter of a million people. Both provincial and regional facilities support the basic units of the system, the polyclinics and rural hospitals which provide general medical care for about 30,000 people each. Patients may be referred to higher-level facilities if their problem requires it, but they go first to their local polyclinic.

[4]   Valuable descriptions and analyses of progress made in Cuban health care can be be found in several recently published articles including John, Kimmelman, Haas, and, Orris (1971), Navarro (1972a), Navarro (1972b) and Stein and Susser (1972).

[5]   It should be noted that the *mutalista* clinics, run for the subscribers of private health plans, continued to exist at least untill 1969, when they accounted for about 3 percent of all consultations (see Danielson, this volume).

Because of the reorganization of services, much-improved health care is now available for the large majority of the population, and use of the services has substantially increased. The number of medical consultations has grown from 13.8 million in 1963 to 29.3 million in 1970 (*Diez años de revolución en salud pública* 1969). A consistent increase in the number of patient visits has occurred despite the fact that nearly half (3,000) of Cuba's physicians left the country between 1958 and 1961. The loss of physicians was made up during the 1960's when close to 30 percent of university students chose medicine as their career.

As of 1972 Cuba had over 7,200 physicians and approximately 20 percent of university students, half of them women, are training to be medical doctors (Navarro 1972b). Most of the physicians who left the country in the early 1960's were based in Havana or other large cities. A factor which has helped to equalize the distribution of medical personnel has been the institution of the requirements of two years of rural service for all new medical and dental graduates. This program was instituted in 1960 and is administered by the rural medical service division of the Ministry of Public Health. In addition, many young physicians come from families of agricultural workers in rural areas to which they are encouraged to return to practice upon completion of their training. In fact, because it is expected that they will return home to practice, deliberate attempts are made to attract people from rural areas into medicine.

As far as allocation of new facilities and hospital services is concerned, the highest priority has been given to rural and indigent areas where services were deficient. One index of the effect of this policy has been a change in the distribution of hospital beds. Havana, with just over one-fifth of the population, had over one-half of the hospital beds; now this proportion has decreased to two-fifths.

There is no doubt that Cuba's health practices and the health status of her citizens are improving, as is attested by critical barometers of change such as rates of maternal and infant mortality. The infant mortality rate was 28 per 1,000 live births in 1972. This compares favorably with the rates of many other Latin American countries.[6] Maternal mortality

[6] According to the *Demographic yearbook of the United Nations, 1971*, Cuba's infant mortality rate, (number of infant deaths per 100 live births) was lower than most in Latin America. In 1970 although Cuba's rate (38.4) was higher than that of the United States. (19.2) and Puerto Rico (28.6), it was lower than, for example, Mexico (68.5), The Dominican Republic (50.1), Guatemala (88.4), Venezuela (48.7), Chile, 1969, (87.5), as well as most others. Cuba also compares favorably with Latin American countries on expectation of life at birth. From 1965–1970 a Cuban could expect to live 66.8 years. In 1970, in the United States, the comparable figure is 70.8 years. Such comparisons, however, are rough because of national differences in the collection, and interpretation of statistics.

has also decreased from 7.5 per 10,000 live births in 1970 to 5.46 in 1972. The fact that deliveries in institutions have increased to 92 percent indicates improved health practices in a country in which a large proportion of children in rural areas had been born at home under unsanitary conditions.

## MASS PARTICIPATION IN CUBAN HEALTH CARE

Particularly illuminating, in illustrating the effect of mass health education and mobilization, has been the Cuban immunization program. This has been carried out largely through the efforts of the People's Commission of Health, which is made up of members of mass organizations: trade unions (CTC) and the Committees for the Defense of the Revolution (CDR), which are local block organizations; the Cuban Federation of Women (FMC); and the Association of Small Farmers (ANAP). Members of mass organizations are elected to health councils at the local, regional, and national levels, thus giving the community and health consumers a legitimate platform for the expression of their needs. It is too early to tell how such participation will ultimately affect the delivery of health care, but the mass organizations do hold potential for the interplay between community interest and central planning.

The health section of the CDR in 1969 mobilized the population so that within seventy-two hours three million children were vaccinated against polio (Navarro 1972b). That virtually 100 percent of the child population has been vaccinated and that there have been no cases of polio in Cuba since 1963, demonstrates the effectiveness with which Cuba has applied its preventive approach (*Diez años de revolución en salud pública* 1969). The significance of this may be measured by the present immunization crisis in the United States, where the combined efforts of the various health institutions have been unable even to approach this achievement.[7] It is in the area of mobilizing and educating the population that the direct contribution of Cuban social science can be seen. The mass organizations have personnel who aid in community health education, such as the sanitary health brigades of the FMC whose work is to educate women in the community and to bring them to the polyclinics for injections or other

---

[7]   *The New York Times*, Oct. 1, 1973, points out that there has been an "alarming decline" in immunization of preschool children in the United States. The Center for Disease Control now feels that "epidemics of polio and other childhood diseases could occur." This crisis is attributed to "public and medical indifference to preventing the disease" as well as to cuts in government funded immunization activities.

preventive care. The FMC is also responsible for the organization and maintenance of child care centers and some members are trained to perform field nurse activities, such as giving injections or vaccinations, especially in emergency situations.

Most health workers from mass organizations have received little formal training other than first-aid information. However, with the recent appointment of a director of health education in the Ministry of Public Health, there are plans to institute a one-year course for health educajors. These will include members from the trade unions and CDR's who will practice in work centers and factories as well as in their own communities. Social science can make a valuable contribution to such training programs in which the trainees' effectiveness is largely based on their understanding of some of the social parameters and problems of the target population.

Inducements offered for specific types of positive health behavior are another example of the emphasis on a preventive orientation as well as an opportunity for the use of social science. In this instance, every worker is supposed to have an annual check-up, including chest x-ray, blood tests, and anti-tetanus vaccination. When the tests are finished, the health unit of the worker's union gives the workers a credit for having been examined. The sum of the total points that a worker has accumulated in a year is the basis on which awards for sociomoral distinction are awarded. (Points are also given for attitude toward work: work discipline; voluntary agricultural work; cultural, sports, and political participation; and commitment to raise one's educational level.) Besides the individual recognition, prizes and honors are also awarded to groups, according to the total number of points accumulated by all members of a work group, such as a department or section. For this reason, if a worker fails to appear for the annual health examination, her or his group will suffer a loss in prestige.

## SOCIAL SCIENCE AND HEALTH IN CUBA

Early in its development as a socialist society, Cuba recognized that social scientific theory and methodology can be a valuable asset for the solution of problems in the organization and delivery of health care. In 1966, seven years after the revolution, a group of psychologists who had just graduated from the national university began to work in public health, and in 1969, a group was officially incorporated into the National Ministry of Public Health, the central health planning agency. The fact that the social scientists involved have been psychologists reflects the tradition and evolution of social science training in the country. The functions of the national group of psychologists include, as part of the program of the Ministry, the planning and supervision of the teaching of behavioral sciences at the School of Public Health, the development and supervision of research projects, and the organization of psychological services at local and regional levels. These psychologists also undertook teaching and research activities which in other countries might have been carried out by people trained in sociology and social anthropology.

Before the revolution no psychologists, sociologists, anthropologists, or economists were trained at the national university. The only career program with a social science component was one that prepared people for employment in diplomacy or public administration. A few psychologists and economists were trained at the Catholic University, but most received their postgraduate education abroad, after finishing their undergraduate studies in pedagogy or philosophy in Cuba. The few with psychology degrees were employed primarily as teachers in secondary schools or at the university, or became psychometricians or guidance counselors in private institutions, or collaborated with physicians in their private practices. With the dubious exception of market research projects financed largely by United States companies, there was virtually no social science research. It should be recalled that a common problem among underdeveloped countries is the fact that many of their professionals receive much of their training overseas or in local institutions with approaches mirroring those of developed nations. Thus, even if they return to their home countries, these professionals often fail to think and teach in terms applicable to their own countries' specific problems, and because they have not been trained in using indigenous techniques and resources, they frequently become dissatisfied with the materials available to conduct their research. As a result their research too often benefits foreign commercial interests rather than their own country.

Shortly after 1959, a degree program in psychology was instituted in the national universities. The program takes five years, and the curriculum contains not only basic subjects, such as neuroanatomy, neurophysiology, general social and developmental psychology, but also sociology, social anthropology, statistics, philosophy, logic, psychopathology, and techniques of diagnosis and treatment. A degree program in sociology has been created very recently, along with the founding of a sociology department associated with the University of Havana, but the program has not yet graduated any students.

The sixty-five psychologists currently working in this field are concentrated in Havana and Las Villas. Between 1959 and 1966 psychologists were used exclusively for diagnosis and treatment of individual cases and as members of psychiatric teams. However, now, consistent with Cuba's very broad definition of health, other forms of application of psychology to the health field have been explored.

The psychologists who work in health care are concerned with clinical, teaching, and research activities. In agreement with Cuba's health ideology clinical focus is now on prevention, and the favored approach is to work with groups and families rather than with individuals. Little had been done previously in community psychology or in isolating elements in the environment that might be detrimental to an individuals' well-being. Psychologists are now integrating psychological concerns into the network of problems defined within the purview of health. Psychological services are being included in basic programs aimed at providing comprehensive health services to the population. This means that a close working relationship must be developed between the psychologists and other members of the medical team, as well as with social workers and members of the health section of mass organizations who function as health educators and sources of referral for the community.

In Cuba, socioeconomic status no longer objectively determines one's access to health service as it does in market-centered societies. However, traditions and modes of behavior shaped by previous inequalities still may limit people's actual use of services. Class-associated factors such as life style and level of education generate different attitudes toward health maintenance, varying reactions to symptoms or the need for hospitalization, and even different ways of adjusting to disabilities. Furthermore, the etiology of illness is in part related to the personality of the patient which in turn depends on psychosocial and cultural factors. Sociopsychological factors are particularly important in countries like Cuba with a health picture which is decreasingly characterized by parasitic and infectious disease and therefore increasingly characterized by chronic morbidity. The courses of such disesaes as heart disease and diabetes are strongly influenced by cultural, social, and psychological factors. The Cubans plan to apply their social science methods and findings to identify areas warranting special effort and to educate better those segments of the population whose health behavior lags most. Detailed surveys on topics such as nutritional practices and studies on the effect of extended periods of hospitalization on young children will have obvious applied value (a few women from the FMC have been trained by psychologists to serve as interviewers on this project).

With limited resources, Cuba has decided that the best implementation of her "preventive rather than curative" policy is to invest heavily in health care for the next generation. There has been building and developing of facilities for children, such as modern schools and child-care centers. While psychologists are traditionally concerned with child development, their concern is now of particular priority, and much of their clinical activity involves aspects of child rearing and development. For example, there is stress on early detection of retardation and behavior problems. One indication of this orientation is that resources have been devoted to experimenting with new computer-based diagnostic methods for detecting brain damage. Because the health care system is interconnected with other social institutions such as the educational system, there are many possible sites for intervention. Follow-up of the psychological development of healthy and low birth-weight babies occurs in polyclinics, day care centers, and both primary and secondary schools.

Some psychologists give prenatal instruction in places of work, schools, and day care centers. Cuba had no widespread programs of parental education but now efforts are made to reach as many people as possible through the mass media as well as directly. A new television series, *Science and Health,* produced by the Ministry of Health, presents psychological information and produces programs on problems of child rearing. Psychologists also become involved in dealing with work conditions through the program of labor medicine. It is recognized that since financial insecurity is no longer a factor, work motivation depends more heavily upon satisfactory relationships between workers and upon the suitability of the job to the worker's personal characteristics (which include such matters as vocation, aptitude, knowledge, and personality). Group discussions, seminars, and advice to supervisors, and diagnosis of the institutional dynamics of the work setting all aim at promoting good psychosocial health.

Since 1966 psychologists have been teaching basic social science, useful to clinicians, postgraduate physicians, nurses, and technical personnel. By designing and running a two-year course for psychotechnicians, psychologists have also been engaged in the training of paraprofessionals. In turn, psychologists are increasingly able to delegate tasks such as data gathering, elementary clinical diagnosis, and group education. Research, which has been secondary to the activities already mentioned, has received more emphasis in the past few years. Current research is aimed at providing immediately useful information. The studies undertaken are either explicitly requested by the health authorities in the different organizational levels or are defined in consultation with the heads of health programs. An unusual example is a current study of the factors influencing driving habits of ambulance drivers.

In the area of child health, the main interest is in socially and culturally influenced differences in approaches to child care and their consequences for health and personality. One area in which it seems especially important to define this relationship is, of course, that of diet. Research is currently underway to establish norms for the psychological and motor development of the Cuban child. Another study is looking at the comparative amount and type of morbidity in the growing number of boarding schools. It is being undertaken by a multiprofessional team consisting of physicians, a psychologist, a statistician, and an epidemiologist.

Research into the utilization patterns of health facilities is of a more sociological nature. Because economic factors no longer are important in the decision to seek health care, current research is concerned with variables such as motivations, beliefs, attitudes, and opinions about health and disease and about the availability of services. Some evaluative research has also been undertaken to establish the effectiveness of programs of health education. A study was recently carried out to discover why being a nurse has become a less popular health career for young people and why trained nurses drop out of the field. This problem relates to an interesting set of questions about the flow of personnel into varying careers when market mechanisms are no longer functioning. The stress in the past few years has been on recruiting students for teaching, agricultural technical specialties, engineering, veterinary service, and other occupations and professions directly connected with economic development. Thus, it may be that there is a limited pool of potential recruits for such professional careers as nursing.

In addition to questions directly associated with health care there is research interest in establishing how psychological health and behavior patterns are influenced by the new socialist way of life. For example, it will be of interest to determine whether raising children in groups and in boarding schools, where intellectual and manual work are combined, has had a noticeable effect on psychological health. Research is also being planned to evaluate how working has affected women who previously stayed in the home and to study the effects of living in new towns on families of agricultural workers who previously lived in rural isolation. These, and many studies of a similar nature await the training of more qualified personnel.

## CONCLUSION

As previously mentioned, Cuba is still in a relatively early phase of her modern development. Her political ideology has had a great influence up-on the elements of the health system and upon health status and behavior. We cannot predict precisely how the society will evolve, but there are many interesting aspects which merit watching, particularly those which con-trast with influences and pressures evident in the United States. The question one might pose concerning Cuba's development might also be asked about other socialist societies, but Cuba is particularly interesting because among the socialist countries she is perhaps the closest to the United States in background and culture, and has most recently changed her political ideology through a popular revolution.

Several Cuban programs are aimed at countering elitism and fostering a sense of interdependence among different types of health workers. At every level of the educational system intellectual work is combined with practical or manual work — this is a matter of basic educational philoso-phy. During their university training, students are also part-time workers in such institutions as factories and child care centers. Medical students are no exception. During their first two years they are assigned to work-study programs as aides in hospitals. One by-product of this measure has been to relieve the shortage of nursing staff. In addition, most professionals still participate widely in voluntary labor projects. These experiences are intended to democratize the attitudes of physicians toward other medical workers and toward their patients.[8] At the same time, a better distribution of services, along with programs of health education, should help overcome the remaining inequalities in the utilization of the health system. A beginning has also been made in reducing hierarchical distinc-tions among health workers.[9]

Perhaps the most interesting aspect of health for most social scientists is health behavior. Since the behavior of a population is influenced by social and economic policy, specific changes in such policy should have a demonstrable effect on behavior. Although there is some government intervention in mixed economies (e.g. through training programs, gov-ernment-funded services, funds for hospital building and research, and controls over food and drug quality), such state intervention has a mini-mal effect. Private industries ranging from medical services to drug companies, to manufacturers of patent medicines sold over the counter, and to the snack and breakfast food industries remain largely unregulated.

---

[8]   The programs, of course, also contribute to production.
[9]   For example, all health workers belong to a single union. This means, among other things, that they participate together in some areas of joint decision making and mutual criticism. It will be of great interest to see how such factors affect job and hierarchical distinctions.

North Americans as well as many Europeans are systematically encouraged to behave in ways, and to purchase products, of dubious value, or even harmful to their health. More than a decade after it was definitely established that smoking tobacco is harmful to health, the cigarette industry continues to grow. Indeed, an apparent industry response to evidence of a link between smoking and heart disease or cancer was the production of a longer cigarette. How the Cuban health behavior evolves now that the private sector has been removed from the society will be of great interest in coming years. The social costs of maintaining her remunerative tobacco industry are becoming a subject of open discussion. Already, cigarettes are rationed and expensive, and Fidel Castro has given up smoking in public. In the area of nutrition Cuba is developing a large and successful fishing industry. Fish has never been a popular food in Cuba. In an effort to induce the people to eat more of it, it is frequently served in the midday meal which most have at school or their place of work.

A major focus of this paper has been on the growing role of social scientists in Cuban society. Further discussion might well focus on certain matters that distinguish their role qualitatively. For one thing, Cuba has largely eliminated the competition among social scientists for shares of the "pie" of research opportunities which generates waste and distorts priorities in the United States. For another, Cuban social scientists bear a direct responsibility to their society both in monitoring attitudes and changes in behavior and in contributing to the planning of services and the delivery of systems; their American counterparts, instead, remain relatively detached. Their work tends to be carried on in isolation, their results tend to be uncoordinated, and their impact on public policy is unpredictable at best. We might speculate that these are largely the reasons for the differing proportions of applied and theoretical social science in Cuba and the United States. The most emphasized, and certainly the most prestigious work done in the United States is abstract or theoretical — the reason may be in part that social scientists in the United States are, in fact, dealing with matters they can little affect.[10] The Cubans, it is true, work within the context of an established Marxist theory and respond to the needs of central planning agencies, but it already seems clear that in terms of theory and practice the development of Cuban social science will affect the thinking of social scientists everywhere.

---

[10]   It is, however, likely that as Cuba develops a larger number of more experienced social scientists, some of them will emphasize theoretical work.

# REFERENCES

ANONYMOUS
  1969   *Diez años de revolución de salud pública.* Havana: Instituto de Libro.
Granma
  1972   Article appearing July 28 in *Granma* (major Cuban newspaper).
JOHN, ROY, DAVID KIMMELMAN, JOANNA HAAS, AND PETER ORRIS
      Public health care in Cuba. *Social Policy* 1 (5).
NAVARRO, V.
  1972a  Health services, and health planning in Cuba. *International Journal
        of Health Services* 2 (3):394–432.
  1972b  Health services in Cuba, *New England Journal of Medicine* 287:954–
        959.
RISKIN, CARL
  1973   Maoism and motivation: work incentives in China. *Bulletin of Concer-
        ned Asian Scholars* 5 (1).
STEIN, ZENA, MERVYN SUSSER
  1972   The Cuban health system: a trial of a comprehensive service in a poor
        country. *International Journal of Health Services* 2 (4).

# Biographical Notes

ENRIQUE ARANETA (1925– ) is a physician and Professor of Psychiatry, University of Florida, Gainesville, and Assistant Chief, Psychiatric Services, Veterans Administration Hospital, Gainesville, Florida. He was born in the Philippines and was educated both in the Philippines and in the United States. He is a diplomate of the American Board of Psychiatry and Neurology and Adjunct Professor of Behavioral Sciences (Psychiatry), Allport College of Human Behavior, Oakland University, Rochester, Michigan. He served as Head of all Mental Health Services, Ministry of Health, Guyana, South America, 1964–1966. His publications are in the areas of anatomy, embryology, and community psychiatry.

MARY BAKSZYSZ BYMEL (1940– ) was born in Chicago, Illinois. She received her B.A. in Anthropology from the Universtiy of Illinois Chicago Circle Campus in 1968 and was awarded a Master's Degree in Cultural Studies by Governor's State University. In her position as an applied anthropologist in the Community Mental Health Program of the Illinois State Psychiatric Institute, Chicago, she has been actively engaged in community development with minority groups in the inner city. In the past several years she has focused on gerontological anthropology and has lectured extensively at professionals' meetings and to community organizations. She serves on the Advisory Council to the Nutrition Program of the Chicago Mayor's Office for Senior Citizens and is a member of the West Side Health Planning Organization Senior Citizens Committee, Chicago. She is the co-author (with Stephen L. Schensul, Ph.D.) of a book entitled *Action research in urban community development: experiences from a Chicano community in Chicago* to be published in 1975 by Scott Foresman.

Ross DANIELSON (1942–   ) combined undergraduate study of Spanish language and Latin American history with advanced training in medical sociology. His research on Cuba will be published by Transaction, Inc. (1975) under the title *Cuban medicine*. He is presently employed as a research analyst in the Department of Public Health and Preventive Medicine, University of Oregon Medical School, Portland, Oregon.

ROBERT G. DYCK (1930–   ) is a native of Blacksburg, Virginia and is currently Chairman of the Urban and Regional Planning Program at Virginia Polytechnic Institute and State University. He studied at Oberlin College (B.A., 1952), Massachusetts Institute of Technology (B. Arch., 1955), University of Pennsylvania (Master of City Planning, 1959), and University of Pittsburgh (Ph.D., Public and International Affairs, 1970). His fields of interest include state and regional planning, environmental policy, and health planning. In 1973 he was awarded a Fulbright-Hays Faculty Research Grant for study of health planning and administration in Yugoslavia.

RAY ELLING (1929–   ) is Professor of Sociology, Department of Community Medicine and Health Care, University of Connecticut, Farmington. He received his Ph.D. in medical sociology from Yale in 1958. He has taught at Harvard, Cornell, and the University of Pittsburgh. He returned to Connecticut in 1973 from a two-year leave of absence with W.H.O. where he served as Chief of the Behavioural Sciences Unit. His work has been primarily on the sociology of medical care organization. His edited volume, *National health care, issues and problems in socialized medicine*, appeared in 1971 and was reprinted in 1973 (New York: Lieber-Atherton). His research monograph with R. F. Martin, *Health and health care for the urban poor*, has just appeared (North Haven, Conn.: Connecticut Health Services Research Series 5). While at W.H.O., he sought to develop a more systematic continuous approach to cross-national studies of health systems. This interest continues and part of the framework for such studies is elaborated in his contribution to this volume.

PHILLIP J. EPLING (1931–1973) was Associate Professor of Health Education at the University of North Carolina at Chapel Hill. An anthropologist who received his education at the Universities of Chicago and of California, he was a life-long student of kinship and of Samoan culture who later developed a deep interest in experimental ethnology and the application of computer technology to ethnographic research.

LESLIE A. FALK (1915–   ) is Professor and Chairman, Department of Family and Community Health at Meharry Medical College, Nashville, Tennesee; M.D. Johns Hopkins School of Medicine (1942), D.Phil. in Medical Sciences at Oxford University, England (1940). His basic field is social medicine, with long-term activities in medical sociology, medical care administration and planning, medical history, international health, consumerism in health care, social value in medical education, primary health care teaching, and rural health. His wife, Joy Hume, was born in Changsha, China; they have collaborated in their research efforts in that area. He has done long-term work with coal-miners, Appalachia, and the rural south. Recent publications include: *History of consumerism* (1974), *Human values and medical education from the perspectives of health care delivery* (1973), *History of occupational health* (1973), *A national system of health care delivery* (1971), *Community participation in the neighborhood health center* (1969), and *Community health programs, industry and the neighboorhood health center* (1968).

LOURDES GARCÍA (1943–   ) was born in Cuba and has a degree in psychology from the University of Havana. She has studied in Mexico and Sweden and currently is the director of the Group of Psychology at the Ministry of Public Health and the President of the Cuban Society of the Psychology of Health.

OMAR J. GÓMEZ (1931–   ) was born in Buenos Aires. He has an M.D. and a D.P.H., both from the University of Buenos Aires. He was a special student at the School of Public Health of Columbia University and has had several appointments as administrator of public hospitals. He was the Hospital Manager of the experimental Health Plan of CEMIC, a Professor of Biostatistics at the School of Public Health of UBA, and a member of the Centro Latinoamericano de Administración Medica (PAHO). Currently, he is a medical care consultant for a private firm in Buenos Aires.

SALLY GUTTMACHER (1941–   ) was born in the United States and has worked with the Group of Psychology at the Ministry of Public Health in Cuba. She received a B.S. from the University of Wisconsin and studied social anthropology at the London School of Economics and Political Science and at the School of Oriental and African Studies in London. She has a M.Phil. from Columbia University and is currently completing her Ph.D. She teaches "The Sociology of Medicine" at New York University.

JOHN N. HAWKINS (1944–　) is Assistant Professor of International and Comparative Education at the University of California, Los Angeles and a member of the Field Faculty of the Department of Family and Community Health, Meharry Medical College, Nashville, Tennessee. He received his Ph.D. in International and Comparative Education from George Peabody College for Teachers and has taught at Vanderbilt University, Meharry Medical College, and the University of Hawaii. He has conducted field research on the problems of education, public health, and economic development in Japan, Hong Kong, and the People's Republic of China. He has published both books and articles on a variety of topics in the field of international education, the most recent being *Mao Tse-tung and education: his thoughts and teachings* (The Shoe String Press, 1974).

PETA M. HENDERSON (1937–　) was born in Northern Ireland and has been a resident of the United States since 1954. She received her B.A. in history from Swarthmore College and her M.A. in anthropology from McGill University in 1969. Her Ph.D. dissertation from the University of Connecticut (in progress) is on "Population policy, female sterilization, and the health system in Puerto Rico." Her major interests are modern health systems analysis and the structure of development and underdevelopment, especially in the Caribbean area. Since September 1974, she has been a member of the faculty of the Evergreen State College in Olympia, Washington.

STANLEY R. INGMAN (1939–　) was born in Pittsburgh, Pennsylvania. He received his B.A. from Miami University, Oxford, Ohio in 1961, an M.S. from Ohio State University in 1963, and a Ph.D. in sociology from the University of Pittsburgh in 1971. He has been Assistant Professor in Community Medicine and Health Care at the University of Connecticut since 1969, and Director of the Social Science and Health Service Training Program for graduate students since 1972. The impact of the interest groups in determining the organization of medical care is his basic research focus. More recently he has become concerned with evaluating the continuum of medical care services needed by the elderly in various societies.

HERMAN D. JAMES (1943– ) is an Assistant Professor of Sociology at the University of Massachusetts at Boston. He received his B.S. from Tuskegee Institute in 1965, an M.A. from St. Johns University in 1967, and his Ph.D. from the University of Pittsburgh in 1972. His dissertation was entitled, "The use of medical services in a Canadian metropolis: a multi-factor analysis." He has served on the Public Policy Committee and on the Sub-Committee to Examine Health Care Delivery Systems of the Medical Sociology section of the American Sociological Association. His other academic areas of interest are research methods and statistics.

FRANK KEHL (1940– ) received a B.A. from Dartmouth College in 1962 and then taught languages at the Chinese University of Hong Kong. As a graduate student in anthropology at Columbia University, he did demographic research in Laos (1966) and studied the social structure of an urban shantytown in Hong Kong (1968–1971). During that period, he directed and scripted an ethnographic film for the University of Hong Kong: *Hungry Ghosts: Chinese Ghost Festival in Urban Hong Kong* (1972). Based on the first visit of scholars to China in 1971, he jointly authored a book with others of the Committee of Concerned Asian Scholars: *China! Inside the People's Republic* (1972). Currently, he is teaching anthropology at Brooklyn College, CUNY, and is an editor of *New China* magazine.

IAN LAWSON (1927– ) is a graduate of the Aberdeen University Faculty of Medicine, Scotland. From 1961 to 1966 he was Consultant Physician in the Middle East of Scotland Regional Geriatric Service. He served two years at the Christian Medical College, Ludhiana, Punjab. He is now Associate Professor in the Department of Medicine, University of Connecticut School of Medicine and Medical Director of the Hebrew Home for the Aged in Hartford, Connecticut.

RANCE PUI-LEUNG LEE (1943– ) was born in Canton, China. He received his B.S.Sc. from Chung Chi College of the Chinese University of Hong Kong in 1965, and a Ph.D. in Sociology from the University of Pittsburgh in 1968. In 1967–1968, he participated in the Stirling County Mental Health Project, directed by Prof. Alexander H. Leighton, in the Department of Behavioral Sciences, Harvard School of Public Health. Since 1968, he has been Lecturer in Sociology at Chung Chi College of The Chinese University of Hong Kong. Currently he is the Director of the Social Research Centre, the Chinese University of

Hong Kong. His present research interest is in the organization of Chinese and Western health services in Chinese societies, especially in Hong Kong and the People's Republic of China.

DOROTHEA C. LEIGHTON (1908–   ) was born in rural Massachusetts. She received her B.A. from Bryn Mawr College in 1930 and her M.D. from Johns Hopkins University in 1936. During training in psychiatry, she and her husband spent a fellowship year getting acquainted with anthropology and doing fieldwork among the Navajo Indians and a group of Eskimos. Subsequently she joined the group doing research in Indian education and prepared a report on this with Clyde Kluckhohn. In the 1950's she joined her husband in his social psychiatric research, leaving this in 1965 to teach at the School of Public Health, University of North Carolina. There she became Professor and later Chairman of the Department of Mental Health. During this latter period, she became involved with others in establishing the Society for Medical Anthropology. Her publications reflect her work with Navajos and Zuñis, in social psychiatry, and in mental health (especially that of children). She retired in August 1974.

JAMES NESBITT (1939–   ) is a Principal Research Assistant, Health Services Research Unit, Graduate School of Public Health, University of Pittsburgh. Prior to that, he was a Senior Systems Analyst for the Pittsburgh Model Cities Program. His primary area of research concerns problems in the delivery of health care, particularly organizational design features relations.

STEVEN POLGAR (1931–   ) is Professor of Anthropology at the University of North Carolina, Chapel Hill. Born in Budapest, he studied anthropology at the University of Chicago and public health at Harvard. His research includes work in action anthropology with the Mesquakie Indians in Iowa, community development in West Africa, schizophrenics at Walter Reed Army Institute of Research, pregnancy and family planning in poverty areas of California and New York City, and library studies on evolution and ecology. He has been a consultant with the World Health Organization and is currently Visiting Professor at the University of Exeter in England.

ALANAGH M. RAIKES (1941–   ) was born in England and has studied and lived in Tanzania for the past eight years (B.A., University of Dar es Salaam, 1971). She taught at the Medical School in Dar es Salaam for two years and is currently working on a comparative study of the home backgrounds and aspirations of the first generation of students in medicine, engineering, and other sciences.

CARLOS RAMOS.   School of Public Health, University of Puerto Rico.

JEFFREY G. REITZ (1944–   ) is Assistant Professor of Sociology at the University of Toronto. He studied at Columbia, where he received degrees in applied mathematics (B.S., 1965) and sociology (Ph.D., 1972). His publications include articles on education, career choice, applied sociology, and ethnic relations. He is co-author of a forth-coming book on applied sociology, and of the report on a major government-commissioned survey on non-official languages in Canada. Recently he launched a new study of ethnic groups and occupational mobility in Toronto.

EDMUND RICCI (1934–   ) is a Research Associate Professor in the Graduate School of Public Health, University of Pittsburgh. He holds appointments in the Departments of Health Services Administration, Biostatistics and Sociology and is Director of the Health Services Research and Evaluation Unit and is Co-ordinator of the doctoral program in Health Services Research. His special interests include evaluative research and medical sociology. He has been associated with the Graduate School of Public Health since 1965 and was awarded the Ph.D. in Sociology in 1967.

STEPHEN L. SCHENSUL (1942–   ) was born in New York City. He received his M.A. and Ph.D. from the University of Minnesota. He has carried out field research in northern Minnesota, among the Banyankole of southwestern Uganda and in a Chicano community in Chicago. From 1968–1974 he was Director of Community Research for the CMHP and Assistant Professor in the Departments of Anthropology and Psychiatry of the University of Illinois at Chicago Circle. In September 1974 he became the Director of the Community Mental Center at Jackson Memorial Hospital, Miami and Associate Professor in the Department of Psychiatry of the University of Miami School of Medicine.

MAX H. SCHOEN (1922–   ) is Dean *pro tempore* and Professor of Dental Health Services at the School of Dental Medicine, SUNY at Stony Brook. He received his D.D.S. from the University of Southern

California in 1943 and his Dr.P.H. from the University of California at Los Angeles in 1969. His special interest is the delivery of dental care and he founded one of the first prepaid group practices in the United States.

BROOKE G. SCHOEPF.   L'Université Nationale du Zaire, Lubumbashi.

JORGE SEGOVIA (1934–   ) was born in Argentina. He received his M.D. and D.P.H. from the University of Buenos Aires. He was a post-doctoral student of Medical Sociology at Pittsburgh University. He was awarded a Milbank Faculty Fellowship for 1965–1970. He has been a pediatrician in a rural area of Argentina, a Professor of Health Education, and of Medical Sociology in several universities in Argentina, a member of the Centro Latinoamericano de Administracion Medica (PAHO), and a Research Associate at the Division of Sociomedical Sciences, School of Public Health, Columbia University. Currently, he is Consultant in Medical Care at the University of Campinas, Brazil.

PHILIP SINGER (1925–   ) is Professor of Anthropology and Behavioral Sciences at the Allport College of Human Behavior, Oakland University, Rochester, Michigan. His special interests include medical anthropology, ethnopsychiatry, community development, and pharmacognosy. He has worked for the United Nations and the Albany Medical Center Hospital and College, New York. Fieldwork has been conducted in America, India, Guyana, and Nigeria. He is a member of the International Committee on Traditional Medical Therapy.

GUY W. STEUART (1918–   ) was born in Durban, South Africa. Currently Head of the Department of Health Education, University of North Carolina at Chapel Hill, he was previously Head of the Behavioral Science and Health Education Program in the School of Public Health, University of California at Los Angeles, coming there from a W.H.O. assignment as Visiting Professor for three years at the Hebrew University, Hadassah Medical School, Jerusalem, Israel.

ANTHONY THOMAS (1936–   ) received his Ph.D. in anthropology from Stanford University in 1971. Previously he held teaching and research posts in eastern Africa: Education Officer in Tanzania between 1962 and 1965; and Research Associate in the Institute of Development Studies in Kenya between 1968 and 1969. Since 1970 he has taught in the Departments of Anthropology and Schools of Medicine at the Universities of Alberta (Edmonton), Connecticut (Storrs and Farmington), and North Carolina (Chapel Hill). His recent publications include *Pilúyekin: the life history of a Nez Perce Indian* (Anthropological Studies 3, Washington, D.C.: American Anthropological Association, 1970); "A struggle for socialist medicine" (in *Bread and roses*, Chapel Hill, N.C., February 1974); and "Oaths, ordeals, and the Kenyan courts: a policy analysis" (*Human Organization* 33: 59–70, 1974).

JANAKI N. TSCHANNERL (1941–  ) was born in Bangalore, South India, and her early education was in India. She received a B.A. in Literature from Swarthmore College in 1966, an M.Ed. from Harvard University in 1969, and is currently completing her doctoral thesis on "Caste and class: a study in a South Indian community" for Harvard University. Since 1972, she has been Lecturer in Sociology and Philosophy in the Department of Education at the University of Dar es Salaam. Her specialties include studies of materialist philosophy, education in class formation, and comparative education in socialist countries.

MARÍA LUISA URDANETA was born in Cali, Colombia, South America; she practiced as a professional nurse and anesthetist in Texas, U.S.A. for several years before receiving her B.A. in 1964 and M.A. in 1969 from the University of Texas at Austin. She is a Ph.D. candidate, Department of Anthropology, Southern Methodist University, Dallas, Texas. Presently she is a Research Associate and faculty member at the Center for Research and Training in Reproductive Biology and Voluntary Regulation of Fertility at the University of Texas Health Science Center at San Antonio, Texas. Her doctoral dissertation explores the relationship of sociocultural factors to attitudes on sexuality and fertility regulating behavior in the Mexican-American female population in a Texas city.

SUSAN VANDALE (1945–  ) is a doctoral student in the Department of Health Education at the University of North Carolina at Chapel Hill. She is currently engaged in a study of infant feeding practices among Spanish-speaking residents in Laredo, Texas.

WILLIE KAI YEE (1944–  ) is a Fellow in Social and Community Psychiatry at the Albert Einstein College of Medicine of Yeshiva University and the Bronx Psychiatric Center. He received his B.A. from Earlham College in 1965, and an M.D. from the University of Pittsburgh in 1969. He completed an internship at St. Vincent's Hospital and Medical Center of New York in 1970, and a Residency in Psychiatry at Albert Einstein College of Medicine in 1972. His present interests include family structure in the People's Republic of China and systems approaches to mental health care in Asian-American communities.

# Index of Names

# Index of Subjects